Revolutions in Communication

2nd Edition

Revolutions in Communication

Media History from Gutenberg to the Digital Age

2nd Edition

Bill Kovarik

B L O O M S B U R Y
NEW DELHI • LONDON • OXFORD • NEW YORK • SYDNEY

BLOOMSBURY INDIA
Bloomsbury Publishing India Pvt. Ltd
Second Floor, LSC Building No. 4, DDA Complex, Pocket C–6&7,
Vasant Kunj, New Delhi 110070

BLOOMSBURY, BLOOMSBURY ACADEMIC INDIA and the Diana logo are
trademarks of Bloomsbury Publishing Plc

First published in India 2023
First published in the United States of America 2011
Second edition published in 2016 by Bloomsbury Academic
Reprinted in 2016, 2017, 2018 (three times), 2019, 2021, 2022

For legal purposes the Acknowledgments on p. vii constitute an
extension of this copyright page.

This edition published with permission from Bloomsbury Publishing Plc,
50 Bedford Square, London, WC1B3DP, UK

Library of Congress Cataloging-in-Publication Data
Kovarik, Bill.
Revolutions in communication : media history from Gutenberg to the digital age / Bill
Kovarik. – 2nd edition.
pages cm
Includes bibliographical references and index.
ISBN 978-1-62892-478-7 (pbk. : alk. paper) 1. Mass media–History.
2. Communication–History. I. Title.
P90.K666 2015
302.2309–dc23
2015022976

ISBN: 978-93-84052-89-8

Typeset by Fakenham Prepress Solutions, Fakenham, Norfolk NR21 8NN
Printed and bound in India by Replika Press

To find out more about our authors and books
visit www.bloomsbury.com and sign up for our newsletters

Contents

Acknowledgments

What follows is a modest attempt to express my deepest gratitude those who have helped with this book and related historical research. Linda Burton, Ben Kovarik, and Nick Kovarik kept the coffee coming and helped me box the compass of issues when I would get lost in the mass of details. Other Kovariks also deserve mention: David, Karen, Daniel, Kitty, Ken, Lisa, and Kim and Andy Acres.

I owe too many friends and colleagues too much to name them all here, but among them are: Moira Baker, Maurine Beasley, Perry Beeman, Hal Bernton, Steven Berry, Venise Berry, Roger Blanchard, Judy Bonds, Chris Bowman, Cabell Brand, James Bruggers, Jeff Burnside, Benji Burrell, Theresa Burriss, Helen Caldicott, Tom Carmichael, John Carter, Saul Chernos, Reese Cleghorn, Lee Daniels, Joe Davis, Lynn Davis, Rob Davis, Jeff Deal, Peter Dykstra, Tricia Easterling, Bill Eby, William Emerson, Mark Ethridge, Michael Evans, Peter Fairley, Keith Ferrell, Fred First, Douglas Fischer, Jon Franklin, Christy George, Larry Gibson, Steve Goldstein, Jamie Goodman, Jim and Laurie Grunig, George Guess, Maria Gunnoe, Janet Hahn, Chris Harrell, Stuart Harrell, Wess Harris, Katherine Hawkins, Pauli Hayes, Vince Hazelton, Tom Henry, Mary Anne Hitt, Cheryl Hogue, William Holmberg, Don Hopey, John Hopkins, Cathy Jackson, Steve Jackson, Taryn Jackson, Tim Jackson, Marsha Johnstone, William Johnstone, Myrl Jones, Detjan Jontes, Steve Kahl, Twange Kasoma, Leigh Ann Kelly, Jamie Kitman, Lenny Kohm, Dianne Kopec, Roland Lazenby, Jay Letto, Francesca Lyman, Mike Mansur, Glen Martin, Robert McClure, Pete Meyers, Cindy Miller, Carlton Minter, Nancy Minter, Sam Minner, Jim Motavalli, Stephen Mulkey, Rita Nardy, Mark Neuzil, Sharon Oosterhook, Paul Pallante, Beth Parke, Chris Rigel, Sam Riley, Mara Robbins, Ann Mary Roberts, Judith Robinson, Jamie Ross, Craig Saunders, Mark Schleifstein, Keith Schneider, Roland Schnell, Debra Schwarz, Fred Singer, Scott Sklar, Dan Smith, Luke Staengl, Joe Staniunis, Bob Stepno, Rick Stevens, Peter Thompson, Greg Tovar, Suzanna Tovar, Pam Trent, Robert Trent, Phyllis Turk, Alice Walker, Jeff Walker, Bud Ward, Ken Ward, Christian Warren, Elizabeth Warriner, Matt Wasson, Tim Wheeler, Carolyn Whetzel, Dale Willman, Mary Wise, Nick Witheford, Roger Witherspoon, and Lynn Zoch.

Special thanks to Astrid Blome of the Gutenberg museum; John Bowles of the Selu Conservancy; Ivanka Knezevic at the University of Toronto; Roland Lazenby, author of *Michael Jordan, The Life*; Sandro Berra of Fondazione Tipoteca Italiana; and Barbara Valotti at the Fondazione Guglielmo Marconi.

Finally, much of this publication would not have been possible without the efforts of countless people in the community of scholars who are making a daily effort to place vital information on the World Wide Web. That sense of community fosters hope for the future of an emerging global culture.

Preface

Working in newsrooms, late into the evening hours, my colleagues and I would sip coffee and sift through stacks of news reports and wire service photos from all over the world. Occasionally, as Atlanta editor Ralph McGill once said, we'd get a sense of the earth wheeling again towards the sun, alive with joys and struggling with sorrows—and all reflected in hundreds of laser photos and wire service stories.

We lived through the last days of hot lead typesetting, chattering Associated Press teletypes, and Western Union telegrams. We fiddled with the first word processors and struggled with the first modems. We saw the media for what it was, and what it was meant to be.

In many ways, we were glad that it was the end of an era. We were all too aware of the media's constraints in the late twentieth century, and we wondered how things would look on the other side of the digital revolution that we knew was coming. We figured that, as with any revolution, we would see both ennobling and corrosive impacts. And that was right.

What we did not expect, and what made the digital revolution so interesting, was that it did not spring from the technology developed by media institutions, big computer companies, and defense industries. Instead, to paraphrase John Adams, we saw the digital revolution first taking place in the hearts and minds of a global community of scientists, engineers, writers, philosophers, artists, and visionaries. The technology emerged from the vision.

Trying to make sense of this, what historians are finding is that a similar sense of community animated most of the great communications revolutions in history. Gutenberg's printing press spread rapidly across Europe in the 1400s thanks to a community of craftsmen; Daguerre literally gave away photographic patents in 1839 and created a world community of photographers almost overnight; and Morse's Code became the first universal software in the 1840s, although his telegraphic patents ended up in the hands of a monopoly. Even so, a community of critics who fought the telegraph monopoly funded Alexander Graham Bell's work to create the telephone, and the global community of scientists investigating electromagnetic phenomena were the ones who created radio, television, and satellite communications.

Studying this pattern, it seems that every communications revolution is circumventing a previous communications bottleneck, and that this sparks social change. Every revolution has its medium, and every new medium creates its own form of revolution.

The benefits of all of these communication revolutions are well known to those of us living in the early twenty-first century. But revolutions come with unexpected costs.

Printing liberated humanity, but also triggered centuries of religious and political struggle; visual communication deepened human empathy but diluted and (some say) degraded public discourse; electronic communication energized the world's nervous system, but in the process, submerged unique cultures and put nationalism on steroids; and now the digital revolution seems to be undermining the literate cultures that were created by the printing press while pulling the world closer together in unpredictable and often uncomfortable ways.

To understand these interesting times, a sense of history is a basic requirement. Without history, we are blind and powerless. With history, at the very least, we are not blind, and occasionally, we may perceive an opening for a real contribution to our common destiny.

Bill Kovarik, Floyd, Virginia

For updates and ongoing information, please see:
http://www.revolutionsincommunication.com.

Introduction

Civilizations rise and fall on the crests of great revolutions in communication, brought on by new technologies and limited only by human imagination.

Well into the first decades of the twenty-first century, we are witnessing these revolutions visibly transforming daily life, not only through new gadgetry but also through shifting modes of communication that shunt aside the older ones. Fortunes are being made and lost, legacies are thrown to the winds, and a new world media is rising in the place of the old, for good and for ill.

To understand and learn from events, and to envision the possibilities of the future, we turn to history. Not just history as a worship of heroes, a cultivation of values, or a defense of tradition. Rather, history in the larger sense: history as investigation; history as a serious search for truth; as Thucydides said, history as a possession for all time.

So, first we'll consider the general issues in history, and then some of the specific issues and patterns in media history and the history of technology.

1 Understanding History

To begin with, history is civilization's memory. Without a sense of the past—without some concept of the lives, triumphs and mistakes of people who have lived before us—we are merely groping blindly into the future.

History is also an active investigation of what happened and what we can learn from the past. The meaning comes from the Greek word, ἱστορία—historia, meaning "inquiry, knowledge acquired by investigation."

Historians are free to explore their topics without expecting to find exact answers, as would usually be required in the sciences or social sciences. While history has a strong duty to accuracy and the truth, history plays by its own rules and answers to its own muse.

History is a powerful tool, not only in terms of analytical ability and scope, but also in the way it can be used to legitimize modern agendas and political projects. As journalist-turned-historian Alan Nevins said, "History is never above the melee. It is not allowed to be neutral, but forced to enlist in every army." Historian Eugen Weber once observed that history is "the dressing room of politics."

Recording and learning from the past is no simple proposition, and history is more than collections of established facts, just as science is much more than an unchanging description of a static physical world. Historical perspectives may change as new facts emerge from research, or as historians use new tools, or as modern perspectives change.

2 Motivations for Historians

Two fundamental motivations for historians are, (1) to remember and honor history's heroes; and, (2) to learn the lessons of history. These were expressed by the two major historians of ancient Greece. The two can be complementary, but they are often at cross purposes.

Herodotus (484–420 BCE) said he wrote *The History* "in the hope of … [p]reserving from decay the remembrance of what men have done, and of preventing the great and wonderful actions of the Greeks and the Barbarians from losing their due need [recognition] of glory." This is "heroic" history.

Thucydides (460–400 BCE) hoped *The History of the Peloponnesian War* would "be judged useful by those inquirers who desire an exact knowledge of the past as an aid to the interpretation of the future … I have written my work, not … to win the applause of the moment, but as a possession for all time." This is "critical" history.

Heroic history often omits the blemishes and controversies, so that when young students are first introduced to history, the heroics get far more attention and controversies are lacquered over. Heroic history has its place—it can help form a basis for cultural or regional pride, or provide, as historian Joseph Campbell once said, "the inspiration for aspiration." Yet heroic history untempered by Thucydides' critical perspective can produce dangerous myths, leading to cultural isolation or extremes of self-righteousness.

Historically damaging myths have included the Dolchstoßlegende, or "stab in the back" myth, that was current in Germany after World War I. That myth blamed Germany's defeat not on military failure, which was the truth, but rather on a lie about unpatriotic people on the home front, and it helped feed anti-Semitism that mushroomed into the Holocaust. Another damaging historical myth is the "Gone with the Wind" myth that portrays the American South fighting for a noble "lost cause" in the Civil War. The truth was far less glamorous.

This may bring to mind the best-known idea about history, which comes from George Santayana (1863–1952), who said, "Those who cannot remember the past are condemned to repeat it." There's always some motive for writing history, and often it is a combination of the heroic and critical perspective and a desire to inform modern policy. Edward Gibbon's (1737–94) *History of the Decline and Fall of the Roman Empire* was an early modern example of a critical history written with the British Empire very much in mind, but also as a celebration of Roman heroes at a time when Britain was looking for its own heroic inspirations.

3 Can History be Objective?

One of the most important questions in the study of history (called historiography) involves the extent to which cultural and personal allegiances can or should be separated from narrative history. People often expect that dry facts, neatly arranged, will speak for themselves, but that idea is at the center of long-standing struggles between contending schools of historical thought.

The best-remembered proponent of the "scientific" historical philosophy was Leopold Von Ranke (1795–1886), a German historian. He thought that historians should report "the way things really were." An account of the battle of Waterloo should be based on facts commonly accredited by French, German, and English historians, he said.

To be sure, Von Ranke was reacting to British historian Thomas Carlyle's quirky and melodramatic 1837 history of the French Revolution, or to American historian George Bancroft's notion that the United States was created more or less as an act of God. Both approaches were heavily influenced by the personal biases of the historian, and this is what Von Ranke's scientific school found objectionable.

Yet there are also flaws in the "scientific" approach to history. For example, while few would disagree on facts about the Battle of Waterloo, larger issues, such as the rise of Napoleon or the European revolutions of 1848, are not seen in the same objective light by all historians. Similarly, Von Ranke's own history of the Protestant Reformation in Germany, although meticulous in most detail, omits at least one important theme: the impact of the printing press in spreading Martin Luther's ideas and helping ensure the Reformation's success.

Von Ranke's contemporary in Britain was Thomas Macaulay (1800–59), but his idea about historical accuracy was to be sweeping and inclusive. Macaulay wrote that history is incomplete if it only involves palace intrigues and great battles.

> It will be my endeavor to relate the history of the people as well as the history of the government, to trace the progress of useful and ornamental arts, to describe the rise of religious sects and the changes of literary taste, to portray the manners of successive generations and not to pass by with neglect even the revolutions which have taken place in dress, furniture, repasts, and public amusements. I shall cheerfully bear the reproach of having descended below the dignity of history, if I can succeed in placing before the English of the nineteenth century a true picture of the life of their ancestors. (Macauley 1848)

Perhaps objectivity is unattainable; perhaps it's quixotic to even speak of it. In *That Noble Dream*, historian Peter Novick describes historians' often futile attempts to attain objectivity in the past two centuries. Not surprisingly, Novick says, many historians disliked the idea of serving up a string of scientifically cold facts as much as they disliked Carlyle's style and Bancroft's American piety. Not everything in human affairs can or should be quantified, and a "science of history" was a farce, some said. Their response was to write history in a way that would be more relevant, or progressive, or uplifting. Prominent among these progressive historians were American historian Charles Beard (1874–1948) and Lord John Edward Acton (1834–1902) of Britain.

Beard used an interesting scientific analogy to describe what he valued in history. It wasn't enough to classify fact after fact, like a botanist's classification of species after species. That approach "does not explain … proximate or remote causes and relations." What was needed was something more interpretive and exploratory, more like the broader study of ecology. So, for example, Beard's most famous and controversial book,

An Economic Interpretation of the US Constitution, argued that American Revolutionary leaders were not merely idealistic, but also were acting in the interests of their social and economic class (Beard 1913).

Lord Acton believed in a moral approach to history. His most famous aphorism is, "Power tends to corrupt, and absolute power corrupts absolutely." The idea comes from an exchange with a colleague about the doctrine of papal infallibility. The colleague had suggested that great men should not be judged too harshly because they were dealing with great issues. Acton disagreed. On the contrary, he said, great men should be held up to an even higher standard, under suspicion that they had become corrupted by power. Acton's *History of Freedom in Christianity* was written with critical ideas about the papacy and uplifting Protestant motives in mind.

Late twentieth-century historian Howard Zinn, like Macaulay, would say that a people's history is far more than an account that tugs on the heartstrings of culture or patriotism. A people's history describes the lives of the powerless as well as the powerful while rejecting, like Action, the myth-making heroics that can obscure the immorality of the powerful.

In the years following World War II, historians moved towards an exploration of the consensus that holds societies together, tending to downplay some of the conflicts. Daniel J. Boorstin was among the leaders in the 1950s and 1960s. But the consensus approach, with the Grand Narrative in the background, did not explain the histories of emerging social movements, especially civil rights of minorities, the women's movement, and the environmental movement. Nor did consensus describe the social turmoil that broke out across Europe and the US in the late 1960s and 1970s. Historians began investigating a variety of new approaches under the heading of social history (Gage 2011).

4 Whig History and Other Fallacies

Scientific objectivity wasn't the only problem, according to historian Herbert Butterfield (1900–79). A larger problem was the tendency of historians to take sides. Butterfield objected to the way historians would "write on the side of Protestants and Whigs, to praise revolutions, provided they have been successful, to emphasize certain principles of progress in the past, and to produce a story which is the ratification if not the glorification of the present." This is often called "Whig" history.

Thomas Macaulay saw these extremes as errors, and advised historians to take a more balanced approach:

> There are two opposite errors into which those who study the annals of our country are in constant danger of falling, the error of judging the present by the past, and the error of judging the past by the present. The former is the error of minds prone to reverence whatever is old, the latter of minds readily attracted by whatever is new. The former error may perpetually be observed in the reasonings of conservative politicians on the questions of their own day. The latter error perpetually infects the speculations of writers of the liberal school when they discuss the transactions of an earlier age. The former error is the more pernicious in a statesman, and the latter in a historian.

A related problem is called the "historian's fallacy," in which we assume that people in the past had the knowledge that we have today, which can lead to unwarranted conclusions about cause and effect. A good historian, avoiding the "historian's fallacy," will take into account the "fog of war," or the limitations on what could have been known at the time.

Another kind of fallacy involves cultural restrictions on historians themselves. Women and minorities were rarely taken seriously as historians until the mid- to late twentieth century, despite outstanding contributions. One who broke through the glass ceiling was Barbara Tuchman, who won a Pulitzer Prize in 1963 for *The Guns of August*, her history of the outbreak of World War I. Another was Elizabeth Eisenstein, whose theories about the influence of printing on early modern Europe changed the way we see the history of communication. Her ideas are discussed in Chapter 1 of this book.

Is there an end of history? To some, such as Francis Fukuyama (1952–present) and Jean Baudrillard (1929–2007), the collapse of ideology or even the end of an *idea* of historical progress represents the "end of history." According to Baudrillard, this comes from the abandonment of utopian visions shared by both the right- and left-wing political ideologies (Fukuyama 1992; Baudrillard 1994).

And yet, ideas about utopian futures re-emerged with the advance of communications technologies, living on in the visions of social networks and free cultures described by Vannevar Bush, John Perry Barlow, Howard Rheingold, Richard Stallman, and others engaged in the digital revolution, as we will see in Chapters 11 and 12.

These, then, are some of the initial issues we encounter when we consider how history is written. The question of objectivity see-saws across the centuries between ideals of accuracy on the one hand and high purpose on the other. It never really ends, but each historian finds points of balance. If there are no final answers, there is at least a need to be conscious of the issues; to attempt to steer one's own best course past the Scylla and Charybdis of historiographic calamity; to write the truth to one's best ability; and to serve the muse of history.

5 The Study of Communication History

The historical study of the whole field of communication is relatively new, but histories of the press and biographies of notable editors have been popular for centuries. These include Joseph Moxon's *Mechanick Exercises* (1683); S. Palmer's *History of Printing* (1733); Isaiah Thomas's *History of Printing in America* (1810); James Parton's *Life of Horace Greeley* (1855); *The Life and Times of Benjamin Franklin* (1864); Frederic Hudson's *Journalism in the United States* (1873); and James Melvin Lee's *History of American Journalism* (1917). (All are available online through Project Gutenberg, Google Books, and others; they are listed on this book's web site.) Moxon and Palmer were intending to strengthen the allegiance of initiates to the profession; Thomas, Parton, Hudson, and Lee all took the heroic approach, although Lee faced criticism in his time for "a complacent and partisan denial" of problems with the news media (Grabo 1918).

Critical perspectives of the news business did begin appearing in the twentieth century, as part of the Progressive Age. No doubt some were inspired by US president Teddy

Roosevelt's 1906 speech denouncing journalistic muckraking, but others thought the news media far too complacent. Will Irwin's *American Newspaper* (1911) appeared in Colliers magazine at a time when the power of the press was "greater than ever before." Irwin noted many problems as well as contributions from the "light of civilization." Another critical approach was socialist reformer Upton Sinclair's *Brass Check* (1920), which focused on the warped reporting of labor struggles and compared journalism to outright prostitution. The *New York Times* reacted by calling Sinclair a "defiling insect" and refusing him editorial space for his views (Goldstein 2007).

Other examples of press criticism are found in Walter Lippmann's 1920 book *Public Opinion* and the Hutchins Commission of 1947—both discussed later in this book—but very few histories of communication saw the light of print.

Edwin Emery and other twentieth-century American media historians focused primarily on a progressive, narrative history of American journalism, following closely behind Hudson and Lee, but updating US media history during the Civil Rights era and the Vietnam War (Emery 1973). The exclusive focus on American journalism, rather than international communication, was typical of the times. Even the American minority press appeared only briefly until Jean Folkerts's book, *Voices of a Nation*, brought a more thorough and long-overdue treatment (Folkerts and Teeter 1989).

In his intellectual history of communication in the US, Daniel Czitrom noted the "surprising dearth of historical precedents." His book, *Media and the American Mind*, covered telegraph, movies, the radio, and historical views of the media. More comprehensive books include *The Story of Human Communication* (1988) by media theorist Wilbur Schramm, and *Social History of the Media* (2002) by Asa Briggs and Peter Burke. Both are strong examples of themed sociological approaches to the history of communication.

6 Parochialism in Communication History

Most students of media history were painfully aware of the narrow outlook that afflicted their field in the early twenty-first century. Not only were media historians barely managing to catch up to great historical issues, such as civil rights and the digital technology revolution, but the attachment to professional and nationalistic heroism was all too obvious. Controversies were often overlooked, especially if they involved complex international issues. This nationalism is contrary to modern trends, according to historian Jonathan Shaw:

> Historians increasingly recognize that trying to understand the past solely within the confines of national boundaries misses much of the story. Perhaps the integration of today's world has fostered a renewed appreciation for global connections in the past. Historians now see that the same patterns … emerge across cultures worldwide through time, and they are trying to explain why. (Shaw 2014)

In his call for an international history of journalism, Mitchell Stephens said,

> To attempt to separate the history of American journalism from developments overseas seems … as foolish as attempting to separate the history of journalism in Ohio or Kansas

> from what was happening in Boston, Philadelphia and New York … A kind of ignorance—which would not be tolerated in literature departments, in theater departments, in art departments, in science departments—is routinely accepted in journalism departments. American journalism history is dangerously and unflaggingly parochial. (Stephens 2011)

The same point should be made across the sub-disciplines of communication. Why should we separate the history of photography from advertising and journalism, or the history of computing from the history of broadcasting? If we do that, we risk missing some of the overlapping effects of the technological revolutions that are having a profound impact on life in the twenty-first century. We also miss seeing the way digital technologies undermined the newspaper industry starting in the 1960s and 1970s; we miss seeing the rise and fall of radio and television broadcasting networks; and we might miss an understanding of the way that artists and reformers have, when confronted by political obstacles, used ever-evolving new media technologies to circumvent the old ones.

This book, *Revolutions in Communication*, attempts to take international, technological, and professional issues as the framework for the narrative structure of media history. Of course, constructing a history that approaches a broad professional and international scope presents an interesting problem of scale; there is far too much to include in a standard encyclopedia, much less a single book.

One solution is to take advantage of the new media that this book describes. We might see this book as an initial structural framework for a much broader international history of the media that is already begun on a variety of collaborative websites such as Wikipedia. Since we live in revolutionary times, we ought to reflect and model those revolutionary new modes of communication in the way communication history is taught—and written.

With that in mind, readers can turn to this book's website—www.revolutionsincommunication.com—for resources that can enhance understanding of the depth, breadth, scope and geographic reach of media history topics.

7 Communication and the History of Technology

The use of tools has often been seen as one of the characteristics that distinguishes humans as a species. The historical study of technology and culture involves questions about the creation, diffusion and social impacts of tools and techniques to extend human power for agriculture, communication, energy, transportation, warfare, and other fields. Which of these techniques and fields have had more influence over civilization is a source of ongoing debate and exploration over the centuries. Technological progress was the primary factor driving civilization, according to some early anthropologists, while others have seen the use of energy or the accumulation of information as central to cultural development.

Mass media technology has had a special influence, according to many historians. We need to ask how this influence has been evident in the past and what is its likely path in the future.

7.1 Harold Innis, Marshall McLuhan, and media technologies

Two mid-twentieth-century historians most concerned with media technologies and their place in history were Harold Innis and Marshall McLuhan.

Harold Innis (1894–1952) was an economic historian who said that Western civilization has been profoundly influenced by communication technologies, while Marshall McLuhan (1911–80) was a media critic who was strongly influenced by Innis and also put communication at the center of history and social life.

Innis had the idea that civilizations using durable media tended to be oriented toward time and religious orthodoxy (Babylon), while, on the other hand, cultures with flexible media (Rome, Greece, modern) were oriented toward control of space and a secular approach to life.

> The concepts of time and space reflect the significance of media to civilization. Media that emphasize time are those durable in character such as parchment, clay and stone. The heavy materials are suited to the development of architecture and sculpture. Media that emphasize space are apt to be less durable and light in character such as papyrus and paper. The latter are suited to wide areas in administration and trade. (Innis 1950)

Figure 0.1
Time, space and communication—Harold Innis (1894–1952), a Canadian historian, noted that flexible or durable communications media had implications for the organization of empires. Photo by William A. James, Jr., Toronto City Archives.

What this implies is both obvious and far-reaching. Clearly, detailed instructions and correspondence over a distance can take place only if medium is light and flexible enough to carry the message. A dozen letters of credit on parchment are far easier to carry than a dozen clay tablets. But rather less obviously, the qualities of media flexibility and durability may be important elements in the way a civilization is organized. The fact that you can have letters of credit means you can have a banking system with branches across large distances.

McLuhan extended Innis's ideas, which he summed up in the statement, "The medium is the message." By that, McLuhan meant that the kind of communication media—print, imaging, broadcasting, or computing—has a strong influence not only on the message itself, but also on the type of thinking and the development of the culture creating the messages. A literate print culture is very different from a visual or radio or television culture, McLuhan said.

Many people thought literate culture would be weakened by television and radio, just as generations before thought that religious oral cultures would be weakened by printing. McLuhan was relatively optimistic, although not utopian, about media technology. Digitally controlled international broadcast media were connecting print and imaging and radio and television through satellites in the 1950s and 1960s, when he was active, and the convergence of media cultures to extend human perceptions would expand exponentially, leading us into a twenty-first-century "global village." This would not lead to universal peace and happiness, he believed, but it would allow humanity to approach a greater degree of cultural maturity.

Figure 0.2 Global villager—Marshall McLuhan (1911–80), a Canadian media theorist, saw changes in communications technology having deep social impacts. Photo courtesy of Michael McLuhan.

7.2 Determinism versus social construction of media technology

When historians consider how a technology is developed, there are often two basic schools of thought at work: determinism and social construction. Determinists see technologies as path-dependent, with inevitable changes and consequently predictable impacts on society. Social constructionists see a stronger influence for economics, politics, and culture that controls technological development. Neither is right or wrong, and both perspectives are often applied to the study of media technology.

Marshall McLuhan took this deterministic view when he said we need to anticipate the process of social change that communication technologies generate. But whether or not we anticipate the change, there will still be an impact.

> Because of today's terrific speed-up of information moving, we have a chance to apprehend, predict and influence the environmental forces shaping us—and thus win back control of our own destinies. The new extensions of man and the environment they generate are the central manifestations of the evolutionary process, and yet we still cannot free ourselves of the delusion that it is how a medium is used that counts, rather than what it does to us and with us. (*Playboy* 1969)

Technological determinism was probably best articulated by historian Charles Beard, who said, "Technology marches in seven-league boots from one ruthless, revolutionary conquest to another, tearing down old factories and industries, flinging up new processes with terrifying rapidity" (Beard 1927). It was simplified into the grim motto of the 1933 Chicago World's Fair: "Science Finds, Industry Applies, Man Conforms."

To a large extent, as I will argue in this book, media technologies have been seen as less deterministic than (for example) technologies in energy or transportation. Still, it's important to realize that many experts see unavoidable impacts in media technologies.

For example, fiber optics, satellites, and digital networks have "flattened" the world, according to *New York Times* columnist Thomas Friedman. They have made it just as easy to process information or do business in India as it is in Europe or North America, he notes in his 2005 book, *The World is Flat*. While social institutions might buffer some of the impacts, the global sharing of semi-skilled information work has brought the world closer but has also destabilized employment in banking, news, entertainment, and other areas.

For example, Eastman Kodak, film and camera company, once employed 140,000 people, but went bankrupt in 2012 after widespread adoption of digital cameras. Where did all that economic value go, asks Jaron Lanier in a 2014 book, *Who Owns the Future?* Digital networks tend to centralize wealth and limit overall economic growth, enriching only a few in the process, he says.

According to Google founder Larry Page, the acceleration of digital technologies might eventually eliminate nine of out ten jobs, but may also make basic living costs much cheaper. "When we have computers that can do more and more jobs, it's going to change how we think about work. There's no way around that. You can't wish it away" (Walters 2014). This is classic determinism, of course, since "wishing" is certainly not the only possible social constraint on technology.

The possibility that technology could accelerate to a point where no social process could exert any control whatsoever is considered to be a technological "singularity" beyond which any future is opaque. For example, futurist Raymond Kurzweil asks what would happen if the global network of computers acquired intelligence. That would be a "singularity," because after that, no one could predict what might happen. The network could even make decisions about ending all human existence (Kurzweil 2005).

The counter-thesis to technological determinism is social construction of technology, which is the idea that social processes (including politics, economics, and culture) have more influence on the development of a technology or on its impacts than the technology's own characteristics.

For example, in most countries during the early to mid-twentieth century, nearly all communication media—from post offices to telegraph companies, to telephone and radio television systems—were socially constructed through national and international telecommunications regulatory agencies, such as the International Telecommunications Union (part of the United Nations) and, on the national level, agencies like the US Federal Communications Commission. Only print media achieved a relatively high degree of freedom, through the First Amendment in the US and similar traditions in Europe and other countries.

The relatively negative experience with over-regulation of electronic media in the US during the mid-twentieth century had a strong influence on the way the world wide web was socially constructed in the 1990s, when innovators successfully argued that the Web should be relatively unregulated, like print media (Rand 1998; *Reno v. ACLU* 1997).

Another perspective on the social construction of technology is that inventors themselves tend to infuse their own values into technology. For example, Steve Jobs of Apple computers wanted to make personal computing possible and then tried to control it when he was successful; Thomas Edison also tried to retain control of the motion picture industry. Sometimes an inventor's values come into conflict with powerful industrial or social forces. Brian Winston, for example, describes the emergence of some media technologies as influenced by what he calls the law of the suppression of radical potential (Winston 2008).

Similarly, values may also be infused in the broad inventive process as people come to believe that things could be done better. Historian Robert Friedel calls these "cultures of improvement," as key technologies are "captured" and become part of a sustained series of changes. The jockeying for power surrounding these technologies is the process by which a technology is controlled (Friedel 2007).

So, is the medium is the message? Or, perhaps we should ask, to what extent is the medium the message? If the dark side of printing was empire, colonialism, capitalism, and the rise of the nation state, what was the dark side of electronic and digital communication? Would the new technology just intensify the same trends? Or would it, as McLuhan believed in the 1960s, produce a qualitative change in society and cultural life, liberating users from the limitations of the past (Blondheim 2007)?

There's no question that, in comparison to McLuhan's era, we are seeing rapid, deep qualitative changes in the media and in society. Old media empires have disintegrated and new kinds of media functions are animating an emerging global culture. Rather suddenly in human history, we have instant language translation, free international encyclopedias, and free media exchanges in text, audio, and video between individuals and groups from anywhere in the world. None of these things was possible a decade ago. We also have unusual public encounters between very different cultures that have never much been in contact before, and as a result, conflicts over closely held values and an increasing drift towards international speech restrictions.

7.3 Utopians and Luddites

When people embrace technology in an extremely optimistic way, they are said to be technological utopians. For example, much of the rhetoric surrounding the development of the telegraph, the early years of radio, and the early years of the internet tended to be influenced by this sort of enthusiasm. The telegraph will make "one neighborhood of the whole country," Samuel Morse wrote about 125 years before McLuhan's idea of the "global village." Similarly, H. G. Wells envisioned the morning television report as a staple of a utopian communal village of the future (Wells 1898).

When people reject technology in an extreme and pessimistic way, they are sometimes called Luddites. The term goes back to 1811, when thousands of British textile workers lost their jobs following the introduction of steam-powered machinery. Mobs of starving workers broke the textile machinery and blamed it on a mythical figure named Ned Ludd, who, according to legend, was a simple-minded boy who accidentally broke textile machinery. Apparently, the Luddites only intended to destroy property, but there were accident deaths of mill owners, and as a result, about two dozen were executed and more were exiled to Australia. French workers with a similar idea of resisting unfair working conditions by breaking machinery with wooden shoes (sabots) led to the term sabotage.

The Luddite movement was very much on the mind of London *Times* owner John Walter II when he promised workers that they would keep their jobs even after steam printing presses were introduced in 1814. Walter's enlightened response didn't work 150 years later, when printing technology triggered a wave of "new Luddite" labor disputes, including the very damaging four-month New York newspaper strike of 1962–3 (Kempton 1962).

Enthusiasm for new technologies has been more the rule than the exception, but skepticism about virtually every technology is not difficult to find in history. One of the chief critics of technology in the nineteenth century was Henry David Thoreau (1817–62), the transcendentalist writer and author of "Walden." He was especially skeptical about the telegraph, which he considered merely "an improved means to an unimproved end."

Another technological skeptic was writer and diplomat Henry Adams (1838–18). He worried that civilization had left behind an old world concerned with religion and had entered a new one, a world concerned with science and technology but morally and philosophically adrift. His point of comparison of the two ages of civilization was between the Virgin, a symbol of old Europe, and the Dynamo, a symbol of new Europe (Adams 1917). This idea has been often repeated in discussions about technology.

7.4. Fallacies and anachronisms

Sometimes predictions for technological directions that do not occur are called technological fallacies. The fallacy that computers would lead to a police state is important to consider in the history of computing because, in the 1970s, it led to a preference for individual, non-networked personal computers.

It was also a partial fallacy for Alexander Graham Bell and other inventors of the late nineteenth century to predict that the telephone would be used more or less as a medium for music and news broadcasting, in the way that eventually occurred with radio in the 1920s. It was a complete fallacy for Guglielmo Marconi, inventor of the radio, to predict that radio waves could stimulate plants and act as a new kind of fertilizer. In the 1950s and 1960s, comic book detectives carried "wrist televisions" like wrist watches to communicate with each other—again, something of a partial fallacy, in that such devices are possible. Following the introduction of the Apple watch, which doubles as a cell phone and personal information assistant, we may now have the return of the comic book detective.

Envisioning the future has always been an interesting and sometimes productive pastime, but the future isn't what it used to be, as many authors have noted. The atomic-powered airplane, the personal helicopter, the robot valet—all have been chalked up by now as technological fallacies (Barbrook 2007; Dregni 2006).

Anachronisms (which means "contrary to time") often confuse two or more time periods. For instance, medieval paintings and Renaissance-era woodcuts often portray biblical figures with fashions or weapons typical of the era when the paintings or woodcuts were made. The usual portrait of Johannes Gutenberg is an anachronism, since it was created to illustrate a different person 100 years after Gutenberg's death and totally misses the typical fashions and style of Gutenberg's era in Mainz, Germany, as noted in Chapter 1.

7.5 Classifying media—hot and cool

Media can be classified by their impacts on audiences, McLuhan said in his 1964 book *Understanding Media*. Some types of media tend to be "hot"—that is, they invite easy participation and less conscious immersion. Others tend to be "cool," and audience members have to take a more active role in constructing meaning.

Just where each medium might fall on a hot-cool spectrum depends on its cultural and technological context. In the 1960s, McLuhan could say that cinema was "hot" because audiences were fully immersed in the medium, suspending disbelief, while television was "cool" because, at the time, it was a low-definition medium that required some effort to enjoy. Yet over time, as television technology improved, the medium became more and more immersive. Today, McLuhan might see television as much hotter than it once was.

The idea wasn't entirely new; for example, Enlightenment philosopher David Hume said in 1742 that a free press should not be feared because the medium could not incite rebellion: "A man reads a book or pamphlet alone, coolly. There is no one present from whom he can catch the passion by contagion" (Hume 1742).

The categories are not really fixed, and McLuhan often said provocative things he called "probes" just to stir up conversation. For instance, he thought of radio as a "hot" medium since it immersed audiences, and yet many others have seen radio as requiring a sense of imagination to fill in the details of the story, which would make it a "cool" medium. Perhaps his most provocative idea was that "hot" new media technology could be so overwhelming that many people would go into a subtle state of shock, a "psychic rigor mortis," as they tried to "cool off" its effects. Modern concerns about addiction to social media and online video gaming systems might be seen as examples of this idea.

In any event, McLuhan's linear view of hot–cool media categories is only the beginning of the study of psychological reactions to media. Studies of brain activity using functional magnetic resonance imaging (fMRI), which was not available in McLuhan's time, show that reading books and watching cinema affect different portions of the brain and deepen our ability to understand the complexities of social life. And yet, for reasons not yet explained, television has less of this effect (Paul 2012).

7.6 Media trajectories: McLuhan's tetrad of technology change

New communications technologies change and grow in familiar patterns that McLuhan said could be mapped out in what he called a "tetrad" of four effects. A new medium can (1) enhance, (2) obsolesce, (3) retrieve, and (4) reverse. For example, the arrival of radio enhanced news and music, it obsolesced (or made less prominent) print and visual media; it retrieved the spoken word and vaudeville-style music hall shows; and it reversed (when pushed to its limits) into television (McLuhan 1992). We might also say that television enhanced the visual, obsolesced the audio, retrieved theatrical spectacle, and reversed into "500 channels with nothing on."

The comparison can help clarify and anticipate some of the social changes that technology creates. We ask:

1 What does the new medium *enhance* or amplify?
2 What becomes *obsolete* or driven out of prominence?

3 What is *retrieved* that had nearly been forgotten from an earlier time?
4 How does the medium *reverse* or flip or diminish into something different?

What about digital communication and the Internet? In his 1964 book, *Gutenberg Galaxy*, McLuhan said, "A computer as a research and communication instrument could enhance retrieval, obsolesce mass library organization, retrieve the individual's encyclopedic function and flip into a private line to speedily tailored data of a salable kind." In other words, networked computers would facilitate memory but allow commercial invasions of privacy.

A further example is the effect of digital networks on print media. The impact of digital media has been to enhance immediacy, obsolesce printed newspapers, retrieve letter writing, and reverse or diminish the political culture of the press.

As media revolutions continue to reverberate, McLuhan's tetrad is a useful way of considering change, although we need to be careful about the uncertainty of historical cause-and-effect relationships. In formal logic, cause-and-effect can involve necessary, sufficient, or contributory causes. Modern historians tend to think mainly in terms of contributory causes because the field is so broad, and so many alternative explanations are possible for complex situations. Historians also tend to consider inter-related levels of impact, such as primary, secondary, and tertiary impacts that may come into play.

A primary impact of printing, for instance, was to make it easier to publish Bibles, and most translations of the Bible into national languages took place after the introduction of printing around 1455. A secondary impact of these translated Bibles was to provide a model for the unification of national languages, which were often quite different from region to region. A tertiary impact of translated Bibles was the ease with which Church doctrines could now be questioned, which contributed to the Protestant Reformation.

7.7 Classifying media services

Another way to understand the changes in mass media is to consider how information is created and channeled (See Figure 0.3). If the source of information and the choice of viewing time and place are all centrally determined, from within a media company, then this is a top-down, traditional mass media service. If the individual controls reception time and place by using a recorder or a video-on-demand service, then that is rich content.

On the other hand, if the individual controls both the content and the time and place of reception, that's social media, where everyone is both a source and a receiver. And if an individual is the source and the control is central, it's probably a virtual market place.

The diagram is an important demonstration of the use of theory in communications history. The idea that rich content, virtual markets and social media could be created with digital technology was an important inspiration for software engineers.

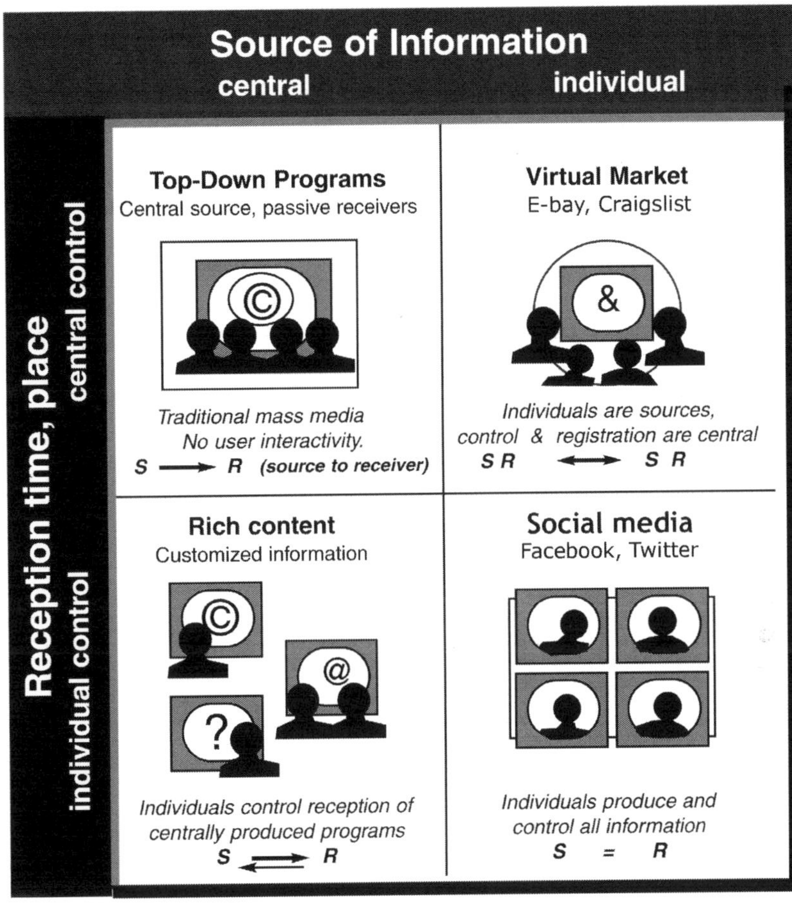

Figure 0.3 Media Traffic—Digital networks have enabled revolutionary changes in the flow of communication, as this chart shows. Traditional media (upper left) is characterized by central control of production at the source as well as central control of the time and place of reception. Other forms of media traffic are characterized by some level of individual control. Illustration by Bill Kovarik; adapted from Sally J. MacMillan, 1999.

For additional reading, discussion questions, links to video, and other suggestions, see www.revolutionsincommunications.com.

Part I

The Printing Revolution

> We should notice the force, effect, and consequences of inventions, which are nowhere more conspicuous than in those three which were unknown to the ancients; namely, printing, gunpowder, and the compass. For these three have changed the appearance and state of the whole world; first in literature, then in warfare, and lastly in navigation: and innumerable changes have been thence derived, so that no empire, sect, or star, appears to have exercised a greater power and influence on human affairs than these mechanical discoveries.
>
> Francis Bacon, *Novum Organum*, 1620

1 Printing

The printing revolution bridged the medieval and modern worlds with enormous force, effect, and consequences. Beginning in 1454, printing technology spread quickly over Europe and played a central role in the great sweep of events—the Renaissance, the Protestant Reformation, the Enlightenment, and the political, industrial, and scientific revolutions from the 1600s to the twenty-first century.

Before printing, people were linked through individual and small group communication, within oral and manuscript cultures, in Asian and then European civilizations. The need to replicate these manuscripts first inspired woodblock printing and then moveable type.

After printing, the sudden acceleration of communication had enormous social and political impacts, leading to even greater acceleration and ever-expanding horizons. The original printing revolution in Europe was followed by the industrialization of media technologies in the nineteenth century—including the telegraph and steam-powered printing—which created the opportunity for larger audiences and new institutions to serve them.

The resulting newspapers and wire services, said Chicago publisher Joseph Medill, were like proud steam ships, "bidding defiance to the tempests, laden with the mails and commerce of the world" (Brendon 1983). Titanic industrial media institutions of all types continued defying the tempests through the nineteenth and twentieth centuries.

Then, by the early twenty-first century, the proud old steamers of the press began sinking, losing two-thirds of their income and most of their value. In city after city, the empty newsrooms were like ghost ships of the press, no longer bidding defiance to anything but their creditors.

The question is not so much about why they faltered. Centuries from now, historians will probably ask instead: how is it that the cultures and institutions growing out of the printing revolution were able to survive so well for five and a half centuries, from 1455 to the early twenty-first century? What cultures and institutions replaced them, and with what force and effect today?

This section on the Printing Revolution compresses these 550 years of publishing into three chapters in order to take the broadest possible view of media history.

- Chapter 1 covers the early printing revolution up to 1814;
- Chapter 2 describes the industrial media revolution in the following century; and
- Chapter 3 describes the central role and rapid fall of print media in the twentieth century.

However, in order to appreciate the printing revolution, we first need to understand the oral culture and manuscript culture that it replaced.

2 Before the Printing Revolution: Oral Culture

Since the emergence of intelligent humanity, groups of people have communicated within what we call an oral culture. Although records of oral culture don't really emerge until the dawn of writing, recent contact with once-isolated cultures and related psychological research has shown that oral cultures have their own forms of wisdom and integrity.

Research has shown, for instance, that humans are born with a natural capacity for complex language with thousands of words and symbols. Most other species, with some possible exceptions, have little capacity for anything beyond a few basic signals. Studies comparing human and primate language abilities using functional Magnetic Resonance Imaging (fMRI) have shown that the human brain has special segments devoted to language (Wolf 2008).

In other words, we are "pre-wired" to talk and communicate, and for nearly all of our natural history, we have communicated songs, folklore, history, and traditions within oral culture.

Storytelling and oral traditions appear all through the world and all through the ages (Campbell 1949). Storytellers, troubadours, and jongleurs carried songs and stories in cultures where people did not read. While the troubadours were lyric poets who dealt mainly with issues of chivalry and courtly love, the jongleurs were the itinerant singers who memorized these poems using verse and other mnemonic devices. A good jongleur or storyteller could memorize long poems or stories after hearing them only a few times (Burke 1982).

Along with the need for memorization, communication researchers such as Walter Ong have found that oral culture tends to be quite different from the print, visual, electronic, and digital cultures that followed. People in oral cultures think in concrete and practical ways, rather than using modern abstract or linear concepts. For example, familiar objects like a plate, or the moon, might be used to refer to the idea of a circle. Asked about themselves, a person in an oral culture would be reluctant to analyze or put themselves in another person's place (Ong 1982; Lerner 1958).

Figure PI.1 Oral Tradition—Storytelling, as part of traditional oral culture, goes back to the dawn of human existence. In this 1902 painting by E. Irving Couse, a Native American storyteller is recounting events around a battle.

Another attribute of people in oral cultures is that they tend to make decisions by consensus, in groups, rather than within a hierarchy. People in oral cultures tend to have polarized world-views, oriented towards good and evil. They also tend to have a love of epic sagas and poetry. Storytellers rely heavily on formulas and themes in order to recall these epics through a tradition of improvisation, mnemonic devices, and rote memory. Using these devices, oral cultures can accurately transmit important information from generation to generation.

We tend to underestimate the effectiveness of oral cultures. We're all familiar with the children's game in which a message is whispered from one person to another until it goes around a room. The message invariably gets garbled—sometimes with hilarious results—when the original message and the final message are compared. But this is misleading. When it is important, oral cultures can accurately transmit information across long distances and through generations. For example, American author Alex Haley was able to discover an oral record of his ancestors in Africa, and his search is described in the 1976 book, *Roots: The Saga of an American Family*. Similarly, the *Odyssey* and *Iliad* were originally heroic oral histories of Greek culture that were only written down many centuries after they were composed.

After the introduction of writing, oral cultures continued to exist alongside manuscript cultures. But oral cultures were considered more reliable, in that messages gained validity through oral delivery. This tradition continues to be important, for example, in the way that legislative proposals are "read" into the record, a sermon is delivered orally in a church, or a lecture is given in a classroom. Similarly, decision by consensus in the modern jury system and the corporate boardroom are vestiges of the consensus orientation of oral cultures.

The move to symbols and then written language profoundly reshaped patterns of human thinking, and it could not have been an easy process. As oral cultures became lost over time, some of the world's most poignant literature emerged in its wake. Examples would include Oliver Goldsmith's 1770 poem, *The Deserted Village*, which lamented rural communities lost to Britain's enclosure acts; Chinua Achebe's 1958 book, *Things Fall Apart*, which described the impact of European colonialism on social structures in Africa; and Anne Pancake's 2008 book, *Strange as This Weather Has Been*, which follows the social disintegration in traditional Appalachian communities created by mountaintop mining. Of course, not everyone takes a sanguine view of traditional oral cultures. "We dream that the country was idyllic in the 18th century, a lost paradise like *The Deserted Village*," said Jacob Bronowski in his *Ascent of Man*. "That is a fable. The country was a place where men worked from dawn to dark ... [i]n poverty and darkness" (Bronowski 1976).

One of the reasons radio may have been so successful as a mass medium, according to communications theorist Marshall McLuhan, was that it revived this sense of community, for example through "fireside chats" and radio drama. To McLuhan, this seemed to be a "re-tribalization" of a culture that longed for an older and more community-oriented communications system.

Another link to the old oral culture is the epic fantasy genre in books, games, and cinema, such as *Harry Potter* or *Lord of the Rings*. These movies may help recover this sense of connection to the heroic epic that was once served by the oral culture (Drout 2006; Campbell 1949).

3 Before the Printing Revolution: Symbols, Seals and Icons

The earliest known enhancements to oral culture involved symbolic Ice Age carvings from ivory and bone from as long as 45,000 years ago. These are not tools—they are intentionally carved and painted objects that are worn and polished by repeated handling over a long period. They don't seem to be related to the Ice Age cave paintings that flourished in some parts of Europe around the same time (Marshack 2003).

We don't know what role these objects played in the oral cultures in this prehistoric time. We can guess that a carving of a mother goddess may have related to fertility, or a carving of a horse might have involved pre-hunting rituals. It's also possible that the objects had some use within the group decision-making process, perhaps being passed around from speaker to speaker to indicate who had the privilege of speaking at a particular moment.

Another class of symbols before printing involved seals and stamps for making impressions on clay, wax, papyrus, or fabrics. The purpose might have been decorative or authoritative, for example, to authenticate a document. Roman historian Marcus Terentius Varro was said to have inserted images of several hundred illustrious persons by the aid of "a certain invention," thus "saving their features from oblivion" and "making them known over the wide world" (Bawker 1887). The invention was probably woodblock printing or some kind of embossing. "As thc inventor of a benefit which will fill even the gods with jealousy, he has clothed these persons with immortality," Roman historian Pliny the Elder said cryptically (De Vinne 1877).

Symbolic and visual communication was also embedded in medieval and Renaissance architecture, sculpture, and painting. These iconic images were the news and educational vehicles of the day. People of the twelfth century would visit Chartres Cathedral to learn religious stories in the same way that scholars would flock to Oxford or the Sorbonne and read books in the following centuries.

We will return to this theme in Section II, The Visual Revolution.

4 Before the Printing Revolution: Writing and Manuscript Cultures

Unlike language, writing is not pre-wired in the human brain. It had to be invented, and because of that, we often see writing as the first communications revolution that extended natural human abilities.

The first kinds of writing involved the use of clay tokens dating back to 8500 BCE to ancient Mesopotamia, and possibly just as early in ancient China (Schmandt-Besserat 1996; Rincon 2003). Meant to keep track of resources like grain and animals, these original clay tokens were three-dimensional solid shapes like spheres, cones, and cylinders kept in clay boxes. At some point along the way, the system changed from keeping 100 clay ox tokens to a symbol for the number 100 along with the symbol for ox. Increasing trade led to a further need to simplify accounting, which spurred the development of writing.

Hieroglyphic symbols emerged in Egypt around 3500 BCE, while formal Chinese writing emerged around 1500 to 1200 BCE, although some early primitive writing apparently goes back to 6600 BCE. Olmec, Zapotec, and Mayan writing emerged in Mexico in the 1000 BCE to 300 BCE era.

Like Egyptian hieroglyphs, Chinese and Mayan written languages are logographic, in that they began with representations of familiar objects through a logo or representation of the object. The simplest type of logograms would be direct representations of the object.

Egyptian, Chinese, and Mayan systems were also partially syllabaric systems, in that the written symbols in the more complex forms of the language can represent the syllables that make up different words. Japanese is an example of a syllabaric system.

Another major type of written language is alphabetic, in which individual characters represent phonemes (sounds) of the spoken language. The first alphabetic writing dates back to about 1800 BCE from the Sinai Peninsula, but its elements seem to have been derived from Egyptian hieroglyphs adapted to language. The alphabet was a democratization of writing, and alphabets in the world today are derived from that original Semitic script (Conner 2005).

Figure PI.2 Medieval Storytelling—Wood carving depicting the Adoration of the Magi at Chartres Cathedral exemplifies the use of sacred iconography in oral tradition. Photo by Lin Burton.

4.1 Impact of writing and manuscript cultures

The introduction of writing brought about a change in thinking for previously oral cultures. Historian Walter Ong noted that writing and printing introduced a more linear, sequential and homogeneous approach to thinking, in contrast to the older oral cultures of heroic epics, songs, and tales told by firelight (Ong 2002). Similarly, theorist Walter Benjamin saw mechanical reproduction of writing and art as contributing to a loss of social ritual and personal identity (Benjamin et al. 2008).

Plato famously warned in his dialogue *Phaedrus* that writing would lead to the loss of memory, which was one of the key elements (canons) of rhetoric:

> If men learn this [writing], it will implant forgetfulness in their souls; they will cease to exercise memory because they rely on that which is written … It is no true wisdom that you offer your disciples, but only its semblance, for by telling them of many things without teaching them, you will make them seem to know much, while for the most part they know nothing, and as men filled, not with wisdom but with the conceit of wisdom, they will be a burden to their fellows.

Although specialized messengers could be trained to remember complex messages to be carried over time and distance, scribes with flexible media could more easily speed messages through empires, and this was vital to their success, according to historian Harold Innis.

Types of Written Language

Logographic: In which the Egyptian hieroglyph  is a duck, and the Chinese logogram 山 stands for mountain.

Syllabaric: In which certain symbols stand for syllables. Complex logographic systems like Chinese, or those derived from logographic systems (like Japanese), have characters that stand for syllables.

Alphabetic: Where individual characters stand for phonemes (sounds) of the spoken langage. For instance, English is based on the Latin alphabet (A, B, C, D ...); Russian is based on the Cyrillic script (А, В, Г, Д, ...).

An important point about these forms of written language is that alphabets can communicate billions of ideas with only about two dozen symbols. In contrast, logographic and syllabaric systems require thousands of symbols. This is not a problem in a manuscript culture, but it was a crucial difference in the development of mass communication through printing, since it is difficult to create and organize thousands of separate permanent symbols to be used in a printing press. So, for example, even though Bi Sheng invented printing with moveable ceramic type in China in 1041–8—about 500 years before Johannes Gutenberg used metal type—the system was too cumbersome to be entirely useful, and Chinese printers continued to use carved wooden blocks until the modern era.

Writing grew naturally from the elite, in early cultures, to the upper and then middle classes in the Greek and Roman empires. Literacy faded in Europe during the early medieval period, around 500–1000 CE, when reading and writing were almost exclusively the province of the clergy. Charlemagne, Frederic Barbarosa, most popes, and most kings and queens of the period were not even able to sign their names. Writing was held in such contempt that when the Crusaders took Constantinople in 1204, "they exposed to public ridicule the pens and ink stands that they found in the conquered city as the ignoble arms of a contemptible race of students" (De Vinne 1877).

At the same time, literacy was nearly universal in other cultures, for example, in Arab nations in the 900–1500 period when great centers of learning flourished from Timbuktu, Mali, to Baghdad, Iraq. Many of the great literary treasures of Greek and Roman civilizations were saved by the literate Arab culture of this era, and appreciated once again in Renaissance Europe only after around 1200–1300 CE.

Writing, said media scholar Wilbur Schramm, is what allowed humans to conserve intellectual resources, to preserve the legacy without having to keep all the details in their heads, and to devote energy to advancing knowledge. This had an enormous effect on human life. "With language and writing in hand, humans had paid the tuition for their own education," Schramm said. Mass media, beginning with the printing revolution, would become their open university.

Figure PI.3: Manuscript Culture—A monk works on a manuscript in this mural from the "Evolution of the Book" located at the Library of Congress in Washington, DC. Mural by John W. Alexander, 1896. Photo by Carol Highsmith, Library of Congress.

Technologies of Writing

Along with language, written communication may require four basic items: an instrument, a carrier (medium), a vehicle, and a way to prepare the vehicle. In Chinese traditional culture these are called the "Four Treasures of the Study," and the specific examples are the brush, the paper, the ink, and the ink-stone.

The earliest civilizations tended to use durable materials, such as clay and stone, to keep track of accounts and send messages through long durations of time.

Stone is the most durable medium but not at all flexible. Carvings and paintings on stone are found throughout the ages, in all parts of the world, as permanent records of empires and faiths. The best-known example is the Rosetta Stone, a decree involving an Egyptian king's divinity, carved on a granite-like rock in 196 BCE and discovered in 1799 by Pierre-François Bouchard, a soldier who was part of the Napoleonic expedition to Egypt. Because the decree was carved in three languages—Hieroglyphic, late Egyptian (Demotic), and ancient Greek—it opened the door for the translation of hieroglyphics.

Clay was the simplest and earliest writing medium. Between half a million and two million clay tablets and markers from ancient Mesopotamia have been recovered in the modern era. Scribes once used a wedge-shaped stylus to make marks in clay, which was then fired in kilns to create a permanent record; or the clay could be recycled for reuse later if the record was not permanent. Early Mesopotamian writing is called Cuneiform, which is Latin for "wedge shaped." Cuneiform translation began in 1835 when Henry Rawlinson visited an archeological site in what is now eastern Iran to see the Bisotun (or Behistun) inscriptions. He realized that, like the Rosetta Stone, the inscriptions consisted of three identical texts.

Papyrus is a plant native to the wetlands of the Nile valley of Egypt. It was originally used by the classical civilizations of Egypt, Greece, and Rome. It is pounded flat and laid crossways to create a sheet of papyrus paper, and is effective because the plant has a glue-like material that holds the sheet together. The first examples are from about 2550 BCE.

Wax tablets on a wooden backing were often used in ancient Greece and Rome for writing that was temporary. Two tablets could be hinged together to protect the wax, which is an idea that probably led to the codex (book).

Parchment was a widely used medium in the ancient Roman Empire that employed the skin of sheep, goats, cows, or other animals. Unlike leather, which is tanned, parchment membranes are soaked and scraped thin to provide a high quality writing surface. The best parchment was vellum, usually from calfskin.

Silk was used since at least the second century BCE in China for transmitting and preserving important religious and civil texts. Silk was flexible but very expensive, and its use was highly restricted to royalty.

Paper is traditionally said to have been discovered by Ts'ai Lun, a Chinese monk who observed paper wasps making a nest around 105 CE. The technique is a huge improvement over hard-to-prepare animal hides, brittle papyrus, and expensive silk. Finely chopped wood or rag fibers are mixed with glue in a vat, and then poured over a screen. The thin layer of fibers on the screen dries into paper.

Figure PI.4 Parchment—Scraping and smoothing animal skins is part of the ancient process of preparing parchment, a long-lasting but expensive medium. Woodcut by Jost Amman (1539–91) from "True Description of all Professions on Earth, exalted and humble, spiritual and worldly," 1568.

Figure P1.5 Paper making—Suspending linen fibers in water, and then pressing the fibers in a layer against a screen, is the technique for making paper, a much cheaper medium for books than parchment. Woodcut by Jost Amman, 1568.

Cheap paper became widely available around 1400 in Europe and was apparently in surplus by the mid-1400s. One contributing factor may have been the increased number of linen rags from cast-off clothing, which people needed to weather the winters in the Little Ice Age (c. 1315–1800).

Scrolls: Parchment, papyrus or paper rolled up on either end. Information is kept sequentially in a scroll; it can't be accessed at random like a codex (book).

Codex (book): The word comes from the Latin for "caudex," meaning the trunk of a tree. A codex is a group of pages of paper or parchment that is gathered from one side at the back. A codex is a book if the pages are separate, but older forms of codex may also have pages folded in series, like an accordion.

1

The Divine Art

My design is to give an historical account of the authors, discovery, improvement and progress of the Art of Printing; an art so highly beneficial to mankind, by preserving and transmitting to posterity the treasures of ancient and modern learning, that its origin has been esteemed divine.

Samuel Palmer, 1733

Figure 1.1 Turning point—The invention of moveable type printing involved a combination of old and new techniques. Johannes Gutenberg, a metalsmith from Mainz, Germany, worked for over 15 years to perfect the process that produced the first Bible in 1454. It was an extraordinary example of craftsmanship, far superior to hand-lettered manuscripts, and it signaled not only the printing revolution, but a turning point in human history. Engraving by Johnson, Fry & Co., 1869, Library of Congress.

1 The Printing Revolution: 1400s to 1814

People were astonished when they saw the first unbound pages of Johannes Gutenberg's Bible at Frankfurt's traditional harvest fair in 1454. There were none of the blemishes, rubricator's marks, or scraped-out ink spots that characterized hand-lettered manuscript Bibles. The linen paper was bright, the edge of the type was crisp, and, at 30 florins, the cost was one-tenth of a manuscript Bible.

"The script was very neat and legible, not at all difficult to follow," wrote an enthusiastic bishop to his supervisor. "Your grace would be able to read it without effort, and indeed, without glasses." He also called Gutenberg a "marvelous man," which is one of the few personal insights we have into the life of Johannes Gensfleisch zur Laden zum Gutenberg (Eisenstein 1980; Fussel 2005).

We know that Gutenberg was born around 1398 in Mainz, Germany, at a time of plague, social chaos, and political upheaval. We think that his father was a cloth merchant and a goldsmith for the Church, and Johannes may well have learned that craft. We have a record of his enrollment at a university around 1418. We know of a will that mentions him in 1419, and there are records of a disputed promise of marriage in 1436. That's about all we know about his early life, except that he ran into problems with an intriguing business in 1439.

Gutenberg's business involved a new way to make the small metal badges that were popular with people who were on religious pilgrimages. The badges, or "pilgrims' mirrors," were four inches high and made from cheap metals such as lead and tin. They would be sewn onto hats or cloaks to show that the traveler was a pilgrim, and they would be held up in the presence of religious relics as the pilgrim's act of devotion. Millions of the badges were sold across Europe between the medieval era and the late Renaissance. Even today, the badges are still being dug up along the old pilgrim trails.

From court records, we know that two investors backed Gutenberg in an improved process for making the metal badges. They expected to sell 32,000 of them, and they were well into production when news came that the Aachen, Germany, pilgrimage was being postponed for a year due to bubonic plague.

With the setback, Gutenberg realized he needed another way to keep investors happy. He started a second enterprise in Strasbourg, France, that used the alloy of lead, tin, and antimony. It also used, according to cryptic court documents, "something required for printing" (McMurtrie 1941). Most likely, then, 1439 is the starting point for what became the first successful printing enterprise. This was the year when Gutenberg first poured metal into a matrix that held the blanks for the different letters of the alphabet. However, like the pilgrims' mirrors, this early enterprise also ended badly. By 1440, one partner was dead from the plague, and one of the important tools—a form for metal casting—could not be recovered from his house.

Gutenberg continued to experiment with metal type and presses during this time, and may have printed several undated works such as a Latin grammar and an astronomical calendar. After a few years, he returned to Mainz to assemble a printing system that would produce the flawless 1,282-page, 42-line Gutenberg Bible. This complex system included metal forges and molds for type; a way to set the type; a long-lasting ink; a new kind of press; contracts for high quality linen paper; methods to stack and order pages; and financing to pull the system together. Sales of the new Bibles were not slow, but in 1456, just as the printing company began to look like a financial success, Gutenberg's investor Johann Fust (or Faust) foreclosed on the loan and took over the business. Gutenberg probably continued in another small printing operation in Bamberg, Germany, and then worked for the Church in other ways in Mainz. He died in 1468.

Meanwhile, Fust and his son-in-law, and former Gutenberg foreman, Peter Schoffer, began the second wave of the printing revolution with a popular form of religious book called a psalter. They also printed two editions of works by the Roman poet Cicero and a "Letter to the Imperial Estates" describing the issues in a war between two contending bishops in Mainz in 1462. It was one of the first uses of the press to disseminate and comment on the news of the day.

Figure 1.2 Johannes Gutenberg—This is the traditional but probably incorrect likeness of the printer from Mainz. The hat and beard would not have been worn by someone from his time and culture. However, no better images exist, according to the Gutenberg Museum in Mainz, Germany. Engraving from John Luther Ringwalt, *American Encyclopedia of Printing*, Menamin & Ringwalt, 1871.

For almost a decade, the printing industry grew slowly and stabilized in central Germany as several dozen people trained in the craft. Then in 1465, two German printers sponsored by a Catholic cardinal started a new printing operation near Rome. By 1469, three other German printing companies had moved to Venice, and by 1471, the number of printing businesses began a dramatic growth. By 1480, every city in Europe had at least one printing company.

Gutenberg and the Pilgrims' Badges

A pilgrim's badge was a small metal medallion worn by people on religious pilgrimages during the Medieval and Renaissance periods. Gutenberg's work on the problem of cheap, durable metals for an Aachen pilgrimage badge was a first step in the creation of effective moveable type. (Gutenberg Museum, Mainz, Germany.)

Figure 1.3 Pilgrim's Badge—These small medallions were manufactured by the thousands around the time moveable type was invented. Like moveable type, they were made of lead, tin and antimony. Each pilgrimage had its own medallion; this one was designed for the Aachen pilgrimage. Wikimedia Commons.

Figure 1.4 Exaltation of Relics—Here we see the exaltation of relics at Aachen Cathedral in 2014—a ceremony unchanged in five centuries, and clearly the same ceremony as depicted in Figure 1.3, the Gutenberg-era pilgrim's badge. Photo courtesy of Domkapitel Aachen, © Andreeas Steindl.

1.1 Precursors of the printing revolution

Gutenberg's system of printing text with moveable type was new in 1454, but the process of making an impression with ink on a raised surface was ancient. The earliest known printed images are from "cylinder seals" used in early Mesopotamian civilizations from around 3500 BCE. Made from hard stone, glass, or ceramic materials, they were rolled across wet clay or textiles to create repeating patterns. Engraved seals and stamps continued to be used for thousands of years to print on clay and cloth.

Chinese artists and scribes used woodblock printing for images, and sometimes text, starting from the sixth century CE. In Europe, similar woodblock images were widely used for playing cards and pictures of saints from the 1200s on. Artists who wanted fine detail and longer press runs shifted to metal plates by the 1400s.

Still, the transition from engraving and woodcuts to printing with moveable type was not easy to make. Woodblock printing is not suitable for more than a few thousand impressions, since images and text start to get fuzzy as the edges of the wood break down under the pressure of the press. Engraving plates are one way around the problem, since text can be engraved on a copper or zinc plate, but they are expensive and difficult to correct. When thousands of impressions are needed for individual letters, something stronger and more flexible than wood is required. Chinese scholar Bi Sheng (906–1126 CE) was the first to come up with a solution to the moveable type problem. Between 1041 and 1048 during the Song dynasty, Bi Sheng cut characters onto the top of thin clay squares, and then baked them into hard ceramic tiles. The difficulty was in keeping the surface height of all of the separate tiles exactly even in order to ensure that the ink would be perfectly distributed. Even one millimeter can mean the difference between a good impression and one that is too light to read.

Bi Sheng came up with an ingenious solution: he placed all the tiles on a board with a thick coat of wax, and then heated up the board. When the wax was soft, he pressed the tiles down from the top with a metal plate, making them all even as they receded into the wax. Then he would let the wax cool.

The idea worked, but there was a larger problem: Chinese language is logographic, with many different symbols required. This is no obstacle for hand-painted text, but a moveable type system required at least 6,000 tiles. So the complexity of a logographic language made it difficult to sort, set, and use moveable type. On the other hand, the Western Latin and Cyrillic alphabets require only about 150 characters. So even though the hardware problem was solved in China, the larger software problem remained, and it was almost as easy to cut woodblocks as it was to set type with a 6,000-character system.

A similar moveable type system was developed in Korea in 1377 using brass characters and woodblock printing, but, Korean, like Chinese, is logographic. While the process worked, it was not a way to drastically cut the cost of communication (Schramm 1989).

A Dutch printer named Laurence Coster (1370–1440) came close to solving Europe's printing problem. The story is that he was playing blocks on the floor with his children when he had the idea to separate parts of the wooden block. The individual wooden characters could then be replaced when they started to wear down. Coster was apparently in the process of switching to metal characters when he died in 1440 (Sonn 2006).

These are just a few of the many rival claims to the legacy of moveable type printing, and the question is often asked whether Gutenberg is in fact the inventor of the technique. From the records and testimony that we have, it does seem clear that Gutenberg was first to solve the key problem of metal type and assemble all the necessary ingredients to create the printing revolution (Taylor 1907; De Vinne 1878; McGrath 2001).

Even so, the printing revolution did not occur because one lone genius invented a single new technology. Printing emerged because Gutenberg's insight into the key problem of moveable metal type occurred at a moment when all of the right conditions and technologies were in place. These included a surplus of paper and ink, as well as presses for printing, foundries for metalsmithing, and a system for business investments.

Most importantly, it occurred because of the rising need for education among the nobility and merchants of Renaissance Europe starting around the 1200s. The purchasing power of the new readership expanded the market to the point where scribes and illuminators were not keeping up with demand.

The printing revolution took place because of "a complex ensemble of many interrelated changes" in social conditions, said historian Elizabeth Eisenstein. "Gutenberg invented moveable type," said historian John Lienhard. "But, it's no exaggeration to say that Medieval Europe worked for 300 years to invent Gutenberg" (Lienhard 1992).

1.2 Diffusion of printing in Europe

Mainz, Germany, was the birthplace of printing; but Venice, Italy, was its cradle. As the most powerful and cultured city in Europe, Venice naturally attracted half of Europe's printing trade during the High Renaissance. By around 1500, Venice had over sixty-five publishing businesses with 200 presses and thousands of people working in printing, paper making, and type foundries.

Two German printers, John of Speyer and his brother Wendelin, were the first to bring printing to Venice in the late 1460s. They produced at least 800 copies of four books—three Roman classics and a book by St. Augustine—in a seven-month period between 1469 and 1470 (Brown 1891). The output of the new printing presses was remarkable for the time; one monk in a monastery might, in that same seven months, have produced only part of one book.

Nicholas Jenson (1420–1480), of Champagne, France, was another printing pioneer in Venice. Jenson's previous job as an engraver at a government coin minting plant in France made him uniquely qualified for the printing trade, since he could design and cut type faces on the metal punches used in type foundries. Jensen had been in Mainz to study under Gutenberg and his successors, and left for Venice in 1468. There he invented "roman" type, which was based on the capital lettering used in Roman architecture, along with a standard lower-case script style developed by monks between 800 and 1200 CE. Roman was more legible than Gutenberg's blackletter (gothic) style, and was quickly adopted as a standard.

Jensen, the Speyers, and other early Venetian printers catered to an elite readership, and they tended to see books as works of art in themselves. They printed the books in small editions on high quality parchment with elaborately illuminated initials at chapter heads and handsomely tooled leather bindings.

Aldus Manutius (1449–1515) changed the high-end business model in the 1490s when he began publishing books for the public at reasonable prices, rather than as works of art for the elite. Between 1494 and 1515, his company produced 157 different books, some with more than 1,000 copies. "While Jenson and his fellows looked upon the press largely as a means for putting out a handsome book [as] a beautiful work of art," said historian Horatio Brown, "Aldus regarded it quite as much as an instrument for the diffusion of scholarship" (Brown 1902).

By 1500, Venice had produced half of the four million first printed books, called "incunabula" (Latin for cradle). But other cities were catching up. By 1500, Paris had seventy-five printing houses and was beginning to surpass Venice, thanks in part to strong royal patronage. By 1533, another 18 million more books were produced by Europe's rapidly expanding publishing industry (Smiles 1867).

Today, only a single plaque on a wall near the Rialto bridge marks the city's once bustling printing center, noting, "From this place spread the new light of civil wisdom." But as Venice declined in power and freedom, the industry moved north to the great printing centers of Amsterdam, Brussels, Frankfurt, Paris, and London.

1.3 Why printing was revolutionary

The rapid diffusion of printing is explained by high demand for books in the Renaissance and their suddenly much lower cost. Printing made books hundreds to thousands of times cheaper to produce. Consider this comparison: a monk or nun could copy one double-sided page of one manuscript per day. But even in the earliest days of printing, a four-person crew of typesetters and printers could print about 1,500 double-sided pages per day.

One specific example comes from Leon Battista Alberti, a noted Renaissance priest, poet, and writer from Florence. Alberti may have understated the case in 1466 when he said that Gutenberg's process involved three men working 100 days to produce 200 Bibles. In contrast, he said, a bookseller in Florence employed forty-five scribes for twenty-two months to copy 200 manuscripts (Richardson 1999). The seventy-fold difference in this one case doesn't quite give an idea of the improvement, since Gutenberg's Bible was huge, and we don't know the size of the manuscripts in Florence.

Modern historian Elizabeth Eisenstein gives an example that brings us a little close to the awesome power of the new moveable type printing press: in Venice before the advent of printing, a monk might charge one florin for copying the eighty pages of Plato's *Dialogues*. In 1483, the Ripoli press charged three florins for printing 1,025 copies of the same number of pages. In any event, it's safe to say that printing was usually hundreds and sometimes thousands of times more cost-effective than hand-lettering (see Sidebar 1.2, Monk Power).

Like other media revolutions to come, the printing revolution regrouped people and skills. The older skills included papermaking, ink manufacturing, leather working, bookbinding and book marketing; and the new skills included press work, typesetting, and foundry type casting. Similar regroupings of skills would be seen, for example, in the visual revolution, when portrait painters like Samuel Morse became daguerreotype photographers and telegraphers; in the broadcasting revolution, when theatrical performers and broadcast engineers created radio drama; and in the digital revolution, when journalists and computer hackers created blogs and collaborative civic information systems.

During the transition from copying to printing in the mid- to late 1400s, the low prices of printed books probably alarmed book retailers who had been selling expensive manuscripts to an elite clientele. But then business accelerated, turning retailers into wholesalers, street vendors into bookstore owners, and copiers into publishers.

Printing continued to expand rapidly throughout the world, reaching as far west as Mexico in 1539 and as far east as Russia in 1553. But the impact of printing was only beginning to be felt (Ferreira 2006). "The printing press precipitated 200 years of chaos, moving from a world where the Catholic Church was the organizing political force to the Treaty of Westphalia, where we finally knew what the new unit was—the nation state," said

Clay Shirky, a sociologist who has described a close connection between communications revolutions and the collapse of institutions. The digital revolution, considered in Section IV of this book, would lead to similar chaos, he predicted (Shirkey 2010).

Monk Power

One interesting way to think about changes in media technology is the amount of work that can be done in one day by one monk copying text by hand all day as compared to one person in a printing chapel or newspaper or broadcasting station. "Monk power" is a concept that helps make that comparison. (With thanks to Roland Lazenby.)

One monk = 1 hand-written page per day
One Gutenberg = 200 monk-days
One Walter (steam press) = 12 kilomonks (12,000 monk-days)
One Pulitzer (high-speed press) = 1 megamonk (1,000,000 monk-days)
One Vannevar (optical typesetting) = 6 megamonks
One Wozniak (desktop publishing) = 12 megamonks

Compared to electronic and digital monk power

One Sarnoff (one radio or TV channel) = 1.15 megamonks
One Berners-Lee (1.3 million websites and posts per day) = 1.3 megamonks
One Brin (2.8 billion Google searches per day) = 2.8 gigamonks

Figure 1.5 Monk—A medieval monk works at a scriptorium. Illustration by William Blades, *Pentateuch of Printing*, 1891.

2 Printing and the Renaissance

The Renaissance was already well under way before the printing revolution. The new desire for knowledge, literacy, art, and wealth; the new institutions such as banks, academies, and universities; the new spirit of exploration; and the new focus on human rather than religious goals—all of these marked the changes that illuminated the human landscape at the dawn of early modern Europe. These conditions opened the way for moveable type printing. If Gutenberg had not invented it, someone else certainly would have.

What impact did printing, in turn, have on the Renaissance? Some scholars have pointed to the "lag" between the start of the Renaissance and the development of the printing industry as an indication that social construction was more significant than technological determinism in the printing revolution. Others, particularly Marshall McLuhan, have taken a more deterministic view. Both perspectives help us understand the intertwined nature of causes and effects as we study complex historical processes. To a greater or lesser degree, printing was a major element in the Renaissance.

The first goal for early printers was to increase the availability of religious texts, especially the Latin Bible. A second and closely related initial goal was to recover ancient Roman and Greek manuscripts. There was, said Samuel Palmer in his history of printing, "a laudable zeal in searching the libraries for those valuable books, which had lain buried in obscurity, and were become extremely scarce, great numbers being lost in the times of ignorance" (Palmer 1732).

Once the recovery of ancient manuscripts was underway during the "incunabula" before 1500, contemporary needs could be placed higher on the printers' agenda, and more books could be published in vernacular (native) languages, rather than only in Latin. This especially included the Bible, but also contemporary literature and scientific books. The publishing agenda of French, Dutch, and English printers increasingly emphasized nationalistic and humanistic goals during the expansion of northern printing in the 1500s and 1600s.

2.1 Initial effects of printing

One of the first effects of printing was seen, at the time, as unifying national languages. Books published in French, German, English, and other languages had the effect of codifying and standardizing far-flung dialects. This, in turn, would become a cornerstone of national identity.

A good example is the first book printed in England—Geoffrey Chaucer's *Canterbury Tales*. The first English printer, William Caxton (c. 1415–92), had moved his printing press from Brussels to a site near Westminster Abbey in 1476. Unlike printers in Venice, Caxton was not as interested in recovering ancient Greek and Roman texts as he was in bringing English authors to an English language market. English at this time, like most languages, had extraordinary variations between regional dialects. Caxton illustrated this with a story about a group of English merchants aboard a ship who sent a boat to a Thames River village to buy some eggs. They asked for "eggys," but the merchant said she did not speak French. Another one of the company understood the local dialect and asked for some "eyren," as eggs were then known in eastern England. "What sholde a man in thyse dayes now wryte," Caxton asked. "egges or eyren? Certaynly it is harde to playse euery man by cause [because] of dyuersite [diversity] and chaunge of langage" (British Library 2015). Later books, especially the Great Bible of 1539 and the King James Bible of 1611, also standardized the language and had a culturally unifying effect.

Standardization of information was another effect of printing; since it allowed exact reproduction of information in a way that manuscript copying did not. This is evident in the contrast between the travel logs of Marco Polo and those of Christopher Columbus. After his return from China in 1295, a century and a half before printing, Polo's narrative was copied in about 150 different manuscripts, with so many differences that we're not sure which version is authentic. In contrast, there is only one version of Christopher Columbus's letters about the exploration of the Caribbean in the 1490s, since they were fixed in printed form and widely distributed at the time they were written. So the certainty of accuracy was another way that printing was an improvement over the old oral–manuscript culture.

Printing itself became standardized in the early 1500s, making possible a new kind of non-linear access to information through title pages and tables of contents and page-numbering systems. Other improvements included better type fonts such as roman and italic, and a standardized printing production process codified in books like Joseph Moxon's *Handy Works* (1683) or Pierre Fournier's *Manuel Typographique* (1764).

Major social impacts of printing included the spread of humanism and individualism. New ideas and explorations about human topics included conservative theologian Sebastian Brant's *Ship of Fools* (1494), a satire about human behavior, illustrated by engraver Albrech Drurer; and *In Praise of Folly* by Desiderius Erasmus, published 1511. Both were veiled attacks on the social and religious structure in Europe. These and other books began to undermine the hold of religion on culture in the years just before the Protestant Reformation. Printing also boosted the Renaissance sense of individualism and achievement by elevating individuals through biography and authorship. For instance, Erasmus was probably the first modern writer to become famous in his lifetime, thanks to printing. And the ranks of Italian Renaissance artists would hardly be known without the 250 biographies in Giorgio Vasari's encyclopedic *Lives of the Most Eminent Painters, Sculptors & Architects*, first published in 1550.

With standardization and individualism came the possibility of personal comparisons: old ideas could be contrasted, contradictions could be revealed, and new ideas could be presented. Perhaps the notion that a culture could change and reach for new horizons remains the deepest impact of the printing revolution.

Figure 1.6: Letter from Columbus—When Christopher Columbus wrote about his explorations, the information spread rapidly across Europe thanks to printing. This woodcut accompanied a translation of the letter that was printed in Florence, Italy, in October of 1493. Library of Congress.

3 Printing and the Protestant Reformation

It is hardly surprising that the Bible was the first book Gutenberg printed. Scripture was at the center of the medieval world, and during mass, priests and bishops would read manuscripts of the Latin Gospels aloud, and then use the sermon to interpret the readings in a liturgical fusion of oral and manuscript culture.

The Church initially welcomed printing as a divine gift. Gutenberg's Latin Bible was seen as a way to diffuse knowledge of scripture, and printing was also seen as a practical aid to the Church. For example, printed posters were helpful in recruiting soldiers to fight against invading Turks in the 1450s, and printing accelerated the Church's ability to trade cash for the forgiveness of sins—a practice known as selling indulgences. Where once the practice was limited to what could be written by hand, the printing press allowed thousands of indulgences to be issued whenever a church ran short of cash.

Figure 1.7 Left him hanging—This 1525 woodcut by Lucas van Leyden (c. 1494–1533) depicts a legend about the Roman poet Virgil. The poet fell in love with the emperor's daughter who pretended to reciprocate. She promised to spend the night with him, and in order to evade her guards, she lowered a basket so he could reach her bedroom. But halfway up, she left him dangling, to be mocked the next morning by the citizens of Rome. The engraving tells us that even wise men can be foolish, and more generally, illustrates the new interest in secular and humanistic thinking ushered in by the printing revolution. Rijksmuseum, Amsterdam.

"There is considerable irony about the enthusiastic reception [first] accorded printing by the church," said historian Elizabeth Eisenstein. "Heralded on all sides as a 'peaceful art,' Gutenberg's invention probably contributed more to destroying Christian accord and inflaming religious warfare than any of the so-called arts of war ever did" (Eisenstein 1980).

This "destruction of Christian accord" began to occur when the Church reacted with alarm to translations of the Bible into vernacular (national) languages such as German, French, and English. Although many of these translations had already occurred before printing, they were not accessible to most people. John Wycliffe translated the Bible into English in the 1390s; Jan Huss helped translate the Bible into Czech in the early 1400s; and a variety of German translations, some created by the Church for missionary purposes, were in existence before printing. But none of these challenged the Church monopoly on knowledge since they were in manuscript form, with only a few copies in existence. Printing changed everything.

3.1 Martin Luther and printing

On the morning of October 31, 1517, a devoted priest and doctor of Bible studies, Martin Luther, wrote a letter to the Bishop of Mainz, and, the story goes, nailed a copy to the doors of a cathedral in Wittenberg, Germany. There was nothing terribly dramatic about the act itself—everybody posted notices by nailing them to doors—but Luther's 95 Theses shocked Europe and kicked off the Protestant Reformation.

Luther's point was that sales of indulgences were gross violations of the original idea of confession and penance. "The people are deceived by that indiscriminate and high-sounding promise of release," he wrote in one of the Theses. You couldn't just sin and pay, he said. You had to truly repent.

If his call for reform simply been shouted from the pulpits, or copied by hand, it could have been easily ignored or suppressed. Similar calls for reform from John Wycliffe of London and Jan Hus of Prague had been put down a century beforehand. But the new printing press amplified Luther's voice to an extent that astonished everyone—including Luther.

Figure 1.8 Printing sparks Reformation—Martin Luther's calls for Church reforms were not the first in Europe, but they were amplified by the new power of the printing press. Luther was depicted around 1525 in this portrait by Lucas Cranach. Library of Congress.

The 95 Theses were printed by his friends in January 1519 and widely distributed (Brecht 1985–93). They were in such demand that crowds surged around printing shops, grabbing for pages still wet from the press (Smiles 1867). The controversy spread quickly. Within a few weeks, everyone in Europe knew about Luther's sharp criticism of the Church. For the first time in history, the power of a revolutionary idea was fully amplified by a mass medium.

In considering Luther's success, it's important to note that technology wasn't the only factor. British Museum director Neil MacGregor points out that, at the time, Germany was divided into regional powers rather than a national government. "You couldn't really have a Reformation in England or in France, because the central power was strong enough to kill it, or at least, make it much harder," MacGregor said. "It happens easily in Germany because of the political diversity" (Attar 2014). While the Catholics from southern German states hunted for Luther, powerful rulers in the northern German states kept him in hiding. He used the time to translate the Bible into German and see it printed—an act that codified and regularized the German language and help provide a stronger foundation for the culture. Luther described printing as "God's highest and extremest act of grace," and his followers began to see the printing press as an agent of freedom, delivering them from bondage to the Roman Church and delivering the light of true religion to Germany.

A decade after the Lutheran revolt started, the Reformation was well underway across Europe, and Protestant leaders took full advantage of the press. In Switzerland and France, John Calvin "played a significant role in the evolution of languages considered appropriate for theological writings," said historian Jean-Francois Gilmont (2005). In the process, Switzerland became something of the European capital of Protestantism, and Calvin's Reformed Church was the source of English Puritanism, Scottish Presbyterianism, and French Huguenot Protestantism.

In England, political power see-sawed between Protestants and Catholics in the early to mid-1500s, and each side used the press. Early in his reign, Henry VIII first suppressed Lutherans and the vernacular Bible translations, but then in 1533, broke away from the Roman Catholic Church and established a separate Church of England. He ordered the printing of an English language Bible, known as the "Great Bible" of 1539. It was based primarily on a translation by William Tyndale that had earlier been suppressed. Tyndale didn't live to see what was essentially his translation in print; he was captured by Catholics in Brussels and executed in 1536. Before he died, he said that he hoped he had opened King Henry's eyes.

Figure 1.9 Execution of William Tyndale—British scholar William Tyndale was executed for heresy in 1536 after printing his unauthorized translation of the Bible from Hebrew and Greek into English. Subsequent English editions of the Bible, including Henry VIII's 1539 Great Bible and the King James Bible of 1611, are primarily based on Tyndale's translations. From Foxe's *Book of Martyrs*, 1563. Library of Congress.

The English throne returned to a Catholic monarch in 1553 when Henry VIII's daughter "Bloody" Mary took the throne and ordered hundreds of executions. Around that time, British Catholic cardinal Reginald Pole expressed the spirit of the Counter-Reformation when he warned Londoners against reading scripture for themselves: "You should not be your owne masters," he said. "Household religion [is] a seed bed of sedition."

When Catholic Queen Mary died in 1558, her half-sister Protestant Queen Elizabeth I took the throne with a promise of religious tolerance. Protestants solidified power with the publication of John Foxe's *Book of Martyrs* a few years later. A shocking piece of Protestant propaganda, Foxe's book depicted the gruesome executions of William Tyndale and many others, bolstering Protestant claims to legitimacy.

3.2 The Counter-Reformation

The gravity of the spreading chaos eventually became clear to Roman Catholic Church officials who fought back with a ruthless Counter-Reformation. As a result, religious warfare broke out across Europe and the fighting continued for generations. In Germany, 25 to 40 percent of the population, already half-decimated by the plague, would perish in religious warfare between 1524 and 1648.

Ordinary people fared badly during the Counter-Reformation. Historian Carlo Ginzburg described the trial of one outspoken Italian miller named Menocchio who in 1584 was accused of heresy for openly expressing simple doubts about a few of the fine points of religious dogma. After an extensive public trial, Menocchio was executed (Ginzburg 1992). Millions of such cases emerged on both sides of the widening chasm between the Catholic and Protestant churches. Sometimes people were executed just for owning the wrong version of the Bible. Giordano Bruno, a philosopher who said the earth revoked around the sun, was burned at the stake in 1600. A more famous scientist who was persecuted for the same thing during this era was Galileo Galilei (1564–1642), an Italian mathematician whose astronomical observations convinced him of the truth of the heliocentric theory. Between 1612 and 1632 he skirted dangerous confrontation with Church authorities, but was finally forced to recant his views publicly under threat of torture.

Meanwhile, Protestant reformers in Switzerland, Germany, and England dogmatically referred to "sola scriptura" as the only authority and then often insisted that they were the only ones who could interpret that scripture. All too often "the rich and varied communal religious experiences of the Middle Ages" were lost as the new authorities demanded obedience. "Open books, in some instances, led to closed minds," Eisenstein observed. The dissidents even suppressed other dissidents. The Church of England attempted to suppress Puritan and Scottish Presbyterian dissent well into the mid-1600s, sparking the "Bishops War" in Scotland and encouraging Puritan emigration to the new colonies in North America. In the end, political pragmatism and a sense of exhaustion helped to deflate religious zealotry in Europe. By the early 1600s, French Catholic Cardinal Richelieu formed pragmatic political alliances with Protestants in order to fight enemies who were Catholic. Religious warfare simmered down after the Treaty of Westphalia in 1648, where the major powers of Europe agreed that each king would determine the religion of his

Figure 1.10 Bibles in a barrel—This Ljubljana Castle exhibit shows Slovenian Bibles hidden in barrels. They were smuggled from a printing press in Wittenberg, Germany, in 1584 to Ljubljana to avoid Church authorities who violently opposed the printing of non-Latin Bibles. Primoz Trubar, the Bible's translator, is a national hero in Slovenia, as is Martin Luther in Germany and William Tyndale in Britain. Photo by Lin Burton.

own nation. But then more religious warfare emerged in France in 1685, forcing French Huguenots (Protestants) to flee the country.

Religion continued to be an important element in conflicts that continued to plague Europe in the late twentieth century, for example, in Ireland and the Balkans. As Elizabeth Eisenstein said:

> We still seem to be experiencing the contradictory effects of a process which fanned the flames of religious zeal and bigotry while fostering a new concern for ecumenical concord and toleration, which fixed linguistic and national divisions more permanently while creating a cosmopolitan Commonwealth of Learning and extending communications networks which have encompassed the entire world. (Eisenstein 1980)

3.3 The slow emergence of religious tolerance

Although printing helped plunge Europe into centuries of religious warfare, it also amplified calls for tolerance and reason. As the horror of religious warfare receded, the need for religious tolerance became a primary ideal among Enlightenment writers.

In France, Sebastian Castellio (1515–63) became one of the first proponents of freedom of conscience. "It is unchristian to use arms against those who have been expelled from the Church, and to deny them rights common to all mankind," he wrote in "Whether heretics should be persecuted," a response to the intolerance of Protestant reformer John Calvin.

In England, John Foxe strengthened Protestantism with his *Book of Martyrs*, noted above, but he also "enunciated a sweeping doctrine of tolerance even towards Catholics, whose doctrines he detested with every fibre of his being" (Dickens 1978).

A British poet famed for writing *Paradise Lost*, John Milton (1608–74) matched the idea of religious tolerance to the historical touchstone of the Athenian senate and marketplace, arguing for a "marketplace of ideas" in his 1644 *Areopagitica*:

> And though all the winds of doctrine were let loose to play on the earth, so Truth be in the field, we do injuriously by licensing and prohibiting misdoubt her strength. Let her and Falsehood grapple; who ever knew Truth put to the worse in a free and open encounter?

Milton insisted that Truth would win out in a free and fair fight, although his argument for freedom of conscience was limited: it did not include "popery" (Catholicism), blasphemy, or impiety.

The North American Protestant colonies of Virginia, Massachusetts, and New York avoided religious war, but were notoriously intolerant of religious deviance in the early years. Yet at the surprisingly early date of 1649, the Catholic colony of Maryland made religious toleration the official position.

Figure 1.11 John Milton—English poet and scholar John Milton argued for tolerance and free speech, insisting that truth would win in the marketplace of ideas. Painting by Pieter Van der Plaas, Library of Congress.

Although Maryland's official tolerance only applied to Christians, and was something of a pragmatic approach for a minority religion in a mostly Protestant set of English colonies, the act is still considered a leap forward for human rights:

> Whereas the inforceing of the conscience in matters of Religion hath frequently fallen out to be of dangerous Consequence in those commonwealthes where it hath been practised … Be it Therefore … enacted … That noe person or persons whatsoever within this Province … shall from henceforth bee any waies troubled, Molested or discountenanced for, or in respect of, his or her religion nor in the free exercise thereof … nor any way compelled to the beliefe or exercise of any other Religion against his or her consent …

Tolerance was a large part of the new creed of printing, and it was within this cultural ferment that the Renaissance gave way to the

Enlightenment. "From the days of Castellio to those of Voltaire, the printing industry was the principal natural ally of libertarian, heterodox and ecumenical philosophers," Eisenstein said (Eisenstein 1980). Printers naturally wanted to expand markets, but the capitalistic motive was not the central point. All Europe was on the move, and "the enterprising publisher was the natural enemy of narrow minds."

In France, for example, Francois Voltaire (1694–1788) railed against "the dreadful folly of religious wars." And Voltaire's friend, Benjamin Franklin, noted that printers themselves could be instruments of tolerance:

> Printers are educated in the Belief, that when Men differ in Opinion, both Sides ought equally to have the Advantage of being heard by the Publick; and that when Truth and Error have fair Play, the former is always an overmatch for the latter: Hence they chearfully serve all contending Writers that pay them well, without regarding on which side they are of the Question in Dispute. (Franklin 1731)

In his *Notes on the State of Virginia* (1787), Thomas Jefferson summed up the Enlightenment view of religious warfare: "Millions of innocent men, women and children ... have been burnt, tortured, fined, imprisoned; yet we have not advanced one inch towards uniformity. What has been the effect of [religious] coercion? To make half the world fools, and the other half hypocrites."

Figure 1.12 Think for yourselves—... And let others enjoy the privilege. That was the advice of François-Marie Arouet (1694–1778), known as Voltaire, one of the most colorful and insightful of the French Enlightenment philosophers. Portrait by Nicolas de Largillière, c. 1725, Wikimedia Commons.

Figure 1.13 Printer and scientist—Benjamin Franklin said that printers had a duty to ensure that all sides be heard in the marketplace of ideas. Painting by Charles Nicholas Cochin, c. 1777, Library of Congress.

4 Scientific and Technical Impacts of the Printing Revolution

Printing was the most obvious and probably the most important element in capturing the scientific and technological revolution from the Renaissance forward. Printing spread news of exploration, descriptions of new technologies, improvements in medicine, insights into astronomy, and information about a host of other discoveries. "The world before printing was one in which the whole pattern of learning, communicating and storing information was defined by what could be written down or drawn or spoken in a singular and immediate fashion," wrote historian Robert Friedel. After printing, it was the exact and repeatable message that "carried authority and influence" (Friedel 2007).

Printing spurred the exploration of physical and mental horizons with the publication of exact maps, charts, and astronomical tables. For instance, news of Columbus's explorations spread rapidly with printing in the 1490s, making him one of the first international heroes, at least until the genocide in the West Indies was understood (Zinn 1980). In contrast, the folkloric accounts of tenth-century Viking landings in North America were little known outside the oral/manuscript culture of Scandinavian nations.

The power of the press also influenced the way geographic discoveries were understood. The travel journals of Amerigo Vespucci were read by mapmaker Martin Waldseemüller, who believed Vespucci's idea that the land to the west could not be India, as Columbus claimed. In 1507, a new world map called the new continent "America" in his honor. The name, amplified by the new power of the printing press, continues to be used.

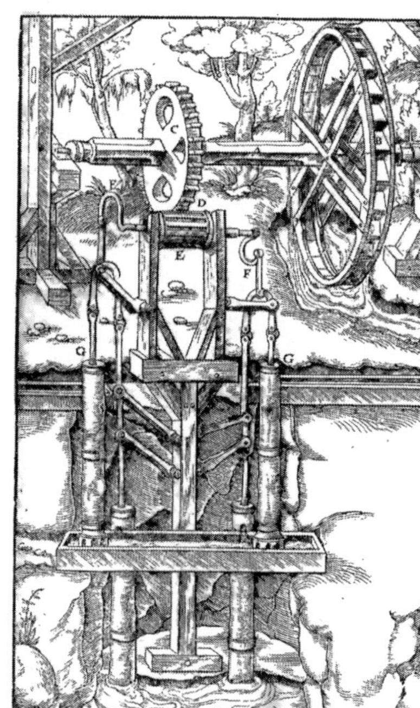

Figure 1.14 Science and printing—Enormous scientific and engineering advances were possible with printing, since detailed information could be transmitted accurately. In this 1556 engraving, Georges Agricola describes a system to pump water out of a mine. Agricola's book *De Re Metallica* (of the nature of metals) remained the authoritative source of information on mining for the next 180 years. Library of Congress.

Early on, the press was not as much an agent of change in the scientific revolution as it had been in the Protestant Reformation. Again, the focus at first was on publishing books from classical Greek and Roman authorities. Scientific publication was also held back by religious intolerance, and the Church's suppression of astronomers Giordano Bruno, Nicholas Copernicus, and Galileo Gallilei is well known.

A new trend was evident in a 1556 book by Georgius Agricola (1494–1555), *De Re Mettalica*, an illustrated exploration of geology, mining, and metallurgy. The book set a standard for scientific and technical books that were to come.

Gradually, scientists adopted the printing press as part of their educational and research efforts. For example, in Denmark, the astronomical observatory established by Tycho Brahe (1546–1601) included a printing shop to help spread new scientific knowledge. While the Church continued suppressing many new ideas, its rear-guard defense of an old way of thinking was doomed by the new media revolution.

Sometimes reformers used the press to challenge the elites. One opponent of the British College of Physicians, an apothecary named Nicholas Culpeper, dared to translate the Pharmacoepia from Latin to English so that medical prescriptions could be widely available. "He hoped it would make every man his own physician, as the translation of the Bible made every man his own theologian" (Conner 2005).

As the horizon of knowledge expanded, the role of printing in forming communities became appreciated. Publishers of all kinds of books encouraged readers to help amend the next edition. For instance, mapmakers and medicinal herbalists called on readers to submit notes about plants and coastlines, and send seeds and maps to the publishers. They "called upon the unlearned to contribute to the knowledge of natural history, geography and physics by communicating their observations on birds and flowers, on ebb and flood tide, on celestial phenomena ... Travelers and mariners especially were invited to do so" (Eisenstein 1980: 236). Eisenstein attributes the advent of participatory media to both idealistic and commercial motives, but there are parallels to crowd-sourcing in the digital age, such as the Wikipedia online encyclopedia with thousands of volunteer writers. "A new form of data collection was launched in which everyman could play a supporting role," she wrote.

5 News in Print

The need to hear and share news is universal in human cultures and a central part of what defines a community (Stephens 2007). Personal news is the first thing most people discuss when they haven't seen each other in a while. People also want to know the latest events in politics, religion, finance, and other areas, whether they are in an oral culture or a literate culture or some blend of the two.

In ancient Rome and China, bureaucrats wrote of political events in the capitals and sent the news out to the provinces. Commercial newsletters were produced as early as 131 BCE, and "armies of scribes" were employed to copy, publish and sell books by the thousands (Schramm 1988). A daily newsletter called the *Acta Diurna* conveyed not only official acts of the Senate but also news of crime, divorce, and other items of general interest (Ward 1996). Intended for both a wide general audience and the upper classes, the *Acta Diurna* is usually considered the first example of a mass media publication.

Aside from individual correspondence and oral communication, there are few known examples of mass communication in Europe between the fall of the Roman Empire in the 400 CE period to the early Renaissance. Around the 1380s, the emergence of banks and international trading made small group communication necessary, and regular handwritten newsletters were copied and sent by messenger.

Book publishing dominated the printing trade after Gutenberg's invention caught on, but a wide variety of small publications were also coming into print. Book merchants offered single-page woodblocks and engravings, along with pamphlets and booklets, such as religious tracts and sermons, exhortations to join causes, or speeches by monarchs and other public figures. Four basic kinds of news publications emerged between the late 1500s and early 1700s (Schramm 1988):

- Relation: a one-time publication about a single event, for example a battle or a coronation, usually printed on a small single sheet.
- Coronto: a small bound book about news from a foreign country.
- Diurnal: a regular publication that covered one subject, typically events in government.
- Mercury: a small bound book that would cover events from a single country for six months at a time.

Each of these types of publication can still be found in various forms. For example, a modern day "diurnal" might be the *Congressional Record* or *Federal Register*, published by the US government. Industry-oriented newsletters from groups like the Bureau of National Affairs might be considered modern day "mercury," in that they are issued daily or weekly but kept and bound by volume, and then used as reference books in specific industry and regulatory areas. Modern-day blogs focusing on a single subject are like "diurnals."

5.1 First newspapers

Johann Carolus, the owner of a French book printing company in Strasbourg, had grown tired of copying business newsletters by hand. In 1605, he decided to use the new printing press to save himself some time and began publishing the first newspaper.

"The copying has been slow and has necessarily taken much time, and since, moreover, I have recently purchased at a high and costly price [a] former printing workshop ... I have set, printed and published the said advice in my printing workshop" (Weber 2006). Other newspapers quickly followed: *Aviso* in Wolfenbuttel, Germany (1609); then papers in Basel, Switzerland (1610); Frankfurt, Germany (1615); Berlin (1617); Amsterdam (1618); London (1621); and Paris (1631).

One early newspaper that was closer in form to the modern newspaper was the *Dutch Courante uyt Italien, Duytslandt, &c.*, first published in 1618. Holland's printing industry introduced many other innovations around this time, including the first newspaper advertisements, the first woodcuts in a newspaper, and the first English and French-language newspapers that were printed in Amsterdam to evade the strict censorship in England and France.

The spread of newspapers and the relationships between printers of various nations is also illustrated by the career of Benjamin Harris, a publisher of small textbooks and Whig reformist tracts in London in the 1670s. From 1679 to 1681, Harris published *Domestick*

Intelligence, Or News from Both City and Country in London. He moved to Boston in 1686 and stared the London Coffee House, modeled on the coffee houses that were becoming popular in England. He also began publishing small almanacs and textbooks and the first newspaper in the United States, *Publick Occurrences, Both Foreign and Domestick*, in 1690. The newspaper reported on a smallpox epidemic, on atrocities by Indians allied with the British, and some local news items. It had no license and was closed after the first edition. Harris took on some Massachusetts government printing work but decided to return London in 1695, where he founded the *London Post.*

Despite the difficulty of publishing news using woodblock printing, a prototype of newspapers, called *kawaraban*, emerged in Japan in the seventeenth century with news about natural disasters, social events, love suicides, and other topical issues. As elsewhere, a growing literacy rate supported the new media (Dentsu 2014).

5.2 Censorship and freedom of the press

The word "censor" comes from the ancient Roman office of Censor, established around 443 BCE, which was responsible for public morals as well as keeping track of the population through a census. In Rome, as in most other countries at most times, censorship of speech and writing was common. Freedom of speech had its early defenders such as Socrates, but his ideas were said to be corrupting the youth of Athens, and he was executed by poison in 339 BCE. Punishment for others who strayed too far from the official view is all too common in history, although freedom of speech and religion have occasionally been prized in some cultures. One notably civilized ruler was Ashoka Maurya of India, 269–232 BCE, who issued the Seven Pillar Edicts promoting religious tolerance and Buddhist principles of compassion and justice.

Free speech was hardly common in early Europe. The Magna Carta of England, for example, written in 1215, guaranteed some rights but not freedom of speech. Parliament in 1275 outlawed "any slanderous News … or false news or tales where by discord or slander may grow between the King and the people …"

The advent of the printing press in Europe presented new challenges to the political and religious authorities, and four basic approaches to censorship were used:

- Licensing of a printing company itself;
- Pre-press approval of each book or edition of a publication;
- Taxation and stamps on regular publications; and
- Prosecution for sedition against the government or libel of individuals.

Often both state and Church censored publications. The Church issued the first Index of Prohibited Books in 1559, and through its control of universities such as the Sorbonne, also controlled all other kinds of publications. The dual system of censorship was widely used in Catholic nations around the world, for example, to prevent the invasion of Protestant ideas in Latin America in subsequent centuries (Newth 2001).

Protestant nations were also engaged in political censorship. In sixteenth-century England, printing was controlled by licensing through the Stationers Company, and punishment for printing unlicensed material was meted out by the Star Chamber. The punishments included the death penalty for printing treasonous articles, for questioning the Church of England, or advocating (or even envisioning) the death of the king. The strictest censorship laws were overturned in 1641, as Parliament demanded reform, and outright censorship ended in 1692, following the Glorious Revolution and ascent of William and Mary to the British throne four years previously.

One of the first countries to put an end to censorship was Sweden, which passed a law in 1766 banning the practice. The law emerged from a controversy over a 1759 pamphlet by Peter Forsskål called "Thoughts on Civil Liberty," in which he echoed John Milton, saying, "Truth always wins when it is allowed to be denied and defended equally."

While printing was often censored locally in central Europe, German states agreed through the Carlsbad Decrees of September 20, 1819, to suppress any seditious writing. The decrees were enforced by what was called the "black commission" located, ironically, in the birthplace of the printing revolution—Mainz, Germany. The Carlsbad Decrees were one of the factors in the European revolutions of 1848, to be discussed in Chapter 2.

The ideas about free speech that took hold in the new marketplace of ideas came from people like John Locke, Jean Jacques Rousseau, Benjamin Franklin, Thomas Paine, and Thomas Jefferson. They insisted that human rights were natural, and not simply handed down by governments or kings. The very structure of government ought to be balanced to allow people to act according to these natural rights, said French philosopher Baron de Montesquieu in arguing for separation of government powers into executive, legislative, and judicial branches. This idea, published in *The Spirit of the Laws*, was to form the basis of most nineteenth- and twentieth-century governments.

In Scotland, as already noted, philosopher David Hume defended freedom of the press by saying that newspapers and pamphlets can't easily incite rebellion. By reading, people can't "catch the passion by contagion," he said (Hume 1742).

Sentiment in favor of free speech and free press echoed back and forth across the English Channel and the Atlantic. In London, on February 15, 1721, popular newspaper columnists John Trenchard and Thomas Gordon, writing under the name of Cato, said:

> Without freedom of thought, there can be no such thing as wisdom; and no such thing as publick liberty, without freedom of speech: Which is the right of every man, as far as by it he does not hurt and control the right of another; and this is the only check which it ought to suffer, the only bounds which it ought to know. (Trenchard 1720–3)

Benjamin Franklin, in his persona as "Silas Dogood," made the identical comment a year later: "Without Freedom of Thought, there can be no such Thing as Wisdom; and no such Thing as publick Liberty, without Freedom of Speech." The motto, written above an entryway to the US Senate, differs only in the placement of a comma from the original by Trenchard and Gordon.

The strongest voice of the French Enlightenment was Francois Voltaire (1694–1778), author of *Candide*, who believed, more than anything else, in toleration, the rule of law, and freedom of opinion. In his *Essay on Tolerance*, Voltaire said, "Think for yourselves and let others enjoy the privilege to do so too." Voltaire also said, in a 1770 letter, "I detest what you write, but I would give my life to make it possible for you to continue to write" (Tallentyre 1907). The idea was later paraphrased as: "I disapprove of what you say, but I shall defend to the death your right to say it."

Naturally, talented printers often moved to nations where they were free to publish, such as Netherlands (Holland), Switzerland, Sweden, and later, Britain and the United States. Freedom of the press drew thinkers like Rene Descartes, John Locke and many others of the early Enlightenment to the publishing houses of the Netherlands. As astronomer Carl Sagan noted, "Because of its tolerance for unorthodox opinions, [the Netherlands was] a haven for intellectuals who were refugees from censorship and thought control elsewhere in Europe—much as the United States benefited enormously by the exodus of intellectuals in the 1930s from ... Europe" (Sagan 1980).

Freedom of the press was also seen as among the natural freedoms, and it was among the "first freedoms" that also included religion, speech, and assembly to be recognized during the American Revolution with the *Virginia Declaration of Rights*, of June 12, 1776, followed by the *Declaration of the Rights of Man and of Citizen*, France, August 26, 1789. Freedom of the press and religion were included in the First Amendment of the federal US Constitution, also called the *Bill of Rights*, in 1791.

These formed the basis of a modern international understanding of human rights, guaranteed in the United Nations *Universal Declaration of Human Rights*, of December. 10, 1948, and the *European Convention for the Protection of Human Rights and Fundamental Freedoms* of May 5, 1963.

5.3 Political revolutions

Just as books helped spark the Protestant Reformation, newspapers triggered political revolutions in England, the United States, Europe and Latin America during the eighteenth and nineteenth centuries. While every revolution has its own unique causes and effects, revolutionary changes in media are often intertwined with rapid changes in the social structure (Billington 1999).

Revolutionaries from the seventeenth to the twentieth century have advocated using the media of their day to advance the political revolutions they created. American revolutionary pamphleteers and publishers were well known as incendiaries. Observers of the French Revolution saw a rapid change in the media before and just after the revolution. Both Lenin and Gandhi began their very different forms of revolution by starting newspapers. And the role of various types of media in dozens of other revolutions has been well documented.

"If a great historical movement such as the Reformation can legitimately said to have started as a quarrel of monks, [late nineteenth-century revolutions were] also, in a certain sense, a tumult of journalists," said historian Aime Dupuy. The same point could have been made about any political revolution.

As philosopher Jurgen Habermas argued, political change is not only marked by a clash of classes or cultures, but is often an outcome of changes in the way people exchange ideas. The period from the seventeenth to the twentieth century was marked by a shift away from authoritarian monopolies over public debate and toward the rise of public opinion. A major factor was the "explosive power" of the periodical press (Habermas 1991).

5.3.1 The English Civil War and the marketplace of ideas

When England's Parliament broke with the monarchy, starting the English Civil War between 1642 and 1646, England's small printing shops quickly expanded into a full-blown industry, with more than 350 periodicals and tens of thousands of other one-off broadsheets, almanacs, ballads, broadsides, and other publications (Friedman 1992).

Both sides—the Royalists and the Parliamentary forces—had their own newspapers, some of them falsely designed to entrap supporters of the other side. Historian Hiley Ward tells the story of "Parliament Joan," a woman who pretended to be selling Royalist newspapers so that the buyers could be identified by their sympathies and turned over to Parliamentary forces (Ward 1996). John Milton's 1644 *Areopagitica* (noted above) was one of the few arguments for tolerance. While it had little contemporary impact, the concept of a marketplace of ideas was taken up by others arguing for freedom of conscience and press in the next century.

While both sides vehemently criticized the other, open discussion of political issues within each faction was not possible. Parliament continued the reign of censorship with the 1643 Licensing Act, which stayed in effect throughout the English Civil War. But the censorship was ineffective against the enormous pent-up demand for news, opinion, and entertainment that had long been suppressed. As Jerome Friedman noted:

> The two tumultuous decades of the English revolution witnessed a virtual tidal wave of cheap pamphlet publication covering every conceivable topic from religion to pornography, from reports of apparitions and monsters to odes describing the beneficial effects of opium and marijuana, from hysterical reports of Ranter blasphemy to accounts of scandalous religious charlatans claiming they were Jesus, Mary, and a host of other Biblical personalities returned from the dead. (Friedman 1992)

The end of censorship in England came in 1694, with the end for the formal licensing system, a result of the "Glorious Revolution" of 1688, when Parliament installed Dutch King William III and Queen Mary II as constitutional monarchs in England (Smith 1988). The revolution marked the end of the English Civil War and the birth of a new period of religious tolerance and press freedom.

In 1778, French Enlightenment philosopher Francois Voltaire compared the civil wars of Rome (49–45 BCE) to the English Civil War of the 1600s:

> The Romans never knew the dreadful folly of religious warfare ... But here follows a more essential difference between Rome and England, which gives the advantage entirely to the later—viz., that the civil wars of Rome ended in slavery, and those of the English in liberty. The English are the only people upon earth who have been able to prescribe limits to the power of kings by resisting them.

5.3.2 Revolutionary press fights for American freedom

Meanwhile in the American colonies, governments initially punished even the mildest criticism with imprisonment. Many colonies still operated with absolute authority. Even though England was convulsed in Civil War at the time, Virginia governor William Berkeley, a royalist, said in 1648, "I thank God there are no free schools nor printing, and I hope we shall not have these hundred years; for learning has brought disobedience and heresy and sects into the world; and printing has divulged them, and libels against the best government. God keep us from both" (Brown and Brown 1964).

As a result, Virginia lagged behind other states. Massachusetts had higher education by 1636, with the founding of Harvard College, and Elizabeth Glover started a printing chapel in Cambridge in 1639. It took Virginia until 1693 to establish its own college—William and Mary, in honor of England's new constitutional monarchs—and three more decades to start a newspaper. Governments continued to suppress printing in the American colonies, closing down the four-page newspaper *Publick Occurrences* after its first edition in 1690 in Boston. Coffee house owner Benjamin Harris had no license for his newspaper, and what's more, had slyly criticized the government. Prosecutions for libeling the government (called seditious libel) continued. Truth was not a defense in such cases, and in fact, truthful criticism was seen as even worse since it more credibly undermined authority. This changed when a New York jury overruled a judge and established truth as a defense in the libel of government in 1735.

The pre-revolutionary period in America was marked by the rise of printing establishments in every major city in the colonies, and new printers were frequently assisted on liberal terms by Benjamin Franklin, who not only owned a newspaper (the *Pennsylvania Gazette*) but also invested in a paper mill, a type foundry, and an ink factory. It was Franklin's assessment of Britain's unwillingness to change that tipped the scales among colonial printers; and the colonial press, in turn, paved the way for the revolution. "The [American] Revolution was effected before the war commenced," said the second US President, John Adams, writing to editor Hezekiah Niles in 1818. "The revolution was in the minds and hearts of the people, a change in their religious sentiments of their duties and obligations … This radical change in the principles, opinions, sentiments, and affections of the people, was the real American Revolution."

The most powerful weapons in this struggle were the colonial newspapers, according to historian Mitchell Stephens. During the decade before the outbreak of revolution,

John Peter Zenger and the Law of Seditious Libel

A landmark moment in American and British press freedom was the John Peter Zenger trial of 1735. Zenger's newspaper, the *New York Weekly Journal*, objected to electoral manipulation by an unpopular colonial governor, who responded by charging Zenger with seditious libel, which means defaming the government. At the trial, Andrew Hamilton, a Philadelphia lawyer, gave an eloquent argument to the jury, insisting that truth should be a defense against seditious libel and that the cause of freedom everywhere was at stake.

> The question before the court and you, gentlemen of the jury, is not of small or private concern. It is not the cause of one poor printer, nor of New York alone, which you are now trying. No! It may in its consequence affect every free man that lives under a British government on the main of America. It is the best cause. It is the cause of liberty. And I make no doubt but your upright conduct this day will not only entitle you to the love and esteem of your fellow citizens, but every man who prefers freedom to a life of slavery will bless and honor you as men who have baffled the attempt of tyranny ...

The jury agreed with Hamilton and bravely returned a "not guilty" verdict. The judges, overruled by the jury, were powerless to continue the case since the jury had, in effect, changed the law. The case had a far-reaching legal and psychological impact in colonies, to the extent that it was later seen as "the germ of American freedom, the morning star of that liberty which subsequently revolutionized America" (Linder 2001).

Figure 1.15 The cause of liberty—New York editor John Peter Zenger's lawyer argues before a colonial court in New York in 1735. Painting by Martha J. Lamb, Library of Congress.

newspapers "festooned themselves with polemical woodcuts: divided snakes, death's heads as mocking substitutes for tax stamps, and coffins designed by Paul Revere to represent the victims of the Boston Massacre" of 1774. Their rhetoric was heated, such as in this line from the *Massachusetts Spy* of 1773: "Shall the island Britain enslave this great continent of America, which is more than ninety nine times bigger, and is capable of supporting hundreds of millions of millions of people? Be astonished, all mankind, at her superlative folly" (Stephens 2007).

Among the most famous agitators for American independence was Thomas Paine (1736–1809), an Englishman who emigrated to Boston in 1774. Paine's pamphlet *Common Sense* argued for a complete break with Britain and independence for the American colonies. In *The Crisis, 1776–1777*, Paine famously said:

> These are the times that try men's souls. The summer soldier and the sunshine patriot will, in this crisis, shrink from the service of their country; but he that stands by it now, deserves the love and thanks of man and woman. Tyranny, like hell, is not easily conquered; yet we have this consolation with us, that the harder the conflict, the more glorious the triumph. What we obtain too cheap, we esteem too lightly: it is dearness only that gives every thing its value. Heaven knows how to put a proper price upon its goods; and it would be strange indeed if so celestial an article as FREEDOM should not be highly rated.

Figure 1.16 Thomas Paine—"These are the times that try men's souls"—The words that turned the spark of rebellion into a campaign for American freedom emerged from the pen of Thomas Paine in 1776 and were spread by the printing press throughout the colonies. After independence, Paine became involved in the French Revolution, then returned to the United States at the invitation of the then-president Thomas Jefferson. From a painting by George Romney, Library of Congress.

The success of the American Revolution, and the role played by the press, meant that press freedom would be protected in a way that would inspire many other countries.

The First Amendment, Thomas Jefferson said, was "a great experiment ... to demonstrate the falsehood of the pretext that freedom of the press is incompatible with orderly government."

5.3.3 France: The call for freedom and the descent into terror

In the decades before the French Revolution, official censors worked hard to contain the circulation of forbidden books, anti-monarchist booklets and the innumerable pamphlets (called "libeles") that floated around Paris and the provinces.

Baron de Montesquieu had to work in secret on his *Spirit of the Laws*; Denis Diderot was hounded as he worked on his *Encyclopdie*; and Franois Voltaire and Jean-Jacques Rousseau had to flee the country at various times in their careers. The idea that these writers were being oppressed by small-minded censors seemed like "a flock of eagles submitted to the governance of turkeys" (Darnton and Roche 1989).

Not all official sympathies were against them. Diderot was once publicly accused of unpatriotic writing, and his apartments were searched by the same official who had previously arranged to hide Diderot's notes in his own apartment. Like the American Revolution, the French Revolution was preceded by a shift in public sentiments expressed in the media. "What took place in 1789 could not have occurred as it did without a press or media revolution," said historian Jeremy Popkin (Popkin 1995).

A new network of "assemblies and clubs, newspapers, pamphlets, broadsides, songs, and other media ... closely and intensely tied to events" was in itself a central part of the "democratic culture" of the Revolution (Reichardt, 1988). In other words, the new form of the press was a symbol of the Revolution; the change in medium was part of the revolutionary message. One of the most interesting moments of the revolution was when journalist Camille Desmoulins (1760–94) was pushed to the front of an angry mob milling on a Paris street on July 12, 1789:

> I was carried upon a table rather than allowed to mount it. Hardly had I got up on my feet when I saw myself surrounded by an immense crowd. Here is my short speech, which I shall never forget: "Citizens! There is not a moment to lose ... This evening all the Swiss and German battalions will sally forth from the Champsde-Mars to cut our throats. We have only one recourse—to rush to arms." I had tears in my eyes, and spoke with a feeling that I have ne'er been able to recapture, no less describe. (Snyder and Morris 1962)

Two days later, Desmoulins helped organize the group that stormed the Bastille; an event commemorated every year as French Independence Day. Later that month his *La France Libre* was published, stating, "A popular and democratic government is the only constitution which suits France, and all those who are worthy of the name of men." His columns were widely circulated during the early years of the French Revolution, but his denunciation of the revolution's excesses led to his execution in 1794. During the first decade after the French Revolution, about 350 newspapers were published in France (Schramm 1988).

Newspapers helped consolidate the gains of the revolution but also split into partisanship over the course of the revolution, with leading papers favoring the Girondists (liberal republicans) or the Jacobins (radical revolutionaries). Newspapers were supported through the Declaration of the Rights of Man and of the Citizen of August 1789, which says in Article 11, "The free communication of ideas and opinions is one of the most precious of the rights of man. Every citizen may, accordingly, speak, write, and print with freedom, but shall be responsible for such abuses of this freedom as shall be defined by law."

The press was needed in the early stages of the revolution, according to historian Robert Darnton, to circulate the Declaration of the Rights of Man, ideas for the new constitution, new currency, a new calendar, a new map, and changes in the language itself. "At every stage in this process they use the same basic tool: the printing press," Darnton wrote. "Without the press, they can conquer the Bastille, but they cannot overthrow the old Regime. To seize power they must seize the word and spread it … When the revolutionaries grasped the bar of the press and forced the platen down on type locked in its form, they sent new energy streaming through the body politic. France came to life again, and humanity was amazed" (Darnton 1989).

Figure 1.17 "Citizens! Rush to arms!"—Camille Desmoulins, an impoverished French journalist and lawyer, is remembered for an impassioned speech that sparked the storming of the Bastille. One of the revolution's most insightful minds, Desmoulins opposed the radical Jacobin faction and was executed in 1794. From a painting by Rouillard, Library of Congress.

Humanity was terrified, too. The violent rhetoric of the French Revolution reached a new extreme with Jean Paul Marat, a Swiss physician who spent most of the pre-revolutionary years in London. He arrived in France to help lead the Jacobins and wrote horrifying predictions about what would happen if the revolution failed. In a July 1790 pamphlet entitled "C'enest fait de nous" ("We're done for!"), Marat wrote:

> A false humanity has restrained your arms and stopped your blows. If you don't strike now, millions of your brothers will die, your enemies will triumph and your blood will flood the streets. They'll slit your throats without mercy and disembowel your wives. And their bloody hands will rip out your children's entrails to erase your love of liberty forever.

As history has so often shown, fanatical rhetoric in the media can lead to bloody deeds in reality. An estimated 40,000 people, including King Louis XVI and Queen Marie Antoinette, were executed by the radical Jacobins at the urging of Marat and others. The Terror worsened when a Girondist (liberal) assassinated Marat at his home in 1793 while he wrote in the bathtub, but then ebbed with the establishment of the Directory in 1795. By 1798, Napoleon Bonaparte assumed power and many of the revolution's noble sentiments, including freedom of the press, lay in ruins. A widespread system of censorship was put in place by 1808, and the number of newspapers in Paris dwindled to thirteen and then finally to four by 1811. Censorship was lifted following Napoleon's defeat, then imposed and lifted again in cycles over the next century.

Figure 1.18 Napoleon—The little corporal, as Napoleon was called, is dwarfed by the printing press. Although he was a novelist and the publisher of several military newspapers early in his career, he also imposed draconian censorship during his reign as emperor of France. Public domain.

5.3.4 Spain, Portugal, and Latin American

The Spanish and Portuguese worlds of Europe and the Americas were yoked to authoritarian political systems from the earliest days of the press, and censorship was strict and relentless. However, like their counterparts in the American and French revolutions, Enlightenment-era Latin Americans also began a long process of political revolution that depended on the press.

Some of the early voices for liberation included Francisco de Miranda (1750–1816), a Venezuelan revolutionary who brought a press and six printers along on an 1806 expedition to liberate Venezuela from Spanish forces. In his Independence proclamation, Miranda said: "The day has come in which our [Latin] America recovers its sovereign independence, where our children will be able to freely express the whole universe of [their] generous sentiments." But the expedition was a failure, and the press fell into Spanish hands and became La Gazeta de Caracas in 1808.

To the west, in Columbia, editor and revolutionary Antonio Nariño (1765–1824) kept escaping captivity and returning to fight for freedom. Five years after the French Revolution, Nariño and a group of others had been jailed during the famous "Trials of 1794" for reprinting the French Declaration of the Rights of Man and other seditious ideas. One Cuban journalist endorsed the government view, saying that Spanish America did not have to accept "the pretentious freedom some people think the French enjoy." To fight royalist sentiments, Nariño established a political newspaper in Columbia, *La Bagatella*, in 1811. With a band of revolutionaries, he fought the Spanish government until he was captured in 1814. He lived to become part of the independent revolutionary government established a decade later.

Simon Bolivar (1783–1830), the liberator of Latin America, was about midway through a twelve-year military campaign when he ordered the creation of two revolutionary newspapers to diffuse ideals of freedom and independence: *Correo del Orinoco* (1818) and *Gazeta de Santafe de Bogota* (1819). Bolivar spent much of his time, even while at war, writing and editing these and other newspapers.

Latin American scholars have seen the press as "an extension of the army" for the other revolutionary movements, such as those in Argentina, Chile, Peru, Mexico, and elsewhere in Latin America, beginning around 1810.

Many insisted on freedom of the press in their new constitutions. Under the heading "Liberated de la Prensa," the *Correo del Orinoco* defended the proposed Constitution of Venezuela, saying it would guarantee "everyone's perpetual right to communicate their sentiments through any possible media ... although with just limits, and making people responsible for their printings, words and writings."

Brazil's press history took a different turn, since presses were prohibited in the early centuries of colonization. In 1808, as Napoleonic forces invaded Portugal, the royal family fled to Brazil and brought a printing press with them. The exodus of Portuguese royalty aligned the old state and military with the constitutionalist movement, and a degree of press freedom was achieved, and lost, and then won back again through a variety of Brazilian governments during the nineteenth century.

"Most liberators and heroes had something to do with the press," said Leonardo Ferreira, author of *Centuries of Silence: The Story of Latin American Journalism*. "They regarded the printed page as the best means of diffusion of their revolutionary ideas. Few revolutionaries, however, were willing to accept a right to freedom of the press without certain limitations ... In the end, all that enthusiasm ... during the early days of the revolutionary war would become, with few exceptions in later times, an exquisite but momentary taste of freedom, an immortal but unfinished revolution" (Ferreira 2006).

6. The Partisan Press before the Industrial Revolution

News traveled slowly before the Industrial Revolution. A newspaper printed in New York might reach Boston in three days, Richmond, Virginia in five, and Cincinnati, Ohio in ten. It would take almost two months to cross the Atlantic from New York to London or Paris until steamships became common in the 1830s, reducing the journey to about two weeks. Newspapers traveling from London to Caracas would take three months.

In Europe, the number of daily and weekly newspapers grew from about 2,400 in 1820 to about 12,000 by 1900, even though publishers there were handicapped by censorship, higher taxes, and higher postal rates. In the United States, newspapers were supported by favorable postal rates as part of a strategy for democratic self-government (Starr 2004). In contrast to Europe, where postal rates held down newspaper circulation, the number of US daily and weekly publications grew from about 800 to nearly 16,000. With fifty newspaper and magazine subscriptions per 100 homes, twice as many publications were available by 1823 to Americans as the British, and the number grew to three times as many by 1900.

The US Postal Service was considered a public service, not a for-profit agency, operating with the idea of unifying a widely disbursed population. Printed information, rather than personal letters, made up 95 percent of the weight carried in the mail, but only 15 percent of the revenue (Starr 2004). Americans were enormously proud of their newspapers. In

1817, Niles Register claimed that New York state, with 96 newspapers, had "probably … a greater number than is published in the whole of Europe" (*Niles Register*, April 26, 1817).

Although the figures are inaccurate, the assumption that Americans depended on newspapers more than other nations was essentially true. "In America there is scarcely a hamlet that has not its newspaper," wrote French aristocrat Alexis de Tocqueville in his 1835 book *Democracy in America* (de Tocqueville 1835). Because "there are no licenses to be granted to printers, no securities demanded from editors, as in France, and no stamp duty, as in France and England … nothing is easier than to set up a newspaper … Hence the number of periodical and semi-periodical publications in the United States is almost incredibly large."

Most newspapers in the United States or Europe were sold to a small circle of subscribers for at least five or six cents per copy, and the optimum economy of scale kept printing operations relatively small. Even national publications in the United States, like Baltimore's *Niles Weekly Register*, had circulations under 5,000. Editors kept in touch with each other by sending their publications through the mails. If the newspaper was being sent to another editor in a small town, it would be considered an "exchange," and other editors were free to print excerpts with attribution. This was seen as so important in the United States that the Post Office did not charge to deliver an exchange.

But the system of low postal rates, editor exchanges and widespread competition would change rapidly, beginning in the mid-nineteenth century, as steam printing transformed local publishing and the telegraph changed the way national news was distributed.

6.1 Partisan papers in Great Britain

The Glorious Revolution of 1688 set the stage for reform in England, and in 1694 the Licensing Act expired. Parliament approved a resolution, drafted by John Locke, noting that prior restraint was impractical: it hindered scholars and hurt the printing trade. Dozens of newspapers emerged at this time supported by two major political factions who opposed each other in the press and every other every aspect of public life. These two parties were the Tories and the Whigs.

The Tory party supported the monarchy over Parliament and tended to resist social reform and support tradition. By the mid-1800s the Tories became the Conservative party. (The name Tory derives from an insulting Irish term for robbers.) The Whig party supported Parliament over the monarchy, and supported free trade, religious toleration, abolition of slavery, and expansion of voting rights. Whigs became known as Liberals and an offshoot became the Labour party in the late 1800s. (The name Whig derives from a nickname for Scottish parliamentarians, Whiggamores, which meant cattle drivers.) Early Tory newspapers included the *Post Boy* and the *Examiner*; Whig newspapers included *The Times*, the *Flying Post*, and the *Observator*.

These newspapers existed in a world swirling with political controversy that also included Whig and Tory political organizations, Whig and Tory coffee houses, and even Whig and Tory fashions in clothing and entertainment. "Party conflict covered almost every aspect of public, professional and even recreational life in post-revolutionary England" (Bucholz 2009).

In 1701, a group of printers wrote to Parliament in protest against a contemplated tax on newspapers. At the time, England had "five master printers" using about 20,000 reams of paper per year, or about 28,000 newspapers in circulation per day nationwide. These sold for one halfpenny "to the poorer sort of people, who are purchasing it by reason of its cheapness, to divert themselves and also to allure … young children and entice them into reading." Hundreds of families, especially blind people, supported themselves by selling halfpenny papers on the streets of London (*Encyclopedia Britannica* 1911). The halfpenny press might have continued in England, but a stamp tax was imposed in 1724, and cheap newspapers vanished into an underground "pauper press" until 1855, when the tax was repealed. It was an extension of this same tax act to the American colonies in 1765 that aroused furor among American printers.

British authorities were finding the press very difficult to control, both at home and in the colonies, in the late 1700s. "For more than a century, newspapers and pamphlets had been strewn across the tables of clubs, inns, taverns and coffee houses and had fueled animated exchanges," wrote historian Jeffrey Smith. No one exemplified this problem better than the editor of the *North Briton*, John Wilkes. Wilkes had been a Member of Parliament for six years when he criticized a speech by King George III. He was convicted of seditious libel in 1764 and fled into four years of exile in France. He returned in 1768 to a tumultuous reception. The crowds in the London streets made it clear that Wilkes was widely supported by public opinion (Smith 1988).

He asserted parliamentary privilege, was released, and won re-election to Parliament in 1768. His treatment by the British authorities was watched carefully in the American colonies, and was considered one reason why American colonial printers believed that the social contract was being undermined by corrupt British leaders. Ironically, just as the revolution was breaking out in America, Wilkes became Lord Mayor of London and spent the rest of his life defending relatively conservative political views.

By the late 1700s, the news business was dominated by the *Times of London*, established by John Walter in 1785. In the beginning, *The Times* favored modest reforms and supported the "unalienable rights" of citizens, including freedom of speech and the right to petition the government (*Parliamentary Reform* 1785). Walter was not immune to the problems experienced by Wilkes, Cobbett, and others, spending 16 months in Fleet Street jail on libel charges. Despite competition from the *Manchester Guardian* and other regional newspapers, *The Times* remained the semi-official newspaper of the nation until 1981, when it was purchased by Rupert Murdoch's News Corporation. (After this, the *Guardian* became the UK's leading newspaper.)

6.1.1 What was the Fourth Estate?

The term "Fourth Estate" was a reference to the growing power of the press by Whig party leader Edmund Burke in a 1787 speech to Parliament. The speech was made when the visitor's gallery was opened to the press for the first time. According to historian Thomas

Carlyle, Burke said that there were three "estates" (walks of life) represented in Parliament: the nobility (House of Lords); the clergy; and the middle class (House of Commons). "But in the Reporters Gallery yonder, there sat a Fourth Estate, more important by far than they all."

This story is disputed. Editors of the *Oxford English Dictionary* say that they cannot confirm Carlyle's statement attributing the phrase "Forth Estate" to Burke. The earliest solid reference is in 1821 to William Cobbett, who was called "a kind of fourth estate in the politics of the country." Another reference is to a different speaker in the House of Commons in 1823 or 1824, and the idea was treated as original at the time.

The point of the historical debate is simply whether the political power of the press was widely recognized in the late 1700s or some fifty years later. Still, by the end of the nineteenth century, there was no doubt about the power of the press. As Oscar Wilde said around the time of his trial for homosexuality in 1895, "In old days men had the rack. Now they have the press … Somebody called journalism the Fourth Estate. That was true at the time no doubt. But at the present moment it is the only estate. It has eaten up the other three … We are dominated by journalism."

6.1.2. Trans-Atlantic connections

Journalists and their ideas traveled back and forth across the English Channel and the Atlantic Ocean as London became Europe's hothouse of political debate. Benjamin Harris, a London publisher, moved to the United States, opened a coffee house, and printed the nation's first newspaper before moving back to London. Benjamin Franklin came to London after leaving his brother's newspaper in Boston, working to learn the trade and earn money to open the *Pennsylvania Gazette* in Philadelphia in 1731.

During the revolutionary period, journalists Thomas Paine and William Cobbett traveled between England, the United States and France. And during the later tabloid press period (late 1800s, early 1900s), publishers in England often adopted agendas and ideas from American counterparts. US publisher William Randolph Hearst and British publisher Alfred Harmsworth, for example, were friends who often traded ideas and techniques.

William Cobbett (1763–1835) was one influential journalist who was constantly in trouble with authorities. He originally wrote from a pro-British perspective in the United States in the 1790s, then returned to England in 1800 and established a Tory publication called the *Weekly Political Register* in 1802. His conservative views changed over the years as he observed the cruelty, poverty, and corruption of the age. In 1809, when he objected to the use of German troops to put down a mutiny, he was sentenced to two years in prison for seditious libel.

Cobbett was in prison when he wrote about the Luddite riots of April 1812. All across the industrial north of England, mobs of starving, unemployed textile workers were seizing grain carts and breaking into factories to destroy steam-powered looms. When *The Times* suggested forceful suppression as the only course, Cobbett reacted: "With what a perfect coolness, with what sang-froid, with what a disregard for the lives of the people this must have been written" (Snyder 1962). After his release from prison, Cobbett continued to edit the *Political Register*, supporting agrarian reform, Catholic emancipation, and changes to the dreaded Poor Laws. But in 1817 he fled back to the US when Britain passed the Blasphemous and Seditious Libels Act. The act gave magistrates the power to seek and seize libelous materials. But the act was not especially effective, and juries were reluctant to convict editors, as Cobbett found when he returned to England. From 1819 to 1835, he fought off at least four more serious libel charges. Cobbett showed that the role of the British press in the social reform movements of the late 1700s and early 1800s could be daring, despite the frequent imposition of jail terms. In the end, his case for reform was largely accepted by British public opinion and reform governments in the mid-1800s.

Figure 1.19 Peter Porcupine—British journalist William Cobbett poured heated rhetoric into his US publications in the 1790s, warning in vitriolic terms of the excesses of the French Revolution and sympathizers like Thomas Paine. He celebrated his sharp personality with the pen name "Peter Porcupine." Returning to Britain in 1800, Cobbett attacked its "smothering system" that led to the Luddite Riots of 1811–12. He vowed to expose Britain's "service and corrupt press" that had become an instrument in the "delusion, the debasement and the enslavement of a people." Engraving by F. Bartolozzi, 1801, Wikimedia Commons.

6.2 Partisan papers in the United States

During the early years of the American republic, newspapers were usually financed and published by partisans of two major factions—John Adams' Federalist party and Thomas Jefferson's Democratic-Republican party. Phillip Freneau's *National Gazette* sided with Thomas Jefferson and the Democratic-Republicans. The paper favored the French Revolution and opposed the Alien and Sedition Acts. Jefferson later said that Freneau saved the country, "which was galloping fast into monarchy." After Freneau retired, Benjamin Franklin's nephew started a newspaper in Philadelphia called *The Aurora* that took up the defense of Democratic-Republican causes.

John Fenno's *Gazette of the United States* was the Federalist publication that sided with George Washington, John Adams, and Alexander Hamilton on great questions of the day, such as the need for a strong federal government. The Federalists were alarmed by the French Revolution.

In an attempt to head off an American version of the French Terror, Congress passed the Alien and Sedition Acts of 1798. Aimed at deporting French sympathizers and quelling criticism of President John Adams, the Sedition Act led to the imprisonment of about 100 people for speaking out against Adams and the government. Thomas Jefferson denounced the Sedition Act as a violation of the First Amendment of the US Constitution, which guaranteed freedom of speech and press. In the Virginia and Kentucky Resolutions, Jefferson and James Monroe argued that the states and not the federal government were ultimately sovereign, and therefore the federal government could not take away the rights of citizens. Although the Alien and Sedition Acts expired in 1801, the two resolutions had unintended consequences as the basis on which the Confederate states justified secession from the Union in the American Civil War (1861–5).

Not all newspapers descended into political partisanship. *Niles Weekly Register*, published in Baltimore from 1811 to around 1844, was guided by what editor Hezekiah Niles called a principle of "magnanimous disputation" (Luxon 1947). Niles was a forerunner of the more objective account of events, and his newspaper covered not only politics but economics, science, technology, art, literature, and population growth.

Niles is sometimes remembered today as the "Editor who tried to stop the Civil War" since he anticipated the conflict as early as 1820 and attempted to outline economic policies like diversification and public works that might lead toward compromise and reconciliation. Remarkably similar policies would resurface in the aftermath of the American Civil War from newspaper editors like Henry Grady and Ralph McGill of the *Atlanta Journal* (Kovarik 1992).

Life in a printing chapel

Figure 1.20 The printing chapel—A young Benjamin Franklin is depicted working in Samuel Palmer's printing chapel, on London's Bartholomew Close, during his apprenticeship in 1725. Engraving by Charles E. Mills, Library of Congress.

Imagine, for a moment, what it was like to work in a printing "chapel," and to live in a world that had barely changed between 1454, when Gutenberg developed moveable type printing, and the mid-1800s, when industrialization changed printing.

If you were an apprentice in a printing chapel, you might find the work tedious, but you would probably find the working environment fascinating. Here, literacy and intelligence were rewarded, women often worked alongside men, and the most interesting people in the city or the nation would show up at all hours.

As an apprentice, you would work under a system of rules much like other trades. You would start out at an early age, perhaps ten, and work your way up to journeyman around age eighteen.

Your work day was long—often twelve to fourteen hours. You worked in a printing company but you called it a "chapel," partly because printing evolved from the scriptoria where monks once labored. And, like the hierarchy of a church, your shop foreman was called a "sextant." In your first week or so, as an initiation ritual, you would receive a "washing," which was a howling maelstrom of noise created by the other apprentices and printers in the chapel. Every person in the chapel joined in, and the drumming, banging, cheering, and roaring could be deafening (Savage 1841).

Apprentices would be assigned unpleasant chores like greasing the presses, preparing the ink for pressmen, and (probably the least favorite) turning over the animal hides that would be soaking outside in vats of urine.

Once you were a journeyman, you might be expected to travel from city to city for two to three years, never coming close to home (except in case of an emergency), and keeping a "traveling book," complete with stamps and notes from various chapels where you stopped off and learned from each master printer. Journeyman years in Germany were called "*auf der Walz sein*" ("to be rolling"), which was sometimes confused by English-speakers as "waltzing," as in the Austrian dance or the Australian journeyman's song, "Waltzing Matilda."

Printing had its own culture, like any craft, but because it was a system that standardized language, many of its own terms and inside jokes have taken on broader meanings over time. In English, words and phrases such as upper case and lower case, out of sorts, by the same token, on the stick, wrong end of the stick, minding your ps and qs, stereotypes, and clichés—all of these come from printing culture. Even different types of meaning of the word "type" are reflections of the pervasiveness of printing culture.

Setting type

Imagine you're in the printing chapel ready to set a few words in type. You would step up to a workbench with two cases, each with dozens of open compartments that hold the individual metal letters. The capital letters are in the upper case and the small letters are in the lower case. Both of these terms—upper case and lower case—are still in use today. The cases have larger openings for commonly used letters, such as e, t, and a, and smaller openings for less commonly used letters.

In order to set the type, you pluck out the pieces of type and place then into a long holder called a "stick." The holder is set at the specific width of a column of type. Holding the wrong end of the stick would mean you'd be setting the type incorrectly.

Let's say you wanted to set the type for the phrase *Life in a print shop*. You would start with the letter "L" in the upper case, placing it into the right hand side of the holder, with the nick up and the letter facing backwards. Then set the i, f, and e—all facing backwards—and then a quadrat (space), then I, n, quadrat, a, quadrat, and so on. This can be confusing at first, and an apprentice typesetter might be told: "mind your ps and qs," because a "p" would look like a "q" when it went in backwards. Ps and qs can also refer to pints and quarts in a tavern, so the double entendre may have kept the idea alive.

The first job of an apprentice typesetter would often involve breaking up the columns of type after they had been set and used to print a book or newspaper. You'd clean them off and sort type back into the type cases according to letter, font, and size. Apprentices would have to be sure that each piece of type went back into the right slot and that the cases were ready for the typesetters. If this took too long, the typesetters might be "out of sorts"—in other words, they would lack the sorted type of a particular font. Later, this came to mean that a person might be upset. Usually, typesetters would work from copy written in longhand on a paper held to the top of the composing case by a spike. When an experienced editor was in a hurry, he or she might set type without even writing out the copy beforehand. This was called composing "on the stick." Today being "on the stick" means being busy with a pressing task (and not being impaled).

By the time you were a journeyman printer, you could probably set around 1,500 letters per hour, or about twenty words per minute. A column of type might take half the day—five or six hours—to set. Once type was set, the columns would be assembled in galleys on the composing stone and then held together inside a frame. The frame would be locked down with quoins and other "furniture." Then the type would be placed on a press.

To print a sheet of paper, one pressman (the "beater") would gently pound an even coat of ink into the type using two soft leather inking balls (this soft leather came from the hides soaking in vats of urine). Another pressman would place a damp page of blank paper into the frisket (a cover to protect the edges of the page from stray ink) and gently fold it over the frame of inked type. The final stage was to roll the type down the carriageway underneath the platen. The pressman would pull on the long lever, and the paper would be pushed down into the inked type. Then the pressman would release the lever, roll the type back, open up the frisket, and hang the page up to dry.

A team of two pressmen and an apprentice would usually print a "token" of 258 sheets per hour. The expression "by the same token" means turning the sheets over once the ink has dried in order to print on the other side of the paper.

Once the pages were printed, they had to be assembled carefully to make a book. This involved placing and trimming the pages in the right order and then sewing up the back of each set of pages, or "signature," which could be from four pages, or sixteen or twenty-four, depending on the size of the page and the kind of book being produced.

It was hard for a publisher to know how popular a book might be. If a book might go into a second or third printing, it would be expensive to reset the type again. But it was also expensive to leave big blocks of pages set in type.

One process to make this cheaper was called a stereotype, and it was developed in England in the 1740s, although not widely used until a century later. A copy of the bed of type would be made with a paper mache mold, and then filled with solid type metal (lead, tin, and antimony) to form a stereotype. This was also called a cliché in France, in part because the lead foundries in the Paris suburb of Clichy served the French printing industry, and also in part because it is an onomatopoeia: molten lead being poured into a mold makes a sound like "cliché."

Figure 1.21 A traditional engraving of the printer's holiday, called a Wayzgoose. Public domain.

Playing quadrats and getting a washing

The work could be tedious and exacting. To make the day go by more quickly, and to contribute to the education of apprentices, one printer might be asked to read aloud from works of literature or the Bible.

Printers had strict social rules. They were not allowed to brag, or to whistle in the presence of a lady, or to leave candles burning when they were not present. Breaking any of those rules would result in a punishment, which they called a "solace," and this could involve performing a nasty chore, or putting money into the entertainment fund, or singing an embarrassing song at the annual printer's holiday, the Wayzgoose, that took place every August 24th.

Printers had fun too. A typical pastime was a game called "quadrats," which uses the square blank type spacers. Each quadrat has a nick, or indentation, on one of its four sides. The game was described in a 1683 book on printing customs:

> They take five or seven Quadrats … and holding their Hand below the Surface of the Correcting Stone, shake them in their Hand, and toss them upon the Stone, and then count how many Nicks upwards each man throws in three times, or any other number of times agreed on: And he that throws most Wins the Bett of all the rest, and stand out free, till the rest have try'd who throws fewest Nicks upward in so many throws; for all the rest are free: and he pays the Bett. (Moxon 1683; Savage 1841)

But watch out! If the sextant (foreman) of the chapel caught you playing quadrats, you would pay the solace (punishment). Sometimes the sextant or master printer also had to pay the solace, since playing quadrats can batter and spoil the type.

If you or a co-worker were in the habit of telling tall tales, sometimes other workers would express their disbelief by giving a washing and making loud banging noises on their presses or type cases. And if, for some reason, an apprentice or journeyman resisted a solace or a washing, and if the other workers in the chapel were determined to enforce it, then the Spirit of the Chapel (sometimes called "Ralph") was said to be "walking" in the shop. Then, whatever mischief was done to the apprentice, such as getting his type "pied" (mixed up) could be blamed on the Spirit.

For additional reading, discussion questions, links to video, and other suggestions, see www.revolutionsincommunications.com.

2

The Commercial and Industrial Media Revolution 1814–1900

The press is "the high priest of history, the vitalizer of society, the world's great informer, the medium of public thought and opinion, and the circulating lifeblood of the whole human mind. It is the great enemy of tyrants and the right arm of liberty, and is destined, more than any other agency, to melt and mould the jarring and contending nations of the world into … one great brotherhood."

Samuel Bowles, 1851 (Brendon 1983)

1 Steam-powered Printing Launches a New Media Era

It's six in the morning on November 29, 1814, and London's Fleet Street is beginning to fill with the cacophony of commerce. But the rows of hand-pulled presses at *The Times*, hardly changed since Gutenberg, have for once stopped their creaking and rumbling. The printers have been standing idle, and they are wondering how the newspaper will be produced today. They were told to wait for important foreign news to arrive.

Then at dawn, John Walter II, owner of *The Times*—a thin man with a beak-like nose and a long black coat—bursts into the pressroom and calls for the printers to gather around. He is holding up this morning's issue of *The Times*—the same newspaper they had expected to be producing. Fearful glances are exchanged around the room. "The Times is already printed—by steam," he announces grandly. He passes the newspaper out to the printers, who regard the boss with anger and suspicion as he explains. Today's *Times* has been printed on a new kind of press designed by Friedrich Koenig, a mechanical engineer, he tells them. It was built in secret by Koenig's men in a guarded warehouse down the street.

It's a tense moment. Workers all over England have been losing their jobs to the steam engine. Three years before, in the industrial cities north of London, the "Luddite" riots broke out when many thousands of textile workers were thrown out of work. Fifteen men were hung in York, and eight in Lancashire, for their roles in sabotaging the cotton mills. Walter warns against any Luddite rebellions in his shop. But he also says that, unlike the textile industry, *The Times* will stand by its workers. There will be no layoffs. In fact, the faster press will mean more work for everyone. The advantage of a steam press is not just speed, he emphasizes, but also less physical labor. This is an important point for the pressmen. Pulling that press lever hour after hour, day after day, leaves many men with one-sided muscle development. In fact, it's possible to tell an experienced pressman just from the loping way he walks. Speed is also important for the business, Walter says. Where a crew of three men on a hand press might print 250 pages per hour, on one side, a crew of six men on the new steam press could produce 1,100 pages, on both sides, per hour—nearly four times the efficiency. (By 1828, it will be 4,000 pages per hour with fewer printers.)

And so, by investing in new technology, and treating its workers with respect, *The Times* scores a worldwide first. The revolution from handcrafted printing to industrial printing production is momentous—costs of production come down, and due to mass circulation, the potential for advertising support goes up. The significance of the moment is difficult to overstate, but *The Times* calls it the "greatest improvement" since printing was invented:

> Our journal of this day presents to the public the practical result of the greatest improvement connected with printing, since the discovery of the art itself. The reader of this paragraph now holds in his hand one of the many thousand impressions of the Times newspaper which were taken off last night by a mechanical apparatus.

Figure 2.1 Steam powered printing—Friedrich Koenig developed a steam-powered press for John Walter II at *The Times* of London in 1814. This Koenig-inspired model was probably built in the 1820s.

Other labor-saving advances were just over the horizon. One was the ability to use molds to produce thin metal copies of whole pages of laid-out type. This was called a "stereotype" in English, or a "cliché" in French. Stereotyping became vital in the 1840s and 1850s because it could be used for cylindrical printing plates on high-speed rotary presses. This in turn allowed circulation to grow from the tens of thousands to the hundreds of thousands for big-city newspapers in the late nineteenth century.

2 The 'Penny' Press: A News Media Revolution

Steam presses and stereotyping created more profits for publishers in two ways: a) better economies of scale on the production side; and b) higher prices for advertising since messages reached more potential customers. Expanding circulation and rising advertising revenues meant that the newspaper could be sold for a lot less—as little as a penny per copy. And that, in turn, could mean more circulation and then more advertising.

Although steam printing was introduced at *The Times* of London in 1814, the penny press business model took off first in the United States in the 1830s, where taxes did not hold back the development of competing newspapers. By the 1850s, the penny press revolution began to have impacts in Britain and the rest of Europe. And the model was also replicated in the broadcasting industry in the 1920s, where advertising supported content development. The penny press model was the dominant business model until the early twenty-first century, when advertising income dropped rapidly, and the circulation–advertising cycle began moving in reverse, as declining circulation meant rapidly declining advertising revenues.

What history remembers best about the penny press revolution is the way it democratized the media. Before steam printing and the "penny press" revolution, most newspapers cost five to six cents each. Circulation was limited to the thousands and oriented toward the social elite. But after the penny press revolution, publishers could serve broad public tastes rather than elite segments of a community. Rather than focusing on the great and powerful, readers could now encounter the daily lives and concerns of ordinary men and women. As historian Richard Kluger said, "a new spirit arose in the common man, who was encouraged to believe that his life, his voice, his vote were of some importance." New expectations were irrepressible once released, and a new literary form encompassing the humble as well as the great was now possible" (Kluger 1986).

At a glance, the "new media" of the 1830s looked a lot like the old media. It was still a newspaper, printed on the cheapest possible paper, with long gray columns of type. But the editorial agenda had changing drastically, shifting from long political discussions to short descriptions of events, crimes, and scandals; from summary essays about social trends to first-person accounts by paid reporters; from long-form descriptions to the "inverted pyramid" that placed key developments in the lead of the news articles. The new publishers who catered to public taste also found that the public was fascinated by bizarre hoaxes, scathing editorials, shocking scandals, and crime with the most lurid possible detail.

Figure 2.2: Printing innovation—Two Boston women assist at a 1822 Treadwell press, a double-acting press that was an improvement over older models. Women often had a role in printing and typesetting, especially in family-run printing shops. Benjamin Franklin and Horace Greeley fought the prevailing prejudice of the times and encouraged women to manage and write for newspapers, but they were not unique. From Robert Hoe, *A Short History of the Printing Press*, 1902.

2.1 New York's penny press: The *Sun*, the *Herald*, the *Tribune* and the *Times*

Four of New York's emerging daily newspapers in the 1830s are remembered as prototypes of the penny press revolution: the *Sun*, the *Herald*, the *Tribune*, and the *New York Times*. Only the *Times* survives in its original form today.

2.1.1 The rise and fall of the *New York Sun*

Benjamin Day's small New York printing business had come to a standstill in the summer of 1833. The financial panic was one reason; another was the cholera epidemic raging through the city. As Day cast about for new ways to earn money, the idea of starting yet another newspaper in the crowded New York market seemed quixotic to his friends. New York already had seven morning and four evening daily papers with circulations between 1,200 and 4,500.

These "elite" papers reported on politics, shipping, and business to select clients. They sold for six cents a copy, over the counter or delivered to subscribers. Day wondered if it wouldn't be possible to print a penny paper and sell it on the streets. It had been tried before—Horace Greeley's *Morning Post*, sold for a penny, had failed the year before after only three weeks. Penny papers in Boston and Philadelphia had also failed.

But with little to lose, Day issued his first copy of the *Sun* on September 3, 1833, noting that the paper's purpose was to provide news of the day "at a price within the means of every one." The leading article was a humorous story about a dueling Irishman. Other items included charges of assault being heard in court; a suicide; three murders; an earthquake in Virginia; and an account of a boy who fell ill from whistling. The paper was a modest success, and Day realized that New Yorkers were far more interested in a man who was arrested for beating his wife than they were in Andrew Jackson and the fight over the United States Bank. He hired a police court reporter and a small army of newsboys to hawk the paper on the streets. Within a month, circulation reached 1,200, and within a year it had reached 10,000 (O'Brien 1918).

Other printers, like Greeley, did not think much of Day's efforts. Although the *Sun* tried to deal with the human condition in ways that the elite papers did not, it had an unprofessional, smirking attitude, as this account shows: "Sudden death—Ann McDonough, of Washington Street, attempted to drink a pint of rum on a wager, on Wednesday afternoon last. Before it was half swallowed Ann was a corpse. Served her right!"

The reaction from the elite papers was predictable. Colonel James Webb, editor of the *Courier* and *Enquirer*, bemoaned the success of "penny trash." Day shot back that the public had been "imposed upon by ten-dollar trash long enough." But there were better penny papers starting to compete with Day. In August of 1835, perhaps in an attempt to catch up with the competition, the *Sun* published six stories about the fantastic discoveries of Sir William Hershel, a British astronomer who was known to be in South Africa at the time.

To make the hoax more credible, the *Sun* invented the "Edinburgh Journal of Science," with elaborate descriptions of new astronomical telescopes and lunar geography, along with descriptions of bat-like winged humans living in the canyons of the moon. While the *Sun* never admitted that the stories had been crafted by its editors, the absence of any confirming reports from England or Scotland soon led people to realize that they had been victims of a hoax.

The *Sun* took on a second life when it was purchased in 1868 by Charles Henry Dana, a Harvard graduate who had served uncomfortably as Horace Greeley's news editor. Dana's *Sun* emphasized the "human interest" story with brief articles about a wide range of activities, evolving into what has been called the first "tabloid" newspaper. Lord Northcliffe (Albert Harmsworth) later said he modeled Britain's first tabloid, the *Daily Mail*, on Dana's editing of the *Sun*.

It was one of Dana's editors, John B. Bogart, who made what is perhaps the most frequently quoted definition of the news: "When a dog bites a man, that is not news, because it happens so often. But if a man bites a dog, that is news."

The *Sun* also earned a prominent place in journalism history with its September 21, 1897 editorial by Francis P. Church, who wrote in answer to a young girl's inquiry: "Yes, Virginia, There Is a Santa Claus."

That same year of 1897, the *Sun* editor Dana died, and the newspaper began drifting out of its orbit. Financially struggling, the *Sun* entered into a series of mergers in 1916 and

Figure 2.3 The Moon Hoax and the *New York Sun*—Benjamin Day (1810–89), editor of the *New York Sun*, was trying to hang onto readers by publishing a fake scientific news item in 1835: "We were thrilled with astonishment to perceive four successive flocks of large winged creatures, wholly unlike any kind of birds, descend with a slow even motion from the cliffs on the western side, and alight upon the plain ... They averaged four feet in height, were covered, except on the face, with short and glossy copper-colored hair, and had wings composed of a thin membrane, without hair, lying snugly upon their backs, from the top of their shoulders to the calves of their legs. The face, which was of a yellowish flesh color, was a slight improvement upon that of the large orangoutang [*sic*], being more open and intelligent in its expression, and having a much greater expansion of forehead ... So far as we could judge, they spent their happy hours in collecting various fruits in the woods, in eating, flying, bathing, and loitering about on the summits of precipices." Engraving by Benjamin Day, *New York Sun*, August 29, 1835. Library of Congress.

was gone by 1920. The *New York Sun* was briefly revived as a conservative alternative to the *New York Times* from 2002 to 2008, but collapsed again with the economic recession of that year.

2.1.2. Bennett and the *New York Herald*

Shocking cruelty and malevolent genius were the trademarks of James Gordon Bennett, editor of the *New York Herald*. An impoverished reporter aged forty, characterized by grim determination, Bennett founded the *Herald* in 1835. He worked out of a cellar and struggled with bankruptcy for a year before the *Herald* became one of the leading national newspapers of the nineteenth century. Success came because every day the *Herald* served up a mix of robberies, rapes, and murders from the criminal courts of New York. In 1836, Bennett became obsessed with the murder of a beautiful prostitute named Ellen Jewett. He visited the scene of the crime, played detective, and even described the corpse: "as

Figure 2.4 Yes, Virginia—Responding to a young girl's letter in 1897, *New York Sun* editor Francis P. Church said, "Yes" to the enduring spirit of childhood. The celebrated letter was part of a revival of the Christmas holiday led by many other writers and by illustrator Thomas Nast, who depicted Santa, caught by a child as he delivers presents, in 1892. Library of Congress. Church wrote: "Yes, Virginia, there is a Santa Claus. He exists as certainly as love and generosity and devotion exist, and you know that they abound and give to your life its highest beauty and joy. Alas! How dreary would be the world if there were no Santa Claus. It would be as dreary as if there were no Virginias. There would be no childlike faith then, no poetry, no romance to make tolerable this existence. We should have no enjoyment, except in sense and sight. The eternal light with which childhood fills the world would be extinguished ... There is a veil covering the unseen world which not the strongest man, nor even the united strength of all the strongest men that ever lived, could tear apart. Only faith, fancy, poetry, love, romance, can push aside that curtain and view and picture the supernal beauty and glory beyond. Is it all real? Ah, Virginia, in all this world there is nothing else real and abiding. No Santa Claus! Thank God! He lives, and he lives forever. A thousand years from now, Virginia, nay, ten times ten thousand years from now, he will continue to make glad the heart of childhood."

white, as full, as polished as the purest Parian (Greek) marble … [with] the perfect figure, the exquisite limbs, the fine face, the full arms, the beautiful bust." Opponents in other newspapers compared him to a vampire or a vulture, but his investigations acquitted the man who had apparently been wrongfully accused of Jewett's murder.

The *Herald* redefined news in other ways, with reports on Wall Street, sports events, and society affairs. Bennett also set up bureaus in Washington, London, and Paris. Bennett's *Herald* carried regular Church news, but its editorial page attacked the Catholic Church, an institution reflecting the "darkness, folly and superstition of the tenth century." Ostensibly a Catholic, Bennett even attacked Americans who "kiss the toe of every debauchee whom the College of Cardinals may elevate to the triple crown [the papacy]." Shortly afterwards he was excommunicated. That meant very little to Bennett. He once horsewhipped the editor of a rival newspaper in the streets, and many victims of his pen felt they had been similarly treated.

Not surprisingly, Bennett was widely disliked. The only chance he had of dying an upright man, said rival editor Benjamin Day, "will be that of hanging perpendicularly from a rope." Charles Dickens saw the *Herald* as "foul mass of positive obscenity," and lampooned Bennett in his portrait of Colonel Diver, editor of the New York Rowdy Journal, in his book *Martin Chuzzlewit.* As his boat arrives at the docks of New York, passengers are assailed by newsboys attempting to sell the "Rowdy Journal," the "Daily Sewer," and the "Family Spy." Looking on the scene with pride was a fellow passenger:

> … a sallow gentleman, with sunken cheeks, black hair, small twinkling eyes, and a singular expression hovering about that region of his face, which was not a frown, nor a leer, and yet might have been mistaken at the first glance for either. Indeed it would have been difficult, on a much closer acquaintance, to describe it in any more satisfactory terms than as a mixed expression of vulgar cunning and conceit.

Figure 2.5 A well-hated editor of the *Herald*—James Gordon Bennett, founder of the *Herald*, brought professionalism and enterprise to the craft, but also caustic editorial attacks. Photograph by Matthew Brady, 1851.

Whatever people thought of Bennett, the newspaper was prodigal in seeking out news and writing it with flair. When Fort Sumter in Charleston Harbor fell to the South Carolina rebels, triggering the American Civil War, Bennett's reporter wrote, "Fort Sumter has fallen. The war has begun. Words have given place to blows. The Gordian knot has been sundered, and the Palmetto State [South Carolina] has taken the final step …"

The *Herald* was by far the leading newspaper during the war, with a circulation of 400,000 daily. Bennett spent huge amounts of money on telegrams from the front lines. Editorially, he was opposed to the war, and often wrote in derogatory terms about President Abraham Lincoln, for example, as the "great ghoul." After his assassination, though, Bennett wrote that in 100 years, historians would still be astounded at Lincoln's greatness. The "real origin" of the assassination, he said, was "the fiendish and malignant spirit developed and fostered by the rebel press, North and South" (Mitgang 1989).

Bennett and his son, James Gordon Bennett Jr., insisted that the newspaper be first with news, rewarding or punishing reporters who scooped (or who failed to scoop) other papers. The *Herald* was the first to report the news of the defeat of General George Custer against the Sioux at the Battle of Little Big Horn in 1876 and the first to report on the sinking of the *Titanic* in 1912. It sent reporters and scientists on numerous expeditions, including Henry Morton Stanley's African expedition of 1871 and the Jeannette Arctic expedition of 1878. The paper was merged with the *Tribune* and eventually purchased by the *New York Times*.

2.1.3. Greeley and the *New York Tribune*

New York readers looking for something above crude sensationalism were relieved when Horace Greeley established the *New York Tribune* in 1841 with the idea of publishing a trustworthy and moral newspaper. Greeley was an eccentric man without much formal education, but his *Tribune* had a profound influence on American politics in the mid-nineteenth century. Greeley said he had "sat at the feet" of Hezekiah Niles, editor of the Baltimore-based *Niles Weekly Register*, whose view of the press was akin to having a sacred trust. Greeley read every issue and absorbed many of Niles' ideas about the abolition of slavery, national economic development, and fairness in news reporting.

Greeley continued the reform tradition by promoting social causes such as women's rights, labor unions, and the end of monopolies. He was also fascinated with the American West, and was long remembered for the admonition, "Go west, young man, and grow up with the country." Greeley took that advice himself, traveling across the Plains to California and recording the trip in "An Overland Journey from New York to San Francisco," published in 1860. Greeley advocated preservation of redwood forests and supported the idea of national parks: "I am sure they [the redwoods] will be more prized and treasured a thousand years hence than now, should they, by extreme care and caution, be preserved so long, and that thousands will then visit them, over smooth and spacious roads, for every one who now toils over the rugged bridle-path by which I reached them.

Greeley also expressed surprise at the way Mormons treated women:

> I have not observed a sign in the streets, an advertisement in the journals, of [Salt Lake City, Utah], whereby a woman proposes to do anything whatever. No Mormon has ever cited to me his wife's or any woman's opinion on any subject; no Mormon woman has been introduced or has spoken to me; and, though I have been asked to visit Mormons in

> their houses, no one has spoken of his wife (or wives) desiring to see me, or his desiring me to make her (or their) acquaintance, or voluntarily indicated the existence of such a being or beings ... The spirit with regard to woman, of the entire Mormon, as of all other polygamic systems, is fairly displayed in this avowal. Let any such system become established and prevalent, and woman will soon be confined to the harem, and her appearance in the street with unveiled face will be accounted immodest. I joyfully trust that the genius of the nineteenth century tends to a solution of the problem of woman's sphere and destiny radically different from this.

Figure 2.6 A moral editor: the *Tribune*—Founder and editor of the *New York Tribune*, Horace Greeley attempted to strike a higher moral tone in the news. Engraving by Johnson, Fry & Co. after a painting by Chappel. Library of Congress.

Greeley was also concerned with events in Europe, and in 1851, hired Karl Marx as London correspondent. Marx wrote 487 articles for the *Tribune*, including this 1862 observation about the resistance by the British working class to the idea of Britain entering the US Civil War on the side of the South:

> The misery that the stoppage of factories and cutting of working time, brought on by the blockade [of Southern cotton from] the slave states is unbelievable and daily on the increase ... English intervention in America has accordingly become a bread and butter issue for the working class ... Under these circumstances, the obstinacy with which the working class keeps silent, only to break that silence to speak against intervention, and for the United States, is admirable. This is new, brilliant evidence of the independence of the English masses, of that excellence which is the secret of England's greatness. (Snyder and Morris 1962)

Like other newspaper editors of the day, Greeley could also be mercurial. The *Tribune* advocated peace before the Civil War but proclaimed "On to Richmond" (the capitol of the Confederacy) when war broke out. Greeley disliked most politicians but promoted Abraham Lincoln's candidacy, then constantly hectored the president on the conduct of the war. He helped form the Republican Party in the 1850s but then ran for the presidency on the Democratic ticket in 1872, losing to one of Lincoln's generals, Ulysses S. Grant.

The *Tribune* merged with the *Herald* in 1924, and the combined *Herald Tribune* continued as one of the most literate and progressive newspapers in America, until 1967.

Some observers said it had been crippled by the New York newspaper strike of 1962–3, which involved demands to slow down the technological changes affecting printing. The *Herald Tribune* continued in Paris as an English language newspaper for American expatriates until 2013, when it was purchased by the *New York Times*.

2.1.4 The *New York Times* as the national paper of record

New York was growing, and publishers like Greeley and Bennett were growing rich. But neither quite caught the spirit of Yankee pragmatism, being either too moralistic or too sensationalistic. So Henry Raymond and a partner had little trouble raising $70,000 and founding the *New York Times* in 1851. It was an immediate success (Talese 1969).

Greeley later said sourly that it gained circulation by pandering to the "ultra abuse" of abolitionists, spiritualists, women's rights advocates, and reformers, but Raymond had a view of news reporting close to Benjamin Franklin's idea that printers need to be amenable to many points of view. And he foresaw a kind of neutrality that would later be called objectivity. In the paper's first editorial on September 18, 1851, Raymond said:

> We shall be conservative in all cases where we think conservatism essential to the public good; and we shall be Radical in everything which may seem to us to require radical treatment and radical reform … We do not mean to write as if we were in a passion … There are very few things in this world which it is worth while to get angry about; and they are just the things that anger will not improve.

Figure 2.7 A dispassionate editor: the *Times*—Henry Raymond founded the *New York Times* in 1851 to provide an alternative to Greeley's moralizing and Bennett's sensationalism. In the process, the *Times* became the country's leading newspaper of record, printing, as his successors would claim in the 1890s, "All the news that's fit to print." Brady-Handy Photograph Collection, Library of Congress.

But even this supposedly neutral, dispassionate newspaper had its sore spots. One incident that provoked Raymond was the Edgardo Mortara affair of 1858, in which a six-year-old boy was taken from his Jewish parents in Bologna, Italy, and handed over by police to Vatican officials. This occurred because a servant in the Mortara household had secretly baptized the boy, and, under religious law in Italy at the time, Christians were not permitted to live with Jews. The boy was never allowed to return home. The affair was an "outrage," Raymond wrote in one of twenty articles carried in the *Times*, a "violation of one of the most sacred natural rights of man." Had the case occurred in another country, or had a Roman Catholic family been similarly treated in a Jewish or Protestant community, "the voice of civilization would have been just as loud in condemnation" (*New York Times*, December 4, 1858).

The *New York Times* continued its moderate but occasionally radical course after Raymond's death in 1869, strongly attacking the corruption of New York's political machine, Tammany Hall, in the early 1870s. The *Times*'s investigative work, along with Thomas Nast's cartoons in *Harper's Weekly*, mobilized public opinion against civic corruption and demonstrated the effectiveness of investigative reporting. Adolph Ochs, a Southern publisher, bought the *Times* in 1896 and coined the paper's slogan: "All the news that's fit to print." Once again, the *Times* was distancing itself from competitors such as Joseph Pulitzer's crusading *New York World* and William Randolph Hearst's sensationalistic *New York Journal*. As the leading newspaper in the nation's largest city, the *New York Times* became the newspaper of record in the United States by the turn of the century.

2.2 The penny press in Britain

By the early nineteenth century, *The Times* of London had become the Britain's leading newspaper, representing a conservative philosophy that opposed most, but not all, reforms or reformers. A classic example is the reaction to heavy-handed environmental cleanup of the London water and sewer systems on August 1, 1854: "We prefer to take our chance of cholera and the rest than be bullied into health," *The Times* said in an editorial column.

The Times' coverage of war and affairs of the empire was deeply intertwined with events themselves. William Howard Russell's dispatches from the Crimea, particularly his reporting on the blundering, bloody charge of the Light Brigade, created political shock waves in Britain. Editorializing on the fall of the British outpost in Khartoum, Sudan, in 1884, after a prolonged siege, *The Times* urged readers to "think only of the grief of England, tortured by the fate of General Gordon" (February 6, 1885). Observers in New York saw "[t]he press demanding action." Readers also found time to think of the fall of the Gladstone government and the subsequent call for new elections (North 2014).

The Times was so important that when a boundary dispute between Britain and Venezuela came up in 1894, the Venezuelan mediators addressed their arguments to the newspaper as well as the British government (Seijas 1896).

The Times was not a popular or "penny" newspaper. That business model arrived late in England, held back by taxes that were designed to hinder the growth of reform-minded publications and protect established newspapers like *The Times*. In fact, the government closed down publications like the *Manchester Observer* that supported protesters in the Peterloo Massacre of 1819. The *Manchester Guardian*, also a reforming newspaper, was established to take its place in 1821. More or less constant calls for the abolition of taxes led, finally, in 1836 to a reduction in the stamp tax but an increase in penalties for those who did not pay it.

The argument against the penny press, from the established British media, was that American newspapers were "wretched and inferior, [given to] flippancy for wit, personality for principle, bombast for eloquence, malignity without satire and news without truth or reliability " (Brendon 1983). In 1842, *The Times* piled on with this: "The once hopeful Eden of liberty remains a wilderness of weeds." But London had its own wilderness, too, in the form of the "pauper press," a group of illegal unstamped publications. Several reform publications like as the *Illustrated London News* were started in the 1840s when portions of the tax were lifted.

Then again, in 1854, there were calls for reform of the "tax on knowledge," and again the tax was supported by prominent publishers and others in the publishing business. Charles Mitchell, an advertising agent with links to *The Times*, said, "Our experience convinces us that such a step [abolishing tax] would completely destroy the respectability of the newspaper press and reduce it from its present position, that of the highest in the world—to that of the American press" (Lee 1937).

"The English press is more concentrated in its means than the German; it is more sober, versatile, and honorable than the French; and it can be more relied upon, and is more decent in its tone, than the American press," said one German observer. "It surpasses all three by the grand solidity of its deportment. It may well be said, that no nation on earth, old or new, could ever boast of such a political press as that of which the English nation can boast" (Schlesinger 1853).

A more recent take on the British press was found in the television series *Yes, Prime Minister*. In a 1987 episode, the prime minister says:

> The *Daily Mirror* is read by the people who think they run the country. The *Guardian* is read by people who think they *ought* to run the country. *The Times* is read by the people who actually *do* run the country. The *Daily Mail* is read by the wives of the people who run the country. The *Financial Times* is read by people who *own* the country. The *Morning Star* is read by people who think the country ought to be run by *another* country [Russia]. The *Daily Telegraph* is read by the people who think it is. (IMDb 1987)

2.2.1 The *Daily Telegraph*

The end of newspaper taxes in the mid-1850s opened the door for the British penny press newspapers, and leading the charge was the *Daily Telegraph*, established in 1855 by Joseph M. Levy. The *Telegraph* immediately confirmed its opponents' worst fears about the penny press, featuring articles about crime, murder, and curiosities modeled after the *New York Herald*, although somewhat muted to better suit British audiences.

In 1869, the *Telegraph* joined the *New York Herald* to back one of the best-remembered stunt reporting sensations of the age, the search for Dr. David Livingstone, a Scottish missionary and explorer. Livingstone had been in Africa twice on British-financed expeditions to chart a navigable river into the interior.

He had not been heard from for over six years; apparently his many letters never made it back to London. British journalist Henry Morton Stanley, working at the time for the *Herald*, proposed the search for Livingstone and, after two years, found him on the shores of Lake Tanganyika on October 27, 1871. He greeted him with the famous words "Dr. Livingstone, I presume?" Ironically, after so much effort had been spent on finding Dr.

Figure 2.8 Dr Livingstone, I presume?—When a Scottish missionary went missing in 1866, *New York Herald* editor James Gordon Bennett, Jr. assigned reporter Henry Morton Stanley to find him. It took eight months of tramping through the East African bush, but on November 10, 1871, Stanley located Livingstone in what is now Tanzania. The encounter took place with several hundred people observing. "I would have run to him, only I was a coward in the presence of such a mob—would have embraced him, but that I did not know how he would receive me; so I did what moral cowardice and false pride suggested was the best thing—walked deliberately to him, took off my hat, and said: 'Dr. Livingstone, I presume?' 'Yes,' he said, with a kind, cordial smile, lifting his cap slightly. I replaced my hat on my head, and he replaced his cap, and we both grasped hands. 'I thank God, doctor, I have been permitted to see you.' He answered, 'I feel thankful that I am here to welcome you.'" This stilted exchange became the stuff of newspaper legend. Illustration by Hachette, 1876, Wikimedia Commons.

Livingstone, the missionary refused to return home with Stanley, insisting that there was more work to be done. He died in Africa in 1873; his body was returned for burial in Westminster Abbey, but his heart was buried in Africa.

In 1908, the *Telegraph* published an interview with German Kaiser Wilhelm II that contributed to tensions before World War I. The main subject was the build-up of the German navy and Germany's imperial ambitions. The Kaiser said: "You English are mad, mad, mad as March hares. What has come over you that you are so completely given over to suspicions quite unworthy of a great nation? … Germany must have a powerful fleet to protect that commerce and her manifold interests in even the most distant seas." The *Telegraph* reporter even suggested that the German Press had placed a very different interpretation, hoping that Germany would flex its imperialistic muscles. "There are mischief-makers," replied the Emperor, "in both countries … But the facts are as I have stated. There has been nothing in Germany's recent action … which runs contrary to the explicit declaration of my love of peace" (*Daily Telegraph*, October 28, 1908).

One of the most interesting moments in the history of the *Daily Telegraph* took place in 1940, when the newspaper helped recruit code-breakers for the war effort. During World War II, the *Daily Telegraph* held its first crossword competition. Hopefuls had to complete it under exam conditions. One winner finished in less than eight minutes. British intelligence invited the entrants to work as code-breakers at Bletchley Park (Rhodes 2006).

The *Telegraph* also had the distinction of launching Europe's first newspaper on the web, on November 15, 1994. The newspaper lives on as the UK's Conservative party flagship.

2.2.2 William Stead and the *Pall Mall Gazette*

The history of the press is full of colorful characters, but few were as unusual and audacious as William Thomas Stead (1849–1912), editor of the *Pall Mall Gazette*. The newspaper was originally founded in 1869 as a highbrow gentleman's publication, but Stead turned the paper on its ear when he assumed deputy editorship ten years later and then became editor in 1883. His promise to his readers was nothing short of Apocalyptic: "To secure the final overthrow of the Powers of Darkness in high places."

This was what Stead called the "new journalism," but as historian Piers Brendon has noted, much of what Stead did was the same lurid treatment of news found elsewhere in the emerging British penny press, with eye-catching crime headlines mixed with crusades for housing reform, expanding the British Empire, and the abolition of the "virtual slave trade"—a Victorian code word for prostitution.

Figure 2.9 An idealistic editor—William T. Stead may have been one of the most idealistic editors of the nineteenth century. His ideas about "government by journalism" never quite caught on, but he is remembered as a strong advocate for a European federation and a world court, both of which took a century to accomplish. Wikimedia Commons.

Stead investigated London's worst dens of iniquity and purchased thirteen-year-old Eliza Armstrong from her mother for five pounds. The series created a sensation, with crowds packing the street outside his office and presses running night and day. The incident inspired George Bernard Shaw to write the play Pygmalion and name the lead character Eliza.

Of course, the idea of crusading against vice, while providing lurid details along the way, has a kind of double appeal guaranteed to lure a broad spectrum of readers. Daniel Defoe used that appeal in his novel *Moll Flanders*, and John Cleland used it in his novel *Fanny Hill*. And it worked for Stead, too, although he served three months in prison for failing to ask the father's permission before buying

Eliza Armstrong. (It's interesting that the lurid crusading approach did not work for the movie industry in New York only a few decades later, as we will see in Chapter 5.)

Denounced by many, praised by many others, Stead tried to employ the techniques of new journalism to support the old Puritanism in a thoroughly contradictory and modern manner. One of Stead's fascinating but grandiose ideas was "government by journalism," in which the press would have its own leaders in Parliament with the power to inspect all government departments. Journalistic "major generals" would be appointed to serve as public opinion pollsters and "interrogators of democracy." But in a sense, he was trying to systematize and normalize a strong existing trend. "For the purpose of molding a constituency into his own way of thinking, the editor has every advantage on his side," he wrote. But the advantages were fleeting and erratic. Stead would have liked to institutionalize them somehow.

Meanwhile, Stead continued bombarding the public with divorce and scandal in high places, but he dissipated his energies in quack cures for cancer, miraculous fertilizers, spirit photography, a process for distilling gold from seawater, and other pursuits. Although considered one of the great editors of the day, Stead did not have the discipline to combine editorial flair with financial independence like James Gordon Bennett or Horace Greeley (Brendon 1983). Stead was the ultimate idealist. He advocated a "United States of Europe" and a "High Court of Justice among the nations"—two great ideas that have actually been fulfilled. He reported the Hague Peace Conferences of 1899 and 1907 and is remembered with a bust (sculpture) at the Peace Palace in The Hague. He was en route to a peace conference in the United States aboard the *Titanic* in 1912 when the ship struck an iceberg. After helping women and children into the few lifeboats, Stead retired to the first-class smoking room and was last seen in a leather chair reading a book (Lord 1955).

2.3 The press in France

The French press played a pivotal role in the Enlightenment and French Revolution, but the on-again, off-again censorship of the post-Napoleonic period held back its development.

Newspapers rose and fell as governments rose and fell, and as censorship rules were imposed or lifted. One newspaper from the 1830s still in existence today, *Le Figaro*, originally began as a satirical weekly.

Technology transformed the French press as quickly as it did the American press, and the penny paper of France was called the *presse bon march*. Two of these—Emile de Girardin's *La Presse* and Armand Dutacq's *Le Sicle*—lowered subscription costs and attempted to make up the losses through advertising as did the *Sun*, *Herald*, and *Tribune* in New York. One French innovation was the serialized novel, called the *roman-feuilleton*.

La Presse began by serializing Honore de Balzac's novel *La Vieille Fille*. While the concept attracted readers, many did not like Balzac's long descriptions and deep prose, and soon more versatile and journalistic novels appeared on the pages. One great success was the serialization of *The Three Musketeers* and *The Count of Monte Cristo* by Alexandre Dumas. Serialization of novels had an enormous impact on the idea of the novel itself, according to Dean de la Motte: "There is no doubt that—because it forced the *hommes de lettres* to write as fast as journalists and because the product of their work had to attract and sustain the interest of as many consumers as possible—serialization had a great impact on narrative discourse and on the structure of the novel" (De la Motte 1999).

Another French innovation of the period was the news agency, which later, with the aid of the telegraph, would become known as a "wire service." The world's first agency was founded by Charles Louis Havas in 1835 with the idea of exchanging and translating news among European nations. Havas used carrier pigeons to carry news of extremely important events to news clients. He also extended its reach to help found agencies in other countries, notably Britain, Germany, and Spain.

By the 1850s, direct censorship was converted into a system of ministerial *avertissements* (warnings) and suspensions, but French journalists considered the system just as deadly to social progress. "The press is the most powerful instrument of government in modern societies," said one French correspondent. Reforms in England, brought about by the press, had calmed social tensions, he said, but repression had made things worse in France: "Frank and open liberty can alone calm the concentrated irritations which have survived our disorders" ("Foreign Intelligence," *The Times*, November 12, 1858: 8). An 1880 law ending censorship put a stop to direct government punishment of news organizations, but libel prosecutions continued to be a problem.

2.3.1 The Dreyfus affair

On the morning of January 13, 1898, the daily newspaper *L'aurore* carried the famous headline in a banner across the front page: "J'Accuse … !"

Emile Zola, one of the nation's leading writers, accused ministers at the highest levels of government of sending an innocent army officer, Alfred Dreyfus, to the notorious prison on Devil's Island in order to cover up a miscarriage of justice. Dreyfus had been falsely convicted of treason and evidence of his connection to a real plot to spy for the German government was fabricated, Zola charged.

The fact that Dreyfus was Jewish, and that anti-Semitism was rife in the army, made him an ideal scapegoat. The affair was deeply divisive, with the church and conservatives on one side and liberals on the other. Following the "J'Accuse" story, Zola was charged with criminal libel and convicted a month later. Rather than go to jail, Zola fled to Britain. He was pardoned a year later when the French president resigned in the wake of the affair. Dreyfus was brought back to France and completely exonerated in 1906.

The editor of *L'aurore* who wrote the "J'Accuse" headline was Georges Clemenceau, who had been in exile in New York during the 1880s for his role in the revolutionary Paris Commune's newspaper. He continued editing newspapers and being involved in French politics until becoming prime minister of France during World War I.

Cinq Centimes

L'AURORE

Littéraire, Artistique, Sociale

J'Accuse...!

LETTRE AU PRÉSIDENT DE LA RÉPUBLIQUE

Par ÉMILE ZOLA

LETTRE

A M. FÉLIX FAURE

Figures 2.10. and **2.10a** "I Accuse"—French writer Emile Zola's headline roared from the pages of *L'aurore* on January 13, 1898, and brought down the French government. It also echoes through media history as the classic example of investigative journalism overturning a wrongful criminal conviction. Wikimedia commons.

2.4 The German and Hungarian press

Newspapers in Germany and Austria-Hungary, like those of Western and Northern Europe, traditionally served political elites. The first newspapers were the *Wiener Zeitung* of Vienna, the oldest surviving German-language newspaper, and the *Hildesheimer Allegemeine Zeitung*, founded in 1703 and 1705, respectively.

The rise in literacy between 1750 and the 1870s—from about 10 percent to over 80 percent—helped drive, and reinforce, the increases in the circulation and numbers of newspapers.

The various German states had a long history of press censorship, interrupted only by a brief period of liberalization during the Napoleonic period, when Prussian authorities tolerated liberal nationalist newspapers such as the *Rheinischer Merkur* (1814–16), if they opposed Napoleon. In 1819, the German states again imposed formal censorship through the Carlsbad Decrees. Over the years censorship became less and less effective, and the number of books and newspapers doubled between the 1820s and the 1840s, and then doubled again during the revolutionary 1840s.

2.4.1 The revolutions of 1848

The revolutions of 1848 in Europe were a series of urban uprisings on the European continent, from France to Poland and from Denmark to Italy. Like the end of the Cold

Central Europe's First Rays of Freedom 1848

Crowds of protesters rallied in the streets of Europe's great cities at the start of the March, 1848 revolution. The novelist Mór Jókai described the scene in Budapest:

> Every one knows ... what followed—how the human avalanche began to move, how it grew, and what speeches we made in the great square. But speech-making was not sufficient, we wanted to *do* something. The first thing to be done was to give practical application to the doctrine of a free press. We resolved to print the Twelve Articles of Pest, the Proclamation, and the "Talpra Magyar" without the consent of the censor. We turned up our sleeves and worked away at the hand-presses ourselves ... Irinyi appeared at the window of the printing-office, for to get out of the door was a sheer impossibility. He held in his hands the first printed sheets from the free press. Ah, that scene! When the very first free sheets were distributed from hand to hand! I cannot describe it. "Freedom, freedom!" It was the first ray of a new and better era! ... A free press! The first-fruit of the universal tree of knowledge of Paradise. What a tumult arose when they actually clutched that forbidden fruit in their hands.

Figure 2.11 Revolution of 1848—Demand for democratic reforms broke out into revolutions across Europe in the spring of 1848. In this contemporary illustration, two boys, Ernst Zinna and Heinrich Glasewaldt, are shown unsuccessfully defending a barricade in Berlin. By Theodor Hosemann, 1848.

War in 1989, or the Arab Spring of 2011–12, Revolutionaries were well aware of each other's efforts through the news media. They formed barricades, printed newspapers, and demanded their rights. Tens of thousands were killed, imprisoned, and exiled, but the uprisings had long-term impacts. In France, for instance, Louis Philippe abdicated in 1848. In Denmark and Hungary, monarchs were forced to share power with national legislatures. In Italy, the 1848 revolution led into a broader fight for unification. In Germany, the "March revolution" of 1848 led to a national constitution, replacing the confederation of loosely allied German-speaking states.

One of the major demands of the revolutionaries in all countries was freedom of the press, and new press laws permitted the founding of the Berlin *National- Zeitung* (newspaper) in 1848 by Bernhard Wolff, a former associate of Charles Louise Havas' news agency of Paris. The paper was a partisan (political party) opinion paper that merged with another paper in 1910.

Another newspaper, the *Bonner Zeitung*, was founded by revolutionary Carl Schurz (1829–1906). When the 1848 revolution collapsed, Schurz fled to the United States and founded a newspaper in St. Louis, Missouri. In 1867, he hired a young Hungarian refugee named Joseph Pulitzer. Pulitzer would buy Schurz's newspaper and combine it with another to form the *St. Louis Post-Dispatch*. Schurz believed strongly in democracy and encouraged Pulitzer to get involved in politics. In 1869, Schurz was the first German-born American to be elected to the US Senate. He is famous for saying, "My country, right or wrong; if right, to be kept right; and if wrong, to be set right."

In Hungary, the uprisings of March 15, 1848 stemmed from a nationalistic desire for independence from Austria. After hearing about revolutions in Paris and Berlin, crowds of Hungarians flocked to the streets of Budapest, singing the national song and insisting on the Twelve Points. The first of these was an end to censorship and freedom of the press.

2.4.2 Karl Marx

The journalist of the 1848 era who is best remembered by history is Karl Marx (1818–93). Marx founded and edited a reformist newspaper, *Rheinische Zeitung*, in 1842 in Berlin. The publication was twice closed by the government, and in 1848, reopened as the *Neueu* [New] *Rheinische Zeitung*. Even then, with more liberal press laws, Marx was tried for incitement to rebellion. In a speech to the jury, Marx argued that the law must reflect social realities and, when those realities change, the law must also change. The jury acquitted him of incitement and even thanked him for expressing his views. Even so, Marx was sent into exile in France and Belgium, where he wrote the *Communist Manifesto* in 1848.

By 1851 Marx was in London, working for Horace Greeley's *New York Tribune*, helping Americans to understand Europe after the 1848 revolutions and informing the influx of European immigrants to America about conditions back home (Chakravorti 1993). When the American Civil War escalated, Greeley stopped publishing Marx's essays.

Marx's writing was usually in editorial-essay form, which was the favored style for the *Tribune*, and it had a relatively modern flavor. His method as a journalist was to present readers with a brief sketch of events or characters, emphasizing hidden interests.

Working as a journalist exposed Marx to deplorable working conditions common at the time and gave him the scope to test out ideas that would "educate the people in preparation for the coming revolution" (Chakravorti 1993).

Marx was originally an advocate of a free press, commenting in 1842, "The free press is the omnipresent open eye of the spirit of the people, the embodied confidence of a people in itself, the articulate bond [between] the individual with the state and the world" (Marxist Internet Archive 2010). Whether or not Marx turned against the idea of a free press in later years, as some have argued, his followers in Russia would later impose harsh censorship in the name of the revolution.

Figure 2.12 European correspondent—One of Horace Greeley's best known European correspondents was Karl Marx, also known for co-authoring the *Communist Manifesto*. Greeley kept him working through the 1850s explaining European politics to American readers, but dropped him when the US Civil War broke out. Portrait by John Mayall, 1875. Wikimedia Commons.

2.4.3 The penny press of Germany

The mid-nineteenth-century German press that Schurz and Marx tried to build was essentially more elite in character than in other nations; most German editors at the time had university degrees and many had doctorates. Most newspapers did not cater to popular tastes and mass audiences, but, rather, were opinion journals containing partisan analysis of political trends.

This changed with the emergence of mass-circulation dailies in the 1870s, according to historian Corey Ross, since increasing reliance on advertising revenue and mass circulation meant increasing concern for public opinion. "What mattered was winning over new readers, and the best means for achieving this was by offering attractive entertainment at the lowest possible price," Ross said (Ross 2008: 23).

One of the most prominent German publishers of the era was Rudolf Mosse, an advertising executive who founded one of Germany's original penny press type newspapers, *Berliner Tageblatt* in 1870, and was involved with many other publications. By the mid-1870s, the *Berliner Tageblatt's* circulation rose to 50,000.

Mosse was challenged by entertainment entrepreneur August Scherl's *Berliner-Lokal-Anzeiger*. Hugo von Kupffer, the paper's editor, had been a reporter at the *New York*

Herald and shared Scherl's view that German newspapers were too dry. Using the British and American formula of popular events and human interest stories, the daily soon rose to a circulation of 150,000 and remained the largest German paper before World War I. Scherl's influence on the German press was so strong that tabloid journalism in Germany was called "Scherlism." Meanwhile, German editors from the elite press, like their contemporaries at *The Times* in London, worried that their profession was being undermined (Green 2001).

American humorist Mark Twain was among many people who thought that German daily newspapers were too dry. In his 1880 book, *A Tramp Abroad*, Twain said:

> A German daily is the slowest and saddest and dreariest of the inventions of man. Our own dailies infuriate the reader, pretty often; the German daily only stupefies him. Once a week the German daily of the highest class lightens up its heavy columns ... with a profound, abysmal, book criticism; a criticism which carries you down, down, down into the scientific bowels of the subject ... Sometimes, in place of the criticism, the first-class daily gives you what it thinks is a gay and chipper essay—about ancient Grecian funeral customs, or the ancient Egyptian method of tarring a mummy, or the reasons for believing that some of the peoples who existed before the flood did not approve of cats ...

3 The Progressive Era: Crusading, Yellow, and Tabloid Journalism

Two important trends converged between the nineteenth and twentieth centuries, a time called the Progressive Era. First, high-speed printing allowed newspaper circulation to reach huge populations and also increased the power of the press in politics. Secondly, modern genres and prototypes of modern public affairs journalism emerged in the 1880–1920 period under a variety of labels—muckraking, yellow journalism, crusading journalism, objective journalism, literary journalism, and others. They flourished under the direction of publishers who tended to put their personal stamp on far-flung news operations. These publishers—sometimes called press "barons"—are a study in contrasts.

Joseph Pulitzer, a high-minded crusader, was also mercilessly critical with his staff. William Randolph Hearst, with a reputation for "yellow journalism," also supported public service journalism—occasionally. E. W. Scripps, a pugnacious and uneducated publisher, also became the country's foremost promoter of science education, both in the press (with the Science Service) and by financing far-sighted research at Scripps Oceanographic Institute in California.

What they all had in common were two overt objectives: to "promote the public good" (as Pulitzer said) and to attract readers and build up circulation. In many cases, the ideal of public service did not live up to the reality, and the press barons were routinely criticized for promoting private interests or personal preferences.

3.1 Crusading journalism and Joseph Pulitzer's *New York World*

Joseph Pulitzer (1847–1911) developed his famous crusading journalism style by studying the editorials of Horace Greeley, the sensational news style of James Gordon Bennett, and the success of illustrated newspapers such as *Harper's* and the *Illustrated London News*. He used these elements in a novel way to increase his newspapers' appeal to working-class readers, especially immigrants to America who needed to understand the politics and culture of the country in a positive light. Pulitzer, too, was an immigrant. He'd left Hungary to join the Union cavalry in the Civil War, and then moved to St. Louis where he met Carl Schurz, a journalist who took part in the European revolution of 1848 and emigrated to the United States in the 1850s. Schurz had become the first German-born American elected to the US Senate in 1869. Pulitzer began working for Schurz in the 1860s at the German-language daily, *Westliche Post*. In 1872, Pulitzer bought a controlling interest in the nearly bankrupt paper and made it a success.

Pulitzer was inspired by Schurz and the European revolutionaries of 1848, according to Hungarian historian Andre Csillag: "Joseph Pulitzer's atavistic love of freedom and the fighting spirit he imported from Hungary accompanied him throughout his lifetime. For his entire life, he was a passionate devotee to the cause of liberty: the liberty of action, of opinion, of government" (Csillag 2008). The *Westliche Post* was a success, and following a series of shrewd business deals, Pulitzer bought the English-language *St. Louis Dispatch* in 1878. The combined *Post- Dispatch* crusaded against gambling and corruption in government. Five years later, building on that success, Pulitzer bought the failing *New York World* and began another set of crusades against corruption and slum housing in the nation's largest city. Pulitzer also enlisted readers in crusades, for example, printing the names of 120,000 people whose contributions helped build a pedestal for the Statue of Liberty in New York harbor in 1885 and 1886.

Pulitzer is often remembered for a bitter circulation fight with William Randolph Hearst's *New York Journal*. Together, Pulitzer and Hearst's newspapers pressured the US government into war against Spain in 1898. The affair was the low point of what came to be called "yellow journalism," named for the yellow ink used to color a comic character called the "Yellow Kid" created by Richard F. Outcault. The cartoon, usually a humorous take on working-class life, was first printed in the *New York World* but also, later, in Hearst's *Journal American* (Moritz 1996).

Pulitzer regretted the role of the press in the Spanish–American War, and was proud that four years beforehand, in 1894, the *World* had helped keep America and Britain out of war. The two nations were on the verge of armed conflict over a territorial dispute in South America and the Monroe Doctrine. Pulitzer worked to avert the war and remind Americans of how much they had in common with Great Britain. One tactic was to publish essays by outstanding writers from both sides of the Atlantic expressing their admiration for the other nation, humanizing the public image of Britain and making them an unlikely enemy.

Figures 2.13 and **2.13a** Crusading editor—With a passion for his adopted country and a fiercely micro-managing style, Joseph Pulitzer was both adored and loathed. His editorial role was often that of a public scold, as in this *Puck* cartoon where he is giving orders to the world. Portrait, 1887, Library of Congress; cartoon, *Puck* magazine, January 29, 1896.

One of the *World*'s most controversial investigations involved charges that US President Theodore Roosevelt and the US government had been involved in a scheme to bribe foreign companies and manufacture a revolution to allow the construction of the Panama Canal. Roosevelt was furious and ordered the attorney general to bring a criminal libel indictment. Pulitzer responded, "The *World* cannot be muzzled," and told reporters he was preparing to go to jail. However, the courts refused to allow the case to go to trial, and the incident was seen as a victory for freedom of the press.

Pulitzer also crusaded against racism. In a 1909 editorial, the *World* railed against President William Howard Taft's decision not to appoint African-Americans to federal positions in the South without the approval of Southern whites. "We cannot agree in drawing such a skin color or race line," he cabled the office (Brian 2001). In the end, Pulitzer's *World* "was a monument to the idealism and patriotism of the many men from Central Europe who went to the United States … turn[ing] their backs upon poverty, persecution and the autocracies of Europe," said Hungarian historian Andre Csillag. His legacy lives on in the Pulitzer Prizes and the establishment of a journalism school at Columbia University in New York.

1889: A Reporter goes Around the World

Sleep was eluding star reporter Nelly Bly. It was 3.00 a.m. on a Sunday night in 1888, and the next morning she would have to pitch a story idea to editors at Joseph Pulitzer's *New York World*. "At last, tired and provoked at my slowness in finding a subject, something for the week's work, I thought fretfully: 'I wish I was at the other end of the earth! ... And why not?' the thought came: I need a vacation; why not take a trip around the world?" The idea was to beat the fictional record of Jules Verne's character, Phileas Fogg, from the novel *Around the World in 80 Days*, published in 1873. At first, there were the usual objections. She was a vulnerable woman. She would have to carry too much luggage. It would take too long to get started. "I can start this minute," she insisted.

She left November 14, 1889, and after a quick visit with Verne in France, she was on the other side of the world. The trip turned into a sensation, as Pulitzer's *World* newspaper printed each telegraphic dispatch with extensive maps and descriptions of the countries she visited. She returned to New York, to a tumultuous welcome, on January 25, 1890, having made the tour in seventy-two days. Historian Brooke Kroeger said Bly was "an exemplar of an age when American women were vigorously asserting their right—indeed, their need—to shape history itself." (1995)

Figure 2.14 *Around the World in Seventy-two Days*—Nelly Bly (Elizabeth Cochran) went around the world for Joseph Pulitzer's *World* newspaper in 1889, beating the fictional record set by Jules Verne's Phileas Fogg in *Around the World in 80 Days*. Library of Congress.

3.2 E. W. Scripps and the first newspaper chain

He called himself a "damned old crank," and more than almost any other newspaper editor, Edward Wyllis Scripps (1854–1926) exemplified the free-spirited industrial age of the press. His enormous size matched an oversized personality, and his wild lifestyle matched his lack of formal education. Yet later, scientists would compare him with Aristotle and Voltaire (McCabe 1951).

In 1872, the eighteen-year-old Scripps helped his brother with a fledgling newspaper, the *Detroit Tribune and Advertiser*. He launched a second newspaper, the *Penny Press*, in Cleveland in 1878 and soon began launching a chain of regional "penny press" daily newspapers. By his death in 1926, Scripps owned twenty-five newspapers and a wire service— the United Press—set up in 1907 to compete with the Associated Press. A famous incident early in his career involved accusations by a competing publisher that Scripps was harboring a mistress. Scripps called a press conference to answer the charges and produced—to everyone's astonishment—the mistress herself. Both made a full confession and then said, in effect, so what?

Scripps was also known for founding the Scripps Institution of Oceanography and the Science Service. He came of age at a time of great opportunity in newspaper publishing, when the voice of the working man was not often reflected in small town newspapers. Using the formula also adopted by Pulitzer and Hearst, Scripps would print sensational anti-corruption stories in the Progressive muckraking style. Unlike Pulitzer, who stuck with St. Louis and New York, Scripps aimed for small Midwestern cities and had a fairly good business sense. His newspapers stayed profitable even through the Depression years when Pulitzer's *New York World* newspaper folded and Hearst's empire began crumbling.

The Scientist and the Crank

It was an unlikely alliance. The famously cantankerous, barely educated newspaper publisher and the zoology professor with a Harvard Ph.D. didn't appear to have much in common when they met in the summer of 1903. But the collaboration between E. W. Scripps and William Ritter changed the American view of science and created two modern mainstays of science: the Scripps Institution of Oceanography and the Science News Service.

For some reason, Scripps got on famously with William E. Ritter, a charming and articulate scientist who had been leading summer lab classes and gathering marine specimens on the California coast when friends brought Scripps by Ritter's lab for a visit in the summer of 1903. What fueled this friendship was a powerful idea the two men shared—a joint vision of a way to improve American life through an understanding of science. By 1907, Scripps helped Ritter set up a permanent research station on 170 acres donated (at Scripps's urging) by the city of San Diego. Permanent buildings were set up in 1910. By 1912 the institution was officially the University of California's Scripps Institute for Biological Research. Scripps, however, called it "bugville" (Pauly 2000).

Nearly every day, Scripps dropped in on Ritter unannounced at the institute. Poking his head through a door, Scripps would remove his cigar and demand of Ritter, "What is this damned human animal anyway?" Ritter would drop everything and they would begin talking, sometimes for the rest of the day. Their conversation could encompass anything on earth or in the oceans. "Ritter started out as early as 1901 with the idea that the biological station should be involved in physical, chemical, hydrographic and biological research," said historian Oliver Knight, "but Scripps conceived a broader role for it." According to Scripps:

> The ideal institution that I had in view was not a school of instruction but a school of research and compilation, and of generalization ... I am convinced that modern civilization is the outgrowth of philosophy, religion and of codes of ethics, of customs and institutions that were founded upon known data far inferior in quantity and in quality to what science can furnish today... As a result of this condition of affairs, the lives of most human beings are unhappy ... I would have a school for the study of life... the organization of which would be divided into three departments. The lowest, the elementary department ... would be engaged in what is called research. The second department would consist of one or more men who would record, correlate, assemble and segregate into groups the facts generated by the first department. The third department would consist of men who would generalize all the information gathered and recorded and there from make deductions which would be passed out to the world as authoritative and as the last word so far uttered concerning what is actually known in order that the people might govern their conduct individually and as social organisms according to so much of nature's law as had been discerned.

Figure 2.15 Science editor—E. W. Scripps, founder of the Scripps newspaper chain—and also the Science Service, the Scripps Institute for Oceanography, and the United Press (later UPI). Wikimedia Commons.

This third stage would be no mere public relations department. The public mission of science was the raison d'être for the scientific research, the driving force behind the institution. Scripps wanted it all to be so original that it would not even have a library, and in 1906 he advised Ritter against buying a collection of books: "The library you should covet should be the one that is yet unwritten and un-cataloged."

Some of the ideas were too much for the University of California, and around 1915 the academics insisted on a more conventional form of organization. Scripps blamed "a bunch of wooden-headed visionless university men" for tearing up his plans and accused them of having "burned down our temple to roast a little pig."

American science was emerging at this moment in history, but few publishers other than Scripps understood what that meant, and partly as a result, few in the public understood it either. If science was even mentioned in a newspaper, "it was in terms of magic or miracles, if not mere ridicule," said historian David J. Rhees. "It was standard practice to assign the staff humorist to cover local scientific conventions." The humorists would typically comment either on the length and luxuriousness of the beards worn by the assembled scientists or on the titles of papers which contained the longest and least familiar words, Rhees observed (Rhees 1979).

Science news in New York at the turn of the century was characterized by sensationalism at both Joseph Pulitzer's *World* and William Randolph Hearst's *Journal*. The *World* ran a column called "Wonders of Science" that focused on exciting and miraculous discoveries. Cures for cancer, especially if they involved radiation or colored lights, were particularly favored. The news about the 1910 return of Halley's Comet, as described by one editor, involved the following elements: a picture of a pretty girl, a "good nightmare idea like the inhabitants of Mars watching [the comet] pass," pictures of scientists, and "a two-column boxed 'freak' containing a scientific opinion that nobody will understand, just to give it class" (Emery 1988). Around the same time in New York, Hearst's editors were headlining lab tests showing that oysters, ice, and milk sold throughout New York city were contaminated by dangerous bacteria. The hysteria would soon lead to the hunt for Typhoid Mary. The sensationalistic media of the era reflected, in part, the sensibilities of the working class.

Yet the more science influenced their world, and the visible world of politics, the more seriously journalists began to take it. Carr Van Anda rose to the top of the *New York Times* in 1901, in part because of his advocacy of serious science coverage. He became famous for his understanding of physics and math, even at one point correcting one of Einstein's formulas that had been badly transcribed.

And by the 1920s, Walter Lippmann, the last editor of Pulitzer's *World*, would advocate a place for science at the heart of American life, alongside—or even instead of—religion. Scripps, however, was the first publisher of this era to see the impact of science on America and was appalled by the news coverage which produced only a "vast quantity of misinformation." The real "adventures," he said, "dramatic as they are, seldom find their way into print." Scripps began thinking about other ways to further the public mission of science:

> It's useless to think of making the world safe for democracy without thinking of making democracy safe for itself. And the only way of making democracy thus safe is to make it more intelligent. But since to be intelligent is utterly impossible without having much of the knowledge, method and the spirit of science, the only way to make democracy safe is to make it more scientific.

In 1918, he and Ritter planned with several national science academies to begin an institution "to translate and interpret science" for the American public. A nonprofit organization was endowed by Scripps and was called the Science News Service. It began distributing the *Science News-Letter* in 1922. (Both the Science Service and *Science News* continue in the twenty-first century.)

The *News-Letter* was often dry and formal and not calculated to appeal to the public. Its editor, Edwin Slosson, was a chemist and a literary critic, not the popularizer Scripps wanted, although he came highly recommended from the scientific societies. Astronomy and archaeology were the most popular topics for the newsletter. Basic sciences were also covered. The most controversial topic of the times, the Scopes trial in 1925, was also extensively covered.

"Peace is possible; famine unnecessary; disease reducible; [and] individual wealth and comfort can be increased enormously," Scripps wrote, and then as an afterthought, added that instead of enormously, "my friend Professor W. E. Ritter would say infinitely" (McCabe 1951).

3.3 Yellow journalism and William Randolph Hearst's *Journal*

Legend and truth are deeply mixed in the many accounts of press baron William Randolph Hearst (1863–1951), the famed "yellow journalism" publisher whose career spanned the late nineteenth to the mid-twentieth century. At its height in 1935, Hearst's media empire included twenty-eight newspapers read by 20 million people, as well as thirteen magazines, eight radio stations and the International News Service. For biographers, Hearst is a fascinating study in contrasts. He was a populist reformer who championed labor unions early in his career but fought bitterly against them when they organized in his own newspapers. He used his inherited millions to get started in publishing and then attacked monopolies under the motto of "truth, justice and public service." He was a huge man with a tiny voice, a war hawk in Cuba in the 1890s but a pacifist in Europe in the 1930s (Nassaw 2001).

Winston Churchill liked him when they met in 1929, thinking of Hearst as "a grave, simple child ... with a strong liberal and democratic outlook." Others disliked him immensely. Senator Sherman Minton (D-IN) said in 1936 that he was "the greatest menace to freedom of the press that exists in this country" because he used his immense media power for propaganda. "He would not know the Goddess of Liberty if she came down off her pedestal in New York harbor and bowed to him," Minton said, adding with sly reference to his personal life, "He would probably try to get her phone number" (Brendon 1983).

After being expelled from Harvard and spending a short time at the *World* newspaper, Hearst began his career as the young publisher of the *San Francisco Examiner* in 1887. The *Examiner* was a small paper that had been purchased by his wealthy father, George Hurst, who owned a string of Western gold, silver, and copper mines and who had began serving a term in the US Senate that year.

Hearst loved running the *Examiner*. He used Bennett's formula of sensationalism, illustrations, and personality features to attract readers. He approached subjects with energy, enterprise, and originality, urging his staff to find illustrations "to attract the eye and stimulate the imagination." Competing papers were mostly interested in politics, and Hearst was determined to create "a revolution in the sleepy journalism" of San Francisco (Nassaw 2001).

For Hearst, said a detractor, journalism was "an enchanted playground in which giants and dragons were to be slain simply for the fun of the thing; a Never-Never Land with pirates and Indians and fairies" (Creelman 1906).

In 1895, Hearst purchased the *New York Journal*, a dying daily newspaper, and began a reckless circulation war with Pulitzer's *World*. For a penny, *Journal* readers could get the same lurid crime reports, scathing editorials, and personality profiles that they would find in the two-cent *World*.

Figure 2.16 Sensationalistic editor—William Randolph Hearst was a notorious editor who appealed to the most lurid instincts in mass audiences. After a career studded with personal and professional scandals, he was an inviting target for the kind of portrait shown in Orson Welles' movie *Citizen Kane*. Bain News Service, 1910. Library of Congress.

Unlike Pulitzer, Hearst had no ethical boundaries. He could be ruthless with people and dishonest in his approach to journalism, having reporters write fake news stories or plagiarize the competition when it suited him. He also "raided" the staffs of the *World* and other competing papers, sometimes doubling their salaries. One who left Pulitzer for Hearst was the *World's* comic strip artist Richard F. Outcault, whose cartoon about life in working-class New York, "Hogan's Alley," featured the Yellow Kid. Yellow ink was something of a novelty at the time, and because it was so heavily used for the comics, it came to symbolize the era's style of tawdry journalism (Moritz 1996). In the fall of 1896, Hearst hired a reporter (Richard Harding Davis) and an artist (Frederick Remington) to cover an insurrection in Cuba against the colonial Spanish government. The insurrection was bitterly fought, with atrocities on both sides, and 200,000 Spanish troops moved tens of thousands of civilians into "re-concentration" camps where many died of disease. The drawings and stories shocked Americans when they ran in 1897, and Hearst, indignant at the brutality, kept up the pressure.

According to one of the Hearst legends, Remington wired Hearst to say there was nothing going on, and Hearst wired back: "You furnish the pictures, I'll furnish the war." The exchange is one of the best remembered anecdotes of journalism and seems in character as a description of Hearst's arrogance. But Hearst later denied writing it, and historians who examined the issue say there is no evidence to support the legend and good reason to believe it was invented (Campbell 2003). Biographer David Nassaw said if Hearst did write the telegram, it would have referred to the existing insurrection, not plans for a coming American invasion (Nassaw 2001). But it was true, at least, that Hearst had already inserted his newspaper into a foreign intrigue in a way that no American newspaper publisher had ever before dared.

When the battleship USS *Maine* blew up in Havana, Cuba, on February 15, 1898, the incident took over the front page of the newspaper for days, with headlines blaring

Figure 2.16a Competing editors—In this satirical cartoon, Joseph Pulitzer and William Randolph Hearst are dressed in yellow baby gowns, symbolizing both yellow journalism and the "Yellow Kid" cartoon. They are also fighting over their roles in promoting the Spanish–American War. William Barritt, *Vim* magazine, 1898. Library of Congress.

"Spanish Treachery" and "Work of an Enemy." Hearst offered a $50,000 reward "for the detection of the perpetrator of the *Maine* outrage." Pulitzer also featured full front page coverage of the disaster, but emphasized the loss of life and noted that the explosion was "Caused by Bomb or Torpedo."

The Spanish-American war and the invasion of Cuba in the spring of 1898 were not caused by Hearst's newspaper coverage, but it was a factor. Hearst's enthusiasm for the war also drew him to Cuba during the war, where he faced gunfire and even personally captured a group of unarmed Spanish sailors—making headlines in the process.

Later, Hearst's involvement in politics included two terms in Congress (1903–7) and then unsuccessful bids for mayor of New York, the Senate, and a US presidential nomination. He became known as William "also-ran-dolph" Hearst. He was a conservative Democrat, supporting and then breaking away from Franklin Delano Roosevelt, lashing out at income taxes and the imposition of labor regulations. Hearst continued to be a sensationalist and sometime reformer as publisher, but his empire started losing money in the mid-1930s. The more his empire slipped away, the more he insisted on total control of each paper's content, down to details of which politicians or film stars to feature and which to ignore.

Hearst was widely despised toward the end of his life for a variety of reasons, especially a 1934 visit with Nazi leader Adolph Hitler which, he said, was an attempt to save Jews. Hitler used the visit to raise Nazi credibility. In 1941, Hearst was caricatured by radio director Orson Welles in the RKO film *Citizen Kane*. Hearst and his media empire fought back in a classic confrontation, keeping the film out of theaters (Cramer and Lennon 2000). In later years, *Citizen Kane* was often placed as the best film of the twentieth century, although *Kane*'s dark and difficult tone would have made it an unlikely commercial success. Ironically, it is Welles' caricature of Hearst, not the real person, that seems to live on in the public mind.

3.4 Tabloid journalism and Alfred Harmsworth's *Daily Mail*

Catching the imagination of the reading public is not easy, but it seemed like a snap for Alfred Harmsworth, one of Britain's most powerful tabloid publishers in the early twentieth century. Can fish speak? Do dogs commit murder? How many people cross London Bridge each day? How much gold is in the Bank of England?

If you mailed in the correct response to Harmsworth's magazine *Answers*, you could win a pound a week for life. Such were the humble arts that brought an Irishman from a modest barrister's family to the heights of British journalism. He started in 1888 as the publisher of a group of small, youth-oriented humor magazines, but by 1894, Harmsworth had two million subscribers and had amassed enough of a fortune to buy a pair of moribund Edinburgh daily newspapers.

Figure 2.17 Can fish speak?—Lord Northcliffe, Alfred Harmsworth, began his meteoric publishing career asking that kind of question in print. With a knack for fascinating the British public, Harmsworth started the London *Daily Mail* and "struck a gold mine." Moffett Studio, 1909. Library of Congress.

In 1896, after agonizing over the basic layout, Harmsworth started the London *Daily Mail*—and "struck a gold mine" with a circulation of 400,000 overnight. Londoners appreciated the same harmless but attention-getting tricks used in *Answers*. As historian Piers Brendon noted, the *Daily Mail* was amusing without being vulgar, and its crime stories were exciting without being lurid. Like Pulitzer and Hearst, Harmsworth backed a small war—the Boer War in South Africa (1899–1902)—and saw circulation numbers rise to one million.

By 1903 he had also started the *Daily Mirror*, originally a newspaper for women. But he found far more success by turning it into an illustrated newspaper for men and women, and within a few years it became the nation's second largest newspaper. In 1908, Harmsworth also became owner of *The Times*.

Meanwhile, the *Daily Mail* continued with stunts and promotions, especially

Media Transitions: Four Stages of the Press

Twentieth-century American journalist Walter Lippmann described what he saw as the four formative stages of the press—Authoritarian, Partisan, Commercial, and Organized Intelligence.

Lippmann saw the commercial (or "penny") press as most beneficial to democracy, in that it freed the mass media from political party allegiances. But that form of press was too flawed to really fulfill its democratic role. Lippmann also foresaw a fourth stage of the press that he called "organized intelligence" (Lippmann 1922). Later, refining the idea, he saw a transition from the "romantic art" of the commercial penny press and yellow journalism era. "The new coming journalism is less temperamental. It deals with more solid realities. Journalism in the next epoch is inclined to become less Napoleonic at the top and less Bohemian at the bottom" ("Lippmann Sees end of Yellow Press," *New York Times*, January 13, 1931).

Another vision of the transition from authoritarian to commercial culture was offered by Jürgen Habermas, a twentieth-century philosopher. Habermas believed that authoritarian press was part of a "representational" culture that was akin to feudalism and designed to overwhelm the audience. The partisan press from the early 1700s onward (in England) and 1800s (in Europe) helped develop the "public sphere" of debate and dialogue, but the shift to commercial media diluted and corrupted the public sphere and undermined social progress. In an ideal speech situation, everyone would have equal access to media and an ability to contribute to social consensus, but commercialization undermined that idea (Habermas 1991).

Figure 2.18 Four stages of the press—In his 1922 book *Public Opinion*, *New York World* columnist Walter Lippmann noted that the media had gone from authoritarian to partisan to commercial models. He hoped that a new model, called "organized intelligence," could be developed. Library of Congress.

The visions of both Lippmann and Habermas would be realized, to some extent, in the late twentieth century as the World Wide Web enabled one-to-one and many-to-many communications. Computers became the most powerful tools for organizing intelligence that had ever been devised. And yet, the deterioration of consensus in the public sphere and the long slow decline of the traditional news media would demonstrate that technological advances do not provide simple solutions to complex social problems.

in the new field of aviation, offering £1,000 in 1907 for the first airplane that crossed the English Channel, and £10,000 for a flight to Manchester. The idea seemed so preposterous that the humor magazine *Punch* offered £10,000 for a flight to Mars. Yet that year, an airplane flew to Manchester and a few years later, another crossed the channel.

Yet there was something tepid about the stunts, which substituted for the bare-knuckled investigative journalism favored by Pulitzer and the scandal mongering of Hearst. The problem, which emerged as he investigated the Lever soap "trusts," was that unlike the United States, British libel laws favored plaintiffs far more than publishers.

Harmsworth's support of the British war effort was so well received by the British aristocracy that he was elevated to the nobility and given the title Lord Northcliffe in 1918. Others despised his shallow patriotism and support for government propaganda. He died in 1922, leaving his brother in charge of the operation. Editorial policy at the *Daily Mail* shifted toward fascism with editorials like "Youth Triumphant" in support of Adolf Hitler in 1933 and "Hurrah for the Blackshirts" in 1934. Its editorial stance remained conservative, but dropped all connections to fascism in the late 1930s.

Phases of Printing Technology

Phase 1: craft printing

1455–1820s—Printing chapels: If Johannes Gutenberg could somehow have come back to a printing shop in 1820, nearly four centuries after the first wave of the printing revolution, he would have been able to get right to work.

Typesetting: Type is set by hand, letter-by-letter, from upper and lower cases, at a rate of about five words per minute.

Printing: Paper is fed manually into hand-pulled wooden (and sometimes metal) presses at about 250 impressions per hour (a "token"). Each impression is one-sided, which means that once the ink has dried, the "same token" has to get a second run.

Circulation: Newspapers and magazines are sent to subscribers through the mail or sold in general merchandise stores. Favorable postal rates help to subsidize widespread publishing in the US.

Figure 2.19: Printing chapel, 1568, Jost Amman, Wikimedia Commons.

Phase 2: steam printing

1820s–1890s: Steam printing and stereotyping.

Typesetting: Type is still set from large cases by hand. A large daily newspaper might employ 100 workers just to set type.

Stereotyping: Hand-set type is too loose to use in higher-speed presses. This problem is solved by casting metal copies of hand-set type into "stereotype" printing plates. The plates are cast in cylindrical sleeves to fit on rotary presses.

Presses: The introduction of steam-powered printing presses speeds up production to thousands of impressions per hour, expanding circulation of newspapers and magazines. The steam press, first used in 1814 at *The Times* in London, allows a new kind of low-cost "penny" papers by the 1830s.

Circulation: Subscriptions by mail are common for magazines, but now children also hawk newspapers on city streets.

Figure 2.20: Women setting type, Germany, 1890s. From a 1991 German Post Office stamp commemorating an organization that promoted professional careers for women. Public domain.

Figure 2.21: Solar steam press, France, 1882. From Charles Henry Pope, *Solar Heat*, 1903.

Phase 3: hot type

1890s–1960s: hot type, Linotype, halftone and high-speed printing.

Typesetting: German-American Ottmar Mergenthaler invents the first successful typesetting machine in 1886. Operators sit at a keyboard that releases blanks, then molten lead is poured over them to create a line of type (hence the name, Linotype). At about thirty words per minute, ready to fit into a page, Linotypes speed up the process by five or six times. Between 1893 and 1968, over 74,000 Linotype machines are sold. In the 1960s, a new Linotype might cost about $50,000 (Holtzberg-Call 1992).

Photo halftones engraving: This process, invented in the 1880s, allows photographs to be etched into metal plates and then printed. Previously, only line drawings could be printed on a press.

Printing: Automated rotary presses use rolls (webs) of paper and can print, fold, cut, and stack the newspaper or magazine. This allows tens of thousands of impressions per hour. Cheap paper is also a factor, with costs declining.

Circulation: Subscriptions by mail are still common for magazines, but circulation is mostly through home delivery carriers and news vendors.

Figure 2.22: *New York Herald*—Composing room and linotype machines, 1902. Bain Collection, Library of Congress.

Phase 4: cold type

1950s–80s: cold type/photo typesetting and offset printing.

Typesetting: Photo-mechanical process invented by Rene Higonnet and Louis Moyroud sets type six times faster than Linotypes at a cost of about $10,000 for a small unit in the 1970s. Photocomposition is increasingly improved by the digital revolution in the 1970s, and by the 1980s, word processing and typesetting are now both handled by mainframe computers.

Pre-press: Sheets of photo-sensitive paper containing separate blocks of type, headlines, and halftones are assembled (laid out and pasted up), then transferred to negatives and burned onto offset aluminum printing plates. Skilled pre-press workers are no longer needed, and the production workforce is cut in half.

Photo halftone prints: Halftones are printed out for paste-up, no longer etched onto metal plates.

Printing: Offset printing uses light aluminum plates instead of heavy cast-lead stereotypes. This allows smaller, cheaper, faster presses that can print color with accurate registration.

Circulation: Home delivery routes become common; postal service subsidies for publishers are reduced.

Figure 2.23: Compugraphic typesetting machine, 1975. Photo by Lin Burton.

Phase 5: digital media

1980s–present: digital production/desktop publishing and pagination.

Typesetting: Personal computers like the Apple Mac (introduced in 1984) and laser printers allowed "desktop" publishing, making it far easier and cheaper to prepare type and photos for the press. By the mid-1990s, a computer and printer might cost $2,000.

Pre-press: Improved computers allow digital layout (pagination), eliminating most pre-press layout and paste-up. Editors can now send pages straight back to the press, and nearly all the production workforce is eliminated.

Digital photos: Associated Press introduces first digital photo handling desks in 1989, eliminating halftone "engraving" shops in printing plants.

Printing: Digital versions of pages are sent through the Internet to large presses in centralized locations, bypassing small printing operations.

Circulation: News of all kinds is now available to billions of people through the World Wide Web and other non-print digital networks.

Figure 2.24: Macintosh computer, 1984. Photo by Lin Burton.

For additional reading, discussion questions, links to video, and other suggestions, see www.revolutionsincommunications.com.

3

Print Media in the Twentieth and Twenty-first Centuries

Th' newspaper does ivrything f'r us. It runs th' polis foorce an' th' banks, commands th' milishy, conthrols th' ligislachure, baptizes th' young, marries th' foolish, comforts th' afflicted, afflicts th' comfortable, buries th' dead an' roasts thim aftherward. They ain't annything it don't turn its hand to ... They used to say a man's life was a closed book. So it is—but it's an open newspaper.

Finley Peter Dunne, 1902

1 The Printing Revolution's Last Century

Publishers were at the top of their games at the beginning of the twentieth century; the technology was mature and the competition was minimal. In the 1970s, following a series of mergers, most cities ended up with only one newspaper. And then, by the early twenty-first century, a familiar story had played out: a profitable near-monopoly had underestimated the digital revolution and missed the curve in the road. American newspapers had lost their readers, their advertising, and most of their stock value. The free press as an institution, created in the Enlightenment to guide the democratic experiment, was all but dead.

If it were some other near-monopoly, the turmoil created by technological change might simply be inconvenient. But a nosedive in US newspaper publishing, along with declines in magazine and book publishing, had far more serious implications. "The loss of newspapers translates to a loss of journalism," said a report by the University of Virginia's Miller Center in 2010. The capacity for public information was being lost, and a greater opportunity for government corruption was fostered when journalists could no longer serve as "watchdogs" of public institutions (Miller Center 2010).

The UVA report echoed concerns from a half-century earlier, expressed by the University of Chicago's Hutchins Commission, that the free press was being imperiled by accelerating technology and irresponsible publishers. To understand what is being lost, we should consider some of the outstanding contributions of the twentieth-century press. During the "muckraking" period, the world wars, and the Civil Rights era, the press served as the eyes and ears of the pubic, the conscience of the nation, and occasionally even heroes to readers. The Vietnam–Watergate era tested that status, and the digital revolution narrowed the ability of the press to function in the way it was originally intended.

But in the twenty-first century, economic problems and declining readership meant increasing concern not only about the press but also the perils of uninformed partisanship.

2 The Muckraking Message 1900–15

Over 100 years ago, a young journalist named Will Irwin took off across the country in search of the American press. In a fourteen-part series published in *Collier's Magazine*, Irwin concluded that the press was "wonderfully able, wonderfully efficient, and wonderfully powerful [but] with real faults." Yellow journalism, especially the tendency of publishers like William Randolph Hearst to trump up news for personal or partisan reasons, counted as one of the faults. But to Irwin, the biggest fault was that the press did not speak to his generation: "It is the mouthpiece of an older stock. It lags behind the thought of its times … To us of this younger generation, our daily press is speaking, for the most part, with a dead voice, because the supreme power resides in men of that older generation" (Irwin 1911).

Irwin put the blame squarely on the Associated Press. No one could start a newspaper without telegraphic news services, and yet existing AP members were blackballing new start-up newspapers: "Until something happens to break the … AP monopoly, the way to journalism will be barred … for the young man of brains, enterprise and purpose." (See Chapter 7 for more about the AP/Western Union monopoly.)

In Irwin's view, the twentieth-century spirit of reform was to be found in magazines like *Cosmopolitan*, *Collier's Weekly*, *McClure's Magazine*, and *Munsey's Magazine*. While there had been a few exposes in newspapers, nothing matched the magazine revelations about child labor, slum housing, tainted meat, political graft, insurance fraud, narcotic medicines, and the corrupt Standard Oil monopoly.

The exposés were needed because the system had failed, Samuel S. McClure wrote in his magazine in January 1903. Lawyers, judges, churches, and colleges—all were failing to uphold the law. The burden of reform had fallen to the people (Kochersberger 1996; Tebbel 1991). But while they were determined to expose the evils of the system, the magazine reformers were not revolutionaries and had no intention of overthrowing the government. In fact, most of them saw then-president Theodore Roosevelt as a strong ally. After all, as police commissioner in New York, he had walked slum alleys with photographer Jacob Riis, and as president, he had responded to the exposés by fighting for legislation that would reign in corporate abuses. He had even written for *McClure's* about social reform (Roosevelt 1901).

Even so, by 1906, reform journalism had shaken the nation's business and political institutions to the core, and questions about social stability were being raised. Roosevelt hoped to ease some fears when he laid the cornerstone of the Cannon Congressional House Office Building on the morning of April 14, 1906. The speech is considered among the most important in American history. Writers who exposed social ills in magazines and

Figure 3.1 Crusaders—Knights of the magazine press are depicted in this heroic 1906 tableau in the political humor magazine *Puck*. Prominent among them are Samuel Hopkins Adams, Ray Stannard Baker, Ida Tarbell, Lincoln Steffans, and S. S. McClure. Illustration by Carl Hassmann, *Puck*, February 6, 1906.

newspapers, Roosevelt said, were useful, but they had to be careful not to go too far. They should not act as the "man with the muck rake" in *Pilgrim's Progress*, a well-known English moral allegory from 1678.

2.1 Impact of the muckraker speech

Roosevelt's "muckraker" speech instantly galvanized a national debate about the role of the press. Some warned that muckraking was being used to stir up agitators. Others said muckrakers were doing much-needed work, performing "an immense and beneficial revolution." The *New York Times* said that he only seemed to approve of journalists when they did not go too far, and that he "was not particularly happy in his inspiration."

McClure's writer Lincoln Steffens, who specialized in exposing political corruption in Midwestern cities, said Roosevelt's speech was misunderstood by the bankers and the railroad men: "They rejoiced. Some of them laughed at me, saying the president had taken a fall out of me." And he told Roosevelt: "Well, you have put an end to all these journalistic investigations that have made [helped] you" (*New York Times*, April 17, 1906).

William Allen White, a nationally famous editor from Emporia, Kansas, wrote humorously that Steffens had been seen riding through Kansas on a special train that carried his enormous muckrake: "It was a fierce looking instrument as it lay on its flat cars,

The Man with the Muckrake

Figure 3.2 President Theodore Roosevelt—In a speech about the excesses of reform journalism on April 14, 1906, Roosevelt warned that the press had shaken the nation's business and political institutions to the core. Library of Congress.

President Theodore Roosevelt, April 14, 1906:

> In Bunyan's "Pilgrim's Progress" you may recall the description of the Man with the Muck Rake, the man who could look no way but downward, with the muck rake in his hand ... The Man with the Muck Rake is set forth as the example of him whose vision is fixed on carnal instead of spiritual things. Yet he also typifies the man who in this life consistently refuses to see aught that is lofty, and fixes his eyes with solemn intentness only on that which is vile and debasing.
>
> Now, it is very necessary that we should not flinch from seeing what is vile and debasing. There is filth on the floor, and it must be scraped up with the muck rake; and there are times and places where this service is the most needed of all the services that can be performed. But the man who never does anything else, who never thinks or speaks or writes, save of his feats with the muck rake, speedily becomes, not a help but one of the most potent forces for evil ...

> At this moment we are passing through a period of great unrest—social, political, and industrial unrest. It is of the utmost importance for our future that this should prove to be not the unrest of mere rebelliousness against life, of mere dissatisfaction with the inevitable inequality of conditions, but the unrest of a resolute and eager ambition to secure the betterment of the individual and the nation. So far as this movement of agitation throughout the country takes the form of a fierce discontent with evil, of a determination to punish the authors of evil, whether in industry or politics, the feeling is to be heartily welcomed as a sign of healthy life. If, on the other hand, it turns into a mere crusade of appetite against appetite, of a contest between the brutal greed of the "have nots" and the brutal greed of the "haves," then it has no significance for good, but only for evil. If it seeks to establish a line of cleavage, not along the line which divides good men from bad, but along that other line, running at right angles thereto, which divides those who are well off from those who are less well off, then it will be fraught with immeasurable harm to the body politic ... The wild preachers of unrest and discontent, the wild agitators against the entire existing order, the men who act crookedly, whether because of sinister design or from mere puzzle headedness, the men who preach destruction without proposing any substitute for what they intend to destroy, or who propose a substitute which would be far worse than the existing evils—all these men are the most dangerous opponents of real reform.

teeth upward and menacing ... Though dulled from recent use, [the teeth] still retain, on their blunted points, the hair and whiskers and fragmentary remains of a number of Congressmen" (*Washington Post*, May 18, 1906).

White's humor approached a difficult subject, but David Graham Phillips, a writer for Hearst's *Cosmopolitan* magazine, was far more blunt. He said that Roosevelt's speech had been politically calculated to ease the fears of Roosevelt's allies in Congress who had come under fire for corruption. The term muckraker was "an easy phrase of repeated attack upon what was in general a good journalistic movement." And a *New York Times* writer, Perry Belmont, noted that the "cue seems now to have been given to assume a tone of indignation at the turning of the searchlight of criticism upon all those holding public positions" (*New York Times*, April 16, 1906).

Like any politician, Roosevelt realized that muckraking investigations could hurt his allies as well as his enemies. Indeed, Roosevelt's Republicans were splintered when *Collier's Magazine* published an exposé on the Pinchot-Ballinger controversy of 1910 involving suspected coal swindles in Alaska. Gifford Pinchot, a Forest Service chief appointed by Teddy Roosevelt, had objected to President William Howard Taft's approach to the issue, and was promptly fired. The controversy probably lost the 1912 election for the Republican reformers.

By 1914, the era of American muckraking was over, ended in part by libel suits, magazine mergers, Roosevelt's criticism, public opinion fatigued by crusading reformers, and the onset of World War I (Miraldi 1988). Historian Mark Feldstein has observed that investigative reporting tends to appear in times when demand is created by social conditions, media competition, and new media technologies. Those conditions were met in the American Revolution and the muckraking era; they did not return until the 1970s with the Watergate-era investigations (Feldstein 2006).

Who were the Muckrakers?

Widely admired for their exposés of monopolies and corrupt public officials, the "muckrakers" were an eclectic group of writers, journalists, and social reformers who led the Progressive reform movement of the early 1900s. They used investigative journalism (muckraking) to go beyond standard inquiries and uncover hidden problems. Social reform was not a new idea for the press in the early 1900s. For example, the *New York Times* investigations in the 1870s helped curb the corruption centered around the city's Tammany Hall politics (Burrows and Wallace 1999). In the 1880s, Henry Demerest Lloyd investigated grain and oil monopolies for the *Chicago Tribune*, and then worked with Jane Addams of the Hull House movement to fight child labor and poor working conditions (Lloyd 1912). Magazines and alternative media were often the only resort for investigative reporters since in many cases the news media was part of the problem. Ida Tarbell found that Standard Oil was paying newspapers in Ohio for continued favorable coverage, and Samuel Hopkins Adams found that patent medicine advertisers had contracts with many newspapers forbidding unfavorable publicity.

Ida B. Wells (1862–1931)— An African-American editor of *Free Speech* newspaper in Memphis, Tennessee, and an influential leader in the early Civil Rights movement. Wells investigated the 1891 lynching of three innocent men at the hands of a white mob. Her newspaper was burned down and she had to flee to New York where worked for civil rights and helped found the NAACP.

Samuel Hopkins Adams (1871–1958)— In "The Great American Fraud," a series for *Collier's Magazine* in 1905, Adams exposed dangerous narcotics and false advertising by the patent medicine industry, contributing to public pressure for establishing the Food and Drug Administration.

Figure 3.3 Ida B. Wells Barnett. Portrait by Mary Garrity, 1893, Wikimedia Commons.

Figure 3.4 Lincoln Steffens, 1894, Wikimedia Commons.

Figure 3.5 Ida Tarbell. Portrait by J. E. Purdy, 1904, Library of Congress.

Lincoln Steffens (1866–1936)—"The Shame of the Cities" investigation was one of Steffens's major exposes of municipal corruption for *McClure's Magazine*.

Cecil Chesterton (1879–1918)—As a reporter for London's *New Witness*, Chesterton exposed stock fraud and insider trading in the Marconi Scandal of 1912. French newspaper *Le Matin* also participated in the investigation.

Ida Tarbell (1857–1944)—Standard Oil Company's rise to monopoly power through corrupt business practices was the theme of Tarbell's 1902 series in *McClure's Magazine*. Her findings were confirmed by congressional investigations and as a result, anti-trust laws were enforced to end the company's monopoly.

David Graham Phillips (1867–1911)—In "Treason of the Senate," a 1906 series in the Hearst-owned *Cosmopolitan* magazine, Phillips exposed senators who had taken direct bribes and campaign contributions by major corporations such as Standard Oil Co.

Upton Sinclair (1878–1968)—*The Jungle*, a 1906 novel about grotesque conditions in the meat-packing industry of Chicago, was based on investigations by Sinclair for the socialist magazine *Appeal to Reason*. The resulting public uproar led to the establishment of the Food and Drug Administration.

Ray Stanard Baker (1870–1946)—Wrote *Following the Color Line*, in 1908, exploring racial issues in the North and South. Baker also reported from the front lines of World War I.

Figure 3.6 Upton Sinclair, Bain Collection, Library of Congress.

3 World War I 1914–1920s

As they skirted French defenses to cross Belgium in August of 1914, German armies carried out carefully planned reprisals, executing civilians and burning entire towns to the ground. Although they intended to bully the Belgians into submission, the Germans, historian Barbara Tuchman said, "shocked the world of 1914, which had still believed in human progress" (Tuchman 1962).

Among the witnesses to the atrocities were a remarkable group of American reporters, including Will Irwin and Richard Harding Davis. Because America was neutral, and had a large German population thought to be sympathetic to Germany, the reporters had been given permission to follow along. What they wrote, however, did anything but encourage sympathy. Davis's report on the atrocities in Louvain, a Belgian town of 42,000, is a classic of vivid reporting:

> Outside the station in the public square, the people of Louvain passed in an unending procession, women bareheaded, weeping, men carrying the children asleep on their shoulders, all hemmed in by the shadowy army of gray wolves ... It was all like a scene upon the stage, unreal, inhuman. You felt it could not be true. You felt that the curtain of fire, purring and crackling and sending up hot sparks to meet the kind, calm stars, was only a painted backdrop; that the reports of rifles from the dark ruins came from blank cartridges, and that these trembling shopkeepers and peasants ringed in bayonets would not in a few minutes really die, but that they themselves and their homes would be restored to their wives and children. You felt it was only a nightmare, cruel and uncivilized. And then you remembered that the German Emperor has told us what it is. It is his Holy War. (*New York Tribune*, August 31, 1914)

The *Berliner Tageblatt* reported the situation in Belgium from a much different perspective:

> German refugees from Belgium are still coming to our office and reporting to us the terrible but true stories of Belgian fanaticism. A German butcher in the Rue Saint-Pierre in Brussels was literally cut to pieces by a wild mob. The crazed people shouted that they would give him a death in keeping with his trade ... (*Berliner Tageblatt*, August 12, 1914, in Snyder and Morris 1962)

Although historians would later show that some atrocities did occur (Horne and Kramer 2001), and that Davis's account of from Louvain was true, many other stories were fabricated out of patriotic fervor. Questions about the stories led to inquiries by the British and Belgian governments and interviews with over a thousand witnesses (Bryce 1914). Their reports, along with eyewitness stories by journalists, had moved public opinion away from Germany in the United States and other neutral countries.

3.1 Censorship in World War I

Although press censorship in various forms is almost as old as the press itself, World War I was a unique large-scale conflict with new situations. For the first time, governments issued blanket censorship regulations and put news correspondents into army uniforms. The Defense of the Realm Act in Britain and similar censorship laws in France literally left "large blank spaces" in newspapers (*New York Times*, October 5, 1917).

The purpose of censorship was to prevent people at home from learning demoralizing information about defeats and difficult conditions. For example, the worst defeat in British history—the Battle of the Somme in 1916—involved troop casualties numbering 600,000. Yet the battle was reported as a victory or kept out of the press altogether. One correspondent, William Beach Thomas of the *Daily Mail*, said later that he was "deeply ashamed" of the cover-up. Several received high honors, including knighthoods, and one publisher was made a lord, as more or less a bribe for silence about the corruption and ineptitude of the war effort. British Prime Minister Lloyd George, in a private conversation with *Manchester Guardian* editor C. P. Scott, said in 1917, "If people really knew [the truth], the war would be stopped tomorrow. But of course they don't know, and can't know" (Greenslade 2014).

Despite censorship, intrepid correspondents could occasionally shake things up. *The Times*' war correspondent Charles Repington reported that a shortage of artillery shells had doomed a March 1915 British attack. The report sent serious shock waves through the government, and advanced Lloyd George to Minister of Munitions, but it also got Repington banned from covering the war (Nicholson 2014).

Censorship also meant that newspapers like *L'Homme Libre* could be suspended from publication by the French government for criticism of war readiness. That paper's editor, Georges Clemenceau, had already spent the 1870s in political exile in New York City, and had returned to edit *L'aurore* during the Dreyfus affair. Despite his struggle against government repression of the media, Clemenceau rode the French political roller coaster to become prime minister in 1917.

It seems ironic that Clemenceau, once an oppressed editor himself, would support censorship as a politician. Yet one wartime scandal—the 1917 Bolo Pasha attempt to insert German propaganda into the French press—explains some of his motivation. The Bolo Pasha affair was a wartime German plot to finance the purchase of French newspapers using millions of dollars funneled through American banks. A German agent, Bolo Pasha, purchased a French newspaper, *Le Journal*, to advocate surrender to the Germans. The plot was discovered, in part by still-neutral American authorities, and the French executed Pasha for treason in 1917. When the war was over, someone asked Clemenceau if he would end censorship. "Do you think I'm a total idiot?" was his response.

Despite supposed neutrality, most Americans sided with the British and French in the 1914–17 period. One exception was newspaper chain publisher William Randolph Hearst, whose pacifism and pro-German stand infuriated the British. Long before the United States entered the war, correspondents for Hearst's International News Service (INS) were banned from France, and INS continued to cover it from behind German lines, sending dispatches back to the United States by way of the powerful radio transmitter in Nauheim, Germany. The Germans also supplied film for Hearst's newsreels, shown in theaters across the United States. After the United States declared war in 1917, the attorney general's office investigated Hearst for his frequent meetings with Bolo Pasha, although no criminal

Figure 3.7 Censored Doughboys—This 1918 photo was banned by US censors because American soldiers were not permitted to be seen drinking alcohol, even though the just-captured German beer steins were empty. Photo by US Army Signal Corps. Heavy-handed censorship had more serious consequences, such as when censors blocked Field Marshall Paul Von Hindenburg's admission that the American military changed the balance of forces and won the war. Later, the Nazis explained the defeat as a stab in the back from the home front. This "Dolchstoss" myth helped propel them to power, according to journalist George Seldes.

charges were ever made. Hearst biographer David Nassaw said Hearst did not realize that Bolo Pasha was a German agent, or that his own correspondents and film distributors were on the German government payroll. Still, when the facts were revealed, the impact on Hearst's reputation and his editorial staff was "devastating" (Nassaw 2001).

The war era in the United States was marked by the arrest and persecution of thousands of dissidents under the Espionage Act of 1917 (Zinn 1980). The Post Office banned German language and dissident newspapers from the mails, which usually meant bankruptcy. The German-language *New Yorker Staats-Zeitung* (one of hundreds of German-language US newspapers at the time) noted constant attacks "upon everything that talks German or sounds German … Our America is to become an America that is strictly English from top to bottom. An America in which but one God, one language, one way of thinking and of living is to be allowed" (*New York Times*, August 23, 1917).

Americans disliked World War I censorship and the morale-boosting, publication-censoring Committee on Public Information (also discussed in Chapter 6). "Why pay for comedy when we have a Creel Committee?" asked a *Washington Post* reporter, complaining about ham-fisted and illogical war censorship.

George Seldes, a reporter with the *Atlanta Constitution* and other newspapers, wrote of one important incident illustrating the counterproductive nature of front-line censorship. On November 12, 1918, the day after the Armistice, Seldes and three other reporters drove through German lines and found Field Marshall Paul von Hindenburg. "The American attack won the war," Hindenburg told the correspondents. The incident is important, Seldes said, because Hindenburg acknowledged that the war was won in the field, and did not make excuses or blame defeat on some kind of betrayal from the home front (Seldes 1987).

When Seldes and the others filed their stories, US censors in Paris blocked them because they had not asked permission in advance. Later, the Nazis would use the Dolchstoßlegende, the "stab-in-the-back" myth by Jews in Germany, to explain away the German defeat in World War I. "If the Hindenburg confession had been passed [by US censors], it would have been headlined in every country … and become an important page in history," Seldes said later. Of course no one realized the full significance of the episode at the time, but in retrospect, Seldes said, "I believe it would have destroyed the main planks of the platform on which Hitler rose to power" (Seldes 1987).

Journalist and novelist Ernest Hemingway also recalled the difficulty of describing the horror of war under censorship. "World War I was the most murderous, mismanaged butchery that has ever taken place on earth," Hemingway wrote. "Any writer who said otherwise lied. So the writers either wrote propaganda, shut up, or fought" (Hemingway, 1942).

4 The Press in the Russian Communist Revolution

The first step in the Russian Revolution, according to Vladimir Ilyich Lenin, was to create a newspaper, and Lenin created a paper called *Iskra* (Spark). Not only would it carry the communist message, but the act of working for a newspaper in itself would transform the revolutionaries. In "Where to Begin," Lenin wrote in 1901:

> The mere technical task of regularly supplying the newspaper with copy and of promoting regular distribution will necessitate a network of local agents of the united party … This work will train and bring into the foreground not only the most skillful propagandists, but the most capable organizers, the most talented party leaders, capable, at the right moment, of releasing the slogan for the decisive struggle and of taking the lead in that struggle. (Lenin 1901)

The significance of the media in the Russian Revolution did not mean that Lenin supported free speech. Quite the reverse, in fact. Leading Russian newspapers like *Pravda*

Figure 3.8 Mysterious photo—This scene of a "mobile newsroom" belonging to the newspaper *Kolhoznik* (agricultural cooperative) near Kiev was staged around 1925. The banner behind the typesetters reads "Let us secure the financial basis for Socialist way of life." The newspaper itself probably served to inform and to engage the workers, but the photo of journalists setting type on a truck in a wheat field is an example of staged events for Soviet communist propaganda. Farm Security Administration, Library of Congress.

(Truth) and *Izvestia* (News) became tightly run organs of the state bureaucracy, and no publication was permitted to print anything remotely critical of Russia or communism. Absolute censorship was enforced with prison sentences and summary execution during Russia's communist period (1917–91). Lenin explained:

> In capitalist usage, freedom of the press means freedom of the rich to bribe the press, freedom to use their wealth to shape and fabricate so-called public opinion ... With the aid of plausible, fine-sounding, but thoroughly false phrases, [people are diverted] from the concrete historical task of liberating the press from capitalist enslavement. (Lenin 1919)

Some, like German communist revolutionary Rosa Luxemburg, argued that the suppression of free speech in Russia was not only wrong but self-defeating. In 1916, Luxemburg said:

> Freedom only for the supporters of the government, only for the members of a party—however numerous they may be—is no freedom at all. Freedom is always the freedom of the dissenter. Not because of the fanaticism of "justice", but rather because all that is instructive, wholesome, and purifying in political freedom depends on this essential characteristic, and its effects cease to work when "freedom" becomes a privilege ... Without general elections, without unrestricted freedom of press and assembly, without a free struggle of opinion, life

dies out in every public institution, becomes a mere semblance of life, in which only the bureaucracy remains as the active element. (Anderson 2004)

Shaking the World

In John Reed's book, *Ten Days that Shook the World*, events of the Russian Revolution of 1917 came alive:

> As we came out into the dark and gloomy day all around the grey horizon, factory whistles were blowing, a hoarse and nervous sound, full of foreboding. By tens of thousands, the working people poured out, men and women; by tens of thousands the humming slums belched out their dun and miserable hordes. Red Petrograd was in danger! Cossaks! South and south-west they poured through the shabby streets towards the Moskovsky Gate, men, women and children, with rifles, picks, spades, rolls of barbed wire, cartridge-belts over their working clothes ... They rolled along torrent-like, companies of soldiers borne with them, bungs, motor-trucks, wagons—the revolutionary proletariat defending with its breath the capital of the Workers and Peasants Republic! (Reed 1919)

Figure 3.9 *Ten Days That Shook the World*—John Reed's classic eyewitness account of the 1917 Russian Revolution won worldwide acclaim, and an introduction by Vladimir Lenin, but was banned by Soviet premier Joseph Stalin. Although Reed sympathized with the revolution, his aim was to tell the story as truthfully as possible. Photo c. 1915, by Bain Service, Library of Congress.

An American journalist who initially sympathized with the communist revolution, John Reed (1887–1920) wrote a first-hand account of the Russian Revolution of 1917 that has become a classic of literary journalism. In *Ten Days That Shook the World*, Reed said he "tried to see events with the eye of a conscientious reporter, interested in setting down the truth."

Reed died in Russia in 1920, and is the only American to be buried in the Kremlin Wall. American diplomat George F. Kennan said later, "Reed's account ... rises above every other contemporary record for its literary power, its penetration, its command of detail ... [It is] a reflection of blazing honesty and a purity of idealism that did unintended credit to the American society that produced him, the merits of which he himself understood so poorly" (Kennan 1989).

Repression of the media in Russia took place against the backdrop of a ruthless suppression of all political dissent known as the "Great Purge." During the dictatorship of Joseph Stalin, from the 1922 through 1953, no fewer than 15 million people died as a result of execution, or at prison camps, or due to forced famine (Conquest 1990).

Although the news media in the United States and Europe frequently reported on the repression, there were some, like *New York Times* correspondent Walter Duranty, who sympathized with Stalin and claimed the reports were exaggerated. A posthumous investigation of Duranty's 1932 Pulitzer Prize ended with the conclusion that he had been a willing tool of Stalinist propaganda and had produced "some of the worst reporting in this newspaper" (*New York Times*, June 24, 1990).

Under subsequent Russian dictators from the 1950s through the early 1980s, repression was lighter but no less real, forcing writers underground, where they fell back on medieval technology: the hand-copying of manuscripts to pass among small circles of readers. These manuscripts were called *samizdats* (same-as-that). In the late 1980s, Soviet Premier Michael Gorbachev began ending repressive policies and by 1991 the Soviet Union of Russia and fourteen other nations was dissolved. Freedom of the press remains an elusive goal in many of these nations, as Reporters Without Frontiers, Article 19, and other international groups continue to document.

5 The Press in India's Nonviolent Revolution

Like Vladimir Lenin, Mohandas (Mahatma) Gandhi also believed that one of the first steps in a revolution was to create a newspaper. In contrast to Lenin, however, Gandhi believed in democracy and nonviolence. He had a deep faith that good ideas would win converts, and that struggle for the liberation of India from British rule could take place with journalism helping to explain the struggle.

Born in India and trained in law in Britain, Gandhi began working as an attorney in South Africa and founded a newspaper called *Indian Opinion* in 1903. He thought it was critical to have the publication in order to explain Satyagraha, the principle behind nonviolent social revolution. Later, when he returned to India, Gandhi founded the weekly *Young India* to promote views on political reform, religious tolerance, and economic self-sufficiency for India. The publication changed its name to *Harijan*, which meant "Children of God." It was published from 1919 through 1948. Gandhi also edited four other journals during his long career (Guha 2003).

"Week after week I poured out my soul in columns expounding my principles and practices of Satyagraha," Gandhi said. "The journal became for me a training in self-restraint, and for friends a medium through which to keep in touch with my thoughts." In his autobiography, Gandhi said that "Satyagraha would probably have been impossible without *Indian Opinion*."

Figure 3.10 Independence leader and editor—Among many other accomplishments, Mohandas (Mahatma) Gandhi edited half a dozen newspapers during his long career as the leader for India's independence movement. This photo by Margaret Bourke-White for *Life* magazine is an example of visual logic and one of the great classics of twentieth century photography. Since Gandhi often said he was just a symbol, Bourke-White put Gandhi's symbol (the spinning wheel) in the foreground. © *Life* magazine, 1946.

Journalism taught Gandhi the discipline of being fair and remaining cool even when he was attacked, said Shall Sinha, a Gandhi biographer:

> It helped him clarify his own ideas and visions, to stay on track, to be consistent, to assume full accountability for his actions and words ... The newspapers brought Gandhi in close communication with many deep thinkers and spiritual leaders. It kept broadening his horizon everyday. Gandhi pursued journalism not for its sake but also as an aid to what he had conceived to be his mission in life: to teach by example and precept. (Sinha 2010)

Chicago Tribune correspondent William L. Shirer covered Gandhi and the Indian independence movement between 1930 and 1932: "For those of us who glimpsed, however briefly, Gandhi's use of [Satyagraha]; and who had the luck, for however short a time, to feel his greatness ... it was an experience that enriched and deepened our lives as no other did" (Shirer 1986). That experience, he said, helped him find the moral courage to describe the Nazi terror creeping over Germany after 1933 when he worked for the Associated Press and CBS radio.

6 The German Press and the Nazi Revolution

It was a scene not witnessed since the Middle Ages: the flames engulfing tens of thousands of German books in May of 1933 seemed ominous harbingers of disaster to William L. Shirer, an Associated Press correspondent in Germany. The descent into barbarism began the moment that Nazi leaders decided that the arts, literature, the press, radio, and films would exist only to serve the purpose of Nazi propaganda, he said.

Following the Reich Press Law of October 1933, the country's 4,700 newspapers were either closed, confiscated, or directly controlled by the Nazi party. Most notably, the Nazis closed *Voissische Zeitung*, a newspaper founded in 1704 and, at that moment in history, comparable to *The Times* of London or the *New York Times*. Other newspapers, especially those with Jewish owners like the *Berliner Tageblatt*, were confiscated by Nazi party leaders. Children of the newspaper's founder, Rudolf Mosse, fled to Switzerland and the United States in 1933. Rudolf's son George Mosse, a historian, helped train US administrators for the post-war German occupation in the 1940s.

Also confiscated by the Nazis was Wolff's Telegraph Bureau, one of the first wire services. Newspaper reporters and editors who dared even the mildest criticism were sent to concentration camps or killed outright (Shirer 1960). Perhaps the only notable dissent involved the printing and distribution of leaflets by German students in the White Rose movement. The pamphlets said "we will not be silent" in the face of "abominable crimes." Three students and a professor at the University of Munich were executed by order of a Nazi court in 1943 (Axelrod 2001).

The Nazis produced some of the most infamous newspapers in history, such as *Der Stürmer*, published 1922–45, which specialized in crude, vivid, and vicious anti-Semitism. "Jewish murder plan against Gentile humanity" was one particularly virulent headline. The only solution, this newspaper often said, was "the extermination of the people whose father is the devil."

The paper's editor, Julius Streicher, was sentenced to death for crimes against humanity at the Nuremburg War Crimes Tribunal in 1946. He was convicted of incitement to murder and extermination, which "clearly constitutes persecution on political and racial grounds ... a crime against humanity" (Bytwerk 2001). Significantly, Streicher was only an editor, not a high party official. The principle of responsibility for media crimes was established with this sentence. Other major figures in the Nazi media, notably film director Leni Riefenstahl, served jail sentences. Nazi propaganda minister Joseph Goebbels only escaped punishment by suicide.

In a similar case from the 1990s, members of the Rwandan media advocating genocide were brought before a criminal tribunal established by the United Nations. Ferdinand Nahimana, head of Radio Rwanda, Jean-Bosco Barayagwiza, chair of the radio board, and Hassan Ngeze, editor of Kangura newspaper, were all sentenced to long prison terms (ICTR 2000; Melvern 2004).

7 The American Press in World War II

The threat to freedom was never more clear than in the 1940s, and news correspondents willingly lent their talent to the Allied war effort to stop fascism in Germany, Italy, and Japan. Censorship was confined primarily to military security, although anything that depicted the enemy as human—for instance, the German army's routine compliance with truce agreements to recover wounded after battles—would be censored by the military.

Censorship barely held down the cantankerous American press. A furious controversy raged on the home front over war preparedness and prewar conspiracies between American and German industries such as Standard Oil (Exxon) and I. G. Farben (Borkin 1978). Incidents from the front lines, such as General George Patton slapping shell-shocked soldiers in hospitals, were picked up by muckraking columnists like Drew Pearson.

Censorship was not as heavy handed in World War II as in other wars. One of the most popular writers of World War II, Ernie Pyle (1900–45), described this scene as the Allied armada sailed from North Africa to invade Sicily in 1943:

> The night before we sailed, the crew listened as usual to the German propaganda radio program which featured Midge, the American girl turned Nazi, who was trying to scare them, disillusion them and depress them. As usual they laughed with amusement and scorn at her childishly treasonable talk. In a vague and indirect way, I suppose, the privilege of listening to your enemy trying to undermine you—the very night before you go out to face him—expresses what we are fighting for. (Pyle 1944)

Pyle had drawn from his experience as a correspondent roving across America in a station wagon with his wife in the 1930s, writing about encounters with people from all walks of life (Pyle 1935), including fishermen in San Francisco, and George Washington Carver at Tuskegee Institute. During the war, Pyle used the same technique, focusing on the stories of ordinary soldiers rather than important generals and big strategies. In one often-quoted piece, "The God-Damned Infantry," Pyle wrote something few can forget:

> There is an agony in your heart and you almost feel ashamed to look at them. They are just guys from Broadway and Main Street, but you wouldn't remember them. They are too far away now. They are too tired. Their world can never be known to you, but if you could see them just once, just for an instant, you would know that no matter how hard people work back home they are not keeping pace with these infantrymen. (Pyle 2000)

Pyle died covering the troops in the fight on the Pacific island of le Shima in 1945. A memorial there reads, "At this spot the 77th Infantry Division lost a buddy, Ernie Pyle."

Women also covered the war, as historians Maurine H. Beasley and Sheila J. Gibbons pointed out in *Taking Their Place* (Beasley and Gibbons 1993). Among the best known was Marguerite Higgins (1920–66), a writer for the *New York Herald Tribune* who witnessed the liberation of the Dachau concentration camp in late April, 1945.

"The liberation was a frenzied scene," she wrote. "Inmates of the camp hugged and embraced the American troops, kissed the ground before them and carried them shoulder high around the place." Higgins went on to win a Pulitzer Prize for coverage of the Korean War.

The African-American press was initially divided over support for World War II. After all, in World War I, critical reporting on military race riots landed a black editor in jail under the Sedition Act. Simple concern for social reform led to investigations for disloyalty by the FBI (Washburn 1986). The African-American press built on the V for Victory campaign with their own "Double V" campaign: Victory over the enemies of democracy, overseas *and* at home.

Figure 3.11 Soldier's scribe—Ernie Pyle's columns for Scripps-Howard newspapers earned a Pulitzer Prize in 1944 and the devotion of US soldiers everywhere. He told stories about the regular guys slogging through the war rather than the great general and the grand strategies. Courtesy of the University of Indiana.

Figure 3.12 War correspondent—Only three years out of journalism school, Marguerite Higgins convinced editors at the *Herald Tribune* to send her to Europe in 1944. She also broke barriers for women reporters everywhere, convincing General Douglas MacArthur to lift the ban on women correspondents in the Korean War in 1950. *New York World-Telegram*, 1950, Library of Congress.

8 Press Responsibility and the 1947 Hutchins Commission

During and after World War II, questions about press responsibility led to a commission financed by *Time* magazine publisher Henry Luce. Leading the commission was Robert Maynard Hutchins, then chancellor at the University of Chicago, whose ideas about education had focused on communication as central to a lifetime of learning.

The Hutchins Commission found that freedom of expression had been imperiled by accelerating technology and by arrogant and irresponsible publishers. The commission urged publishers to "regard themselves as common carriers of information and discussion" and recommended five major points that it said society was entitled to demand of its press:

1 A truthful, comprehensive, and intelligent account of the day's events in a context which gives them meaning.
2 A forum for the exchange of comment and criticism.
3 The projection of a representative picture of the constituent groups in the society.
4 The presentation and clarification of the goals and values of the society.
5 Full access to the day's intelligence.

"Where freedom of expression exists, the beginnings of a free society and a means for every extension of liberty are already present. Free expression is therefore unique among liberties: it promotes and protects all the rest," the commission said (Hutchins 1947).

The commission's point about projecting a representative picture of constituent groups in society was especially troubling for the press in the 1950s and 1960s as it grappled with new demands for equality from African-Americans. The commission had said that it "holds to the faith that if people are exposed to the inner truth of the life of a particular group, they will gradually build up respect for and understanding of it." In effect, civil rights was the crucial test of what Thomas Jefferson had called the great experiment.

9 The Press and Civil Rights

One of the finest moments in the history of the American press was its response to the Civil Rights movement that peaked in the 1950s and 1960s. To understand that moment, however, it's important to understand that civil rights advocates had a long history of pleading their own cause in their own press for a century and a half before the cause was appreciated.

Starting in 1827 with the founding of *Freedom's Journal* in New York, the African-American press fought slavery and prejudice with low budgets and high expectations. "We wish to plead our own cause," said John Russworm, the short-lived journal's editor. Several other small papers emerged in the pre-Civil War era, but none better known than the *North*

Star, published from 1847 through the mid-1860s by former slave Frederick Douglass. A fiery orator and passionate writer, Douglass wrote, "The white man's happiness cannot be purchased by the black man's misery. Virtue cannot prevail among the white people, by its destruction among the black people, who form a part of the whole community. It is evident that the white and black must fall or flourish together" (Douglass 1849).

Altogether some 2,700 African-American newspapers came to life during the nineteenth and twentieth centuries, but they tended to survive only nine years on average. Despite its lack of financial power, the African-American press became "the greatest single power in the Negro race" (Roberts and Klibanoff 2007).

The two most influential newspapers in the African-American media were the *Chicago Defender*, a weekly founded in 1905 by Robert A. Abbott, and the *Pittsburgh Courier*, founded by Robert Lee Vann and Edwin Harleston in 1907. Circulation of the two papers would eventually top 300,000, in part because both were circulated nationwide. They called on African-Americans to move North, where there was more opportunity. Between 1910 and 1930, about 1.75 million left the South in what was called "the great migration"—with the *Courier* and *Defender* lighting the way.

As the nation's strongest voices for civil rights, the *Courier*, the *Defender*, and the rest of the African-American press provided a forum for the African-American community. They employed gifted writers like Langston Hughes and Ida B. Wells; they campaigned for integrated sports; they organized boycotts of racist films like *Birth of a Nation*; they covered race riots and investigated lynchings; and they debated tactics and helped clarify the early goals of the Civil Rights movement. Another important milestone for the African-American press was the establishment of *Ebony* magazine in 1945 by John H. Johnson. Designed to look like other glossy magazines, *Ebony* emphasized entertainment and the success of African-Americans, but also covered difficult issues of racism and segregation. The success of these and other publications gave a voice to millions of people who were not usually heard in the mainstream media.

At the time, the mainstream media paid little attention to civil rights. In 1944, Swedish journalist Gunnar Myrdal toured the American South and wrote that if the press ever did tell the story, the rest of the nation would be "shocked and shaken" and would demand sweeping changes. A decade later, Myrdal's prophecy came true.

One event that brought civil rights into the national spotlight was the May 17, 1954 *Brown v. Board of Education* decision by the US Supreme Court. The court unanimously decided that racially segregated schools were "inherently unequal" and that African-American students had been "deprived of the equal protection of the laws guaranteed by the 14th Amendment."

Public opinion was strongly galvanized the next year with the 1955 murder of Emmett Till, a fourteen-year-old Chicago resident visiting relatives in Mississippi. Till was brutally beaten, shot, and dumped in a river in apparent retaliation for supposedly talking in a sassy way to a white woman.

His mother demanded that his body be sent home for burial in Chicago. When the coffin arrived, she had it opened "to show the world what they did to my baby." Photos of Till's horrifically beaten face were first printed on the front page of the *Chicago Defender*, and in *Ebony* and other magazines. "It gave a real picture to the brutality and terrorism against African Americans," said Roland Martin, editor of the *Chicago Defender*, in 2005 (Goodman 2005). Reporters from around the world attended the trial of his accused white murderers. Despite considerable evidence of guilt, the men were quickly acquitted by the racially prejudiced Southern judicial system. The slaying brought "strong criticism of [Mississippi's] white supremacy practices from other sections of the country," a *New York Times* reporter wrote (Roberts and Klibanoff 2007).

As African-Americans pressed for equality with bus boycotts, lawsuits, lunch counter sit-ins, and other nonviolent tactics, the mainstream press wondered how to cover rapidly unfolding events. At first the media settled into what seemed at first to be a gentlemanly debate over schools and desegregation. But by misreading the sentiments of political extremists in 1955, the *Times* "failed to see that the extremes would soon be in control," said Gene Patterson and Hank Klibanoff in *The Race Beat*, a 2006 Pulitzer Prize-winning history of civil rights news coverage.

9.1 *New York Times* advertising libel lawsuit

One of the most important media-related issues from the Civil Rights era involved a lawsuit filed against the *New York Times* in 1960 and decided, in favor of the *Times*, in 1964.

The issue emerged when, as part of a fund-raising effort, a group of Southern ministers ran a full-page advertisement in the *Times* under the headline "Heed their Rising Voices." The ad included descriptions of events that had minor inaccuracies. Louis B. Sullivan, police commissioner of Birmingham, Alabama, sued the *Times* and won at the state court level. However, the US Supreme Court reversed the state court decision, and cleared the way for media coverage not only of the civil rights issue but of government in general.

"We consider this case against the background of a profound national commitment to the principle that debate on public issues should be uninhibited, robust, and wide open, and that it may well include vehement, caustic, and sometimes unpleasantly sharp attacks on government and public officials," the Supreme Court said in its 1964 opinion in *New York Times v. Sullivan*. (The suit is also discussed in Chapter 6.)

9.2 Press divisions on civil rights

The mainstream press, like the country, was divided on the Civil Rights movement. Editors James J. Kilpatrick of the *Richmond Times*, Virginia, and Thomas Waring of the *Charleston Courier*, South Carolina, advocated "massive resistance" to integration and encouraged Southerners to fight for "states rights."

More temperate Southern editors advised gradual change. These included *Atlanta Journal* editor Ralph McGill, Greenville, Mississippi, editor Hodding Carter, and Little Rock editor Harry Ashmore.

Ralph McGill was especially known for crafting carefully balanced editorials to depict the Civil Rights movement as a sometimes uncomfortable but necessary and even inevitable

Figure 3.13 Robert Lee Vann—A Pittsburgh, PA, attorney, Vann helped found the *Pittsburgh Courier*, an important African-American publication. This World War II-era government illustration was meant to remind African-Americans that their contributions were valued, despite continued discrimination. Illustration by Charles Henry Alston, Office of War Information, 1943, US National Archives.

process—a process that would help build a South that would be, he said, too busy and too generous to hate. After an Atlanta bombing, McGill wrote in a 1959 Pulitzer Prize-winning editorial, "This … is a harvest of defiance of the courts and the encouragement of citizens to defy law on the part of many Southern politicians." McGill also urged journalists to cover the rising demands for equality as a struggle for "civil rights"—a term we take for granted today, but which at the time struck journalists as a self-fulfilling prophecy. Still, it was far better than the alternative term and self-fulfilling prophecy: "race war."

McGill's protégé, Gene Patterson, wrote a front-page editorial after Dr. Martin Luther King's assassination in 1968 in the *Atlanta Journal*. He called on white Americans to cease "the poisonous politics of hatred that turns sick minds to murder. Let the white man say,

'No more of this ever,' and put an end to it—if not for the Negro, for the sake of his own immortal soul."

Between the 1950s and 1980s, ultra-conservative Southern editors resisted any coverage of civil rights rallies or demonstrations. If a news reporter turned in a civil rights story, it would often be killed. When that happened, Southern reporters knew that they could circumvent their editors and send their stories to the *New York Times*, and a glance through the *Times* civil rights coverage shows a large number of stories without bylines. (This is one reason why the *Times* was a target in the *New York Times v Sullivan* libel case.) Similar ultra-conservative attempts to block civil rights coverage took place with the television media, as we will see in Chapter 9. In the end, the success of the nonviolent Civil Rights movement was closely connected with the media's ability to witness events. "If it hadn't been for the media—the print media and the television—the civil rights movement would have been like a bird without wings, a choir without a song," said civil rights leader John Lewis in 2005 (Roberts and Klibanoff 2007). Eventually, even conservative editors such as Kilpatrick admitted that they had been wrong about civil rights, and the South changed.

In witnessing the suffering of American civil rights demonstrators, the press came to be regarded with gratitude as an agent of national reconciliation.

10 Vietnam, Watergate and the Adversarial Press

National reconciliation never really took place following the Vietnam War. Unlike the Civil Rights movement, the aims and conduct of the war in general—and the role of the press in particular—remained vexed political questions long after events had run their course.

The Vietnam War began with the end of World War II and the French attempt to re-establish their former colonies. American assistance grew as the French lost control of the northern part of the country in the late 1950s. The United States created a weak regime in the South through the 1960s. After a protracted guerrilla war, and a series of military defeats, the US withdrew all forces in 1975. Two major points of media controversy included the skepticism of the press corps and the impact of television images on public opinion.

The American experience in World War II informed, to a large extent, the US government's lack of censorship of press coverage during the Vietnam War. Very few restrictions were imposed in Vietnam. In the early years, the press corps was skeptical about the war, but the reporters themselves saw skepticism as part of their responsibility. One reporter in particular, World War II veteran reporter Homer Bigart, had never played the role of cheerleader for the home team, even in World War II. As colleague Malcolm Browne said, "However critical his reporting of such military blunders as the Anzio beachhead [in World War II] could be, there was never any doubt which side had his sympathies. In Vietnam, by contrast, Homer could never wholeheartedly identify himself with an American team that often looked arrogant and wrongheaded and whose cause seemed questionable to him" (Browne 1993).

Others, including Bigart's colleague and World War II *Herald-Tribune* veteran Marguerite Higgins, saw sensationalism and pessimism overwhelming the more optimistic assessments of the Vietnam War, which in turn provoked a politically defensive escalation of the war in its early stages (Higgins 1965).

The later generation of reporters had a different take. David Halberstam initially believed that a US victory was needed to discourage "so-called wars of liberation" but eventually came to the conclusion that the war "was doomed," and that the United States was "on the wrong side of history" (Halberstam 1965). Neil Sheehan, a UPI reporter, saw the war as being lost on the ground long before it was lost in American public opinion (Sheehan 1988). And studies of US media coverage showed that the news media tended to be neutral while public opinion was increasingly opposed to the war (Vaughn 2008).

Questions about the impact of television images on public opinion were raised during the war and long after it ended, with the idea that bloody images proved too horrible for sensitive Americans and had a morale-sapping effect. However, analyses of war coverage has shown that view to be unsupported by the data. (Note: For more on television and the Vietnam War, see Chapter 9.)

For the military, the main lesson of Vietnam was that reporters would need to be managed. Press "pools" in conflicts ranging from the Falklands (1982), Grenada (1983), and Panama (1989), to the Iraq conflicts (1991, 2003) and Afghanistan (2000s) were kept away from war's gruesome scenes and troubling questions about civilian casualties.

10.1 The Pentagon Papers and Watergate

One of the major turning points in the public opinion about the Vietnam War was the publication in 1971 of the "Pentagon Papers," a secret history of the war drawn up by the US military and leaked to the *New York Times* by Pentagon consultant Daniel Ellsberg. The papers showed that three administrations had "systematically lied, not only to the public but also to Congress, about a subject of transcendent national interest and significance" (Apple 1996). Three days after the leak became public, President Richard Nixon asked the courts for an injunction to halt publication.

A temporary injunction was granted, but after a week of examining the papers, and amid a dozen other leaks to other newspapers, the US Supreme Court lifted the injunctions, finding that the government had not met the heavy burden of proving that publication would cause "grave and irreparable" danger— proof that would be necessary to enforce censorship (*New York Times v. United States* 1971).

Concern about this and other leaks to the press from inside the government led the Nixon administration to assemble a team of former CIA employees as "plumbers" who would fix the "leaks." One of their assignments was to break into the Democratic National Committee offices at the Watergate apartment and office building in Washington, DC. When the burglars were arrested, two young *Washington Post* reporters—Bob Woodward and Carl Bernstein—investigated ties between the burglars and the White House. In the process, Woodward and Bernstein unraveled a web of illegal activities in the White House and the Justice Department, including extortion and bribery.

This led to the resignation of President Nixon in 1974 and criminal convictions for seven high-level members of his administration. Woodward and Bernstein were just starting their careers when they began investigating Watergate. Many senior reporters did not believe that a scandal of that magnitude could unravel, and were astonished at the success of the investigation.

As we will see in future chapters, sometimes individuals who don't know enough to be discouraged can change the course of history. This was as true for telegraph inventor Samuel Morse and Apple computer inventor Steve Wozniak as it was for Woodward and Bernstein.

The combination of events surrounding Watergate and the Vietnam War led to a perception, especially among American conservatives, of an irrationally "adversarial press," rather like the reaction in Teddy Roosevelt's era to the muckraking press. But investigative journalism also aroused a sense of admiration for the extent to which the press could fulfill its constitutional role as a check on government power. These views, although not mutually exclusive, never reconciled in the coming decades with partisan political scandals of the Reagan, Clinton, and Bush presidencies. Polls showed that trust in the press, at near 40 to 50 percent levels in the 1980s, declined to half those levels by 2015.

Figure 3.14 Watergate reporters—Two young reporters, Bob Woodward (left) and Carl Bernstein, exposed the connection between President Richard Nixon and the burglars who broke into the Democratic National Committee offices during the 1972 election campaign. Nixon resigned two years later, unable to cover up the widening scandal. Photo by the *Washington Post*, 1973.

11 Literary and Gonzo Journalism

The Civil Rights movement, the Watergate scandals, and the anti-war movement all played against a backdrop of a changing society where conventions of all kinds were being challenged. One of the more important conventions of journalism was the idea of objectivity and the "inverted pyramid" form of writing. Magazine and newspaper writers took a different approach in the 1960s with the "literary journalism" movement. While still telling a factual story, writers used novelistic devices like dialogue, omniscient narration, and scene-by-scene construction to form a more interesting and personal narrative.

Sometimes "literary journalism" had the confusing label of "new journalism," but the narrative form wasn't so new after all. It had been used by Daniel Defoe, Charles Dickens, Stephen Crane, Ernest Hemingway, Richard Harding Davis, Ernie Pyle, and many others. One significant example of literary journalism was John Hershey's August 1946 *New Yorker* article "Hiroshima" that was subsequently published as a book. Previous descriptions of the bomb's impact tended to be impersonal, but Hershey traced the experiences of six survivors hour by hour on August 6, 1945. He adopted a neutral style designed to let the personal stories of the survivors come through. As a result, Americans understood the horror of nuclear warfare in a way that had deep, long-term impacts on public policy.

One particular cause of the explosion of literary journalism in the 1960s may have been the New York newspaper strike, when many of the "new journalism" writers out on the streets for four months—among them, Tom Wolfe, Gay Talese, Nora Ephron, Calvin Trillin, and others (Sherman 2012). Wolfe was one of the main advocates for the new literary journalism movement of the 1960s. He was a newspaper feature writer who broke away from conventions and captivated readers with rich descriptive style in books such as the *Electric Kool-Aid Acid Test* (about San Francisco in the 1960s) and *The Right Stuff* (about astronauts and the space race). In *The New Journalism*, Wolfe described what he saw as a reversal of the old hierarchy of literature. In the old days, he said, news and feature-writing journalists were at the bottom, columnists and essayists were in the middle, and novelists were at the top. But the novel was dead, and the new literary journalism had now reached the apex of literature (Wolfe 1975).

Wolfe's ideas set off a serious debate. Some journalists thought that Wolfe and company had lost their bearings in the fervid environment of 1960s counterculture. Especially controversial during this experimental era was what *Rolling Stone* writer Hunter S. Thompson called "gonzo" journalism. At best, the gonzo approach was a hilariously critical, first-person view of people twisted by political and social institutions. But at its worst, Thompson's drug-crazed writing churned grimly through a mélange of psychotic episodes.

Despite the criticism, literary journalism was a strong break from inverted-pyramid "telegraph-ese," and became a widely used writing style as the press struggled to keep up with, and serve, a rapidly changing society.

12 The Story of the Century: Covering Science and the Environment

Perhaps the most influential magazine article series of the twentieth century was Rachel Carson's 1962 *New Yorker* series and subsequent book, *Silent Spring*. A biologist and accomplished science writer, Carson warned that overuse of pesticides such as DDT threatened bird populations and human health. The book set off a firestorm of controversy and reignited the conservation movement from earlier generations (Neuzil and Kovarik 1997).

Silent Spring was published in an era when people were beginning to take science and the environment seriously, but it was not always that way. In earlier generations, if science was even mentioned in the press, said historian David J. Rhees, "it was in terms of magic or miracles, if not mere ridicule" (Rhees 1979).

A series of killer smogs and burning rivers in the 1950s and 1960s, along with medical advances and the space race, led to increasingly serious coverage of science and the environment. In 1969, the *New York Times* created a permanent environment beat, and other newspapers and magazines followed suit. The need to create a larger cadre of reporters to handle specialized beats was reinforced in the chaos of the Three Mile Island nuclear explosion in Harrisburg, Pennsylvania, in April 1979. Despite the significance and popularity of the articles, *Times* news writers were constantly under assault by well-organized corporate lobbies for a supposed lack of objectivity. By the twenty-first century, most science and environment beats in the press had been scaled back. In 2008, Cable News Network even laid off its entire nine-person science unit. The decline in reporting on complex but vital topics was decried by scientists and journalists alike. Carl Sagan, a noted astronomer and public scientist, said that we had approached a moment in history where "no one representing the public interest can even grasp the issues," due to a disdain for education and the "dumbing down" of the American media (Sagan 1995). The trend Sagan spotted intensified into the twenty-first century. By 2015, the economic foundation of the American and European press was greatly weakened, and political debate became increasingly polarized.

13 The End of the Printing Revolution

Five and a half centuries after Johannas Gutenberg, the printing revolution seemed to have run its course. Between 2007 and 2014, US newspapers and magazines lost two-thirds of their traditional advertising income, one third of their circulation, and three-quarters of their stock value (Pew 2014; Edmunds 2014). Over half of newspaper employees were laid off, and the job outlook for all journalists was a long-term decline (Johnson 2011; BLS 2015). Many publications declared bankruptcy or moved to online-only publication.

Globally, the newspaper industry saw circulation increases in Asia, Africa, and Latin America, but steep declines in Europe and the US. Revenues dropped from $183 billion in 2008 to $163 billion in 2013, according to the World Association of Newspapers (WAN 2014, 2015).

The problem was not a simple recession or a switch to consumer spending on television, video games, or other media. Media spending in non-print categories was on the rise by 2015. Instead, the problem was a broken financial model for newspapers. This, in turn, undermined journalism, which is traditionally a key function of a working democracy.

"Now for the first time in modern American history, it is entirely plausible that we will not have even minimally sufficient resources dedicated to reporting and editing the news and distributing the information and informed analysis that citizens require," said John McChesney in *The Death and Life of American Journalism*. "Already much of government activity is conducted in the dark. Investigative journalism is on the endangered species list" (McChesney 2010).

"By undermining the economic basis of professional reporting and by fragmenting the public," said Paul Star, the digital revolution "has weakened the ability of the press to act as an effective agent of public accountability." What's more, said former *Washington Post* editor Robert G. Kaiser, the media is accelerating the fragmentation. "Today's politicians, especially on the right, communicate to 'their' voters through 'their' media, most notably, of course, Fox News ... So 'the news' that once helped unify the country is now just another source of division" (Kaiser 2014).

Many other voices have joined the chorus of concern, but few have any idea what can be done. "What if it is simply impossible to generate commercially viable popular journalism online, let alone journalism adequate for a self-governing people?" McChesney asked in the book *Digital Divide* (McChesney 2014).

13.1 Who killed the American newspaper?

The complex chain of events that led to the collapse of the American publishing industry began with ideal business and political conditions. Nearly all mid-sized city newspapers were comfortable monopolies. They were family-owned operations, making 5 to 10 percent annual profits, and free from much (if any) competition, thanks to an arrangement with the Associated Press. (This lasted until 1945, as we'll see in Chapter 7.) And to make things really easy, Congress passed the Newspaper Preservation Act of 1970, legally allowing newspapers to become local monopolies.

In effect, all the business and political forces aligned to grease the skids as publishers coasted through the twentieth century. Yet, with all that momentum, the publishing industry was unprepared for the effects of changes in technology, and it was allowed to drift into one of the most colossal and consequential business failures in history.

The first technological changes were quite beneficial. That story begins in 1942 when two electronics engineers from Lyon, France, happened to visit a printing plant using massive Linotype machines—a kind of cross between a giant typewriter and a lead type foundry—that poured boiling lead into matrices to produce a line of type.

These clanking machines were used worldwide, and they were faster than setting type by hand. But the process seemed dangerous, even "insane," to the engineers—Rene Higonnet and Louis Moyroud. By 1946, they had developed an alternative system that used a small strobe light to rapidly flash characters onto photo-sensitive paper. When developed with ordinary darkroom chemicals, the paper could be pasted onto a photo-mechanical flat and transferred to an aluminum printing plate.

Higgonnet and Moyroud called their new machine a "Lumitype" because it used a strobe light and also, perhaps, in recognition of the Lumier Brothers. (The Lumiers were also from Lyon, and had invented theatrical cinema in1894, as we'll see in Chapter 5.)

With the help of MIT's Vannevar Bush and a publishers' cooperative, Higonnet and Moyroud commercialized a photo-mechanical process in the 1950s. It set type six times faster than Linotypes at one-fifth or less of the cost. The photomechanical process eventually took on more and more computerized controls, and eventually digital systems like Compugraphic, Atex, and SII used transistors to control light exposure on photosensitive paper. Around the same time, even more savings were achieved with the switch from letterpress to offset printing, which involved lighter aluminum printing plates.

These savings meant that sleepy old family operations that earned a few hundred thousand dollars a year in profits could now be making millions, with a return on investment in the 20 to 40 percent range per year.

These new processes saved on labor, too, which meant that thousands of pressmen could be laid off. This led to the bitter New York newspaper strike of 1962–3, among many others in the next two decades. But the new profitability also meant that family-owned newspapers became the target of Wall Street acquisitions. The shift from regional public service enterprise to profitable acquisition reflected the tension between contending ideas about the modern media corporation. On the one hand, media experts like those on the Hutchins Commission insisted that publishers have a social responsibility (as we have seen here in Chapter 3). On the other hand, economists like Milton Friedman maintained

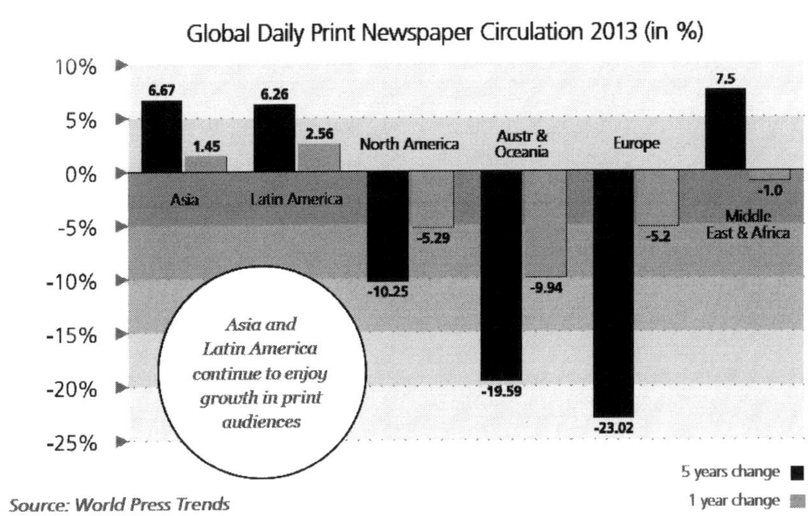

Figure 3.15 Circulation—Newspapers in North America and Europe are declining in circulation, but there are some advances in the rest of the world. Courtesy of the World Association of Newspapers, 2015.

that the only social responsibility that any corporation really had was to increase its profits (Friedman 1962). Wall Street preferred Friedman's view and pushed the publishing industry to keep pulling in 20 to 40 percent annual returns on investment.

In most other industries, a substantial portion of the profits are invested to keep up to date with new technologies. Wall Street managers, anxious to maximize media profits, refused to allow those investments on anywhere near the scale that was needed.

The picture is complicated by the fact that hundreds of weaker second dailies and afternoon newspapers failed and went out of business in the 1970s–1990s. But investors expected that the dominant newspapers would continue to produce high profits, whether their contents were first class or third class, as industrialist and media investor Warren Buffet said in 1985: "That is not true of most businesses: inferior quality generally produces inferior economics. But even a poor newspaper is a bargain to most citizens simply because of its 'bulletin board' value" (Shafer 2009).

When the savings that came with cold type and offset printing had been exhausted, publishers turned to newsroom staff cuts, generating enormous controversy in the 1990s. In *The Vanishing Newspaper*, Philip Meyer noted that Wall Street tended to support quality when newspapers had competition, but tended to demand cuts in editorial staff as competition declined. "There is no shortage of historical studies showing a correlation between quality journalism and business success … [even in] monopoly markets," Meyer said (Meyer 2009). But the reverse was also true: declining quality also strongly correlated with declines in circulation (Lacy and Martin 1998).

Economists have long observed that the general problem with monopolies is that the lack of efficiency makes the product overpriced, and cuts in quality lead to declines in consumer demand—a phenomena known as deadweight loss. As demand falls, prices stay high, and the downward spiral in quality leads consumers to search for alternatives and talented writers to search for circumventing media.

"Newspaper publishers might believe that the abnormally high profit margins that they enjoyed relative to other businesses in the twentieth century are their birthright, but they're not," Meyer said. "They were the result of a condition that no longer exists—their near monopoly control over retailers' access to their consumers" (Meyer 2009).

Other trends were beginning to work against newspaper publishing monopolies as well. Direct mail advertising, free newspapers, and other unbundled press services were already starting to steal the show.

13.1.1 Digital media challenges newspaper profit centers

When the digital revolution made going online easy for everyone in the late 1990s, all kinds of specialized online networks were becoming viable enough to challenge newspapers in its three profit centers:

- circulation (mostly paid subscriptions);
- classified advertising (selling cars, houses, looking for employees);
- display advertising (from businesses with products or services to sell).

All three were strong around 2000, and were under assault by 2005. First, the ability to read news for free, online, cut into circulation revenue. Readers could get national news directly from national media, and often the value of local news was marginal. Also, newspapers were a "bundled" product, and now readers could just find what they wanted without paying for the whole bundle. One answer was to set up a "pay wall" so that online readers pay something to subscribe, but this has only been moderately successful for major national newspapers such as the *New York Times* and *Washington Post*.

Second, classified advertising revenues dropped from about one-third to only a fraction of overall newspaper revenue after consumers became aware of free bulletin boards like Craigslist. In the 1990s, a number of publishers had been warning about this. Digby Solomon of the Tribune Media Services gave regular talks about what he called "category killers" that were going to "eat our lunch." Far earlier, Marshall McLuhan saw the possibilities. "The classified ads and stock-market quotations are the bedrock of the press," McLuhan said. "Should an alternative source of easy access to such diverse daily information be found, the press will fold" (McLuhan 1966).

Finally, display-advertising revenues were down because general advertising is far less effective than targeted advertising. In the past, someone selling a specific product would hope that interested people would see the ad in the newspaper. Search engines like Google can now sell retailers access to targeted audiences that are already searching for that specific product. And as newspaper advertising revenue in the US dropped from $50 billion to under $20 billion, Google revenue rose from nothing to $50 billion.

13.1.2 Early digital

The best that can be said of the corporate publishing industry's response to the digital revolution is that a few organizations made a feeble attempt to meet the challenge. There was no serious attempt to retool and adapt the industry, since that would have meant cutting into profits.

Even though the press had a long history of technological change, in the post-World War II years, very few people thought that the press would fundamentally change. In 1983, for example, the *New York Times* thought so little of the possibilities for digital sales that it sold off its online copyright to another company, only to have to negotiate to get it back in 1995. In a phrase that has aptly described the response of other major corporations to the digital revolution, publishers kept going in the same direction as always, and missed the curve in the road.

There were a few scattered attempts to anticipate the future. For example, the Knight-Ridder newspaper chain began an experiment with online news called "Viewtron" in 1979. But the barrier to entry was high, with receivers costing over $500, and the graphics were far worse than television. Worst of all, the Viewtron box was not much more than a dumb terminal. The most important feature of digital media—that it enabled people to participate—was not appreciated.

The Viewtron experiment ended in 1986, just as a similar project in France called Minitel was catching on. The French experiment had no barriers (terminals were free for phone users) and participation was open, as people could easily read and place classified and display advertising. There were also new sorts of options, such as discussion groups and open bulletin boards (Kovarik 2001).

Newspapers also tried partnerships with online service providers to replace classified newspaper advertising, but many were dropped because "the feared competition [from digital media] never developed" (Peterson 1998). One partnership that survived for a time was Real Cities (1999–2008), a network of local portals featuring news, email, search services, e-commerce, and site-building tools launched by Knight-Ridder in 1999. The newspaper chain spent $25 million per year, then sold Real Cities between 2006 and 2008.

One of the few to make a difference was originally called Classified Ventures (1997–2014), an auto and real estate classified service including Cars.com and Apartments.com. It was owned by major publishing chains like Gannett, the *Tribune* and the *Washington Post.* Gannett kept Cars.com and is spinning it off into its broadcast division—not the print division, where it was originally intended to supplement declining advertising (Haughney 2014).

Another early innovation was Knight-Ridder's experiment with the "information tablet" in the 1990s at the Information Design Laboratory. The tablet idea was ahead of its time, and the lab was shut down in 1995. Eventually, digital technology developed to the point where Apple Computers could create a version of the iPad tablet in 2010. Its main advantage is that it is more portable than a personal computer, but the iPad, like Knight-Ridder's tablet, was designed to be a top-down information utility (Rusbridger 2010). As Roger Fidler said in the 1997 book *Mediamorphosis,* "The idea that people will be leisurely reading

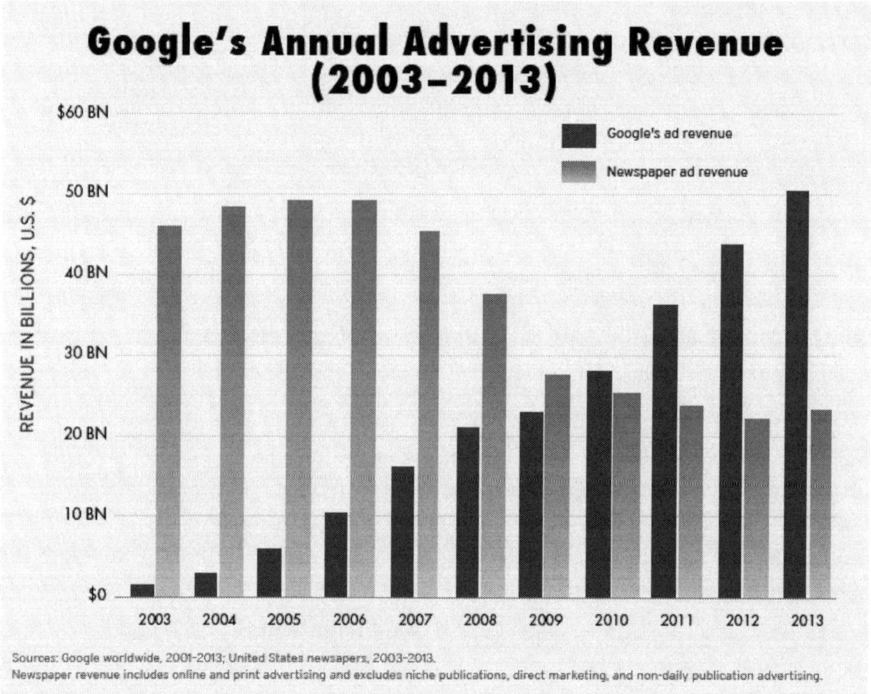

Figure 3.16 Advertising—US newspaper advertising had declined as the Google Corp.'s revenue has grown. Courtesy of the Brookings Institution, 2014.

documents on portable tablets by the year 2010 may seem unrealistic given the present state of computer and display technologies, but it is no more fantastic than was the 1980 vision of people routinely using mobile cell phones." Fidler was not only right, he called the year.

Among the many curves in the road was the moment when *Washington Post* business managers briefly considered investing in a new search engine called "Google" back in 1998. One editor met with Larry Page and Sergi Brin in their garage offices. The Post "kicked it around," but decided not to pursue that investment. (Kaiser 2014). Only fifteen years later, the *Post* would be sold for $250 million; Google would be worth $104 billion.

Experiments like Viewtron and Real Cities allowed users to read regular daily updates of news, but they had a major shortcoming—they did not enable creative uses of the technology. They were "top-down" technologies, not "generative" technologies.

"From the beginning, newspapers sought to invent the web in their own image by repurposing the copy, values, and temperament found in their ink-and-paper editions," said media analyst Jack Shafer. "Despite being early arrivals, despite having spent millions on manpower and hardware ... every newspaper web site [was] instantly identifiable as a newspaper web site. By succeeding, they failed to invent the Web" (Shafer 2009).

The decline in newspaper journalism accelerated through the first decade and into the second decade of the twenty-first century. By 2014, some of the most hopeful signs for a still-floundering news media were that new digital organizations like Buzzfeed, Vine, and Vice were starting to hire several thousand full-time employees. In its 2014 "State of the News Media" report, the Pew Research Center for Journalism and Media noted "a new sense of optimism—or perhaps hope—for the future of American journalism" (Pew Project 2014).

If the traditions of the press could be transferred into the digital revolution, it would depend on new business models such as non-profit news companies, consumer news co-ops, crowd-financed journalism and training for citizen journalists. It might also depend on universities taking on market experiments as part of an ethical responsibility, although they could not hope to fill the rapidly expanding gap in news coverage, nor would most be able to take on the responsibility of an independent government critic.

14 Conclusion

There's one obvious lesson to be drawn from the collapse of publishing in the twenty-first century: that a public service industry can be lost when subjected to overwhelming financial pressures. We may also observe that the financial system is not well equipped to support the media functions that help guide democratic government.

While the continuing consumer need for public service information probably means that some new institutions will emerge, the proud steamships of the press have hit their iceberg. For now, the long-term damage to democracy is only visible below the water line, but the steamships are settling and the holds are flooded. Some will try a reversion to the old partisan models of the press, but the future lies in finding new models of what Walter Lippmann called "organized intelligence." This organization can mean rationalization of content, in other words, eliminating duplication, and there hardly seems any reason to prefer reading the wires on a local newspaper than on a regional or national or international paper. And reorganization is not necessarily the death of all content creation.

At a some point, people will pay for the content they love. But then, what does that say about journalism? The popularity of the profession has gone down, and few people today would see journalists as knights of the press, as they did a century ago. Journalists have always been the gadflies of their communities, and perhaps as unwelcome today as in the days of William Cobbett or Joseph Pulitzer.

The old Scottish printer William Blackwood probably said it best in 1834: "The press, a machine than can no longer be broken, will continue to destroy the old world 'till it has formed a new one.'" In the process, it will have to find a place in this new digital world.

For additional reading, discussion questions, links to video, and other suggestions, see www.revolutionsincommunications.com.

Part II

The Visual Revolution

> People have not only ceased to purchase those old-fashioned things called books, but even to read them! ... [In the future] Books, the small as well as the great, will have been voted a great evil. There will be no gentlemen of the press. The press itself will have ceased to exist.
>
> William Blackwood, 1844

The power of images worried people, even before the visual revolution moved into high gear with the arrival of printed photos and movie theaters. As early as 1844, people worried that the press itself would not survive the onslaught of images. They could see that a new media technology was having an impact on the old media.

Punch magazine and the *Illustrated London News*—and similar publications in Paris, Berlin, and New York—were only a few years old and already immensely popular when William Blackwood said they were swallowing up the old press. Soon they would be followed by a host of other publications that featured engravings and cartoons. Louis Daguerre's photographic process for capturing images was also new, although it wouldn't be possible to print photographs until the late 1880s.

This section on the Visual Revolution organizes the history of two imaging technologies, and the image-making industry of advertising and public relations, into three chapters in order to take a panoramic view of media history:

- Chapter 4 covers photography from the 1830s to the present.
- Chapter 5 covers cinema from the 1890s to the present.
- Chapter 6 describes the history of advertising and public relations as image-making enterprises from the 1800s to the present.

1 Images before Photography

1.1 Cave paintings and human psychology

In the autumn of 1879, an eight-year-old named María de Sautuola followed her father Marcelino into a cave near Altamira, on the northern coast of Spain. He was searching the floor of the cave for ancient artifacts, but his daughter looked up and noticed a ceiling full of red, ochre, brown, and black images.

"Papa. Look, oxen," she said.

De Sautuloa lifted his torch, and became the second person in thousands of years to see the oxen, horses, deer, boar, and bison painted with amazing artistic skill on the ceiling of the Altamira cave.

"I was overcome with amazement," De Sautuola wrote, "What I saw made me so excited I could hardly speak" (Spivey 2006).

He realized that the paintings resembled bone carvings that he had seen in museums, and he hired a university archaeologist to help publish his findings in 1880. The idea that these were ancient paintings, however, proved controversial. Professional archaeologists, surprised at the artistic power and the well-preserved state of the paintings, accused Sautuola of fraud. Later, as similar paintings were found in other caves, Sautuola's scientific adversaries apologized, and archeologists began to take prehistoric images seriously.

Today, the Altamira cave is recognized as one of the great archaeological finds of the modern era, with paintings over 35,000 years old. But the story of its discovery illustrates

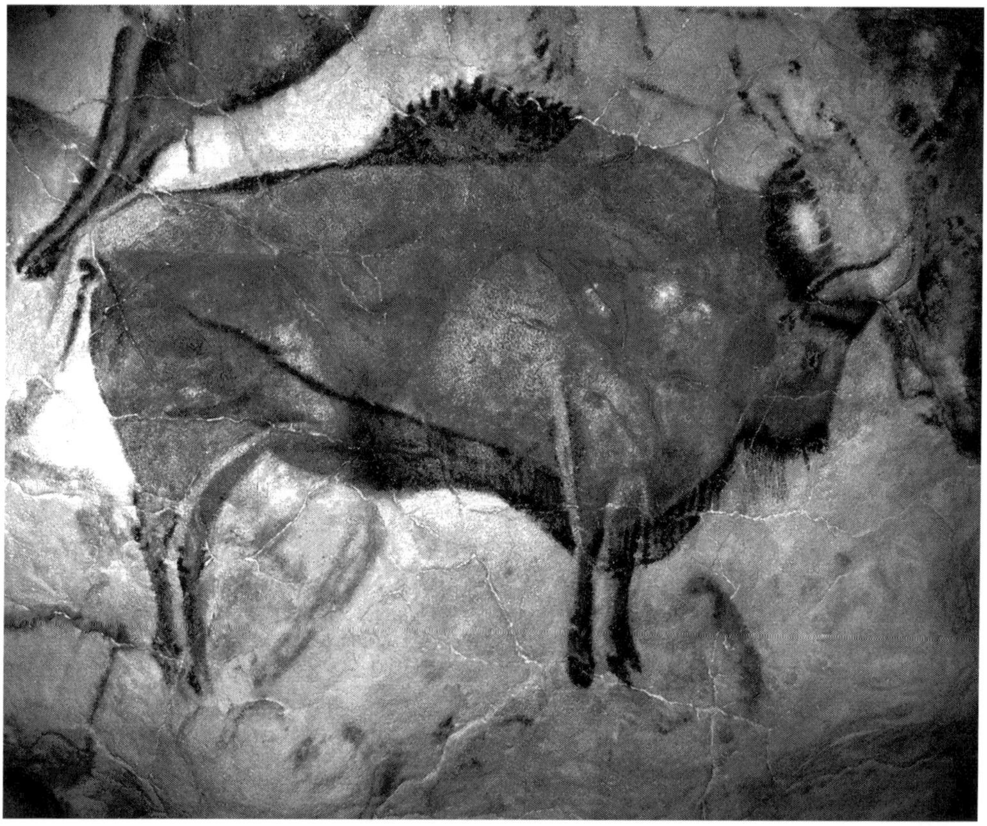

Figure SII.1 The power of the image—The discovery of the Altamira cave paintings in 1880, and the controversy over the paintings, reflects the power that often surrounds visual communication. By Rameessos, Wikimedia Commons.

the power and controversy that often surrounds visual communication. And the idea that a child was the first to notice the paintings says something about the significance of visual imagery deep in the human psyche.

1.2 Psychology of visual communication

Anthropologists and psychologists believe that over the long span of human evolution, the human brain has become specialized in recognizing and remembering images. And, for tens of thousands of years, prehistoric humans have themselves crafted images for unknown rituals.

Visual images are the keys to memory and the guideposts to the terrain of human psychology. The first experimental psychologists, Wilhelm Wundt and William James, observed in the 1890s that images—not words—were the building blocks of human psychology (Thomas 2010). The insight was confirmed by twentieth-century experiments on the "picture superiority effect" showing that concepts are much more likely to be remembered when they are presented as images rather than words (Nelson et al. 1976).

We now realize that visual communication predates writing by at least 35,000 years and that visually symbolic communication is found scattered across the ancient landscape. These symbols are sometimes expressed as stone circles, sometimes as paintings preserved in caves or tombs, and sometimes as small carvings whose microscopic markings show repeated use. The symbols become more complex with proximity to modern times.

A small carving might have been used in a rite of passage ceremony, or as a token of privilege, or as a way to count natural cycles. The closer in history that these carvings come to modernity, the more complex they seem to become (Marshack 2003).

People have always had a knack for symbol making, according to psychologist Carl Jung. A person "unconsciously transforms objects or forms into symbols, thereby endowing them with great psychological importance, and expresses them in both his religion and his art" (Jung and von Franz 1964).

1.3 Images from the Middle East and Asia

The earliest known printed images, with the potential for mass distribution, are from "cylinder seals" used in early Mesopotamian civilizations from around 3500 BCE. Made from hard stone, glass, or ceramic materials, they were rolled across wet clay or textiles to create repeating patterns. These had decorative, authoritative, or symbolic uses, or occasionally all three.

In China and Japan, woodblock prints of Buddhist images were printed on silk earlier than 400 CE. Buddhist woodblocks combining text and images are known from about 627 onward. Woodblocks were often used for printing books on silk from 1000, and while moveable type was known, woodblocks of full pages were used because of the complexity of the Chinese character set, with thousands of pictographic images.

The world's earliest remaining woodblock printed book, the Diamond Sutra, is a Chinese scroll dating from 868. Woodblock printing is also found on textiles in the Arabic

Mediterranean around 1000, and was transmitted to Europe before the 1300s. Color printmaking of non-religious art emerged around 1700 with the Torii school and continued through the 1800s with the complex and Zen-like art of the Utagawa school.

Techniques for reproducing visual images were known in the ancient world of the Middle East, India, China, and Japan. It is possible, some believe likely, that all kinds of printing techniques were transmitted between Europe and Asia even earlier, during the 1200–1300 CE era through the Mongol Empire (Christensen 2006). While some printing techniques, like woodcut, could have been adapted during this period by Europeans in the Renaissance, others, such as metal plate engraving and lithography, were invented as part of the printing revolution.

European interest in Japanese and Chinese art styles resurged in the 1860s and influenced a broader discussion about art. Artists questioned the older formal styles of painting that merely reproduced landscapes or religious and historical events. Photography, they said, could accomplish that. But photographers would also try to show that their work was also a form of art.

1.4 Early visual communication in Europe

Visual communication, like written communication, went through a process of transformation during the European Renaissance. Where public art and architecture were once the only forms of visual communication, with manuscripts available only to the elite, the printing press allowed images to be multiplied by the thousands and tens of thousands. Just as printed Bible stories helped spread religion, these printed images dramatized and democratized concepts of spirituality, politics, exploration, technology, medicine, and science.

The first mass produced images were printed with woodblocks in the 1300s, and, as is typical in a communications revolution, they borrowed subject matter from previous forms of media. At the start of the imaging revolution, artists borrowed from illustrated Bible stories that had been created in manuscript form during

Figure SII.2 *Nuremberg Chronicles*— A crowning achievement in the early years of printing, the illustrated *Nuremburg Chronicles* (*Die Schedelsche Weltchronik*) provides a fascinating glimpse into the medieval mindset. From Hartmann Schedel's *World Chronicle* of 1493, Wikimedia Commons.

medieval times. For instance, the "Biblia pauperum" theme came from hand-illuminated manuscripts as early as the 800s in Germany, but was popular enough to be among the first items printed in woodcut in the early 1400s. A similar illustrated book of Bible stories called the *Mirror of Human Salvation* was illustrated in manuscript form and then became popular as woodblock prints around the same time. After moveable type printing arrived in the 1450s, both books were printed with a combination of woodblock and metal type.

One of the most important early books using woodcuts was the 1493 *Nuremberg Chronicles* (in Germany: *Die Schedelsche Weltchronik* or *Schedel's World History*). As many as 2,500 copies may have been produced in Latin and German. The book offers a fascinating glimpse into the medieval sense of history, following five biblical ages from the creation to the birth of Christ, then one age to the present and a seventh age leading to the Last Judgment. With over 1,800 woodcuts, the *Chronicles* was a crowning achievement in the earliest years of printing.

Figure SII.3 *Gin Lane*—William Hogarth (1697–1764), a British artist, illustrated allegorical stories intended to improve public morals. Hogarth's 1751 *Gin Lane* was part of a social and legal movement to counter alcoholism. Wikimedia Commons.

The publisher of the *Chronicles,* Anton Koberger, was one of the world's first media barons, owning twenty-four printing presses in cities from Lyon to Budapest. He was also the godfather of Albrech Durer (1471–1528), one of the finest painters and engravers of the high Renaissance. Durer is remembered for both religious and secular art, and for blending Italian classical composition with the practical style of northern Europe. A gifted artist from an early age, Durer's work was so skilled that he was imitated for centuries.

Artistic engraving and etching added immensely to the visual landscape of post-Renaissance Europe. Names of many famed artists are among those who used this printing technique to circulate their work more widely. They include Rembrandt (Harmenszoon) of the Netherlands, Hans Holbein of Germany, Francisco Goya of Spain, Honore Daumier of France, and William Blake and William Hogarth of Britain. Hogarth, especially, is noteworthy as taking advantage of an age in which the visual environment was becoming increasingly complex.

Artistic prints were widely circulated and shown on walls in homes, taverns, shops, and public buildings, and Hogarth used printing and engraving to tell stories. "My picture was my stage," he once said. Hogarth's heavy-handed moral crusade used symbols to tell stories such as the *Harlot's Progress*, the *Rake's Progress*, *Marriage*, *Industry and Idleness*, *Beer Street*, *Gin Lane*, and the *Four Stages of Cruelty*.

2 Visual Communication and the Press

The mass production of images had enormous social effects, and savvy publishers, aware of the power of images, launched illustrated publications that succeeded in attracting large audiences.

One of the first newspaper illustrations in the United States was the *Join or Die* woodcut depicting a snake cut in pieces corresponding to the thirteen colonies. The illustration, published by Benjamin Franklin in the *Pennsylvania Gazette* in 1754, encouraged greater unity among the colonies.

Most newspapers did not go in for illustration, or only rarely used it. Yet in May of 1842, a new illustrated newspaper was founded by Herbert Ingram, who was "seized with the belief" that it would be possible to publish a newspaper entirely devoted to illustrations. The idea was so successful at first that with a year, Ingram licensed versions of the *News* in Berlin, Leipzig and Paris.

When the novelty started to wear off in the late 1840s, Ingram sent free copies of the paper to every clergyman in England. Prominently illustrated in that issue was the installation of the head of the Anglican Church, the Archbishop of Canterbury. The ploy bolstered the respectability of the new approach to media, and its circulation. Even greater heights of circulation were reached with coverage of major events. Circulation reached 300,000 when the *News* ran engravings based on Roger Fenton's photos from the Crimean War in 1852.

Illustrated publications soon sprang up in US as well—the *National Police Gazette* in 1845, *Harper's Weekly* in 1850, and *Leslie's Illustrated Newspaper* in 1852. Pictorial newspapers followed with the development of halftone processes in the 1880s and 1890s, including the London *Daily Graphic*, the *Daily Mirror*, and the *Daily Sketch*.

2.1 Lithography allows faster, cheaper reproduction of images

Figure SII.4 Colonial Unity—The message in Ben Franklin's woodcut was that the colonies could not survive if separated. *Pennsylvania Gazette*, 1754, Library of Congress.

One important advance in the mass production of images was lithography, invented in 1796 in Germany as a way to publish music and posters at low cost. The process, a forerunner of offset printing invented a century later in Britain, takes advantage of the tendency of oil and water to separate. The image is first sketched onto a smooth limestone slab and then finished with a wax stylus, and the stone is treated to absorb water in the blank areas. An oily ink is applied, which sticks to the waxy surface and not to the water-soaked surface, allowing the image to transfer to paper.

The process became one of the cheapest and most popular ways to distribute prints, posters, and book illustrations. Among the most important lithography companies between 1834 and 1907 was Currier & Ives. The company produced over 7,000 titles, with millions of copies, depicting everyday life, battle scenes, famous people, and usually conservative political commentary. Depictions of women and African-Americans were often highly objectionable by modern standards, although at the time they were considered more clownish than hateful. The company's low prices and wide circulation meant that they outlasted many of their competitors, but the company closed when the photo halftone processes became widely adopted in the early years of the twentieth century.

Figure SII.5 Audubon Lithographs—John James Audubon's bird paintings were not initially popular in America, but British art and scientific circles were enthusiastic. His paintings were transferred to lithographs and published in London from 1827 to 1838 in four volumes. Original copies of *Birds of America* are the second most valuable printed book in the world, after the Gutenberg Bible. Library of Congress.

Another example of popular lithography was John James Audubon's *Birds of America*, printed in 1860. Based on Audubon's paintings made while traveling through the country, the 436 life-sized, hand-colored prints resulted from Audubon's painstaking collaboration with a master lithographer.

3 Precursors of Photography

Lithography was a better printing method than engraving or woodcut, but preparing the litho stones was time-consuming work. French lithographer Joseph Niepce started looking for a way to speed things up. He began experimenting with light-sensitive chemicals in the 1820s and stumbled upon some of the key techniques needed in photography. Niepce's collaboration with Louis Daguerre led to the first practical method of taking photographs, as we will see in the next chapter.

Another technology that set the stage for photography was the silhouette. Named for a French government official who liked to doodle, silhouettes caught on in France during the 1700s as a popular way to remember the exact likeness of a family member. A silhouette could be done quickly by using a "camera obscura"—a dark room (called a "camera," similar to the English word "chamber") with a pinhole opening in the wall, allowing light through from the outside.

The pinhole acts as a lens, and an image can be projected upside down on the far wall, making it easy to trace. The combination of a camera obscura with a light-sensitive negative became the photographic camera by the 1840s.

3.1 Social impacts of the visual media revolution

As we will see in Chapter 4, Mathew Brady's exhibit of Civil War photos shocked New Yorkers in 1862. As the *New York Times* said, "If he has not actually brought bodies back and laid them on our dooryards and along the streets, he has done something very like it … There is a terrible fascination about it that draws one near these pictures … You will see the hushed, reverend groups standing around these weird copies of carnage" (*New York Times*, October 20, 1862). Similarly, as we will see in Chapter 5, movies about the war in the trenches shocked and fascinated London audiences in 1916: "If women had sometimes to shut their eyes to escape for a moment from the tragedy of the toll of battle which the film presents, opinion seems to be general that it was wise that the people at home should have this glimpse of what our soldiers are doing and daring and suffering" (*The Times*, August 22, 1916).

The question about the appropriate use of media is age-old. "We have not sufficiently recognized the power of moving images," said Mitchell Stephens in his book *The Rise of the Image* (Stephens 1998). In previous times, reading was one of the few ways of experiencing the wider world, but in the modern world, "the image is replacing the word as the predominant means of mental transport."

This is hardly a new issue. Publishers worried about the abundance of visual images emerging in popular culture as early as the 1840s, long before it became possible to print photographs. As we saw at the beginning of this section, William Blackwood, a publisher in Edinburgh, Scotland, said in 1844, shortly after the success of the *Illustrated London News*, that the "new art of printing" threatened the old habit of reading:

> Who has leisure to read? Who cares to sit down and spell out accounts of travels which he can make at less cost than the cost of the narrative? Who wants to peruse fictitious adventures, when railroads and steamboats woo him to adventures of his own … We are not told, but shown how the world is wagging… The beauties of Shakespeare are imprinted on the minds of the rising generation in woodcuts … Views of the Holy Land are superseding even Holy Scriptures … [In the future] Books, the small as well as the great, will have been voted a great evil. There will be no gentlemen of the press. The press itself will have ceased to exist. (Blackwood 1844)

What's interesting about this rather crabby complaint from an old Scottish printer is that it sounds so familiar. Similar things have been said about film, about radio and television, and about the Internet. Producers of older media rarely welcome competition from new media, especially when the new media seems, to them, shallow and yet more powerful than the old media.

Neil Postman (1985) summed it up neatly in a book called *Amusing Ourselves to Death*. The social problem for the media isn't simply that it can lead to the tyranny envisioned by George Orwell in 1984, but also that it can lead to the "Brave New World" envisioned by Aldous Huxley. In Huxley's world, an abundance of superficial distractions degraded individual and social responsibility. So it's not surprising that those who defended new media forms in their early days would use arguments about their educational and moral value to deflect criticism. We'll see this in photography, in film, in broadcasting and in digital media.

3.2 Stereotypes: Injury and inspiration

Like any powerful tool, the power of images has been used in a variety of ways to elevate, to inspire, and, all too frequently, to injure. Walter Lippmann, borrowing a technical term from the printing industry, said that we all use "stereotypes" or "pictures in our heads" as mental shortcuts that allow us to make quick judgments.

In the nineteenth century, demands by women for the vote and social equality were often seen as ludicrous (as in Figure SII.6) or as fitting, since women were just as capable as men, even in the Wild West (as in Figure SII.7).

Figure SII.6 Stereotypes—This 1869 perspective on the right of women to vote is part of the Currier & Ives lithographic portfolio of 7,000 subjects with millions of copies. The firm went out of business after photo halftone printing was developed in the late 1800s. Many of its older ideas were also going out of fashion. Women finally overcame stereotypes like this one and secured the right to vote in 1918 in Britain and Canada, and 1920 in the United States. Library of Congress.

The power of the mass media to create these stereotypes and shape public opinion is well known. From the wave of American race riots that followed the film *The Birth of a Nation* in 1915 to genocide in Rwanda and Bosnia in the 1990s, the impact is clear. The path to genocide can be paved by a complicit media. And the question naturally arises, should the media be held responsible? Is hate speech a form of speech that should be free?

Julius Streicher, publisher of *Der Stürmer*, attacked German Jews without mercy in the 1930s, as we have seen in Chapter 3. He was convicted of crimes against humanity after the Nazi defeat in World War II. But Leni Riefenstahl's film *Triumph of the Will* only helped glorify the Nazis and solidify Adolf Hitler's power grab in Germany. She endured a few years in prison, but escaped Streicher's fate. While she maintained throughout her life that she was merely naive and not political, she evaded the key ethical question: to what extent are individuals in the mass media responsible for the use of their artistic or literary gifts? Aside from these extreme cases, stereotypes of gays, of African-Americans, and many other social groups have been known to injure in more subtle ways.

Figure SII.7 Wild West—The exuberant image of the "Wild West," and its appeal to newspaper readers back east, is reflected in this May 22, 1886, *Police Gazette* account of the jailbreak of real-life outlaw "Belle" Myra Maybelle Shirley Star. Library of Congress.

"Media promulgated stereotypes of various and diverse groups of people cause harm in both direct and indirect ways by presenting oversimplified, mostly negative, and often deceptive depictions," said Paul Martin Lester in his book, *Images that Injure* (Lester 1996).

Sometimes, an outrageous image can injure a worthy target. Such was the case with Thomas Nast's 1871 *Let Us Prey*, a caricature of the Tweed ring, a notoriously corrupt gang that ran City Hall in New York. Nast's cartoons led to reforms that swept through the city.

While images can injure, they can also inspire. We will see Louis Hine and Jacob Riis using photography in campaigns for child labor laws and the clean-up of slums. And in a similar sense, the documentary photography of the Farm Security Administration from the 1930s was an attempt to demonstrate the determination of the American people to come out of the Depression.

Often what is best in human nature is expressed at the worst of times, and an image, rather than many thousands of words, is needed. This was the thought behind the *London Illustrated News*'s image of the Christmas Truce of 1914, in which the guns of World War I fell silent for just one day.

3.3 Advertising and public relations as image-making

Advertising and public relations are functions that are as old as humanity, but the two professions emerged forcefully in the visual media revolution. Creating a positive image of a product or company can often spell the difference between success and failure, even for the most powerful companies.

As we will see in Chapter 6, advertising with images, especially powerful artistic images that evoked emotional responses, became common in the early 1900s. Even more than the physical artifact of an image, the idea of image-making also had a social impact, to the point where ideals were replaced by the personal and corporate image. Similarly, politicians and others in public life have always relied on mental images and symbolism to make their point. In the mid-twentieth century, however, there seemed to be an increasing distinction between use of a symbol or stereotype to understand a position or event, and the use of imagery to create a bewildering set of impressions on the public debate. Librarian of Congress Daniel J. Boorstin is especially remembered for his concern about the rise of imagery in public relations:

> While [corporate logos] have become more important with each decade, a more abstract kind of image is the peculiar product of our age. Its tyranny is pervasive. An image in this sense is not simply a trademark, a design, a slogan or an easily remembered picture. It is a studiously crafted personality profile of an individual, institution, corporation, product or service. It is a value-caricature, shaped in three dimensions, of synthetic materials. Such images in every increasing numbers have been fabricated and re-enforced by the new techniques of the graphic revolution. (Boorstin 1961)

Figure SII.8 Let us prey—One of the most iconic images of nineteenth-century America, this Thomas Nast editorial cartoon depicted the corrupt administration of New York City political boss William Tweed and cronies in the most unflattering light possible. *Harper's Weekly*, September 23, 1871.

Some have argued that advertising and public relations professions have some responsibility for undercutting the social meaning. French sociologist Jean Baudrillard has argued that the abundance of visual communication in the modern era has caused an effacement of reality in which symbolic value ("sign value") becomes more important than exchange value. "Conspicuous consumption," once possible only among the leisure class, has been extended to everyone in the consumer culture. And so, in a world where everything is a commodity that is up for sale, psychological alienation is total (Kellner 2009).

Yet advertising supports media financially in a way that government cannot, and public relations is, to a large extent, the voice of businesses competing in both financial markets and the marketplace of ideas. Questions of social impacts of media are profound, and the ability of a free society to regulate corporate political speech and spending by law is a point of serious, and ongoing, contention.

Figure SII.9 Christmas Truce—Well into the twentieth century, illustrations took precedence over photography in graphic magazines. This illustration by Frederic Villiers shows the "light of peace" as a German soldier approaches the British lines on Christmas Eve, 1914. Wikimedia Commons.

4

Photography: Giving Vision to History

At first we did not dare look long on at the images he [Daguerre] produced. We were frightened by the clarity of these men, imagining that these small, indeed, tiny, faces, fixed on a plate, could turn back and look at us.

Charles Dauthendey, c. 1850 (Johnson 1991)

1 The Arrival of Photography

Unlike most other technologies, photography was a true overnight sensation. Although chemists had been trying for years to fix an image on well-known light-sensitive materials, it was clear in 1839 that a French artist had achieved the impossible.

The artist—Louis Daguerre—presented the entire photographic process, with detailed instructions, as a gift, "free to the world," on August 19, 1839. There were no patent fees or devices to buy. Anyone could begin using photography; everyone did. Within weeks, dozens of entrepreneurs had set up "daguerreotype" studios in major cities in Europe, the Americas, and Asia

2 Foundations of photography

Daguerre's efforts grew out of a long-standing artistic tradition and many small advances in chemistry that set the stage for photography.

For example, Thomas Wedgewood is sometimes called the "first" photographer because he experimented with light-sensitive chemicals and created the first unfixed photographic picture in 1792. British scientist Humphrey Davy wrote about experiments he shared with Wedgewood in 1802, noting that he was able to find chemicals so sensitive to light that even dim rays from a camera obscura would leave an imprint. However, he did not find a way to fix the images (Litchfield 1903).

Many others attempted to solve the problem, but French lithographer Joseph Nicephore Niepce was the first to make any progress in his experiments that started in 1814. By 1826 he tried coating a tin plate with asphalt and leaving it in a camera obscura pointed out of the window for eight hours. Areas of asphalt that had not been hardened by sunlight washed off with turpentine. His image, "La cour du domaine du gras," is the first surviving photograph in history. But it was not a practical process, since the image was grainy and only buildings or fixed objects could be photographed.

2.1 Daguerre's breakthrough

Louis Daguerre was a Parisian artist whose work initially involved painting elaborate theatrical scenes, called dioramas, that depicted history and fantasy with painted backdrops, props, and wax figures.

Like Niepce, Daguerre was obsessed with finding a quicker way to get his work done and accurately depict his subjects. He began to study photography—so much that he neglected his painting. In 1824, his wife went to see a famous French chemist to see if he could talk Daguerre out of spending all his time and money on his foolish experiments. The chemist agreed to help out, but after talking with Daguerre, he was so impressed that he offered to help instead (*Photographic Times* 1910).

Daguerre also heard about Niepce's experiments, and rather than becoming rivals, the two men began collaborating around 1829. Niepce died four years later, and Daguerre persisted in trying to solve the problem of fixing the image permanently.

Figure 4.1 First photograph—Joseph Nicephore Niepce took this image from the window at Le Gras, France, over an eight-hour period in 1826. He gave the image to an English friend the following year, and it was lost until 1951. Wikimedia Commons.

By 1838, Daguerre settled on a process using a highly polished silver plate, exposed to iodine fumes. Once the plate was exposed to light through a camera, it was covered with mercury and then the image was fixed with sodium thiosulfate (hypo). He called the images "heliographs" (sun writing); but the rest of the world called them Daguerreotypes.

"Daguerre's plates … aroused awe and fear of a radically new way of presenting the world in two dimensions," observed historian Paul Johnson (Johnson 1991). But they were also widely hailed as a great scientific breakthrough.

Daguerre did not attempt to make a fortune with his process, nor did he attempt to control its use for profit or for a moral purpose, as later inventors would do with telegraph, telephone, cinema, and radio. Instead, in return for a pension from the French government, he disclosed the exact details of the process through the French Academy of Sciences and gave the invention away.

Figure 4.2 Inventor of photography—After years of experiments, Louis Daguerre found a practical way to take photographs. He shared the technology without patents or charge, as a gift to the world, in 1839. Library of Congress.

2.2 Competition and improvements

The Daguerrotype process produced a detailed image, but it was a one-of-a-kind image. There was no negative and so there were no subsequent prints on paper. Another process called a calotype was invented in 1841 by William Henry Fox Talbot. Although it could produce negatives, the images were too soft or fuzzy to be competitive with Daguerreotypes. And since Talbot had patented his process, it was cheaper for photo studios to continue with Daguerrotypes.

The process that replaced the Daguerrotype was invented in 1851 by Frederick Scott Archer. It was the "wet plate" collodion process, and it produced a detailed glass plate negative that could generate thousands of positive prints. The collodion process was also far more light-sensitive, and required only a few seconds of exposure. That meant no more agonizing five-minute poses in front of the daguerrotype camera.

The only drawback was that preparation and development had to take place just before and just after the photo was taken. This wasn't a big problem for portrait studios, where everything was fixed in place. But to take images in the field with the wet plate process, the entire darkroom, its large format cameras and racks for glass negatives, had to travel along with the photographer in a wagon.

Still, it was an advance. The wet plate negative process, combined with new ways to make positive prints, meant that cheap photos of popular people or places could easily be made by professionals, and purchased at a low price by the public.

Figure 4.3 Daguerreo-typo-mania—The year after Daguerre disclosed the photo process to the world, France was gripped by "Daguerro-typo-mania." This engraving shows long lines of people waiting to be photographed and teaching photography and selling equipment. The gallows are available to rent for artists, and symbolize fear that photography would mean the death of art. Théodore Maurisset, 1840. Library of Congress.

3 Diffusion of Technology

Photo studios sprang up around the world in the mid to late nineteenth century. Among the many who deserve to be better known are: Lala Deen Dayal who documented life in India; Felice Beato, an Italian photographer who traveled throughout Asia; Guillermo Kahlo, a German-Mexican photographer who was the father of artist Frida Kahlo; William Carrick, whose photos depicted life in Russia in the 1870s; and many more.

Samuel Morse is usually known for his Morse code for the telegraph, but he also imported the first photographic equipment from France after watching Louis Daguerre announce his process in 1839. One month later, he was teaching the art of photography in New York. One of his students was Mathew Brady, who became a famed US Civil War photographer:

"I was introduced to Morse [in 1839], who was then painting portraits at starvation prices in the university rookery on Washington square," Brady wrote. "He had just come home from Paris and had invented upon the ship his telegraphic alphabet of which his mind was so full that he could give but little attention to a remarkable discovery one Daguerre, a friend of his, had made in France" (Horan 1955).

Figure 4.4 Traveling Darkroom—An entire wagon-load of equipment was needed in the field just to take "wet plate" photos in the 1850s and 1860s. Here Marcus Sparling, assistant to British war photographer Roger Fenton, is having his picture taken just before venturing into the "Valley of the Shadow of Death." Roger Fenton, 1854. Library of Congress.

In 1844, Brady opened his portrait studio over a saloon on New York's busiest street—Broadway. Not only did he offer daguerreotypes at a reasonable price, but he also sought advice from the best chemists to help refine his techniques. His portraits soon began taking first place in competitions, and by the late 1840s he was a household name: "Brady of Broadway."

Brady also made a point of documenting the likenesses of the most famous people of the day for the Gallery of Illustrious Americans. His subjects were everyone still living who was important, including presidents Andrew Jackson and James Polk, and many other actors and politicians famous in their day.

In 1860, when an Illinois politician gave an important speech in New York's Cooper Union lecture hall, he also stopped into the Brady studio for a photo. It was reproduced by the thousands and became the best known image of the 1860 presidential campaign.

"Brady and the Cooper Institute made me president of the United States," Abraham Lincoln said (Horan 1955).

Brady is most often remembered as the man who photographed the US Civil War, but he was not the first war photographer. He was preceded by an unknown photographer who captured images from the Mexican–American War of 1848. He was also preceded by Roger Fenton, a British photographer, who traveled to the Russian Crimean region with British troops in 1855. Some believe that Fenton's photographs were meant to offset anger from the British public over the disastrous Crimean War (Sontag 2003: 126). He was under orders not to take photos of the dead or wounded soldiers. A controversy about his photos of a road covered with cannon balls emerged in recent years, and experts say Fenton probably tampered with the scene to enhance the image of danger (Morris 2007).

A few years later, Brady did not hesitate to reveal the macabre aftermath of the battle to the public. When Brady exhibited photos of the Antietam battlefield in 1862 at his New York studio, the effect was sensational. The *New York Times* said that Mr. Brady "has rendered us a real service … By this work of his, undertaken so courageously and carried forth so resolutely" (*New York Times*, September 26, 1862). "If he has not actually brought bodies back and laid them on our dooryards and along the streets, he has done something very like it … There is a terrible fascination about it that draws one near these pictures … You will see the hushed, reverent groups standing around these weird copies of carnage" (*New York Times*, October 20, 1862).

Figure 4.5 Presidential candidate—Abraham Lincoln, running for president in 1860, stopped by Matthew Brady's New York studio on February 27 for a photo. The image showed Lincoln's strength and honesty. It was widely circulated and helped him win the election. Matthew Brady, Library of Congress.

Brady, like Fenton, was not averse to staging photos for more artistic effect. But like Fenton and others before and since, Brady endured hardships and risked everything for history. "No one will ever know what I went through," Brady said. "Some of these negatives nearly cost me my life."

The negatives were nearly lost after the war, and Brady lost his studio and his fortune. Still, he had lived up to his ideals. "The camera is the eye of history," he said. "From the first, I regarded myself as under obligation to my country to preserve the faces of its historical men and women" (Horan 1955).

4 A Question of Art and Copyright

As photography became popular in the 1840s and 1850s, the question of whether photography was art or simply some form of mechanical reproduction became important, not only for abstract and cultural reasons, but also for legal and economic reasons.

In the beginning, the high culture of the mid-nineteenth century looked down on photographers. For example, in 1859, when a group of artists and photographers finally succeeded in getting photography shown at the Paris Salon, patrons had to use a back entrance.

"Some painters, especially miniaturists, quickly began to feel threatened and intimidated by the new 'art' of photography," said historian David Haberstich. Honore Daumier, a noted artist of the day, depicted portrait photographers of Paris as lazy louts in a print entitled *Patience is the virtue of fools.*

By 1862, the legal question of whether photography was fine art or merely mechanical reproduction had to be settled because of conflicting copyright claims, and a series of French and British cases were vehemently argued in the courts and salons. One of the most celebrated involved the re-sale of images of famous people originally taken by photographers working with Mayer and Pierson publishers in Paris. Another case involved a photographer who was originally commissioned to help a painter get an exact likeness for a portrait, but who then sold prints of the photograph.

Figure 4.6 Brady's war—Mathew Brady, or one of his assistants, took this photo of the dead being recovered on the field at Gettysburg in July 1863. War photos shocked the public when exhibited in Brady's New York gallery. Library of Congress.

Artists were furious, not only for what they thought was obvious theft, but also about the larger issue of "likening photography to art." In the Mayer and Pierson case, a lower court judge ruled that Daguerre's invention of photography was in the public domain, and so too were any products of the invention. When the case was appealed to the French high court, attorneys arguing for artists said "Photography lacks the qualities which are necessary to constitute a work of art: it is not a creation, [and] does not have originality."

On the other hand, Mayer and Pierson's attorneys argued:

> Photographic images, too, have their inspiration. This inspiration belongs entirely to the artist, and the sun is merely his compliant and splendid collaborator! Let us then give the mind its rights and limit the equipment to its proper role. It appears that there is a reliable criterion for judging this matter. The work of a machine may be identified by its uniformity. The work of man is identifiable by its variety, its diversity, its progress.

Figure 4.7 Mathew Brady—This June1861 photo shows him just after one of the first big battles of the US Civil War. "The camera is the eye of history," he said. Library of Congress.

The French high court took a middle course, deciding that while photographs "are not … creations of the mind or genius," certain images could be considered artistic and therefore could have copyright protection (Bentley and Kretschmer 2010; also Freund 1980). A similar controversy erupted in the United States in the 1884 when a photograph of playwright Oscar Wilde by the New York photographer Napoleon Sarony was widely reproduced.

Sarony sued a lithographic company that reproduced this and other celebrity photos, and the case went to the US Supreme Court. In court, the company argued that the original wording of the US Constitution only allowed Congress to protect the "writings" of "authors," and so the Copyright Act of 1870, which included protection of photographs, was unconstitutional. However, the court ruled in favor of the photographer, endorsing not only the power of Congress to regulate photography but also the concept that the law should be read as being adaptable to challenges posed by new technologies (*Burrow-Giles v Sarony* 1884).

5 Photography for the People

Until the 1880s, photographs had to be developed right after they were taken. In a studio this wasn't a problem, but out in the field, it meant that photographers literally had to take along wagon-loads of darkroom equipment. Few, other than professionals, could afford it. This changed with the introduction of two new improvements: dry plate photography and celluloid film.

The "dry plate" process allowed an exposure to be made and then set aside and developed later. British scientist Richard Maddox is usually credited with the advance in 1871, although Louis Lumiere of France, later famous for developing cinema with his brother Auguste, commercialized dry plate photography in Europe in 1881.

The second improvement was the use of flexible celluloid film. Celluloid was the first early form of plastic made by combining cellulose with nitric acid. It was dangerous and could catch fire easily, but flexible celluloid film meant that detailed images could be taken with much smaller cameras.

New Yorker George Eastman saw the possibilities for celluloid film, and in 1884, he patented the first film in rolls for cameras. By 1888, Eastman created the Kodak camera, the first designed specifically for roll film.

The Eastman Kodak Company started with the idea that everyone could be a photographer. For one dollar, anyone could buy a Kodak "Brownie" model camera that was sold loaded with film and ready to take 100 pictures. After taking the pictures, customers would bring the camera back to the store where they bought it and pick up their developed, printed photos in a week. "You push the button, we do the rest," was the Kodak slogan.

Figure 4.8 Is photography art?— It is not just an aesthetic argument; money is an issue here too. This portrait of playwright Oscar Wilde, taken in 1884, was copied without permission by a New York lithography company. When the photographer sued, Burrow-Giles lithographers said that only the arts were covered by copyright law, and photography was not an art. But photographers argued that they brought a sense of art into the photographic process, and won the precedent-setting US case. Photo by Napoleon Sarony, 1882. Library of Congress.

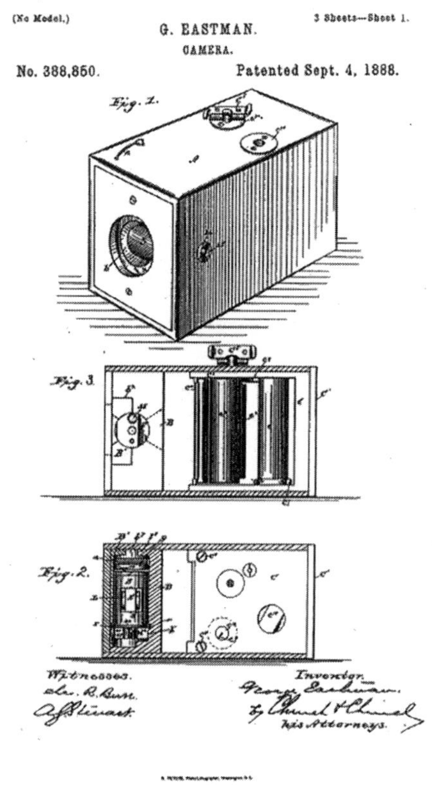

Figure 4.9 Key patent—George Eastman's patent for a box camera using rolled up flexible celluloid film represents a major advance for consumer photography. US Patent Office, 1888.

Figure 4.10 Democratizing photography—Before celluloid film, large cumbersome cameras were needed to hold glass plate negatives. George Eastman, founder of the Kodak Corporation, made photography accessible to everyone with a line of small easy-to-use cameras in the 1880s. Hartman Center, Duke University.

By simplifying what was once a complex process, Eastman Kodak created an enormous empire of 150,000 employees and hundreds of thousands of outlets in every grocery and chain store in the world. But the company did not weather the digital revolution and went into bankruptcy in 2012.

6 Turning Photography into Art: Pictorialism

The debate over the legitimacy of photography raged on long after the Mayer and Burrow-Giles cases were settled in France and the United States. A series of artistic movements and counter-movements inspired new approaches by new generations of photographers and artists. "The pressures of industrialization pushing against the bedrock of agrarian and artisanal tradition were threatening to split apart the old orders, whether political, economic, or aesthetic," said one art historian (McCauley 2008).

The snobbery of Parisian portrait painters over what was legitimately artistic helped to spur the "pictorialist" photographic movement. In defense of their art, pictorialists depicted subjects with soft visual effects in artistic poses. One part of the movement was the "The Brotherhood of the Linked Ring" founded in Britain in May 1892. Similar clubs were formed in Vienna and Paris to promote the artistic side of photography.

American pictorialists included Alfred Stieglitz and Edward Steichen, who started the "Photo Secessionist" movement and opened the 291 Gallery in New York. They were determined that photography would find its place "as a medium of individual expression," as Steiglitz said. The gallery proved successful in selling fine art photography, taking the forefront of modern art in the pre-World War I period. Among the best-known photos of the period is the Flat Iron Building, taken by Steichen.

The success of the 291 Gallery inspired another reaction in the Straight Photography movement. Photographers like Paul Strand thought pictorialism was too apologetic, and did not take advantage of the new medium. Strand took photography into advertising and abstract work with the idea of "absolute unqualified objectivity" rather than artistically manipulated photos. Strand was politically liberal, and like other photographers of the era used the camera to advance social causes as well as present artistic subjects.

Figure 4.11 Atmospherics—The Flat Iron Building—taken on a damp winter afternoon in 1905, Edward Steichen's atmospheric photograph epitomized the pictorialist movement in photography. Library of Congress.

The overbearing architecture and isolation of people in his 1915 Wall Street photo is a social comment as much as an artistic expression. Like many American artists, Strand suffered from blacklisting during the post-World War II reaction to communism, and spent the last three decades of his life in Europe.

On the US west coast, a group of photographers who sided with Strand's Straight Photography movement formed the f/64 Group in the early 1930s. The name is a reaction to Stieglitz's 291 but is also a technical description of an approach to photography. F/64 is a narrow lens aperture setting. It requires long exposure times and intense lighting, but it results in strong, clear images with extraordinary depth of field. The modernistic approach to photography is also seen in attention to underlying geometrical patterns. Ansel Adams's work is probably the best example. Other members of the group included Imogen Cunningham and Edward Weston.

Figure 4.12 Straight photography—A perfect contrast with pictorialist atmospheric photos was Paul Strand's 1915 Wall Street photo, where alienated people seem to be dwarfed by the buildings and institutions of modern society. Library of Congress.

7 Photojournalism and Social Reform

Photography was a serious art by the 1890s, but could it be used for journalism, to help to expose injustice and corruption? Could it spur social reform?

One man who was convinced that it could was Jacob Riis (1849–1914), a Danish-born police reporter for the *New York Tribune* who often roamed the streets with his friend Theodore Roosevelt, who was then commissioner of police.

Riis used two new innovations to get his message across: flash photography and photo halftone printing.

Until the invention of flash photography, low light conditions were difficult to photograph. The solution was a magnesium compound, invented in the 1880s, that would produce a flash of bright light to capture subjects in dark conditions.

Halftone printing of photos involved breaking up an image into little dots which could hold patterns of ink on a printing plate. The process was invented in Britain in 1882 but not widely used until the end of the decade. Riis used halftone photos in his 1890 book, *How the Other Half Lives*, but he also mixed in drawings of starving street children, thugs waiting for a victim, and immigrants crammed into unsanitary slums. His photos greatly magnified the effect of his scathing indictment of New York's indifference to its suffering population. The book was an instant success and generated a storm of controversy. It set a standard for muckraking reporting and spurred investigations that changed the building codes and health rules for New York.

Another example of photography for social reform involved Lewis Hine (1874–1940), a photographer who joined the National Child Labor Committee in 1907. Hine's stunning portraits of children working with dangerous machinery proved to be more powerful arguments than anything that could be said or written. By 1916, child labor reform laws had been enacted in the United States.

Hine's work has been carried on by many photographers, in recent years notably by Sebastio Salgado, a photographer who works in the UN Global Movement for Children.

"More than ever, I feel that the human race is one," Salgado said. "There are differences of color, language, culture and opportunities, but people's feelings and reactions are alike. People flee wars to escape death, they migrate to improve their fortunes, they build new lives in foreign lands, they adapt to extreme hardship ..."

Figure 4.13 Muckraking photography—Jacob Riis, a muckraking journalist, told the story of poverty in the New York slums in his 1890 book, *How the Other Half Lives.* Theodore Roosevelt commented, "The countless evils which lurk in the dark corners of our civic institutions, which stalk abroad in the slums, and have their permanent abode in the crowded tenement houses, have met in Mr. Riis the most formidable opponent ever encountered by them in New York City." Riis, 1890, Library of Congress.

The economic depression of the 1930s was another great social problem, involving a lack of confidence in the economic system and, for some people, the very concept of democracy. One response from Franklin Delano Roosevelt's New Deal administration involved the rural rehabilitation efforts of the Farm Security Administration.

Among its other jobs, the FSA was supposed to boost national morale by sending photographers and writers out into the country to document the national spirit. FSA photographers took over 200,000 photos documenting the condition of the country. The result was not always a morale-boosting portrait, but rather, one of a people struggling to cope and not always managing. While the intent was to "introduce Americans to Americans," the underlying argument of the photos was for social reform. "The compassionate optimism of so many of the FSA photographs was not created solely by

Figure 4.14 Breaker boys—The hopelessness on the faces of these Pittston, Pennsylvania, children who were forced to work in the coal mines is what photographer and reformer Lewis Hine hoped to depict. "If I tell you what child labor has cost a few of these children," Hine said, "you will ask how, in view of the terrible cost, we can afford child labor." Hine, 1911, US National Archives.

government decree," said historian Vicki Goldberg. "The belief was abroad in the land that with sufficient will, technology, and the proper kind of government intervention, even the problems of the Depression could be licked" (Goldberg 1991: Curtis 1991).

8 Photographic Magazines

Henry Luce (1898–1967) founded a publishing empire in 1923 with the conviction that busy people needed a news magazine to help keep them informed. *Time* magazine, started in 1923, compressed the week's news into what one writer called a "capsulized abridgement of a condensation" (Swanberg 1972).

The magazine had an exuberant writing style that reminded readers of young men just out of college, which is a fair description of Luce and his colleagues. Unlike the established magazines such as *Literary Digest*, *Time* magazine spoke to its generation. And as he achieved success in the 1920s, Luce launched other ventures. *Fortune*, a magazine for the business community, was his first in 1930. But *Life* magazine, launched in 1936, became the star attraction, creating the platform for some of the most brilliant photography of the twentieth century.

Figure 4.15 Modern child labor—Documenting child labor in the twenty-first century, Sebastio Salgado carries on the work of reformers like Riis and Hine. This photo shows children carrying sacks of coal from a mine face to a train in India. Salgado continues working with UNICEF to fight child labor. Courtesy Sebastio Salgado.

The idea of a photographic magazine was not new. Probably the most direct influence on *Life* magazine was the *Berliner Illustrirte Zeitung* (*BIZ*), founded in Germany in 1891. The magazine was originally illustrated with engravings, but made the switch to photographs early in the twentieth century. Under Kurt Korff as editor-in-chief (1905–33) the *BIZ* developed a new brand of magazine layout featuring photojournalism. Korff said the magazine's success came from a general shift toward a more visual culture and a "new relationship" with images themselves as conveyors of news (Ross 2008). Korff fled Germany in 1933 when the Nazis took over, eventually working for Luce. Meanwhile, one of his most talented photographers—Robert Capa (Endre Friedmann)—fled to Paris. He would later become famous as one of the world's great war photographers.

Life magazine editors also took cues from the *Illustrated London News*, which emphasized photos over text even more than *BIZ*, and from *Vu*, a French magazine, with modern typefaces and in-depth photo essays that told complex stories. The *Life* magazine manifesto, written in exchanges between Luce and poet Archibald MacLeish, begins, "To see life, to see the world; to eyewitness great events; to watch the faces of the poor and the gestures of the proud; to see strange things—machines, armies, multitudes, shadows in the jungle and on the moon; to see man's work … to see and to take pleasure in seeing" (Brinkley 2010).

Life was an overnight success when it was first published in 1936, and its fifty weekly pages of photos spawned many imitators, such as *Look* and *Paris Match*. It lost momentum in the television age, struggled through the end of the twentieth century in various forms, and is now published primarily as an online archive.

Figure 4.16 Power House—Along with his child labor crusade, Lewis Hine also made "work portraits" that emphasized the human contribution to modern industry. This iconic photo was also an inspiration for Charlie Chaplin's 1936 comic film *Modern Times*. Library of Congress.

9 The Corner of Her Eye: Dorothea Lange

The most famous portrait of the twentieth century was taken by Dorothea Lange, a photographer who visited migrant farm camps while working for the FSA in California. Her classically composed *Migrant Mother* photo, taken in March 1936 in Nipomo, California, resulted from a combination of intuition and professional determination.

As Lange told the story, she had been on assignment for a month and was driving home when she said she noticed a "pea pickers camp" sign "out of the corner of my eye." She drove on in the rain for another twenty miles, convincing herself that she didn't need to go back to take one more set of photos. And then:

> Almost without realizing what I was doing, I made a U-turn on the empty highway. I went back those 20 miles and turned off the highway at that sign, PEA-PICKERS CAMP. I was following instinct, not reason; I drove into that wet and soggy camp and parked my car like a homing pigeon. I saw and approached the hungry and desperate mother, as if drawn by a magnet. I do not remember how I explained my presence or my camera to her, but I do remember she asked me no questions. I made five exposures, working closer and closer from the same direction. I did not ask her name or her history. She told me her age, that she was thirty-two. She said that they had been living on frozen vegetables from the surrounding fields, and birds that the children killed. She had just sold the tires from her car to buy food. There she sat in that lean-to tent with her children huddled around her, and seemed to know that my pictures might help her, and so she helped me. There was a sort of equality about it. (Lange 1960)

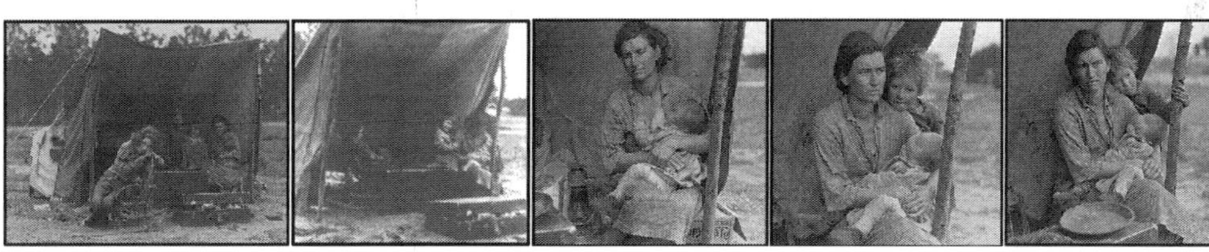

Figures 4.17, **4.18**, and **4.19** Migrant Mother—One of the most iconic photos of the twentieth century was Dorothea Lange's 1936 portrait of a migrant farm worker and her children. Lange took a series of shots, ending with the most famous one. The woman, Florence Owens Thompson, had just sold the tires from her car to buy food for the children. Lange told relief authorities about the situation, and they brought food to the camp the next day. The photos also helped John Ford envision the 1940 film, *The Grapes of Wrath*. Library of Congress.

The next day, Lange and her editors alerted federal relief authorities, and food was rushed to the camp. The subject of the *Migrant Mother* photo, Florence Owens Thompson, survived the Depression and raised her children in California. Thompson's daughters said she had avoided publicity until 1978 because she was ashamed at having been an icon of poverty. But FSA photos like the *Migrant Mother* gave no hint that the subjects had brought misery on themselves through any fault of their own. Instead, they portrayed good people as victims of a flawed system.

9.1 Parks and other *Life* magazine photographers

Another FSA photographer, Gordon Parks, made a similarly iconic photo. Parks, a northern-born African-American, was unaccustomed to the racism of the American

South, so when he was hired in 1942 in Washington, DC, his first assignment was to leave his camera behind and go to a lunch counter and the movies. He was turned away from both establishments, which was the reason he was given the assignment.

Later that afternoon, as the somewhat angered Parks was settling into his new job, he noticed Ella Watson cleaning the building. He asked her to pose in front of a flag, broom in one hand and mop by her side, in the style of a famous painting called *American Gothic*. Parks's boss, FSA chief Roy Stryker, said he had the right idea but had overdone it, which could get them all fired. Parks went on to work for *Life* magazine for twenty years. He also became the first major African-American director in the United States with films like *The Learning Tree* (1969) and *Shaft* (1971).

Working for *Life* magazine was the way many great photographers stayed in the field. Along with Parks, the *Life* photography crew included some of the twentieth century's best photographers: Margaret Bourke-White, Dorothea Lange, Robert Capa, Alfred Eisenstadt, W. Eugene Smith, Edward Steichen, and many others.

Figure 4.20 American Gothic—Gordon Parks had just been hired by the Farm Services Administration in August, 1942, when he took this photo of Ella Watson, who worked on the cleaning crew in the federal building. Parks was feeling angry after having encountered racism in Washington, DC. The photo shows a woman who has been victimized but who also has a deep personal resilience. Library of Congress.

10 Twentieth-Century War Photography

While photography was tightly censored in World War I by the Creel Committee, World War II was a different kind of war, involving fully mobilized civilian populations. Propaganda was important and the image meant everything.

Among the most dynamic photographers of the war years was Robert Capa, a Hungarian-born refugee from Nazi Germany originally named Endre Friedmann, who found he could not get work as a photographer in Paris in 1933. With two friends, he advertised a new Paris photo agency being opened by the famous American photographer Robert Capa. At first, Friedmann was the non-existent Capa's assistant, but soon he was using the name as his own. "I invented that Bob Capa, a famous American photographer who came over to Europe," Capa admitted in 1947 (Kershaw 2002).

One of Capa's famous photos is that of the Spanish Civil War soldier at the exact moment of death in 1936. Although some have alleged that the photo was faked (Knightly 2004), others insist that clues in the photo, along with corroborating evidence, demonstrate its veracity (Whelan 2002). Capa fled to the United States when the Germans invaded France in 1940, and worked on assignment for *Collier's* and *Life* magazines covering the war. He parachuted into Sicily with the Allied invasion and followed the grim Italian campaign of 1943–4.

He was reassigned to Britain and, after a round of parties with friends like Ernest Hemingway and John Steinbeck, Capa followed the invasion across the English Channel. He was the only photographer on Omaha Beach on D-Day, and his photos were mishandled by darkroom assistants. Yet they were widely published and, in their hazy and overdeveloped way, seem to paint a moment of sharp contrasts and great confusion. Capa was killed in Vietnam in 1954 covering that unfolding war.

Margaret Bourke-White was already famous for her photos of the "dust bowl" of Oklahoma when she documented the liberation of Buchenwald concentration camp in 1945. The pictures were so stark that then-US general Dwight Eisenhower toured the camps to confirm that they were real. Of course, they were horrifyingly real, and Bourke-White later said that it helped to have a camera in between her and the pitiful victims of the camps. She also took a deceptively simple portrait of Mahatma Gandhi in 1946.

Figure 4.21 Falling soldier—Taken at the very moment of death, this 1936 photo of a soldier in the Spanish Civil War made Robert Capa an international celebrity. Robert Capa, Magnum.

Gandhi is shown with a spinning wheel in the foreground of the photo, which implied that a person can, with modesty, be a symbol of change and put the symbol forward, rather than themselves.

Joe Rosenthal was another great photographer of the war era, and his Associated Press shot of US Marines planting the flag on Iwo Jima is among the best-known photos of the era. Like Lange when she shot *Migrant Mother*, Rosenthal had a feeling that drew him on. He kept going up Mount Suribachi even when he met other photographers and reporters coming down the mountain. They said the flag had already gone up. As it turned out, Marines were preparing to raise a second, larger flag, and Rosenthal captured a well-remembered photo that earned a Pulitzer Prize. Asked about the photo later, Rosenthal would reply with typical modesty: "I took the picture. The Marines took Iwo Jima" (Leary 2006). Rosenthal worked for the AP until his retirement in 1981.

Another iconic photo of the war was taken on VJ Day, August 14, 1945, in Times Square. Exuberant crowds were reacting to the announcement of the official end to World War II when prolific *Life* photographer Alfred Eisenstaedt noticed a sailor kissing every woman he came across. The photo became a widely known symbol of the jubilation at the end of the war. "We are only beginning to learn what to say in a photograph," Eisenstaedt once said. "The world we live in is a succession of fleeting moments, any one of which might say something significant."

11 Celebrity Photography

Abraham Lincoln was the first president whose photographic image was known to the entire country, thanks to Brady of Broadway, but celebrity photography really became part of the American scene with the advent of picture magazines in the 1910s and 1920s. The feedback between Hollywood film and celebrity magazines had enormous power to make people like Italian-American actor Rudolph Valentino into superstars.

Photographer Alfred Eisenstaedt's specialty, he said, was people. "It is more important to click with people than to click the shutter," he was fond of saying. From Marilyn Monroe to Joseph Goebbels, Eisenstaedt seemed to use the camera to peer deeply into the human soul.

Another photographer famous for deeply perceptive celebrity photos is Annie Liebowitz. She was chief photographer of *Rolling Stone* in the 1970s and is well known for her photo of John Lennon and Yoko Ono taken only hours before Lennon was killed. The photo was "10 years in the making" because she had known Lennon and Ono, along with the rest of the global rock and roll scene, for many years. She had seen a cover for their *Double Fantasy* album and it involved a kiss. She said:

> I was so moved by that kiss. There was so much in that simple picture of a kiss. So, for the photo I wanted to take, I imagined them somehow together. And it wasn't a stretch to imagine them with their clothes off, because they did it all the time. But what happened at the last minute was that Yoko didn't want to take her clothes off. So, we went ahead with the picture. (Liebovitz 2008; Nudd 2013)

Figure 4.22 Iwo Jima, 1945—Associated Press photographer Joe Rosenthal took this photo of the US Marines raising the flag over Mount Suribachi during heavy combat on Iwo Jima. The photo became a symbol of the US Marine Corps. Joe Rosenthal, the Associated Press.

Perhaps one of the darkest moments in the history of photography was the car chase that led to the death of Britain's Princess Diana in 1997. The paparazzi—freelance photographers who sensationalize celebrities—had been hounding Diana without mercy in the decade before her death, even risking their lives to pursue her car. But on August 31, her driver, in an attempt to elude the paparazzi, crashed the car and Diana was killed. A coroner's jury rejected claims that she was murdered and blamed the driver of her car for recklessness. One result of the Diana tragedy is that laws restraining invasions of privacy by photographers are easier to enforce. Even so, the basic commitment to freedom of the press, along with the fact that celebrities are voluntary public figures, makes it difficult to draw the line.

12 Conservation And Environmental Photography

If photography has the power to change the way we look at ourselves, it also has the power to change the way we look at our environment. One of the most dramatic examples is

Earthrise, a photo of the earth from 240,000 miles out in space, taken on Christmas Eve, 1968 by US astronaut William Anders aboard the Apollo 8 in orbit around the moon.

The photo was printed in thousands of newspapers, magazines, and books, and was the cover for the *Whole Earth Catalog.* Wilderness photographer Galen Rowell called it "the most influential environmental photograph ever taken." Photos taken from space remind us, said astronomer Carl Sagan, that we are all in this together: "In all this vastness, there is no hint that help will come from elsewhere to save us from ourselves."

Another NASA photo, taken from the TOMS satellite in 1984, showed clearly that the protective layer of ozone was decreasing in the atmosphere. The photo had a dramatic political impact. Within a few years, the United States signed the Montreal Protocol, an international treaty pledging to eliminate chlorofluorocarbon chemicals that were causing ozone depletion.

Photography inspired by the beauty of natural landscapes or remote corners of the world is a recurrent theme. Among the first to take advantage of the camera for this point of view were the Bisson brothers, who adored alpine hiking in the 1850s and took stunning shots of mountaineers on glaciers.

Carleton E. Watkins was known as an accomplished field photographer in the American West in the 1860s, hoping to give everyone "the best seat in the house." William Henry Jackson accompanied the Hayden Geological Survey of 1871. His photos helped persuade Congress to create Yellowstone National Park.

In contrast, Margaret Bourke-White's photos of the Oklahoma "dust bowl" brought back the misery of the experience in the 1930s. She wrote in *The Nation*:

> By coincidence I was in the same parts of the country where last year I photographed the drought. [Then] there was an attitude of false optimism. "Things will get better," the farmers would say. "We're not as hard hit as other states. The government will help out. This can't go on." But this year there is an atmosphere of utter hopelessness. Nothing to do. No use digging out your chicken coops and pigpens after the last "duster" because the next one will be coming along soon. No use trying to keep the house clean. No use fighting off that foreclosure any longer … (Bourke-White 1935)

The increasing concern about environment and preservation of nature was a consistent theme of photography in the mid- to late twentieth century. While Ansel Adams's photos of Western landscapes spoke of the need for conservation, other photographers documented the increasing human cost of environmental degradation. One of the most prominent photographer-filmmakers was Jacques Cousteau, who became known for his 1953 bestselling book *The Silent World* that described the beauty of underwater photography:

> The world … was twilight blue [and] flesh was a greenish putty color. The far-off sun gleamed on the chromed regulators, winked on the frames of the masks and ensilvered our exhaust bubbles … The Athenian marbles were dark bluish shapes, blurred with blankets of marine life. We dug under with our hands, dog fashion, to pass cargo slings under them. As the stones ascended, color grew on the crust and, at the surface, they swung into the air ablaze with life. As they drained on deck, the Joseph's coat of flora and fauna faded into the earth shade of death.

Figure 4.23 Earthrise—on Christmas Eve, 1968, US astronaut William Anders snapped this shot of earth rising above the moon's horizon while aboard the Apollo 8 spacecraft. US National Aeronautics and Space Administration.

Cousteau went on to win Academy Awards for his films; today his son and grandchildren are carrying on the struggle to save the world's oceans.

Another of the world's great photographers, W. Eugene Smith, must be mentioned. His photos of Pittsburgh, Pennsylvania, taken between 1955 and 1957, at the height of the smokestack era, reveal the grit and human costs of the steel industry. His portraits of the victims of mercury poisoning in Minimata, Japan, published in *Life* magazine on June 2, 1972, shocked the world. The most famous of the photos shows Ryoko Eumura holding her severely deformed daughter, Tomoko, in a style similar to Michelangelo's sculpture, *La Pieta*. The photo was so good that Tomoko became an international symbol of the impacts of unregulated chemical industry. But the encroachment on the victim's privacy was too much, and the Eumura family asked Smith's heirs to withdraw the photo from circulation. Smith also suffered for daring to document a chemical factory's impact. He was seriously injured in an attack he believed was ordered by the chemical industry and never recovered before his death in 1978 (Smith and Smith 1975).

Photographers are routinely targets of outrage, and nowhere more so than on the front lines of environmental conflict. Repeatedly arrested for covering environmental conflict in the Appalachians, photographer Antrim Casky said in 2009, "It's OK to pick sides.

Photo journalists like Robert Capa were against Fascism. He supported the soldiers that he covered. In a sense, it's not much different here" (Roselle 2010).

Eliot Porter should not be overlooked among nature and conservation photographers. His bird photography and site-specific work on Glen Canyon, before it was flooded by Lake Powell, had a strong influence on the environmental movement. Porter worked with Ansel Adams (mentioned previously in connection with the f/64 Group) and David Brower of the Sierra Club to invent the "exhibit format" photo book which carried a message to conserve a particular place. Another photographer who worked to save Glen Canyon in the 1950s was Philip Hyde.

Two significant photographic journeys include Frans Lanting's Journey Through Time, for *Life* magazine in 2006, and Michael "Nick" Nichols' journey on foot across central Africa for *National Geographic* magazine in 1999. Among many other great photographs in this category are Gary Braasch's portraits of climate change; Joel Sartori's glistening shots of endangered species; and Edward Burtynsky's vistas of frighteningly polluted landscapes. Other important conservation efforts include Jack Dykinga's desert landscapes; David Muench's photos of nature; David Doubilet's underwater photography; and C. C. Lockwood's portraits of bayou country.

Because conservation photography is so vital, an International League of Conservation Photographers was formed in 2003 (see www.ilcp.com). Another effort to inspire a new generation of photographers was the Environmental Protection Agency's "Documenting America" project, digitizing and posting photos from 1971 to 1977 on the web.

Figure 4.24 Environmental photography—This photo of an expedition to a glacier was taken in the 1850s by the Bisson Brothers. Library of Congress.

13 Photography and Ethics

Increasing concerns about the ethics of photography have also played a role in public appreciation for photography. For example, "spirit photographers" of the nineteenth century took advantage of gullible people by superimposing fake ghosts over the images of living people. Similarly, the *New York Daily Graphic* was able to use cut-and-paste techniques to alter news photos in the 1920s.

News photographers have always tried to strike a balance between public service on the one hand and sensationalism on the other. When AP photographer Nick Ut took a famous photo of children fleeing from a village in Vietnam in June of 1972, editors debated whether or not to use it, since it showed a young girl (Phan Thị Kim Phuc) whose clothes had been burned off by napalm. AP editors decided that the news value outweighed modesty. After taking the photo, Ut took the girl to the hospital. He remained in touch with her over the years as she found a new life.

The new ability to digitally manipulate photos made fraud harder to detect in the late twentieth century. New concerns even showed up in debates about old photos, such as those by Robert Fenton and Robert Capa, as we have seen.

One of the most controversial decisions to manipulate a photo was made by *Time* magazine editors following the arrest of O. J. Simpson on murder charges in 1994. *Time* and *Newsweek* magazines both ran the same police photo on the cover, but *Time* darkened the photo to make Simpson look more sinister. If the identical photo had not been on the same newsstands that same week, the controversy might not have broken out. *Time* later apologized to its readers. Similar controversies broke out over digital manipulation of *Los Angeles Times* photos from the Iraq War in 2003 and over an *Economist* magazine manipulation of a shot depicting President Barack Obama standing on the shore of the Gulf of Mexico in 2010.

The American Press Photographers Association code of ethics takes a strong position on digital manipulation of photos and advises photographers to "respect the integrity of the photographic moment."

14 Digital Photography

Digital imaging technologies have brought the world together in ways that exchanges of text never could. Ironically, they came out of research for the Cold War and the US–Russia space race during the 1950s and 1960s.

The basic technology that turned photons into digital images was called a charge-coupled device (CCD). It was developed at Bell Laboratories in Princeton, New Jersey, as part of a secret US government satellite surveillance program and patented by Willard Boyle and George Smith of Bell Labs in 1973. Electronics firms like Fairchild semi-conductor and Texas Instruments began building the devices, and in 1975, Kodak engineer Steven Sasson used a Fairchild CCD in a prototype of a consumer digital camera (Dobbin 2005).

With basic research funded through government programs, CCDs improved during the 1970s and began to make inroads in the professional markets in the early 1980s. CCD-based video cameras were especially valued in the television industry. In the studio, heavy analog cameras would often need repairs at inconvenient moments. In the field, using 16mm film cameras meant that the film had to be developed in time for the six o'clock news, a process that took at least half an hour. Video camcorders (as they were called) could deliver video instantly.

Digital images were originally too large for the average home computer until the late 1980s, when one of the first online networks, CompuServe, developed a format called the Graphics Interchange Format (gif) in 1987. The format was geared to the consumer market with 8-bit processors and only 256 possible colors within the image. Kodak also developed a digital format called the Photo CD in 1992, but it was superseded by international developments.

During the twentieth century, the world was divided into three main regions for television technologies. The US used NTSC television encoding, Europe and the Middle East used PAL codes, and Asian nations used SECAM codes. Consumers could not translate TV programs and DVDs from one format to another.

More universal formats came out of two international groups working in Geneva, Switzerland, in the 1980s: the Joint Photographic Experts Group (JPEG) and the Moving Picture Experts Group (MPEG). The groups set standards for compression and transmission of images within computers and storage devices, and also through cable and satellite systems. The first JPEG (or JPG) standard was released in 1992, and unlike the GIF format, JPG had three channels of 256 colors each, for a total of over 16 million colors. JPG was also an open source format, which meant that it could be used without charge, and improvements could come from all kinds of users and be incorporated in new versions. (For more about MPEG, see Chapter 8.)

News organizations around the world had been using analog photo exchanges for decades, first with grainy photo faxes and then with the laser photo system developed by the Associated Press in the 1970s. By 1988, AP had a "Leaf Desk" system using the 1986 TIFF format. Not only could a Leaf Desk scan, send, and receive photos, it could also create a camera-ready halftone for the pre-press process. It was the last piece of the puzzle in the development of the all-digital newspaper.

Similar tools would become available to consumers in applications like Adobe Photoshop during the mid-1990s. The need to prepare photos for printing would drive the high end of the digital imaging market before the need to compress photos for the World Wide Web.

14.1 Kodak: The rise and demise of a photo giant

Eastman Kodak was the photographic behemoth, producing everything from film to x-rays to cameras to flash bulbs. The company had over 140,000 employees and hundreds of thousands of outlets in nearly every grocery and chain store in the world, making it the undisputed leader in consumer and industrial photography. It had a near-monopoly of the US market during most of the twentieth century.

Kodak also led the industry in technology development, with defense contracts for advanced film and digital imaging and unlimited budgets for government work in aerial and satellite reconnaissance. Some of the company's digital imaging technology was used in satellites by the 1970s, decades ahead of the first consumer digital cameras. And the world's first unclassified digital camera was developed at Kodak in 1975. It was bigger than a pair of shoeboxes and took low-quality images—but it worked.

So Kodak wasn't just affected by the digital imaging revolution: the company helped create it. And yet, Kodak went bankrupt in 2012 for complex reasons. The Kodak story is not similar to the traditional "curve in the road" story that is usually told about the digital revolution, in which big companies like IBM and Xerox are outmaneuvered by smaller companies with a larger vision, like Microsoft and Apple (see Chapter 10).

Kodak management knew perfectly well how the digital revolution would play out. In a 1979 report to the Kodak board, a Kodak manager of advanced consumer equipment development, Larry Matteson, predicted that film, cameras, and other products would shift in stages from analog to digital (Dickinson 2012; *Economist* 2012).

"The analysis was a projection of the improvement in integrated circuits performance and cost based on Moore's Law," Matteson told the board. "The assumption was that different Kodak businesses would adopt electronic imaging at different rates based on the performance benefits each business would derive from adopting electronic imaging. Consumer photography was predicted to be the last of Kodak's businesses to make the transformation to electronic imaging. Consumer electronics generally has a return on sales of around 5 percent. This was far below Kodak's historic profit margins." For a 1979 prediction, it was amazingly accurate.

Figure 4.25 Relocation Camp—This Ansel Adams photo from 1942 shows editor Roy Takeno reading a copy of the *Manzanar Free Press* in front of the newspaper office at the Manzanar War Relocation Camp in California, one of the ten major centers where 110,000 Americans of Japanese ancestry were held during World War II. Adams is well known for atmospheric photos, and the mountains in the background show his style; but like Dorothea Lange and other photographers of the era, Adams was also concerned about the injustice of the relocations. Library of Congress.

In response, Kodak's modernization strategy involved moving into the digital imaging business, and by 2005, the Kodak EasyShare camera models were leading US markets. But the business model for the EasyShare involved selling chemicals for printing photos which, as it turned out, were not as valued by consumers. Kodak also did not envision the rise of cell phone cameras, which cut into another part of their market.

Despite efforts to create new markets for digital cameras, the nature of digital technology was such that the market would not generate the same kinds of profits. "The mistake, if it was a mistake," Kodak executive Matteson told

Der Speigel, "was that Kodak could never separate itself from the notion of being a company about images" (Fitchner 2012).

Kodak's other competitors also went bankrupt as digital photography replaced analog. Polaroid, which produced expensive instantly developing photos, ended business in 2001. Agfa Photo, the German film company, and Ilford, the British film company, both declared bankruptcy in 2005. Only Japanese filmmaker Fujifilm stayed in business by shifting to chemistry and cosmetics, rather than staying in imaging and photography.

14.2 Democratizing impact of digital photography

The replacement of film with digital photography shook up the industry, but it did not pose the kind of threat to democratic information systems as did the collapse of newspapers and magazines. Instead, the fluidity and rapid transmission of digital images improved access and participation in the mass media. One development was the advent of photo sharing with companies like Flickr, created in 2004, and Instagram and Pinterest, both launched in 2010.

A dramatic example of the impact of digital photography and networks took place following a massive 7.9 magnitude earthquake that killed 70,000 people in Sichuan Province of central China on May 12, 2008. "The earthquake was reported as it was happening," said media analyst Clay Shirkey. "People were texting from their phones, they were taking photos from their phones, taking video from their phones … and uploading it to QQ, China's largest internet service." The BBC got the news from Twitter networks of friends connected to people in China. "The last time China had a quake that size [in the 1970s], it took them three months to admit that it had happened."

In contrast, photos of the 2008 earthquake were impossible to censor because they were produced by Chinese people inside China. Censors were relying on the Great Firewall of China, a surveillance and content control system set up in 2000. The system was designed to stop messages sent by foreigners into the country. It was not capable of filtering out the vast number of connected people and cell cameras inside China.

Just as George Eastman once built an business empire out of the idea of making it easy to take pictures, companies like Flickr, Instagram and Pinterest are growing by making it easy to share digital photos.

15 The Future of Photography

In 1889, a speaker at a New York photographers club said that within fifty years, the audience would marvel at stored solar energy lighting up buildings in the evenings; reporters attending meetings remotely; color photography; and push-button instant print cameras (*New York Times*, "Talks of Photographers," March 6, 1889). Each of these innovations took place, but almost in the reverse order.

Edward Land patented the Polaroid instant camera in 1937; Kodak made color film available in 1935; reporters began attending meetings remotely via internet applications in the early twenty-first century; and solar energy was becoming the most cost-effective long-term energy option in the 2010s.

In *Who Owns the Future*, author Jaron Lanier noted that Kodak, at the height of its power, was worth $28 billion. "Today Kodak is bankrupt, and the new face of digital photography has become Instagram." Lanier points out that when Facebook bought Instagram in 2012, the company only employed thirteen people. "Where did all those jobs disappear to? And what happened to the wealth that those middle-class jobs created?" That wealth now comes from the millions of users who are part of the network that uses Instagram. So digital technologies are centralizing wealth and limiting overall economic growth, Lanier says.

A web search for the "future of photography" turns up many interesting ideas, including improvements to digital cameras, GPS signatures and other information embedded in photos, three-dimensional and moving photos on reusable plasma screens, and the return of Polaroid-type instant prints.

Still, the technology in any form is just the vehicle for the enduring image. "In an era of information overload, the photograph provides a quick way of apprehending something and a compact form for memorizing it," said Susan Sontag. "The photograph is like a quotation, or a maxim or proverb." (Sontag 2002) This deflection of reality makes us all detached spectators, she says, and although we can't imagine what it was like to be in the image, we are, nevertheless, always drawn towards it.

For additional reading, discussion questions, links to video, and other suggestions, see www.revolutionsincommunications.com.

5

Cinema: The Image Comes Alive

Whoever controls the motion picture industry controls the most powerful medium of influence over the people

Thomas Edison, *New York Times*, May 16, 1923

Other [media] have sprung up in a night, almost unheralded; these too have fallen first into the hands of men of vigorous imagination and ruthless temper [and] ... aroused frenzies of fear and crusades of repression. The theater in the time of Shakespeare, the novel in the 18th century, the newspaper a century later, were also extravagantly hailed and extravagantly anathematized ...

Thomas H. Dickinson, *New York Times*, July 6, 1923

1 Introduction

Cinema clobbers the senses, influencing the way people perceive each other and their world like nothing else. It's a very "cool" medium, in the sense that a well-crafted succession of images leads people to suspend disbelief with little effort. No other medium requires so little active personal involvement or delivers ideas so deeply into the human psyche.

Cinema is hotly controversial as well. Some films generate heated debate for decades, while others are so warmly remembered that they become generation-spanning clichés.

Although other types of media may have the power to reflect, deflect, and drive social change, none have achieved it with the artistic sweep and social force of cinema. The story of cinema, from the Lumiere brothers to the Cohn brothers, from Hollywood to Bollywood, from the Oscars to Cannes, is a story that parallels the social revolutions of the twentieth and twenty-first centuries.

When cinema first arrived, it was instantly seen as more powerful than any other media, and the first glimpse of a "movie" astonished some people so much that they would occasionally duck to avoid a head-on locomotive, or shout out warnings to images of endangered actors flickering across theater screens.

People were ready for cinema. As early as the mid-1600s, long before cinema technology arrived, audiences would watch "magic lantern" shows that provided narration, music and moving images in darkened theaters. Magic lantern shows could also be visually complex, with a dozen slots for slides to project a foreground, middle, and background. Some of the later model lanterns had several lenses to allow for effects such as dissolves and wipes. The

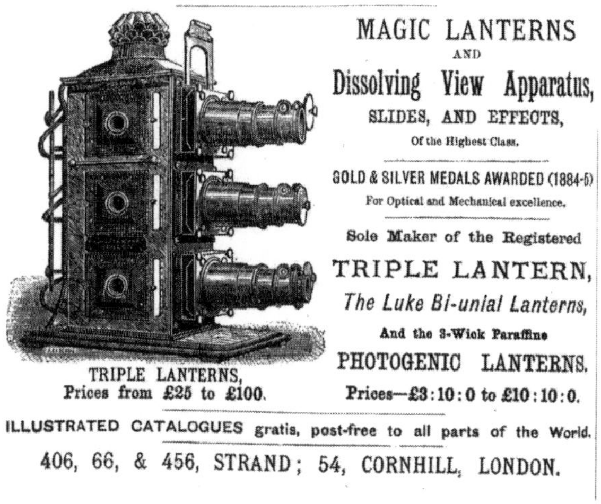

Figure 5.1 Magic Lantern—Centuries before motion pictures, audiences could look at painted pictures on screens and, by the 1850s, photographs as well. Wikimedia Commons.

Figure 5.2 Slides for magic lantern. Photo by Lin Burton.

story of a great naval battle, for example, could have waves in the foreground, ships in the middle, and a seascape in the back, and could dissolve to another slide set of close-ups of the action. Technically, early cinema drew from existing media such as toys like flip books, the Zoetrope (US) and the Daedalus (Britain). They were the forerunners of the Kinetoscope and the Mutoscope systems, where lone viewers would crank handles on a machine. The "scopes" and the toys worked because the persistence of vision phenomena, in which a succession of images flashed in front of the eyes would appear to take on motion, to become "animated."

Early cinema also drew from the experience of Eadweard Muybridge, a San Francisco photographer, who used glass plate photos to sequence images. Muybridge got his start in motion studies in 1877 when California governor Leland Stanford hired him to settle a bet about the way horses run. Stanford bet that there is a moment when a horse, at a full gallop, is not touching ground. Muybridge set up an experiment involving a series of cameras with shutters hooked to trip wires, showing that a galloping horse does indeed leave the ground, and helped the governor win the bet.

Figure 5.3 Moving images—Eadweard Muybridge, a California photographer, set up a series of cameras in 1877 to take pictures of a galloping horse, winning a bet for then-governor Leland Stanford. The governor had bet that all four feet leave the ground when a horse is running. Library of Congress.

2 Inventing the Movies

2.1 Thomas Edison's Kinetoscope

Muybridge inspired other inventors, especially Thomas Edison, who had begun to consider ways to overcome the technical problems of animated pictures. In a February 27, 1888 meeting at the Edison labs, Muybridge proposed that he and Edison work together on the problem of synchronizing sound and pictures. But Edison was never one to share the limelight, and he filed his own preliminary patent application in October 1888.

By the next summer, Edison was experimenting with some of George Eastman's new flexible celluloid film, and he realized that the key problem was allowing a regular advance and momentary halt of the film. Edison's mechanical engineers solved the problem with a stop-and-go disk mechanism, which was the first practical system for shooting and displaying film.

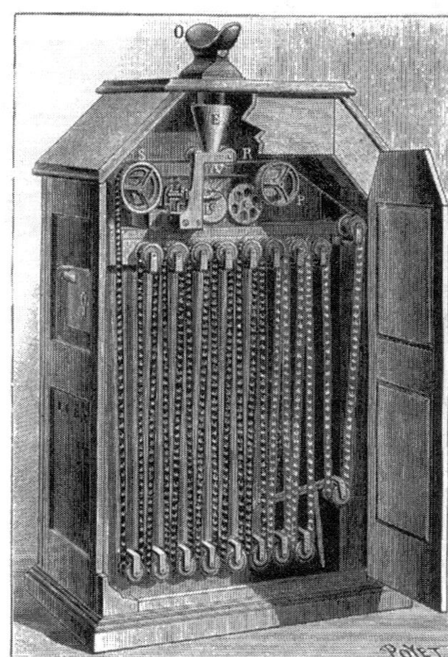

Figure 5.4 Kinetoscope—Thomas Edison's vision for cinema was a one-person, hand-cranked viewer for short films. A viewer would drop a penny (or nickel) into the slot and watch the shows in halls lined with the machines. W. K. L. Dickson, 1894. Wikimedia Commons.

Both the camera (the Kineto*graph*) and the viewing system (the Kineto*scope*) were first exhibited on May 20, 1891. The system was among the highlights of the Chicago World's Fair in 1893. During the next few years, Edison engineers shot dozens of very short films in the "Black Maria" studio in Orange, New Jersey, showing people doing rather ordinary things—sneezing, dancing, talking, working, kissing.

Kinetoscope projectors allowed people to watch individually, and one person would get to see a short film after putting a penny or a

Figure 5.5 Fathers of film—George Eastman (left) and Thomas Edison pose behind a World War I-era movie camera. Library of Congress.

nickel (five US cents) into the machine's slot. "Nickelodeon" halls, as they came to be called, quickly spread in the United States, much like video game parlors in the 1970s and 1980s. The technology spread slowly but then took off all at once. Fourteen years after the World's Fair, there were only eighteen Nickelodeon halls in downtown Chicago. By 1910 there were hundreds in Chicago and over 500 in New York. While Edison's Kinetoscope and a rival machine called a Mutoscope may have been popular, everyone knew their prospects were limited. Theatrical performances to large audiences watching one large screen together were much more interesting than individual viewing machines. By 1896, Edison's group developed the Vitagraph projector to show films to theatrical audiences. But Edison was just catching up with the Lumiere Brothers.

2.2 The Lumieres: Getting the picture out of the box

Cinema is simply too big a concept to be confined to little Nickelodeon boxes. That, at least, is what Antoine Lumiere concluded when he saw one of Thomas Edison's Kinetoscope machines exhibited in Paris in September 1894. He returned to his home in Lyon, France, with a big project for his sons Louis and Auguste. "Get the picture out of the box," he told them. Put it on a big screen, in a theater, where everyone can see it.

The Lumieres were already the leading name in French photography. Louis had patented a method for dry plate photography at the age of seventeen, and the Lumiere factory in Lyon employed dozens of workers churning out photo chemicals, plates, and papers.

All through the fall of 1894, the brothers worked on the problem. Then one night, when Louis was unable to sleep, a solution came clearly to his mind. The film could be advanced, held, and exposed, using a mechanism similar to a sewing machine (Toulet 1995). They tried it using a perforated paper tape, and then using a perforated light-sensitized film running at sixteen frames per second. With refinements, it worked, and on February 13, 1895, the Lumiere Brothers patented the first Cinematographe. In March 1895, they showed their first film of workers leaving the photo factory.

From the standpoint of cameras, the Lumieres were behind Edison, who had already used perforated film and similar kinds of advancing and escapement mechanisms. But by creating a system of projecting motion pictures in theaters, the Lumieres developed a much larger vision for cinema.

On December 28, 1895, the Lumieres first exhibited ten short films in the Grand Cafe in Paris. The films were projected on a theatrical screen, and the subjects were all filmed

Figure 5.6 Lumiere Brothers—Auguste and Louis Lumiere were already running one of Europe's major photographic factories when they invented a system for filming and showing motion pictures. They called it the Cinematographe. Wikimedia Commons.

Figure 5.7 Cinematographe—The system designed in 1894 by the Lumiere Brothers had both a film camera and projector for theatrical performances. Wikimedia Commons.

outdoors or on location, in contrast to Edison's "Black Maria" indoor movies. Outdoor locations were possible because of the light-weight and portability of the Cinematographe system.

In fact, the system was so portable that the Lumieres were able to send seventeen photographic ambassadors around the world to shoot and show films. One of these was Gabriel Veyre, a pharmacy graduate from the University of Lyon, who traveled to Mexico, Latin America, Canada, Japan, and China in 1896–8.

Veyre not only took films, he also showed the films he took to audiences in the countries where the films were taken. He finished filming in Mexico on August 15, 1896, and the next evening, showed the films to an audience of 1,500 guests. "The applause and bravos make us foresee big potential," he wrote later. "Everyone exclaimed 'Muy bonito,' or 'How beautiful, how beautiful!' (Jacquier, 1996).

Figure 5.8 First ambassador of film—Gabriel Veyre was one of seventeen Lumiere company operators who traveled the world to shoot film and bring it back to France. Wikimedia Commons.

When they returned to Paris, Veyre and other operators showed their films at the 1900 Paris international exhibition on a 70-foot-wide screen to an audience of 20,000 people. For the first time it was possible to get a glimpse of life, in motion, around the world. It was a magnificent achievement that underscored the vitality and possibilities of documentary cinema in a way that Edison, for all his technical genius, never quite approached.

Alice Guy-Blaché, the First Director

Only a few months after the Lumieres premiered their ten short subjects in Paris, Alice Guy-Blaché produced one of the first fictional film narratives. Called *The Cabbage Fairy*, this 1896 film is only 50 seconds long, and it depicts, in the French theatrical *féerie* tradition, a woman finding babies growing under cabbage leaves.

Although predated by Louis Lumiere's short film *The Gardner*, *The Cabbage Fairy* was the first fictional film to be created by a full-time director at a film studio, which would give Guy-Blaché a claim to be the first director in cinema, perhaps in competition with George Méliès. In any event, Guy-Blaché produced hundreds of films while working as the head of production at the Gaumont in Paris. Among these were the 1906 *Life of Christ*, a major production for the era. She was an early pioneer in special effects such as masking, double exposure, and synchronized sound.

Guy-Blaché left France for the United States in 1907 and worked for Gaumont with her husband in New York, and in 1910 the couple formed Solax studios, where the motto was "Be Natural."

The studios produced hundreds of films, including *Falling Leaves*, based on a popular O. Henry short story, about a sick woman who thinks she will die when the last leaf falls from a tree. Later, when she is cured, she learns that the leaves had been re-attached and painted onto the tree by her sister. She also directed *Matrimony's Speed Limit*, which concerned a wealthy woman's attempt to allay her poor boyfriend's fears before their marriage. And she directed *Algie the Miner* about a gay man coping with life on the frontier. "She understood that telling a narrative story in film was going to require following the perspective of a single character," said Alison McMahan in a documentary film about Guy-Blaché. "And it took a good ten years for other film directors to figure out exactly what she had done" (Green 2013).

Figure 5.9 First film director—Alice Guy Blaché was put in charge of film development for Gaumont films in Paris in 1896. About ten years later, she set up one of the first film studios in New York. Wikimedia Commons.

Overall, Guy-Blaché produced more than 1,000 films in her two-decade career. Only a few of her films survive, and Guy-Blaché herself has long been neglected by film historians. Still, she was the first director, and well admired by Alfred Hitchcock, among others, for expanding narrative techniques in cinema.

Figure 5.10 Méliès' moon—A 1902 film by French director George Méliès, *A Trip to the Moon*, had memorable special effects and a plot based on Jules Verne's book by the same name. Wikimedia Commons.

3 The New Theater

3.1 The business emerges

Watching the earliest of the silent films is a lot like watching a theatrical performance or a magic lantern show. The camera, like the audience, is fixed, and the grammar and logic of film is barely visible.

For example, George Méliès' 1902 film, *A Trip to the Moon*, is known for its early special effects, such as in-camera effects, miniatures, and matte painting. But the film is also known for its lack of close-ups, medium shots, or complex transitions from one scene to the next, showing that the language of film was still being discovered. This is typical of the early stages of any media revolution as the new media starts by following the form of the old media. As we have seen, the first printed books were designed to look like hand-lettered manuscripts, and the first photographs were often taken in the style of portraiture or landscape paintings. Similarly, radio followed the theatrical variety show format in the early years, and the first web pages resembled the prefabricated formats of newspapers and Internet service providers.

The earliest movies featured visualizations of then-familiar themes, including the lives of the saints, religious figures, Jules Verne's science fiction stories, and some geographic and educational topics. But as the commercial prospects for film mushroomed, the topics became socially riskier—burglaries, train robberies, or a stolen kiss in a shoe store—and these themes were threatening to the old cultural elites.

The very fact that young people were congregating in dark, crowded theaters instead of churches or lecture halls was alarming to advocates of refined culture, especially in the older generation. Some who were alarmed, like social reformer Jane Addams, worried that the "corrupt" art of movies was replacing true drama, which was needed to satisfy the craving for a higher conception of life. If young people "forecast their rose colored future only in a house of dreams," Addams said, society would founder on a "skepticism of life's value" (Czitrom 1983). A more immediate cause for trouble was the carnival atmosphere and sexually suggestive songs and dances found in movie districts.

Thomas Edison thought he had the cure. He filed a patent lawsuit in 1908 against Biograph, Pathé, and other moviemakers, forcing them to work with his Vitagraph company in the US. "One result of this combination will be a cleaning up of the lower class of moving-picture shows," said a February 12 report in the *New York Times*. "The Edison interests are said to be determined to force the issue on this line." The result was the Motion Picture Patents Company, also known as the Edison Trust (trust in this case is synonymous with monopoly).

Apparently the increased control was not enough to satisfy moralists. The showdown came on Christmas Day, 1908, in New York. Reacting to testimony from religious groups that movies involved "profit from the corruption of the minds of children," the mayor revoked the licenses of 540 motion picture halls. Mayors in other cities quickly followed suit. In response, movie theater owners formed an association and sued the city. "This sort of treatment can go in Russia, but it can't go in this country," one of the theater owners said (*New York Times*, December 29, 1908).

By January 7, 1909, the moralists lost when the courts ruled that the mayor had no power to close all movie theaters, even though reasonable regulations over fire hazards and indecency could be imposed (*New York Times*, January 7, 1909).

3.2 Racism and film censorship

Another round in the early fight over film censorship involved the first African- American heavyweight boxing champion, Jack Johnson. In a well-publicized July 1910 match, Johnson won the title, beating James Jeffries, a white boxer who had been styled as the "great white hope." Word of a black man's victory led to rioting in fifty US cities and an estimated 20 deaths. The film's ideological significance alarmed racists in Congress who passed a federal ban on interstate sales of all boxing films in 1912 (Berry and Berry 2007; Streible 2008). Historian Robert Niemi called it an "exceedingly ugly episode in the appalling annals of American racial bigotry" (Niemi 2006).

Another controversy blew up over films about prostitution a few years later. Filmmakers used the pretext of a 1912 report on vice in New York to show supposedly moralistic films depicting the evils of the "white slave trade." These "vice films" outraged moralists in the media. Films like *Damaged Goods*, *The House of Bondage*, and *Guilty Man* "will pour oil upon the flames of vice," the *New York Times* editorialized on November 4, 1913.

The contrast, if not hypocrisy, is interesting. When newspaper publishers used the same sensationalistic tactics a generation before, they were well rewarded. William T. Stead, who published London's *Pall Mall Gazette*, made an enormous profit exposing the "virtual slave trade" of London in 1883, treating the subject as a moral lesson but providing plenty of salacious detail on the side. Pulitzer and Hearst also used the cloak of morality to present shocking tales of vice and intrigue.

But film was new, and as a New York judge said in 1913, "tends to deprave the morals of those whose minds are open to such influences" (*New York Times*, December 29, 1913).

Independent filmmakers insisted that they were fighting for freedom of expression and wondered why the newspapers were not on their side. Newspaper editorials cast the issue in terms of films being "withdrawn" rather than "censored," and some of the worst offenders by the standards of the day were retired by the Edison Trust's national censorship board.

Figure 5.11 Winning boxer—US boxing champion John Jackson's victories in the ring set off a string of race riots. The official reaction was to censor boxing films in 1912 to prevent more riots. Wikimedia Commons.

Independent film companies, especially Solax Co. and the founders of Universal, Paramount, and Twentieth Century Fox studios, never accepted the Edison Trust's control. They moved away from the East coast to California, where mild weather and distance from the Edison Company allowed the film industry room for creative expansion. Then, too, the dominance of European films such as Méliès, Gaumont, and Pathé ended abruptly with the outbreak of World War I in 1914.

The emerging film industry once again went to the courts for protection. In 1915, independent producers, contending that Edison's MPPC was an illegal monopoly, won a Supreme Court decision in *United States v. Motion Picture Patents Company*.

That same year, the court also opened the door for censorship in *Mutual Film v. Industrial Commission of Ohio* by ruling that films are not protected by the First Amendment. States were then free to set standards and film censorship boards of their own, and many did. A week before the decision, director D. W. Griffith inserted a "Plea for the art of the motion picture" in his film *Birth of a Nation*:

> We do not fear censorship, for we have no wish to offend with improprieties or obscenities, but we do demand, as a right, the liberty to show the dark side of wrong, that we may illuminate the bright side of virtue—the same liberty that is conceded to the art of the written word—that art to which we owe the Bible and the works of Shakespeare.

Fearing a patchwork of state censorship boards, and reacting to a series of Hollywood scandals sensationalized by the Hearst newspapers, the film industry formed the Motion

Pictures Production and Distributors Association in 1922 (which became the Motion Picture Association of America in 1945). Headed by Will H. Hays, the MPAA fought both federal proposals for film censorship and critics within the movie industry who charged that it was a way to establish a "complete monopoly" of major film producers over independent theater owners ("Theater Owners Open War on Hays," *New York Times*, May 12, 1925). This fight over control of theaters began an antitrust lawsuit that was finally settled in the *United States v. Paramount* case two decades later.

The MPAA code said, "No picture shall be produced that will lower the moral standards of those who see it." Under the code, criminals could never win, and nudity, steamy sex scenes, and homosexuality were all strictly banned. The code survived numerous court challenges until the 1960s, then changed to a rating system (G, PG, PG-13, R, and NC-17) that is still administered by the MPAA. As a product of its times, the code did not prohibit narratives encouraging racism or anti-Semitism that came to be considered far more immoral in the later twentieth century.

The code also made it more difficult for independent filmmakers to compete against the big studios, and it contributed to the Hollywood domination of international cinema well into the twenty-first century. Critics contend that a secretive private ratings system, without an open appeals process, still amounts to a form of censorship. (For example, see the 2006 documentary *This Film Is Not Yet Rated.*)

4 The Silent Film Era

Now freed from the hobbles of Edison's monopoly and with the horrifying experience of World War I in the past, world cinema embarked on an era of innovation and development. Four early films that set the pace were those by D. W. Griffith, Lois Weber, Charlie Chaplin, and Sergei Eisenstein.

4.1 D. W. Griffith: *Birth of a Nation*

The most innovative and controversial film of the silent era was D. W. Griffith's *Birth of a Nation* (1915), a film that told the story of families torn apart by the US Civil War. The movie featured broad panoramic views of battles and full command of the now emerging logic of cinema. The plot was based on Thomas Dixon's book *The Clansmen*, which romanticized the slavery-era antebellum South and depicted Reconstruction-era African-Americans in the worst possible light as drunkards, rapists, and murderers. They were only thwarted from their evil designs when a heroic white vigilante group, the Ku Klux Klan, rode out to oppose them.

Critics were outraged, some saying the film was "unfair and vicious" (*Outlook*, 1915). Riots broke out at theaters in major cities (*Washington Post,* April 18, 1915). Performances were shut down in eight states, and many others were picketed by the National Association for Colored People.

Then-president Woodrow Wilson watched the film at a White House performance and said "It is like writing history with lightning. And my only regret is that it is all so terribly

Figure 5.12 and **Figure 5.13** Racism on film—One of the least admired films of all time was D. W. Griffith's *Birth of a Nation,* depicting post-Civil War Southern women as victims of African-Americans who needed to be rescued by secret terrorist societies like the Ku Klux Klan. A wave of violence against African-Americans followed the release of the film in 1915. The National Association for the Advancement of Colored People (NAACP) mounted numerous and strenuous protests about the message the film conveyed. Library of Congress.

true." Many versions of the film carried this remark in the opening credits. Although Wilson later denied the remark, film critic Roger Ebert said, "My guess is that Wilson said something like it in private, and found it prudent to deny when progressive editorialists attacked the film" (Ebert 2003).

The romantic view of the American South, also expressed in later movies like *Gone With the Wind,* is called the Dunning historical school. Wilson's own historical work was partly in this category. The Dunning school was a defensive, monocultural, one-sided and pro-Southern perspective that reanimated virulent racism in America and encouraged a culture of lynchings and intolerance. As such, it also demonstrated the destructive power of historical myths amplified by media.

Griffith was aware that his film had done more damage than intended, and in 1916 made *Intolerance,* a film showing the damage that intolerance can do. Although depicting the intolerance of white lower-class people, it omitted a long list of injustices perpetrated by the Ku Klux Klan and other groups that he had glorified in 1915.

4.2 Lois Weber: *The Blot*

Far less recognized than D. W. Griffith, but equally talented, was Lois Weber (1879–1939), another of the early American directors with a unique creative vision.

She started out as an evangelistic singer and musician, but started acting with Alice Guy-Blache's Gaumont studios in New York. After appearing in several movies, she wrote a film called *Hypocrites,* directed by Guy-Blaché, and *A Heroine of '76,* which she co-directed with her husband Phillips Smalley and Edwin S. Porter (who directed the famed *Great Train Robbery*).

By 1912, Weber and Smalley had all taken over the small New York studios of Rex Motion Picture Company, which was merged with others into Universal films. They moved to Hollywood and made popular films using innovative techniques. In 1913, Weber produced *The Jew's Christmas*, telling the story of a rabbi's daughter who marries a Gentile man and is ostracized. Twelve years later, the rabbi meets an impoverished small child who turns out to be his granddaughter. The message of the film is to fight anti-Semitism with the idea that love is stronger than any religion or ideology.

Figure 5.14 *The Blot*—US director Lois Weber made hundreds of films but received little credit later in life. One film, *The Blot*, involved romance across the classes. Wikimedia Commons.

By 1917, with dozens of films completed, Weber began her own production company and was the only woman in the Motion Picture Directors Association. She was influenced by the trial and imprisonment of Margaret Sanger for indecently advocating scientific birth control, and produced that year's top money-maker for Universal, *Where Are My Children?*

One of the best films she produced during this era was a 1921 masterpiece, *The Blot*. The story follows the wife of a college professor whose meager income puts the family on a near-starvation diet. When the couple's daughter becomes sick, the professor's wife steals a chicken. A rich suitor for the daughter, who is also the callow son of the college president, rescues the professor's family. He also tells his dad that the paltry salaries paid to college professors are a "blot on the present day civilization."

In her day, Weber was widely considered to be the leading female director in Hollywood. Yet, as Hollywood changed in the 1920s, Weber's jobs involved smaller films, less income, and less independence. She directed her last of 135 films in 1933 and died five years later.

4.3 Charlie Chaplin: *The Immigrant*

The most famous icon of the silent era was Charlie Chaplin, whose "tramp" delighted audiences worldwide with a down-at-heel character who was refined but bewildered. He said he created the character for film producer Mack Sennett when he was asked to put on a comic costume for a 1914 film:

> I had no idea what makeup to put on ... However, on the way to the wardrobe I thought I would dress in baggy pants, big shoes, a cane and a derby hat. I wanted everything to be a contradiction ... I had no idea of the character. But the moment I was dressed, the clothes

> and the makeup made me feel the person he was. I began to know him, and by the time I walked on stage, he was fully born. (Chaplin 1964)

By 1916, Chaplin had become one of the first great stars of the Silent Era, signing a contract with Mutual Films for over half a million dollars. Soon he owned his own studios, producing classic silent films like *The Gold Rush* and *The Kid*. Chaplin would often begin filming with only the barest outlines of a concept and no written script (Brownlow 1983).

His film *The Immigrants* began as a comedy sketch about restaurant waiters, but ended as a film about a family's difficult journey across the Atlantic, through US immigration and a reunion in the restaurant. At one point, Chaplin gives a US immigration official a sneaky kick in the pants and then whistles innocently as the official looks in vain for the culprit. The scene expressed Chaplin's own frustrations with the US government, and his impoverished youth. It also endeared him to a generation of downtrodden workers. "The Immigrant touched me more than any other film I made," Chaplin said (Chaplin 1974).

Some of Chaplin's other work, such as *Modern Times*, showed frustration with the dehumanizing pace of modernization. His humane approach is also seen in the way he made fun of the stuffy and overwrought high culture in sketches like "Dance of the Cleaning Ladies."

Chaplin was also an innovator in business, founding United Artists in 1919 along with D. W. Griffith, Mary Pickford, and Douglas Fairbanks. The distribution company provided an important alternative to the studio system, through which a few executives at five big studios dominated the industry in its early years. By the late 1940s, United Artists pioneered the backing of independent films—a business model that eventually toppled the big studios (Balio 1987).

Figure 5.15 *The Immigrant*—This 1917 Charlie Chaplin film began as a comedy sketch about restaurant waiters, but turned into an allegory about the American experience. Wikimedia Commons.

Charlie Chaplin, Superstar

Chaplin drew a crowd wherever he went, such as this plea for Liberty Bonds in Washington, DC, in 1917. Charlie Chaplin's celebrity reached such heights that he could set off near-riots by his mere presence. Historian Corey Ross described a visit to Berlin in 1931 in which frenzied crowds surrounded the hotel and besieged the train station when he arrived. Left wing newspapers of the day celebrated the working-class genius. Conservative newspapers said it was inappropriate that he should be so highly celebrated. And Nazi papers said they were disgusted by the reception given to the "Jewish film clown," even though Chaplin was not Jewish; when asked, he would respond, "I do not have that honor" (Schickel 2006).

The episode shows the rising power of media and the way political parties started defining themselves in relation to a film star, not the other way around. "Chaplin's trip to Berlin ... highlights not only the vital importance of the media to social and cultural life in the 1930s, but also their political impact, the challenge they posed to traditional values, their transcendence of social and national boundaries, and the complex relationship between cultural producers and their audiences" (Ross 2008).

Figure 5.17 Chaplin draws a crowd. US National Archives & Records Administration.

4.4 Sergei Eisenstein: *Battleship Potemkin*

By the 1920s cinema had begun to emerge as the dominant art form of the age as directors discovered that cinema has its own language and logic. One of the most significant new directors in the 1920s was Sergei Eisenstein (1898–1948), a Russian whose 1925 film, *Battleship Potemkin*, glorified an early episode in the Russian Revolution.

Potemkin was among the first films to use montage, which is a compilation of shots, including extreme close-ups and details, to convey a strong overall impression. The montage of the Odessa Steps in *Potemkin* is considered must-viewing for students of film history and production. In the montage, Eisenstein would continue the motion of different objects from one shot into the next, or punctuate the visual impression of a shot with a different shot, or, in later films, music written specifically to accompany the montage.

Eisenstein led a challenging life; first as a Soviet film director, whose credits also included a 1927 film version of John Reed's book *Ten Days that Shook the World* (described in Chapter 3). Between 1928 and 1933 he traveled through Europe and the US, and collaborated with muckraker Upton Sinclair on a film about the Mexican Revolution. Artists Diego Rivera and Frida Kahlo were also involved.

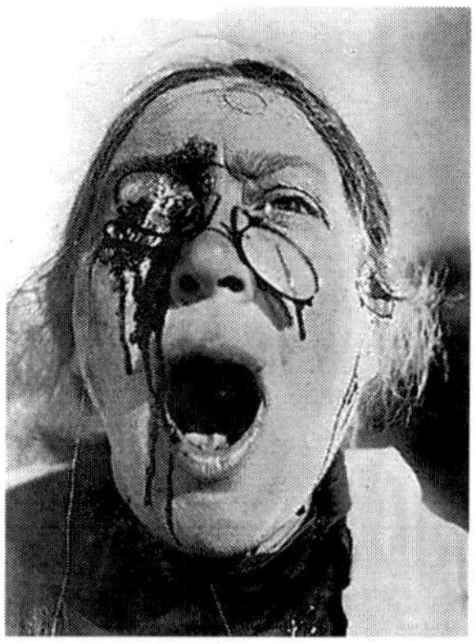

Figure 5.16 Bullets in Odessa—The nurse in Sergei Eisenstein's famous 1925 *Battleship Potemkin* film is shot during the famous Odessa Steps sequence. Wikimedia Commons.

Eisenstein returned to the Soviet Union at a time of turmoil, Communist party purges, and ideological violence. Although he managed to avoid the wrath of dictator Joseph Stalin, like other artists under the Russian thumb at the time, Eisenstein's every move was scrutinized for ideological deviance.

In 1937, Eisenstein was allowed to make *Alexander Nevsky*, a film about the thirteenth-century war between the Teutonic knights of Germany and Russia. With brilliant music by Russian composer Sergei Prokofiev, the film was a critical hit, and was especially welcomed by the Kremlin within the political context of rising tensions between Communist Russia and Nazi Germany. Eisenstein continued making films and teaching, but his health was failing. After completing most of his *Ivan the Terrible* trilogy, he died in 1948.

4.5 Expressionism and experimental film

In the years following the devastating aftermath of World War I, German artists and filmmakers moved away from traditional historical, romantic, and adventure themes and began pursuing darker topics of crime, madness, and betrayal (MOMA 2015).

Members of this artistic movement embraced new and dramatically different styles of film production, including sets with bizarre jarring angles and painted shadows that contradicted the films lighting. Among leading examples of Expressionist films are Robert Wiene's *Cabinet of Dr. Caligari* (1921), a dream about an insane doctor, and F. W. Murnau's *Nosferatu*, a 1922 adaptation of the Dracula story.

Fritz Lang's *Metropolis* (1927) was one of the most sophisticated films from the Expressionist movement, using expensive matts and models to give the impression of a giant city in the year 2000, where clashes are taking place between striking workers and an authoritarian industrialist. The industrialist builds a robot to substitute for a young woman who has inspired the workers. In end, the industrialist's son and the young woman symbolically unify workers and capital on the steps of a cathedral.

Figure 5.18 *Cabinet of Dr. Caligari*—One of the leading films of the German expressionist movement, the 1920 film explored the issue of how to define sanity in an insane world. Wikimedia Commons.

German Expressionism is significant in film history because it had a major influence on mainstream cinema. Famed British director Alfred Hitchcock, for example, worked on films for British companies in Germany during the 1920s, met some of the other directors (Murnau, for instance), and absorbed some of the Expressionist techniques. Murnau and others migrated to Hollywood, first for better opportunities, and later, in the 1930s, to avoid Nazi oppression. These directors made or influenced the style of cinematic genres such as horror (*Phantom of the Opera*, *Dracula*) and film noir (*Citizen Kane*, *Maltese Falcon*).

Because the language of cinema had not been well developed at this point, all kinds of other film experiments flourished in this era. One of the most interesting was *Man with a Movie Camera* (1929) by Dziga Vertov, a montage of urban life in the Russian cities of Kiev, Kharkov, Moscow, and Odessa. Another experimental film that same year was American artist Ralph Steiner's short film *H2O*, a cinematic "tone poem" about flowing water. And, also in 1929, in Spain, director Luis Bunuel made *Un Chien Andalou*, a surrealistic film starring Salvador Dali and following a kind of free-association dream logic.

5 End of the Silent Film Era

Hollywood moguls believed that they had reached the pinnacle by the mid-1920s and saw no reason to change things. When Jack Warner agreed to spend $10,000 to build a sound stage in 1927, those who knew him got construction underway within minutes. When he changed his mind a few hours later, he found that construction was already too advanced to stop.

The new sound stage used Vitaphone equipment, developed over the previous years by AT&T. It was used for a film about a vaudeville entertainer, and despite low box-office expectations, *The Jazz Singer*, starring Al Jolson, turned out to be a major hit. Although Jolson's blackface act is stereotypical and offensive by modern standards, it was meant to be clownish and sentimental at the time.

The combination of sound and film changed everything, said film historian Scott Eyman. "It changed how movies were made, of course, but more importantly, it changed what movies were." Where silent film demanded participation in the experience, talking films were immersive but stylistically shallow. "Talkies were not an evolution, but a mutation, a different art form entirely; as a result, an art form was eliminated and hundreds of careers were extinguished" (Eyman 1997).

Early sound film technology limited camera movement and actors gestures, and often forced shooting indoors. "Cinema became far less cinematic," said Mark Cousins in his epic *Story of Film*. The emphasis on flexibility in studio work meant more generic lighting and shot composition (Cousins 2011). Some of the narrative sweep of silent films was lost for the time being.

Figure 5.19 First "talkie"—Al Jolson's routine in *The Jazz Singer* was a cinematic hit in 1927 because audiences could hear him sing. The blackface routine is offensive by today's standards but was meant to be clownish at the time. Library of Congress.

Talking pictures produced new stars in the late 1920s. These included Walt Disney's Mickey Mouse, whose debut in the first fully-synchronized sound cartoon made Disney the nation's leading animator. And sound led to fame for new directors like Alfred Hitchcock, whose first sound film, *Blackmail*, was also an enormous hit with audiences.

The last major silent film, *Modern Times* by Charlie Chaplin, was originally written as a "talkie," but Chaplin balked, fearing that his tramp character would hardly seem as romantic or wistful. Although *Modern Times* was a big hit in 1936, the motion picture audience had come to expect music and dialogue, and Chaplin's film was seen as the last of the silent era.

6 Golden Age of Cinema

By the 1930s, cinema was one of the most visible businesses in America, and most people were going out to movie theaters at least once a week. With better sound and film technology emerging, the industry was able to pursue new directions, entering a golden age of creativity and exploration. Although partly fettered by censorship, the American film industry epitomized glamour and attracted audiences with strong narratives, romantic characters, and hair-raising exploits.

Hollywood was the incubator for six primary genres in the 1930s, according to historian Mark Cousins: comedies, musicals, cartoons, horror films, gangster films, and, most American of all, the western.

Products of the Golden Age include a long list of movies that are now seen as classics: *The Wizard of Oz, Stagecoach, Mr. Smith Goes to Washington, Casablanca, It's a Wonderful Life, It Happened One Night, King Kong, Citizen Kane, Some Like It Hot, All About Eve, The Cocoanuts, Duck Soup, Singin' in the Rain,* and many more.

At the time, Hollywood was operating like a factory, and the "studio system" churned out thousands of films, permanently employing tens of thousands of actors, extras, and technicians. The studio system offered stable incomes and long-term contracts, and as a result, studios like Paramount (formed in 1912), Columbia Pictures (1920), Warner Brothers (1923), Metro-Goldwyn-Mayer (1924), RKO Pictures (1928), and Twentieth Century Fox (1935) were able to draw talent from all over the nation and the world.

The studio system provided stability but it had many faults as well. Actors and directors who did not comply with the demands of studio executives found that their stars could fall as quickly as rise. Theaters that were owned by individual studios did not serve audience interests as they promoted their lower grade films along with the hits. Independent theaters were often forced to sign "block booking" contracts that guaranteed screens for unpopular films along with the popular ones. A lawsuit started in 1938 over block booking reached the US Supreme Court as *United States v. Paramount Pictures, Inc.* in 1948. The court's order to break up the link between theaters and film studios under antitrust law was the beginning of the end for the studio system.

Many of the same genres once explored in silent films were repeated and more fully explored in the Golden Age. Westerns, costume dramas, musicals, comedies, cartoons, and horror films all found enthusiastic audiences. New genres, like "film noir," involving hard-bitten but soft-hearted detectives, such as Humphrey Bogart in *The Maltese Falcon,* found niche audiences before attaining cult-like status for later generations.

It's interesting that the most widely discussed film of the Golden Age was produced not only through the studio system, but also in spite of it. *Citizen Kane,* voted the most influential film of the twentieth century by the American Film Institute, was produced and directed for RKO Pictures in 1941 by Orson Welles, a brash and volatile radio and theater director famed for scaring American radio listeners with his *War of the Worlds* broadcast

Figure 5.20 *Citizen Kane*—A parody of the life of William Randolph Hearst by Orson Welles, *Citizen Kane* used innovative techniques that were decades ahead of the times. Hearst hated the movie and forced RKO to retire it to the vaults, where it remained until rediscovered in the 1960s. In the American Film Institute's top 100 movies of all time, *Kane* is number one. Wikimedia Commons.

Chaos on the Set

What it was like when the Marx Brothers filmed The Cocoanuts *in 1929*

"Our first picture *Cocoanuts* was shot in New York," Harpo Marx said in a 1974 book, *Harpo Speaks*. He continued

Figure 5.21 Marx Brothers—Chico, Harpo, Groucho, and Zeppo Marx, 1931. Library of Congress.

> Shot was just the word for it. All they did was point the camera at us while we ran through our old stage version ... There were many long delays in the shooting, due mostly to the unexcused absences of Chico from the set. Since nobody had bought tickets to watch him, Chico figured there was nobody to squawk when he ducked out to consult with his bookie or play a few hands of pinochle. Trouble was, Chico would forget to come back if the action was good. Then Groucho, Zeppo and I would wander off looking for him. Sometimes Chico would return while we were gone, and he'd say the hell with it—if that's all we cared, he'd take the rest of the day off too.

When all four of the Marx brothers were on the set at the same time, and the camera got rolling, the directors would start laughing and ruin the scene. So the producer put the directors in a glass booth and set up four jail cells for the actors. The cell labeled "Chico" even had its own phone.

> Now Chico could call his bookie any time he felt like it, without bringing production to a standstill. Between takes, we were locked behind bars and the directors were let out of the booth. When the shooting resumed, the directors were put back in their glass cage and the stars were let out of their jail cells. Too bad they didn't film the filming of *Cocoanuts*. It would have been a lot funnier than the movie was.

of 1938. Welles had never before produced or directed a film in his life, but he threw all of his genius into making the movie.

Citizen Kane is about the search for the identity of a newspaper tycoon who used his family wealth to build a powerful empire, promote his mistress, and crush his opponents. The film was intended to be a biting parody of the life of William Randolph Hearst, a powerful newspaper publisher who did in fact use his newspapers to promote his mistress and crush his opponents. Hearst saw the movie as a frontal assault on his reputation, and he did everything in his power to wreck the emerging career of Orson Welles. RKO "retired" the film after a few weeks, and both Welles and Hearst ended up losing, according to an excellent documentary, *The Battle Over Citizen Kane*.

Another Golden Age film worth a special mention is *The Grapes of Wrath*, starring Henry Fonda as a farmer who takes his family from the "dust bowl" of Oklahoma to the promised land of California. Based on the novel by John Steinbeck, the film used a style of cinematography based closely on the Depression era photography of Dorothea Lange, especially her *Migrant Mother* series. Even the few critics who scoffed at the Depression-era social message conceded that the film transcended the issues of the time with an enduring human story.

6.1 A Global Golden Age

Film historians with a more international perspective believe that it is a mistake to consider the 1930s as the golden age of Hollywood, rather than as a golden age of world cinema. The emergence of British cinema, with Hitchcock's *39 Steps* (1935) and *The Lady Vanishes* (1938), and French cinema, with Jean Renoir's *Grand Illusion* (1937) and *Rules of the Game* (1939), are as significant as any Hollywood production of the era.

So, too, was French director Marcel Carne's beautiful and haunting *Shadows on a Pier* (*Quai des Bromes*) (1938), although it was said to be so defeatist that someone accused Carne of helping France lose the opening battles of World War II. Carne replied: "You'd blame a storm on a barometer" (Cousins 2011).

The 1930s marked the beginning of the golden age of Mexican cinema with Ferdanando de Fuentes' *Alla en el Rancho Grande* (1936) involving a conflicted love triangle, and the unfinished Sergei Eisenstein film of 1930, *¡Que viva México!*

At the same time, China was going through its own "golden age" with films like *The Goddess* (a.k.a. *Shen Nu*, 1934), written and directed by Wu Yonggang and starring Ruan Ling-Yu. It is a story about a prostitute (known as a "goddess" in slang at the time) who is trying to protect her son (Christian 2006). The film is known for a heartbreaking plot and exquisite montages of pre-war Shanghai at night. Another from the era is *Classic for Girls* (1934), a melodrama describing the hard life of a young Shanghai woman. The *Fate of Graduates* (also known as *Plunder of Peach and Plum*, 1934) is another describing attempts by educated people to reform a corrupt system.

In other countries, the "golden age" of cinema took place following World War II. In Japan, for instance, the 1950s are called the "golden age," and three films stand out in world cinema history: *Rashomon*, *Tokyo Story*, and *The Seven Samurai* (1950, 1953, 1954).

Italian cinema also flourished after WWII in its golden neorealism period, with films such as Roberto Rossellini's *Open City* (1945), and Federico Fellini's *La Strada* (1954) and Vittorio De Sica's *Bicycle Thieves* (1948), along with De Sica's *Two Women* (1960), for which Sophia Loren won an Oscar for Best Actress. All used low-budget location shots and non-professional actors to depict the everyday struggle for survival.

Similarly, the golden age for "Bollywood" —India's cinema—is considered to be the 1940s and 1950s, after Indian independence from Britain. The era started on a high note with a Cannes Festival Best Film award for the social realist film *Neecha Nagar* (*Lowly City*, 1946), a story about the gulf between rich and poor featuring sitar music by Ravi Shankar. Among the best known directors of the era was Guru Dutt, with two movies in the *Time* magazine top 100: *Pyaasa* (*Thirsty*, 1957), about a poet and a prostitute, and *Kaagaz Ke Phool* (*Paper Flowers*, 1959), about a director who falls in love with the leading lady.

7 Animation and the Cinema

Perhaps the earliest surviving stop-motion animation was a call to support British troops in the Boer War of 1899. Made by Arthur Melbourne Cooper, the animated short film showed matchsticks writing an appeal on a black wall. Cooper was a decade ahead of animation pioneers in the United States, where, for example, Windsor McCay's animated cartoon *Gertie the Dinosaur* debuted in 1914. McCay had to redraw every background scene in every frame of the five-minute cartoon—a tedious process that made the film look jittery.

Cel animation was a way to get around the jitters. Invented at the John Bray studios in 1914, celluloid ("cel") animation allowed backgrounds to remain stable while moving characters were inked on transparent sheets. Another innovation was the introduction of cartoon "stars" like Felix the Cat by Otto Mesmer and Mickey Mouse by Walt Disney.

The innovation that catapulted Disney to success was the marriage of sound with animation in 1928. Only a year after *The Jazz Singer* amazed audiences with synchronized dialogue and music, Disney produced a Mickey Mouse cartoon called *Steamboat Willie*, with tightly synchronized sound effects and orchestrated background music. The cartoon was a takeoff on Buster Keaton's silent classic, *Steamboat Bill*, released earlier that year.

Short animated films preceded a main feature movie at the time, but Disney achieved another first with the first feature-length animation, *Snow White and the Seven Dwarfs*, released in 1938. The cartoon used naturalistic figure drawing (as opposed to the unrealistic "rubber hose" approach used in other cartoons). It also was the first to use full color. Despite early doubters (even Disney's wife Lillian said no one would ever pay to see 'a dwarf picture'), the film premiered to wildly enthusiastic audiences. *Snow White* was followed by animation classics like *Pinocchio* in 1940, *Dumbo* in 1941, *Bambi*, *Cinderella*, and many others.

Disney was by far the most successful, in both artistic and commercial terms. Still, the Disney studio's factory approach shows "the studio system's best and worst effects on the development of animation as an art form," said Michael Crandol in his *History of Animation*, since many talented animators were eclipsed by Walt Disney himself (Crandol 2010). Attempts to increase recognition and salary at the Disney studios were ignored and, in the animated film *Dumbo*, parodied by a parade of drunken clowns singing "Oh, we're gonna ask the big boss for a raise." Many of Disney's talented animators went on to create their own cartoons or found their own studios: Ub Iwerks left Disney during the 1930s to create Flip the Frog and Porky Pig; Hugh Harman and Rudy Ising went on to create Loony Tunes for MGM in the 1930s; Don Bluth left the Disney studios in 1979 to create *The Secret of Nimh* (1982), *An American Tale* (1986), and *The Land Before Time* (1988), among others.

Figure 5.22 Cartoon King—Walt Disney founded a studio that produced thousands of cartoon shorts and features, including the first full-length animation, *Snow White and the Seven Dwarfs*, in 1938. Library of Congress.

Hugh Harman's 1939 animated short, *Peace on Earth*, was another break from the Disney tradition of animation. The cartoon was a serious plea for peace on the eve of World War II. It depicted never-ending wars and the last people on earth killing each other, followed by animals rebuilding society using the helmets of the soldiers. The cartoon was nominated for an Academy Award—and the Nobel Peace Prize. Other animators departed from Disney's naturalistic storytelling techniques to create physics-defying characters. Tex Avery, for instance, created Red Hot Riding Hood in 1943, in which a wolf's mouth is seen dropping down to its feet, while its eyes bulge out and its tongue unrolls. "That is the most wonderfully liberating spectacle," said Monty Python animator Terry Gilliam in a review of his ten favorite animations (Gilliam 2001).

Another wave of animation began in the 1940s in Japan with the release of Osamu Tezuka's *Astro Boy*, the first anime cartoon. Japanese animators like Hayao Miyazaki, inspired by Tezuka and Disney, developed dozens of popular cartoons such as *My Neighbor Totoro* (1988) and *Princess Mononoke* (1997).

8 Propaganda Films

The World War II era might be considered the "golden age" of propaganda films. While silent films (such as the 1915 US film *Birth of a Nation* and the 1925 Russian film *Battleship Potemkin*) could be effective in advancing reactionary or revolutionary agendas, sound-on-film could be more effectively used to play on emotions and deceive audiences.

A classic of the propaganda genre is Leni Riefenstahl's *Triumph of the Will*, made to glorify the Nazi party in 1935 and celebrate Germany's return to power after its defeat in World War I. Using long tracking shots, triumphal music, and masterful montage, the film depicted the 1934 Nazi party rally at Nuremburg. Given the Nazi control of all German media at the time, *Triumph of the Will* was the only image the German people had of the Nazi party, and Riefenstahl's film helped Hitler consolidate power in the years before World War II.

Riefenstahl later claimed that she had no choice in making the film, and that she had no knowledge of Nazi concentration camps. She also claimed that artists should not be held responsible for the political problems their art causes. She spent several years in detention after the war but was never convicted of war crimes.

"Leni Riefenstahl is a monster," the *New Republic* (1994) said, mincing no words in reviewing a documentary about her life. We can admire her work, the magazine said, in the same way that we admire Soviet masterworks of film "for their art despite the heavy irony of their now blood-drenched enthusiasm."

Even more monstrous was the 1940 Nazi propaganda film *The Eternal Jew*, a violently anti-Semitic pseudo-documentary that provoked racial hatred in Germany with its comparisons of Jews to rats and other vermin. It was directed by Fritz Hippler, head of the film department in the Nazi government. "If one compares the directness and intensity of

Figure 5.23 Glorifying evil—Leni Riefenstahl's *Triumph of the Will* is a feature-length depiction of the 1934 Nazi party celebrations in Nuremberg, Germany. It is considered a classic in technique but monstrous in its social impact. Riefenstahl denied that she was anything but naïve for having given so much support to the Nazis, but her three years of imprisonment demonstrated a link between social responsibility and artistic creations. Library of Congress.

the effect that the various means of propaganda have on the great masses," he said, "film is without question the most powerful" (Hippler 1937). After the fall of the Nazis in 1945, Hippler was sentenced to two years in prison for his propaganda work against Jewish people. Months before his death in 2002, he added this postscript to his life: "If it were possible to annul everything [about the film] I would. Terrible things happened and I had many sleepless nights because of this."

By depicting Jewish people as subhuman, Nazi cinematographers like Hippler and Riefenstahl opened the floodgates of barbarism and encouraged the Holocaust. Similar dehumanization through media has paved the way for genocide at other times in history, most recently in Rwanda and Bosnia in the 1990s, explaining, perhaps, why *The Eternal Jew* is still banned in Europe.

8.1 Fighting fascism with film

Counter-propaganda involved both comedy and serious documentary work in the US and Britain during the time of World War II. In 1940, Charlie Chaplin's film *The Great Dictator* used biting sarcasm and hilarious slapstick to attack the cruelty of the Nazi regime. At one point, dictator Adenoid Hinkle of Tomania carelessly tosses a balloon globe into the air, only to have it pop at the end. Hinkle's lookalike, a Jewish barber, is mistaken as the dictator and gives a speech at the end that reverses fascist ideology. "We are coming out of the darkness into the light," Chaplin's character says at the end of the film. "We are coming into a new world, a kindlier world, where men will rise above their hate, their greed and brutality."

Chaplin's moral courage in satirizing Hitler and defending Jewish people should not be underestimated, since few people in 1940 would have predicted the end of Nazi rule only five years later. Film critics have seen *The Great Dictator* as Chaplin's way of symbolically reclaiming the Little Tramp's moustache from Hitler, but it was far more than that. His was a small and courageous voice standing up at a time when Hollywood was shackled by fear, isolationism, and the Hays Code, which supposedly discouraged political messages in films and required that the "people and history of other nations ... be presented fairly" (Herschthal 2008).

Other comedies were also heavy-handed and perhaps equally courageous. The Three Stooges, for instance, released a film called *You Nazty Spy* lampooning events in "Moronia." The film was released nine months ahead of Chaplin's *Great Dictator*, in January of 1940. Two of the actors, Moe Howard and Larry Fine, said that *You Nazty Spy* was their favorite.

Disney also released a cartoon called *Der Fuehrer's Face* in 1943 that was circulated for a limited time during the war. Another set of cartoons, produced by Warner Brothers between 1943 and 1945, showed "Private Snafu" doing everything wrong—and helping educate soldiers and sailors about how to handle the challenges they faced.

The most significant American documentary of the era was *Why We Fight*, first released in 1942 and directed by Frank Capra, who was chosen by the War Department because, they said, the director of *Mr. Smith Goes to Washington* and *You Can't Take It With You* understood American ideals. Capra said he was challenged by Leni Riefenstahl's propaganda films and tried to create a stylistic as well as ideological alternative. Rather than refute enemy claims, Capra worked with writers to craft a positive message. The documentary was intended as a substitute for morale-building lectures by army officers, but it became emblematic of the beliefs of the nation. Although loaded with plodding patriotic music and gimmicky devices, the film lived up to Capra's ambition to combat Nazi propaganda and help win "a fight between a slave world and a free world." The film was thought so important that President Franklin Roosevelt ordered it released to the general public.

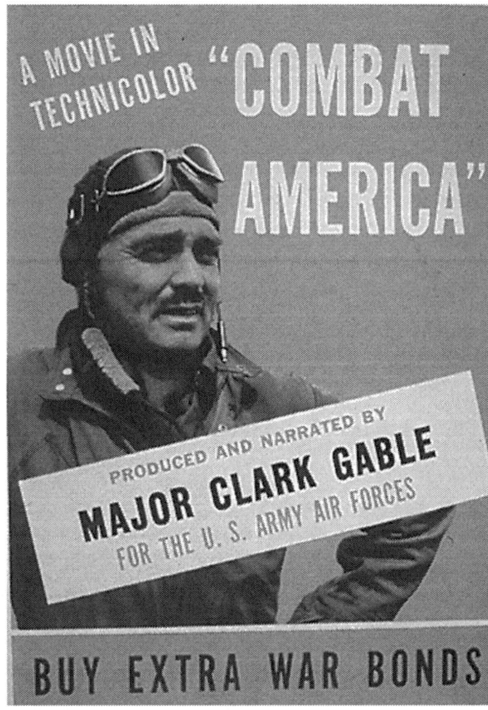

Figure 5.24 Giving a damn—Unlike John Wayne, Ronald Reagan, and other WWII-era actors, Clark Gable went into real combat and risked his life, then made training films for pilots. US National Archives and Records Administration.

Films made for entertainment during World War II usually also had a moral about the war. *Mrs. Miniver*, produced in 1942, depicted an ordinary British family caught up in the Dunkirk evacuation and other war scenes. It concluded with a sermon in a bombed-out church emphasizing the novelty of a "people's war," that involved everyone. British Prime Minister Winston Churchill said the film was "more powerful to the war effort than the combined work of six military divisions" (Parish and Mark 1981).

Also significant as a war film was *Casablanca*, a 1942 film featuring Humphrey Bogart who encounters his lost love (Ingrid Bergman) fleeing the Nazi occupation of France to North Africa in the hope of finding passage to the United States. In one stirring scene, a group of Nazi officers try to sing "Die Wacht am Rhein," a patriotic German song. In response, a French patriot asks the house band to play "La Marseillaise," the French national anthem. It's one reason—and there are many others—why film critic Roger Ebert called *Casablanca* the best-loved film in cinema history (Ebert 1996).

Despite fears that propaganda films like *Why We Fight* would make post-war Americans unwilling to be gracious in victory, the line-up of films of the late 1940s and early 1950s emphasized light entertainment. But there were also reconciliation stories about people caught up in the war years, such as *It's a Wonderful Life* by Frank Capra about a guy who stayed on the home front and held life together for his community.

Similar reconciliation films would be seen after Vietnam (*Forrest Gump*), the end of the Cold War (*K-19*, *The Hunt for Red October*) and the fall of the Berlin Wall (*Goodbye Lenin*).

9 The HUAC Hearings and Hollywood Communism

Back in the United States, concerns about the influence of communists in Hollywood led to an investigation by the House Un-American Activities Committee beginning in 1947. As the hearings began, Walt Disney, Ronald Reagan, and other prominent Hollywood actors and directors testified, and, without evidence, agreed that the threat of communism to the film industry was serious. The committee also called a number of writers and actors and asked the question, "Are you now or have you ever been a member of the Communist party?"

Ten of these who tried to answer by framing the question as a breach of their constitutional rights were convicted of contempt of Congress the following year and barred by the MPAA from employment in the film industry—a practice known as "blacklisting." As the investigation rolled on, no evidence concerning attempts by actual communists to influence Hollywood productions was ever uncovered. Yet by 1951, a booklet called *Red Channels*, produced by the FBI, listed 151 names to be blacklisted. Most were forbidden from working in the US film industry, including Charlie Chaplin, Zero Mostel, and writer Dalton Trumbo, who was jailed for eleven months.

Figure 5.25 Blacklisted—Dalton Trumbo, a brilliant scriptwriter, refused to testify in 1947 congressional hearings about suspected communist influence in Hollywood films. After spending eleven months in jail, Trumbo was not permitted to write for Hollywood studios. Unofficially, Trumbo wrote dozens of award-winning scripts after being blacklisted for films like *Exodus* and *Spartacus*, eventually winning two Oscars. Library of Congress.

Some actors courageously stood up to the HUAC investigations. These included Humphrey Bogart, Lauren Bacall, Danny Kaye, and director John Huston, who organized the Committee for the First Amendment to protest the hearings. Bogart explained his position in an article entitled "I'm No Communist" in the March 1948 issue of *Photoplay*. He reminded readers, "liberal-minded folks are pure Americans … devoted to our democracy" (Bogart 1948).

It's important to remember that most of those blacklisted were simply liberals and young people of the 1930s who saw the communist movement reflecting idealism. Russian communists were US and British allies during World War II, and were lionized in Hollywood productions like *Days of Glory*.

Hunting for communists in the post-war Hollywood seemed to be little more than an excuse to victimize innocent people in order to gain political power. The highly publicized committee hearings dovetailed with witch hunts in other areas, and led to the "McCarthy era" in which US Senator Joseph McCarthy made wildly paranoid accusations about communist influence in government. The real victim, in the end, was Hollywood. Despite the eagerness of Hollywood executives to root out supposed communists, many came under fire themselves. One studio owner, RKO's Floyd Odlum, was so unnerved by the controversy that he simply sold his company. The chaos at RKO led to its early settlement of the Paramount antitrust case of 1948.

10 Movies bring Empathy to the Racial Divide

One of the most important stories about Hollywood takes place not in a single film or production company, but over a span of decades in hundreds of films. It's the story of how African-Americans came to be treated as equals on and off the screen, and how their contributions to cinema came to be respected. But the story is still one of a lack of serious influence in Hollywood or other mainstream media institutions in America, according to historians S. Torriano Berry and Venise T. Berry (Berry and Berry 2007).

In the earliest days, films featuring white actors in "blackface" portrayed disgusting, degrading, and ridiculous themes, such as the *Watermelon Eating Contest* and *The Wooing and Wedding of a Coon*. The 1914 film *Uncle Tom's Cabin* should have been an exception, since the original book was an indictment of slavery and the original Uncle Tom was beaten to death for refusing to reveal the location of runaway slaves. However, in the film, the main character is transformed into a subservient stereotype. Independent productions by black filmmakers included the 1912 *Railroad Porter* and others, and the new talking pictures led to studio productions in 1929 like *Hearts in Dixie*, the first all-black musical. One star from *Hearts in Dixie* was Lincoln Perry, whose character Stepin Fetchit exaggerated stereotypes of African-Americans as ignorant, shiftless, and witless.

Fighting these stereotypes, black entertainers showed they could perform with dignity and style. When Bill "Bojangles" Robinson tap-danced alongside white child-star Shirley Temple in the 1930s, the underlying message was that the races could set aside their differences. The Nicholas Brothers' spectacular dancing abilities were also widely recognized as a serious contribution. Yet often these dance numbers would be cut out of films shown in the American South by movie owners who were all too aware that humane images of African-Americans could speed reconciliation between the races.

Strong images of African-Americans were often stereotyped in the 1930s and 1940s. Paul Robeson's *Emperor Jones*, in 1933, produced by United Artists, depicted an ex-convict who takes control of a remote Caribbean island and is caught up in voodoo and dishonest scams. Hattie McDaniel, who played the Oscar-winning role of Mammy in *Gone with the Wind*, is an example of a strong but still stereotyped image of black Americans.

In the World War II era, the expression of ideals in films like *Why We Fight* required that some of those same ideals be better honored at home. One film that featured the first fully glamorized African-American woman was Twentieth Century Fox's movie, *Stormy Weather*, with singer-actress Lena Horne. "They didn't make me into a maid, but they didn't make me anything else, either," Horne said later. "I became a butterfly pinned to a column, singing away in Movieland."

Horne was an important figure "because she was able to bridge the gap between black and white in a way that others could not," said Eugene Robinson (Robinson 2010). Social issues were gingerly explored in the aftermath of the war, for example in the 1949 film *Pinky*, in which a black woman with light skin passes for white, but then realizes that she had almost lost her sense of humanity. Fully realized human characters emerged slowly, but are evident in films like Daryl F. Zanuck's *Island in the Sun* (1957), starring Harry Belafonte and Dorothy Dandridge. The film featured some light interracial romance.

One of the most significant attempts to bridge the racial divide was *To Kill a Mockingbird* (1962), a film about a Southern American town torn apart by racial injustice. The film stars Gregory Peck as a lawyer who defends a black man falsely accused of raping a white woman. Author Harper Lee said the book was based on events from her childhood in the 1930s but also on many actual events in the South, such as the trial of the Scottsboro Boys.

Important racial reconciliation films included the1963 film, *Lilies of the Field*, for which Sidney Poitier was awarded an Oscar, and the 1967 *Guess Who's Coming to Dinner*, starring Poitier, Spencer Tracy, and Katharine Hepburn. This film depicted an interracial couple who were intent on obtaining their parents' permission to get married. Like Horne, Poitier bridged the black–white gap in a way that attracted and educated audiences.

11 Social Upheaval and Antiheroes

Movies from the 1960s onward tended to both reflect and lead a major shift in world culture, away from patriotism and simple heroics toward tolerance, introspection, and personal growth. The era is often described as post-classical cinema, characterized by an undermining of cultural hubris and a devolution into artistic chaos. But the edgier new approach also gave audiences something that could not be seen on television.

Many films reflected relatively new social themes, for example *Rebel Without a Cause* (1955) about teenage rebellion, and *Easy Rider* (1969) about a drug-fueled motorcycle quest for personal freedom. Heroes were now seen as mere mortals, and life was depicted in many shades of gray instead of black and white. *Bonny and Clyde*, an oddly sympathetic

1967 film about two 1930s gangsters, was one of the films that showed this change of intellectual climate. Another was *The Graduate* (also 1967), about an after-college romance.

11.1 War movies: No more cowboys and Indians

The cultural shift is seen early in war movies that explored personal tragedy and human values more than heroics or the glory of combat. For example, where the 1941 film *Sergeant York* depicted an unvarnished backwoods hero of World War I, American cinema began exploring more nuanced themes of betrayal, unwilling sacrifice, and personal doubts. These include *From Here to Eternity* (1953), *The Bridge on the River Kwai* (1957), *The Guns of Navarone* (1961), *Dr. Strangelove* (1962), and *The Dirty Dozen* (1967).

Moral ambiguity is evident in this line from *The Guns of Navarone*, when Captain Keith Mallory (Gregory Peck) says, "The only way to win a war is to be just as nasty as the enemy. The one thing that worries me is we're liable to wake up one morning, and find we're even nastier than they are."

One 1968 film, *The Green Berets* with John Wayne, tried to maintain that unvarnished Hollywood heroism, but it didn't work. Film critic Roger Ebert said at the time, "The Green Berets simply will not do as a film about the war in Vietnam. It is offensive not only to those who oppose American policy but even to those who support it ... We certainly do not need a movie depicting Vietnam in terms of cowboys and Indians. That is cruel and dishonest and unworthy of the thousands who have died there" (Ebert 1968).

What was needed, Ebert and other critics suggested, was a more realistic view of the complexities of war, not simple-minded propaganda. More realistic anti-war films about Vietnam did come along in the late 1960s and 1970s, including *Platoon*, *The Deer Hunter*, *Full Metal Jacket*, and *Apocalypse Now*.

11.2 Westerns: Print the legend

Western genre movies also emerged from the wooden plot structure with a new kind of antihero. *The Magnificent Seven* (1960) was a direct takeoff from Akira Kurosawa's 1954 Japanese film, *The Seven Samurai*, in which a group of down-on-their-luck samurai defend a poor farming village from marauding bandits. *The Man Who Shot Liberty Valance* (1962), directed by John Ford, featured actors John Wayne and Jimmy Stewart and tells the story of a heroic legend who wasn't as much of a hero as his friend. Its classic line is, "When the legend becomes fact, print the legend."

An "anti-establishment" take on the western genre was also seen in *Little Big Man* (1970). The movie follows a naive Dustin Hoffman as he moves back and forth between white and Indian societies, finding both to be attractive and yet difficult. It was one of the first films that portrayed American Indians with any depth or sympathy.

The problem of the portrayal of American Indians came home to Hollywood when Marlon Brando turned down his Oscar for *The Godfather* in 1972 and said: "The motion picture community has been as responsible as any for degrading the Indian and making a mockery of his character, describing his as savage, hostile and evil. It's hard enough for children to grow up in this world. When Indian children watch television, and they watch films, and when they see their race depicted as they are in films, their minds become injured in ways we can never know" (*New York Times*, March 30, 1973). Later films about Indians such as *Jeremiah Johnson* (1972) and *Dances with Wolves* (1990) tended to romanticize the frontier experience.

Although the western genre was fairly well exhausted by the twenty-first century, variations such as the sci-fi and space western resulted in popular fusion films like *Back to the Future* (1990) and *Serenity* (2005).

11.3 Science fiction

Science fiction and horror genre films also moved from Cold War proxy threats attacking from outside, as in the film *Invasion of the Body Snatchers* (1956), to the monsters lurking within apparently ordinary human beings, as in Alfred Hitchcock's *Psycho* (1960), featuring Anthony Perkins as a schizophrenic motel owner.

An early outstanding example of the science fiction genre is *The Day the Earth Stood Still* (1951), a story about an ambassador from outer space who tries to deliver a warning about self-destruction to the nations of earth.

Despite the popularity of the science fiction genre, most films had poor special effects and plot, and few equaled the quality of *The Day the Earth Stood Still* until the release of *2001: A Space Odyssey* (1969) and *Star Wars* (1977).

11.4 Blockbusters and special effects

With the demise of the Hollywood studio system, and the increasing erosion of old distribution models in the cinema business, two basic market approaches were apparent: the high-stakes, big budget "blockbuster" movie, and the lower budget independent films that would reach for the remaining market share.

Blockbusters are expensive because of stars and marketing, but also, increasingly, because of the need for elaborate special effects. Creating the "wow" moment in a film with special effects was one way to stand out and present audiences with something new and different.

Special effects had always been a part of cinema, from George Méliès' 1902 film, *A Trip to the Moon*, to Fritz Lang's 1927 *Metropolis*, which also featured effective miniatures and mattes. Stop motion animation reached a new peak with Willis Obrien's work in the 1933 movie *King Kong*. Ray Harryhausen extended the technique in adventure movies like *Jason and the Argonauts* (1963), with animated monsters and skeletons fighting live actors. Although extraordinarily influential, Harryhausen's films tended to be box office disappointments. Ironically, most studios closed down their special-effects units by the mid-1970s just as the digital revolution was knocking on Hollywood's door (Zoglin 1986).

A new generation with interests in fantasy and science fiction made special effects a major element in developing the "blockbuster" film of the late twentieth and early twenty-first centuries. And independent film producers, with more independence and new special-effects technologies, were in a better position to create blockbusters than the old studios where they rented back lots.

Star Wars, which started as a back-lot experiment with new modeling and special effects techniques to bring viewers closer to the action, grossed $4.3 billion in the thirty years since the first film was made in 1977. The relatively low-budget first film was successful, in part, because of special effects supervisor John Dykstra, who used large models and lightweight cameras to give a more realistic look to space exterior shots. The effects crew went on to become Industrial Light and Magic Co., creating special effects for blockbusters such as *Harry Potter, Indiana Jones, Back to the Future, Terminator, Avatar*, and many others.

The transition away from animated models to full digital special effects took place around 1991 during the production of *Jurassic Park*. Originally, director Stephen Spielberg intended to use stop-motion animation from Stan Winston Studio, while Industrial Light and Magic was to add a few minor digital effects. But ILM animator Steve Williams roped together a computer system that created a highly realistic digital dinosaur. One of the stop-motion animators watching the first trials said, "I think I'm extinct" (Watercutter 2014).

An interesting related issue came up with *Avatar* in 2010. The film won three Oscars—for Art Direction, Cinematography, and Visual Effects—but nothing for the actors. The movie, made with "performance capture" technology, placed human actors into computer-animated scenes. Director James Cameron insisted that the actors deserved to be considered, arguing that the process was "actor-driven," and not simply made up in the computer as an effect (Abramowitz 2010).

12 Independent and International films

With the advent of on-demand video, viewers by the second decade of the twenty-first century had increasingly broad choices of content. This meant that the once dominant Hollywood system was now competing with, and sometimes promoting, films made in Asia and Europe. Films like *Crouching Tiger, Hidden Dragon*, a martial arts film made in China in 2000, proved enormously successful in US and European markets. Other foreign-language films that have achieved hit status in English-speaking markets included the loveable, color-saturated *Amelie* (French); *Lagaan*, an Indian film about poverty in the time of British rule; *Spirited Away*, a Japanese anime that was the first to win an Oscar; and *Slumdog Millionaire*, an Indian film about modern poverty.

Film production companies are increasingly considering international audiences. *Inglorious Bastards*, a violent 2005 fantasy by Quentin Tarantino, was created in German, French, and English to broaden its appeal. In 2014, the song "Let It Go" in Disney's *Frozen* was produced in forty-one languages before it was released. The song was so well known from advance publicity that people sang along with the film on its opening weekend.

European films have made a worldwide comeback by virtue of an artistic content that is often superior to formulaic Hollywood approaches. One interesting development in Europe was the Dogme 95 group, which has attempted to prove that high-quality films can be made without huge Hollywood budgets. Directors using the Dogme 95 approach use hand-held shots and on-location sounds only, avoiding gimmicks and special effects.

India overtook the US and Europe as the world's largest film producer in the 1970s. The Indian film industry is centered in Mumbai, and is informally called "Bollywood." Like film industries everywhere, Bollywood caters primarily to mass audiences. Productions range from crime and action dramas to family-oriented comedies and musicals. However, an alternative to commercial Bollywood is the socially realistic Parallel Cinema movement.

In the early twenty-first century, Nigeria overtook the US as the world's second largest film producer after India, according to UNESCO (2012). Known as "Nollywood," the Nigerian movie industry is based mostly in the capital city of Lagos and shares a tradition of filmmaking with Ghana ("Ghallywood"). Nollywood movies deal with issues of poverty, culture, justice, and moral dilemmas facing Africans, but most of all they are about love and passion. One popular film, *One God One Nation*, is about a Muslim man and a Christian woman who plan to marry but find that their tribal and religious differences are keeping them apart.

The Nollywood system is an example of technological leapfrogging. From the early 1990s, Nigerian movies have been made "straight to video" without the far more expensive celluloid production or distribution systems. The system is also more closely aligned with home viewing and VHS/DVD video exchanges, along with on-demand cable and internet viewing through systems like MultiChoice, with 24-hour channels dedicated to African content, which means predominantly Nigerian productions.

An important influence on international cinema is the Cannes Film Festival, held every year since 1946 in the resort town of Cannes, France. Other film festivals, especially Venice, Berlin, and Sundance (US), also showcase the desire to produce higher quality cinema (Forbes 2001). The increasing participation of American and Asian films and stars shows a rising sense that a global cinema is emerging.

The next big cinema sensation may not come from Hollywood, or Bollywood, or the storied studios of Lagos or Shanghai. But it will come from someone with a great idea. "The money men don't know the secrets of the human heart or the brilliance of the medium of film," says Mark Cousins in *The Story of Film*. "It's images and ideas that excite us, not money or show biz."

13 Legal Issues Around Film Distribution

The first controversy over home viewing of movies emerged with the use of videotape to copy whole programs or films—a practice that, according to the Motion Picture Association of America, would destroy the movie industry. In 1984, the MPAA sued electronics manufacturer Sony Corporation over use of videotaping machines. The case made it to the US Supreme Court, which said that legal use of home video recorders for "time-shifting" was a "fair use" and not a violation of copyright. Video stores flourished and home video sales became a movie industry mainstay rather than an instrument of its demise.

More powerful home computers introduced in the 1990s presented a new sort of challenge, allowing high-quality copying of music and video. Hollywood and the music industry moved quickly to protect their markets from copyright piracy, and Congress passed the Digital Millennium Copyright Act of 1998 (DMCA). The act made music and video piracy a more serious offense, but it also contained a "safe harbor" clause that insulated Internet service providers and search engine operators who allowed users to upload music and videos. The idea was that the users, but not the websites, would be responsible if the sites took down material when copyright owners objected. Websites that were primarily intended for copyright piracy could be taken down entirely. The DMCA's legal doctrine was enforced following a suit by A&M Records against music-sharing website Napster in 2001. Other lawsuits stopped widespread sharing of copyrighted music through websites such as Kazaa and Pirate Bay in the following years.

As web user bandwidth increased in first decade of the twenty-first century, the music-sharing controversy spread to video-sharing sites, especially YouTube, purchased by Google in 2006. Viacom, owner of Comedy Central, MTV, and other television and movie production companies, filed a suit arguing that Google had deliberately ignored copyright violations and profited from widespread video piracy.

Google countered that it did not ignore the violations, pointing out that when Viacom presented a list of 100,000 violations in 2007, virtually all were removed within a day. In June 2010, a lower court found that YouTube was primarily intended to host user-generated content, and could not have known which videos were posted with permission and which were not. Since the DMCA put the burden of copyright enforcement on the music and movie industries, and since YouTube complied with take-down notices, the DMCA's "safe harbor" provisions shielded them from Viacom's lawsuit.

But as it turned out, the audiences did not mind paying a fair price for home access to digital video. The problem was that this price did not create the same level of profits that the industry once enjoyed.

14 The End of the Mass Audience

Going to a movie was a weekly ritual during the 1920s, and even during the height of the Great Depression in the 1930s, 95 million Americans—nearly 75 percent of the population—went to see a movie once a week. This figure declined somewhat by 1948 to 90 million Americans—about 65 percent of the population—buying about 4.6 billion tickets per year.

Television cut deeply into movie ticket sales by the 1960s, with sales dipping below two billion per year, despite attempts by Hollywood studios to entice theater-goers with epic productions, special effects, and more contemporary themes than were possible with television. By the 1980s, sales were half again, at about one billion US tickets per year. The number rose again and peaked in 2002 at 1.5 billion, and has steadily declined to about 1.3 in 2013 (MPAA 2014).

Driving the trends were the proliferation of home entertainment and video game systems. To make up for the decline in ticket sales, Hollywood counted on video rentals and, later, DVD sales to make up losses. The strategy worked for most of the early years of the twenty-first century, but by 2010, the DVD strategy was in trouble. MGM's film library generated $558 million in revenue in 2007, but fell by more than half by 2010 (*New York Times*, September 9, 2013). Meanwhile, Blockbuster LLC, a video retail store, had 60,000 employees and more than 9,000 stores at its peak in 2004. By 2010 it had declared bankruptcy, and the last remaining stores closed in 2014. Other video retail chains, such as Hollywood Video, also declared bankruptcy. DVDs could now be ordered by web and delivered through the mail, or even through high-bandwidth Internet connections, and companies like Netflix and RedBox put retail video rental companies like Hollywood Video and Blockbuster out of business.

As the Hollywood financial model eroded in the digital era, major studios increasingly turned to risky high-stakes blockbuster productions to stay in business. Massive changes were afoot, Steven Spielberg said in a 2013 appearance: "The big danger … is an implosion where three or four or maybe even a half-dozen mega-budget movies are going to go crashing into the ground, and that's going to change the paradigm" (Bond 2013).

Nicholas Negroponte, former head of the MIT Media Lab, once noted a feeling of frustration, driving videotapes and DVDs back to the rental stores at night, trying to get them in without paying late fees. It was ironic, he thought, that he was using massive amounts of steel, glass, and petroleum just to move bits and bytes around. He predicted in 1996 that the first entertainment industry to be displaced by digital transmission technologies would be the video rental business. "And it will happen fast," he predicted.

One man who shared this frustration about the midnight video drive was Reed Hastings, who, as founder of Netflix, took Negroponte's advice and started moving bits and bytes around in ways that were more convenient for consumers, as we will see in Chapter 11.

For additional reading, discussion questions, links to video, and other suggestions, see www.revolutionsincommunications.com.

6

Advertising, Public Relations, and the Crafted Image

> Historians and archaeologists will one day discover that the ads of our time are the richest and most faithful daily reflections any society ever made of its whole range of activities.
>
> Marshall McLuhan, Rothenburg, 1999

1 Creating the Image

What goes into a Super Bowl ad, a Google campaign, a national promotion? How do people decide to buy a product, or buy into an idea? What motivates our fellow humans?

When tennis champion Andre Agassi used the line "image is everything," in ads for Canon cameras in the 1990s, it was more than just a slogan. It was the credo of a century, reflecting an increasing preoccupation with both physical and mental images—a major theme in the history of advertising and public relations.

The rise of the image as the central focus of consumer and political culture was noted with concern in 1961 by historian Daniel Boorstin, who said the public landscape had been altered to the point where reproductions were becoming more "real" than originals, and where pseudo-events were replacing real ones (Boorstin 1961). The power of images to promote products has been well known for millennia. Romans in the classical era used logos and symbols to promote everything from taverns to gladiatorial games. The Catholic Church first used woodcuts to promote piety in the early days of printing, then banned certain images that undermined Church authority.

The industrial media that emerged in the mid-nineteenth century depended on advertising for most of its revenue, and advertisers increasingly discovered that the power of imagery was what attracted consumers and built fortunes.

The idea of imaging changed the psychology of advertising around the turn of the twentieth century. Late nineteenth-century soap advertisements, for instance, tended to focus on the cleanliness of a factory or the purity of the product. But as images became more prevalent, and more professional, advertising shifted to a more appealing, image-building, consumer-centered message. A soap ad, for example, might feature an image of a beautiful woman endorsing the product, implying that you, too, can be beautiful if you use this soap. Dramatic photos of people using products, influenced by the pictorialist and straight photography movements, increasingly dominated advertising.

Even radio ads asked listeners to visualize the product's benefits. As advertising became increasing image-oriented, the messages changed from product quality to product image. "Sell the sizzle, not the steak," became a byword of the business. Brand images, unique selling propositions, and product positioning were among the core advertising strategies of the twentieth century.

Advertising plays an important role in a free market as the financial lynchpin supporting independent media. Ads for cars, soap, toothpaste, and the myriad of other products and services have financed the independent news and entertainment media far better than government subsidies or consumer subscriptions.

Yet by the twenty-first century, the traditional model of mass media supported by broad-spectrum image advertising was breaking down. New approaches to advertising—such as Internet metrics, social networking, and "viral" web videos—became part of the new creative strategy.

Public relations also changed from simple advocacy and press agentry to image building. Railroads, petroleum, tobacco, and other major industries turned to public relations experts to help sort out problems of adverse legislation and criticism from Progressive-era reformers in the early twentieth century. Politicians, too, became more concerned with image in the early twentieth century, and "image politics" is often said to be a question of style over substance and personality over policy.

Public relations history shows that polishing images—metaphorical and visual—is useful in some cases—for instance, in diplomacy and the Edison–Westinghouse war of the currents. But it is not a remedy for real problems. When international public health groups criticized the Nestle Corporation for deceptive infant formula advertising in developing nations, Nestle found that despite public relations efforts, the company continued to face consumer boycotts and deep-seated criticism well into the twenty-first century. BP's handling of the 2010 Gulf of Mexico oil well blowout is another example of an instance where public relations can't gloss over obvious disasters.

2 Early Advertising

Advertising is among the world's oldest professions. Street barkers loudly calling attention to products are typical in almost any market from antiquity to modern times. Advertisements painted on walls or wooden signs have been found by archaeologists in the ruins of ancient Egypt, Babylon, Greece, and other ancient civilizations.

One of the best-preserved glimpses into ancient advertising during the time is found in the ruins of Pompeii, a Roman city with a population of 20,000 that was suddenly inundated with volcanic ash in 79 CE and preserved for centuries. Pompeii's streets featured signs with logos and advertisements for wine, condiments, taverns, brothels, gladiatorial games, and political candidates. These included "the quick surveyor," "Publius Cornelius Faventinus, barber," "Phoebus the perfume dealer," "Cresces the architect," and

"Marcus Vecilius Verecundus, the tailor/clothes dealer" (Rokicki 1987). Similar signs posted or painted on walls are still found in busy cities.

Another ancient form of advertising is the town crier. In medieval England, the town crier, or bellman, would ring a bell and shout "Oyez, oyez, oyez" (listen) to command attention and silence. After reading an official proclamation, the crier would post the notice on the doorpost of a local public house. The archaic phrase "oyez, oyez, oyez" is still used in some courts to begin official proceedings. A variation on the town crier was the human billboard "sandwich man," described sarcastically by Charles Dickens as "a piece of human flesh between two slices of paste board." Before the advent of the popular industrial press in the mid-1800s, London streets were choked with people employed in this form of advertising.

Advertising through printed woodcuts is older than moveable type. From the 1400s on, churches distributed handbills to advertise religious fairs and to recruit soldiers to fight the Turks in the 1450s. Columbus used a woodcut image as the cover for his 1493 public relations pamphlet describing his voyages. The Protestant Reformation was successful, in large part, because of the power of printed text and images seventy years later.

The first printed text advertisement in English is often attributed to William Caxton who distributed a handbill promoting a newly printed book in the 1470s. Small announcements became one of the most common features of the emerging newspaper business from the early 1600s, and personal or "classified" advertising was also evident. The first newspaper ad may have been a notice about a stolen horse in *The Weekly Newes* in 1622.

Figure 6.1 Sandwich men—Human billboards on the Strand in London take a break from their advertising duties in this sketch, 1884. Library of Congress.

Short notices of commercial or personal significance filled the back pages of newspapers until the early twenty-first century (Sampson, 1875). Some are particularly moving, such as this ad from London in the 1830s: "To A.M. Your brother implores that you will immediately return home … or write me and relieve the dreadful distress in which our parents are at your absence" (Knight 1851).

Ads for brand-name products are found as early as the 1600s. One ad appeared in a newspaper for Robert Turner's dentifrice in 1661. When the bubonic plague hit England, ads for all kinds of remedies ran in newspapers: "Anti-Pestilential Pills," "Incomparable Drink Against the Plague," "The Only True Plague Water," "Infallible Preventive Pills Against the Plague," and "Sovereign Cordials Against the Corruption of the Air" (Rothenberg 1999).

With billboards, posters, newspapers, sandwich men, and other advertising, London became so cluttered that Charles II proclaimed, in the 1660s, "No signs shall be hung across the streets shutting out the air and the light of the heavens" (Rothenberg 1999).

As the population of London grew, passing the one million mark in 1800, an extraordinary riot of costumed advertisers shouted from horse-drawn wagons made up to look like tins of boot polish, or hats, or famous architecture, in order to advertise products and theatrical performances.

> Behold, rolling down from Oxford Street, three immense wooden pyramids—their outsides are painted all over with hieroglyphics and with monumental letters in the English language … [and] portraits of Isis and Osiris, of cats, storks, and of the apis; and amidst these old-curiosity-shop gods, any Englishman may read … that there is now on view a panorama of Egypt—one more beautiful, interesting, and instructive than was ever exhibited in London … In no other town would such tricks be necessary conditions of existence; but here, … where all press and rush on to make money or to spend it—here, where every one must distinguish himself in some way or other, or be lost and perish in the crowd—where every hour has its novelty—here, in London, even the most solid undertakings must assume the crying colour of charlatanism. (Schlesinger 1853)

Another advertising wagon on the London streets was a horse-drawn carriage built in the shape of a seven-foot-tall hat to advertise a hat maker. Historian Thomas Carlyle said the hat was not quite as large as the comic effect it produced, and yet, it also struck him as somewhat tragic: "To me this all-deafening blast of puffery, of poor falsehood grown necessitous, sounds too surely like a dooms-blast … God's blessing is not written on all this" (Puffing 1852).

2.1 P. T. Barnum and the art of ballyhoo

One of the most celebrated showmen and public relations agents of the 1800s was P. T. (Phineas Taylor) Barnum. Founder of Barnum's American Museum in New York and a popular traveling circus, Barnum understood the public's taste for hokum and ballyhoo.

Barnum's enormous museum opened in 1842, covering half a block of lower Broadway. It was decorated with flags, banners, painted animals, and murals. Inside, curious spectators who paid a small fee could find a zoo, wax museum, dioramas of famous events, scientific instruments, and all kinds of curiosities and hoaxes. And always, something going on.

One of Barnum's first hoaxes was a taxidermical concoction called the "Feejee Mermaid," sporting the tail of a fish and the head of monkey. Barnum himself advertised that he didn't believe it, but the exhibit drew enormous crowds. The museum burned down in a spectacular fire in 1865, along with tens of thousands of exhibits.

Figure 6.2 Ballyhoo and Barnum—The king of boisterous advertising, called "ballyhoo" in the 1800s, was Phineas Taylor Barnum, owner of Barnum's Museum and a traveling circus. Barnum's philosophy was expressed in the phrase "There's a sucker born every minute." Library of Congress.

The *New York Times* said that, despite the "innumerable sensations with which the intelligent public were disgusted and the innocent public deluded, and the ever patent humbuggery … the Museum still deserved an honorable place in the front rank of rare and curious collections of the world" (*New York Times*, July 14, 1865).

Barnum did not coin the phrase often attributed to him: "There's a sucker born every minute." Instead, a rival hoaxer whose "Cardiff Giant" hoax had been called into question by Barnum coined that memorable phrase after Barnum promoted his own version of the Cardiff Giant in 1869. The "giant" was a 10-foot statue of a man created for the hoax and weathered with acid to seem ancient in order to show the "giants" described in Genesis. Barnum opened the door to blatant hucksterism and ballyhoo in many areas of advertising and public relations.

Figure 6.3 Biscuit campaign—The National Biscuit Company's "Uneeda Biscuit" ads were astonishingly successful for such a transparently hyped message. Hartman Center, Duke University.

Another example of American ballyhoo was the National Biscuit Co. (Nabisco) Uneeda biscuit campaign of 1898. Planned by N. W. Ayer advertising agency, the first packaged ready-to-eat food had a compelling name: Uneeda. The Uneeda biscuit marketing campaign would come to a town with just one word on a billboard and in newspaper ads: "Uneeda." The next day, the ad would read "Uneeda biscuit." The following day it would read: "Do you know Uneeda biscuit?" And next: "Of Course Uneeda biscuit."

The Nabisco campaign was a smashing success, and was followed by Fig Newton, Animal Crackers, Lorna Doone, and the Oreo. Interestingly, Oreo cookie was one of a trio of new products in 1913 and added as an afterthought. The other two new products—the Mother Goose Biscuit, depicting nursery rhyme characters, and the Veronese Biscuit, a sort of upscale Uneeda—were Nabisco's picks for success. But the Oreo caught on, eventually becoming the best selling cookie in the world (Burrough and Helyar 1990). By 2005, 490 billion Oreo cookies had been sold (Toops 2005).

British opinion of all this American ballyhoo was not high. British historian Henry Sampson wrote in 1875 that Britons "have not yet learned to sacrifice all that should be dear and honorable to humanity" as some of his American counterparts had. "The Americans are a truly great people," Sampson wrote, "but they have not yet settled into a regular system so far … as newspapers and advertisements are concerned" (Sampson 1875: 14).

2.2 Merchandising and advertising

The idea of customer-oriented merchandising doesn't seem so radical today, but in an era when shops were small and customers stayed on their own side of the counters, the combination of large "department" stores, retail marketing, and aggressive advertising was entirely new. In London, Bainbridge's became the first department store in 1849. In Paris, there was the famous Le Bon Marché, opened in 1850 and made famous in the Emile Zola novel, *The Ladies' Paradise*, in 1883:

> The greatest power of all was the advertising. [Store owner Octave] Mouret spent three hundred thousand francs a year in catalogues, advertisements and bills … illustrated with engravings, even accompanying them with samples, gummed between the leaves. It was an overflowing display; The Ladies Paradise became a household word all over the world, invading the walls the newspapers even the curtains at the theaters … (Zola 1883)

Figure 6.4 British Ballyhoo—Thomas Lipton, a Scottish grocer, catapulted to world fame through shrewd marketing and strong advertising messages. Library of Congress.

British grocer Thomas Lipton took the ballyhoo approach to advertising with his rapidly growing chain of stores in the late 1800s. He printed fake currency that could be redeemed for low-cost produce, especially Irish ham. Lipton also hired a cartoonist who depicted an Irishman with a pig in a sack. "He's an orphan, so, out of pity, I'm taking him to Lipton's." Once the joke was known, pigs with ribbons tied in their tails would be paraded through the streets with signs showing that they were "Lipton's orphans" (Wood 1958).

In 1881, Lipton announced that the company would import the world's largest cheese from New York to Glasgow, Scotland, for Christmas. The cheese would be sold in the Christmas custom with coins placed inside. "The streets were lined with spectators cheering the giant cheese on its way to Lipton's new store in High Street," according to a Glasgow city history. Police were called out to hold back the crowd. A few years later, Lipton staged a parade to announce his new line of packaged tea, for which the company is now known. An elephant led an army of 200 men dressed in Chinese garb, wearing sandwich boards with messages about the tea as they paraded through the streets of Glasgow (Waugh 1950; Wood 1958).

Back in America, a Chicago department store manager named Harry Gordon Selfridge worked tirelessly to make the Marshall Fields store profitable, coming up with merchandising gimmicks such as reminding customers that there were only so many more shopping days until Christmas.

Selfridge visited Paris and admired Le Bon Marché, and then noticed that such "cathedrals of shopping" didn't exist in London. He opened Selfridge's department store in London in 1909 with bold illustrated advertising that drew attention, and followed it up with exhibits of the first airplane to cross the English Channel. Selfridges was a safe experience for a middle-class woman, a way to meet friends, have tea, go window shopping, look at new fashions, and try new perfumes, all without having to actually walk on the streets of London.

3 The Advent of Advertising Agencies

In the four centuries between the 1450s and the 1830s, newspaper, magazine, and book publishers depended mostly on direct sales and subscriptions, also known as circulation revenues. Advertising was a service that editors could provide or, in some cases, might not, as they saw fit.

With the advent of industrial presses and greatly expanded circulation, penny press editors realized that they could sell their newspapers at one or two cents, actually losing money on circulation, but more than regaining it with advertising revenue. This shift in business models is one of the most important in media history. Within the penny press model we can identify four kinds of advertising agencies developed in the nineteenth and twentieth centuries: (1) the newspaper agency (taking orders for ads); (2) space jobbing (selling space to clients and then buying the ad space); (3) space wholesaling (buying large amounts of advertising space at a discount and then reselling the space to clients at regular rates); and (4) advertising concession (contracting for advertising space and taking the risk of selling the space).

Before the penny press revolution, clients who needed to place ads in newspapers and magazines would simply go to the printing establishment and place their orders. But as commerce began to speed up, specialists who offered advertising services began to emerge.

The first advertising agency appeared in London in 1812, established by George Reynell, to handle legal advertising for lawyers and their clients. In the United States, Volney Palmer established the American Newspaper Advertising Agency in 1841 and quickly branched out with offices in New York, Boston, and Philadelphia.

Others followed, and most early advertising agencies, like Palmer's, were buyers and brokers, either simply passing the orders along or placing ads into spaces they had already purchased.

In the 1870s, however, newer advertising agencies turned to a full service model, helping clients develop trademarks, package designs, and marketing plans as well as advertising. Around the turn of the twentieth century, when big business was under fire from reformers and muckrakers, public relations was added to the full service suite.

As advertising specialists played an increasing role in commerce, advertising also began to draw critics. In 1850, Palmer decided to do something about it, and ran a contest for the best essay on the "Philosophy of Advertising." The winner was Horace Greeley, the well-known editor of the *New York Tribune*, whose business owed everything to advertising. Greeley said:

> Men of business are hardly aware of the immense change which a few years have wrought in the power of the public press … He who would build a business must be like the times … To neglect [advertising] is like resolving never to travel by steam nor communicate by telegraph. It is to close one's eyes to the light and insist on living in perpetual darkness … He who neglects the advantages of advertising not only robs himself of his fair advantages, but bestows the spoils on his wiser rivals. (Greeley 1850)

Reaction to the essay was not uniformly positive. In "The Philosophy of Puffing," the *Circular* magazine was alarmed that every man could be his own trumpeter with the "vast amount" of newspaper advertising that had suddenly appeared: "Nature requires no man to make proclamation of his doings … There is not a man born into the world but feels that he is degrading himself if he speak of his excellencies and … supremacy in his craft" (Puffing 1853).

Media critics of the era also noticed "a real evil … [in] the attempt to serve two masters: to sell space for the publisher and, at the same time, to act as an expert and impartial counselor for the advertiser" (Appel 1939).

3.1 Full service agencies: J. Walter Thompson and N. W. Ayer

Publishers who needed to find advertisers often sent sales agents into the streets. This was the origin of the J. Walter Thompson agency when, in 1864, William Carlton began canvassing for some of the New York City newspapers. Carlton hired Thompson, a Civil War veteran, in 1868, and ten years later, Thompson bought the company and renamed it for himself.

Thompson focused on the "full service" agency approach, helping clients craft and place ads. The agency specialized in ads with magazines like the *Century*, *Scribners*, *Godey's*

Lady's Book, and *Lady's Home Journal*. The company's portfolio included household and women's products like Ponds cold cream, Quaker Oats, and Gerber baby food.

In 1899, Thompson's *Red Book on Advertising* echoed Greeley in its philosophy of advertising: "The merchant who does not believe in advertising does not believe in banks, insurance or other modern institutions. He is a relic of the lost ages ... Advertisements cannot be too strong. You cannot catch the public eye too skillfully or too often." It also helped clients develop trademarks and package designs. As the company grew, J. Walter Thompson pioneered testimonials, photography, psychological research, and broadcast advertising. The agency's name was changed to JWT in 2005.

Around the same time, another agency that established a full service approach to advertising was N. W. Ayer & Son. The name itself was a bit of a ruse, since the young Francis W. Ayer was not really in business with his father. As a twenty-one-year-old starting off in Philadelphia in 1869, he just wanted it to appear as if the business was already established.

Ayer had purchased some of the remnants of Volney Palmer's old newspaper network, and also took a page from Greeley's "philosophy of advertising" when, in his own company promotional, "The Ayer Idea in Advertising," he wrote:

> Suppose you were to say "I do not believe in darkness; I do not want darkness." Will it not grow dark tonight quite the same? ... You may not like the idea of the telephone or typewriter or adding machine ... but these are established instruments ... To refuse to use them stamps you as being behind the times, and competition with the man or business who does use them is no longer possible. (Ayer 1912)

Behind this lofty rhetoric was F. W. Ayer's determination to serve the client first. Ayer took an "open book" approach to clients, allowing them to see exactly how much money was being charged by the publication where the advertising was purchased. This assured clients that they came first, and not the need to sell advertising space that the agency had already contracted.

Figure 6.5 The Commodore—J. Walter Thompson created the first full service advertising agency in 1878. Hartman Center, Duke University.

"As Ayer saw it, he was working for the advertiser and the other agencies were working for the publisher," said historian Joseph Appel. Some of the company's early clients included seed companies, Montgomery Ward, John Wanamaker Department Stores, and Singer Sewing Machines. Even with his religious background, Ayer participated in some of the worst forms of advertising of the day. At one point, one quarter of the Ayer

Figure 6.6 and **Figure 6.7** The new face of advertising—Throughout the 1800s, newspaper and magazine ads extolled the virtues of their products. It was only around the turn of the century when advertisers realized that simple "ballyhoo" was not enough, and that subjective approaches that appealed to user needs could be more effective. Library of Congress.

business was for " patent medicines." Ayer dropped the accounts in 1906, long after others had done so, when strong federal regulations were looming.

4 The Dawn of Public Relations

The idea that public opinion can be swayed, and that politics can be influenced, is at the foundation of most of the study of rhetoric and public speaking from classical Greece and Rome. Politicians and political leaders in all times have used traditional techniques. Public relations was a factor in the American Revolution, when Samuel Adams developed symbols such as the Liberty Tree, and staged events like the Boston Tea Party, and spread propaganda like the idea of the Boston "massacre."

Professional public relations in the mass media is a nineteenth- and twentieth-century phenomena. The first American PR professional is considered to be Amos Kendall, a Kentucky lawyer and editor. Following Andrew Jackson's election as US president in 1828, Kendall became a member of Jackson's group of informal advisors called the "kitchen cabinet." His specialty was writing speeches, dealing with the press, and articulating policy for Jacksonian Democrats. Kendall lost money while serving as Jackson's Postmaster General but later made a small fortune as attorney for telegraph inventor Samuel Morse.

Another early PR professional was Thurlow Weed, a former newspaper editor and Republican party organizer who served in the crucial position as an advisor to Abraham Lincoln's ambassadors to Britain and France during the US Civil War. Had either country decided to join with the Confederacy in the early 1860s, the outcome of the war could have been quite different. Knowing this, Weed lobbied, wrote letters, and worked to keep the Confederacy isolated. Henry Brooks Adams, grandson of John Quincy Adams, worked with him at the US embassy in London, and later wrote the description of what appears to be a perfect public relations practitioner:

> Thurlow Weed was a complete American education in himself. His mind was naturally strong and beautifully balanced; his temper never seemed ruffled; his manners were carefully perfect in the style of benevolent simplicity, the tradition of Benjamin Franklin ... The trait that astounded and confounded cynicism was his apparent unselfishness ... The effect of power and publicity on all men is the aggravation of self, a sort of tumor that ends by killing the victim's sympathies; a diseased appetite, like a passion for drink or perverted tastes; one can scarcely use expressions too strong to describe the violence of egotism it stimulates; and Thurlow Weed was one of the exceptions; a rare immune. He thought apparently not of himself, but of the person he was talking with. He held himself naturally in the background. He was not jealous. He grasped power, but not office. (Adams 1918)

Figure 6.8 Thurlow Weed—As an American diplomat in London during the US Civil War, Weed was considered to be the perfect public relations practitioner. Harper's Magazine, 1861.

The term public relations appears to have been first used by Dorman Eaton, an American attorney who fought Boss Tweed and was active in reforming the US Civil Service in the 1870s. He spoke at Yale in 1882 about the "Public Relations and Duties of the Legal Profession," encouraging fellow attorneys to speak out in favor of reform (Heath 2004).

Another milestone of public relations took place at Westinghouse Electric when the first in-house corporate public relations department was established in 1889. The company was locked in the "war of the currents" with General Electric over the establishment of electrical distribution networks. Westinghouse

Company founder George Westinghouse favored alternating current, which was more efficient over long distances. Thomas Edison had patents in direct current transmissions, and for commercial reasons, went out of his way to portray alternating current (AC) as far more dangerous than direct current (DC), embarking on a smear campaign that included public killings of animals with AC current (Brandon 1999). Edison and his spokesmen told audiences that DC was "like a river flowing peacefully to the sea, while AC was like a torrent rushing violently over a precipice" (Tesla 2003).

By far, the worst stunt in this early public relations war was the execution of convicted murderer William Kemmler in 1890. Edison employee Harold P. Brown built the first electric chair for criminal executions in New York State using AC power. When it was first used, on August 6, 1890, someone apparently underestimated the voltage needed to kill the condemned prisoner. "The stench was unbearable," said a *New York Times* reporter who also quoted telegraph report by a technician (possibly Brown): "Execution was an awful botch. Kemmler was literally roasted to death" (*New York Times*, August 7, 1890). One newspaper, following Edison's lead, said the prisoner had been "Westinghoused" (Brandon 1999).

Westinghouse realized that the public knew very little about electricity and that Edison was winning the battle. He hired Ernest H. Heinrichs, a journalist from Pittsburgh, to write pamphlets and op-ed articles in favor of AC and in opposition to its use in the electric chair. It was the first in-house public relations department for a major industry. The process took about three years, but Westinghouse was able to overcome Edison's public relations blitz, convincing people that AC was a better technology and securing crucial initial contracts at the Chicago World's Fair in 1893 and Niagara Falls in 1896.

5 Advertising and Patent Medicine

Until about 1906, advertising in the United States resembled nothing so much as a lawless frontier. Especially troubling were ads for opium-based syrups designed to soothe children with toothaches.

"Poison for the poor" was how *Collier's* magazine depicted the patent medicine business in a 1905 muckraking series of articles by Samuel Hopkins Adams. "Gullible America will … swallow huge quantities of alcohol, an appalling amount of opiates and narcotics, and a wide assortment of varied drugs ranging from powerful and dangerous heart depressants to insidious liver stimulants," Adams said in the opening to "The Great American Fraud" (Adams 1905).

The bottles of syrup and boxes of powders were called "patent" medicines because the brand names were often trademarked, although the ingredients were not actually patented.

Cocaine and opium may stop pain, Hopkins argued, but narcotics are not safe, particularly when they are hidden under the label of "cough remedies," "soothing syrups," and "catarrhal powders." And it was a grave injustice, Hopkins said, that people could be hoodwinked into thinking that extract of witch hazel could cure meningitis, or that concoctions based on cocaine and opium could cure cancer, or that mildly acidic formulas could prevent yellow fever. Even worse were the "soothing syrups" made of opium, given to children to keep them tranquil.

Adams also charged that the American newspapers and magazines were in league with the patent medicine advertisers. A "red clause" in the advertising contracts allowed the patent medicine makers to void the contract in case of adverse legislation or publicity. This meant that newspaper publishers had a strong financial interest in ensuring that people did not learn about patent medicines, and that no laws regulating patent medicine were passed at the state or federal levels.

Adams was not the first to point out that unregulated pharmaceutical and advertising industries had turned millions of ailing people into drug addicts. As early as 1892, the *Ladies Home Journal* had banned advertising for "patent" medicines. And Coca-Cola, a popular drug-store tonic drink, stopped including cocaine in the formula around the turn of the century.

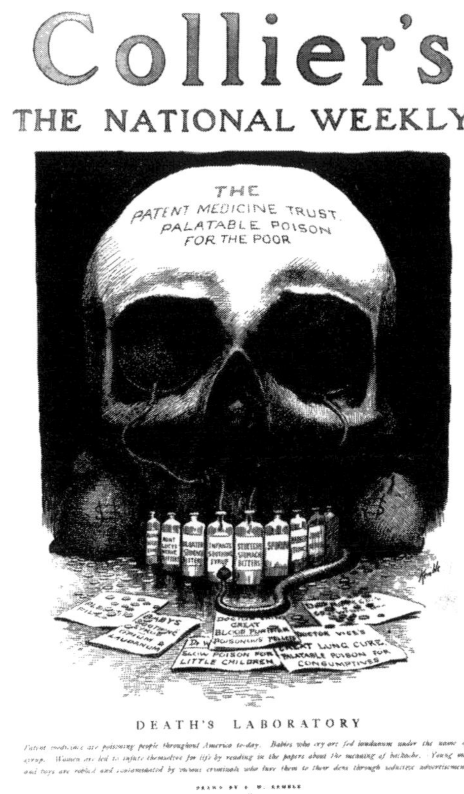

Figure 6.9 Patent medicine—In 1905, a muckraking series of articles by Samuel Hopkins Adams in *Collier's* magazine exposed fraud and abuse in the patent medicine business. Along with *The Jungle*, about the Chicago meatpacking industry, the *Collier's* article helped create the political momentum for reform. US advertising regulation started at this point, with none of the constitutional protections enjoyed by newspapers until after the 1964 *New York Times v Sullivan* case. E. W. Kemble illustration, *Collier's*, 1906.

Adams' articles came at a time when Americans were awakened to injustice and clamoring for reform. By 1906, Congress passed the Pure Food and Drug Act requiring federal inspection of meat and labeling of the drug content of medicines. The act paved the way for the creation of the Food and Drug Administration (FDA), which monitors pharmaceutical advertising as well as food safety.

In another series of articles, Adams wrote about the deadly impacts of misleading advertising for Grape-Nuts, a popular cereal made of bran, molasses, and salt. One advertisement read, "No Appendicitis For Those Who Use Grape-Nuts." Another said, "It is a practical certainty that when a man has approaching symptoms of appendicitis, the attack can be avoided by discontinuing all food except Grape Nuts."

"This is lying—Potentially deadly lying," Adams wrote in a *Collier's* editorial. In response, Postum Company ran an ad in other publications saying that Adams and *Collier's* magazine were attacking them with "out and out falsehoods" in an attempt to win

Figure 6.10 Killem Quick Pharmacy—Cocaine, opium, and other dangerous drugs could be sold legally as part of the patent medicine industry in 1900, when *Puck* magazine published this cartoon. Here a bartender (left) watches the pharmacist with envy. "I can't begin to compete with this fellow," he says. It's notable that magazines led the charge for reform; newspapers depended so heavily on patent medicine advertising that many had agreed, by contract, never to say anything negative about the patent medicine business. The reform movement culminated in the establishment of the Food and Drug Administration in 1906 and the Federal Trade Commission in 1914. Library of Congress.

back their advertising contracts. In return, *Collier's* sued Postum for libel in 1907 and won, but the verdict was overturned on a technicality in 1912 (*New York Times*, September 7, 1907; February 17, 1916).

The upshot of the libel trial, said historian Clark Gavin, was that advertisers realized they didn't need to make extravagant claims for their products. "It was enough to show … a Hollywood star … using the product—Copy was unnecessary" (Gavin 1962). In other words, the power of the image was far more effective than the power of the word.

6 Public Relations versus Muckraking

As we saw in Chapter 2, the "muckraking" era of the American press involved exposes such as Adams's "Great American Fraud" along with Upton Sinclair's book, *The Jungle*. Both of these influenced Congress to pass the Food and Drug Act of 1906.

Other muckrakers also had major social impacts. Ida Tarbell's 1906 *History of Standard Oil* showed how John D. Rockefeller used bribery and underhand tactics to absorb competitors into his oil monopoly. Others, like Charles Edward Russell, Ray Stannard Baker, and Lincoln Steffans, took on the railroad monopolies and corruption in politics.

At the time, reformers in government, led by President Theodore Roosevelt, had passed laws to break up monopolies and restore competitive markets. To help corporations craft a response, public relations experts such as Ivy Ledbetter Lee emerged. Many business leaders did not see the necessity of public relations, and to some extent, Lee and other public relations experts fought a battle on two fronts. They worked for the corporations, but spent a lot of time and energy convincing the corporations they were needed. The traditional nineteenth-century corporate response to calls for government regulation and concern for public opinion had been openly defiant. "I owe the public nothing," banking tycoon J. P. Morgan said in this context. Similarly, William Vanderbilt became instantly infamous when, asked about public opinion of his railroad in 1882, he roared, "The public be damned" (Gordon 1989).

Lee began in 1904 by forming the Parker and Lee Company with experienced journalist George Parker. Lee's philosophy was that the companies and their public relations practitioners had a responsibility beyond obligations to the client: "Our plan is frankly, and openly, on behalf of business concerns and public institutions, to supply the press and public of the United States prompt and accurate information concerning subjects which it is of value and interest to the public to know about" (Tuney 2010).

Lee's early work for the Pennsylvania Railroad turned the tables on the Vanderbilt approach, providing press releases and accurate information about a 1906 railroad accident before details reached the media from elsewhere. It was the first time that reporters had been given access to accident scenes and witnesses by a railroad (Princeton 2010).

Figure 6.11 Ivy Lee and public relations—Ivy Ledbetter Lee was one of the first to set up public relations agencies to help industrialists deal with critics and political problems. Prompt and accurate information was the goal, but Lee did not always live up to his ideals. Library of Congress.

In 1914, a state militia killed nineteen people, including two women and eleven children, during a coal miners' strike in Ludlow, Colorado. Ivy Lee was dispatched to the scene by the mine's owner, Standard Oil tycoon John D. Rockefeller. Lee quickly blamed the victims for carelessness in starting an accidental fire, and then circulated a bulletin, "How Colorado Editors View the Strike," quoting eleven editors who supported the coal industry. All eleven worked for newspapers owned by the coal industry—the rest of the state's 320 editors were not quoted (Olasky 1987). Lee also had Rockefeller's son attend a social event in the mining camp and dance with the miners' wives to show he was a regular guy (Hiebert 1966). Muckraking journalists, such as Upton

Sinclair, said Lee tried to mislead them about the massacre. They labeled him "poison ivy" Lee.

Around this time, laws forcing the break-up of monopolies (such as the Sherman Antitrust Act of 1890) had passed Congress and were being enforced by the Supreme Court. Standard Oil Co., for instance, was broken up in 1911 following a civil trial showing that it had engaged in anticompetitive practices (*Standard Oil Co. of NJ v. United States*, 1911).

AT&T, the phone company founded by Alexander Graham Bell, was also under investigation by the Justice Department for buying up its competitors. Unlike oil, however, the telephone company argued that it was a "natural monopoly" and could provide service to every American.

As an AT&T president said in 1909, "The public does not know us ... It has never seen us, never met us, does not know where we live, who we are, what our good qualities are." To change that, Ivy Lee worked with James Ellworth of AT&T, and N. W. Ayer advertising company. Ayer created a series of standardized ads that aimed at public familiarity and long-range corporate image building. It set the "right tone" of restrained but straightforward friendliness, not one of gaudy low appeal, like Prince Albert tobacco, but not high toned, like Steinway pianos. The hope was to make people understand and love the company, "to hold real affection for it" (Marchand 1998).

Figure 6.12 Promoting monopoly—The advertising campaign that helped American Telephone and Telegraph hold on to its regulated monopoly in the antitrust era was designed by Ivy Lee and N. W. Ayer. It emphasized reliability and universal service. Hartman Center, Duke University.

The first of the AT&T ads, "Twenty Million Voices," began appearing in late June, 1908. "The usefulness of the telephone is in its universality as one system," the ad copy says. "Where there are two systems you must have two telephones—and confusion" (Griese 1977). In the long list of great public relations campaigns, AT&T was called "the granddaddy of them all" (Marchand 1998: 49). The campaign paid off, and in 1913, AT&T and the Justice Department signed the "Kingsbury Commitment" which allowed the monopoly to continue under government regulation.

Lee continued to work for AT&T and the railroads, insisting that external public relations was also good for employee morale. He also served as the publicity director of the American Red Cross during World War I. But Lee's true allegiance was with Standard Oil Co., and he helped it through numerous crises in the 1920s.

One of Standard Oil's biggest public relations problems was its agreement with I. G. Farben, the German dye and chemicals trust, to protect each other's patents and interests in the years leading up to World War II (Borkin 1978). Lee traveled, at Standard Oil's request, to Germany in January of 1934. He met with Adolf Hitler and advised German Propaganda Ministry officials to take an "equality of armaments" line with regard to breaking their rearmament treaties. When he returned to the United States in July 1934, a congressional "Un-American Activities" committee called Lee to testify. Lee insisted that he told the Nazis that Americans would never be reconciled to their treatment of Jewish people. But he had a difficult time explaining why this advice would be worth over $25,000 (*New York Times*, July 12, 1934). Lee died later in 1934 from a brain tumor before the contradiction could be cleared up.

7 Tobacco Advertising

When R. J. Reynolds, the famed tobacco baron from Winston-Salem, NC, decided to market a brand of pipe tobacco nationwide, he called the N. W. Ayer creative team in 1907. They came up with the name "Prince Albert," after the popular son of British Queen Victoria who became King Edward VII. They found a photo of the prince with Mark Twain, copied it, and put it on a tin can filled with tobacco. The ad caught on, and American Tobacco sales went from one-quarter million to 14 million pounds in four years. In 1913, American Tobacco took the financially risky approach of marketing prepackaged cigarettes, which at the time were not popular. Reynolds used local and Turkish tobaccos, and, playing up the mysterious Eastern connotation, called the cigarettes Camels.

Again, the Ayer Company led the account and, like its Uneeda biscuit campaign, the cigarette would be introduced into each market with teaser ads. First, "Camels" and then "The Camels are coming" and then "Tomorrow there'll be more camels in this town than in all Asia and Africa combined!" and finally "Camel Cigarettes are here."

"It was breathless and brazen, and by modern standards, hokey," said historian Bryan Burrough. "But it made the first national cigarette a major event." At 20 cents a pack, Camels undercut other brands, and within a year, 425 million packs were sold (Burrough 1990).

After World War I, tobacco companies began to look for new markets and began thinking about women as an overlooked market. At the time, social conservatives considered the idea of women smoking as a sign of low morals. Early ads featuring women smoking took an indirect approach. In 1926, for example, Liggett & Myers, owners of the Chesterfield brand, ran an ad with a young woman,

Figure 6.13 Breathless and brazen—Camels were the first cigarettes to be mass marketed through advertising. Hartman Center, Duke University.

who was not smoking, saying to a young man, "Blow some my way." American Tobacco, hoping to get in on "a new gold mine right in our front yard," hired Lord & Thomas advertising firm, which specialized in delicate issues (such as feminine hygiene products). They also hired another public relations expert, Edward Bernays.

Bernays was called the "father of scientific public relations," in the sense that he would use social science research techniques to inform his campaigns. In his book *Crystallizing Public Opinion*, Bernays equated "manipulation of the public mind" with the "social purpose" of speeding change and preventing chaos (Olasky 1987). He found that, even after winning the right to vote in 1919, women were concerned with freedom and independence. His idea was to promote cigarettes as symbols of freedom. Bernays organized demonstrations of women smoking Lucky Strike cigarettes in public, culminating in the 1929 New York Easter Parade. They carried placards identifying their cigarettes as "torches of liberty." Photos and articles were distributed to small town newspapers across the nation (Schudson 1978). The Lucky Strike campaign grew to $19 million a year by 1931, and included themes of sex appeal as well as freedom. Ads featuring slim women were headlined, "Reach for a Lucky instead of a sweet."

A congressional committee expressed its outrage over women smoking. "Not since the days when the vendor of harmful nostrums was swept from our streets has this country witnessed such an orgy of buncombe, quackery and downright falsehood and fraud as now marks the current campaign promoted by certain cigarette manufacturers to create a vast woman and child market," one senator said (Schudson 1978).

Figure 6.14 Scientific PR—Edward Bernays pioneered a more scientific approach to public relations, using polling and focus groups to help companies understand public opinion before being committed to a position. Library of Congress.

Around this same time, Bernays helped another company deal with a crisis. U.S. Radium Corporation had been severely criticized for legal tactics and delays in a case involving the "radium girls" watch dial painters who had radiation poisoning. In 1928, the *New York World* newspaper criticized U.S. Radium and the courts for barring the doors of justice to the dying women. While the company was negotiating an out-of-court settlement, Bernays worked to ensure that medical uses of radium were kept in the public eye (Neuzil 1997).

"The implications of Bernay's public relations paradigm … alarmed some political, academic and religious observers during the 1930s, as concern about the political effects of mass manipulation … [b]ecame more widespread," said historian Marvin Olasky. "For instance, in a 1934 letter to President Franklin Roosevelt, Supreme Court Justice Felix Frankfurter referred to Bernays and Ivy Lee as 'professional poisoners of the public mind,' exploiters of foolishness, fanaticism and self interest."

8 Madison Avenue goes to War

In April of 1917, a few days after the United States formally entered World War I, President Woodrow Wilson created the Committee on Public Information, also known as Creel Committee for its leader, George Creel. The committee also included Edward Bernays, who later remarked that "the essence of democratic society" was the "engineering of consent."

The committee used all available media to spread its message, and historians estimate that 6,000 government ads and news releases found their way into the press (Mott 1966). Some of these even advised Americans to beware of people speaking German, creating a climate of fear in German-American communities in the upper Midwest.

The committee also served a role that would later be filled by radio and television when it recruited about 75,000 "four minute men" (Ward 1996: 449). These were volunteers who would stand up at the beginning of movies, church services, and other public

Figure 6.15 Who needs comedy?—George Creel's committee on public information was not universally popular, as this *Washington Post* cartoon from 1917 shows. Despite censorship in World War I, it's notable that open criticism of the censors could still slip by. *Washington Post*, October 7, 1917.

events to speak for four minutes about subjects ranging from the draft to rationing, war bond drives, victory gardens, and the reasons America had entered the war. By 1918, the four-minute men made more than 7.5 million speeches to 314 million people in 5,200 communities.

Creel later wrote in his memoir, *How We Advertised America*, "In no degree was the Committee an agency of censorship … Our effort was educational and informative throughout, for we had such confidence in our case as to feel that no other argument was needed than the simple, straightforward presentation of the facts." Yet many journalists at the time saw the work as ham-fisted censorship and illogical posturing.

Commercial advertising did not dry up during World War I, even though consumer goods were in short supply. Business owners were able to buy ads that also stressed the role of their business in helping the war effort and promote sales of government war bonds. The successful campaigns led the advertising trade journal *Printers' Ink* to recall that "it is possible to sway the minds of whole populations, change their habits of life, create belief, practically universal, in any policy or idea."

During World War I, as the US government assumed unprecedented power, large corporations that had been under fire in the muckraking age could now gain legitimacy through war advertising. Many felt it helped break down "imaginary, artificial barriers" between the corporations and the national cause. Advertising professionals also believed that their efforts in the war helped them gain new prestige as professionals (Marchand 1998).

After the war, the advertising industry went through an enormous period of expansion and a change in emphasis. "There is a major shift from trying to inform the public of a product's existence, and what it supposedly can do," said historian Mark Stoler, "to playing on psychological desires and needs, such as acceptance, prestige, sex, and popularity" (Stoler 2012).

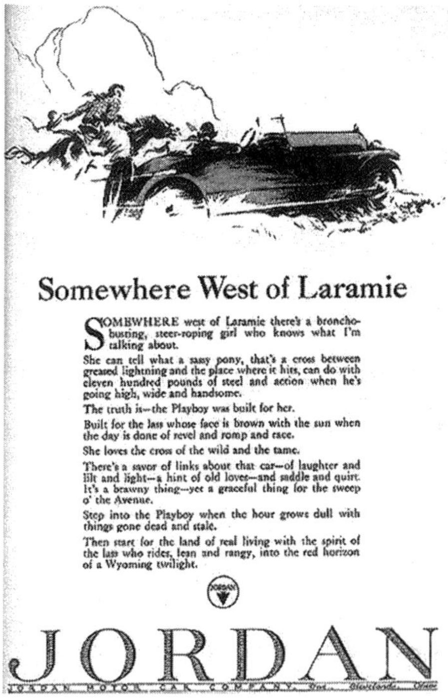

Figure 6.16 Appealing to women—Cigarette makers weren't the only ones appealing to women. One of the most colorful pieces of copywriting ever written, the Jordan car ad of 1923, lived on long after the actual company vanished. "Somewhere west of Laramie, there's a broncho-bustin' steer-roping girl who knows what I'm talking about." Library of Congress.

9 World War II

By the 1940s, when World War II broke out, public relations and advertising were ready once again to support the war effort and show the role corporations were playing. This time they started with a serious handicap. In the years after World War I, American oil and automotive industries had grown close to their German counterparts in terms of technology, politics, and long-term business strategy. General Motors and other major companies helped rebuild Germany's defense industries in the 1930s. IBM helped the Nazis with a census that tracked Jewish populations (as will be noted in Chapter 10). Texaco, an American oil company, helped fascists win the 1930s civil war in Spain and provided a New York haven for German spies and diplomats in the months before the US entered World War II (Sampson 1975). Standard Oil (Exxon) had allied with German chemical giant I. G. Farben and helped support production of key war materials such as synthetic rubber (Borkin 1978).

Some of this information came out before the war, but as the US entered World War II, the British security agencies provided the evidence to expose the companies in the US press and in congressional investigations (Stevenson 1978). The resulting public anger was a serious problem for companies who were suddenly anxious to prove their patriotism. "Once problems and scandals are revealed, corporations are often faced with negative public reactions and perceptions," said historian Deborah Petersen-Perlman. "It is common for these corporations to engage in public relations campaigns which highlight these corporations' good deeds" (Petersen-Perlman 1994).

Texaco began sponsoring the Metropolitan Opera Broadcasts in 1940 "as atonement for past sins," Petersen said. Standard Oil hired Roy Striker, the famous former head of the Farm Security Administration photography effort, to document the role that petroleum was playing in the war (Plattner 1983).

The War Advertising Council was organized in 1942 to help prepare voluntary advertising campaigns for wartime efforts. *Advertising Age* saw a connection between the fervent patriotism exhibited by the advertising industry and investigations by then-Senator Harry Truman. "The industry launched a frontal campaign to protect itself, promoting its importance to the war effort and construing

Figure 6.17 War Advertising Council—The campaign to save rubber was one of the War Advertising Council's big projects and one way that civilians were engaged in during the early years of World War II. Natural rubber supplies from Southeast Asia had been cot off and synthetic rubber from petroleum had been blocked by the oil industry. Walter Richards, 1942, Library of Congress.

itself as the information industry" (Rothenberg 1999). Overall, the council garnered $350 million in free public service messages. After the war it was renamed the Advertising Council.

Figures 6.18(a) to **6.18(d)** Recruiting posters—Four recruiting posters for the Navy show the evolution of style over the nineteenth and twentieth centuries. The first is designed to recruit volunteers for the Confederate Navy in 1863. The second was a highly successful "I want you" direct appeal that was widely copied in World War I. The third, from World War II, shows a heroic figure in action. The fourth, from the Vietnam era, emphasizes training and opportunity with a low-key personal appeal. US National Archives and Records Administration.

10 Broadcast Advertising

The idea of putting advertising on the radio in order to pay for programs is usually attributed to David Sarnoff and his radio memo to the American Marconi Corporation in 1916. But it's worth noting that the concept was already being tested by several amateur groups in the upper-Midwest.

Radio advertising seemed like a perilous venture at first, said historian Roland Marchand, because it would intrude into family home life. But when RCA and other radio manufacturers found they could not finance radio programming simply through sales of radio equipment, and when the US decided not to follow Britain's 1922 lead with a subsidized radio network like the British Broadcasting Corporation, then advertising was the only route forward.

Early broadcasters soon adopted the print media model of advertising support for programs. Sometimes a single advertiser would support a program: Orson Welles' Mercury Theater radio program went without advertisers for a few years before the *War of the Worlds* broadcast in 1938, but was then supported by Campbell's Soup; and the *GE Theater* television program was supported by General Electric in the 1950s. Most programs were supported by a variety of advertisers who would package their messages in 15- to 30-second commercials that were priced according to the size of the audience they could reach.

Radio may have been limited to sound, but it opened the doors to imagination as well. Often radio advertisers took advantage of this "theater of the mind" concept. Comedian Stan Freberg demonstrated the effect on his radio show in 1957, using sound effects to dramatize the towing of a 10-ton cherry onto a 700-foot mountain of whipped cream floating in hot-chocolate filled Lake Michigan, with 25,000 extras cheering. The bit was later used by the Radio Advertising Bureau to promote radio advertising.

Both radio and television were regulated by the Federal Communications Commission, and worked under additional ethical codes as well. The National Association of Broadcasters code prohibited the use of profanity, any negative portrayal of family life, irreverence, alcoholism, cruelty, detailed techniques of crime, and negative portrayal of law enforcement officials, or use of subliminal messages in advertising, among other things.

This did not, however, prevent broadcasters from promoting tobacco, even to children. Lucky Strike cigarettes sponsored many radio and television comedies, for instance, including the Jack Benny Show, the Kollege of Musical Knowledge, and the Lucky Strike Hit Parade, which featured teenage singers like Frank Sinatra. Tobacco companies also sponsored TV shows such as *I've Got a Secret* and the *Flintstones* cartoon series. At one point, cigarettes were the dominant factor in television advertising sponsorships. In 1963, teenagers were exposed to 1,300 cigarette commercials per year (Elders 1994).

The most significant ad icon of the twentieth century, according to *Advertising Age*, was the Marlboro Man cigarette campaign. First conceived by the Leo Burnett agency in 1954, the Marlboro Man image involves cowboys, often riding horses in a Western setting.

Originally the ad campaign was seen as a way to increase the popularity of filter cigarettes, since unfiltered cigarettes were considered more masculine. Sales went up 300 percent in two years. That same year, tobacco companies released "A Frank Statement," the first in a campaign to counter reports that smoking cigarettes could cause lung cancer. But within a decade, a Surgeon General's report concluded that lung cancer and other serious health effects were, indeed, caused by smoking. Tobacco advertising was banned from broadcasting by Congress starting January 2, 1971. All printed tobacco advertising must now display a health warning from the US Surgeon General.

11 Public Relations and Crisis Communications

After World War II, Ivy Lee's one-way press agent concept expanded into a two-way concept of public relations advocated by Edward Bernays. Corporations should listen to public opinion and tailor some activities with the public in mind, Bernays said. Still, the symmetry of the communication varied considerably.

For some companies, public relations was nothing more than a defensive tactic to be used when under fire from public opinion and potential regulators. Others with longer-range vision used ethical principles and accepted corporate responsibility, which in turn made their public relations efforts far more successful.

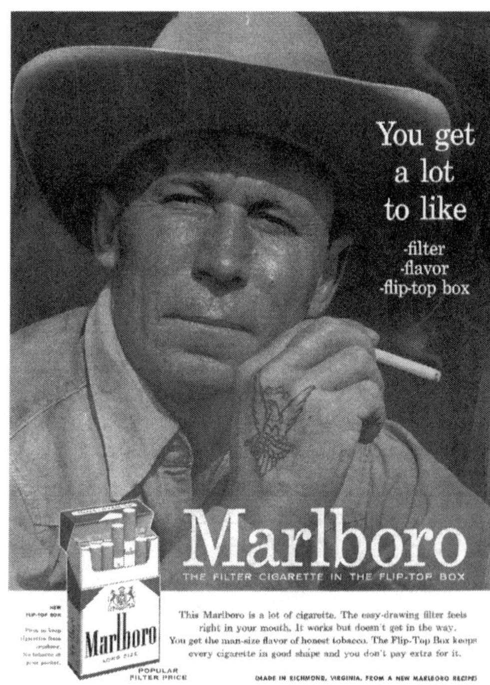

Figure 6.19 Marlboro Man—This image was crafted in 1954 to embody the rugged American spirit and sell filtered cigarettes to men. The Marlboro Man was considered the top advertising campaign of the twentieth century. Hartman Center, Duke University.

Several controversies from the era showed how varied the approaches could be. In the 1970s, public health officials in developing countries noticed a disturbing trend. Infant mortality rates were rising as mothers switched from natural breast feeding to infant formula. A major factor in the switch included advertising techniques designed to convince mothers from Aruba to Zimbabwe that infant formula was cleaner and safer. In Europe and the United States, these tactics might not have been entirely honest, but they were at least not damaging. In the developing world, switching to infant formula was like "signing the death certificate of a child," according to a United Nations health committee. That was because mothers in poorer regions lacked clean water to mix with formula powder, and often couldn't afford to keep buying baby formula (*Time*, 1976).

In 1974, Nestlé sued the publishers of a twelve-page pamphlet entitled *The Baby Killer* for libel. After a two-year trial in Switzerland, Nestlé won a settlement of 300 Swiss francs. The paltry award upheld Nestlé's view that it hadn't directly broken Swiss law, but emphasized that, in the eyes of the court, Nestlé had acted unethically. An international boycott of Nestlé products was launched in response. At one point the Episcopal Church even contacted the mother of a Nestlé executive to encourage a change in behavior—without success. In 1984, Nestlé agreed to abide by an international health code, but the boycott was reinstated in 1988 after an investigation showed continued patterns of violations. In 1999, Nestlé insisted in a public relations campaign that it was acting ethically and responsibly, but a British Advertising Standards Authority found that the contention was not supported (Ferriman, 1999). As this book went to press in 2015, the boycott was still in effect (Babymilkaction.org/nestlefree).

In contrast, a 1982 crisis involving Tylenol poisoning showed how a major business ought to handle a disaster. The crisis began when seven people died after taking Tylenol pain reliever due to malicious tampering with Tylenol packages. Although the company was not at fault, Tylenol maker Johnson & Johnson issued an immediate recall for all of its products, refunded all consumers, staffed phone banks, and announced it would develop tamper-proof packaging (Rehak 2002).

Often a company's reaction would do more harm to its reputation than the original incident. The 1979 partial meltdown of the Three Mile Island nuclear reactor was one such event. During the ongoing disaster, neither the utility nor the Nuclear Regulatory Commission (NRC) had a way to get information from people who had it (in the control room and at the site) to the public and the press, with enormous confusion resulting (President's Commission 1979). The public was not informed about the accident itself until hours after it took place, nor was it informed of gas or water releases containing high levels of radiation (*Washington Post*, 1999).

Similarly inaccurate information and attempts to control media access fueled public outrage about the explosion on a BP oil-drilling rig in the Gulf of Mexico in 2010. The outrage was even more widespread due to the new ability of the web to spread many-to-many communication, and also as something of a backlash to the attempts to create a business personality. While these efforts worked for AT&T in the early twentieth century, they seemed to have backfired on BP in the early twenty-first century. "The more successful they are in creating such a personality, the more there is to love—and hate," said a *Financial Times* analyst (Kelloway 2010).

Public relations expert James Grunig, who developed the idea of the "two-way symmetrical flow" of communication, contends that ethical public relations helps a company avoid problems in the first place by alerting management to the seriousness of a problem and encouraging responsible reactions (Grunig 1989). "By working to implement a symmetrical system of internal communication, public relations professionals can, in turn, affect organizational culture" (Sriramesh et al. 1996).

Ongoing controversies tarnished the public images of Nike, Nestlé, BP, the nuclear industry, and many other businesses, and continue to demonstrate that public relations alone cannot obscure irresponsible corporate behavior. Personalizing a corporate image may help in good times, but when things go wrong, the personality becomes a target of consumer outrage.

12 Ad Agencies in the Late Twentieth Century

As consumer culture caught on in the years after World War II, advertising agencies began developing psychologically based marketing theories that would give them an edge over their competition and frame their efforts to reach audiences. It was a time of personality, creativity, and opportunity (Cappo 2005). Among the creative personalities were the following:

- Leo Burnett (1892–1971) believed in personalizing and sentimentalizing products, creating icons like the Jolly Green Giant, the Pillsbury Doughboy, Charlie the Tuna, Tony the Tiger, and most famously, the Marlboro Man.
- Norman B. Norman (1914–1991), one of New York's original ad men, tied advertising to theories of empathy for clients including Colgate-Palmolive, Revlon, Ronson, Chanel, and Liggett & Myers.
- Helen Lansdowne Resor (1886–1964), worked for J. Walter Thompson to help market products to women. Woodbury Soap's ad, "The skin you love to touch," was typical of her use of personal appeals to attract interest.
- David Ogilvy (1911–1999) believed that "brand personality" drew consumers to products. At the height of his career in 1962, *Time* magazine called him "the most sought-after wizard in today's advertising industry." He was known for a career of expanding the bounds of both creativity and morality in advertising. Ogilvy's campaigns included "The man in the Hathaway shirt" (featuring a model with an aristocratic eye patch) and "The man from Schweppes is here." In 1989 The Ogilvy Group was bought by WPP Group, a British parent company which, by 2010, was the largest ad agency in the world.
- Rosser Reeves (1910–1984) was a pioneer of broadcast advertising who saw repetition of a "Unique Selling Proposition" (USP) as the key theory. These were often translated into slogans (such as M&M's candy that "melts in your mouth, not in your hand") or dramatic demonstrations. Reeves was famous for annoying pain reliever commercials with cartoons that would depict anvils inside people's heads being hit with hammers. In one commercial, a nerve-wracked daughter shouts "Mother Please! I'd rather do it myself." Reeves was the model for the protagonist in a television series about advertising called *Mad Men*.
- William Bernbach (1911–1982) rejected the "USP" idea and developed off-beat, attention-getting campaigns that made him a leader in the "creative revolution" of the

1960s and 1970s. His "think small" campaign for Volkswagen was the top campaign of the twentieth century according to *Advertising Age* (Klein and Donation, 1999). Emphasizing that creativity was the path to audience interest, Bernach warned against thinking of advertising as some kind of science.

- Maurice and Charles Saatchi (b. 1946 and 1943, respectively) were among the first to take a global approach to advertising when they founded Saatchi & Saatchi in 1970. Through a series of mergers and acquisitions in the 1980s, the company became the world's largest advertising super-agency by 1988. The Saatchi brothers split off from the main agency, now owned by Publicis Groupe, to run a smaller creative agency, M&C Saatchi.
- Lee Clow (b. 1942) took Bernbach's creative revolution of the 1970s into the next generation, crafting television ads like the famous Apple "1984" commercial. He is also known for the Energizer Bunny, Taco Bell Chihuahua, and California Cooler campaigns.

13 Advertising Regulation: Europe and the United States

Advertising regulation in Europe has traditionally been more paternalistic, yet advertising graphics tend to be far more explicit than in the United States. For example, ads for tobacco and alcohol are tightly regulated in Europe, and yet ads with nudity or suggestive themes are not considered as offensive to European tastes.

UK advertising regulation was assumed by the Advertising Standards Authority, which consolidated advertising regulatory authority from television, radio, and print commissions. The code is described as a mixture of self-regulation for non-broadcast advertising and co-regulation for broadcast advertising. Like US advertising laws, ads cannot be misleading or cause "physical, mental, moral or social harm to persons under the age of 18."

Controversies about advertising in France often revolve around attempts to maintain French traditions amid an increasing internationalization of both advertising and language. French advertising laws discriminated against non-French products until around 1980, when Scotch whiskey manufacturers sued France in the European Court of Justice. By 1991, French laws prohibited all tobacco advertising and alcohol advertising on TV or in cinemas. Some relaxation of restrictions on wine advertising took place around 2008.

The view of advertising as a free speech right has changed dramatically in the United States. Before 1976, US courts drew a sharp distinction between the right to political speech and the right to advertise. While local and state governments could not prohibit strictly political dissent without running afoul of the First Amendment, they could control the content of commercial messages.

This meant, for example, that when laws were passed to curb the abuses of patent medicine advertising, there was no basis to complain that the First Amendment rights were being violated. But it also meant that in 1928, when the United Mine Workers of

America wanted to place ads in local newspapers during a coal strike, state courts could grant the coal industry an injunction to stop them (*Washington Post*, February 28, 1928).

The idea that advertising could be regulated as states and localities saw fit was reinforced by the courts in a case called *Valentine v. Christensen*. The dispute started in 1940, when a surplus World War I submarine was being exhibited for profit, and the city of New York stopped the owner from passing out advertising on city streets. The US Supreme Court heard the submarine case in 1942 and ruled that the city was free to regulate advertising because commercial speech did not have First Amendment protection (*Valentine v. Christensen*, 316 US 52, 1942).

A much more difficult case was presented in 1964, when a lawsuit over a Civil Rights ad became the focus of a major national decision on the right to criticize public officials (see sidebar captioned "A landmark advertising and libel case"). The Sullivan case involved an advertisement that was clearly political, and the US courts tried to maintain a sharp distinction between commercial and political speech. However, ten years later, several advertising cases came up that presented both political and commercial dimensions.

In one case, a Virginia law prohibited advertising for what had become legal abortion services (*Bigelow v. Virginia*, 421 US 809, 1975). In another case, a citizens' consumer council asked the court to overturn a Virginia state ban on advertising for generic drugs. Although the case was primarily commercial, the citizens' group argued that this was a case of discrimination against the elderly, who needed price information to make better choices, and therefore the argument had a political dimension (*Virginia State Board of Pharmacy v. Virginia Citizens Consumer Council*, 425 US 748, 1976).

At this point, the Supreme Court began ruling that while state or federal agencies could prohibit false or deceptive advertising, they could not prohibit truthful advertising about lawful products in most cases (tobacco advertising was one important exception). A state or federal agency could only regulate the time, place, and manner of advertising, but the regulations had to be content neutral and narrowly tailored to meet a compelling government interest.

Subsequent cases confirmed the link between the First Amendment and the right to advertise, while still upholding the ability of governments to regulate false advertising.

A difficult case involved shoe manufacturer Nike Inc. in 1997. Investigators alleged that people making Nike shoes in Vietnam and other Asian nations were subject to dangerous and abusive working conditions. When Nike responded with a public relations campaign that denied such abuses existed, an activist named Marc Kasky sued Nike under California laws prohibiting false advertising. The state Supreme Court agreed, saying, "when a business enterprise, to promote and defend its sales and profits, makes factual representations about its own products or its own operations, it must speak truthfully." The case was sent to, and then sent back from, the US Supreme Court, without resolution. Eventually the case was settled out of court, and while both sides were not entirely satisfied, the validity of regulating untruthful advertising in a commercial area was upheld.

14 Corporate Consolidation

The creative revolution of the 1960s and 1970s gave way, in the 1980s, to a deeply depressed business climate for advertising agencies. Before the 1980s, agencies would take care of all creative work and also handle media buying, getting a 15 percent commission in return. If a client bought $100 million in advertising, the agency would collect $100 million from the client but only be charged $85 million by the publication or broadcast network where the ad was placed. "It was a sweet deal," remembers advertising historian Joe Cappo.

European agencies led the way in the 1980s toward a split in the creative and buying functions. A client could now purchase advertising directly through media brokers who only charged from 2 to 5 percent, and hired ad agencies to do the creative work. The idea of the agencies as a full service-marketing partner vanished. As a result of the contraction in business, major corporate advertising mergers began to take place. The economies of scale that appealed to publishers and broadcasting companies also made sense in an advertising business that was rapidly contracting. Out of 20 major ad agencies in the 1980s, only one was still independent by 2005, according to Cappo. Four major agencies dominated 80 percent of the market in the United States and 50 percent of the market worldwide.

15 New Advertising Models in the Digital Age

The collapse of the newspaper and magazine publishing industries in the first decade of the twenty-first century was not a complete surprise. Advertising executives had been worried that digital information systems would undermine traditional forms of classified and display advertising for at least a decade. The surprising part was how rapidly the change began taking hold.

Between 1950 and 2010, the newspapers and magazines lost more than half their shares of US advertising revenues, with the steepest decline coming in the 2005–10 period (Varian 2010). Newspaper ad revenues dropped from a peak of $47 billion in 2005 to less than half of that by 2010 (NAA 2010).

Radio and television advertising also dropped in the face of market fragmentation and a wider variety of alternative news and entertainment sources. On a typical night in 1976, about 92 percent of all viewers were watching the three networks, but by 2010, four networks could attract only 46 percent of TV viewers (Auletta 2010).

Broadcasting also experienced declines in advertising, although not as severe as the print media, although the same forces that undermined the print media business model are at work for broadcast media as well. Advertisers in both media counted on a "bundled" package of information that would appeal to mass audiences. A person might buy a newspaper to read garden advice or the comics, but mass advertising also supported news and public affairs programming. Publishers and broadcasters never had to keep track of whether enough people were tuning in to reports on parliamentary elections, fashion news, or Brazilian business.

Internet search engines effectively "unbundled" the content, allowing those with interests in politics, fashion, or business to find exactly the stories they wanted without having to buy information they didn't ask for. As a result, the business model of an independent media with a variety of information types, supported by mass advertising, faded rapidly in the twenty-first century. Nearly two centuries after the penny press business model was adopted for print, and almost a century after it was adopted for broadcasting, the old business model could no longer support the traditional news and information system.

In contrast, Internet advertising rose rapidly from its beginnings. After Congress first permitted commercial use of the Internet, the first banner ad campaigns appeared on the web in October 1994. Twenty years later, Internet advertising stands at about $23 billion in the US (IAB 2014).

What's new about Internet advertising is that it is not aimed at mass markets, but rather at individuals and small groups of consumers. The Nike plus campaign is an example. Using a small sensor in a Nike running shoe connected to an iPod, runners can keep track of their progress and connect with other runners in their area. As a result, customers are coming to the company, rather than the other way around, and Nike is spending less money with traditional media. "We're not in the business of keeping the media companies alive," Edwards said (Story 2007).

The vast majority of the new Internet advertising revenue comes to one company—Google—which began as a search engine for the Internet in 1996 and expanded into a marketing and data mining giant. Google's AdWords system offers pay-per-click (PPC) advertising, in which a client is charged when users click through to the client's site. The fact that advertisers are charged only when consumers take action is revolutionary.

John Wanamaker's quip was once a standing gag in the advertising business. The department store founder once said, "I know I waste half the money I spend on advertising. The problem is, I don't know which half " (Rothenberg 1999). With Google, not only does a company know which half is being wasted, it also knows all kinds of other details about its consumers, from demographics to purchasing history to web-surfing behavior. As a result, precisely targeted advertising can be used in a way that is far more effective than mass-market advertising.

Google's approach to advertising is being mimicked by others in various ways. Organizations like Demand Media and Associated Content produce thousands of "pieces of content" that are created in response to web searches and other measurements of topic popularity. "We can predict the return on investment on each of these pieces of content," says Demand CEO Richard Rosenblatt (SXSW 2010). Writers who make less than the minimum wage in some of these start-ups are not so sanguine (Carr 2010).

Google is also working on ways to streamline demand management for information by monetizing high-value ad space and auctioning lower-value. From a one-way advertising model, the company expects to develop far more user-centered advertising and information servicers that create new opportunities for quality information. The concept will take a decade to fully develop, as the traditional media copes with increasing chaos (Fallows 2010).

The new models seem to fit some of the old media theories. As Marshall McLuhan said, "If the audience can become involved in the actual process of making the ad, then it's happy—Sort of like quiz shows. They were great TV because they gave the audience a role, something to do" (Hirshberg 2007).

McLuhan's optimism about audience interaction was increasingly questioned as new forms of individually targeted advertising emerged in the second decade of the twenty-first century. Coupons, once clipped from newspapers and magazines to allow consumer discounts, could now be downloaded onto mobile phones, along with personal information about the consumer. The convenience of an instant discount is offset, consumer advocates said, by increasing concerns about invasions of privacy through "behavioral targeting." Groups like the Center for Digital Democracy have asked the Federal Trade Commission to regulate the flow of personal information to marketers (Cha 2010).

It's interesting that a 2002 science fiction film, *Minority Report*, depicted highly invasive advertising techniques of the year 2054. In the story, a police captain walks through a shopping mall and is bombarded by holographic ads calling him by name. It is a mark of the rapid acceleration of communications technology that ideas about a distant future would be within reach only a few years later.

A Landmark Case about Free Speech and Advertising

As the Civil Rights movement began gaining ground in the United States, arrests of leaders became more frequent. In March, 1960, a group of ministers hoping to raise money for the defense of Martin Luther King placed an ad in the *New York Times* asking for donations and urging Americans to "Heed Their Rising Voices." The ad described repression faced by the movement in a critical tone, noting that many demonstrators had been expelled from their schools and that police had taken hostile action against them. In some cases, the descriptions of events had minor inaccuracies, and these provided the basis for Montgomery, Alabama, Police Commissioner L. B. Sullivan to sue for libel. Sullivan was successful in the Alabama state courts, as was expected since the power structure of the Old South was unsympathetic to the Civil Rights movement and to what was often seen as outside criticism.

However, when the US Supreme Court heard the case, there was unanimous agreement that the *New York Times* had not libeled the police commissioner. On the contrary, the criticism in the ad was considered to be valuable political speech in the tradition of a "profound national commitment to the principle that debate on public issues should be uninhibited, robust, and wide-open."

The Sullivan standard did three things: it put the burden of proof on the plaintiff in a libel case, not the defendant; it said citizens had not only a right but a duty to criticize public officials; and it said the plaintiff had to prove "actual malice" (defined as when a defendant knowingly published or broadcast a falsehood or acted in reckless disregard for the truth).

The case cleared the way for "sharp, even caustic" debate in the United States, permitting nonviolent reform movements the maximum amount of latitude to make their arguments. It also had a profound impact on law in other nations, such as the United Kingdom, Australia, New Zealand, and many European nations, where libel laws were reformed in subsequent years. Only Canada seems to have maintained an older, more paternalistic view of libel and resisted the Sullivan standard in the first decades of the twenty-first century.

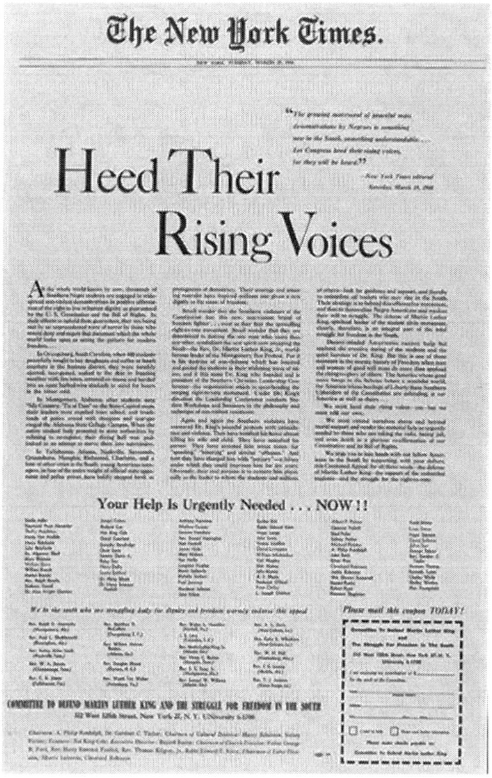
The New York Times.

Heed Their Rising Voices

Your Help Is Urgently Needed . . . NOW!!

Figure 6.20 *New York Times v Sullivan*—One of the most significant free speech cases of the twentieth century involved the reaction to this March 29, 1960 advertisement in the *New York Times*. Alabama state officials who opposed the Civil Rights movement sued for libel, but the Supreme Court said that political advertising was protected by the First Amendment and that everyone had a right, and even a duty, to participate in open public debate. *New York Times*, March 29, 1960.

For additional reading, discussion questions, links to video, and other suggestions, see www.revolutionsincommunications.com.

Part III

The Electronic Revolution: From "National Neighborhoods" to the Global Village

It would not be long before the whole surface of this country would be channeled for ... a knowledge of all that is occurring throughout the land, making, in fact, one neighborhood of the whole country.

Samuel Morse, February 15, 1838

1 The Significance of the Electronic Revolution

Rapid communication over long distances has often been associated with divine forces, for example, in Greek and Roman mythology, with Nike, Hermes, and Mercury. For ordinary mortals, communication has historically been confined to the speed of a running horse or fast ship. History and literature are full of references to the role of messengers bringing the long-delayed news of victory or defeat. The runner from Marathon, the messenger in Shakespeare's *Henry IV*, the signal flags of Trafalgar are among many examples of the problems with communications in pre-industrial history and culture.

Perhaps the classic example of news failing to arrive in time involves the needless loss of life at the Battle of New Orleans. When the armies of the United States and Britain fought the battle on January 8, 1815, the generals could not have known that a peace treaty had been signed before Christmas of 1814. It took seven weeks for the fastest sailboat to carry the message from London to Louisiana.

Yet in about fifty years, the same message would have taken less than an hour to be relayed by electronic telegraph using Morse code. The unique combination of hardware (electric wires) and software (a simple arrangement of dots and dashes) changed the world, brought down the barriers of time and distance, and opened the door to the electronic and digital mass media revolutions. No other development since printing had so many impacts in so many different walks of life.

This section on the Electronic Revolution organizes the history of three technologies:

- Chapter 7 covers the telegraph and telephone from the 1830s to the present.
- Chapter 8 covers radio from the 1890s to the present.
- Chapter 9 covers television from the 1920s to the present.

2 The Telegraph and Telephone as Mass Media

Historians usually see the telegraph and telephone as one-to-one personal media, entirely separate from mass media—at least until the late twentieth century, when individual and mass media were converged in digital networks.

Yet media can't be so easily separated. Although the telegraph carried private, one-to-one communications in the form of telegrams, it also allowed news agencies and wire services to carry political and economic news between mass media outlets. Between the 1850s and the 1980s, it provided the essential infrastructure in a two-stage mass communications system. Wire services like Reuters, Havas, and the Associated Press served an essential function distributing news via telegraph.

The telephone system, although originally designed for private one-to-one communications, also served as the essential infrastructure of national radio networks when they emerged in the 1920s. News, drama, comedy, and other programs originating in one place would usually be carried to the rest of the country by static-free telephone lines and then broadcast by regional radio stations. Like the telegraph, the telephone was indispensable to the two-stage mass communications system until satellites arrived in the 1980s. The business models for the telegraph and telephone also had an impact on the overall shape and diversity of the mass media.

In the United States, a joint Western Union–Associated Press monopoly shaped the economics of publishing, creating barriers to entry and making it difficult for alternative newspapers to compete. The very device that expanded the spatial and temporal reach of communication seemed to weaken its depth and flexibility. Younger journalists like Will Irwin complained that the newspapers spoke in the voice of an older generation, as we have seen in Chapter 3. Meanwhile in Europe, the competitive economics of publishing took different forms since government-owned telegraph and telephone systems did not favor any one particular group of members, and this contributed to a greater diversity of expression.

While the electronic revolution began with the telegraph and telephone, these prototype electronic technologies were the basis from which radio, television, and satellite broadcasting developed. Their scientific origins and business models are intertwined. Industrial print and early radio and television grew up in an interdependent network, around the telegraph and telephone, from the beginning. The concept of media convergence is not just an artifact of the digital age, but rather, a constant condition of overlapping technological influences in mass media history.

3 Cycles of Open and Closed Technologies

Innovation in communication technology often follows a cycle that can be described in three stages: open, closed, and alternative. The first stage of the cycle involves open experimentation, competition, and development of a new media. It may be followed by a second stage in which stakeholders close the technologies around profit-generating activities protected by patents. If the stakeholders are successful, they may be able to dominate the market. In a third stage, successful monopolies become stagnant, charging more and more money for fewer and fewer services. The downward spiral often spurred the search for circumventing technologies as alternatives to the old monopoly. Once a promising new avenue is found, the open competition starts again.

Although the cycle of open–closed–alternative technologies is a useful generalization, it doesn't fit every media technology exactly. As we've seen in Section II, photography was born as an open source technology, with its exact secrets revealed from the outset. In contrast, the earliest cinema companies attempted to control the industry through patents and industry associations. Although direct industry control failed, indirect content control through the Motion Picture Production Code become the norm.

As we will see in Chapter 7, telegraphy also went through a period of open experimentation, and Samuel Morse, for one, wanted it to stay that way. Like Daguerre, he also hoped that the government would own the hardware. But in the US, as over 500 telegraph companies emerged, fought, and then merged by 1866, telegraphy became a national monopoly under the Western Union company. Operating without regulation, Western Union and its sole partner in the Associated Press exerted an enormous amount of control over which ideas and people would compete in the information system of the nineteenth century.

One response was a US campaign for legislation to transfer the telegraph to the Post Office, which was already taking place in Britain. When that failed, the same campaigners who fought the telegraphic monopoly helped create the telephone system in the 1870s. Through its control of patents and market manipulation, the Bell telephone system also became a monopoly around the turn of the twentieth century. Anxious to avoid problems that had surfaced with Western Union, the US Justice Department forced AT&T to take a neutral "common carrier" position with respect to content and charges for services.

As we will see in Chapters 8 and 9, broadcasting also began with a cycle of open innovation among scientists like Heinrich Hertz and James Clerk Maxwell. Entrepreneur Guglielmo Marconi attempted to control the emerging radio telegraph system, and was initially successful, but the US and UK governments curbed the monopolies in the pre-World War I period. American Marconi eventually became the Radio Corporation of America, which in turn created the National Broadcasting Company.

Meanwhile, inventors like Reginald Fessenden turned to radio telephony, and some of their key patents were purchased by AT&T. By the 1920s, radio technology had more or less closed, and television technology was opening. By the 1950s, television technology was closed, and the search for circumventing technologies would lead to satellite and cable systems by the 1980s and to digital imaging systems in the 1990s and twenty-first century.

4 Re-tribalization and the Global Village

Electronic communication through radio and television arrived relatively quickly, over the course of only a few decades from the late 1920s to the early 1950s. Print oriented societies that had once been organized around slower, linear forms of culture were now facing what seemed like a chaotic set of changes. Many regular people felt utterly swamped by modernity. And even Thomas Edison, George Eastman, Guglielmo Marconi, and other inventors never felt comfortable with the twentieth-century world their own inventions helped to create.

Marshall McLuhan characterized the social changes created by electronic media as a "re-tribalization" into a "global village." Radio and television had created new "tribal" forms of art and entertainment with an emphasis on inclusiveness and nationalism. Winston Churchill's speeches on radio, Franklin Roosevelt's Fireside Chats, and, on the dark side, Adolf Hitler's use of radio in the 1930s and 1940s—all of these were examples of the new tribalism and nationalism. Other examples included the way radio became the medium for rock 'n' roll in the post-World War II era.

Meanwhile, the old print culture continued to dominate politics, law, education, and commerce, with its emphasis on individuality and linear thinking. The coexistence of the two contrasting forms of society and experience were, McLuhan thought, "a formula for complete chaos" (McLuhan and Powers 1989).

With society changing so quickly in McLuhan's era, in the 1950s and 1960s, it's easy to see why people would search for explanations. But it turned out that the chaos wasn't so complete. Audiences select media based on their own preferences; cultures can construct their technologies, not just react to them, if they have the freedom to do so.

How they constructed these technologies, and the extent to which they are free, has been a wide-open controversy. In Ray Bradbury's novel, *Fahrenheit 451*, people watched television to be part of a family and cared very little if the state banned their books. There is something of that search for community and tribalism in the way people watch television today. But that's not the whole story. There is the possibility of participating in, and generating, our own media systems. McLuhan's fear of chaos in the coexistence of print and electronic cultures turns out to be conservative, deterministic, and not quite in step with the twenty-first-century experience.

5 Social Responsibility

From the 1920s on, the power of amplified sound and moving images, in the form of cinema, radio, and television, were suddenly available to national leaders, creating new opportunities to both abuse and elevate the human condition.

Certainly the tragedies of the Holocaust, the Rwandan and Bosnian genocides, and countless others, would not have been possible without a mass media to incite hatred. Radio and television may have had a particularly deep role in this, although the print media shows up in the record as well, for example, in the way the *Dur Sturmer* newspaper carried grotesque and virulent anti-Semitism in the 1930s in Germany.

Radio and cinema delivered very strong messages of hatred in Germany in the 1920s and 1930s; radio and newspapers were the vehicles for inciting genocide in Rwanda in 1994; and television was the vector for hatred in Bosnia in the late 1990s.

The consequences for responsible publishers and managers in the German, Bosnian, and Rwandan media included long prison sentences and (in one case in 1945) execution. So the idea that social responsibility is expected of media professionals is certainly bound up in the punishments that have been meted out for criminal behavior.

Like the printing press, however, the new electronic media also provided many opportunities for expanding tolerance, diversity, and freedom. Radio rallied the public and was a key ingredient in elevating sentiment to fight the Nazis in the 1930s and 1940s. Televised news helped crystallize empathetic public opinion around civil rights issues in the 1950s and raise appropriate questions about the Vietnam War in the 1960s.

Still, the international distortions of the mass media have proven difficult to counteract. The imbalance in the media power of developing nations, as compared to the industrialized West, created what is sometimes termed "Hollywood hegemony." And the apparent threat of Western modernity to traditional cultures has created violent reactions in recent decades.

Today, with instant, global, full spectrum communication possible through dozens of media, we are indeed a global village, although not a peaceful one, as McLuhan accurately predicted. We are not yet reconciled to each other's differences, aware of each other's strengths, or tolerant of each other's weaknesses.

As Henry David Thoreau once observed, communication technology can be nothing more than an improved means to an unimproved end. And yet, a larger and more positive vision for the role of mass media technology, not fully cast, is still being articulated.

7

The First Electronic Revolution: Telegraph and Telephone

It is obvious, at the slightest glance, that this mode of instantaneous communication must inevitably become an instrument of immense power, to be wielded for good or for evil ...

Samuel Morse, 1838

There are only two forces that can carry light to all corners of the globe—the sun in the heavens and the Associated Press down here. I may seem to be flattering the sun, but I do not mean to do so ...

Mark Twain, 1906

1 The Telegraph as the First Electronic Network

The telegraph arrived in the mid-1840s as part of a widespread revolution in communications that included mass production of newspapers, magazines, and books, along with improvements in transportation such as canals, steamships, and railroads. The invention marks the beginning of the electronic revolution, which led to telephones, radios, and televisions. It was also one source of the digital revolution, since Morse code, based on a dot-or-dash signal, is a binary software system.

Socially, the telegraph was the first electronic network, or as historian Tom Standage said, the "Victorian Internet." Telegrams were delivered within hours and responses could be sent right away, with an effect somewhat like an e-mail system (Standage 1998). Politically, the Western Union telegraph system, in tandem with the Associated Press, became the first monopoly in America. In Europe, governments took over the telegraph companies to avoid the abuses of a monopoly system apparent in America. Meanwhile, inventors worked on a way to circumvent the monopoly through a system called the telephone.

1.1 Signals over distance

The problem of signaling over a distance is an ancient one, and some of the most complex systems have been used in military campaigns. Greek historian Thucydides described naval flag systems in the Peloponnesian War that may have been similar to those still in use today. The Roman army used a complex "box cipher," according to historian Polybius. The cipher used a system of two torches whose positions could be used to indicate twenty-five letters, with 1-1 representing A; 1-5 representing E; and 5-5 representing Z (Kahn 1967).

The term "telegraph" was first coined for a 1792 French invention, also called the Napoleonic semaphore, by Claude Chappe. This original mechanical telegraph was a system of pivoting shutters placed atop signal towers to send coded messages. The system was used extensively by the French and British military during the Napoleonic era to carry signals from Paris and London to the fleets at naval bases along the coast.

Telegraph towers were used only by the government, but they were widely known, and the word "telegraph" quickly entered the popular lexicon. When Admiral Horatio Nelson sent a ship-to-ship message using traditional naval signal flags just before the Battle of Trafalgar in 1805, newspapers at the time said he "addressed his fleet by telegraphic communication" with the famous message: "England expects that every man will do his duty" (*Times*, London, December 2, 1805).

Figure 7.1 First telegraph—The "optical" telegraph was developed by Claude Chappe in France forty years before Samuel Morse began thinking about using electricity for signals over distance. The optical telegraph was too expensive for routine use and could not be used in bad weather. 1805 illustration, Library of Congress.

Businesses were not able to use military systems, so when events were pressing and a few hours' advantage could mean large profits, news would be sent by carrier pigeon. In 1815, a group of London stock speculators learned of Napoleon's defeat at Waterloo by carrier pigeon, allowing them to buy stocks in advance of the rapid rise in value when the news became official. Carrier pigeons remained a useful tool for news agencies like Havas in Paris until the advent of the telegraph in the 1840s. For most people, couriers or the regular mail were the only ways to send messages, and important information could easily be delayed.

2 Samuel Morse and his Code: The Software of Telegraphy

It's often said that Samuel F. B. Morse invented the telegraph. But as we have seen, there were many kinds of "telegraph" in use during the early 1800s. What Morse really invented was the software—the Morse code—that made it easy to use telegraphic devices. It was a key insight, similar to Gutenberg's invention of moveable type, and Tim Berners-Lee's idea for a world wide web. In these and many other cases, a rising technical capacity is held back until inventors arrive at the key insights.

What obsessed Samuel Morse about long-distance communication was not military power or the stock exchange, like other telegraphic inventors. Instead, he was motivated by his wife's sad death in 1825 following childbirth. He was in Washington, DC, painting a portrait of the revolutionary war hero Marquis de Lafayette, and she was dying in Connecticut. The letter informing him of her death took five days to reach him. It was a cruel blow, made worse by the gap in communication (Morse 1914). After his wife's death, Morse spent years studying art in Europe. On a ship homeward bound in October 1832, he began talking with other passengers who were interested in electromagnetic experiments. Pacing the deck after dinner one night, he came up with the idea of sending signals through wires and sketched out his ideas in a notebook.

2.1 Foundations of telegraphy

The idea of an artist like Morse becoming an inventor may seem far-fetched, but Morse was a Yale University chemistry graduate and came from a university tradition that saw "arts and sciences" as parallel and interrelated pursuits. Morse's technical insight was not to overcome the mechanical problems of transmitting bursts of electricity; that had already been accomplished by many others.

Steven Gray first sent electric current 700 feet through a line in London in 1727. Benjamin Franklin in the United States was famous for his experiments with electricity. And in England, William Fothergill Cooke and Charles Wheatstone, unknown to Morse, were working on a complex telegraph sending-and-receiving system that was patented on June 12, 1837. The Cooke and Wheatstone system used five wires and a pattern of letters that could be selected or read through indicator needles on either end (Munro 1891). And in British India, an inventor named William O'Shaughnessy invented an improvised telegraphic system in the 1840s.

Figure 7.2 Franklin's kite—In June of 1752, American printer and scientist Benjamin Franklin raised a kite to test his theory that lightning was similar to the charge that could be generated with chemical batteries. This extremely dangerous experiment was one of many being conducted at the time into the nature of electricity. Henry S. Sadd, c. 1840, Library of Congress.

Fortunately, Morse was not well informed about other inventors at the time, and persisted despite many obstacles. He developed a working mechanical system that was an improvement over other electrical telegraphs. And like Cooke, Morse originally tried a system of numbers for individual words and used electric signals to mark a paper tape. Morse patented his device on October 3, 1837.

Working with a collaborator, Alfred Vail, Morse continued to develop the simplified set of dots and dashes known as Morse code. To create the code, Vail and Morse puzzled over the problem of the relative frequency of letters in English. They wanted to match the simplest signals with the most frequent letters. A visit to a nearby printing firm helped solve the problem. In a typical type font, printers stocked 12,000 letter Es and 9,000 Ts, and these were assigned the simplest signal: E was one dot and T was one dash. Morse and Vail also found that the letters Q and Z were rarely used, with 400 and 200 letters in the type case, and so Morse gave them the most complex symbols: Q --.- and Z --..

Morse's unique contribution, then, was an extremely simple way to transmit information using bursts of electricity. In effect, it was an elegant software solution to a hardware problem that others like Cooke and Wheatstone had not solved. Morse had a difficult time finding investors, but he clearly understood the significance of his invention. In a remarkably prophetic letter to Congressman Francis Smith in 1838, Morse wrote:

> It is obvious, at the slightest glance, that this mode of instantaneous communication must inevitably become an instrument of immense power, to be wielded for good or for evil, as it shall be properly or improperly directed. In the hands of a company of speculators, who should monopolize it for themselves, it might be the means of enriching the corporation at the expense of the bankruptcy of thousands; and even in the hands of government alone it might become the means of working vast mischief to the Republic.

2.2 Development of telegraphy

Figure 7.3 Morse code—Samuel F. B. Morse invented not just an electromagnetic telegraph, which was well known, but more importantly, a simplified code that made it easy to use the telegraph. Within a decade the Morse code had been adopted for international use. Photo by Matthew Brady, c. 1850, Library of Congress.

Morse suggested that the government buy the patent and license it to private companies, creating "a systems of checks and preventatives of abuse ... to permit only the good and neutralize the evil" (Morse 1914). Between 1838 and 1842, Morse approached hundreds of potential investors in the United States and Europe. In the hope of financing more experiments on telegraphy, he attended an 1839 lecture in Paris by Louis Daguerre, and returned with the equipment and know-how to teach photography in New York.

Inventors thought the idea of an electric telegraph to be more like a conjuring trick than a useful invention, let alone a profitable one. But in 1842, Congress surprised Morse when it agreed to fund an experimental line from Washington, DC, to Baltimore, Maryland. On May 1, 1844, news from a Whig party convention reached Morse's headquarters in the capitol building an hour ahead of the train, and crowds waiting for news were jubilant, praising Morse for his invention. In a formal demonstration later that month, Morse sent the famous message: "What Hath God Wrought" (*New York Times*, May 1, 1894).

Meanwhile in Britain, Cooke and Wheatstone had finally managed to set up an ongoing public demonstration along a section of railway track between London and Windsor. It was a curiosity at first, but the speed with which royal announcements could be made, and the coordination of police forces in catching criminals fleeing by train, eventually convinced conservative Brits that the Cooke–Wheatstone telegraph was useful. The view was reinforced when the Royal Navy contracted a telegraph along the same route between the Admiralty in London and its main base in Portsmouth—a route once noted for the Navy's optical telegraph.

By the fall of 1845, Morse formed the Magnetic Telegraph Co. in Washington with the help of Amos Kendall, an attorney and former press secretary for President Andrew Jackson. Cooke and Wheatstone, meanwhile, formed the Electric Telegraph Co. in London. With regular service, public enthusiasm soon replaced skepticism, and telegraph lines began doubling yearly. By 1850, in the United States, 12,000 miles of line were run by twenty different companies. At the height of the speculative fever, some 500 telegraph companies were competing.

The telegraph also took off quickly in other countries. By 1852, Britain had over 2,000 miles of line, and Germany had 1,500 miles radiating out from Berlin. France lagged because their early lead with the optical telegraph meant that they were less willing to adopt a new system (Standage 1998). Yet the French also created the first wire service: the Havas Agency.

As continental America and Europe became increasingly connected, links across the ocean were attempted. The first long undersea cable linked Paris and London in 1850, but was then damaged and replaced in 1851. The first dispatches from Britain's war in the Crimea arrived through this system in 1853.

A much greater effort would be needed to connect the New World and the Old. In 1854, New York paper company owner Cyrus W. Field, working with Samuel Morse and others, completed the first leg of the North American portion of the cable, from New York to Newfoundland. The next 2,000 miles across the Atlantic proved difficult, but was completed in 1858.

The first trans-Atlantic cable carried a transatlantic message on August 16, 1858, and fireworks, parades, speeches, and prayers greeted the news. But twenty days later, the cable burned out and the messages stopped. Field went from national hero to laughing stock

Figure 7.4 Yanks and Brits—John Bull and Johnny Yank shake hands across the Atlantic through the celebrated 1858 telegraphic cable, which only lasted three weeks. It took another eight years to lay a more permanent trans-Atlantic cable. Baker & Godwin, 1858, Library of Congress.

overnight, and a British board of inquiry found that the entire project had been poorly designed. Trial and error technology had led to disaster in 1858. Clearly, a new approach was needed, and the new company turned to a Glasgow mathematician and engineer William Thompson (Lord Kelvin). Similar limits to trial-and-error work would be seen in other areas, particularly radio, in later years. It took until 1866 to lay another working cable, but other submarine cables followed in rapid succession.

3 Telegraph ushers in a New Era of Communication

The advent of the electric telegraph promised "universal interests and the worldwide victory of Christianity," enthusiasts said. "The public mind will be stimulated to greater activity with the rapid circulation of news … The whole nation will be impressed with the same idea at the moment. One feeling and one impulse are thus created from the center of the land to the utmost extremity" (Czitrom 1983).

Enthusiasts outnumbered critics, but naturalist and writer Henry David Thoreau was one of the minority voices. Thoreau considered the telegraph little more than an "improved means to an unimproved end":

> [As] with a hundred "modern improvements"; there is an illusion about them; there is not always a positive advance … Our inventions are wont_to be pretty toys, which distract our attention from serious things … We are in great haste to construct a magnetic telegraph from Maine to Texas; but Maine and Texas, it may be, have nothing important to communicate … As if the main object were to talk fast and not to talk sensibly … (Thoreau 1854)

Figure 7.5 Not impressed—Naturalist and author Henry David Thoreau was not impressed when the telegraph arrived in New England, considering it to be merely an "improved means to an unimproved end." Library of Congress.

Occasionally, other critics worried that too much had been made of the telegraph. One felt compelled to write that the telegraph "can neither rescue a man from sin nor transport him to heaven" (*New York Times*, August 24, 1858). Another said the telegraph was "superficial, sudden, unsifted, too fast for the truth" (Lafrance 2014).

The telegraph did more than ease the spread of information. Like any communications revolution, it made new *functions* of communication possible. "Telegraphy gave rise to both the modern conception of news and methods of news gathering," said historian Daniel Czitrom. Before the telegraph, colonial newspapers printed news as it arrived in the mail, or by word of mouth, seldom seeking out news. Timeliness was

Telegraph Changes News Writing

The telegraph changed basic styles of news writing as the costs of telegrams forced journalists to condense their facts and fit the most important information into the very first few words of the dispatch, in case it was cut off by accident or censorship. The change illustrates McLuhan's idea that the medium *is* (or at least *has* a major influence on) the message.

For instance, compare these two news reports. The first is from William Howard Russell's famous 1854 dispatch about the Charge of the Light Brigade, a unit of the British army, written from the Crimean Peninsula of Russia before telegraph lines were available. The second is the lead of a wire dispatch from Washington to New York only seven years later:

Before the telegraph

"If the exhibition of the most brilliant valor, of the excess of courage, and of a daring which would have reflected luster on the best days of chivalry can afford full consolation for the disaster of today, we can have no reason to regret the melancholy loss which we sustained in a contest with a savage and barbarian enemy."

William Howard Russell, writing about the Charge of the Light Brigade, *The Times*, London, November 13, 1854

After the telegraph

"Our troops, after taking three batteries and gaining a great victory at Bull Run, were eventually repulsed, and commenced a retreat on Washington."

Henry Villard, writing about an opening battle of the US Civil War, *New York Herald*, July 22, 1861

Figure 7.6 Before the telegraph—Dispatches written by *The Times* correspondent William Howard Russell (above) from the front lines of the Crimean War in 1854 were not limited by the pressing demands of telegraphic systems. Howard's report on the famous Charge of the Light Brigade, delivered by letter, was long, flowery, and patriotic. In contrast, dispatches from the front lines of the American Civil War tended to be factual and terse. Photo by Roger Fenton, 1854, Library of Congress.

secondary to record keeping. For instance, the pre-telegraphic *Niles Weekly Register's* motto was, "The present and the past, for the future."

After the telegraph, the emphasis tended to be on timeliness and on standardization of information rather that storytelling, especially for news transmitted via telegraph by wire services like the Associated Press (AP). The AP dispatches were "more free from editorial comment than most reporting for single newspapers" (Schudson 1978). The model of AP reporting was, according to the AP's Kent Cooper, "the finest moral concept ever developed in America and given the world ... that news must be truthful and unbiased" (Siebert 1963). But the ideal of unbiased news took root slowly among the newspapers that depended on the AP, according to historian Michael Schudson.

While Russell exemplified the finest moments of early English journalism in his letters to *The Times* from the Crimean War, the effect of the telegraph was to reduce the value of the individual war correspondent and their lengthy dispatches sent from the front.

The wire service's condensed style became a journalistic gold standard, emphasizing facts over opinion. But it did not always obscure opinion, as seen, for instance, in the "our troops" comment by Villard. The short, punchy style of writing was lionized by writers such as Ernest Hemingway, for example, who called it "telegraphese" (Baker 1972).

Nor did the new medium guarantee that the news would be truthful and unbiased, as AP often claimed. In fact, the AP's hand-in-hand monopoly with Western Union proved controversial for nearly a century.

3.1 Telegraph changes the news business

Before the advent of the telegraph, newspapers could compete with each other by catering to select audiences, and every city usually had several newspapers. But the telegraph forced newspapers into a new business model.

When the Mexican–American war began in 1846, telegraph lines from New York and Boston only stretched as far south as Richmond, Virginia. Because communication from the front lines of the war was so difficult, five New York newspapers, including the *Times* and the *Herald*, agreed to share an express service to quickly bring home war news.

This agreement was the beginning of a permanent news gathering cooperative that also included cooperation through an 1848 Harbor News Association in New York, leading to the formation of the New York Associated Press in 1851 (Pyle 2005). By then, the few hundred miles of wire had turned into a telegraph network of over ten thousand miles (Howe 2007). A second "Associated Press" formed around Chicago and St. Louis in 1862. This western Associated Press cooperated with the New York group and eventually merged with it in 1900.

By the mid-1860s, Western Union and the two AP groups agreed on low rates, exclusive use of AP and Western Union services by all members, and a mandatory refusal to transmit or print any "hostile" information about AP or Western Union. One of the most objectionable features of the monopoly was that existing members could veto the entry of new members. Attempts to start newspapers in San Francisco, Chicago, and other cities failed when AP membership was not granted. The situation generated a continuous storm of controversy through the end of the nineteenth century.

3.2 Monopoly in the US: AP–Western Union

Twenty-five years after Samuel Morse's demonstration, the United States had built over 120,000 miles of telegraph line. Within that same time, nearly all of the independent telegraph companies had been purchased by or consolidated under the Western Union company. Given the power of telegraphy, and the potential for disclosure of private business matters, many people were alarmed.

"By the combination of the Western Union, the Associated Press and the railroad monopolies, almost every daily paper in all our large cities is brought under the dominion of the monopolies and extortionists," said San Francisco Herald editor Charles A. Sumner. It is a "disgrace to our country and a standing menace to freedom." (Sumner 1876).

Sumner went on to serve a term in the US Congress and helped bring some of the 96 bills and resolutions, along with forty-eight committee reports, that concerned the AP–Western Union monopoly over the next forty years.

"The issue of telegraph regulation was very prominent in the public sphere," said legal historian Menahem Blondheim. "It was debated extensively in the press and even constituted a favorite topic for college exercises in rhetoric and debating" (Blondheim 2003–4).

Figure 7.7 Learning Morse code—This Western Union telegraph delivery boy was photographed in 1910 by Lewis Hine learning Morse code between deliveries. Hine criticized Western Union, along with coal mines, newspapers, textile factories, and others, for abusive child labor practices. Library of Congress.

AP argued that it could not be regulated, since the First Amendment guaranteed freedom of the press. Although Western Union could not make a similar argument, its relationship with the press meant that public opinion was constantly tilted in its favor. Gardiner G. Hubbard, the leading lobbyist for a postal telegraph service and father-in-law of Alexander Graham Bell, said the AP–Western Union monopoly was "a power greater than any ever wielded by the French Directory, because, in an era when public opinion is omnipotent, it can give, withhold, or color the information which shapes that opinion. It may impart an irresistible power to the caprice of an individual" (United States Senate 1884).

The complex controversy was never resolved at the congressional level, although an enormous amount of testimony accumulated about the AP–Western Union monopoly's underhand business practices, such as theft of secret information for stock trading and exclusion of competitors from key newspaper markets (Parsons 1899; United States House, HR 3010 1912).

Among many instances of underhand business practices was the AP role in forming its supposed competitor, the United Press, in 1882, with a secret agreement funneling profits back to AP. When the agreement was exposed in 1891, AP withdrew its support and began enforcing its non-competition clause, forcing newspapers to choose between AP membership and UP service. In some cases, the courts forced AP to back down and permit newspapers to subscribe to more than one wire service. But UP went bankrupt in 1897, in part because at that point, AP had an exclusive deal for European news with Reuters.

Opposition to the monopoly eventually grew to the breaking point. The state of Texas, for example, passed an antitrust law in 1899 specifically "aimed at the Associated Press" with stiff daily penalties for any organization that refused to sell news to competitors (*New York Times*, May 28, 1899). The AP also lost a 1900 antitrust case brought by Inter-Ocean News when it was refused membership in the AP. In ruling against AP, the Illinois courts said:

> No paper could be regarded as a newspaper of the day unless it had access to and published the reports from such an association as [the AP] ... For news gathered from all parts of the country, the various newspapers are almost solely dependent on such an association, and if they are prohibited from publishing it or its use is refused to them, their character as newspapers is destroyed and they would soon become practically worthless. (*Illinois/Inter-Ocean v Associated Press*, 1900)

Figure 7.8 Wire service—This teletype machine, used by the Associated Press for most of the twentieth century, allowed member news organizations to send and receive dispatches. While AP had a strong commitment to quality journalism, the organization's structure helped members hold down competition until an antitrust suit in 1945. Photo by Lin Burton.

When AP lost the case, the company packed up and moved from Illinois to New York State, where business laws against restraint of trade, barriers to entry, and refusal to deal were far more lenient.

The AP–Western Union news monopoly was a product of the times, but as one of the first major monopolies, it also set the pace for others to follow. Virtually every other industry was consolidating in the late 1800s. Oil, railroads, whiskey, sugar, grain, and other commodities all developed a "trust" in which stock was held by a monopoly combination to control trade and keep prices high. In some cases, the increased efficiency lowered prices for consumers and helped widespread adoption of new technologies. But the trusts also ignored customer needs, drove competitors out of business, and raised or lowered prices as they pleased. Antitrust laws, passed first by states and then by the US Congress in 1890, began to force break-ups in the commodity trusts.

Critics of the AP monopoly pointed out that news was far more important than a simple commodity. Americans had a long-standing commitment to a "robust sharing of ideas," long before the telegraph, as seen for example in low postal rates for newspapers and magazines (Starr 2004). For example, labor and public health news could easily be downplayed or suppressed by newspapers owned by the offending industries, and AP would simply pass along their reports. Labor organizers in West Virginia coal regions found it so difficult to get recognition for issues like dangerous working conditions and economic feudalism that *The Masses* published a cartoon showing an AP executive dripping poison into a reservoir of "The News" with the label "poisoned at the source." AP sued for libel, but later dropped the suit in the face of public criticism.

Despite its deserved reputation for high quality journalism, AP's resistance to competition would not end until 1945, when it lost an antitrust suit brought by the US Justice Department. AP argued that it was protected by the First Amendment, but the Supreme Court rejected that argument. "Freedom to publish means freedom for all and not for some," the court said in its decision. "Freedom to publish is guaranteed by the Constitution, but freedom to combine to keep others from publishing is not" (*Associated Press v. United States*, 326 U.S. 1, 1945).

3.3 European wire services

Specialized newsletters go back to the Renaissance and the birth of banking and stock markets. No matter how the news of major events is carried—by telegraph or messenger

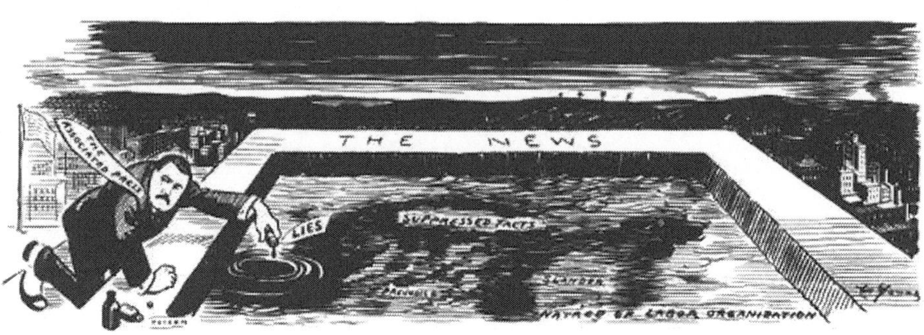

Poisoned at the Source

Figure 7.9 Poisoned—This cartoon depicts the Associated Press pouring lies into "The News." Labor unions in Appalachia objected to the way the AP passed along reports from newspapers owned by the coal industry, with suppressed facts and inaccurate reports about labor organizations. By Art Young, 1913, for *The Masses*. Wikimedia Commons.

or carrier pigeon—even a few hours of advance notice can be profitable on a stock market or in commodities trading. But these news services were meant for an elite audience. For most readers, news from other countries came from newspapers carried in the mail, translated, edited, and then reset into type. The process could take days or sometimes weeks. Charles Louis Havas, Paul Reuter, and Bernhard Wolff changed the world by creating news agencies that used the telegraph to rapidly transmit information.

Charles-Louis Havas (1783–1858) started his working life as a supply officer for the French military, serving in Nantes, France. Later he was a banker, a cotton importer, and a newspaper entrepreneur. Because of his work in both imports and news, he found it easy to view information as an international commodity. In 1830, following the July Revolution, Louis-Philippe succeeded to the French throne. Having strong liberal tendencies, Louise-Philippe proclaimed freedom of the press, and Havas saw the need for better organization of information and news traffic (Havas 2015). His first step was to set up a foreign newspaper translation bureau in Paris. The bureau was also a bookstore and a focal point of international politics and information. Three years later it became Agence Havas, the world's first news agency (Shrivastava 2007).

In the beginning, Havas used carrier pigeons to bring news from the morning's British newspapers to Paris by 3.00 p.m., in time for the evening editions. When the telegraph arrived in France in 1845, Havas was the first to use it. The Havas agency became a publicly traded company after the death of Charles-Louis Havas in 1858, and was the largest of the world's news agencies for almost a century.

Bernhard Wolff and Paul Reuter were two Havas employees who, with the help of Havas, founded two other major telegraphic news agencies.

Wolffs Telegraphisches Bureau started in Berlin a year after the Revolution of 1848 and the liberalization of press laws. Wolff was manager of the National Zeitung, founded that year, which started a policy of carrying news dispatches by telegraph from Paris, London, Amsterdam, and Frankfurt. By 1869, WTB was so closely associated with the government that it had offices in the main postal and telegraph building.

Paul Reuter was a journalist and bookstore owner who married a British banker's daughter. He and his wife left Germany after the collapse of the revolution of 1848 and he began working for Havas in Paris as a translator. Seeing opportunity in the expanding telegraph, Reuter moved to Aachen, Germany, in October of 1849 and opened a news and stock service. Aachen, that year, was the end of the line for the telegraph from Berlin. When the French opened a telegraph line from Paris to Brussels, Reuter was in the middle. He began filling in the 140-kilometer (90 mile) gap across the border by using carrier pigeons and express riders. As the telegraph network expanded, Reuter stayed ahead. He moved to London and opened an office in the heart of the city's financial center one month before the new London–Paris submarine telegraph cable started operating.

Havas was also influential in the creation of other news agencies. Guglielmo Stefani (1819–61) was a journalist from Venice who joined the 1848 revolution and fought for Italian independence from Austria. He was imprisoned by the Austrians but then exiled, and in 1853, with help from Havas, he set up Agenzia Telegrafica Stefani. After his death, Havas acquired half of the agency, which continued as the major Italian news agency until 1945.

Havas also linked up with a Spanish news agency established by Nilo Maria Fabra, a Barcelona journalist, in 1865. The Agencia de Noticias (news agency) Fabra merged with two other agencies in 1939 to form EFE, the world's largest Spanish-language wire service.

European telegraphy tended to be more diverse than the US, and so international cooperation was necessary. In May 1865, a convention decided to adopt Morse code as the international telegraph alphabet and to protect the right of everyone to use international telegraphy. The group continued to meet regularly, and eventually became the International Telecommunications Union (ITU), the oldest organization incorporated into the United Nations system in the mid-twentieth century (ITU 2010).

Figure 7.10 Paul Julius Reuter—Founder of Reuters, the world's oldest continuous news and wire service. Rudolph Lehnmann, 1869. Wikimedia Commons.

The big three European wire services were able to dominate the competition. In 1870, Havas, Reuters, and Wolff formed a cartel that dividing up territories for exclusive news services. Wolff's Telegraph Bureau (WTB) would serve northern and eastern Europe; Reuters would serve the British Empire; and Havas would serve the Mediterranean and Latin American regions (Storey 1951). The cartel agreement was extended into the US with a deal between Reuters and the AP.

The European wire services were often seen as semi-official agencies of their respective governments. Wolff 's had little choice in 1933 when the Nazis merged the agency with smaller competitors. Havas and Stefani were also left without choices when faced with fascist governments. After the war, Havas was replaced by Agence France Press, Stefani was replaced by Agenzia Nazionale Stampa Associata (ANSA), and Wolff's was replaced by Deutsche Presse-Agentur (DPA).

Today a dozen major news agencies from the era of the telegraph—especially AP, Reuters, AFP, EFE, and DPA—compete in twenty-first-century global news markets.

The World's Major Wire Services and News Agencies.

Name	*Dates*	*Country*	*Founder*	*Modern Name*
Havas	1835–1945	France	Charles-Louis Havas	Agence France Press, **AFP**
Associated Press	1846–present	US	Moses Beach	**AP**.
Wolff's	1849–1933	Germany	Bernhard Wolff	Deutsche Presse-Agentur, **DPA.**
Reuters	1851–present	Britain	Paul Reuter	**Reuters**.
Stefani	1853–1945	Italy	Guglielmo Stafani	Agenzia Nazionale Stampa Associata, **ANSA**.
Fabra	1865–1939	Spain	Nilo Maria Fabra	**EFE**.
Itar-Tass	1925–present	Russia	From St. Petersburg Tel. Agency (1904)	**ITAR-TASS**.
Press Trust of India	1947–present	India	From AP India (1909)	**PTI.**
Xinhua	1937–present	China	Red China News Agency (1931)	**Xinhua.**
Kyodo	1947–present	Japan	Domei News Agency (1936)	**Kyodo.**
United Press Int'l	1958–2000	US	From United Press (1907) and Int'l Press (1909) **UPI.**	
Inter-Press Service	1964–present	International	Roberto Savio	**IPS.**

3.4 United Press and International Press begin competition

Publishers who were not included in the Associated Press monopoly in the US were in a difficult position, and in the early twentieth century, two of them decided to create separate news agencies. E. W. Scripps, publisher of the first US newspaper chain, created a competing news service called United Press Association in June 1907. (UPA was unrelated to the United Press that had been driven into bankruptcy ten years earlier.) Then in 1909, William Randolph Hearst created the International News Association for his newspaper chain.

"One result of these successive changes was to encourage new papers by making it easy for them to secure a comprehensive news service," said diplomat and former *New York Tribune* editor Whitelaw Reid in an *Encyclopedia Britannica* article in 1911. "The almost official authority with which the public formerly attributed to an Associated Press dispatch declined."

Congressional hearings in 1912 established that a long history of attempts to regulate telegraphy had failed, and that prices in Europe were less than half of the same prices for telegraphic messages in the United States. While this was only one of many congressional investigations into monopolies at the time, it represented a changing legal climate. In 1913, Western Union's parent company AT&T agreed to an out-of-court settlement with the US government called the Kingsbury Commitment (discussed later in this chapter). One result was that UPA and IP wire services were able to use the telegraph at the same cost as AP from that point forward.

Newspaper publisher E. W. Scripps later said, "I do not believe in monopolies ... I do not believe it would be good for journalism in this country that there should be one big news trust such as the founders of the Associated Press fully expected to build up" (Shrivastava 2007). He also said, "I regard my life's greatest service to the people of this country to be the creation of the United Press."

Lucian Carr, a beat generation writer who served as a UPI editor in the 1950s, once said, "UP's great virtue was that we were the little guy [that] could screw the AP." United Press and International Press merged in 1958 to become United Press International. At its peak in 1978, the organization served more than 7,000 news clients. UPI fell on hard times by the 1990s, and in 1999 its news service contracts were sold to the AP. The organization itself then went through a series of owners, including a cult church, and vanished as a news organization.

The US telegraph system, in the end, did not develop as a widely distributed system of small independent providers, as Morse envisioned, nor as a branch of government, following the European business model. Instead, the telegraph became a commercial monopoly. Later, Guglielmo Marconi and Thomas Edison attempted to take the same route using patent rights to monopolize radio and film. But they would be thwarted by antitrust laws that were, in part, a reaction to the AP–Western Union situation.

4 The Telephone as a Circumventing Technology

The invention of the telephone in 1876 was a direct reaction to the monopoly power of Western Union. Angered at the control over financial and political information, Boston lawyer Gardiner Hubbard—called the "national nemesis" of Western Union—first tried to have the telegraph system nationalized as part of the Post Office through an act of Congress. When that attempt failed, he financed a set of promising experiments by Alexander Graham Bell, who was working on systems to amplify sound for people with hearing loss.

When Bell secured patent rights to the new telephone in 1876, it was Hubbard who organized the financing to create the Bell Telephone Company. Bell married Hubbard's daughter Mabel, who had been one of his hearing-impaired students, in 1877.

The telephone would have been invented without Bell and Hubbard—Elisha Gray of Chicago filed a similar patent only a few hours later on the same day as Bell at the US Patent Office, and controversy still remains concerning details of their patent applications. But the courts decided that Bell had the best claim.

As Hubbard organized the company, Bell launched a series of lectures to popularize the new invention, starting with a description of the telephone and then pointing out a telegraph line that he had leased. A few miles away, Thomas A. Watson, Bell's assistant, would be waiting. "I had at my end one of our loudest telephones specially adapted for the purpose," Watson said in his autobiography. On Bell's signal, he would have to tell a brass band to start playing. But that was just the warm-up, because the audience really wanted to know whether the telephone could talk.

> I shouted such sentences such as "How do you do?" and "What do you think of the telephone?" which the audience could hear … [Also] I had to do something of importance for Bell's audiences, called by courtesy, singing … I sang Yankee Doodle and Auld Lang Syne … My singing was always a hit … [and] I was usually encored to the limit of my repertory. (Watson 1926)

At one point in 1876, Hubbard and Bell attempted to sell the Bell patents to Western Union. Skeptical Western Union businessmen were aghast:

> Hubbard and Bell want to install one of their "telephone devices" in every city. The idea is idiotic on the face of it … Why would any person want to use this ungainly and impractical device when he can send a messenger to the telegraph office and have a clear written message sent to any large city in the United States? (Pershing 2010)

After Western Union rejected the phone proposal, Hubbard focused on the organization and Bell focused on showmanship. The work paid off, and the Bell telephone system began stringing wires in 1877. Within ten years, 150,000 people owned telephones. While Bell continued working on improvements, such as Thomas Edison's carbon microphone, some of his patents expired in the mid-1890s, and some 6,000 phone companies created their own phone systems. Research into telegraph and

Figure 7.11 Inventor and his family—Alexander Graham Bell, Mabel Hubbard Bell, and two daughters c. 1885, the year he patented the telephone system. Bell's father-in-law, Gardiner Green Hubbard, was one of the country's chief opponents of the Western Union telegraph monopoly. He originally financed Bell's experiments with the telephone. Grosvenor collection, c. 1885, Library of Congress.

telephone electronics paved the way for other developments to the point where some historians have seen the telephone as the "father of broadcasting" (White 2010).

While the telephone was intended for one-to-one conversations, home entertainment was an option before radio. In 1893 a Hungarian system called Telefon Hirmond began operation in Budapest. A similar system, the United States Telephone Herald Company, was a failure (White 2010).

4.1 Antitrust law and AT&T

American Telephone and Telegraph, created by the Bell Company in 1885 to build long-distance lines, became Bell's parent company in 1899. At that point, only about half of the nation's telephones were part of the Bell system (Starr 2004). In order to control the market, AT&T waged a ruthless campaign to undercut competition. AT&T denied access to long-distance lines and undermined competitors credit (Marchand 1998). For example, in 1907, the Bell system secretly bought a company that built switching equipment and used components that were claimed under Bell system patents. Once the "infringing" equipment was purchased, Bell would seize the equipment and force the independents out of business (Telephony, 1907).

The tactics led to an antitrust investigation by the US Justice Department, and the possibility emerged that AT&T could be broken up or that the United States would follow the European model and nationalize telephone and telegraph services under the Postal Service.

In response, AT&T launched one of the strongest public relations campaigns in history, placing thousands of newspaper and magazine ads with the slogan "One System, One Policy, Universal Service." The claim was that telephony was a "natural" monopoly that would work better than a patchwork system to provide service to everyone. As noted in Chapter 6, the campaign succeeded, and in 1913 the Justice Department negotiated a deal with AT&T called the Kingsbury Commitment that allowed AT&T to continue as a regulated monopoly. The deal, named for AT&T vice president Nathan Kingsbury, also forced Western Union to carry competing wire services such as United Press and International Press at the same rate, allowing them to compete with the Associated Press.

The Kingsbury Commitment also meant that AT&T had to stop the trade war and guarantee system access for all independent phone companies. However, the government allowed AT&T to keep buying up independent companies and manufacturing telephone equipment through Western Electric, which had been Western Union's manufacturing arm. In effect, the regulations slowed but did not stop AT&T's quest for monopoly. By the mid-twentieth century, Bell owned 80 percent of the US phone market.

4.2 Breaking up "Ma Bell"

In 1974, the Justice Department sued AT&T under antitrust laws, and in 1982, courts ordered the company to break up into regional carriers, opening the door to more competition and lower long-distance rates for individual consumers. The company that was semi-affectionately known as "Ma" (mother) Bell would no longer be permitted an exclusive monopoly on telecommunications.

The decision came as part of a double blow to the telephone business, because AT&T was also losing the radio and television broadcast networks that were switching to cheaper, higher quality satellite service—a circumventing technology they developed to replace AT&T's costly long-distance lines.

The AT&T break-up also led to the decline of Bell Labs, once a leading international research center, with seven Nobel Prizes to its credit and vital work on radar in World War II and photovoltaic solar cells for satellite systems.

Perhaps the most significant of the Bell Labs inventions was the transistor, which changed radio from a complex household item using radio tubes to a far more portable device. The transistor was also a milestone in the digital age, changing the computer from an expensive military system to an affordable information processing system for banks, insurance companies, and telecommunications systems. Bell Labs also developed communications satellites, the Unix computer operating system, digital switching, and cell phones. But there were also commercial flops, such as the 1964 picture phone that debuted at the Seattle World's Fair. Despite its achievements and the public relations campaigns, not everyone was fond of "Ma Bell." During the heyday of its monopoly, phone "freaks" developed ways to avoid paying for expensive long-distance phone calls.

It was the challenge of beating this system that helped draw Steve Wozniak, a co-founder of Apple computers, into electronics. In 1975, just as a prank, Wozniak and friends used the circumventing technology to make a free call to Rome, Italy. Wozniak called the Vatican and, with a thick German accent, claimed to be then-Secretary of State Henry Kissinger wanting to speak with the pope. The Vatican asked him to call back, and an hour later, refused to connect him with the pope. "So I guess they checked up on my story," Wozniak told a documentary filmmaker (Cambeau 2006; Wozniak 2006).

5 Conclusion

The peak year for the telegraph was 1930, when 211 million were exchanged in the United States. The very last telegraph was sent in 2009, and by then, Western Union changed its business model to become an international financial service.

The impacts of the instant electronic communication, according to media theorist James W. Carey, included new forms of writing, new concepts of standard time, new spatial boundaries, new forms of language, new structures in social relations, and new futures markets for agriculture that led to a break-up of patterns of city-state capitalism. It meant the end of the tall tale and the hoax as newspaper staples, but the beginning of a new concept of rapid-fire political debate that reverberates in the twenty-first century (Carey 1992).

With the introduction of cell phones in the 1990s, and the addition of text, photos, and video on demand, the telephone also changed from a one-to-one medium to a mass medium virtually overnight. Old-fashioned landline phones went from a necessity, with 97 percent market penetration in 2001, to something of a luxury, with 60 percent market share in 2013. Exclusive cell-phone use was at 40 percent of the population and rising rapidly (Blumberg 2013).

Controversy over the roles of AT&T's spin-off companies, such as Verizon Corp., and the uniformity and neutrality of access to telecommunications services, remain permanent fixtures of the regulatory environment, as we will see in Section IV.

The Western Union–Associated Press monopoly was the first controversial and highly contested monopoly, but it was also the first to begin linking the world together. Along with AT&T, the communications technologies of the nineteenth and twentieth centuries served important social purposes, albeit imperfectly.

"We need a good network to pull together the community of humans," said Robert Miller, Director of Communication Technology Research at AT&T. "I think in the end, it [communication] will probably keep us from blowing ourselves up" (Cambeau 2006).

For additional reading, discussion questions, links to video, and other suggestions, see www.revolutionsincommunications.com.

Figure 7.12 New media—Alexander Graham Bell is wearing headphones in order to listen to the radio, which at the time was the latest development in new media. The photo was probably taken in 1922, the year Bell died. Underwood & Underwood, Library of Congress.

8

The New World of Radio

It's of no use whatsoever.

Heinrich Hertz, 1888, in response to questions by students about the practical value of his experiments

Oh, the Humanity.

Herbert Morrison, radio reporter at the scene of the *Hindenburg* disaster, 1937

This … is London.

Edward R. Murrow, 1940, reporting the blitz for CBS

1 Auroras and Equations

The mysterious forces surrounding electric currents fascinated scientists of the eighteenth and nineteenth centuries—from Luigi Galvani and Alessandro Volta in Italy to Benjamin Franklin in America and Michael Faraday in Britain. When telegraph lines began stretching across continents, the mystery deepened as scientists tried to explain occasional fluctuations in electrical current that seemed to be associated with the Aurora Borealis and solar flares.

Particularly mysterious were the events of September 2, 1859, when the sky filled with auroras of writhing purple and red colors unlike anything ever seen before. "Around the world, telegraph systems crashed, machines burst into flames, and electric shocks rendered operators unconscious," said Stuart Clark in a book about the auroras of 1859. "Compasses and other sensitive instruments reeled as if struck by a massive magnetic fist" (Clark 2007).

"I have cut my battery off and connected the line with the earth," tapped out a Boston operator on the morning of September 2. "We are working with current from the Aurora Borealis alone. How do you receive my writing?" The other operator, who had also cut off his batteries, responded, "Much better than with batteries on" (*New York Times*, September 6, 1859).

In New York, a telegraph operator having trouble the evening of September 3 happened to look out the window and saw "broad rays of light extending from the zenith toward the horizon in almost every direction."

We now know that the worldwide auroras of 1859 were the same as the "northern lights" usually seen in polar regions, and that the auroras expanded for a few days due to a giant solar flare. We also know that electromagnetic fields travel invisibly through the atmosphere. And we call the solar storm a "Carrington event" for the English astronomer, Richard C. Carrington, who observed the solar flare and described it at the time.

2 Like Discovering a New Continent

Scientists wondered how electricity could be related to magnetism, and how the great auroras of 1859 could create electricity in telegraph wires. One piece of the puzzle was solved a few years later, when James Clerk Maxwell, a British mathematician, published a paper describing the electric and magnetic forces that could be carried through space without wires. Maxwell called it "displacement current." Another part of the puzzle involved Thomas Edison's observations about the behavior of one electrical circuit when it was near a similar circuit. The phenomenon, when one circuit mimics another without actually touching it, was called the "Edison effect." Some historians think Edison's labs could have created radio, had he not focused on a sound-recording device (the phonograph, patented in 1878) and the electric light (patented in 1879).

In the 1880s, Heinrich Hertz, a German scientist, found a way to test Maxwell's theory by generating electromagnetic waves, detecting them, and measuring their velocity. When he published his findings in 1888, Hertz thought he had simply verified an interesting scientific speculation (Aitken 1992). "This is just an experiment that proves Maestro [teacher] Maxwell was right," he said. "We just have these mysterious electromagnetic waves that we cannot see with the naked eye. But they are there." Asked about the value of the experiment, Hertz told students: "It's of no use whatsoever."

If Hertz saw no practical value in radio telegraphy, others were racing to lay claim to what seemed like a new continent that was just being discovered. In the United States, Nikola Tesla began giving demonstrations of short-range wireless telegraphy in 1891. In Britain, Oliver Lodge transmitted radio signals at a meeting of a British scientific society at Oxford University. Similar experiments were being conducted by Jagadish Chandra Bose in India at the same time. Radio experiments are also recorded in Germany, Russia, and Brazil. All faced the same problem: usually the signals would not travel more than a few dozen meters.

2.1 Guglielmo Marconi

An unlikely inventor is often credited with making radio telegraphy practical. Guglielmo Marconi, a twenty-year-old from a wealthy Irish-Italian family with little formal education, had become fascinated with electronic waves while attending a friend's scientific lectures at the University of Bologna.

In 1894, Marconi was able to duplicate Hertz' experiments in his home laboratory, but he faced the familiar problem: he was not able to receive a signal over any great distance. At the time, most research was focused on the higher-frequency part of the radio spectrum, and physicists hoped to understand the relationship between radio waves and light waves. Marconi moved down the spectrum, using lower-frequency waves. He also used high-powered transmitters and larger, grounded antennas.

Marconi was not the first to think of using what we now call a "ground," but he was the first to use it specifically for radio signaling, and he was also the first to fully describe the commercial potential of long-distance signaling. He arrived at just the right time, with the right financial and political backing connected with his family's Jamison Irish whiskey fortune.

In 1896, Marconi was introduced to officials in the British Postal Service who, just that year, were finalizing the purchase of the last remaining commercial British telegraph company. This was being done to avoid the information bottlenecks created by monopoly systems like Western Union in the United States. Having nationalized the telegraph system by merging it with the Post Office, postal officials now saw a duty to fully investigate what they saw as an entirely new communications system.

Figure 8.1 Radio entrepreneur—Using trial and error techniques, Guglielmo Marconi found a way to transmit radio over long distances. With influential backing, Marconi patented early radio technology and commercialized radio telegraphy. Photo by Pach Brothers, 1908, Library of Congress.

In 1897, on a windy day on Salisbury Plain, near the ancient Stonehenge monument, Marconi showed government officials a practical radio telegraph system that could send a signal for 6 kilometers (3.7 miles). Over the next few years, the range of Marconi wireless systems expanded with higher-power amplifiers, and their value became obvious when radio helped rescue ships' crews in distress off the English coast.

As radio began saving lives and money, insurance companies like Lloyds of London ordered ships to install the new devices. By 1900, the Marconi radio telegraph could be found on most large ocean-going vessels. In several cases, Marconi operators saved the lives of many passengers. For example, in 1910, an operator named Jack Binns became famous for using radio to save passengers on the HMS *Republic*—a sister ship of the ill-fated *Titanic*.

3 Radio and the *Titanic*

Problems with radio played a major role in the *Titanic* disaster of April 14, 1912, when the British passenger liner sank after hitting an iceberg in the mid-Atlantic. These problems delayed and complicated the rescue, contributing to the deaths of 1,514 passengers and crew, and very nearly sealing the fates of those who managed to survive.

Although its owners boasted that the *Titanic* was the most modern ship of its day, the Marconi radio system that had been installed in the weeks before the disaster was already obsolete. It was not, as was claimed at the time, the best radio technology available.

Instead, the system devised by Guglielmo Marconi in 1897, and still in use in 1912, had long since been superseded by other radio pioneers—Reginald Fessenden and Lee DeForest in the US, and others in Europe. Still, Marconi used his patents, research, and monopoly power to hold back competition from other systems. And in the end, even Marconi himself admitted he was wrong to do so.

The *Titanic* was on its first voyage from Britain to the United States, and had just crossed the point where messages from ships at sea could be exchanged from the easternmost North American wireless station at Cape Race, Newfoundland. After sending personal messages from the *Titanic*, the operators were taking down news and stock reports for the passengers to read the next morning.

Just minutes before the *Titanic* hit the iceberg, Cyril F. Evans, a wireless operator on the *Californian*, which was about 20 miles away, attempted to contact the *Titanic* to tell them they were surrounded by dangerous icebergs.

The captain of the *Californian* told Evans: "Better advise [the *Titanic*] we are surrounded by ice and stopped. So I went to my cabin, and at 9:05 p.m. New York time I called him up. I said, 'Say, old man, we are stopped and surrounded by ice.' He turned around and said 'shut up, shut up, I am busy; I am working Cape Race' [Newfoundland] and at that I jammed him."

When questioned, Evans explained to a US Senate inquiry: "By jamming we mean when somebody is sending a message to somebody else and you start to send at the same time, you jam him. He does not get his message. I was stronger than Cape Race. Therefore my signals came in with a bang, and he could read me and he could not read Cape Race." "At 11:35 I put the [ear] phones down and took off my clothes and turned in." He was awakened by the *Californian*'s captain at 3:40 am when the crew observed distress rockets coming from the *Titanic*'s position. By that time, it was too late to help.

Figure 8.2 Marconi cutting the wires—Poster from a celebration in spring 1903 in Bologna, Italy. Courtesy of Marconi Museum, Bologna, Italy.

Members of a British commission of inquiry were incredulous. "Do I understand rightly then that a Marconi operator ... can only clearly hear one thing at a time?" one asked. It was, unfortunately true, and as the *New York Times* said a few weeks later, "Sixteen hundred lives were lost that might have been saved if the wireless communication had been what it should have been" (*New York Times*, May 2, 1912).

The official cause of the disaster was the negligence of the *Titanic*'s captain in ignoring iceberg reports. However, the delayed rescue effort was also a crucial issue, a US Senate committee found: "Had the wireless operator of the *Californian* remained a few minutes longer at his post ... that ship might have had the proud distinction of rescuing the lives of the passengers and crew of the *Titanic*" (*New York Times*, May 29, 1912).

The *Titanic* used wireless technology that was rapidly becoming obsolete. Marconi was not a scientist, and when he found an effective system based on previous scientific work and his own trial-and-error results, he used the patent system to freeze the technology into place and buttress his commercial monopoly. While research on better systems was taking place in smaller companies, such as Reginald Fessenden's National Electric Signaling Company, none of these had the commercial power of the Marconi company.

Technically, the problem with the radio telegraph systems on the *Titanic* was that Marconi's "spark" system soaked up large segments of the bandwidth and created

Figure 8.3 RMS *Titanic*—The radio system in use when the RMS *Titanic* sank on April 14, 1912 could have been much better, and a better system could have saved lives. This photo shows the ill-fated ocean liner departing Southampton, UK, on April 10, 1912. Wikimedia Commons.

interference even when there were only a few ships on the vast ocean. As many engineers were realizing at the time, it was far better to use continuous wave radio transmitters (where signals were carried inside the wave) rather than intermittent spark transmissions (where interruptions in the wave *were* the signal). A continuous wave could be "tuned" to allow a variety of frequencies, and it could use shorter-wavelength radio transmissions, which carried over long distances by bouncing off the electrically charged outer layer of the atmosphere called the ionosphere—the region where auroras form. This more modern approach uses the ionosphere as a resource, rather than as an obstacle to be overcome, as was the case with Marconi's approach.

With large profits from international radio sales, Marconi could have investigated a variety of technical paths to improve radio. Instead, the company focused on a narrow technical path—low-frequency, spark transmission, high-power transmitters—that was initially successful but not flexible enough in the long run. In effect, said historian Hugh Aitken, the personal stubbornness that made Marconi a commercial success prevented him from envisioning a wider variety of engineering solutions to obvious problems.

"Now I have realized my mistake," he told an audience of radio engineers in a 1927 speech in New York City. "Everyone followed me in building stations hundreds of times more powerful than would nave been necessary had short waves been used" (Aitken 1992). After the speech, Marconi laid a wreath at a small Battery Park memorial for Jack Phillips, the wireless operator who had gone down with the *Titanic*, still sending out distress calls to the last (*New York Times*, "Marconi Describes Beam to Engineers," October 18, 1927).

The *Titanic* disaster illustrates the limitations of monopolies that form early in the cycles of technological adaptation. Because the *Titanic* used wireless technology that was already obsolete, within an industry-dominated regulatory framework, many people lost their lives.

3.1 Radio Act of 1912 is passed

US regulation of radio telegraphy had already been contentious in the years before the disaster for two major reasons. In the first place, antitrust law had not been applied to telecommunications in the same way that it had been to commodities. American Telephone and Telegraph Co. had successfully lobbied the government and the public to be considered as a regulated "natural" monopoly, and was in the process of working out an agreement with the Justice Department that would be called the Kingsbury Commitment. Similarly, the Associated Press and Western Union monopolies had been frequently called into question but very little had been done. On the other hand, commodities, especially petroleum, were seen as a major object of antitrust law, and the year before the *Titanic* disaster, the US Supreme Court confirmed a Justice Department order breaking up the Standard Oil Trust into thirty-four separate companies.

Secondly, there had been very little in the way of radio regulation, and what there was had been extremely weak. Federal regulation of radio began with the Wireless Ship Act of June 24, 1910, which forbade any steamer carrying or licensed to carry fifty or more persons to leave any American port unless equipped with a radio and staffed by a skilled operator. But the 1910 act did not regulate frequency allocation or require radio licensing, which was an extremely unpopular idea among radio amateurs. Nor did it require round-the-clock radio monitoring, which would have prevented the *Californian* from steaming off that night of April 12, 1912, instead of stopping to help. Nor did it interfere with the Marconi monopoly on radio equipment. All of these issues would be on the table in the wake of the *Titanic* disaster.

Six bills were presented to the House Merchant Marine and Senate Commerce committee to give the Secretary of Commerce "control over wireless operation." Various features of the bills would come together in the Radio Act of 1912, passed exactly four months later, on August 13, 1912. The law provided for the setting of radio frequencies, for penalties against interference with emergency communications, for an international distress signal (SOS), and for interoperability of radio stations "without distinction of the radio systems adopted by each station, respectively." In other words, Marconi operators could no longer be instructed to ignore those using other kinds of radio sets. The law also required that ship radios be monitored for distress calls 24 hours a day.

4 Early Radio Technology

On Christmas Eve, 1906, operators in the "radio shacks" of ships around Cape Cod were sending and receiving routine messages in Morse code over the airwaves.

Suddenly their headphones picked up a strange sound ... Through the static, they heard a violin, playing "O Holy Night." Even more astonishing ... the voice of Reginald Fessenden reading a passage from the Bible. The Canadian radio inventor and entrepreneur had developed a continuous wave system to broadcast voice and music after years of experimentation in universities and with the US Weather Service. With the help of investors, he built a high-power continuous wave transmitting station in Brant Rock, Massachusetts, designed to compete with Marconi's spark transmitting system. Fessenden's financial backers hoped to sell the telephonic radio system to AT&T, but the company was deeply involved in antitrust litigation and may have misunderstood the opportunity.

Around the same time, the problem of tuning the radio and broadcasting voice and music was solved with the invention of the "audion" (triode) tube by Lee DeForest, but the device would undergo many improvements before it became part of commercial radio broadcasting in the 1920s.

The electronics engineer who contributed the most to the development of radio was Edwin H. Armstrong, who devised and patented a new kind of radio tuning circuit in 1914. Bypassing DeForest's audion patents, Armstrong developed a system that took part of the current and fed it back to the grid, strengthening incoming signals. As a young man testing this concept in his house in Yonkers, New York, Armstrong began receiving distant stations so loudly that they could be heard without headphones, which had been necessary until then. The story is that he was so excited he woke up his sister, Cricket, shouting, "I've done it! I've done it!"

Figures 8.4 and **8.5** First voice broadcast—On Christmas Eve, 1906, operators in the "radio shacks" of ships around Cape Cod were sending and receiving routine messages in Morse code over the airwaves. Suddenly their headphones picked up a strange sound … Through the static, they heard a violin, playing O Holy Night. Even more astonishing … the voice of Reginald Fessenden reading a passage from the Bible. The Canadian radio inventor and entrepreneur had developed a continuous wave system to broadcast voice and music after years of experimentation in universities and with the US Weather Service. Marconi, then dominant in radio telegraphy, stayed with spark technology until the *Titanic* disaster of 1912. Wikimedia Commons.

Armstrong later found that when the feedback was pushed to a high level, the tube produced rapid oscillations acting as a transmitter, and putting out electromagnetic waves. He also developed FM (frequency modulation) radio, which had far less static than older AM (amplitude modulation) radio technology. Although Armstrong developed the electronic key to continuous-wave transmitters that are still at the heart of all radio and television operations, a bitter patent fight with RCA broke out. The fight was one reason that AM radio technology dominated commercial broadcasting until the 1960s.

Commercial radio was still a dream when, in 1914, amateur radio operators across the country formed the American Radio Relay League (ARRL). Soon afterwards, legend has it, a young Marconi employee, David Sarnoff, wrote a "radio music box memo" about the possibility of commercial broadcasting to Marconi:

> I have in mind a plan of development which would make radio a "household utility" in the same sense as the piano or phonograph. The idea is to bring music into the house by wireless. While this has been tried in the past by wires, it has been a failure because wires do not lend themselves to this scheme. With radio, however, it would seem to be entirely feasible.

The new system would be supported with advertising, rather than by subscription or government subsidy, Sarnoff said. While there is some historical controversy about the memo itself, there is evidence that Sarnoff pushed for commercial radio at the time. Ideas about commercial radio had to be put on hold, however, with the outbreak of World War I, and all radio operations were suspended. Armstrong donated all his patents and know-how to the government to help fight the war, and served as a captain in the US Army Signal Corps.

Figure 8.6 Exuberant inventor—Edwin H. Armstrong, inventor of FM radio and many other improvements to radio, was fond of climbing radio towers. He is seen here atop the 115-foot-tall RCA radio tower in New York on May 15, 1923, the opening day of RCA's Radio Broadcast Central. US Army photo.

5 The 'Radio Craze' of the 1920s

They called it the "radio craze," and after World War I, millions of young people put on headphones and tuned into the weak signals from a handful of small radio stations and individual broadcasters. The sets were so popular that Radio Corporation of America—the new US company created from American Marconi at the end of World War I—pushed its radio tube manufacturing from an average of 5,000 tubes per month in 1921 to over 200,000 by June of 1922. (By 1930, the number would rise to 125 million per month.)

Radio listeners originally heard a haphazard and eclectic schedule of literary readings, church sermons, foreign news, and musical recitals put together at the whim and convenience of local radio stations. Only four station schedules were listed in the *New York Times* "radio section" when it was included in the newspaper in May, 1921, and of these, only one was near New York. The others were in Pittsburgh, Chicago, and Springfield, Massachusetts.

Consumer demand surprised everyone, especially the electronics industry, which was preoccupied with a complicated set of patent lawsuits between Edwin H. Armstrong and RCA, Westinghouse, and AT&T. Their original plan was to freely broadcast educational music and high-toned programming, making money by marketing home radio receivers. But since demand for the receivers was already so high, the focus turned to a business model for radio broadcasting. Some 732 radio stations were on the air in 1927, among them, the two stations owned by RCA in New York and Washington, DC. Other affiliates would form the two networks for RCA's National Broadcasting Company division. The affiliates were either in the Red network, offering commercial entertainment; or the Blue Network, originally to have news and cultural programs without sponsors. Also in 1927, a small group of radio stations formed the Columbia Broadcasting System headed by the young heir of a cigar company, William S. Paley.

5.1 Radio licensing

Before radio could be a commercial success, the chaos in the airwaves had to be straightened out. After a failed attempt at voluntary regulation, Congress created the Federal Radio Commission (FRC) in 1927 with the idea that radio should serve the public interest, convenience, and necessity. But the commission found "public interest" to be an elusive concept, and on August 20, 1928, the FRC issued General Order 40, a set of regulations that split radio licenses up into three classes.

Third-class amateur radio operators were not permitted to broadcast news, weather, sports, information, or entertainment, but instead were confined to an undesirable part of the AM spectrum. Medium-sized radio stations were assigned low broadcasting power and limited hours. Many of these were educational stations owned by unions, universities, and churches. They were labeled "propaganda" stations by the FRC and given the lowest priority.

Twenty-five "clear channel" radio stations were given strong frequencies, and of these, twenty-three were affiliated with NBC. They were not permitted to play recorded music, which meant that all music had to be live on the air. Only a very large company could afford its own in-house orchestra. In this way, radio became a centrally controlled national medium rather than a widely distributed locally controlled medium (McChesney 1994).

Publicly, FRC commissioners said the educational stations differed greatly in their technical qualities. But privately, they hoped to do away with these "small and unimportant stations" by requiring four license renewals per year and by assigning them poor low-power frequencies. Within a year of the 1927 regulations, 100 radio stations had folded up, and by 1930 only a handful of the original educational stations remained.

WNYC, a station owned by the city of New York, was among those assigned a part-time, low-power channel. The city appealed to the FRC and lost. Other stations, such

Figure 8.7 Radio legend—David Sarnoff was a pivotal figure in twentieth-century broadcasting. According to one legend, now proven mostly false, Sarnoff stayed by his telegraph key for days relaying news of the *Titanic*. Another legend, possibly true, was that Sarnoff envisioned the future of commercial broadcasting in 1915. However, there's no question that, as a long-time executive with RCA and NBC, Sarnoff put his personal stamp on the way radio and television broadcasting developed. Harris & Ewing, 1939, Library of Congress.

as a handful of Brooklyn-based Jewish community stations, also lost in the rush to create a large central network.

The US process failed to make the best possible use of the medium, noted legal analyst Philip J. Weiser (2005). In contrast, Britain, Australia, and Canada created hybrid systems where both commercial and non-profit educational stations coexisted and were funded by taxes on radio.

6 Radio Licensing and Censorship

Fear of the power of the new media was one of the reasons that the US government excluded small non-profit stations, but censorship was already taking place on many levels. Complaints about the treatment of controversial speakers were typical in the early days. Congressman Emanuel Celler of New York noted that speakers had been cut off in mid-sentence, plays had been censored, and even political speeches had been edited before air time (*New York Times*, May 29, 1927). Norman Thomas, a leading US democratic-socialist, warned that radio had lost the capacity for genuine discussion of great ideas in the rush to commercialism (*New York Times*, March 30, 1934).

In idealizing radio policy, former President Calvin Coolidge insisted that control remain in the hands of the government:

> In its broad aspects, radio is a new agency brought by science to our people which may, if properly safeguarded, become one of our greatest blessings. No monopoly should be allowed to arise, and to prevent it, the control of the channel through the ether should remain in the hands of the government, and therefore of the people, as the control of navigation upon our waters; that while we retain the fundamental rights in the hands of the people to the control of these channels we should maintain the widest degree of freedom in their use. Liberty is not license in this new instrument of science. There is a great responsibility on the part of those who transmit material over the radio." (*New York Times*, Nov 20, 1938)

But the reality was far from the ideal. The government promoted a monopoly radio network and shoved the small independent educational stations off into a corner. Most of these gave up or joined NBC or CBS.

It is not surprising that a system favoring tight content control would be the original framework for the new medium. Film, also relatively new at the time, was similarly regulated for similar reasons. No one was sure what the social effects of new media would be.

Some of the new programs and stations posed serious challenges to the emerging radio system. Licenses for two radio stations were revoked in the early 1930s by the FRC, which said that the stations were "sensational rather than instructive" in nature. John R. Brinkley, a Kansas City surgeon, used his radio station, KFKB, to advocate medically fraudulent implants of supposedly rejuvenating animal organs. When his medical license was revoked in 1930, the FRC also revoked the radio station's license. He moved the operation to Mexico, where his station was one of the most powerful in North America.

Two years later, the FRC also revoked the license of KGEF, a radio station owned by Rev. Robert P. Shuler and the Trinity Methodist Church. Shuler was a shrill muckraker who mounted extreme anti-Semitic attacks on corrupt politicians in Los Angeles. In denying the church's legal appeal, a federal court said radio was only an "instrumentality of commerce." The First Amendment did not apply to broadcasting, the court said, and the license revocation was simply an "application of the regulatory power of Congress."

This broadcast licensing case stands in sharp contrast with the 1933 newspaper censorship case, *Near v. Minnesota*, in which a state tried to shut down the *Saturday Press* of Minneapolis. The Supreme Court said that printed media, no matter how offensive, could not be censored outright. But radio, on the other hand, could be censored.

7 The Golden Age of Radio

Radio became the first "electronic hearth," bringing families—and nations— together to face the crises of the 1930s and 1940s. Media theorist Marshall McLuhan said radio was having a "re-tribalizing" effect, creating an electronic return to oral culture and representing a departure from literacy. Radio was also an extension of, and new twist on, vaudeville and theater, and during its golden age in the 1930s and 1940s, radio attracted the best entertainers in the world.

Originally, the NBC network, led by David Sarnoff, took a high-minded approach to public service. An advisory group of seventeen prominent citizens helped shape the programming schedule with lessons in music appreciation, productions of Shakespeare, political debates, and symphonies. By 1928, the network made its first profits (Smith 1990: 73).

Sarnoff "had a vision of what radio and television could become in terms of being informational, educational, cultural, relevant," said his great-nephew, Richard Sarnoff, in 2008. "He said 'OK, we've got radio, let's put Tchaikovsky on!' ... The reason the broadcast media didn't end up being this public trust type of programming ... is that radio and television is just so good at delivering audiences to advertisers. Business being what it is, whatever you're good at, you concentrate on, you maximize, and that ends up delivering value to your shareholders" (Auletta 2010: 222).

While "high-brow" symphonic and theatrical productions drew modest audiences, people were far more interested in popular entertainment. Vaudeville, the variety entertainment genre of theater, became the model for many local and national radio programs, and provided a platform for comedians, musical variety, and short dramas. Children's and family-oriented programs were also especially popular, and these included Western dramas and comic-book heroes.

The most popular show on radio at the end of the 1920s and all through the 1930 was *Amos 'n' Andy.* The show shamelessly stereotyped two African-American taxicab owners. At first in 1926, white actors Freeman Gosden and Charles Correll syndicated the show by distributing recorded episodes. Despite its offensive nature, the show proved to be an unexpected hit, within a few years attracting 40 million listeners per episode—far more than any other program at the time. NBC signed contracts with Gosden and Correll in 1929.

"*Amos 'n' Andy* profoundly influenced the development of dramatic radio," broadcast historian Elizabeth McLeod said:

> Working alone in a small studio ... [the performers] created an intimate, understated acting style that differed sharply from the broad manner of stage actors ... The performers pioneered the technique of varying both the distance and the angle of their approach to the microphone to create the illusion of a group of characters. Listeners could easily imagine that that they were actually in the taxicab office, listening in on the conversation of close friends. The result was a uniquely absorbing experience for listeners who, in radio's short history, had never heard anything quite like *Amos 'n' Andy*. (McLeod 2005)

The show was not only offensive by modern standards—it was also offensive to some people by the standards of the 1920s. Bishop W. J. Walls of the African Methodist Zion

Church said it was "crude, repetitious, and moronic." A petition drive was taken up to have the show taken off the air. But *Amos 'n' Andy* was only mildly controversial in the African-American community, and the show's two white actors were favorite guests at Bud Billekin picnics and parades in Chicago. Nor is there any mention of controversy in several references to the show in *Chicago Defender* (Ellett 2010).

This may have been because the show provided occasional glimpses into the real world of African-Americans. For instance, at one point, the show depicted an innocent Amos undergoing brutal interrogation by police—an event not at all uncommon at the time. The National Association of Chiefs of Police took *Amos 'n' Andy* so seriously that they protested to the network, and the story had to be rewritten to show that it was nothing more than a dream. Still, it's interesting to note that the show proved too controversial to make the transition to television in the 1950s. After two seasons it was taken off the air and kept out of circulation until 2012.

Figure 8.8: Controversial radio—Actors Freeman Gosden and Charles Correll created the first big radio hit, *Amos 'n' Andy*, depicting comic slices of life in an African-American taxi company. Although offensive, the show also provided occasional glimpses into the real-world dilemmas of American minorities. *New York World Telegram*, 1935, Library of Congress.

Following the success of *Amos 'n' Andy*, highbrow symphonies and educational programs were pushed off the air, and radio comedies and dramas began to dominate. The public, anxious to escape the grim realities of the Depression, bought radios by the millions. NBC and CBS worked hard to keep up with the demand for programming.

One of the favorite and best-remembered radio dramas of the 1930s was *The Shadow*, a melodrama concerning a crime-fighter with psychic powers. Its opening line, delivered with manic and sinister laughter, was, "What evil lurks in the hearts of men? Who knows? The Shadow knows."

Apparently the FCC knew as well. The FCC objected when a Minneapolis, Minnesota, radio station allowed "certain words" (damn and hell) to go on the air when they broadcast Eugene O'Neill's play *Beyond the Horizon*.

Give me Trouble

The FCC was "outraged" when, on December 12, 1937, NBC's *Chase & Sanborn Hour* carried a skit featuring Mae West and Don Ameche in the Garden of Eden. The skit depicts Eve as adventurous and hoping to "develop her personality." She was seen as bored with life in the Garden and encouraged Adam to "break the lease." At one point Adam asked what's wrong with life in the Garden.

Figure 8.9 "Give me trouble"—Mae West got more trouble than she anticipated with a 1937 NBC comedy sketch about the Garden of Eden. *New York World Telegram*, c. 1938, Library of Congress.

> Eve: You don't know a thing about women.
>
> Adam: You apparently forget you were one of my own ribs.
>
> Eve: Yeah, I'm ribbed once, now I'm beefin'.
>
> Adam: Me? I know everything about women.
>
> Eve: That's covering a lot of territory. Listen long, lazy and lukewarm. You think I want to stay in this place all my life?
>
> Adam: I do, and I tell you, you're one of my ribs.
>
> Eve: Yeah, but one of your floatin' ribs. A couple of months of peace and security and a woman is bored all the way down to the bottom of her marriage certificate.
>
> Adam: What do you want, trouble?
>
> Eve: Listen, if trouble means something that makes you catch your breath, if trouble means something that makes your blood run through you veins like seltzer water, mmmm, Adam, my man, give me trouble.

These provocative words led the FCC to issue a "stern reprimand" for violating "the ethics of decency." The agency began considering how to deal more effectively with content on the radio networks—not just allowing or taking away station licenses, but reaching more into the core of the program development process.

8 Radio and the News

As radio became more popular, radio broadcasters were able to bring fascinating new sounds to the American public. From the volcanoes of Hawaii to the acoustics of a submarine, the microphone could go everywhere and try everything. Its power was particularly noticed during a prison riot on April 21, 1930, in Columbus, Ohio. A line to the radio station, which had already been installed months before to pick up the prison band, now carried the sound of a prison riot and fire. One prisoner, identified only by number, described the fighting and confusion that killed 317 men. "The microphone was at the heart of the grim tragedy, at times no more than thirty feet away from the crackling flames," said a *New York Times* account.

Radio gained audience and advertising power during the Depression, increasing ad revenues 40 to 50 percent per year as newspaper advertising dropped. American newspaper publishers began to fear radio, fanning the "smoldering fires of opposition" to the new medium, as NBC radio president M. H. Aylesworth warned in 1930. Yet he argued that radio and newspapers are natural allies: "Gutenberg's conception of printing, coupled with Marconi's perfection of the radio, has armed society with its greatest weapon against darkness" (*New York Times*, April 25, 1931).

NBC's olive branch did not win the friends NBC needed, and in 1933, the three wire services (Associated Press, United Press, and International Press) agreed with the publishers association to boycott radio news. AP began with lawsuits against radios broadcasting their news without permission the next year.

CBS radio, at that time a far smaller organization than NBC, responded by creating its own news service. William Paley, president of CBS, found a sponsor for a news program and CBS had gathered 600 part-time reporters in major cities across the world. But in December of 1933, CBS and NBC succumbed to pressure from publishers and wire services to scrap individual broadcast news divisions and form a "Press-Radio" bureau. Under what was called the "Biltmore Agreement," the bureau would air two 5-minute broadcasts per day, except when issues of "transcendent" importance came up. The broadcasts would not be in prime time and they would refer listeners to their newspapers for more details.

Local radio stations more or less ignored the Biltmore Agreement, even though they now had no wire service access to national and international news. But the networks held back on news coverage until the 1936 elections. Tensions began running high between the networks and the publishers. For instance, when CBS gave *all* presidential candidates airtime—including an unlikely candidate from the Communist party—the Hearst *Journal-American* ran an editorial cartoon of CBS president Paley on a soapbox waving a red flag.

One incident proving the value of radio news involved the May 6, 1937, *Hindenburg* disaster. Herbert Morrison was narrating the airship's landing, which was being recorded to be broadcast the next day on Chicago's WLS radio station. Morrison talked as the airship, arriving from Frankfurt, Germany, burst into flames as it attempted to land at the Lakehurst, New Jersey, airfield. His exclamation, "Oh the humanity," as he helplessly watched passengers die, shows the deeply emotional nature of radio. The phrase has become an idiomatic cliché of the twentieth century.

Demand for radio news grew with the rise of tensions in Europe, and one of the talented young CBS news producers, Edward R. Murrow, was tapped in 1937 for the job of heading the network's European offices. Murrow was initially frustrated that his plans for wider coverage of Europe were not supported, but events on the ground were moving quickly. The Nazi takeover of Austria on March 11, 1938 was the first time that Murrow and other correspondents, such as William Shirer, were able to broadcast a full report from the field. NBC also broadcast the event, doing a better job than the CBS team. CBS president Paley, at this point, began to come around to Murrow's point of view, and then claimed to have invented the "World News Roundup" himself. Murrow

Figure 8.10 Radio news—Edward R. Murrow and William L. Shirer fought with the CBS bureaucracy to create a news program from European capitols. With Murrow in London and Shirer in Berlin, Americans by 1938 began hearing some of the disturbing developments first-hand. Murrow's radio and television work would later be seen as legendary in broadcasting, while Shirer went on to write a ground-breaking history of the Third Reich and a memoir of his years covering Mahatma Gandhi in India. *New York World Telegram*, c. 1938, Library of Congress.

and Shirer were hardly in a position to argue when they finally got the okay for their project.

As radio proved its worth, cooperation between radio news organizations and the wire services grew. By 1938, as major events began overtaking minor disputes, AP stopped worrying about whether radio was carrying their news. Now all news organizations started focusing on the increasingly irrational demands of Nazi leader Adolf Hitler. In September 1938, war was temporarily averted when Britain and French leaders met with Hitler in Munich, Germany, and agreed to cede the Sudetenland in western Czechoslovakia to Germany. Radio reports were now coming in daily, and audiences were becoming attuned to urgent news announcements for the first time. Yet people were not accustomed to taking a critical view of the media, and could easily be misled by hoaxes.

Martian Invasion Panics Millions

The whole thing began as a Halloween prank. A brilliant but immature young theater director named Orson Welles hoped he could scare some of the CBS listeners. Like the sorcerer's apprentice, he got a lot more than he bargained for.

Welles had been hired by CBS to present non-commercial dramas such as adaptations of *Treasure Island, Dracula, The Count of Monte Cristo*, and *Huckleberry Finn*. CBS management hoped the productions, which had no sponsorship and no advertising, would help ward off FCC concerns about over-commercialization. Welles and the under-funded Mercury Theater were always under tremendous pressure to present these Sunday night programs, and when the idea for an adaptation of H. G. Wells's *War of the Worlds* came up, Welles and others worried that it would be their least successful program to date. They decided to frame the narrative inside a series of newscasts to make it seem a little more realistic.

John Houseman later recalled that the scriptwriters for the *War of the Worlds* did not believe the show would be quite up to standard. They studied Herbert Morrison's *Hindenburg* disaster reporting as they rewrote it so that they could achieve the live news effect. "We all felt its only chance of coming off lay in emphasizing its newscast style—its simultaneous, eyewitness quality," Houseman said.

The show aired on October 31, 1938. Over the course of an hour, the Martian invaders traveled from their home planet, landed in New Jersey, released clouds of lethal gas and then took over New York. In the end, of course, the Martians were defeated by the humblest of earth's creatures, the bacteria. All within an hour.

Listeners panicked as they heard what seemed to be a news broadcast about an invasion. Without interruptions for commercial sponsors, station identification, or even any warning that it was all just in fun, hundreds of thousands of listeners took to the streets, especially in New Jersey, as they attempted to flee the approaching Martians.

Figure 8.11 Martian invasion—radio and theater producer Orson Welles panicked millions of Americans with an hour-long program that used news bulletins to depict an invasion from Mars. Welles went on to produce and direct the movie *Citizen Kane*. Wikimedia Commons.

Although no deaths or major incidents were reported, reaction to the prank was fairly strong. Within a month, some 12,500 newspaper articles were written about the broadcast (Hand 2006). Houseman attributed the press reaction to its disdain for radio itself. "Having had to bow to radio as a news source during the Munich crisis, the press was now only too eager to expose the perilous irresponsibilities of the new medium" (Houseman 1948).

A similar Spanish-language radio drama based on the original Orson Welles script was broadcast in 1949 in Quito, Ecuador, with a much more serious effect, according to historian John Gosling. The broadcast was interrupted when a full-blown panic emerged in the city streets. Thousands mobbed cathedrals, hoping to receive last rites. When the infuriated listeners realized they were victims of a prank, a mob set the radio station on fire, killing as many as twenty people (Gosling 2009).

9 Censoring Hate Speech on the Radio

If radio could convince people of a Martian landing, how much more damage could it do? As Adolf Hitler said, "By clever, constant propaganda, a people can be convinced that heaven is hell or that a miserable life is paradise" (Brown and Brown 1939).

One American who attempted to prove Hitler right was Father Charles Coughlin, a Catholic priest with a syndicated radio talk show and 16 million listeners. Coughlin started out as a democrat, a union supporter, and a champion of the oppressed working class. But by the middle of the 1930s, he had become so disgusted with Depression- era capitalism that he embraced fascism and anti-Semitic rhetoric, for example, calling FDR's "New Deal" the "Jew Deal." He also repeated German Nazi propaganda nearly word for word in his newspaper columns and secretly took money from Nazi front groups (Warren 1996).

In the summer of 1938, throwing his arm out in a Nazi salute, he told a rally of supporters, "When we get through with the Jews in America, they'll think the treatment they received in Germany was nothing" (Manchester 1974). The "treatment" got even worse in November 1938, as Nazi party members destroyed synagogues and killed Jewish people across Germany in a pogrom called "Kristallnacht." Coughlin tried to defend it, saying that persecution was only natural since Jews had been "numerous among radical leaders" on the left, and that many Christians had been persecuted by communists in Russia.

It was a moment of truth for many Americans, who reacted with horror. And it was a turning point for Coughlin as well, since from that point forward, the NBC and CBS networks refused to pass along "errors of fact" and demanded Coughlin's advance radio scripts. Coughlin refused, and continued his broadcasts through independent radio stations for another year. The Nazis trumpeted the censorship, saying Coughlin was not

Figure 8.12 Fascism on the air—Charles Coughlin, a Catholic priest, ran a syndicated talk show that drew 16 million listeners in the mid-1930s. He began as a pro-labor reformer, but when he openly backed the Nazi party and its treatment of Jews, radio networks and the US government pulled the plug. *New York World Telegram*, 1935, Library of Congress.

being allowed to broadcast the truth. This was of course the rankest hypocrisy, since censorship in Nazi Germany had long since risen to totalitarian levels.

While the FCC wondered how to approach content regulation, the National Association of Broadcasters changed the code of ethics to bar the sale of airtime for the presentation of controversial issues except in political races. The effect was to take Coughlin and others like him off the air permanently in 1939. "This new rule closed the one loophole that remained in the networks' and stations' ability to censor controversial opinion: the dollar loophole," said historian Michelle Hilmes. "The ability to pay was no longer [enough] … In fact, now broadcasters had an obligation to restrict all those outside the broad mainstream of political views" (Hilmes 2006: 129).

A few months later, in January of 1940, the FBI raided the secret New York hideout of seventeen armed Nazi saboteurs who had been associated with Coughlin's group. Although he tried to defend their ideas, it was clear that Coughlin had totally misunderstood American public opinion. He was forced by the Church to retire from public life.

Coughlin also inspired counter-propaganda efforts. Rachel Du Bois, a New Jersey high school teacher, started an influential radio program on diversity because she was infuriated with Coughlin when he yelled things like "This is a country for White Christians!" She proposed a series, financed by the Department of Education, entitled *Americans All, Immigrants All* that described the variety of ethnic streams that made for a diverse and stronger country (Hilmes 2006).

Coughlin was one of several popular fascist Americans whose views were marginalized and undermined by network regulation during the years before World War II. The process was disconcerting to many who felt, at the very least, that Americans needed to understand what they would soon be fighting. But the security threat was real. German attempts to keep America neutral had been exposed in the Bolo Pasha-Hearst affair in 1917 (see Chapter 3), and similarly well-financed attempts to influence the American public were also taking place in the 1930s (Shannon 1995).

"To permit radio to become a medium for selfish propaganda of any character would be shamefully and wrongfully to abuse a great agent of public service," said US President Franklin D. Roosevelt. "Radio broadcasting should be maintained on an equality of freedom which has been and is the keynote of the American press" (*New York Times*, November 20, 1938).

9.1 Developing a governing philosophy of broadcasting

By the late 1930s, the power of radio was being seen as far greater than anyone originally imagined. To give First Amendment freedoms to the very enemies of the First Amendment raised the question of how much faith one could have in the wisdom of the American public. On the one hand, many argued for freedom of speech and trust in the public. "The American people are not boobs," as one pundit picturesquely said (Saerchinger 1940). On the other hand, the FCC had become increasingly concerned about controlling the content

Figure 8.13 Fireside chats—US President Franklin D. Roosevelt's "fireside chats" were an innovative use of media at the time. Roosevelt used them to reassure Americans during the Great Depression and rally the country during World War II. *New York World Telegram*, 1937, Library of Congress.

of the media. The Coughlin problem, the Mae West episode, the War of the Worlds panic, and dozens of other issues provoked calls for outright censorship. In FCC hearings in 1938, regulators talked about "the right of free speech and liberty of thought." The FCC chairman said censorship was "impracticable and definitely objectionable," and then called for self-regulation of radio as the only traditional American way to avoid a plague of innumerable and unimaginable evils (*New York Times*, November 20, 1938).

The National Association of Broadcasters responded with changes in its voluntary code of conduct in 1939, effectively taking Father Coughlin off the air permanently and advanced the idea of greater scrutiny of radio programming. While controversial ideas would still be heard on the air, they would be part of news programs or balanced panel discussions. A formal FCC policy on fairness and objectivity, known as the Mayflower Decision, came in January 1941. The context was a contested radio station license in Boston, Massachusetts. Mayflower Broadcasting Corp. challenged the existing license holders because they endorsed political candidates. While not siding with Mayflower, the

FCC agreed that the station (WAAB) had made a mistake when "no pretense was made at objective, impartial reporting."

"Radio can serve as an instrument of democracy only when devoted to the communication of information and the exchange of ideas fairly and objectively presented," the FCC said. "A truly free radio cannot be used to advocate the causes of the licensee [owner]. It cannot be used to support the candidacies of his friends. It cannot be devoted to the support of principles he happens to regard most favorably. In brief, the broadcaster cannot be an advocate. The public interest—not the private—is paramount" (*New York Times*, January 18, 1941). This policy was the precursor of the 1947 Fairness Doctrine, which applied to both radio and television, as we will see in Chapter 9. Since it was based in part on the idea of the scarcity of radio frequencies, courts upheld the Fairness Doctrine until 1984, when competition from other media undermined the scarcity rationale and opened the way to deregulation.

10 Radio in World War II

The long-expected shooting war arrived in Europe on September 1, 1939, when Nazi Germany's armies invaded Poland, although America would remain neutral for another two years and four months. Radio became the way that Americans best understood what was at stake for the British as they faced the Blitz. Edward R. Murrow is particularly associated with giving a human and dramatic flavor to news from London during the bombings of the early 1940s. His signature opening, "Hello America: This is London calling," was heard by millions around the world. Murrow would often report from rooftops with the sound of bombs and anti-aircraft fire in the background, describing the gritty determination of Londoners and the hardships of the war.

Radio also carried some of the best remembered speeches in history, such as Winston Churchill's June 4, 1940 address: "We shall defend our island, whatever the cost may be. We shall fight on the beaches, we shall fight on the landing grounds, we shall fight in the fields and in the streets, we shall fight in the hills; we shall never surrender." And Americans gathered around the radio when, on December 7, 1941, the Japanese bombed the US Naval base at Pearl Harbor, Hawaii. The next day, 81 percent of American homes listened to the radio as Roosevelt asked Congress for a declaration of war.

A fireside chat later that week is remembered for its eloquence: "We are now in this war. We are all in it—all the way. Every single man, woman and child is a partner in the most tremendous undertaking of our American history."

The war hardly meant unanimity of opinion in all things. Debates about the best way to go about defeating the Nazis, and how best to mobilize the American public, took place at many levels of society. As Hilmes notes, a group of prominent writers in the Office of War Information resigned in 1943 after objecting to advertising-agency and publicity-style tactics that were aimed at manipulating rather than informing the public. They also objected to the way that home-front controversy was censored from news sent to the soldiers through radio and newspapers (Hilmes 2006).

On the front lines, radio news reporters carried each twist and turn of the war to the home front. Radio news reporters were a brave and storied lot, climbing into bombers and broadcasting from the front lines of the war. Among them were Edward R. Murrow; Walter Cronkite, later to become the famed news anchor for CBS television; Chet Huntley, who became the NBC television news anchor; and William L. Shirer, whose 1960 history, *The Rise and Fall of the Third Reich*, would become a classic.

Cronkite's February 26, 1943 CBS broadcast gives a feel for the air war. Parts of the broadcast were obscured by static, so a full transcript was never made:

> In what should be the peaceful [unintelligible], up where the blue skies begin fading into only a haze, I witnessed a man-made hell of bursting anti-aircraft shells, of burning tracers, of crippled Fortresses, and exploding Nazi fighters, of men parachuting to a [unintelligible] plunge in the North Sea, and of other men not so lucky, plunging to death in fiery planes ... those who made the supreme sacrifice for their country. For two hours I watched a vicious gun duel, so excited I had no time to be scared. That came later. I have seen what it's like to [unintelligible] in the dark, what it is like to fight German airmen and dodge German flak. We put our bombs just where they were supposed to go, but we paid a price. As you know, seven of our bombers did not come home. I guess we were lucky. Other formations felt the brunt of German fighter blows, and we watched Fortresses and Liberators plucked from formations around us as if an invisible hand had reached out and pulled them to the ground.

Cronkite wrote about the experience for United Press the following day, but the newspaper dispatch had only some of the immediacy and personal drama of the radio Report (Cronkite 1943).

Figure 8.14 Women in radio—The contribution of women in World War II was often as courageous as its depiction in this US Navy poster. John Falter, 1942, Library of Congress.

10.1 "If I have offended you ..."

In an outstanding broadcast at the war's end, Murrow has described the notorious Buchenwald concentration camp:

> There surged around me an evil-smelling stink, men and boys reached out to touch me. They were in rags and the remnants of uniforms. Death already had marked many of them ... As we walked out into the courtyard, a man fell dead. Two others, they must have been over 60, were crawling toward the latrine. I saw

> it, but will not describe it … I pray you to believe what I have said about Buchenwald. I reported what I saw and heard, but only part of it. For most of it, I have no words … If I have offended you by this rather mild account of Buchenwald, I'm not in the least sorry …

Murrow and colleagues had proven the value of radio news in ways that could have hardly been imagined a decade before. One indicator of how far radio news had come in the war is this: Colleagues in the print media did not even allow Murrow to join the London Correspondents Club in 1937. By war's end, he had been elected the club's president (Sperber 1998).

But radio news had its own particular problems that would extend into television after the war. A single company would sponsor a news or entertainment show and expect the show's stars to attend the company's business functions, cut ribbons at factory openings, and even invite company executives to their summer homes. Murrow had this relationship with the Campbell Soup Company, and the company followed his work very closely.

In a post-war *Hear it Now* show, Murrow described people in the town of Anzio, Italy, now recovering from heavy combat a few years beforehand. In the course of the report, Murrow mentioned that the mayor happened to be both Catholic and communist. The soup company started getting complaints from American listeners and even threats to boycott company products. A company advertising executive wrote to warn Murrow to be more pro-American in his reporting. "There are comments … that you are pink," the man warned, asking him to give "careful thought as to what to do about it." ("Pink" here meant slightly "red," which is to say, sympathetic to communism.)

11 The Post-war Blue Book Controversy

The structure of the news media has always been a contentious issue. During the 1920s, under a Republican administration, the FRC helped NBC and CBS networks establish dominance over the airwaves. But under the democratic administration of Franklin D. Roosevelt, concentration of media power was considered to be a problem by the new Federal Communications Commission. In 1939, following a lengthy controversy, NBC was ordered to sell the Blue Network. It became the American Broadcasting Company (ABC), and the Supreme Court backed the FCC order up in 1943.

Attention turned once again to the structure and performance of radio at the end of the war. Since only a limited number of radio stations could use the publicly owned broadcast spectrum, the question became how well they were serving the public interest.

On March 7, 1946, the FCC issued *Public Service Responsibility for Broadcast Licensees*, also known as the "Blue Book" report. The report expressed disappointment in the over-commercialization of radio, it high wartime profits, its lack of public service programming, and the generally lax quality standards in the industry. The report also insisted that broadcasters had an obligation to serve the "public interest, convenience, and necessity," and that obligation could be enforced by revoking station licenses (*New York Times*, September 18, 1947).

"Shabby commercialism" and a "listeners be damned" attitude is how *Kiplinger* magazine depicted the issue in 1947 (*Kiplinger*, 1947). "Wayward" radio executives will not be punished by forcing them to listen to their own programs, said Charles R. Denny, FCC chairman, because that would be cruel and unusual punishment (*New York Times*, 1945).

Meanwhile, a report by Robert Hutchins' Commission on Freedom of the Press devoted a chapter to radio (although it had primarily been concerned with newspapers and magazines, as we have seen in Chapter 3). The commission joined the FCC in its concern about commercialism in radio, saying that the networks and electronics companies had a responsibility to do more. "Unless broadcasters themselves deal with over-commercialism, the government may be forced to act. So far this challenge has produced little from the National Association of Broadcasters except outraged cries about Freedom of Speech and suggestions for a new code, which, of course, would not go to the heart of the problem" (Hutchins 1947).

Broadcasters "howled" about free speech and encroaching communism, and said that a peril to press freedom could emerge when new technologies, such as newspaper by fax, allowed newspapers to be delivered via broadcasting (*Washington Post*, June 19, 1947). But newspaper publishers sided with the FCC, saying that broadcasters had to get their own house in order.

The controversy died down when the broadcasters issued a new code and Denny resigned in 1947 to take a job with NBC. But the complex question remained over how much pressure the FCC could put on broadcasters to improve their public service when station licenses were only rarely suspended or terminated.

Another regulatory issue emerged around the same time. Newspapers were refusing to accept advertising from businesses that also advertised on radio. The US Justice Department brought a case against the *Loraine Ohio Journal*, questioning its "refusal to deal" as a violation of antitrust laws. The Supreme Court agreed in the case *Loraine Journal v. United States* (1951), and the principle that advertising had to be accepted in competitive situations was established. Both cases would come up in subsequent media antitrust actions, such as the when the US Justice Department sued Microsoft in 1999 over its alleged refusal to deal with competing web browsers (see Chapter 11).

12 New Competition for Markets

Radio was at the center of news and entertainment during the first half of the twentieth century. But in the 1950s, the rise of television meant that radio's original role as the "electronic hearth" and prime source of news and entertainment had become obsolete.

At this point, radio reverted to more local content as the broadcast networks focused their efforts on television. Sometimes radio's move to local content focused on news and sports, but increasingly it turned to music that could be heard while driving or doing other things. It was inexpensive to program and, station owners found, it was increasingly appreciated by the post-World War II baby boom generation.

With universal technical standards for what was called high-fidelity music in the 1950s, a market for record sales began driving the content of a new kind of locally produced radio.

The radio format was called Top-40, and its theme was a kind of competition between music artists to see whose record could become the best-selling top of the charts hit.

Typically, radio DJs (disk jockeys) would "count down" from the top 40, inserting commercials, announcements, and wise-cracking commentary between three-minute songs. Some DJs became celebrities in their own right; probably the most famous in the 1960s was a New York DJ, Murray the K (Murray Kaufman).

As the recording industry income grew, the pressures to promote records to teenagers grew as well. Underpaid DJs began taking various kinds of bribes to promote records or big name bands coming to their city. Investigations in the 1950s and 1960s led to criminal prosecutions for what was nicknamed "Payola" (Hilmes 2006). Congressional hearings looking into radio and television programming practices also found that television quiz shows had been rigged. Stronger regulations against bribery for music promotion or programming followed.

The recorded music industry, boosted by radio, doubled in size between 1960 and 1970 from $600 million to $1.2 billion in the United States and more than doubled again by 1980. Similar acceleration was seen in Britain, France, Germany, and Japan (Gronow 1983).

As the radio audience grew, content expanded into a variety of new formats. By the 1970s a fair-sized city might have a dozen separately owned radio stations, each with a distinct approach to music and culture, including Top 40, heavy metal, classic rock, golden oldies, middle of the road and classical symphonic music, and "talk radio" programming.

This broad variety of programming was expensive to maintain locally, and in the 1980s and 1990s, station owners turned to syndicated radio shows. Starting around 1981, radio stations could buy music program packages delivered by satellite at costs geared to market sizes. While this produced profits in the short term, over the long term, radio again drifted into national syndication and began losing its local news, audiences, and advertisers.

Ownership rules for broadcasting began changing during the 1980s and 1990s. Under the original FCC rules, ownership of radio and TV stations was limited to the "rule of sevens"—seven AM, seven FM, and seven TV stations. During the 1980s, more consolidation of station ownership was permitted under various deregulatory initiatives.

Then, in the 1996 Telecommunications Act, ownership regulations were lifted almost entirely as part of a sweeping reform of telephone, satellite, cable, and broadcast industry regulation. In theory, the act was supposed to allow more competition and better efficiencies of scale. In practice, however, the new regulations allowed a much higher concentration of radio stations under single owners, a homogenization of programming, and loss of minority-owned radio stations.

Technically, the high concentration of radio station ownership is not a monopoly, and statistically an argument can be made that radio is more competitive than most other kinds of businesses. Even at the height of media consolidation, around 2005, one company (Clear Channel, now iHeart Media) owned only about 10 percent of all radio stations (Thierer 2015). But the argument also involves the loss of a diversity of voices, including the declining ownership by women and minorities and the decline in community and local service radio.

Advocates for media reform point out that people of color—36 percent of the US population—own only 8 percent of commercial radio stations, typically small, with lower quality frequencies, representing only 1 percent of the total assets. "The *real* reasons for the decline in minority [radio] ownership are well known," said David Honig, co-founder and president of the Minority Media and Telecommunications Council (MMTC). They include access to capital; advertisers' "no urban" and "no Spanish" instructions to ad agencies to avoid customers they don't want patronizing their stores; employment discrimination; sampling deficiencies in radio ratings; and many other problems that could be remedied at the FCC level (Honig 2012).

"Imagine a US media landscape even more viciously unfair, more drastically tilted to favor greedy, irresponsible and immensely powerful media corporations than the one we already have," said Bruce A. Dixon in a Black Agenda Radio commentary about removing "the few remaining limits on how many radio and TV stations and newspapers giant media companies are allowed to operate in a single market."

Another issue is the influence over live entertainment markets that comes with concentration. For instance, in a 2004 antitrust lawsuit against Clear Channel, a Denver promotions group said the radio station was refusing to sell advertising for its concerts. The suit was settled out of court (*Billboard*, 2004). More issues involving diversity of voices include the banning of music by groups that disagreed with the Iraq War and the inability of pre-programmed local radio to respond to life-threatening local emergencies, such as train wrecks and the release of killer clouds of chemicals.

One area of media reform that has been at least partially successful has involved the expansion of low-power FM community radio stations. Following decades of advocacy and protests, in 2000, the FCC issued regulations for the LPFM category of non-profit education radio station. But with resistance by traditional radio and after a decade of filings, notices, and rule changes, the FCC will have the LPFM "right back where it started—small, isolated, and rare" (Skorup 2012).

With all kinds of alternative sources of music and entertainment, including podcasting and satellite radio, the fight over radio ownership concentration almost seemed moot by the second decade of the twenty-first century.

13 Emergence of Talk Radio

Among important developments in radio during the late twentieth century was the distribution of "talk radio" shows to older AM radio stations and mainstream FM stations. With 400 radio stations around 1990, talk radio grew to nearly 3,000 stations by 2010 (Pew Research, 2010).

A typical talk radio show would last from one to three hours daily and focus on political issues, often with telephone call-ins from listeners. Research by the Pew Center in 2004 showed that 17 percent of the public were regular talk radio listeners and tended to be male, middle-aged, and conservative.

The talk radio format had partisan precursors in Father Charles Coughlin's Sunday talks, but also in the more balanced panel programs such as *America's Town Meeting of the Air*, put on by NBC from 1935 to 1956. The end of the "Fairness Doctrine" in 1987 gave a green light to partisan political radio shows that became popular in the 1990s, when passionate conservative viewpoints connected with a popular market. One of the first of the conservative talk radio success stories was Rush Limbaugh, whose show was carried on 600 Clear Channel network radio stations. Other conservative talk show hosts included Bill O'Reilly, Michael Savage, and Glenn Beck. Yet conservative talk shows began facing major problems as an aging audience demographic made old-guard conservatism increasingly irrelevant (Ungar 2014).

Liberal talk radio was relatively rare in comparison, with hosts such as Ed Schultz, Stephanie Miller, Randi Rhodes, and Bill Press. A network designed to carry liberal talk shows, Air America, started in 2004 but went bankrupt by 2010, partly because overall radio revenue fell by 20 percent or more per year in the economic recession. But Air America itself had problems. It was based on a broader and more expensive concept of audience service, business observers said. Conservative talk radio programs are sold to individual radio stations and have their own individual following. Progressive radio "remains a solid business proposition" said Bill Press, but it takes business and radio experience first, and not ideology (Press 2010). *Ring of Fire*, a progressive show starring Robert F. Kennedy Jr., survives as one of the foremost liberal talk shows.

14 New Radio Technologies

The idea for direct satellite radio service for consumers dates back to the 1980s, when new telecommunications satellite link-ups allowed programs produced in Los Angeles or New York to be broadcast through local radio stations. Bypassing the "middle man"—the small local radio station—seemed like an attractive business strategy. Broadcasting directly to the consumer was technically feasible by the early 1990s, and the idea attracted great hopes. "A new technology will eventually compete with local stations," said media writer Edmund L. Andrews (*New York Times*, January 13, 1995).

But it was not until 1997, over the strong opposition of the National Association of Broadcasters, that the FCC finally approved satellite radio, with the condition that the two major entrants in the field—XM Radio and Sirius—never merge. Despite a wide variety of programming, with hundreds of channels ranging from shock jocks to sports to all kinds of music genres, consumer barriers included the need for a specific satellite radio receiver in the car or at home, and the monthly subscription costs were relatively high. Within a decade, competition from other digital media was so strong that both satellite radio companies were on the brink of bankruptcy, and the FCC allowed the two companies to merge into one monopoly service that would compete against traditional radio.

Meanwhile, in the rest of the world, satellite radio became significant for its ability to promote development and international interconnections. Radio is the only accessible medium in many rural and developing areas, and several low-earth orbit satellites carry development and peacekeeping information programs from the United Nations to rural Africa, Asia, and Latin America. Peacekeeping missions involve a mix of terrestrial and satellite transmissions for the Congo, Kosovo, Liberia, Haiti, Timor-Leste, and other conflict regions.

14.1 Podcasting and Internet radio streaming

In the spring of 1993, when the possibilities of the Internet were just beginning to dawn on most people, an enterprising author and public domain advocate named Carl Malamud began the first Internet radio station, the Internet Multicasting Service. His "Geek of the Week" program featured interviews with European and US internet experts, including a then-obscure British programmer named Tim Berners-Lee who went on to develop the world wide web.

At the time, audio file formats were clumsy and Internet speeds were slow, even for text exchanges. Malamud used a Sun Sparc computer to send and receive audio files, and joked that he owned either the world's cheapest radio broadcasting station or the world's most expensive radio receiver.

Even with high-tech equipment, file sizes were large and download speeds were excruciatingly slow. A three minute uncompressed audio file might be 50 megabytes in size, while a 56 kilobit-per-second download speed would be the best available. So, up to two hours could be spent waiting for a three-minute file to work its way through the system.

But improvements were on the way. During the late 1980s, the International Standards Organization (ISO) had been hosting meetings of digital technology coordination groups such as the Joint Photographic Experts Group (JPEG) and the Motion Picture Experts Group (MPEG). The motion picture group developed a standard for audio compression that allowed a controlled loss of data in order to compress a large file into a smaller one. By 1995, a free software compressor could turn an audio file in the of 50 MB size into a 5 MB file, or smaller, in the new MPEG-1 Layer 3 (or "mp3") format.

The MPEG compression technologies were effective because they first removed data in audio ranges that tended to be less audible to the human ear. The speed and ease of audio file exchanges, especially music downloads, became appreciated in the late 1990s when digital versions of popular music were exchanged through services like Napster (see Chapter 11). This free exchange of copyrighted music was opposed by the Recording Industry Association of America, and Napster was out of business in 2001.

Around the same time, Apple computers offered music files in mp3 and other easy to use formats that could be played on a small player called the iPod. They also introduced a network that allowed the sale of copyrighted music at reasonable prices. The iPod freed audiences from passive roles and allowed them to create their own playlists and even send their own podcasts back into the system. It was an instant hit.

As people began using iPods and other MP3 players more and more, radio audiences have begun to shrink, affecting both traditional radio stations and satellite broadcasters.

Since nearly two-thirds of radio audiences are listening in their cars on any given day, the introduction of iPods is shrinking both terrestrial and satellite radio audience size.

Other mobile devices, such as cell phones, are also allowing consumers to receive both live "streaming" and stored audio files in their cars and cell phones, wherever they go. These developments probably spell the end of the traditional radio broadcasting station. The people formerly known as the "audience" will now have the technology to easily pick and choose their own music playlists and talk programs without the intervening broadcast medium. Once again, a circumventing technology was used to undermine a monopoly.

14.2 Copyright and music on the Internet

The introduction of mp3 audio compression made it far easier to digitally store, rearrange, and share audio files. One effect was to unbundle songs that had been thrown together into standard 70-minute "album" sets to be sold on CDs. With mp3 technology, listeners could isolate their favorite songs and play them in whatever order they wanted. At the same time, musicians did not have to conform to a list of ten to twelve songs. They could have more flexibility and control over how their music was created and when and where their songs were released.

"There is a whole universe that already exists on line, built around the mp3," said Neil Strauss in the *New York Times*. "It is not a world of pirated music, as the record industry would have you believe, but one in which you can choose and design the look and feel of your music" (Strauss, 1999). Yet "piracy"—the illegal sharing of music—did become a problem for the industry, which began the debate in 1999 by insisting on full digital rights management (DRM) so that mp3 players could not be used for copied songs. Consumers rejected DRM, and younger music lovers began sharing music files by the millions over the Internet.

Napster was one of the first sites to freely share copyrighted music. It was developed by Shawn Fanning while at Northeastern University in Boston in 1999. By 2001, Napster had over 26 million users worldwide, but lost a copyright suit brought by A&M Records and other music companies. By 2002, Napster was bankrupt. While some established musicians, including Dr. Dre and Metallica, were vehemently opposed to having their music given away for free, other emerging musicians, such as Radiohead and KidA, found that the exposure helped their sales and concerts.

Once Napster was shut down, other point-to-point music-sharing sites, such as Limewire, Gnutella, Kazaa, and Pirate Bay, emerged between 2000 and 2010. Most were closed down after various legal battles; the owners of Pirate Bay, for instance, were sentenced to one year in jail in Sweden in 2010.

Meanwhile, legal music websites, especially iTunes by Apple, emerged to take advantage of legal music sales through the Internet. Apple also managed to pull back from near-bankruptcy with its popular iPod, a player for digital music in MP3 and other formats. By 2010, iTunes was selling 312 million songs per year for one dollar each. But the music industry notes that this was only a fraction of its $10 billion US annual (and $27 billion international) revenue in 2008—a figure that had come down 25 percent from the recording industry's peak sales ten years earlier.

The Recording Industry Association of America (RIAA) said that musicians were suffering. "Piracy doesn't even begin to adequately describe the toll" that music theft takes on the industry, it said, claiming that global music theft "causes $12.5 billion of economic losses every year" (RIAA 2010).

To reduce the losses, the RIAA sued 17,000 individuals who simply downloaded music in the decade between 2000 and 2010. Only a few chose to fight the lawsuits; most settled with the RIAA and paid a few thousand dollars. Those who did fight faced serious consequences. In one 2009 case, *Capitol Records v. Jammie Thomas-Rasset*, the RIAA persisted through a jury trial and was awarded a fine of $80,000 per song or $1.9 million for twenty-four songs. Later, the judge cut the fine to $54,000 for Thomas-Rasset, a working mother with four children. In another case, *Sony v. Tenenbaum*, courts upheld a verdict of $675,000 for a young man who illegally downloaded thirty copyrighted songs.

Neither defendant has any hope of paying the fines, which were widely seen as so far out of proportion to the individual impacts of the infringements that it was highly contrary to the spirit of the law. Critics said the existing copyright system was flawed, and that excessive fines and overly long copyright terms should not be imposed on new digital media. Elected representatives, deeply out of touch with younger music-lovers, maintained stiff fines for infringements without regard for the harm it caused relatively innocent people, critics said.

The debate had the familiar sound of previous media controversies. Two prominent critics of the copyright law, Harvard University law professors Lawrence Lessig and Jonathan Zittrain, questioned the way copyright and communications law affected creativity and freedom. Lessig compared copyright law to the original idea of property ownership that extended from the ground all the way out into space. That idea was fine until the invention of the airplane, he said. At that point, a new technology made the old law irrelevant:

> We come from a tradition of free culture. Not "free" as in "free beer" ... But "free" as in "free speech," "free markets," "free trade," "free enterprise," "free will," and "free elections" ... A free culture is not a culture without property, just as a free market is not a market in which everything is free. The opposite of a free culture is a "permission culture"—a culture in which creators get to create only with the permission of the powerful, or of creators from the past. (Lessig 2005)

One of the impacts of digital media technology on the music recording industry was the reduced support that recording companies were able to give their musicians. This change in media structure was rather similar to the way the Hollywood studio system collapsed with the advent of television. As they began to lose constant, dependable income, the broad based systems began shrinking, which opened the way for a more independent productions, but, at the same time, made it more precarious to try to make a living as a musician or producer.

15 The Future of Radio

From its earliest days, predictions about the future of radio involved many ideas that today seem impractical or even absurd. Some predicted that radio would help speed up crops growing in fields with a kind of fertilizing effect. Others predicted that radio microwaves could be used to send electric power over long distances without wires, an idea that is possible in theory but extremely dangerous in practice. Over a century after the birth of radio, it turns out that its enduring value is its ability to accompany people as they do other things, such as walking, driving, and working, in situations where video would be too distracting.

To the extent that music and talk programs are now available through new wireless technologies, the connection between telephones, cars, and home computers will allow people to program a wide variety of music, news, or educational experiences before or during these activities.

And so, one frequently made prediction for radio is coming true. The future of radio, Guglielmo Marconi said in 1928, involved its ability to avoid the expense of cable wiring. “The value of the cables has been very great,” said the man who helped create wireless, “but I would hesitate to express an opinion about their future” (*New York Times*, February 25, 1928).

For additional reading, discussion questions, links to video, and other suggestions, see www.revolutionsincommunications.com.

9

Television: A New Window on the World

> If there are any historians about 50 or 100 years from now ... they will find recorded in black and white, or color, evidence of decadence, escapism and insulation from the realities of the world in which we live ... This instrument can teach, it can illuminate; yes, and it can even inspire. But it can do so only to the extent that humans are determined to use it to those ends. Otherwise it is merely wires and lights in a box. There is a great and perhaps decisive battle to be fought against ignorance, intolerance and indifference. This weapon of television could be useful.
>
> Edward R. Murrow, 1958

1 Television Embodied the Dream

As the central source of information and entertainment since the 1950s, television has reflected and shaped the hopes and fears of the age.

From its crude beginnings in the 1920s, television electronics rapidly improved with color, high definition, cable, and satellite delivery systems in the late twentieth century. Through this electronic cornucopia came stories of conflict and reconciliation, reports of war and peace, parades of comically lowbrow stuff, and, occasionally, works of genius.

Television embodied the dream of universal international communication more than its electronic predecessors. And yet when these dreams did come true, it exposed and compounded the clash of cultures as much as it contributed to peace and understanding.

In 1954, the United States had only three television channels (NBC, CBS, and ABC) and Britain had two (BBC and commercial ITV). The range of programming and possibilities for television seemed limited. Nevertheless, the American radio industry threw everything it had into television, from talent to engineering, while the British held back, and retained radio as a significant medium for news and entertainment well into the twenty-first century.

But as the television medium crossed the millennia mark, long-standing trends undermined its once central position in the political world, while new digital technologies fragmented its channels, empowering its audiences—and its critics.

2 Early Concepts of Television

Advances in telegraphic and radio technology in the late nineteenth century led visionaries to imagine that, like electricity, light itself would soon be sent through wires. The "telephonograph" was just around the corner, and French artist Albert Robida, among others, imagined flat screen televisions that would soon be entertaining Parisians in their living rooms.

In 1898, British science fiction writer H. G. Wells wrote about a man waking up 200 years in the future and being introduced to new technology. "There is an optical contrivance we shall use … It may be novel to you. You stand in a very bright light, and they see not you but a magnified image of you thrown on a screen—so that even the furthest man in the remotest gallery can, if he chooses, count your eyelashes" (Wells 1898).

Even in 1925, with television on the threshold of feasibility, futurists were trying to imagine life with television. A British college professor, A. M. Low, drew this scenario in the *New York Times*: "At breakfast, which may come up by tube from a communal kitchen, a loud speaker will take the place of a morning paper, giving him all the news, while a 'television' machine will replace the daily pictorial newspapers …"

Science fiction was not that far ahead of reality, as it turned out. Building on work involving the light-sensitive properties of the element selenium, German inventor Arthur Korn developed a way to scan photographs and send the signal through wires—an early fax machine. A series of demonstrations around Europe in 1907 convinced police departments to use the device to exchange photographs of wanted criminals. "We can now send a not-too-complicated photograph over very long distances in six or seven minutes," Korn said. "The problem of television is not yet solved … The great difficulty is the speed required" (*New York Times*, November 24, 1907).

"Now that the photo-telegraph invented by Prof. Korn is on the eve of being introduced into general practice," said *Scientific American*, "we are informed of some similar inventions in the same field, all of which tend to achieve some step toward the solution of the problem of television" (*Scientific American*, June 15, 1907).

The principles Korn developed would be tried in a dozen different ways before a gifted Idaho high school student named Philo Farnsworth conceived of a television system using

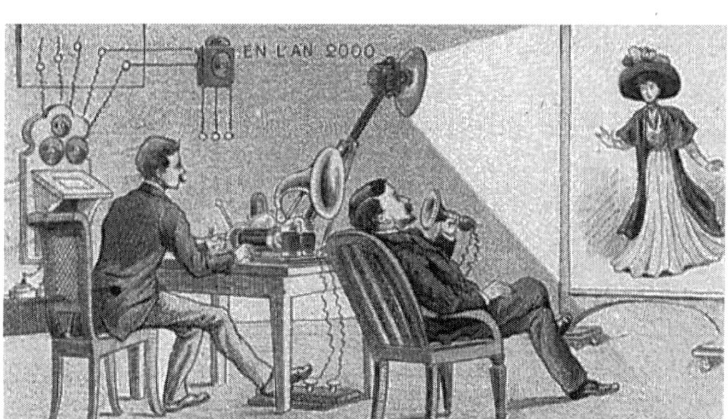

Figure 9.1 Cinema-phono-telegraph—An operator helps a man talk with a woman through a cinema-phono-telegraph as envisioned in 1910. Villemard, Wikimedia Commons.

an electronic scanning principle that lit up phosphorous on the back of a glass screen. Farnsworth demonstrated the television in 1928, but found he was in competition with Westinghouse engineer Vladimir Zworykin. A patent fight between RCA, Westinghouse, and Farnsworth was eventually decided in Farnsworth's favor, but he is sometimes seen as the last of the lone inventors in the mold of Thomas Edison. Invention now was becoming a group effort and a company product, especially in electronics.

Originally, Zworykin estimated that it would cost $100,000 over a year and a half to develop commercial television. Ten years later, after an engineering team spent $50 million, Sarnoff announced the "birth of television" at the World's Fair in New York on April 20, 1939: "Now we add radio sight to sound … [Television is] a new art so important in its implications that it is bound to affect all society. It is an art which shines like a torch of hope in a troubled world. It is a creative force which we must learn to utilize for the benefit of all mankind" (Sarnoff 1968).

Zworykin's RCA team developed four models that were first put on sale at the fair. Westinghouse, General Electric, and other manufacturers also had competing versions, but prices were high—about the equivalent of a new car. Few of these television sets sold, and marketing plans had to be put on hold with the outbreak of World War II. Newspapers, radio, and newsreels would inform the public during the war, but television audiences had to wait for the duration.

Figure 9.2 Inventor of TV—Philo T. Farnsworth (right) is seen directing a television production in Philadelphia in 1934. Courtesy J. Willard Marriott Library, University of Utah.

The transition from radio to television was not an easy one. The earliest programs simply broadcast a view of an announcer or live theatrical productions staged for the camera. News was particularly difficult. "The notion that a picture was worth a thousand words meant, in practice, that footage of Atlantic City beauty winners, shot at some expense, was considered more valuable than a thousand words ... on the mounting tensions in Southeast Asia," said historian Erik Barnouw. Television news broadcasters also had to cope with network expectations of high profits to cover the costs of developing television technology.

3 FCC and the Structure of Post-World War II Television

At war's end, the question of how to deal with controversial issues in the content of broadcasting was revived. The FCC's Mayflower decision of 1941 banned radio broadcasters from taking sides in controversies (see Chapter 8). Radio was seen as a neutral forum for the views of others, not a vehicle for the owners' political viewpoints. This changed somewhat as the war ended. One influence was the 1947 report from the privately funded Hutchins Commission. The report said that the underlying theory of media regulation

Figure 9.3 Commercializing TV—Vladimir Zworykin (1888–1982) fought with Philo Farnsworth over television patents for RCA and Westinghouse as television moved slowly towards commercialization. Here Zworykin is shown demonstrating TV to Mildred Birt in 1934. The tiny round window is the television screen. Science Service Records, Smithsonian Institution.

should involve the duty of social responsibility in general. Especially important was the broadest possible access to information with fair representations of minorities (see also Chapter 3).

Following this reasoning, the FCC reversed the Mayflower decision in 1949, allowing TV and radio broadcasters to take sides on issues so long as they also gave audiences a balanced presentation from all sides. This "Fairness Doctrine" became, until the mid-1980s, the guiding philosophy for rationing the publicly owned broadcast frequencies. The Fairness Doctrine was upheld by the courts through the years, for example in the 1969 *Red Lion Broadcasting v. FCC* case, but fairness proved difficult to enforce in the 1970s as contentious new issues emerged. Particularly difficult were demands by environmentalists to secure equal access to the airwaves and counter advertising claims of the oil and automotive companies.

The FCC also disagreed with the Hutchins Commission recommendations in another area—how to deal with the scarcity of broadcast frequencies for television. The Hutchins Commission recommended that more stations be licensed to prevent the concentration of ownership. Instead, the FCC took the opposite approach in the 1940s and 1950s, continuing a policy from the 1920s that constrained the number of broadcasters with the idea of producing higher quality content. Critics countered that the strategy had not worked with radio and probably would not work with television (Hilmes 2006).

As prosperity increased in the post-war years, television programming and home television set sales boomed. By 1948, the United States had 108 television stations under construction or on the air, and most were affiliated with the big three networks or a few independent start-ups like the DuMont network. At this time, the FCC froze television station licensing in order to re-examine the technology. Yet at the same time, manufacturers kept churning out television sets that were not compatible with possible new higher quality technologies.

By 1952, one-third of all homes, or about 15 million, had television sets. Color television technology could have come online at this point, but the problem of "backward compatibility" meant that existing television sets would have to be considered. The technical problem, although somewhat arcane today, meant that the FCC had to choose between two rival systems—one advanced by NBC and the other advanced by CBS. The NBC system, with lower quality but high-powered lobbying, eventually gained the upper hand.

4 Confrontation on Television: Murrow and McCarthy

The most important global political development of the post-World War II era was the start of the "Cold War" between Western democracies and communist China and Russia. While communist leaders embraced a totalitarian ideology that suppressed freedom of speech, the Western democracies, including the United States, France, Britain, and the Commonwealth nations, were determined to preserve individual human rights and free market economies.

Figure 9.4 American viewers—A familiar scene in 1958, as US families gather around the tube. The Depression, World War II, and fights over technical standards delayed TV adoption, but when this photo was taken, four out of five US households had a TV. Evert F. Baumgardner, National Archives and Records Administration.

Communism was not particularly popular in the United States in the 1920s and 30s for a variety of reasons. Even so, the reaction to the Russian communist military threat grew into a media-fueled national witch-hunt in the post-WWII years. One of the first episodes was the 1947 investigation of communist influence in Hollywood movies by the House Un-American Activities Committee, as we have seen in Chapter 5. While no actual communist conspiracy was found, the political atmosphere had become highly charged with partisanship.

Amid growing tension, a relatively unknown US senator named Joseph McCarthy (Republican, Wisconsin) catapulted to national fame in February 1950 when he claimed to have a list of communist spies operating in the US State Department. The reckless accusations were widely repeated in the media, but a Senate investigation led by Democrats that year labeled McCarthy's charges a "fraud and a hoax." The committee said that McCarthy's charges did nothing but "confuse and divide the American people … to a degree far beyond the hopes of the Communists themselves." Republicans backed McCarthy and responded to the committee report with accusations of treason.

Figure 9.5 Anti-communist crusade—Wisconsin Senator Joseph McCarthy carries on a reckless crusade against exaggerated communist threats in Senate Hearings in June 1954. Joseph Welch (seated left) and Senator Joespeh McCarthy (standing right) during the 1954 Army–McCarthy hearings. United States Senate Historical Office.

Radio and print media exposure fueled McCarthy's continued accusations during the early 1950s. Specific accusations were usually made from the safety of the Senate floor. But two major instances of television exposure dramatically changed public opinion about the corpulent, beetle-browed senator, in part because few had ever seen McCarthy up close or heard his arguments for more than a few minutes at time. McCarthy's first major television exposure involved thirty-two days of Senate hearings concerning charges that McCarthy had used his influence to obtain favors for friends in the army.

During April 1954, ABC television carried the hearings live from the US Senate, and many previous charges by McCarthy about spies in the Pentagon were exposed as fabrications that damaged innocent individuals. The high point of the hearings was the moment when the legal counsel for the US Army responded to a McCarthy charge by saying, "You've done enough. Have you no sense of decency, sir, at long last? Have you left no sense of decency?"

The second instance of extended television exposure was a classic confrontation between a journalist and a politician. CBS News broadcaster Edward R. Murrow, famed for his radio reports from London during World War II, had made the transition to television with a program called *See it Now*. In one episode of the program, Murrow told the story of a young Air Force officer named Milo Radulovich who had been classified as a security risk simply because his sister and father read a Serbian-language newspaper. In

Figure 9.6 Sparring with McCarthy—CBS News editor Edward R. Murrow seen through a studio window. Murrow responded to Senator Joseph McCarthy's charges by urging that Americans not allow themselves to be driven into an age of unreason. 1957 photo, University of Maryland Broadcasting Archives.

another, Murrow focused on McCarthy himself and the lack of substance behind most of his allegations. Murrow concluded:

> We must not confuse dissent with disloyalty. We must remember always that accusation is not proof and that conviction depends upon evidence and due process of law. We will not walk in fear, one of another. We will not be driven by fear into an age of unreason, if we dig deep in our history and our doctrine, and remember that we are not descended from fearful men.

McCarthy demanded equal time, and Murrow was happy to oblige, turning over the entire half-hour program. McCarthy directly attacked Murrow for friendships with left-of-center figures and supposed ties to communist groups. With no evidence and astonishing bluster, McCarthy succeeded only in exposing himself as a political bully. Conservatives with genuine concerns about communism began to see him as a liability, and in December 1954, the US Senate passed a motion to censure Senator McCarthy. He died in 1957, abandoned by his party and his supporters. Murrow, hailed as a champion of free speech, also came to be regarded as a liability by CBS network executives. News stories about cigarettes and lung cancer, about segregation and schools, about apartheid in South Africa were controversial. Some entertainment-oriented higher-ups thought Murrow was trying to "save the world every week" (Friendly 1967).

In 1956, *See it Now* lost its sole sponsor (Alcoa Aluminum) and was transformed into an irregularly scheduled documentary series. By 1958 the program had been taken off the air. Simple controversy was one problem, but another factor was the profitability of easily produced quiz and game shows on other networks in adjacent time slots. "It was as though an highly successful amusement park had gone up across the street from a school, said CBS producer Fred Friendly. "Suddenly the property values had changed" (Friendly 1967: 77).

Murrow went on to work in the Kennedy administration as head of the US Information Agency. When he died in 1965, a colleague said, "We shall live in his afterglow a very long time … we shall not see his like again" (Emery and Emery 1997: 369).

5 Satellites Build Bridges Among World "Archipelagos"

The news on October 6, 1957 that the Soviet Union had launched a satellite around the world came as a shock to the United States and Western Europe, long accustomed to seeing themselves in the vanguard of science. The feat was hailed as a triumph of the communist system but denounced in the Western press as "political rather than scientific" (*Washington Post*, October 10, 1957). The "Sputnik crisis," as it was called, revealed cutbacks in scientific research programs and gaping deficiencies in American scientific education.

The reaction to the crisis in the late 1950s and 1960s led to a chain of events and initiatives that had a profound international impact. Among the best known initiatives was President John F. Kennedy's goal of sending astronauts to the moon by 1970. Others included the creation of the National Aeronautics and Space Administration (NASA) in 1958, new federal funding for science education, and new investments in computer hardware, software, and networks that would, in time, form the basis of the internet (see Chapter 11).

The most visible side of the US space program was the competition with the Russians to put astronauts in orbit around the earth (the Russians were first with the spaceflight of Yuri Gagarin on April 12, 1961) and to land on the moon (which the United States accomplished in July, 1969). Also fairly visible were non-defense satellite projects such as the 1958 SCORE satellite and the Telstar communications satellite, launched in 1962 as a cooperative venture between the United States, Britain, and France.

The first geostationary satellite was launched in 1964 and was used to send television broadcasts to the United States from the Summer Olympics held that year in Japan. The

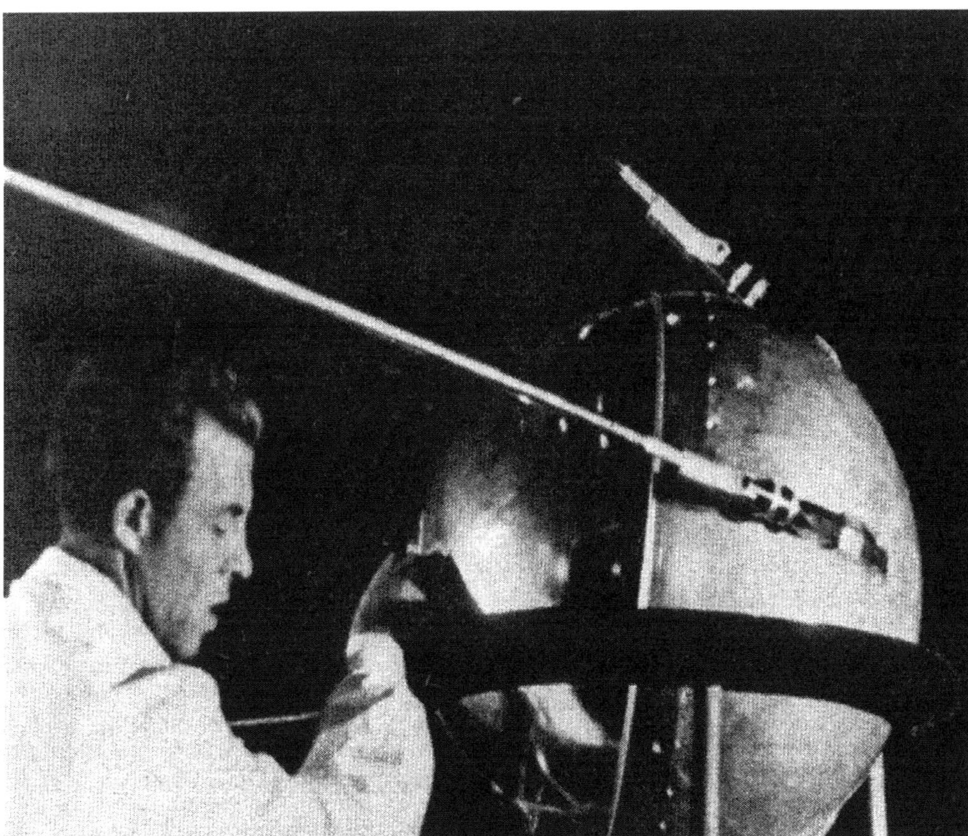

Figure 9.7 Sputnik launch—A Russian technician prepares the Sputnik satellite for launch October 4, 1957. As the first satellite in space, the launch was a victory for Russia in the Cold War and a wake-up call for US science. It marked the beginning of the space race, promoted international telecommunications, and inspired the defense computer networks that formed the technical foundation of the Internet. Photo via National Aeronautics and Space Administration.

advantage of geostationary satellites, as first conceived by British science fiction writer and mathematician Arthur C. Clark in 1945, was that they were ideal telecommunications relays. Rather than pushing a signal through thousands of miles of wire, a broadcast signal could be sent through a dozen miles of atmosphere, and then through space without interference. An important milestone was the 1964 formation of the International Telecommunications Satellite Consortium (INTELSAT), an international satellite organization with 143 member countries.

By the 1970s, satellites were being routinely launched to help broadcast unions and networks around the world uplink and downlink programs to affiliates. These allowed consumer television offerings to expand in the United States with Cable News Network, the Weather Channel, and Home Box Office, and also allowed regional broadcasters to exchange programs at far lower cost than ever before. These satellites allowed the exchange of broadcast information from all over the world for the first time. They also had an important secondary effect in that they required international cooperation in all kinds of standard formats for information interchange through United Nations groups (such as the International Telecommunications Union and the International Standards Organization).

Some of these standards, such as those for photos and motion pictures, had an important influence on computer networks that are well known today. These included picture files called JPEGs (from the Joint Photographic Experts Group) and audio and video files called MPEGs (from the Motion Picture Experts Group).

"Young people today find it difficult to imagine how far we were ... from the global view that now seems so familiar," said Raymond Frontard of the International Standards Organization in Geneva, Switzerland. "The earth did not yet shake at the slightest tremor in its most remote region. It was, instead, an archipelago of distinct worlds" (Frontard 1997).

6 Television Culture: Golden Age or Vast Wasteland?

The popular myth is that television of the 1950s and early 1960s reflected a golden age of a prosperous and contented time in American life. Yet the same complaints once vented about radio were heard again, with more force, about television. These included the lack of quality, over-commercialization of the public airwaves, under-representation of minorities, and the unwillingness of the networks to sacrifice any profits for public interest programming in return for their use of a public resource.

An early platform for television critics involved hearings by Senator Estes Kefauver on juvenile delinquency, starting around 1955. A host of witnesses testified about the many negative social influences on young people, including comic books, movies, and violence on television. Network executives defended themselves by pointing to the National Association of Broadcasters Code of Conduct, most of which had to do with avoiding controversy over moral issues. The code also limited commercials to 6 to 10 minutes per hour at night and 10 to 14 minutes per day, but these limits were not always observed, especially among segments of the television industry that were less profitable.

Controversy continued over the effects of having single sponsors for television programs, one prime example being the impact on CBS News when Alcoa dropped its sponsorship of *See It Now*, as noted above. Eventually, the networks stopped the decades-old practice of having one sponsor per program and sold advertising by the time slot rather than on a single program basis.

6.1 Quiz show scandals

The most serious crisis for network television in the 1950s came with the quiz show scandals. In a 1959 congressional investigation, witnesses testified that the shows had been fully scripted and that contestants had been coached to give right or wrong answers. Americans were shocked. Even President Dwight Eisenhower said it was "a terrible thing to do to the American public." One of the contestants, Charles Van Doren, confessed to the committee, "I was involved, deeply involved, in deception … I realize that I was really giving a wrong impression of education. True education does not mean the knowledge

Figure 9.8 Quiz scandal—Quiz show *21* host Jack Barry turns toward contestant Charles Van Doren in 1957 as fellow contestant Vivienne Nearine looks on. Two years later, Van Doren would confess to a congressional committee that he was "deeply involved in deception." Orlando Fernandez, *New York World Telegram*, Library of Congress.

of facts exclusively. I wrote articles trying to express this feeling but few were interested. Instead, I was referred to as a 'quiz-whiz, a human book of knowledge, a walking encyclopedia'" (*New York Times*, November 3, 1959).

No federal laws had been broken by the deception, although that soon changed as the FCC wrote new regulations to enforce a more honest approach in such shows. But it was also the abundance of cheap, easy to produce, yet highly profitable quiz and game shows that bothered media critics.

6.2 Vast wasteland

Most of what television presented to the public over the first few decades of its life was not memorable or even significant for its time. An endless parade of trivial entertainment was enough to capture eyeballs and boost network profits. But there were notable exceptions.

Perhaps the most popular entertainment program of the age was *I Love Lucy*, a situation comedy that concerned Hispanic band leader Desi Arnaz and his ditzy but loveable wife Lucille Ball. The show's themes often verged on controversial areas, such as alcohol content in medicine (which made Lucy drunk when she filmed a commercial) or sweatshop labor (in a scene where she couldn't keep up with the conveyor belt, much like a similar scene in Charlie Chaplin's *Modern Times*). Other comedies of the time, such as *Gilligan's Island* and *Donna Reed*, reflected white American values but not much in the way of substance.

The Western was the popular genre for social commentary, and shows like *Bonanza* and *Gunsmoke* (which evolved from a radio series) frequently involved themes of justice and the treatment of minorities and women. Still, violence was the usual solution for problems, and minorities were badly stereotyped. While mild controversy was tolerated and sometimes even celebrated, real social issues and serious change were rarely considered until the 1970s, when programs like *Archie Bunker* and *MASH* went on the air.

The idea of television as a "vast wasteland" came up in a speech by a newly appointed FCC commissioner Newton Minow as he addressed an audience of the National Association of Broadcasters on May 9, 1961. The phrase became a cliché for television critics who advocated more public interest programming. Minow said:

> When television is good, nothing—not the theater, not the magazines or newspapers—nothing is better. But when television is bad, nothing is worse. I invite each of you to sit down in front of your own television set when your station goes on the air and stay there, for a day … until the station signs off. I can assure you that what you will observe is a vast wasteland. You will see a procession of game shows, formula comedies about totally unbelievable families, blood and thunder, mayhem, violence, sadism, murder, western bad men, western good men, private eyes, gangsters, more violence, and cartoons. And endlessly commercials—many screaming, cajoling, and offending. And most of all, boredom.

Television executives worried about the speech, saying that while there was always room for improvement, having the chair of the FCC as their chief critic was uncomfortably close to government censorship. "At what point does criticism become coercion?" asked NBC president Robert Sarnoff in 1961. "Where does freedom leave off and interference begin?" (*New York Times*, December 8, 1961). Despite the protests, broadcast journalism as a public service expanded greatly by 1962, with over 400 documentaries produced that year by the three networks (Hilmes 2006). By 1963, the 15-minute evening news programs had expanded to half an hour.

Minow was happy but not entirely satisfied with the scope of the improvements in public service programming. However, the only tools the FCC had were license revocations (extremely rare) and the ability to encourage competition. One way to boost competition was to expand the available channels to UHF, and under Minow, the FCC passed a regulation that new television sets would have to be capable of picking up the higher-frequency channels. Many of these independent television stations would, by the 1970s, be linked together in satellite and cable television systems that Minow also championed.

Another form of competition was the introduction of a public education channel. The Corporation for Public Broadcasting was first authorized in 1967, and PBS went on the air in 1970.

7 Television and the US Presidency

Television was not taken too seriously in its early days, and advertising for the 1952 Eisenhower presidential campaign featured a cartoon of Uncle Sam and an elephant leading a brass band in a parade with a catchy musical jingle. His opponent, Adlai Stevenson, took a dim view of campaign ads on television. "The idea that you can merchandise candidates for high office like breakfast cereal is the ultimate indignity to the democratic process," he said. He had the same idea in 1956, when he ran, and lost, again.

But television was serious. In 1952, vice- presidential candidate Richard Nixon was accused of taking $18,000 in bribes for campaign expenses and other loans. Eisenhower was just on the verge of replacing Nixon, six weeks before the election, when, on the advice of aides, Nixon bought a half-hour of prime time TV. From the well-lit set of a Los Angeles theater, Nixon explained that the fund was legal and intended for campaign expenses. He also spent time explaining his personal finances and work-ethic background and praising Eisenhower. The speech was remembered because, to clinch public support, Nixon said that he had only taken one gift—a cocker spaniel dog named Checkers that had been sent to his children. Most Americans were impressed by the sentiment of the speech. Public opinion overwhelmingly shifted to Nixon, but the huge wave of support was, to Walter Lippmann, "disturbing ... with all the magnification of modern electronics, simply mob law" (Morris 1991).

After a few years in office, Eisenhower opened the doors to television cameras at press conferences. The print and radio media were not happy, because the presence of television tended to formalize meetings that had been relatively informal until then. The new realities of television also meant that important political announcements had to be made by 2.00 p.m. eastern standard time in order to be reported on the evening news. "After Eisenhower, television was no longer a novelty, but a central premise in all political logic," said Roderick P. Hart (Hart and Triece 2010).

Figure 9.9 Confrontation in Moscow—Then US Vice President Richard Nixon (right) pokes a finger at Soviet Premier Nikita S. Khrushchev in 1959 at a US exhibit in Moscow depicting the average American home with a stove, washing machine, radio, and other appliances. With television cameras rolling, Khrushchev said he didn't think the average American could afford such a home. Nixon responded, "Diversity, the right to choose, the fact that we have 1,000 builders building 1,000 different homes is the most important thing." Thomas J. O'Halloran, *New York World Telegram*, Library of Congress.

Although he was one of the first politicians to effectively use television with his "Checkers speech," Nixon performed poorly during television debates with John F. Kennedy during the presidential campaign of 1960. It was the first time that candidates of the two major parties faced each other on TV, and the contrast between Kennedy's calm demeanor and Nixon's apparent unease on camera was apparent. The series of four nationally televised debates moderated by members of the press would not be repeated until 1976, but the presidential debate has become a fixture of US presidential races ever since.

The significance of television as the central medium of the post-World War II era came into sharp focus with the assassination of President John F. Kennedy on November 22, 1963. CBS news anchor Walter Cronkite was eating lunch at his desk when a wire editor burst in with the news that Kennedy had been shot in Dallas. Someone must have

Figure 9.10 Presidential debate—The first presidential debates on television took place in 1960 between Richard Nixon and John F. Kennedy. The debates were crucial in the election, and most people believed that Nixon did not come across well on television. Nixon avoided debates in the 1968 and 1972 presidential campaigns. Wikimedia Commons.

asked him what he would write, because he yelled, "The hell with writing, just give me the air." When Kennedy's death was confirmed an hour later, Cronkite choked up on the announcement and paused to wipe away tears, quietly expressing the profound sense of grief and shock shared by the nation and the world. People gathered around television sets, finding not only news but also a sense of social cohesion and resilience in the face of catastrophe.

"Before that, TV had been a theater and a sports stadium," said CBS producer Don Hewitt. "All of the sudden it became a sort of chapel where Americans went to hold hands with Cronkite. He was everyone's anchor, and everyone's clergyman" (Garvin 2009). Similar scenes, where people gathered for days around their television sets, would be repeated worldwide in subsequent disasters, such as the September 11, 2001 attacks that destroyed the World Trade Center.

If television could be a chapel, it could also be a political wrestling arena, as President Lyndon Johnson proved with one of the first negative campaign ads aired briefly during the 1964 presidential campaign. It only aired once, but the publicity surrounding the ad brought it to everyone's attention, and it was a factor in President Lyndon Johnson's victory over Barry Goldwater. The ad was targeted at Goldwater's idea of using nuclear weapons in Vietnam. It begins by depicting a young girl picking the petals off a daisy and counting. But when she reaches nine, she looks up in the sky as an ominous male voice counts down to a nuclear explosion. Johnson's voice says, "These are the stakes! To make a world in which all of God's children can live, or to go into the dark. We must either love each other, or we must die." Another voice then says, "Vote for President Johnson on November 3. The stakes are too high for you to stay home."

A similar ad attacking Democratic candidate Hubert Humphrey in 1968 had positive images and bandwagon music dissolving into headache-inducing reverb effects and photos of riots and the Vietnam War. Attack ads in other campaigns included the infamous "Willie Horton" ad of the 1988 campaign, in which Democratic candidate Michael Dukakis was attacked for being the governor in a state where a convicted murderer got out on parole; and the "swift boat" ads that attacked presidential candidate John Kerry in the 2004 campaign in an area where he was strongest — his military record. Similarly, in the 2012 campaign, some veterans groups attacked successful candidate Barack Obama for, they claimed, politicizing the attack on Osama Bin Laden (Bacevich 2012).

In most countries, political advertising during electoral campaigns is highly regulated. But a case that equated campaign spending with free speech, called *Citizens United v the Federal Election Commission*, decided by the US Supreme Court in 2010, essentially deregulated political spending. Corporations and secret donors are now able to flood the airwaves with advertising about issues that affect them, without having to identify their real interests or objectives. Over 83 percent of Americans are not happy with the decision and believe that limits should be placed on campaign spending (Little 2012).

Overall spending on political advertising keeps rising in the US, with each four-year presidential election cycle breaking new records. Political advertising in the 2012 cycle rose to $9.8 billion, with about 57 percent going to television advertising, which was a decline from 2008 (Watson 2012; Borrell 2012). Online advertising in political campaigns is rising because it is more effective and generates more activism.

8 Vietnam: The First Living Room War

The impact of television on public opinion during the Vietnam War remained a contentious issue well into the twenty-first century. The traditional myth was that the "living room war" proved too horrible for sensitive Americans and had a morale-sapping effect. Then-president Richard Nixon said, "Our worst enemy seems to be the press" (Hammond 2007). "Public support for U.S. involvement in Vietnam declined drastically once the television networks began suggesting that the war was a stalemate" said media critic Stephen J. Farnsworth (Farnsworth and Lichter 2007). The idea that the press "lost the war" through its negative coverage has an eerie similarity to the Dolchstoss "stab-in-the-back" myth that Germans used to explain their defeat in World War I. "The entire vernacular of American politics has been altered" by the use of the Dolchstoss myth about Vietnam, observed Kevin Baker in 2006 (see Baker 2006; Lembecke 1998).

Closer studies of television and public opinion in the Vietnam era show a far more complex picture, and the steady drop in public support for the war seems unrelated to any one set of events or images, but rather to highly public national debates about its overall purposes and conduct which were carried in the media as a matter of course. One controversial incident involved a 1965 report about the burning of the small village of Cam Ne. CBS news correspondent Morley Safer watched as American soldiers burned thatched-roof huts while elderly Vietnamese stood by helplessly. "This is what the war in

Vietnam is all about," Safer said to the camera, as a soldier set an old man's roof on fire in the background. "The marines are burning this old couple's home because [gun] fire was coming from here. The day's operation burned down 150 houses, wounded three women, killed one baby, and netted four prisoners."

The incident sparked immediate public controversy and an outraged phone call to CBS president Frank Stanton from President Lyndon Johnson, indicating the important role that television images had taken on in the national debate over the war.

Other dramatic television and photographic images from the war included a napalm attack on a village that resulted in injuries to children and the street execution of a suspected Viet Cong insurgent. Television news tended not to broadcast more serious images of the US massacres, such as My Lai, and tended to support the US position on the extent of Viet Cong atrocities such as the Hue massacres of 1968. Historians Daniel Hallin and William Hammond reviewed years of television coverage of the war and found that most television news was upbeat in the early years. The occasional negative report, although inevitable in war coverage, was greatly outweighed by the sympathetic light in which American soldiers were invariably seen (Hallin 1986).

Hammond, a military historian, challenged assertions that the media lost the war by swaying public opinion. In an encyclopedic set of books, Hammond said the media

Figure 9.11 Bowing out—President Lyndon Johnson makes a surprise announcement that he will not run again for president in 1968. The impact of the televised Vietnam War was a factor. Courtesy Lyndon B. Johnson Presidential Library.

tended to follow rather than lead public opinion. While government and the press shared a common vision of containing communism in the early years of the war, upbeat government press releases were challenged by journalists' experiences in the field. As public sentiment shifted, presidents Lyndon Johnson and Richard Nixon both tried unsuccessfully to manage the news media to project an image of success even though the military and strategic picture was discouraging.

One turning point in the war was the 1968 in-depth report from experienced World War II correspondent Walter Cronkite, then anchor of CBS news. While nuanced and respectful, Cronkite concluded that the military was not winning or losing the war, but rather the "bloody experience of Vietnam is to end in a stalemate." Johnson took Cronkite's disaffection with the war so seriously that he told advisor Bill Moyers that if he'd lost Cronkite, he'd lost middle America (Halberstam 1979; Murray 1999). Was this a factor in Johnson's decision not to run in the 1968 election? Some historians say the influence of television was exaggerated, and Johnson had other things on his mind (Campbell 2010).

9 Civil Rights and Television

Television was the medium through which the Civil Rights movement needed to get its message to the American people. As we have seen in Chapter 4, gruesome photographs of Southern brutality (such as the body of Emmett Till) had been widely circulated in the 1950s and earlier. Yet nothing caught the conscience of the world like the televised images of snarling police dogs turned on demonstrating children in Birmingham, Alabama, or the cruel clubbing of Civil Rights demonstrators amid clouds of tear gas at the foot of the Edmund Pettus bridge in Montgomery, Alabama on March 7, 1965. Meanwhile, churches, homes, and shops with ties to the Civil Rights movement were being bombed.

At a time when American soldiers were fighting communism in Vietnam, the images of embattled Civil Rights demonstrators flashing around the world were deeply embarrassing for the administration of President Lyndon Johnson. A renewed commitment to Civil Rights, and national legislation stiffening laws against voter intimidation, were among the direct results of the new awareness brought about by television.

"The ascendancy of television as the new arbiter of public opinion became increasingly apparent at this time to Civil Rights leaders and television news directors alike," according to the Museum of Broadcast Communications (MBC). Yet the television audiences in the South closest to events of the Civil Rights era were often kept in the dark. Many Southern TV stations routinely cut national network feeds of Civil Rights coverage, often pretending that they were having technical difficulties. Newspapers were also neutral or quite often hostile to Civil Rights in the 1950s and 1960s, and usually omitted wire service coverage of Civil Rights issues unless there was a white "backlash" angle. (Important exceptions included the *Atlanta Constitution* or the Greenville, Mississippi, *Delta Democrat-Times*.)

While newspaper publishers were free to do as they pleased under the First Amendment, broadcasters had an obligation to fairness under the Fairness Doctrine, and their station licenses were controlled by the federal government. Broadcasting offered more opportunity to force change than the print media.

9.1 The WLBT–United Church of Christ case

Beginning in 1954, a group of Civil Rights activists began studying the pattern of racially biased news and public affairs programming on television in the South. The Jackson, Mississippi chapter of the National Association for the Advancement of Colored People (NAACP) filed repeated complaints with the FCC about one particularly racist television station, WLBT in Jackson. Requests for a public hearing when the station license came up over the years were consistently turned down by the FCC.

Figure 9.12 Television and Civil Rights—The impact of television on the Civil Rights movement was profound, not only from the standpoint of live coverage of the 1963 "I have a dream" speech by Rev. Martin Luther King at this march on Washington, but also in terms of conveying the suffering and brutality of white Southern resistance. But the Civil Rights movement also changed television, and Southern TV stations could no longer black out or ignore national news about Civil Rights issues. US National Archives and Records Administration.

In May 1963, the pressure led WLBT to make one small concession. The station allowed a charismatic Civil Rights leader, Medgar Evers, on the air to speak about the need to end segregation. Three weeks later he was assassinated at his home in Jackson. Around this same time, the United Church of Christ, a liberal national church from the Congregational tradition, met with Martin Luther King, Andrew Young, and others to work on methods for challenging the Southern broadcast media. Dr. Everett Parker, a professor at Yale Divinity School, became involved because he had developed a method of content analysis that would hold up under the FCC review process.

"I really looked at stations throughout the [region], from New Orleans to the East Coast, and found that it was a very bad situation," he said in a 2008 interview. "When Thurgood Marshall won the *Brown v. Board of Education* and was on NBC, [WLBT] put up a sign—'Sorry, cable trouble'—and blamed it on the telephone company. But anyway, I hit on WLBT, simply because of the terrible things that it was doing" (Goodman 2008). WLBT also blacked out an award-winning three-hour NBC documentary on Civil Rights, *The American Revolution 1963*.

When WLBT applied for what it thought would be a routine renewal of its broadcasting license in 1964, the church and a coalition of Civil Rights leaders formally challenged the license. They charged that the station blacked out nationally produced Civil Rights news about nearby events; had promoted race-hating points of view without balance or regard for the Fairness Doctrine; and refused to feature African-American speakers in any context, even on Sunday morning church service broadcasts.

The WLBT response was typical for stations whose licenses were challenged: it drew up a list of all its public service activities from its logbooks, including service to the African-American community. Usually complaints would stop at this point, and in effect be buried in red tape. But the coalition had an ace up its sleeve—it responded that the station's logbooks were highly inaccurate, and presented evidence from Parker's content analysis, which had been kept secret up until that point.

The back-story behind the content analysis group is that white faculty members at nearby Millsaps College kept detailed logs and recordings of WLBT's programs. The group met in secret and kept their names confidential; even Parker could not reveal their identities if he were to be captured by the white power structure of Mississippi. "Don't forget, this was almost immediately after the murder of Medgar Evers," Parker once told an interviewer.

In a formal hearing, the FCC denied the United Church of Christ "standing" in the case, meaning that they had no formal right to come into the agency's legal process and argue their case. Without remarking on the facts of the case, the FCC renewed the WLBT license for one year. Usually, the bureaucratic procedure at this point would be for the station to show evidence that it was mending its ways, but the WLBT management had a deep ideological commitment to segregation and remained defiant (Horwitz 1997).

The church appealed the decision to a federal court. The UCC attorneys did not really expect to win both the case and the much larger battle over FCC's regulatory procedure. Yet in 1966, the appeals court ruled that the FCC would conduct public hearings on the license and that the citizens would have standing before the FCC. The court decision, written by Judge Warren Burger (who would later become the Chief Justice of the US Supreme Court) eloquently restated the long-standing tradition of broadcast regulation:

- "A broadcaster is not a public utility … but neither is it a purely private enterprise like a newspaper or an automobile agency. A broadcaster has much in common with a newspaper publisher, but he is not in the same category in terms of public obligations imposed by law. A broadcaster seeks and is granted the free and exclusive use of a limited and valuable part of the public domain; when he accepts that franchise it is burdened by enforceable public obligations. A newspaper can be operated at the whim or caprice of its owners; a broadcast station cannot. After nearly five decades of operation the broadcast industry does not seem to have grasped the simple fact that a broadcast license is a public trust subject to termination for breach of duty …
- Under our system, the interests of the public are dominant. The commercial needs of licensed broadcasters and advertisers must be integrated into those of the public. Hence, individual citizens and the communities they compose owe a duty to themselves and their peers to take an active interest in the scope and quality of the

> television service which stations and networks provide and which, undoubtedly, has a vast impact on their lives and the lives of their children ... The 1964 renewal application [for WLBT] might well have been routinely granted except for the determined and sustained efforts of Appellants [the Civil Rights–church coalition) at no small expense to themselves. Such beneficial contribution as these Appellants, or some of them, can make must not be left to the grace of the [Federal Communications] Commission." (*United Church of Christ v FCC*, 1966)

The public hearing ordered by the court took place in May 1967 in a small room in the Jackson, Mississippi, Post Office, because state officials refused access to other public buildings. The room was overflowing with WLBT supporters waving Confederate flags, and the FCC hearing examiner treated the church coalition with obvious contempt.

In the face of this official prejudice, Charles Evers testified that WLBT had created the atmosphere that led to the assassination of his brother Medgar four years earlier (Horwitz 1997). After considering the evidence from the hearing, the FCC commissioners renewed WLBT's license in a bitterly split 1968 decision. But the decision made the Court of Appeals furious, and in a 1969 ruling, the higher court said the FCC's conduct was "beyond repair."

In an unprecedented move, the Court of Appeals ordered the FCC to vacate WLBT's license and hold hearings to consider new applicants. The coalition organized an integrated group, Communications Improvement Inc., and proposed a unique arrangement, splitting station profits between public broadcasting in Mississippi and Tougaloo College in order to teach communications to African-American students. Communications Improvement Inc. got the license, although the continuing legal battles would not be resolved until 1983.

The success of this one case in which a license was revoked for public interest reasons did not lead to long-lived reform, said communications scholar Robert B. Horwitz. "The really sobering thought is that the old broadcast reform coalition has clearly collapsed, and a new ... conservative movement ... seeks to limit standing, curtail the ability of citizens to bring legal actions and diminish public intervention in general." It has become increasingly difficult to approach reform with a non-market theory of public interest, he said (Horwitz 1997).

Although television's powerful images of the Civil Rights struggle helped Americans understand its human dimensions, TV news coverage of rioting following the assassination of Martin Luther King in 1968, and of other riots in Watts, Detroit, and Washington, DC in the 1960s "provoked a reaction by the end of the decade, marked by the presidential campaign slogans calling for law and order," said the MBC. "Consequently, many of the very images that supported the movement simultaneously helped to fuel the national backlash against it" (MBC 2010).

Television Stars Join Activists

In the wake of the Medgar Evers assassination and the controversy over racism at television station WLBT, students at Tougaloo College began a letter-writing campaign to ask performers visiting Jackson, Mississippi to cancel their appearances in protest against segregated music halls and fairgrounds. Many did, including Original Hootenanny USA, trumpet player Al Hirt, and piano player Gary Graffman.

The cast of *Bonanza*—Lorne Greene (Ben Cartwright), Michael Landon (Little Joe), and Dan Blocker (Hoss)—also agreed with the students and canceled a contracted appearance at the county fair in January 1964. Blocker even sent a telegram to the *Jackson Daily News* explaining that he was disgusted with residents of the town. In response, Jackson's two daily newspapers started a "black out *Bonanza*" campaign, but local ratings remained unchanged. "Most white viewers, when pressed to choose between enjoying a favorite television show or upholding the claims of racial segregation, chose the former," said historian Michelle Hilmes.

Only a few months later, in April 1964, a *Bonanza* episode featured the story of an opera singer who had been invited to come to Virginia City. When the singer arrives, people realize for the first time that he's an African-American, and a variety of prejudiced reactions result. He's also jailed on a mistaken warrant as an escaped slave, and the Cartwrights have to help straighten out the problem. "The importance of appealing to the uncommitted middle in achieving a solution to the racial problem was related in the final scene, when the singer forgets his humiliation and gives his concert," a *New York Times* reviewer said. The show "added to the stature of popular TV entertainment." General Motors, the sponsor of *Bonanza*, was concerned about potential controversy, but NBC executives, for once, stood firm against the sponsors (Gould 1964).

The science fiction show *Star Trek* was another whose themes and characters envisioned solutions to racial and cultural tensions. One of the first African-American stars on TV was Nichelle Nichols, who played Lieutenant Uhura on the show. But after the first season's success in 1966, Nichols thought about resigning and going to work on Broadway. She changed her mind when she happened to run into Martin Luther King at a fundraising dinner. King said he and his family were huge fans of the show.

"I was speechless," Nichols said in a radio interview. "He complimented me on the manner in which I'd created the character. I thanked him, and I think I said something like, Dr. King, I wish I could be out there marching with you. He said, no, no, no ... You are marching." So Nichols stayed with the show. "I was projecting in the twenty-third century what should have been quite simple," she said (Martin 2011).

Although many TV and film stars joined the Civil Rights movement in the 1960s, few had the impact on public opinion as the shows themselves and the depictions of human reconciliation in Western and science fiction genres like *Bonanza* and *Star Trek*.

10 Public Broadcasting

Forty years after the Federal Radio Commission shoved educational and public broadcasters out of the way to create the RCA/NBC radio network, an act of Congress created a framework for the Public Broadcasting Service and other educational efforts. It took 40 years for the broadcast reform movement to finally find a national home on the airwaves. One major focus for the reform movement was the National Association of Educational Broadcasters (NAEB), which began as an alternative to the NAB in 1934. Their studies and lobbying led the FCC to reserve radio frequency space for educational channels in the 1940s. Because it was so expensive to lease telephone lines, a "bicycle network" of taped educational radio programs allowed stations to share programs.

When the FCC thawed out the frozen television frequency allocation system in 1952, one innovation was the reservation of 242 channels nationwide for non-commercial education use. New ideas about educational programming also began emerging at various universities at this time, aided by new momentum from the "Sputnik crisis" of 1957. The next year, Congress passed the National Defense Education Act to aid direct school-to-home and other instructional TV projects. The act got unexpected support from Southern congressmen who were opposed to school integration and were looking for a way to maintain education outside the public school system.

By the 1960s, networks of regional educational stations were springing up and new federal funding was helped them expand. Innovative programs like Julia Child's *The French Chef* series and Fred Rogers' *Mister Rogers' Neighborhood* made the networks increasingly popular. Also significant was the creation of the Children's Television Workshop in 1968, which produced *Sesame Street* for PBS (first aired in 1970) and other children's programs like *The Electric Company*.

Educational programs from the British Broadcasting Corporation (BBC) also padded out the broadcast schedule for public television in the United States. The BBC's educational programs had a dual purpose of both improving broadcasting quality in Britain and strengthening the "open universities," which were the equivalent of American community colleges. Costume dramas that depicted nineteenth-century literary classics, along with television lecture series like Jacob Bronowski's *The Ascent of Man* and James Burke's *Connections* series were funded as supplements to university education.

The major milestone in educational broadcasting, and the culmination of 40 years of the broadcast reform movement, was the 1967 Public Broadcasting Act authorizing federal operating aid to educational stations. But the act was flawed in that it depended on year-to-year funding rather than other more permanent funding mechanisms. (An alternative, suggested by the Ford Foundation, would have been the use of profits from satellite communications to finance educational television.)

The year-to-year funding was an ongoing political problem for PBS. As early as 1971, President Richard Nixon vetoed a two-year authorization bill, and in 1981, President Ronald Reagan started making drastic cuts in CPB funding, but in 1984, the FCC loosened the rules for public broadcasting, allowing advertising under the name of "enhanced underwriting."

Other controversies included a variety of confrontations over liberal versus conservative social issues in programming. Conservatives objected to a 2004 cartoon called *Postcards from Buster* in which the child has "two mommies." They claimed that PBS documentary producer Bill Moyers was too liberal, pressuring him to resign in 2005. (He did, but returned when PBS invited him back in 2007.)

In the twenty-first century, about half of PBS revenues come from state and federal taxes and another half come from private donations. Some believe that public broadcasting has outlived its usefulness, since it started as an alternative to the three major networks. Others point to a long history of educational and public broadcasting and maintain that commercial television is not capable of consistently producing educational programming.

Figure 9.13 Big Bird and the First Lady—One legacy of the broadcast reform movement was an increasing emphasis on educational television for children through shows like *Sesame Street*. In this 1993 photo, Big Bird meets then-First Lady Hilary Clinton. US National Archives and Records Administration.

11 Television Advertising

11.1 Tobacco advertising

Television advertising is powerful, more so than radio or print, and the images it presents can be highly influential. When the US Surgeon General issued a report in 1964 summarizing 7,000 studies on the destructive effects of tobacco smoking on health, some of the first recommendations involved warning labels on cigarettes and a ban on television advertising.

The Federal Communications Commission considered that since the topic of smoking was controversial, broadcasters were breaking the Fairness Doctrine when they aired cigarette commercials since they didn't provide air time for opposing viewpoints. Although anti-smoking ads stared appearing on television in the late 1960s, the glamorization of smoking was itself controversial. This included advertising campaigns featuring the "Marlboro Man"—a rugged cowboy depicted in a Western setting smoking a cigarette—and even children's cartoon characters like the Flintstones. Congress passed the Public Health Cigarette Smoking Act, banning cigarette advertising on television on January 2, 1971.

Tobacco companies shifted advertising to magazines and sports events, but new US laws and regulations in 2010 prohibit companies from sponsoring sports, music, and other cultural events.

An international treaty banning all tobacco advertising was approved by 168 nations, not including the United States, in 2005. The treaty, called the World Health Organization Framework Convention on Tobacco Control, is seen as a watershed moment for global public health.

11.2 Advertising to children

A variety of controversies over television advertising to children emerged in the 1970s and continue to the present. Among them are the sheer volume of advertising; the advertising of unhealthy foods; and the psychological and programming approaches used by advertisers to engage children.

The average child watches about 25,000 TV commercials a year (Holt 2007), and the rate has risen slightly since the 1970s. Ads for foods with high amounts of sugar and fat are the most troubling to consumer advocates, who have seen a connection to childhood obesity.

Consumer advocates argued that children are trusting and vulnerable, and that advertisers were taking advantage of that innocent frame of mind. In 1974, the FCC issued new guidelines for children's advertising that separated program content from commercial messages and limited the number of commercials. "If our policy against over-commercialization is an important one," the FCC said, "it is particularly important in programs designed for children." The same year the advertising industry put together the

Children's Advertising Review Unit (CARU), a voluntary regulation agency that dealt with complaints and made recommendations to advertisers.

Organizations and grass-roots groups concerned about advertising asked the FCC for tightened regulations. But in the 1980s, with the Reagan administration's deregulatory approach, the FCC took the opposite stand and began deregulating all advertising, saying "the market will regulate itself." One of the groups, Action for Children's Television (ACT), petitioned the FCC for a rehearing about the specific question of children's advertising, presenting evidence that the market had already failed to regulate advertising for children. The FCC refused to reconsider children's advertising, and ACT filed a federal lawsuit.

A federal court examined the issue and found that the FCC had changed the regulations without considering the problem at all, which it found "profoundly wrong" (*ACT v. FCC*, 1987). In 1990, Congress passed the Children's Television Act, noting that market forces alone had not created an adequate amount of children's educational programming and that government action was needed. The act limited ads to twelve minutes per hour on weekdays and 10.5 minutes per hour on weekends, along with limiting program length advertising (shows that depicted a character also being sold as a toy).

Since the 1990 act, media choices have exploded, with cable satellite and Internet services. But advocates say the amount and quality of educational programming has not really increased (Conley 2010).

One effect of top-down regulation has been an increase in alternative advertising approaches, such as running contests and events where the advertiser has only a subtle presence. This was "exactly the opposite of what some of the advocacy groups were aiming for," a *New York Times* article noted (Clifford 2010).

12 Controversy over Television Violence and Indecency

The question of whether television influences people, especially children, to commit violent acts has been hotly debated for decades. Hundreds of commissions, studies, lobbying groups, and regulations emerged since then, with two major recommendations: better approaches to the way television is produced for young children; and the development of a rating system that parents can use to evaluate programs that may be unsuitable.

The regulatory saga began with the Commission on the Causes and Effects of Violence, started in 1968 by President Johnson. A panel of industry and academic experts looked at previous studies and commissioned twenty-three more social science and psychological studies of the effects of television. The panel's report in 1972 was controversial, as industry struggled against academics to tone down the report's conclusions. The National Association of Broadcasters code prohibited gratuitous violence or pandering to morbid curiosity, but the public appetite for violent programs brought home a long-standing dilemma: what's in the public interest is often not what the public is interested in. The gravity of the problem of violence on TV was reinforced with a 2002 report by the

American Academy of Child and Adolescent Psychiatry. The report said that violence on TV was not the only cause of violent behavior, but that hundreds of studies had shown that children were becoming numb to the horror of violence; were gradually accepting violence as a way to solve problems; and were imitating what they saw on TV (AACAP 2002).

Also in the closing decades of the twentieth century, as indecent talk shows and comedy routines became increasingly popular, the problem of children's exposure to casual indecency on the air remained. Two approaches were taken to address the problems. First, under the "safe harbor" concept, FCC regulations are intended to keep patently offensive material off the air from 6.00 a.m. to 10.00 p.m. Second, the idea of using technology to allow parents to block objectionable programming was written into the Telecommunications Act of 1996. Television receivers sold since 1999 have to have "V-Chip" as part of the circuitry. V-Chips can detect information about a program's rating and block it if parents desire. Yet according to a 2007 FCC survey, only 27 percent of parents could figure out how to program the V-Chip. And in a separate poll that year, only 12 percent of parents were using parental controls such as the V-Chip, and the conservative Parents Television Council called it a failure.

13 Broadcast Deregulation: The End of the Media Reform Era

The big change in broadcasting policy from the 1980s to the twenty-first century was a greater emphasis on marketplace competition and reduced emphasis on social responsibility theory. The milestone was the Telecommunications Act of 1996, which deregulated ownership rules for radio, television, and cable companies, leading to a host of mergers and consolidations that concentrated the broadcast industry.

The advent of new technologies like cable and satellite television challenged the original reason for FCC regulations, which was the idea that broadcasting depended on government allocation of the broadcast frequency spectrum—a limited public resource. In other words, now that the resource was not so scarce, the "scarcity rationale" that justified government regulation had been undermined. What this meant was that broadcasters pushed for—and got—a deregulation of the content and the structure of broadcasting.

One casualty of the new market approach was the Fairness Doctrine. Originally created by the FCC to ensure that all sides of controversial issues could be heard, the doctrine was used to assure that anti-smoking advertising balanced tobacco advertising in the 1960s. The doctrine was affirmed by the Supreme Court in cases like *Red Lion Broadcasting v. FCC* (1969), which involved a station's attack on an individual book author. But the courts did not agree that environmental issues such as leaded gasoline advertising deserved balance from the environmental perspective (*Friends of the Earth v. FCC*, 33 FCC 2nd 648 1972).

By the 1980s, the view of broadcasters as community trustees was replaced by a conservative view of broadcasters as marketplace participants. The courts also noted the complexities of enforcing balance that emerged in a case involving the League of Women

Voters, and a few years later, the FCC said it would no longer enforce the doctrine. Calls for a return of the Fairness Doctrine are frequently heard, such as one from environmental lawyer Robert F. Kennedy Jr:

> The airwaves belong to the public. They were public-trust assets, just like our air and water, and broadcasters could be licensed to use them but only with the proviso that they use them to promote the public interest and to advance American democracy ... Today six giant multinational corporations now control all 14,000 radio stations in our country, almost all 6,000 TV stations, 80 percent of our newspapers, all of our billboards, and now most of the Internet information services. So you have six guys who dictate what Americans have as information and what we see as news. The news departments have become corporate profit centers. They no longer have any obligation to benefit the public interest; their only obligation is to their shareholders. (Kennedy 2004)

Another casualty of the market-oriented approach was the "News Distortion Rule," which says that as public trustees, broadcast licensees may not intentionally distort the news, and that "rigging or slanting the news is a most heinous act against the public interest." However, in cases where the rule was invoked, the FCC took no action. For example, in 1997, two Florida reporters said their investigation on the dangers of a synthetic growth hormone (BGH) used by dairies was distorted, but complaints to the FCC were not upheld (*WTVT v Akre*, 2003).

14 Cable and Satellite Home Television

Cable television was originally created in the 1940s to serve remote communities where broadcast signals were weak. When the cable systems began to use microwave relays in the 1960s to import more programming, independent non-network stations operating on the UHF bands were afraid that would be driven out of business. Broadcasters mounted a "fight pay TV" campaign, and the FCC effectively blocked the expansion of cable systems.

When satellite communications became available in the early 1970s, thousands of community cable systems began merging to take advantage of new channels such as Home Box Office (HBO) and Music Television (MTV). "Superstations" such as WTBS in Atlanta began serving more of the cable market through satellites and grew into larger organizations such as Cable News Network (CNN). In the process, cable service grew from a small percentage of the market to about 60 percent by the year 2000.

The majority of cable TV services were owned by five or six large integrated companies, ranging from Comcast and Time Warner to Cox and Charter. But local franchises are administered by cities and counties, which have not been prepared to deal with major corporations. Cable companies took advantage of their monopoly status, according to the Consumer Federation of America, noting that deregulation of cable in the Telecommunications Act of 1996 meant that cable rates rose at three times the rate of inflation.

Meanwhile, hobbyists who did not want to pay for cable TV in the 1980s could order kits to build a large (three-meter) satellite dish and pick up some unscrambled transmissions from satellites. At one point the market was growing so quickly that a congressman joked that they had become the "state flower of West Virginia." Small dish direct broadcasting (DBS) home satellite TV, introduced in 1994 by Hughes DirecTV, was followed in 1996 by EchoStar. Proposals to merge the two satellite TV companies were rejected by the FCC in 2002 because television audiences would then only have the choice between a local cable monopoly and a satellite TV monopoly.

By 2010, cable TV had peaked at about 60 percent of all US homes, while satellite TV had about 30 percent of the market. New digital systems would quickly undermine the old monopolies.

15 Hard Times for Traditional Media

Television networks and other content providers went into a tailspin similar to that of newspapers in the first decade of the twenty-first century. Smaller audiences meant declining profits, which led to lower quality programs, which led to smaller audiences. At its peak in 1976, the three US networks (ABC, CBS, and NBC) attracted 92 percent of all viewers. By 2008, the four main networks (including Fox) attracted only 46 percent of viewers. Over the previous decade, NBC's ratings dropped 37 percent, ABC's 35 percent, CBS's 33 percent, and PBS dropped 37 percent. Network news was especially hard hit, overwhelmed by the financial demands of corporate owners who have "little appreciation for the sacred trust that goes with owning a news organization," said Philip S. Balboni in *Nieman Reports*, noting the "near extinction" of the kinds of television documentaries produced by Edward R. Murrow and others in the 1950s and 1960s (Balboni 2001).

Staffs cuts of half or more of a newsroom made once-thriving network news offices look empty, and news bureaus closed down in most cities outside Washington and New York. The new austerity meant that the reporters who managed to keep their jobs had to perform at a higher level. They would no longer be accompanied by a producer or camera crew, but would now set up their own camera, record their own news story, edit it, and send it back to the newsroom on their own. While the technology made this process easier, it didn't make it any less time-consuming. "They're getting away from substance," said one journalist. "They're not covering the statehouse, the city council, the county board. They do whatever's quick and easy" (Kurtz 2010).

One of the quickest and easiest ways to attract audiences was through television talk programs. Usually TV talk shows are hosted by a celebrity, conducted in the present tense, and highly structured. They are fairly inexpensive to produce, compared to network dramas, and can bring in high returns for networks (Timberg 2002). They also involve a relatively neutral figure moderating the conflict. The US political debate became less moderated as audiences and channels fragmented in the late twentieth and early twenty-first centuries. On the one hand, more channels meant that viewers could simply click the remote to hear a different point of view. And because there were more channels, there was no "scarcity rationale" for government-imposed content boundaries, such as the Fairness

Doctrine. Under heavy commercial pressures, network news and public affairs became increasingly shrill and partisan.

Traditional television networks, losing audiences and desperate for a return to their once-lucrative market positions, retreated into a level of vitriolic partisanship not seen for a century. Fired up by the deregulation of political advertising, partisan television especially seemed to be fragmenting the political center in the United States.

In a speech reminiscent of Edward R. Murrow's NAB address (quoted above), John Stewart, a television comedy show host, noted:

> The press can hold its magnifying glass up to our problems, bringing them into focus, illuminating issues heretofore unseen, or it can use its magnifying glass to light ants on fire, and then perhaps host a week of shows on the sudden, unexpected dangerous flaming-ant epidemic. If we amplify everything, we hear nothing … The press is our immune system. If it overreacts to everything, we actually get sicker … And yet, with that being said, I feel good. Strangely, calmly good, because the image of Americans that is reflected back to us by our political and media process is false. It is us through a funhouse mirror. (Burnett 2010)

The image was false, Stewart said, because in everyday life, people cooperate and work together in ways that belie the media image of constant partisan politics.

16 The Impact of Digital Networks on Television

As usual in the history of media technology, the reaction to a monopoly is the development of new technologies. We've seen the trend in printing, for example, when magazines led the early twentieth-century Progressive-era charge for broad social reforms in the US at a time when newspapers were too monopolized to take risks. We've seen it in the way that Alexander Graham Bell's financiers wanted to replace the telegraph monopoly with the telephone in the 1870s. We've seen it in home satellite delivery television, introduced in the 1990s, that was intended to circumvent local monopolies of cable television systems.

Similarly, in the second decade of the twenty-first century, home broadband Internet technologies expanded to the point where consumers could access television programs without paying high satellite or cable fees, as a wide variety of news and entertainment programs became available through computers. But the economic impacts of connecting the Internet to the home television posed problems for both delivery systems and content providers.

New types of delivery systems included Netflix, a subscriber service which offered instant movies by internet access; and Hulu, an advertising-supported experiment by three big networks (NBC, ABC, and Fox) to deliver their content over the internet. Technically, it was easy around 2010 to begin distributing television through the internet to home television sets. Set-top boxes from providers Apple TV, Google TV, and Boxee became available around 2010. However, content providers like NBC, ABC, Fox, and others, worried about profits, blocked the new set-tops from carrying their programming. The largest cable provider in the United States, Comcast, bet on creating its own on-demand programs in a bid to compete with on-demand models like Netflix and Google TV.

Broadcasters in Europe were much quicker to embrace the internet TV model, offering "catch-up" television where the original broadcast would be available for a week or so on the internet through services like itvPlayer in the UK and M6 in France. Audiences found they didn't need to pay for a bundle of network programming schedules when what they really wanted was just a few favorite programs. The ability of to unbundle news, sports, and entertainment had impacts in other areas, such as newspaper readership, as we have seen. Yet by 2010, it seemed inevitable that cable and satellite television would shift, in part, to the Internet, breaking up old monopolies and allowing new forms of competition.

17 Broadcasting as Re-tribalization

One interesting issue was the possibility that social evolution had taken a turn toward what Marshall McLuhan called "re-tribalization" through broadcasting. McLuhan used the term as a way to describe the tendency of radio and television to enhance the post-literate culture, making it more passionate while, at the same time, craving a harmonious and unified sense of social balance. In a 1969 interview, McLuhan said:

> The instant nature of electric-information movement is decentralizing—rather than enlarging—the family of man into a new state of multitudinous tribal existences. Particularly in countries where literate values are deeply institutionalized, this is a highly traumatic process, since the clash of the old segmented visual culture and the new integral electronic culture creates a crisis of identity, a vacuum of the self, which generates tremendous violence—violence that is simply an identity quest, private or corporate, social or commercial.

Although McLuhan observed the trend with concern for violence, there are others who have seen changes in the individual ties to society as simply emerging in new forms. Tribes, according to business writer Seth Godin, have always been a natural focus for social change. What the Internet has done, and what mass marketing through one-way broadcasting media never could do, is allow the development of small groups that could lead social change (Godin 2008).

"Narrowcasting" of video through the web can empower global innovation, according to Chris Anderson, a media entrepreneur behind the TED conference (Technology, Education and Design). Anderson believes that the expansion of video on the web will make up for the decline in public information from network television and printed media.

"This is the technology that's going to allow the rest of the world's talents to be shared digitally, thereby launching a whole new cycle of crowd-accelerated innovation," he said in a 2010 TED talk. Noting that 80 million hours of YouTube are seen every day, it's possible to imagine an internet-fueled learning cycle "capable of carrying all of us to a smarter, wiser, more beautiful place."

"If it's all puppies, porn and piracy, we're doomed," Anderson said. "I don't think it will be. Video is high-bandwidth for a reason. It packs a huge amount of data, and our brains are uniquely wired to decode it" (Anderson 2010).

YouTube, Music, and Cultural Curators

Although MP3 technology allowed music sharing in the late 1990s, video sharing was not easy until after around 2005, when a site called YouTube allowed free video uploads to the web. At that point, people with small cameras or camera phones could directly upload unedited clips.

Figure 9.14 Embedding Rube Goldberg—Members of the rock band OK Go disputed the way their record label allowed access to promotional videos on YouTube. Here, in black and white but with embed tags restored, are OK Go's Andy Ross, Damian Kulash, Dan Konopka, and Tim Norwind after a workout with the *This Too Shall Pass: Rube Goldberg* video on YouTube. Courtesy Andy Gershorn.

The idea for YouTube came from the difficulty several of its founders had in sharing video files over email. By 2011, it was the third most accessed website in the world after Google and Facebook (Alexa 2011). While most of YouTube's videos are uploaded by individuals, many music videos are professionally produced. In some cases, musicians who are happy to encourage fans have come in conflict with their record labels. For example, in 2006, a rock band named OK Go uploaded "Here It Goes Again," a song with a humorous video. The video became popular (or "went viral," as people said at the time), bringing in 10,000 hits per day. This happened because fans put the video's <embed>

code on their own web pages so that the video would play on their websites. The group's record label, Capitol/EMI, realized they were losing advertising money from the ads that are automatically placed by YouTube. So EMI pulled the plug on the embed tags. Fan hits quickly dropped from 10,000 to 1,000 per day, and EMI's revenue from YouTube dropped from about $80 a day to only $8 per day. "This isn't how the Internet works," said Damian Kulash of OK Go. "Viral content doesn't spread just from primary sources like YouTube or Flickr. Blogs, Web sites and video aggregators serve as cultural curators, daily collecting the items that will interest their audiences the most. By ignoring the power of these tastemakers, our record company is cutting off its nose to spite its face" (Kulash, February 20, 2010).

While respecting EMI's need to recover its investment in musicians through its studio system, Kulash also felt that the group's use of the new media was in the record company's long-term best interest. Eventually, the record label restored the embed code on the group's YouTube video, but the issue shows how difficult it can be for traditional media to anticipate the problems posed by new digital media.

"It's been like a corporate version of the Three Stooges: absurd flailing, spectacular myopia and willful ignorance of reality," Kulash added. "Now that the big record companies have made themselves obsolete, bands such as mine can make a better living without their help than we can with it" (Kulash, August 29, 2010).

For additional reading, discussion questions, links to video, and other suggestions, see www.revolutionsincommunications.com.

Part IV

The Digital Revolution

> Changes in the information age will be as dramatic as those in the Middle Ages in Europe.
>
> James A. Dewar, 1998

> The Digital Revolution is whipping through our lives like a Bengali typhoon.
>
> Louis Rossetto, *Wired* magazine, 1993

The power of the digital revolution was not anticipated in the decades before computers graced every desktop and "desktops" opened every computer. The popular early visions of computers featured machines that were cunning, inhuman, and dangerous. George Orwell's *1984* (published in 1948) described a totalitarian state where history is erased on demand and where people are constantly monitored. Stanley Kubrick's *2001: A Space Odyssey* (produced in 1969) is a film in which a computer takes over a spaceship and kills most of the crew. William Gibson's *Neuromancer* (published in 1984) described a nightmarish world of totalitarian control over human–computer interfaces.

It might have been easy to dismiss these as fantasies at the beginning of the digital revolution; after all, they were projected on a technology that nobody quite understood. But the fears were taken very seriously at the time, and that had an impact on the way the technology developed.

As we will see in this fourth section of *Revolutions in Communication*, the digital revolution was conceived early in the nineteenth-century Industrial Revolution and born in the twentieth-century chaos of World War II. This section on the Digital Revolution organizes the history of these technologies into three chapters in order to take the broadest possible view of media history:

- Chapter 10 describes the *origins of computing*, from the 1830s to the present.
- Chapter 11 traces the development of *digital networks* from the 1960s to the present, and how they helped in the creation of new ways to distribute information and new approaches to businesses.
- Chapter 12 describes the *emerging global culture* that digital technologies have enabled, including civic and social networks.

We'll also consider questions still hanging in the balance: for instance, whether the digital revolution will ultimately prove to be a liberating technology after all, or whether its enormous power will be harnessed for lesser purposes.

1 Social Construction of the Digital Revolution

A revolution is a dramatic, wide-reaching change in conditions or an overthrow of the established social order. The first three media revolutions—printing, imaging, and broadcasting—helped create social revolutions on a vast scale. Each revolution had an impact on the one beforehand. Imaging changed publishing, making it more visual, emotional and mass oriented; broadcasting changed both, co-opting visual media and pushing print publications into news cycles with more immediacy and geographic reach.

Digital media, as the fourth wave of revolutionary technology, created revolutionary change in the first three media types, making production and distribution far more flexible. It also opened doors to new information functions and traffic patterns. Media was no longer a one-way deal, from top-down to mass markets. It was networked, allowing many-to-many conversations. It didn't have to be centrally produced. Users, readers, and/or viewers all had highly individualized choices. And, as a result, all kinds of new and revolutionary applications emerged. People with new ideas radically changed old business models, inside the old media, and in many other kinds of business.

Why did that happen? Why did we end up with a kind of new media structure that entailed so many new dimensions for information content? Couldn't it just as easily have become a tightly controlled, top-down information system, perhaps with a little bit more flexibility? What made the digital revolution different? Was it the technology itself? Or was it the way people adopted the technology?

1.1 Early perceptions of computers

Technically, early digital computers of the 1940s were a cross between adding machines and radios. They were originally meant to serve the code-breakers, weapons designers, and rocket scientists who needed to manipulate complex calculations in World War II. The networks that linked them by the 1950s were originally meant to warn of pending nuclear attacks and provide the capability to launch retaliatory strikes.

Yet computer engineers thought their machines were capable of greater things, and they tended to have a far more positive vision than writers and artists like Orwell, Kubrick, or Gibson. Engineers at SRI, PARC, and other research organizations saw an enabling technology that could help reorganize the way people used information. Their vision spread slowly across the decades, from nerd engineers in the 1960s to hipster hardware developers in the 1970s to the rebellious cyberpunk programmers of the 1980s and 1990s.

What gave these visionaries hope was that the technology itself seemed to be so malleable that it had no single or obvious trajectory. Unlike most other technologies, computing could have gone in a million different directions.

Perhaps it could have been used to help build a nightmarish totalitarian society. Perhaps it still can be, although some don't believe that computing so easily adapts to the service of totalitarianism.

1.2 Curves in the road

The advent of digital technologies in the mid-twentieth century had enormous impacts on previous communications revolutions.

In print media, disputes over the adoption of digital technologies in typesetting and printing led to serious labor problems and long-term structural change, starting in the 1950s and 1960s, as we saw in Chapter 3. Imaging technologies lagged behind typesetting and printing, but when the Associated Press introduced the "Leaf Desk" in 1988, the most complex analog job in the newspaper—photo-engraving—became entirely redundant, as we saw in Chapter 4. Electronic technologies, especially recorded music and radio, changed dramatically with the digital revolution in the 1990s and early 2000s as we saw in Chapter 8. And where digital technologies helped create a system of international satellite broadcasting networks, those networks became fragmented and financially unstable in the second decade of the twenty-first century, as we saw in Chapter 9. There were a few people in the traditional media who saw it coming. Derek Daniels, chief editor of the Knight newspapers (*Miami Herald, Detroit Free Press*) predicted in 1970 that multimedia technologies would become the future of the media business. Kodak executives knew their business model would change in the digital world and worked to adapt. But most other media executives just didn't get it. As late as 1994, Viacom CEO Sumner Redstone said the emerging internet was "a road to fantasyland"—and not a game changer. "To me it seems apparent that the information superhighway … is a long way coming if it comes at all," he said (Auletta 2010).

As it turned out, the publishing and broadcasting industries maintained business as usual, and, by driving their business in a straight line, they "missed the curve in the road," as programmers would say in California's Silicon Valley. On the few occasions when big media did attempt to cope with the digital revolution, it somehow managed to miss the mark.

Few in the American public seemed to feel that much was at stake. Gallup polls showed journalists with public confidence ratings higher than members of Congress but far lower than doctors or teachers (Gallup 2015). The unpopularity of mainstream media in the twenty-first century is worth noting, since a major motivation for new media technologies has been to circumvent the old, dominant media technologies. As we have seen, telephone technology was financed by people who hoped to get around the telegraph monopoly; radio and film were attractive new media in their day because newspapers (as Will Irwin famously said) spoke in the voice of the older generation. The new digital media spoke to a new generation because it allowed members of that generation to speak with each other.

"For generations, the leading newspapers, networks and magazines have served as the nation's information gatekeepers, deciding which of the many millions of news stories will move through the gate and out into the country. Armed with relatively inexpensive new technology, millions of Americans are now finding that they don't need the gatekeepers any more" (Katz 1993). It took almost twenty years for this idea, and many more like it, to work its way through the social and technological system. When it did, the publishing business was in collapse and the profession of journalism so out of fashion that universities started closing down journalism schools, apparently not recognizing that the problem had nothing to do with shared information but rather the obsolescence of an older media form.

Like big media, the big telecommunications corporations also missed many of the curves in the road. As we will see in this section, three of the largest US companies -- AT&T, IBM, and Xerox—lost out to far smaller rivals. AT&T engineers disliked the idea of data transmission interfering with their voice telephone lines in the early 1970s. The company refused the Defense Department's request that they own and administer the Internet. Instead, a consortium of universities ran the network haphazardly and kept it open to innovation.

Perhaps two of the best-known and hotly disputed traditional stories about computing history involve Microsoft and Apple. As often noted, IBM was not prepared for the personal computer market, and allowed Microsoft to develop an operating system that could be used in "clone" computers. Xerox didn't appreciate its own research at the Palo Alto research center and lost creative staff and big ideas to Apple Corp. in the early 1980s.

By missing the curve in the road, big corporations left digital technologies open to competition from smaller, more creative and more inclusive companies.

2 Determinism and Social Construction

The digital revolution proved amazingly fluid and very difficult to predict, let alone control. It allowed the creation of new forms of information at the center of new kinds of communities. No single person can be credited with kicking off the digital revolution. Instead, hundreds of thousands of engineers, programmers, and visionaries shared the idea of liberation through concepts like "open source" software, "crowdsourcing," and individuals as information producers as well as consumers.

How that happened, and why, is the historical question. Was it something fundamental in the digital technology itself, or was this a case where social construction mattered more? Or was it both? Did this process of creating a vision change the path of what could have been a more controlling technology?

Not according to J. David Bolter, who saw digital media as more open in his book *Turing's Man*: "The premise of George Orwell's *1984* was the marriage of totalitarian purpose with modern technology. But … computer technology may well be incompatible with the totalitarian monster … Computers make hierarchical communication and control far easier, but they also work against … the absolute dedication to the party line" (Bolter 1984).

Inside the computer revolution, the idea of social construction dominated, as we will see. Steve Jobs of Apple often said his mission was to "change the world" in a way that empowered more freedom and individualism. Echoing this in 1993, *Wired* magazine's editor said this about the cyberpunk revolution: "the digital counterculture will reject [the old] bleak vision [in exchange] for a future where technology enlarges the human spirit as a new tool for consciousness" (Rossetto 1993).

It's possible to find similar rhetoric in the history of other media technologies. Take the telegraph, for example: "One feeling and one impulse are created from the center of the land to the utmost extremity," said an enthusiast in the 1840s. Or take the radio and television, or cinema. But the question is why did computers have such an impact? Why did a machine that was originally designed to compute artillery trajectories and bank deposits become a Thomas Paine of the new media revolution?

One thing to observe is how social construction of technology played a major role in the vision for computing and how the media experience stands in sharp contrast to other areas of technology.

In energy and environmental debates, for instance, a constant comment from traditional utilities and fossilized industries is that "you don't get to pick and choose" technologies. But why not? What is a democracy if the fundamental technological foundations of a society are so far removed from popular choice?

No one in the telecommunications industries takes that particular line, that people don't get to choose their technologies. Choice is not up in the air in debates over regulating the digital media revolution; all discussions about media are pre-freighted with concerns about protecting freedom of speech, based in part on the First Amendment in the US, and Article 19 of the UN Human Rights charter globally. But how can, or should, the structure of media technology protect freedom? The details have become contentious as the cycles of innovation close up behind the digital media revolution and as a wider variety of cultures are affected worldwide. So the story of computers and digital media is the story of creative cultures patching together an improbable system. It's the story of innovation and cooperation winning over competition and hierarchy. It's also the story of how the world's largest computer and media businesses missed their moments, while the smallest companies, guided by a larger vision, created a vehicle for a global culture and media with a new ideal of service.

If there is any one lesson of history to be appreciated from revolutions in communication, it is that without a positive vision for a technology, dystopian tendencies can become self-fulfilling prophecies. On the other hand, people with a positive vision can—as computer pioneers predicted—change the world.

2.1 Regulating the digital media revolution

As he was leaving one of the secretive meetings of the US Constitutional convention in 1787, Benjamin Franklin was asked what form of government the delegates were creating. He famously responded, "A republic, if you can keep it."

Keeping revolutionary freedom in the aftermath of any revolution has always been daunting, and no less so in this case. The digital revolution entails multiple dimensions of structure and content regulation, on national and international levels, within both the drastically altered business models of media and the continued expectations of public service to democratic institutions.

In terms of structure, the idea of treating digital networks like phone networks—using the "common carrier" model—was endorsed in 2015 on the executive level in the US, but challenged by telecommunications companies that had hoped to be able to guide information traffic to preferred sites. Similar structural issues revolve around copyright protections and how they are to be enforced, with huge controversies over US proposals that were seen as overly broad with the potential for freezing out freedom of speech.

Although international media structures differ from region to region, the totalitarian governments have an increasing ability to filter out specific content and to punish dissidents. The idea that the communications technologies within the global villages would become "technologies of freedom" as de Sola Pool said in 1983, is possible, even probable, but not necessarily inevitable, as we will see in Chapter 12.

10
Computers

Computing is not about computers anymore. It is about living.

Nicholas Negroponte, *Being Digital*, 1995

1 Charles Babbage's Victorian-Era Computer

The computer age traces back to the surprisingly early date of 1821, when Charles Babbage, a mathematician working at the Greenwich Observatory near London, found an error in a set of astronomical tables used by navigators to fix the position of ships at sea. Babbage was alarmed, but then he found another error. And then dozens more.

Naturally, the errors bothered Babbage because lives depended on the accuracy of these tables. Errors could take a ship miles off course and lead to a wreck on an unseen reef. In the process of correcting the tables, it occurred to Babbage that a mechanical device might avoid the errors entirely. He began to envision an analytical device that could handle all kinds of problems, not just astronomical calculations. Soon the idea took shape as a vision of a "difference engine": the world's first analog computer that could accept instructions, process calculations, store information, and print answers with unerring accuracy.

Babbage spent much of his life working on the project, which was blueprinted and partially built, but never entirely completed. He claimed that in its final design of 1849, the difference engine could solve complex equations with answers of up to 31 decimal places.

The historical mystery was whether it could have actually worked and whether it could have been built in his time. Some, like MIT's Vannevar Bush, said yes, it could. "His idea was sound enough, but construction and maintenance costs were then too heavy," Bush said. Others thought not.

Then, in the late 1980s, London Science Museum curator Doron Swade built the Babbage machine, taking care to use machining techniques available in Babbage's time. Working from twenty drawings, Swade built a 5-ton, 11-foot-long machine with 8,000 cams and cogwheels made from bronze, cast iron, and steel. "It's a design of extraordinary elegance and economy," he said. The solutions to polynomial equations could not only be printed in hard copy but also punched into a soft card for hot lead stereotypes in order to completely eliminate typographical errors.

"We know he could have built it in that time," said Nathan Myhrvold, a former Microsoft executive whose interest in history led him to help finance the computer's re-creation. The problem, he said, was that Babbage "didn't know how to manage a large complicated project." Even so, the historical issue was settled when the final version of the Babbage machine showed that basic principles of computing were well understood long before electronic computers were built in the 1940s.

There had been other attempts at mechanical devices to help with calculations. One of these was an ancient Greek astronomical device brought up from the Aegean Sea off the island of Antikythera in 1900. The device turned out to be a modestly accurate model of the solar system that would have been useful for navigation (Price 1959).

Figure 10.1 Victorian-era computer designer—Charles Babbage (1791–1871). Wikimedia Commons.

French scientist Blaise Pascal also created a mechanical adding machine in 1642, and German mathematician Gottfried Leibniz produced the "stepped reckoner" in 1694. The Leibniz machine was an improvement over Pascal's since it could not only add, but also multiply, divide, and extract square roots. Leibniz used a binary system, typical of electronic computers of a later age, rather than Pascal's decimal system.

However, Babbage is often called the "father of computing" because his system could handle polynomial equations needed for astronomical tables and artillery ballistics calculations. He not only created a processing system using gears and cog wheels, but he also designed an input device, a memory system, an output device, and other features of a modern computer.

Although visionary, Babbage's difference engine was also a product of its times. Babbage wanted to mechanize intellectual work in the same way that steam-powered mills were mechanizing hand looms during the Industrial Revolution. He felt frustrated that his vision of a computer seemed so far away. He once said he would give the rest of his life just to spend a few days 500 years in the future. As it turned out, he would not have had to travel quite so far ahead in time to see what the difference engine would become.

Another visionary worked with Babbage on what is today called computer "software." She was Countess Augusta Ada King Lovelace (1815–52), the daughter of the famed British poet Lord Byron and his wife Anne Byron. Her father died when she was eight years old, and her mother, fearful that his wit and madness might overtake her, strongly encouraged an interest in logic and mathematics.

Lovelace turned out to be a mathematical prodigy early in life, and was introduced to Babbage and his difference engine in 1836. She worked on a translation of an Italian mathematician's memo on the difference engine in 1842 and added her own notes,

Figure 10.2 Reconstructing Babbage's difference engine—Doron Swade, a curator at the Science Museum of London, stands next to a reconstruction of Charles Babbage's 1847 difference engine, built from original architectural drawings. With 8,000 cams and cogwheels, it can handle polynomial equations and calculate to 31 decimal places. Courtesy Science Museum of London.

longer than the translation, in which she proposed a method for calculating a sequence of Bernoulli numbers. At the time, the achievement was seen as remarkable but not terribly significant. Today it is considered the first computer program.

Like Babbage, Lovelace had a vision for computing that stretched far beyond mathematics. "Supposing, for instance, that the fundamental relations of pitched sounds in the science of harmony and of musical composition were susceptible of such expression and adaptations," she wrote. Then "the engine might compose elaborate and scientific pieces of music of any degree of complexity or extent."

But Lovelace did not believe that computers would ever take on a life or intelligence of their own. "The Analytical Engine has no pretensions whatever to originate anything … It can follow analysis; but it has no power of anticipating any analytical relations or truths" (Gleick 2011). In other words, the ever-practical countess said it could do great things, but it was still just a machine.

Figure 10.3 First programmer—Countess Ada King Lovelace, daughter of famed poet Lord Byron, was a mathematician who developed algorithms for Charles Babbage's early computers. Portrait by Alfred Edward Chalon, 1848. Wikimedia Commons.

2 Tabulating Devices

The search for a solution to another kind of problem led to a different approach to computers. As the US Census Bureau approached the national census of 1890, a young mathematician named Herman Hollerith was trying to make it easier to search through massive amounts of data for specific facts, such as how fast manufacturing was growing, or how many Irish now lived in New York, or the birth rate in Chicago.

Figure 10.4 Computing pioneer—Herman Hollerith, a US Census employee in 1890, developed a tabulating machine to more accurately read and sort census data. Hollerith founded the company that became IBM. Photo by C. M. Bell, 1888. Library of Congress.

Hollerith tried punching holes in rolls of paper, like a player piano, but what seemed to work best were individual cards, patterned after cards used as textile guides. Census operators could use a tabulating machine to read 8,000 cards a day.

Hollerith went on to improve mechanical computers and create the Tabulating Machine Company in 1896, which became International Business Machines (IBM) in 1924. The company focused on large-scale projects for government and business, including census, social security, military, insurance, and banking operations. IBM's electro-mechanical tabulators from this period were extremely useful in keeping track of many numbers, but they were not programmable computers. In the 1940 US Census, for example, IBM tabulators—or Hollerith machines—could process cards containing census information at the rate of 400 a minute, and from these, twelve separate bits of statistical information could be extracted and summarized.

Figure 10.5 Hollerith machine—Ann Oliver of the US Census demonstrates a "Hollerith machine" in this 1939 picture. Harris & Ewing, Library of Congress.

Tabulating and calculating machines were so useful that IBM machinery was sold around the world. The most controversial use of census tabulators involved the IBM's German subsidiary, which in the 1930s played a role helping the Nazi government of Germany identify Jews and organize the Holocaust. Evidence exists that technical support also came from US headquarters (Black 2002), but IBM officially denies the inference (IBM 2001). Researchers have not accessed IBM archives, and the controversy remains unsettled.

The tabulating and calculating machines typical of the 1930s used mechanical relays. They were reliable but very slow, using mechanical switches not much improved since Babbage's day. The machines weren't even called computers. Before the 1940s, a "computer" was the person who computed mathematical problems, just like a painter was someone who painted and a baker was someone who worked in a bakery. Thousands of "computers" were employed by census bureaus, banks, insurance companies, engineering firms, and the military. Sitting in log rows of desks, they might use mechanical adding machines to calculate artillery ballistics, or actuarial tables, or bank reconciliations. The work was slow and painstaking. In contrast, even the earliest electronic/digital computers, such as the 1945 ENIAC, would take only a few hours to do the work of 100 human "computers" working for an entire year.

It was only the 1940s, towards the end of World War II, that the term "computer" came to mean an electronic device that could quickly carry out mathematical or logical operations automatically.

3 Bletchley and the First Digital Computers

As the threat of war loomed in the late 1930s, engineers raced to create faster ways to crunch numbers and analyze problems. The electronic digital computer, made from radio tubes, could work much quicker than the tabulating machines with mechanical relays.

The world's first electronic computer was probably the Z3, developed by an engineer named Konrad Zuse in Berlin in 1941. It was used for aircraft engineering problems, like calculating the stresses on airplane wings. Although it was much faster than mechanical tabulating machines, it was not used for the wider array of problems that mathematicians were just beginning to envision. It was destroyed by Allied bombing in 1943.

Meanwhile, in a mansion fifty miles north-west of London, a family of computers with a very different mission was under construction by a group of social misfits and theoretical mathematicians. The computer, in its various incarnations, was called the Colossus and the mission was the "Ultra" secret deciphering of coded German military messages. The mathematicians were recruited from Oxford, Cambridge, and puzzle contests run in the *Daily Telegraph*.

"I told you to leave no stone unturned to get staff," said Winston Churchill as he inspected Bletchley Park with its director early in 1941, "but I had no idea you had taken me so literally." Yet these famously eccentric and dedicated geniuses managed to reconstruct coding machines based on small clues and detailed computer analysis of the intercepted messages.

At its peak, 9,000 women and men worked on signals intelligence and computer development at Bletchley Park. Because of secrecy requirements, and short-sighted post-war policies, most of the records for the Colossus were destroyed at the end of the war. But many of the people involved in the Bletchley Park program went on to make contributions to computing.

Figure 10.6 Colossus—A Colossus Mark 2 computer being operated by Dorothy Du Boisson (left) and Elsie Booker. The slanted control panel on the left was used to set the "pin" (or "cam") patterns of the Lorenz. The "bedstead" paper tape transport is on the right. UK National Archives.

Among these was Alan Turing (1912–54), a British mathematician and cryptographer who led the most difficult German naval code breaking effort. He became a key figure in designing computing systems on mathematical principles, formalizing concepts of "algorithm" and "computation" for example. He also proposed the idea of evaluating the completeness of a general purpose computer, now called a "Turing complete" computer.

Citing Ada Lovelace, he wrote a 1950 paper, "Computing Machinery and Intelligence," in which he proposed the "Turing Test" of artificial intelligence. The test involves a situation where a person communicates with what may be a computer, or a human, and the computer is responsive enough and apparently intelligent enough that it can be mistaken for another human. Turing's personal life proved difficult in the homophobic world of post-war Britain, and it ended tragically with suicide in 1954. In 2009, the British government made a public apology for what Prime Minister Gordon Brown said was "the appalling way he was treated."

Another set of veterans from the Colossus project were the parents of Tim Berners-Lee, the visionary who developed the idea of the world wide web in the early 1990s (see Chapter 11).

The largest computer developed during the war years was the ENIAC, the electronic numerical integrator and calculator. Built at the University of Pennsylvania, the ENIAC used 17,468 radio tubes, weighed 30 tons, measured 100 feet long and 8 feet high, and, on a good day, could perform 100,000 calculations per second. Technically, the ENIAC has been described as a processor with twenty register positions. Yet in two hours it did the work of 100 human mathematicians working one year.

Harry Reed, who worked with ballistics lab in the early 1950s, thought of the ENIAC as very personal computer: "Now we think of a personal computer as one which you carry around with you. The ENIAC was one that you kind of lived inside … You could wander around inside it and watch the program being executed … So instead of you holding a computer, this computer held you" (Reed 1996).

Another important influence in early military computing was Grace Hopper, a US Navy computer scientist who worked on the Mark I computer at Harvard and developed the COBOL computer language.

Figure 10.7 Allan Turing (1912–54), the genius behind World War II code-breaking efforts and early computer architecture. Wikimedia Commons.

Figure 10.8 ENIAC—The first large-scale electronic computer in the US was made for the Army Ballistics Research Lab at the University of Pennsylvania. Here, Glen Beck checks wiring to the some of the 17,486 vacuum tubes while Frances Snyder Holberton stands in front of a set of function tables on wheels. As ungainly as it looks, in an hour the Electronic Numerical Integrator and Computer could perform the tasks of fifty human "computers" (mathematicians) working for a year. Photo 1945 by US Army.

Figure 10.9 Navy programmer—Grace Hopper, a computer programmer and (by her retirement) Admiral in the US Navy, developed the COBOL computer language and worked on Defense Department computing during a long career. She also came up with the term "debugging" computer programs after a moth got stuck in the Harvard computer in 1947. Photo with three other unidentified programmers, 1960, Smithsonian Institution.

4 The New Frontiers for Science

One of the most important figures in the long-term development of the computer was President Franklin Roosevelt's science advisor, Vannevar Bush. In the years after World War II, Bush outlined the relationship between science and the democratic system and suggested new goals for scientists who had been freed from wartime research needs. He said that while discussions about politics and crops at the corner store might not explicitly involve democracy and its relationship to science and technology, those elements are constantly in the background. "They determine our destiny, and well we know it." Bush also expressed hope that the need for democratic influences on science and technology could be recognized.

"In a free country, in a democracy, this [path taken] is the path that public opinion wishes to have pursued, whether it leads to new cures for man's ills, or new sources of a raised standard of living ... In a dictatorship the path is the one that is dictated, whether the dictator be an individual or part of a self-perpetuating group" (Bush 1949).

Bush was specifically concerned with the problem of information overload and suggested a high priority for new information systems to extend human wisdom. In a 1946 article published in *Atlantic* magazine, Bush predicted the development of a computer that he called a "Memex."

> It consists of a desk, and while it can presumably be operated from a distance, it is primarily the piece of furniture at which [a person] works. On the top are slanting translucent screens, on which material can be projected for convenient reading. There is a keyboard, and sets of buttons and levers ... Wholly new forms of encyclopedias will appear, ready made with a mesh of associative trails running through them, ready to be dropped into the memex and there amplified. The lawyer has at his touch the associated opinions and decisions of his whole experience, and of the experience of friends and authorities. The patent attorney has on call the millions of issued patents, with familiar trails to every point of his client's interest. The physician, puzzled by a patient's reactions, strikes the trail established in studying an earlier similar case, and runs rapidly through analogous case histories, with side references to the classics for the pertinent anatomy and histology ...
>
> The historian, with a vast chronological account of a people, parallels it with a skip trail which stops only on the salient items, and can follow at any time contemporary trails which lead him all over civilization at a particular epoch. There is a new profession of trail blazers, those who find delight in the task of establishing useful trails through the enormous mass

Figure 10.10 Science and democracy—Vannevar Bush, science advisor to President Franklin D. Roosevelt, was at the center of a revolution in computing in the 1940s and 1950s. His widely shared perspective was that the technological path taken in a democracy is the one that is led by public opinion. Library of Congress.

> of the common record. The inheritance from the master becomes, not only his additions to the world's record, but for his disciples the entire scaffolding by which they were erected ... The applications of science ... may yet allow [mankind] truly to encompass the great record and to grow in the wisdom of racial experience. (Bush 1946)

The essay had a profound influence on scientists and engineers at the time, particularly J. C. R. Licklider, who envisioned the Internet, and better human–computer interfaces at MIT, and Doug Englebart, who invented the computer mouse and the graphical user interface at Stanford Research Institute.

5 Early Days for Computer Technology

5.1 First public test of a computer

By 1952, the ENIAC had spun off into a private company and was dubbed the Sperry-Rand Univac computer. Its public debut was on election night, 1952, on CBS television. With early election returns from key precincts, the Univac was able to project that Dwight Eisenhower would win 438 electoral votes and his opponent, Adlai Stevenson, would win 93. The official count would turn out to be 442 and 89 electoral votes (Goff 1999). Although Eisenhower seemed likely to win at the time, the landslide was unexpected. The data seemed so out of line with other predictions that the CBS network news team and the computer programmers held it back, claiming that they had some kind of computer malfunction.

The next morning, reviewers found it charming that computers had such a hard time replacing humans. "The CBS pride was called the Univac, which at a critical moment refused to work with anything like the efficiency of a human being," TV reviewer Jack Gould wrote in the *New York Times* the morning after the election. "This mishap caused the CBS stars, Walter Cronkite, Edward R. Murrow and Eric Sevareid to give Univac a rough ride for the rest of the evening, in a most amusing sidelight to the CBS coverage." Actually, the computer's projections were so accurate that it frightened not only the CBS news producers but also the Univac programmers.

According to the National Academy of Engineering (NAE), the projection was so unequivocal that Univac's operators grew nervous and altered the program to produce a different result. "They later confessed that the initial projection of electoral votes had been right on the mark," the NAE said (NAE 2010). Computer problems also popped up on subsequent election nights, and the wonder is that the Univac did so well under deadline pressure. It used radio tubes that were fragile, failing at the rate of one every seven minutes.

5.2 From tubes to transistors

Since radio tubes were essentially just electronic switches, a lot of research went into the idea of creating smaller and more efficient switches. This could be done if the switches were placed

Figure 10.11 Computer of the future—CBS news anchor Walter Cronkite demonstrates a prototype of a "television communication set" that was a prototype, "a globally connected library system," in 1967. *New York World-Telegram*, Library of Congress.

inside a semi-conductor environment such as silicon. William Shockley and others at Bell Labs invented the semiconductor transistor as a way to miniaturize the radio tube in 1947. This made computers, radios and other electronic devices much smaller and easier to manage.

A transistor-based computer called the TRADIC (for TRansistorized Airborne DIgital Computer) was developed for the military in the 1950s. It processed a million operations per second. At the time, a transistor cost $20 and a radio tube cost about one dollar, so it was an expensive machine. But it could perform thousands more calculations without failing and it was light enough to be used in aircraft.

By the early 1950s, Texas Instruments Company had developed a cheaper transistor, making far more powerful computers possible. But transistors were destined to remain expensive, since all of the circuitry was linked by an individual hand-soldering process, and flaws were bound to emerge somewhere as computers became more complex.

IBM continued to dominate the market for mechanical adding machines, typewriters, and other business equipment, and it was coming to dominate the computer market as well. IBM's first computer using an integrated processor, the IBM 360, was marketed in 1964 and has been mentioned alongside the Boeing 707 and the Ford Model T as a technological milestone. One reason for the success of the IBM 360 was that it was based on the idea of scalable architecture, which means that a variety of capabilities and add-ons could run on one system. According to Bill Gates of Microsoft, the concept drove away many of IBM's competitors until other companies like Amdahl, Control Data, Hitachi, and Intel also delivered computers in the 1970s that could run on IBM system software (Gates 1995).

Along with the military, IBM's computers served the insurance and banking industries, which had a need to create actuarial tables and complex banking reconciliation statements. As computing power grew, and the cost of computers declined, other industries began sharing time on computers to run their numbers and calculations. These "time sharing" arrangements meant that every company could take advantage of the power of mainframe computing in the 1960s–80s.

Not many people saw anything revolutionary in these developments, least of all IBM. Their personal business culture was one of strict conformity. Precise haircuts, dark suits, narrow black ties, and a strong sense of company loyalty made the IBM world, for some, a harrowing glimpse into the totalitarian future of computing. For others, the problem was just that the old-fashioned IBM culture simply failed to glimpse the possibilities of the technology it dominated.

5.3 From transistors to integrated circuits

In the late 1950s, a number of electronics engineers realized that there was no need for transistors to be separately soldered onto circuit boards. The idea of the integrated processor, or "chip," occurred independently to Jack S. Kilby of Texas Instruments and Robert Noyce of Fairchild Semiconductors at around the same time. In 1958, Kilby used a small germanium slab and interconnecting wires to create an integrated chip. He was awarded the Nobel Prize in Physics in 2000. The following year, Noyce developed a set of circuits and transistors that could be printed onto each layer of a silicon chip. The ability to print circuits and transistors allowed mass production. Like Gutenberg's original printing system, the printing of computer transistor systems reduced costs and helped spark a communications revolution (Reid 2001).

In 1969, Noyce and Gordon Moore established the ultimate Silicon Valley company: Intel. From the beginning, Intel was an engineer's company, with business decisions being made by engineers and not professional managers. Intel was known for creating a new kind of corporate culture, one where offices had no doors and where managers stayed in touch with researchers by working part of the year in the labs or on the factory floor.

One of Intel's early clients was NASA and the Defense Department. Rockets needed guidance systems, and integrated chips were powerful and lightweight. Even paying several thousand dollars just for one small chip was no problem.

Rapid increases in the power of the computer chip seemed to be following a predictable path, and in 1965, Gordon Moore published a paper predicting that computer power would keep doubling about every year. It was later called "Moore's Law," although unlike a law of nature or physics, it was simply an observation that computing power, in the form of transistors per chip, was doubling every 18 months to two years (Moore 1965). It proved to be accurate, or even slightly pessimistic, as the computer industry boomed.

Moore counted computer power in the number of transistors per chip, but there are several other ways to gauge computer power. One is IPS, instructions per second, which is an older way to gauge computer processing power. Typically, in the 1980s, a chip might be rated by MIPS (Million Instructions per Second). Another way to calculate speed is FLOPs, or Floating-point Operations per Second.

By 1971, Intel's first commercial chip—the 4004—used four-bit processing, and it contained the equivalent of 2300 transistors and ran at 0.092 MIPS at 2.25 MHz. It was the size of a fingernail and performed as many calculations as the 30-ton, 100-foot long UNIVAC in 1946 (Intel 2015).

By 2015, a commercially available Intel chip had over two trillion transistors and ran at nearly 300,000,000,000 IPS at 3GHz.

Another way of looking at the improvement in computing power is the cost per Gigaflop. In 1961, a single gigaflop would have cost $8.3 trillion in constant 2013 dollars,

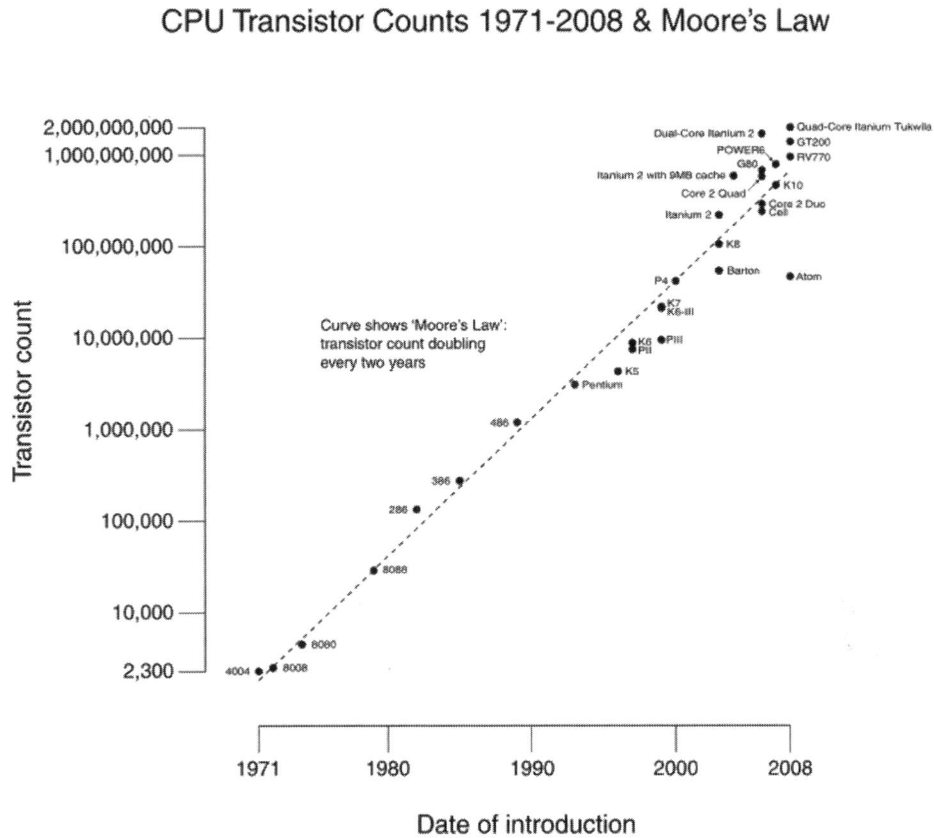

Figure 10.12 Moore's Law—Gordon Moore of Intel observed that computer power was rising quickly in 1965, and projected the trajectory of improvements in processing power. The prediction proved amazingly accurate. Wikimedia Commons.

although it would have taken 17 million of IBM's best chips to achieve it. Computing power dropped below the $100 per gigaflop level in 2003. By 2015, computing power was operating in the teraflops (trillions of calculations per second) and a gigaflop cost only 8 cents.

6 Social Reaction: Fear of 1984

Rocketry, ballistics and accounting were not the first things that came to mind when people thought about computers in the 1960s and 1970s. Instead, there was a sense of unease that accompanied the increasing power of computers. They became associated with totalitarian governments and George Orwell's book *1984*, which described government monitoring people through their "telescreens," which were actually two-way television sets.

Another idea about computers was that artificial intelligence would threaten humanity. That theme found an early expression in Stanley Kubrick's 1968 film *2001: A Space*

Odyssey, in which the computer kills astronauts on a space mission. The computer was named HAL, a single shift up the alphabet from IBM.

"In the 1950s and 1960s there existed the notion that the computer not only could but would control all aspects of our lives," said MIT management expert Edgar H. Schein. "Images of the fully computerized home that automatically turned the lights on and off and that prepared meals and controlled daily diets were popular. And the fear that computers might, as in the movie *2001: A Space Odyssey*, even try to take charge altogether was widely experienced" (Shein 2004).

Ironically, Arthur C. Clark—the author of the book *2001: A Space Odyssey*— did not personally think that computers were dangerous. In a 1974 interview, Clark predicted that within twenty-five years, people would be using small consoles in their homes to talk with their "friendly local computers" to take care of banking, theater tickets, and other information needs. Although there might be problems, he said, "computers will enrich our society" (ABC 1974)

Realistic or not, fear of computers led to a social reaction that influenced a generation of programmers and engineers to attempt to push the technology into directions that were less about control and more about individual empowerment. Computers had to be liberated from the IBM way of life, according to publisher Stewart Brand and programmer Ted Nelson.

Nelson especially, in a series of books starting in 1973, was among those advocating "Computer Lib" (liberation) through socially conscious engineering. Nelson advocated a vision of a network of computers that would inform, entertain, and make information sharing possible in ways that had never been considered before. For that reason he was called the "Don Quixote of computing."

Nelson's thinking influenced many up-and-coming programmers in the 1970s, including Steve Jobs of Apple. But it also reflected thinking that was coming from inside the Department of Defense, as we will see in the next chapter, and the idea among satellite engineers and communications specialists that they, too, had been advancing "technologies of freedom" (de Sola Pool 1984).

The computer had a special place in all this, according to historian James Burke. In a 1979 BBC documentary, Burke said that innovative people have always had to struggle against oppressive systems. Yet, ironically, a product of that system could blow everything wide open:

> With this [microchip] … we might be able to lift the limitations of conforming to any centralized representational form of government—originally invented, because there was no way for every body's voice to be heard. [But] with it, we could operate on the basis that values and standards—and ethics and facts and truth—all depend on what your view of the world is—and that there may be as many views of that, as there are people.

So the focus on personal computers—as opposed to mainframe computers—was a social construction as much as it was a natural part of the technology's trajectory. A personal computer was one that you could use without "big brother" looking over your shoulder. Also, for computer nerds, the personal computer was a way to have some access to computers in order to develop software. Many hobbyists who later became software developers were happy to have a more user-friendly machine available After all, it was hard to get computer time on a mainframe, regardless of "big brother."

7 New Business Cultures and the Personal Computer

7.1 Liberating machines

The idea that computers could liberate and not tyrannize was shared across several innovative centers at the time. One was located in Cambridge, Massachusetts, and associated with the Massachusetts Institute of Technology (MIT). Another culture emerged in the 1970s around Stanford University in Palo Alto, California—a region also known as "Silicon Valley." Among the many problems these two different centers encountered was the human–computer interface.

J. C. R. Licklider, an MIT professor who became head of the Defense Department's research team for information processing in the 1960s, was fascinated by the problem. His 1960 paper, *Man–Computer Symbiosis*, discussed the need for interactive computing.

One of Licklider's ideas was that computing should be interactive. When you typed something into a terminal, the computer should come back with an instant response. Licklider is considered one of the most important figures in computer history because, like a kind of intellectual Johnny Appleseed, he planted the ideas and inspired dozens of young protégés with a vision for the future. He also envisioned the development of something he called the "intergalactic computer network," which we will explore in Chapter 11. When Licklider moved to the Department of Defense, he was able to fund early efforts in time-sharing, which helped mainframe computers be more interactive. He also had a hand in starting the Augmentation Research Center at Stanford Research Institute in Silicon Valley.

The human–computer interface problem also fascinated researchers in Silicon Valley, especially Douglas Engelbart, who, like Licklider, thought computers had a potential to change the world for the better, although making the world better through computing was considered to be a wild and somewhat dangerous idea in the 1960s. Engelbart joined SRI and in 1962 wrote *Augmenting Human Intellect: A Conceptual Framework*, which contained ideas inspired by Vannevar Bush and J. C. R. Licklider. By augmenting human intellect, Engelbart did not mean isolated clever tricks that help in particular situations: "We refer to a way of life in an integrated domain where hunches, cut-and-try, intangibles, and the human 'feel for a situation' usefully co-exist with powerful concepts, streamlined terminology and notation, sophisticated methods, and high-powered electronic aids."

These gains in human thinking could be as significant, he said, as the gains made in personal geographic mobility since horseback and sailboat days. He presented a plan for research that would look into ways to improve interactivity with computers. The paper led to funding from Licklider's office at the Advanced Research Projects Agency to launch Engelbart's work at the Associative Research Center.

On December 9, 1968, the previously unknown Engelbart launched into history with a 100-minute multimedia presentation of the mouse, the graphical user interface (GUI), and the possibilities for networking. Most impressive was Engelbart's implementation of Bush's Memex machine, showing how a user could select a word in one document and bring up a second relevant document instantly—a forerunner of the hypertext link. The 1,000 computer engineers assembled at the conference gave Engelbart a standing ovation. Today the presentation is known as the "Mother of All Demos."

William K. English was involved with Englebart in the "Mother of all Demos." He left SRI and moved, in 1971, to Xerox PARC, taking a dozen researchers with him, to develop other new advanced applications including the "what you see is what you get" (wysiwyg) interface, the desktop, Ethernet, and object oriented programming. PARC put the concepts together into the first working personal computer—the Alto—developed in 1974. Thousands were manufactured and used in corporate offices and universities, but never sold commercially.

7.2 Apple takes a bite out of the market

The excitement surrounding the work at MIT, SRI, and PARC spilled over into Stanford University in Palo Alto, California. One of the informal groups that sprang up was the eclectic "Home Brewed Computer Club," a learning club that met weekly at Stanford to hear lectures and share ideas about computing. Steve Wozniak and Steve Jobs were among the computer enthusiasts who attended these early meetings.

As high school students, Jobs and Wozniak were originally motivated by a desire to use their knowledge of electronics as a way to make free phone calls, but Wozniak found he was fascinated by the intricacies of electronics. He became the "Mozart of computer engineers" (Cringley 1996). Teaming up with Jobs, a technically adept and dynamic leader, the two founded Apple computers in 1977. The name Apple was chosen at random, probably after working on a California farm, Wozniak said, and they just never came up with anything better (Linzmahyer 2004).

Figure 10.13 Xerox Alto—The first working personal computer was developed at Xerox Palo Alto Research Center (PARC) in 1974. Thousands of prototypes were manufactured. Although never a commercial product, the Alto had an enormous influence on personal computing with attributes like a graphical user interface and a computer "mouse." Photo by Lin Burton.

Apple's first personal computer sold fifty units, and with venture capital, they marketed the Apple II, the first personal computer designed to look like a consumer product that could be used in a small business. Primitive by modern standards, the Apple II was nevertheless an instant hit, and eventually five to six million units were sold. Meanwhile, Jobs, and Wozniak were multimillionaires by the time they celebrated their twenty-fifth birthdays. Apple hit the market at exactly the right time with a good product that was several steps ahead of the competition.

The Apple II looked like a home appliance, not a piece of electronic equipment. It was like a typewriter, but it was also programmable, like the IBM 360. And anyone could write software for it. One of the independent software innovations for the Apple II was a spreadsheet program called VisiCalc, created by Dan Bricklin, then a business graduate student at Harvard. The idea was to create a "visible calculator" that would help small businesses "run the numbers" for the weekly payroll or inventory or supplies. It was copyrighted but, due to issues with the legal system at the time, not patented (Bricklin 2010).

Spreadsheets cut the workload so dramatically that VisiCalc became the first "killer application" — that a software application is so useful that people would buy the computer just to be able to run the software (Cringley 1996). It sold 700,000 copies in six years, and it helped make the Apple II a success.

7.2.1 Apple and the curve in the road at Xerox

One of the enduring legends of the computer industry is the way that Xerox Corp. missed the "curve in the road" by allowing Steve Jobs of Apple Computers to "steal" the research products from Xerox PARC. The reality is far more complex, as Michael Hiltzik's history, *Dealers of Lightning*, points out (Hiltzik 2000).

Xerox established the Palo Alto Research Center next to Stanford University in January 1970 to pursue research in computing and physics. Xerox was oriented more towards paper and chemistry, originally founded in 1906 as a photographic paper and chemicals supplier competing with Kodak in Rochester, New York. Originally called Haloid Photographic, the company became Xerox in 1958 and introduced plain paper photocopying in 1962. The copiers were very profitable, and the company dominated the market until 1970,

Figure 10.14 Apple founders—Steve Wozniak (left) and Steve Jobs, around 1978, examine an Apple I computer. The design was elegant and the product flew off the shelves, helping to start the personal computer revolution. Photo by Joe Melina, Getty.

when IBM introduced a plain paper copier. Other competitors were following quickly, and some far-sighted Xerox executives hoped that PARC would help the company find new products.

With a strong research budget and an extraordinary staff, PARC was a hothouse of innovation. Most of the shape of the modern personal computer industry was first envisioned by engineers sitting in the famous PARC bean-bag chairs, sipping coffee, talking, and jumping up to scribble new ideas on whiteboards. Despite all the excitement, PARC became an island of innovation in a sea of stranded ideas. Proposals for a small business and personal computer called the Alto were not well received by Xerox managers. A plan to market the Alto III had been put on hold and an electro-mechanical typewriter with a small amount of correctable memory was marketed instead. Senior management were not convinced that PARC's highly advanced computer would make the company money. "If there's no paper to be copied … how will I get paid?" That was the thinking inside management (Hiltzik 2000).

When Jobs, Wozniak and the Apple engineering team were invited to a Xerox PARC presentation in December 1979, they were widely hailed as the kids who had hit the big time. But their Apple II computer had a build-in keyboard, no mouse, a poor word processing interface, and low-resolution graphics. They had began working on a project called "Lisa," a next step in personal computing that would make it easier and more useful, and they were looking for ideas.

The invitation to visit PARC was not unusual. PARC engineers often hosted tours and briefings for potential customers. But some of the engineers inside PARC worried that Apple was a potential competitor, not a customer. This worry seemed a little misplaced at the time—Xerox had invested in Apple earlier that year, with the understanding that Apple would look at its technology, give advice on its marketability and possibly license some of its products. Nevertheless, it is a grain of truth behind the legend.

Jobs and company were given a short demonstration in December 1979 and went away apparently satisfied. But Jobs, often described as a man with an intense and demanding personality, returned a few days later, unannounced, insisting on the full briefing. After hurried calls to headquarters in New York, and handwringing by some of the staff, Jobs and the Apple team got their briefing (Hiltzik 2000).

Jobs and the Apple engineers saw four important concepts:

1. Ethernet, a system for a networked office, with email and links to printers and copiers.
2. A graphical user interface (a "GUI") with a "desktop" and windows arrangements for different files, using a mouse that points at anything on the screen.
3. "Wysiwyg" text editor (what you see is what you get), a computer screen that shows exactly what the printed product will look like.
4. An object-oriented programming language called Smalltalk that made it easy to create a GUI with bitmapped graphics on the computer screen.

"After an hour looking at demos, [Jobs] understood our technology and what it meant more than any Xerox executive understood it after years of showing it to them," said Larry

Tesler, who worked for Xerox PARC at the time but soon moved to Apple.

Within four years, all except the object-oriented programming language would be part of the Apple Mac. Falling back on the theme that set the personal computer revolution in gear, Apple introduced the Macintosh with a Super-Bowl television ad that depicted an athletic woman eluding masked police while everyone else is marching in step. The woman throws an athletic hammer and smashes a giant telescreen while workers in identical uniforms out of Orwell's book *1984* gape in astonishment. "You'll see why 1984 won't be like *1984*," the ad promised.

Figure 10.15 Apple II—The Apple II computer had dual disk drives (one for the application and one for storage), along with a built-in keyboard and an auxiliary number pad. Photo by Lin Burton.

The Apple Mac, with its GUI, wysiwyg desktop, and mouse, featured the second "killer application" to hit the market: desktop publishing. With desktop publishing, users could set type, create graphics, design newsletters and newspapers. In effect, anyone could enter the publishing business for less than the cost of the chemicals needed to run photo-optical systems in the big newspaper and publishing companies.

Sales soared at first, but flattened out later when consumers balked at the $4,000 price tag. Meanwhile, Apple's board of directors, unhappy with Steve Jobs' manic management style, decided to relieve Jobs of his position at the head of the Macintosh division. Jobs went to work on a new Unix-based computer system called NeXt and on digital animation techniques by helping form the Pixar Corp until he returned to Apple in 1996.

7.3 IBM, Microsoft, and the clones

Meanwhile, alarmed that it had missed the market for personal computers (PCs), IBM introduced its own PC in 1981. In their haste to market a competitive product, IBM approached a small Seattle software company called Microsoft to write the underlying operating system.

The moment, like the Apple–Xerox saga, has been called Microsoft's "coup," and the point where IBM "missed the curve in the road" (Segaller 1998). "The Microsoft connection made the IBM PC possible, and the IBM connection ensured Microsoft's long term success as a company," said Robert X. Cringley (Cringley 1996: 134). It was the deal of the century.

Microsoft founder and president Bill Gates saw it differently: "We gave IBM a fabulous deal—A low, one-time fee that granted the company the right to use Microsoft's operating

Figure 10.16 Why 1984 won't be like *1984*—This award-winning advertisement for the Apple Macintosh played off the association of computers with totalitarianism as depicted in George Orwell's book *1984*. The Mac, and this ad, were introduced in the year 1984. With a graphical user interface and a mouse, the Mac changed personal computing. Taken by Joi Ito. Wikimedia Commons.

system on as many computers as it could sell." Two other computer systems were also available for the PC then, but the Microsoft system, at $50,000 was by far the cheapest (Gates 1995).

The main goal for Microsoft at the time was to establish a software standard that would reach a tipping point, just as VHS tapes had helped standardize the video rental industry. "Our goal was not to make money directly from IBM, but to profit from licensing MS-DOS to other companies," Gates said. "It has become popular for certain revisionist historians to conclude that IBM made a mistake working with Intel and Microsoft to create its PC." But if IBM was "king of the hill" in the mainframe market, in the volatile world of the personal computer, IBM's position was more like a front runner in a marathon (Gates 1995).

IBM thought that the sale of hardware would be the key to the future of the business, but they had not counted on "reverse engineering," which is the legal ability to take a product apart, write exact specifications for it, and build a similar product from scratch. Only two years after the IBM PC was introduced, Compaq computers introduced the first PC "clone" that could run any software that an IBM PC could run.

That didn't detract from IBM's success at first. In 1984, IBM's PC sales reached two million, instead of the half million projected, and the PC team was euphoric (Segaller

1998). IBM had reached the height of its corporate power, with record profits of $6.6 billion on sales of $46 billion. But sales peaked in 1990, stock prices fell, and in the coming years over 100,000 employees left the firm.

And so, IBM lost the race by focusing on hardware rather than software. The "suit" culture of IBM had lost to the nerd engineers. Like Samuel Morse with his Morse Code, software turned out to be the key to technological success in the personal computer business.

7.4 Desktop publishing and nonlinear editing

Mechanized typesetting reached its technical peak in the 1950s with a "hot" type system called a Linotype (see Chapter 3). Reporters turned their "copy" in to the news desk, on paper, and then they would be taken "over" to the copy desk, where the copy would be proofread and sent down to typesetting. "Copy over" and "copy down" were frequently heard calls in a busy newspaper or magazine organization. A Linotype operator would key in a line of reversed type and then release a stream of molten lead. The steaming metallic lead would form a positive raised impression from the reversed type and, after trimming, would fall into a stick just like hand-set type. From there it would be composed on a page that would then be prepared for printing.

Figure 10.17 The IBM Personal Computer, introduced in 1981, was followed by hardware clones that still needed the Microsoft operating system and other spreadsheet and word-processing applications. Photo by Lin Burton.

The Linotype machines were based on a century of experimentation with mechanized typesetting technology and cost around $50,000 each in the 1950s. The machines were hot, dirty, and dangerous, and lead poisoning was a frequent problem in the publishing trades.

Two French inventors, Rene Higonnet and Louis Moyroud, thought hot-lead Linotypes were archaic technologies. With the help of Vannevar Bush and a publishers' cooperative, they developed a photo-mechanical process in the 1950s that set type six times faster than Linotypes at a cost of about $10,000 for a small unit. The photomechanical process eventually took on more and more computerized controls, and eventually digital systems like Compugraphic, Atex, and SII used transistors and then computer chips to control light exposure on photosensitive paper.

The paper was developed through a photographic process, cut, and then pasted onto a page. Large news organizations saved money using this photo-mechanical process but found the "cold type" system unpredictable and difficult to maintain. In the words of Virginia publisher Roger Haebeck, it took "a bishop, five priests and a dozen acolytes to keep the things running."

The "desktop publishing" revolution involved much simpler technology for setting type. The Apple Mac, introduced in 1984, and other PC systems later in the 1980s, made it possible to set type in wysiwyg format using laser printers and Postscript technology developed by Xerox PARC researcher John Warnock, who founded Adobe Systems in 1983.

Less than twenty years after the last Linotype machine was sold for $50,000, and ten years after a Compugraphic sold for $10,000, it was possible to produce camera-ready pages for printing with an investment of $5,000 in a computer and a laser printer.

When the Berlin Wall came down in 1989, newspapers across the Eastern Bloc rushed to set up their own typesetting operations, which had been centrally controlled by the Communist publishing system. News organizations like the *Washington Post* offered their older ATEX and SII systems without charge to newspapers like *Lidov Noviny* in Prague. But an economic analysis for the American Press Institute showed that it was actually cheaper to buy new desktop publishing systems than to keep the old behemoths going (Kovarik 1990).

Nonlinear video editing systems also changed the movie and television news business. Although experimental units were available as early as the 1970s, the breakthrough came with the Lucasfilm EditDroid, developed in the mid-1980s to replace film editors like the Moviola system. EditDroid used laserdiscs and lacked processing power to deliver clean edits, but it was a harbinger of high quality editing systems that would be developed in the 1990s, such as Sun and Silicon Graphics, and later, the Avid and Media100 applications for Macintosh and PC computers.

7.5 Sun Microsystems workstations

Personal computers caught on quickly in the 1980s, but generally they were not powerful enough to handle complex tasks such as three-dimensional mechanical designs, engineering simulations, and medical imaging. Such tasks could be performed by a mainframe computer before PCs, but that was expensive. Since the 1960s there had been a niche for another kind of computer called a workstation that was smaller in scale and suited to scientific and technical work. The earliest workstation was a 1959 unit by IBM called the Cadet, and it rented for $1,000 a month—far less than a mainframe but still far more than any average person could afford. It lacked logic circuitry, leading some to claim that that Cadet meant "Can't Add, Doesn't Even Try."

IBM also developed several other small-scale scientific computers, but the leader in the workstation field was the Digital Equipment Corp.'s PDP-8. Even the Xerox Corp.'s Palo Alto Research Center used a PDP-8 in preference to Xerox's own Sigma computers in the 1970s. All in all, about twenty-five companies competed for the workstation market in the 1980s and 1990s.

One of the most successful was Sun Microsystems. The company was founded in 1982 by four Stanford University students: Scott McNealy, Vinod Khosla, Bill Joy, and Andy Bechtolsheim. They created the Sun computer as part of the second wave of successful start-ups (after the Apple/Microsoft wave) that included Silicon Graphics, 3COM, and Oracle Corporation. The Sun workstation was among the first to reach the "3M" goal—1 MIPS (million instructions per second)—1 Megabyte of RAM, and 1 Megapixel of display (1280 x 800). While twenty-first-century home computers have surpassed the 3M goal, at the time, the IBM personal computer had only 16 Kilobytes of memory, a text-only display, about 1 kiloflop/second performance, and a 320 x 200 pixel display.

So in other words, the Sun workstation ran rings around the personal computer of the 1980s, performing sixty-three times faster with displays that were sixteen times more complex. It also had networked file sharing and graphics acceleration, which meant that it was useful for computer animation and special effects that were coming to dominate movies. Sun workstations animated the popular movie *Toy Story*, for example. Sun's Sparc workstation sold for three to four times more than personal computers.

By 1993, over a million units were shipped and Sun had taken its place next to Apple and Microsoft as an enormously successful system. By 1995, Sun introduced a software package called Java, with the motto "write once, run anywhere." It was a software system that allowed interactive graphics to be shown on the web on any platform. And Sun partnered with Netscape to make web browsers Java compatible (see Chapter 11).

The company was also a proponent of open systems in general and Unix system software, and was a major contributor to the open source movement. Despite their advantages and contributions, Sun workstations became less useful in comparison to the increasing power of the personal computer, and the company moved increasingly into providing Unix-adapted mainframe hardware for networked systems. In 2010, Sun was acquired by the leading networking hardware company, Oracle, for US $7.4 billion.

8 Apple Dominates the Twenty-first Century

Microsoft had all but won its race against IBM in the late 1980s when another major challenge emerged: a copyright infringement lawsuit brought by Apple Computers Inc. Apple contended that the Microsoft Windows system copied the "look and feel" of the Apple system. Microsoft responded that the Windows idea really came from Xerox PARC and was never licensed to Apple (although Xerox was an Apple investor).

Apple lost the suit in 1993, and the company teetered on the verge of bankruptcy. At one point around 1995, Apple was so desperate that it experimented with licensing its operating system to lower-priced clone manufacturers, such as Power Computing. But in 1997, with the end in sight, Apple brought back its original visionary, Steve Jobs. Jobs ended the licensing program right away and began asking engineers to rethink computers, networks, and applications people would want in the future.

The key to market success was complicated in the first decade of the twenty-first century by the fact that the dot-com market "bubble" had burst. Silicon Valley start-up companies, once the darlings of Wall Street, went bankrupt by the dozen. Even the once-mighty Microsoft descended from the lofty heights of nearly $600 billion in market capitalization to around $300 billion for most of the decade, and then under $200 billion during the financial crisis of 2009–11. Microsoft's strategy, to diversify into computer games with the Xbox, helped keep the company solvent, but profits stayed relatively flat through the first decade and a half of the twenty-first century.

Steve Jobs and the engineers at Apple, on the other hand, bet the farm on mobile communications, introducing a new line of non-computer products starting with the iPod in 2001, the iPhone (2007), and the iPad computer tablet (2010). The company even changed its name from Apple Computers Inc to just Apple Inc.

The bet paid off. By 2012, Apple was the world's largest corporation in terms of market capitalization, with a peak capital of $559 billion (with a "b"). By 2014, Apple was worth over $700 billion. The company had more capital than Exxon-Mobil petroleum, more than any banks, and more, in fact, than any other country on earth except the United States. Because of Steve Jobs' vision, it had, indeed, become a fabulously successful enterprise.

Yet part of that success came from subcontractors who ran inhumane, high-pressure sweatshops that made workers sick in order to keep profit margins healthy. The story

Figure 10.18 Former rivals—Steve Jobs, former CEO of Apple Computers, and Bill Gates, former CEO of Microsoft, enjoy a moment at a 2007 forum. More than any others, Jobs and Gates shaped personal computing technology in the twentieth and twenty-first centuries. Photo by Joi Ito, Creative Commons.

Thinking About the "Computer of the Future" Photo

The caption on the photo reads: "Scientists from the RAND Corporation have created this model to illustrate how a 'home computer' could look like in the year 2004. However the needed technology will not be economically feasible for the average home. Also the scientists readily admit that the computer will require not yet invented technology to actually work, but fifty years from now scientific progress is expected to solve these problems. With teletype interface and Fortran language, the computer will be easy to use."

According to historian John Tosh, there are three components of analysis when examining an historical document: textual authentication; validity of factual information; and weighing alternative interpretations (Tosh 2000).

1. Textual authentication—The photo and the text are part of the same image, as would be typical of a wire service photo sent to news organizations. However, checking the Associated Press photo transmission guide, we see that many elements are missing, including date, location, photographer's name, photo agency, and metadata about the transmission itself and intended publication date range. There are also grammar issues—"how a home computer could look like ..."

2. Validity of factual information—It's possible that scientists from RAND Corp. were working on computers of the future, since as we learn from a simple Google Search, the RAND Corp. was founded in 1945 as a policy and technology institute. But we don't know that they anticipated, or even could have anticipated, a home computer. Most of the work on computers had been taking place at MIT and the University of Pennsylvania with the Univac system. Predictions about home computers were much more typical of the late 1960s and 1970s.

Figure 10.19 Computer of the future? Photo from Fark.com and Snopes.com.

3. Alternative information—Rather than a news agency photo of a home computer being demonstrated at the RAND Corp., could this photo and caption be something else? The visual information seems suspect. For instance, why would a computer have a steering wheel? This leads us to ask whether this could be a control panel for something other than a computer.

Now let's re-evaluate. Using search engines to find this image, we learn that it is not a vision of a computer of the future from the year 1954, but actually a caricature from the present poking fun at supposed miscalculations of the past—a classic blunder in understanding history.

This apparent vision of a twenty-first-century home computer is in fact a full-scale mock-up of a control room in a nuclear submarine from 1954. The original photograph was taken at a Smithsonian Institution exhibit called "Fast Attacks and Boomers: Submarines of the Cold War." It became the basis of a Fark.com photo editing contest in September 2004.

came out in 2006, when investigative reporters looked into Foxconn, an Apple subcontractor in Longhua, China. About 200,000 workers lived in closed-off factory dormitories and worked fifteen-hour days for $100 a month (*Daily Mail*, 2006). Suicides by fourteen workers in 2010 drew fresh attention to Apple's human rights issues. Although Apple promised to reform its contractors, a late 2014 report by the Institute for Global Labour and Human Rights said that the same abuses were persisting (IGLHR 2014).

There were also long-standing concerns that iPhone and iPad had been closed to applications that did not meet the company's political approval process. Like Thomas Edison and Guglielmo Marconi, who attempted to control film and the radio, Steve Jobs and his successors were regulating content delivered through iPhone and iPad "apps."

"If you want to criticize a religion, write a book," the *App Store Review Guide* said. "Any app that is defamatory, offensive, mean-spirited, or likely to place the targeted individual or group in harm's way will be rejected."

By way of explanation, Apple said, "We view apps different [*sic*] than books or songs, which we do not curate" (Apple 2015). The use of the word "curate" as opposed to "censor" is interesting. "Curate" means "to look after and preserve," which is what British Museum officials did with the Babbage computer. To "censor" is defined as "official or officious supervision over morals and conduct" Clearly the latter is what is intended with Apple Apps.

By 2014, over 1,200 apps were submitted per day for review, compared to only about thirty-eight per day in 2008. Open-architecture systems, such as the Google Android for mobile phone/information devices held the promise of a more flexible system. By 2015, 43 percent of US mobile phones were using Apple systems.

For additional reading, discussion questions, links to video, and other suggestions, see www.revolutionsincommunications.com.

11

Digital Networks

> The message that changed the world: By the power vested in me by nobody in particular, alpha/beta version 0.5 of NCSA's Motif-based networked information systems and World Wide Web browser, X Mosaic, is hereby released …
>
> Marc Andreessen, Saturday, January 23, 1993 at 7.21 a.m.

Marc Andreessen, a grad student in computer science, was half joking when he said that the power was vested "by nobody in particular." Actually, Andreessen's group was funded by the National Center for Supercomputing Applications, which was trying to develop non-commercial software to aid scientific research. Releasing software was routine. But no one had any idea how much impact this particular piece of software would have.

Andreessen's software was called a "browser" for a network system designed by Tim Berners-Lee, a computer engineer at a major European physics project called CERN. Berners-Lee designed a network that he called the World Wide Web a few years before, in 1990. But at that point, the web was a structure without much of a navigational system, rather like a highway without on-ramps or maps. So Berners-Lee distributed Andreessen's message through the international academic email system with this comment: "An exciting new World-Wide Web browser has come out, written by Marc Andreessen of NCSA. Using X/Motif, and full of good features, it [Mosaic] installs very easily."

Mosaic was the first easily available web browser that could be used to view websites, but it was remarkable in that it was also released with its own web server. It was as if Andreessen distributed free eyeglasses to help read books, and then threw in a printing press as well.

Computer users who had grown accustomed to network screens full of numbered lines of green text now had what looked like a book page in front of them, with formatted text, pictures, and—coolest of all—clickable hyperlinks to an infinite number of pages in a rapidly expanding world library.

Mosaic caught on in a matter of months, and the concept of a world wide web was on the minds of everyone in the media business by 1994. Clearly, the web was a first class enabling/generative technology; enabling people to do far more than just passively receive media from centrally produced sources. It was a door into the future. Andreessen's Mosaic was the key that opened the door, making it easy for everyone to access and generate content for an open and unregulated world wide web.

By the mid-1990s, with just a little knowledge of html coding, anyone could be a global publisher. Within a few years, the web exploded: by 1998 there were 26 million pages. By

2000 there were a billion (Alpert and Hajaj, 2008). And by 2015, three billion people—nearly half the world's population—were using the internet and the World Wide Web (Miniwatts 2015).

Early Visions of a World Wide Web

H. G. Wells, science fiction author:
Both the assembling and the distribution of knowledge in the world at present are extremely ineffective … [We] are beginning to realize that the most hopeful line for the development of our racial intelligence lies rather in the direction of creating a new world organ for the collection, indexing, summarizing and release of knowledge, than in any further tinkering with the highly conservative and resistant university system. (Wells 1937)

Figure 11.1 H. G. Wells. Library of Congress.

Vannevar Bush, White House science advisor:
Consider a future device for individual use, which is a sort of mechanized private file and library … A "memex" is a device in which an individual stores all his books, records, and communications [which] may be consulted with exceeding speed and flexibility … Wholly new forms of encyclopedias will appear, ready made with a mesh of associative trails running through them … There [will be] a new profession of trail blazers … who find delight in the task of establishing useful trails through the enormous mass of the common record. (Bush 1945)

Figure 11.2 Vannevar Bush. Library of Congress.

J. C. R. Licklider, MIT and ARPA, 1960:
"It seems reasonable to envision, for a time ten or fifteen years hence, a thinking center that will incorporate the functions of present day libraries together with anticipated advances in information storage and retrieval." (Larry Roberts said: "Lick had this concept of the 'intergalactic network' in which … Everybody could use computers anywhere and get at data anywhere in the world. He didn't envision the number of computers we have today by any means, but he had the same concept.) (Segaller 1998)

Figure 11.3 J. C. R. Licklider. Library of Congress.

Martin Greenberger, computer science professor: Barring unforeseen obstacles, an on-line interactive computer service, provided commercially by an information utility, may be as commonplace by 2000 AD as telephone service is today. By 2000 AD man should have a much better comprehension of himself and his system, not because he will be innately any smarter than he is today, but because he will have learned to use imaginatively the most powerful amplifier of intelligence yet devised. (Greenberger 1964)

Figure 11.4 Courtesy of Martin Greenberger.

Ted Nelson, inventor of hypertext, network designer: Forty years from now (if the human species survives), there will be hundreds of thousands of files servers. And there will be hundreds of millions of simultaneous users. All this is manifest destiny. There is no point in arguing it, either you see it or you don't (Nelson, *Literary Machines*, 1981). By "hypertext" I mean non-sequential writing— text that branches and allows choice to the reader, best read at an interactive screen. (Nelson, Computer Lib 1987/74)

Figure 11.5 Ted Nelson. Photo by Wikimedia Commons user Dgies.

The Internet Versus the World Wide Web

The Internet is a global confederation of computer-to-computer networks that send digital signals through telephone, cable, satellite, and fiber optic systems. The signals are interpreted with standardized protocols such as TCP/IP which are regularly checked and updated through an international governance process. Many different kinds of computer applications run through the Internet, for example telnet, chat, email, and file transfer protocol (ftp), along with the World Wide Web. At times, the "internet" may also refer to a concept of free-flowing communications around the globe.

The World Wide Web is a multimedia information system that runs on the internet and allows exchange of documents through hypertext links. It was invented by Tim Berners-Lee in 1989 and is the most widely used application on the Internet. Internet domain names (like revolutionsincommunication.com) are regulated through the Internet Corporation for Assigned Names and Numbers (ICANN), formed in 1998. In 2011, the ICANN opened up the ICANN process to all languages (not just English) and to all registrants.

1 Vision Precedes Reality

The basic idea of a technology often precedes the hardware. People dreamed about flying, about riding in horseless carriages, and exchanging instant audio-visual communication long before the airplane, the automobile, the television were possible.

Engineers and software nerds with dreams also blazed the first conceptual pathways into the Internet and World Wide Web. Among the early problems that early visionaries wanted to overcome was information overload—the storage and retrieval of large volumes of reference information. Other problems involved optimal sharing of data between computers and messaging systems that came to be known as email.

The computer networking system could have taken any one of a number of technological paths. Like other communications revolutions, there were curves in the road where giant companies bought up small organizations, and other instances where the giants lost to smaller visionaries. Unlike other communications revolutions, computer networks began with a very strong government role, which then, over time, proved so useful in civilian applications that it sidelined the original military functions.

The networking revolution was unusual in the history of technology. It did not just replace top-down content from large companies. Instead, networking allowed bottom-up, user-to-user communication. It was an "enabling" or "generative" technology. It let people do things that had never been done before, and its capabilities quickly stretched far beyond the original idea of a giant reference library.

In the early years of commercial networks, from the 1980s to 1990s, Internet Service Providers (ISP) created their own databases, reference materials and interest group networks. The big question was which one of them would come out on top. But these ISPs were like gated communities without access to the broader World Wide Web. In the end, none came out on top.

"They [the ISPs] were crushed by a network built by government researchers and computer scientists who had no CEO, no master business plan, no paying subscribers, no investment in content, and no financial interest in accumulating subscribers," observed Jonathan Zittrain (2006).

Attempts to control the Internet through the Federal Communications Commission were also defeated. "The interest in encouraging freedom of expression in a democratic society outweighs any theoretical but unproven benefit of censorship," said the Supreme Court in a 1997 decision that ensured the freedom of the internet (*Reno v. ACLU*, 1997).

The end result was that the Internet and web were considered "protected speech" and left mostly unregulated, unlike the radio and television industry. Today there is no Federal Internet Commission with endless debates about content issues, as is typical of the Federal Communications Commission. (However, the FCC does have a role in structural issues, as we will see below in the discussion of network neutrality.)

The story of networked computing revolution, of the internet and the world wide web, is a story of the link between an enabling technology and the moments in history when innovators unite around a common vision.

2 The First Networks

Just as massive electronic digital computers were a product of World War II, computer networks grew up in the Cold War atmosphere in which scientific researchers had unlimited funds. One of the top priorities was to use computers to link radar systems across the Canadian and Alaskan north to anticipate Russian warplanes. The system was called the "Defense Early Warning" (or DEW) line. One priority for this DEW line and other networks was to develop a system that could survive a Russian nuclear attack. When the Advanced Research Projects Agency was established in 1958, engineers began considering how to improve communication systems. One idea was to use phone lines for digital signals—an idea that AT&T resisted as too competitive with the then-monopoly Bell System (Segaller 1998: 116).

Instead, the research focused on analog signals. But digital signals had many advantages, among them that they could be sent in "packets" through a distributed network and could be automatically re-routed around trouble spots, stored, and then reassembled in case of network problems. In case of a nuclear war, a digital network could be more flexible and durable than a centralized analog network. Networking could also solve other technical problems, according to J. C. R. Licklider, the legendary computer information chief at the Defense Department's Advanced Research Projects Agency (ARPA).

First, digital networks would allow computers to work in real time, continuously rather than processing batches of instructions on cards; and second, a network could allow "time sharing" on computers to maximize their efficiency. As a bonus, networks could also create an advanced library, according to Licklider.

Licklider's colleague at ARPA was Rob Taylor whose Washington, DC office in the mid-1960s had three computer terminals: one for the computer at the University of California, Berkeley; one for a computer at MIT in Massachusetts; and a third for a computer at Systems Development Corp. in Santa Monica, California. "To talk to MIT I had to sit at the MIT terminal," Taylor said. "To bring in someone from Berkeley, I had to change chairs to another terminal. I wished I could connect someone at MIT directly with someone at Berkeley. Out of that came the idea: Why not have one terminal that connects with all of them? That's why we built ARPAnet" (Softky 2000).

To move forward with the networked computing idea, ARPA sent out a request for proposals in 1968. The winner was a small Cambridge, Massachusetts company called BBN that had the idea of creating an Interface Message Processor (IMP) between the different kinds of computer systems. Within a year, BBN connected four universities' computer systems to create the first computer network called ARPANET. Only a few people saw the revolutionary impact of this achievement when it was completed, relatively quickly, in December 1969.

One of the contractors for ARPA, Len Klienrock, predicted that with more sophisticated computer networks, "we will probably see the spread of computer utilities ... like the present electric and telephone utilities" (Segaller 115). An important milestone was the development of electronic mail (email) in 1972. Electronic messages were not new, of course. Operators of mainframe computers were able to place electronic messages to other operators of the same computer since the 1960s. Ray Tomlinson at BBN wanted to extend this capability to the expanding ARPA network, and wrote a program allowing computers to send and store individual messages. In order to individualize the message address, Tomlinson selected an obscure symbol used for accounting—the @ symbol—to indicate the destination domain of the email.

Scientists and academics who first used email in the 1970s started to enjoy the free and fast information exchanges. They found it easy to keep up with distant colleagues, arrange conferences, exchange ideas, and collaborate on research. And they also started having fun writing to friends and trading advice and jokes. Email quickly became the "killer application" of networked computers, but in the early 1970s, preliminary designs for email applications were too weak to handle the growing network. Better packet-sharing protocols and standardized systems were needed.

2.1 TCP/IP and ethernet

Some computer scientists believe that the development of a common computer data transfer protocol was far more significant than ARPANET itself. They also note that it was an international effort; collaboration with researchers in Europe was crucial to its success (Hauben 2010).

The need to standardize digital packet switching networks was recognized early on by Vint Cerf, at Stanford University, and Robert Kahn at ARPA. They began envisioning a system of protocols that would link both satellite and ground-based data networks together.

Networking issues were also recognized by other researchers at the same time. Louis Pouzin was developing the French packet switching network Cyclades/Cigale network. In Britain, Donald Davies and others were working on the NPL network. "The question became how could these networks be interconnected, i.e., how would communication be possible across the boundaries of these dissimilar networks," said Ronda Hauben. International conferences not only brought many together to discuss their work, but also showed how collaboration could make incremental improvements in what became TCP/IP (Hauben 2004).

The TCP system that emerged allowed the network itself to route only the data from "nodes" and have no central control function. The "IP" or Internet Protocol would provide the address that allowed packets to be transmitted. The system was supposed to be simple enough that it would run through "two tin cans and a string."

Making the system work for personal computers was Bob Metcalfe's contribution. Metcalf had worked at BBN and helped tie MIT's computer into the ARPANET in 1969. By 1972 he was at Xerox PARC working on the same problem that Cerf and Kahn had been navigating. Metcalf 's answer was "Ethernet," a term he coined in 1973, envisioning a network that used cable to route a local area network of personal computers together.

Ethernet was the perfect addition to PARC's small personal computer called the Alto; it already had a graphical user interface and a computer "mouse" developed by Doug Engelbart at SRI.

But in the mid-1970s, the academics from Palo Alto and Stanford University found their vision of the future of computing had diverged from the Defense Department's vision. For example, the Defense Department's ARPA asked private company AT&T to take over ARPANET, more or less at cost. But AT&T refused out of fear that data networks would somehow create problems in the phone system. This would later be seen as another instance of a big company missing the "curve in the road," especially when it became far more efficient to translate analog voice signals into digital data. Development was left to the academics.

Ethernet and TCP/IP had some short-term commercial applications. For example, high-quality printers, such as laser printers developed at Adobe systems in the 1980s, were three to four times more expensive than the computers they served. Few people would buy a $2,000 computer and then add on a $6,000 laser printer. Ethernet solved the problem by allowing small offices to network personal computers with an office printer.

However, in the early years, the engineering work on what was to become the Internet remained embedded in small academically affiliated research groups rather than large corporations and defense contractors. The work was accomplished by people who did not have the usual corporate loyalties, freeing them to create a system that had few controls and much potential, unlike anything that had been seen before.

3 Networks Expand in the United States and Europe

In the late 1970s, various pieces of the academic and military networks were brought together into one National Science Foundation network and merged with a university network called "Bitnet." Both were really patchworks of several dozen networks that were able to join together using TCP/IP.

From this patchwork, two major types of network activity emerged in the 1980s: university internet systems, where users had email, ftp (file transfer protocol), and text-only files accessed through "gopher" servers; and commercial Internet Service Providers (ISPs), again, a text-only system, designed for non-academics and hobbyists to exchange email and use chat rooms, and for games played in "multi-user dungeons."

Although capabilities lagged, the basic framework of the Internet was in place and the future direction of networking was fairly obvious in 1978. Yet when IBM began planning a personal computer that year, the idea of networked computers seemed outlandish to the corporate suit culture.

When the IBM executive in charge of the PC project, William Lowe, asked Ted Nelson and Doug Engelbart to talk with computer executives about the future of networking, they were treated like dreamers. According to computer historian John Markoff, the two network designers "sketched out a world in which computer users would be able to retrieve information wherever they were, [and it] came as a shock to the blue-suited I.B.M. executives … It gave a hint of the world that the PC would bring, and even though

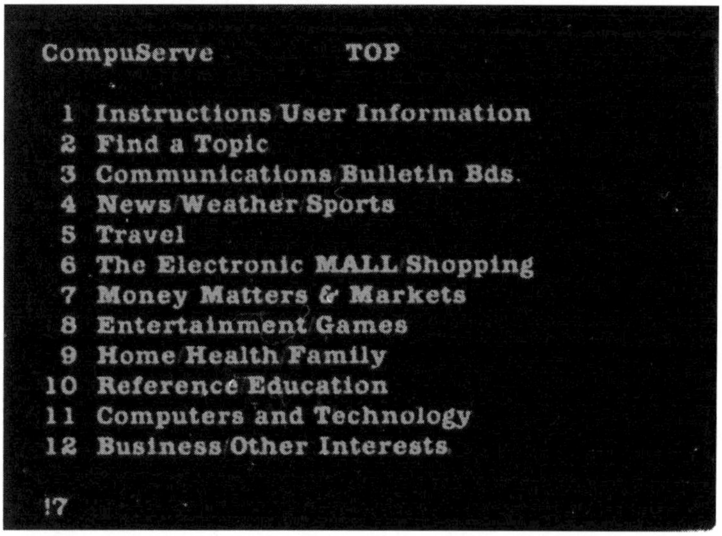

Figure 11.6 Early Internet—This screen from the Compuserv ISP around 1984 shows the interface of the early text-only Internet. That same year, Apple was introducing the first computer with a "what-you-see is what-you-get" (wysiwyg) screen interface. It would take another decade before the Internet could handle a wysiwyg interface through early web browsers. Author's collection.

the I.B.M.-ers were getting ready to transform a hobbyist business into one of the world's major industries, they had no clue of the broader social implications" (Markoff 2007).

3.1 University-based computer networks

By the early 1980s, the center of gravity for the digital revolution had shifted to an extensive set of networks linking major US and European universities. The network accounts were free to students and faculty, had no time limits, and were very useful for communication within disciplines. Computer science students were especially encouraged to share their software projects.

One of the first innovations was a method to send a group email called a "listserv." (The limit of eight characters for file names in early computers explains some of the strange spellings of terms like "listserv" and "videotex.") Users could "subscribe" to any discussion group, and hundreds formed around topics from network protocols to science fiction. Anyone could start a listserv on any discussion topic. Another network function was FTP (file transfer protocol), used for downloading all kinds of programs and documents.

Adventurous Internet users could join "Internet Relay Chat," a real-time text exchange where anyone could set up a "channel" on any topic at any time. In its heyday you could find a thousand channels going with participants from Australia to Sweden holding forth on topics ranging from world politics to video games. There was even an IRC channel called "hot tub" for those who enjoyed racy and sexually suggestive talk.

Another development that shook some media professionals was the Usenet "news group" system. It usually involved collections of email threaded by topics ranging from recreation to computing to professional interests. Few had anything to do with traditional news topics, and none were moderated by professional journalists.

Discussion group topics were dominated by computing and networking issues but also included topics from archery to zoology. Usenet postings usually took a day to be distributed because the network was designed to operate at night and take advantage of what would usually be computer downtime. Anyone with access to university networks could start their own group.

One system that closely anticipated the web was a hierarchical structure of read-only files called the "gopher" system, developed at the University of Minnesota. Between 1990 and 1994, hundreds of thousands of gopher sites served up text files in numerical hierarchy. But it was clear that a more visually oriented, easy-to-navigate system was needed.

3.2 Minitel and other European networks

Interactive networks caught on in Europe much more quickly than the United States, since they were backed by governments that had a tradition of running subsidized and more reliable telecommunications services. In the early 1970s, the British Broadcasting Corporation (BBC) began offering a service called Teletext, a closed-caption interactive news service carried over the television broadcast signal in the vertical blanking interval.

In 1980, the British Post Office launched a videotex computer service called "Prestel" amid a chorus of enthusiastic predictions. Prestel offered online news and services such as banking and travel ticket sales. It was linked directly to television sets. However, it was expensive and conservative British politicians in the 1980s were not inclined to continue subsidies. When attempts to market the service to business did not pan out, it was finally suspended in 1994.

The French telecommunications ministry was far more successful with an ambitious project called Minitel, rolled out experimentally in 1978 and launched nationwide in 1982. Minitel featured a small, low- resolution terminal that could be hooked up to a telephone line at little or no cost to the consumer. In the beginning, Minitel carried online phone

Figure 11.7 Early British internet—Teletext, a closed-captioned text service delivered through television broadcast signals, was available from the 1970s through the BBC. About two million Teletext sets were in use in 1982. But the system was slow to respond and not capable of high-resolution graphics, as this screen shot from July 1990 shows. Courtesy of Dr. William Johnstone.

listings and saved the cost of publishing phone directories. But by the mid-1980s, Minitel blossomed into the world's largest e-commerce marketplace, with banking, shopping, and all kinds of services. At its height around 2000, Minitel had about nine million terminals in operation.

Similar Minitel services were offered through postal and telephone services throughout Europe, especially in Italy, Ireland, and Spain. In most cases, the terminals were not given away, as they were in France, so consumer barriers were significant.

The Minitel experience was early proof that interactive networked media could catch on and be valuable. But on June 30, 2012—thirty years to the day after the project began—French engineers reluctantly shut down the obsolete Minitel system. In the end, some saw the project as hopelessly out of date and bureaucratically top-heavy. For example, any service that wanted to use Minitel had to ask permission from French Telecom. But many of the ideas that proved successful on the Internet were first tried out on Minitel (Schafer, 2012).

3.3 The Internet takes off with ISPs

If you wanted to explore online sites in the 1980s, and you were not a university student or faculty member, you couldn't just call your local telephone company. Instead, you would join an individual bulletin board or ISP service, call a local number, and then connect to the Internet with a series of bell-like noises surrounded by static. This was called a

Figure 11.8 Early French internet—An ambitious telephone-based information service called Minitel was used by about 25 million people in the 1980s and 1990s for business services, advertising, and telephone directories. Minitel also had chat features available that allowed the creation of virtual communities. The system was an early demonstration of the value of large-scale networks when prices were within reach of most people. The service started on June 20, 1982 and ended June 30, 2012.

Lessons from Early Networks

Valuable lessons came out of Prestel, Minitel, Viewtron, and other early experiments:

- ***Navigation is important.*** The back button and site history lists, which became standard on web browsers in the 1990s, came from the confusion of having to navigate endless chains of numbered topics in the 1980s.
- ***News is not enough.*** People wanted to be able to communicate in small groups and generate their own grass-roots content. Access to news and other "top-down" information is not sufficient for consumers to overcome price barriers.
- ***Graphics matter.*** Users wanted a graphical display for networked communications to match new GUI interfaces on their computer desktops. People wanted, at the very least, to experience the first two media revolutions—movable type and visual communication—through their computer networks. Audio and video, from the third media revolution, arrived faster than most people anticipated.
- ***Networks can help business.*** With enough people participating, even small businesses can use networks to efficiently sell specialized goods and services, developing what would become known as "long tail" marketing.

"dial-up" ISP service. It took several decades, but by the early 2000s, Internet connections were available from the phone companies.

Text was the only communication method possible in the early days of the Internet. Images, audio, and video files were far too large to send through network connections (a problem that led to the development of MPEG a/v and JPEG photo compression technologies). Early modems ran at very low speeds—around 300 bits per second, and by the year 2000, modem speeds still remained as low as 28,000 bits per second (or 28.8 kilobits). It wasn't until around 2004 that DSL modems with speeds in millions of bytes (MBs) per second became commercially available. Still, in the early 1990s, about 70,000 independently operated small bulletin boards were operating in the United States (Rheingold 1996).

These ISPs were, in effect, entirely separate islands of data. Not until the mid- to late 1990s would ISPs themselves connect to the broader Internet or web. One reason for the isolated ISP approach was that the backbone of the Internet at the time was the National Science Foundation's data network. Access was limited by the NSF's Acceptable Use Policy that prohibited commercial traffic, requiring that all information have educational, scientific, or research value.

Legislation to open the NSFnet to links with commercial networks, called the Scientific and Advanced-Technology Act, was championed by Senator Al Gore and Representative Rick Boucher and passed in 1992.

The first large ISP was CompuServe, which grew from several hundred thousand subscribers in the late 1970s to about four million in the early 1990s. Users paid an access fee and an hourly rate. It was expensive: an hour online every day could cost over $100 a month.

One of the lessons from an early 1981 partnership between CompuServe and the Associated Press was that not many people were interested in paying a premium fee for news. Only about 5 percent of the demand involved information needs; most of the rest involved person-to-person communication about personal interests and games.

"Someday everybody will communicate by computer," said Art Kleiner in a 1984 *Whole Earth Catalog* review of computers, modems, and online services. "Personal computer networking—exchanging text and pictures between terminals, over phone or cable—is so convenient that many expect it to become as widespread eventually as the telephone and television are now." Kleiner noted that networks involved "uneasy compromises between computers and phone lines, which weren't designed to work together. In practice, that means every computer network and software package you use will take a bit of fiddling until you get your connections right" (Kleiner 1984).

An early experimental dial-up "bulletin board" network was the Whole Earth 'Lectronic Link (WELL), a computerized counterculture meet-up started by *Whole Earth Catalog* publisher Stuart Brand in 1985. One of the early advantages of WELL membership was the ability to keep track of concerts by music groups like the Grateful Dead, sharing travel plans and bootlegged music tapes. But all kinds of other exchanges were taking place, from jokes to political activism. ISPs like the WELL allowed person-to-person communication and provided safe places where people could socialize, extend their personal lives, share photos, and find avenues for self-expression. Some allowed free classified advertising for jobs, used cars, real estate, and garage sales, beginning to replace the way newspapers had once served as a central bulletin board for small-scale community commerce.

There was fun in discovering all these new functions; people enjoyed becoming part of a virtual community. Journalist and author Howard Rheingold was so fond of his first experiences with social networks in the 1980s that he described the excitement in his book *The Virtual Community*:

> Finding the WELL was like discovering a cozy little world that had been flourishing without me, hidden within the walls of my house; an entire cast of characters welcomed me to the troupe with great merriment as soon as I found the secret door. Like others who fell into the WELL, I soon discovered that I was audience, performer, and scriptwriter, along with my companions, in an ongoing improvisation. A full-scale subculture was growing on the other side of my telephone jack, and they invited me to help create something new. (Rheingold 1993)

Another advantage of virtual community was the ability to create political momentum quickly. Art Kleiner noted that in 1982, the Colorado Springs city council proposed a bill outlawing professional work at home. "Instead of tracking the bill down at City Hall, residents could dial in at their convenience and read the bill at home. Within a week, Hughes had gathered enough angry readers to storm the next city council meeting and influence council members to defeat the measure" (Kleiner 1984).

"Ben Franklin would have been the first owner of an Apple computer. Thomas Jefferson would have written the Declaration of Independence on an IBM PC. But Tom Paine would

Figure 11.9 Falling into the WELL—Journalist Howard Rheingold fell into the Whole Earth 'Lectronic Link (the WELL) in 1985 and described in his book *The Virtual Community* how "[a]n entire cast of characters welcomed me to the troupe." Photo by Joi Ito, Creative Commons.

have published *Common Sense* on a computer bulletin board," Rheingold quoted David Hughes as saying.

In 1989, a commercial ISP named Prodigy attempted to cut the high cost of online services with a new business model that included advertising. IBM and Sears invested over a billion dollars in Prodigy with the idea that it would be the litmus test for the online industry.

Prodigy billed itself as a family-oriented ISP and used editors to screen sexual and other potentially offensive content. As a result, the courts held that Prodigy was responsible for everything published on its websites, and the company lost an expensive libel case as a result (*Stratton-Oakmont v. Prodigy*, 1995).

Prodigy eventually merged with CompuServe, which in turn merged with America Online. One problem that ISPs faced in the early 1990s, before the introduction of the World Wide Web, involved low-resolution graphics due in part to very slow networks then in existence.

3.4 The short, turbulent life of America OnLine

America OnLine (AOL), founded in 1992, was the most successful of the many ISPs in part because it had the best graphical user interface (GUI), which was helpful in navigating a new and complex internet system.

It wasn't easy to deliver graphics at this time. Given the large relative size of pictures, and low speed of the internet in handling anything but text, AOL came up with interesting workaround: The company distributed monthly packages of updated graphics data through the US mails, and these put permanent frames and navigation buttons around the interactive text windows to make it seem more user friendly.

AOL also simplified the process of connecting to an Internet system for consumers who had few other options at a time when the telephone companies were not providing Internet connection services.

The number of AOL subscribers grew from half a million in 1993 to a peak of around 27 million by the year 2000. That year, at the peak of its over-capitalized value, AOL purchased Time-Warner, a giant media conglomerate, for $350 billion. It was the largest merger in corporate history. "This is a historic moment in which new media has truly come of age," said chairman Stephen Case at the time.

The train wreck that followed is the stuff of legend. First, the "dot-com bubble" burst on March 13, 2000, probably caused by a coincidental influx of sell orders processed that day. The sell orders triggered a chain reaction of selling that fed on itself as investors bailed out of speculative bets on information technology stocks.

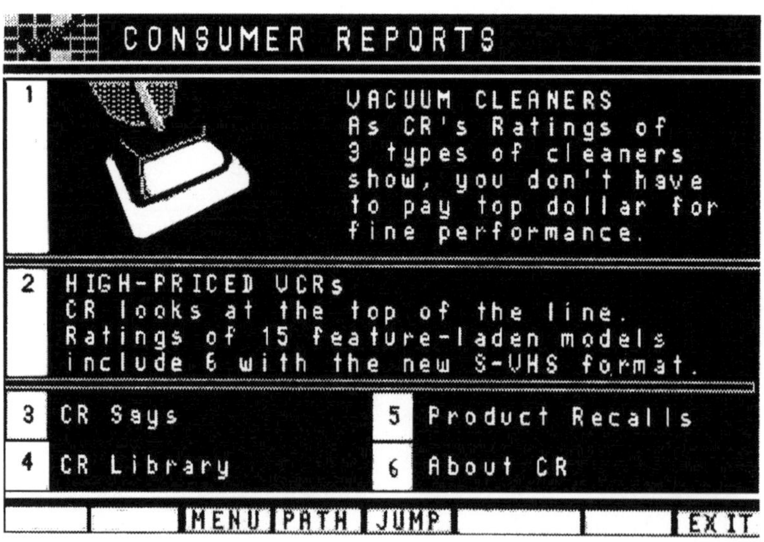

Figure 11.10 Prodigy service in the United States—In an attempt to cut costs to consumers, IBM and Sears invested in Prodigy, an information service supported by advertising. Prodigy screens had low-resolution graphics and better navigational controls than most other services at the time. Author's collection.

Contributing to the panic was a court finding that Microsoft was operating as a monopoly. Around the same time, a federal investigation showed that AOL had been inflating earnings statements in order to get into position to buy Time-Warner. When the dust cleared two years later, Case had left the building, and AOL was worth $200 billion less in shareholder value.

Some analysts blamed the disaster on the clash of business cultures, AOL's financial irregularities, and Time-Warner's inability to carry out the vision. Yet the disaster wasn't entirely unpredictable. AOL was already becoming obsolete since fewer consumers needed an ISP to access the Internet. The regular phone companies were starting to wake up to the business opportunity.

Another problem with the AOL merger was that computer users were not so interested in simply extending their television habits into some sort of web interactivity. While AOL offered hobby groups, online markets, and other community oriented resources, many users did not find the network worth the $30 per month subscription price. AOL was often compared to a "walled garden" on the edge of the enormous World Wide Web frontier.

In 2009, Time-Warner sold off AOL for a fraction of its original value, and by 2010, the combined value of both companies was a fraction of what it had been (Arango, 2010). "In their single-minded quest for power, Steve Case and Jerry Levin were at each other's throats even before the deal was announced," said Nina Munk in a book, *Fools Rush In*. Worse, "with a remarkable sense of timing, Steve Case had used grossly inflated Internet paper to buy Time Warner" (Munk 2004).

3.5 Mass media and the Internet, 1980s–1990s

The mainstream mass media attempted to keep up with all the changes, but digital technologies had already caused painful transitions in previous decades. These included

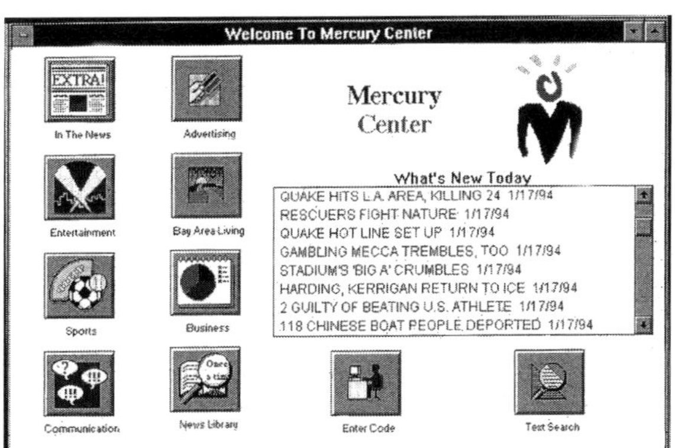

Figure 11.11 America Online—One of the most innovative early Internet Service Providers was America Online (AOL), a company started in 1992 and merged with Time-Warner in 2000. AOL's graphics and fixed navigational buttons were pre-loaded from discs sent through the mail. The approach was highly successful in the 1990s, but the company failed to keep up with changes in technology in the early twenty-first century. Author's collection.

Al Gore and the Internet

Did Al Gore really say he invented the Internet? Not according to Snopes.com and other fact-verifying services. While a US senator in 1992, Gore introduced several key bills expanding and allowing commercial uses for the National Science Foundation network, which became the backbone of the US Internet. Then, during the 2000 presidential campaign, he said this: "During my service in the United States Congress, I took the initiative in creating the Internet. I took the initiative in moving forward a whole range of initiatives that have proven to be important to our country's economic growth and environmental protection, improvements in our educational system."

Although the quote does not reflect precision or eloquence, he is clearly not claiming to have been the inventor of the Internet, but rather, to have helped with legislation. The canard that he falsely claimed to have "invented" the Internet is just politics.

Figure 11.12 Al Gore—Former senator and vice president Al Gore never claimed to have "invented" the Internet. As a US senator in 1992, Gore introduced legislation that helped clear the way for commercial use of the Internet. Photo by Tom Raftery, 2010, Creative Commons.

the switch from "hot" lead typesetting to "cold" computer-set type and an expensive switch from film cameras to videotape in the broadcasting business. As a result, publishers were cautious about new technology investments despite the high profits the mainstream media enjoyed at the time.

In the 1980s, two kinds of experiments in new interactive media backed by news organizations turned out to be expensive failures: teletext and videotex. Around 1978, television networks experimented with the idea of inserting text and graphics into the TV signal (technically, into the vertical blanking interval). Several hundred pages could be broadcast in sequence to viewers who owned a special receiver and a small keypad. Stations and networks in the United States, Japan, and Europe experimented with the teletext system, but the system was slow and highly limited.

Another approach involved what was generically called "videotex." Early prototypes included an Associated Press/CompuServe partnership in 1980 and the Times Mirror "Gateway" and Knight Ridder "Viewtron" experiments of 1982–6. Viewtron was ahead of its time with electronic banking, games, chats, and other non-news services. Another experiment was the CBS–IBM–Sears venture called Trinitex, which started in 1984 and ended in 1988. It was revived in 1989 as Prodigy without CBS as a partner.

The US experiments did not succeed partly because the technology was expensive. Users had to buy the Viewtron terminal, at a cost of $600, and then pay monthly fees of over $20. Viewtron tried to bring down the expense with advertising, but the system did not allow high-resolution graphics, and the poor graphical-user interface was not attractive to advertisers or users.

By the end of the 1980s, news media analysts concluded that videotex was "not a threat" to the news business. Editors in the traditional media said that they were in the news business, not in business to help users connect or chat with each other. Although ISPs like Compuserv, Prodigy, and America Online still offered news from newspapers and the Associated Press, the media companies turned down most opportunities to invest in the ISPs and experiment on their own.

The Times Mirror Company, still bruised from the Gateway experiment, and others like Cox Communications in Atlanta, Georgia, tried partnering with Prodigy between 1992 and 1995. But editors worried that computer experts and site designers were more in control of the news than they were. They believed that with the complexity of the technology, quality news was taking second place to packaging.

One of the publishing industry's last attempts to anticipate market changes was launched at Knight Ridder's Information Design Lab in Boulder, Colorado, in 1992. The idea was to create "touch-tablet" technology with a look and feel similar to a newspaper. "For the first time, we're going to be seeing an alternative to ink on paper," said lab director Roger Fidler. "It may be difficult to conceptualize the idea of digital paper, but in fact, we believe that's what's going to happen." But the concept was ahead of its time—and the technology. The lab closed in 1996. "Fidler's dream never quite got airborne before the hurricane blowing through the American newspaper industry killed off the Knight Ridder lab and all its hopes," said Alan Rusbridger in 2010 (Rusbridger 2010).

4 The Arrival of the World Wide Web, 1989–93

Tim Berners-Lee said he never really had a "Eureka" moment about the World Wide Web. Instead, the idea grew and coalesced over the years as he worked at CERN, the European Laboratory for Particle Physics based in Switzerland. "Suppose all the information stored on computers everywhere was linked," he thought. "Suppose I could program my computer to create a space in which anything could be linked to anything" (Berners-Lee 1999).

Berners-Lee was aware of a previous attempt at network building called Xanadu by Ted Nelson. Like many projects, it was too early and too complex, but it had valuable ideas. One of these was "hypertext," the ability to embed links that could lead from one document to another. Berners-Lee called the basic protocol for the web a "hyper-text transfer protocol," also known as "http." Another important idea was the Universal Resource Locator, "URL," that would help locate web pages.

The first website built was at the European Organization for Nuclear Research (CERN), and was first put "on line" on August 6, 1991. The idea was to exchange charts and other graphic data more easily by using a computer program that interpreted text and pictures in one window. It was originally developed for scientists to collaborate on high-energy physics projects as they worked at different universities and institutes all over the world, but Berners-Lee believed it could also be useful for all kinds of communication. The program could read pages of text which had special commands or "tags" that automatically brought pictures into the browser window. Several different kinds of tags were used initially, but HTML (Hyper Text Markup Language) was what caught on. Berners-Lee shared his idea freely with users around the world and a number of early browsers emerged.

The first widely popular web browser, Mosaic, was created (as noted above) between 1992 and 1993 by Marc Andreessen and fellow computer students at the National Center

Figure 11.13 World Wide Web pioneer—Tim Berners-Lee, as an employee at the European Organization for Nuclear Research, conceived the idea of using hypertext with a code that combined text formatting and a graphical-user interface. His idea went online in August 1991, but took off in 1993 when the Mosaic browser and server software, developed by Marc Andreessen and others at the University of Illinois, became freely available. The web allowed anyone to publish virtually anything, revolutionizing international communications in a few years. Photo by Uldis Bojārs, Creative Commons.

for Supercomputing Applications (NCSA) at the University of Illinois. Mosaic could run on Windows, Unix, and Mac platforms and it had navigation buttons, a memory, and seamless graphics. It also came with server software, which allowed anyone to not only read but also publish on the World Wide Web.

Because Andreessen's research project was funded specifically for developing free scientific applications, he gave Mosaic away, and in the process fueled a surge of interest in this new form of communication. The original Mosaic browser was rather clunky and network connections were still fairly slow, but the combination of text and visual communications was instantly recognized as revolutionary. By March 1994, the phenomenal success of Mosaic led Andreessen and others to create a company that became Netscape. Among the early investors were news media giants like Knight Ridder. As it turned out, a handful of visionaries at universities and research institutions had transformed the Internet from a valuable but limited text delivery service into a new window on the world.

As Berners-Lee said: "We are slowly learning the value of decentralized, diverse systems and of mutual respect and tolerance... My hope and faith that we are headed somewhere stem in part from the repeatedly proven observation that people seem to be naturally built to interact with others as part of a greater system"(Berners-Lee 1999).

4.1 News on the web

The news media does not usually get credit for a quick response to the web, but in some cases it should. Knight Ridder and NBC, for example, jumped in with both feet in 1994 and 1995. "They brought [Mosaic] up on the screen— graphics, text, data. I was blown away. It didn't take long to see that this was going to be a revolution," Chris Jennewein, Knight Ridder News Media vice president for technology and operations, told *American Journalism Review* in an article about the web. In January of 1994, Jennewein was

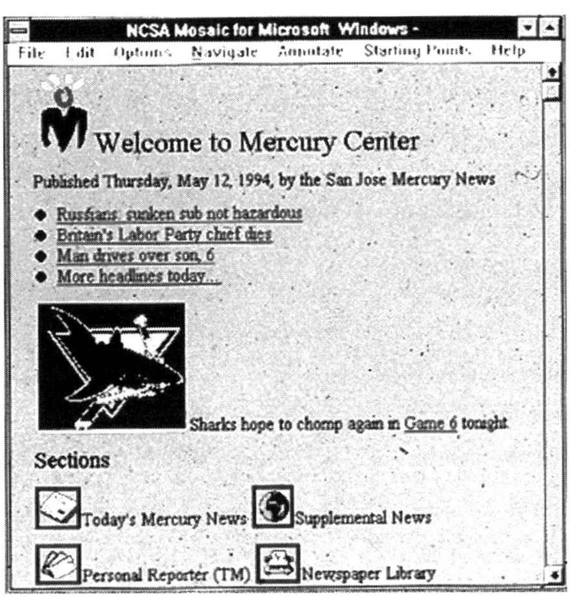

Figure 11.14 First news web page—The *San Jose Mercury News* put the first news web page online in May of 1994. While the graphics capabilities were limited, at least the entire content of the web page could be downloaded at once, unlike America Online, the dominant ISP at the time. Screenshot courtesy *San Jose Mercury News*.

working with Knight Ridder's *San Jose Mercury News*. Since the *Mercury* is located in the heart of Silicon Valley, its editors and reporters had been more aware than most of the digital revolution. They had already developed a faxed newspaper and an Internet bulletin board.

In 1994 the newspaper had a news site available through America Online, but the disadvantage was that readers had to subscribe to AOL. Also, the graphics were pre-downloaded from a disc weeks or months in advance, not from the site update. News photos could not be sent through the network.

And so, Jennewein said, developing a website was the logical next step. In fact, Knight Ridder also became one of the original investors in Netscape as Marc Andreessen and the other inventors of the Mosaic browser broke off to form their own browser company. Following the *Mercury* by early 1995 were the *Washington Post*, the *Raleigh News & Observer*, and many others.

By 1996, every major publication and broadcast network had a website. However, most of them didn't do much more than "shovel" the same news from the paper or broadcast onto their pages. A few began to innovate with interactive forums, audio, and video clips, and other services. The idea that new media could help traditional media deliver better services, faster, to a growing audience, had a general appeal but did not lead to serious investment.

5 Building the Web

5.1 When content was king

A joint partnership between NBC and Microsoft to create a new MSNBC cable channel and the msnbc.com website started off with high hopes in December 1995. But it floundered, for a time, as ratings remained low. Critics quipped that CNN and Fox were cable channels with websites, while MSNBC was a website with a cable channel. The website/cable channel idea was based on the widely accepted idea, best articulated by Bill Gates, that "content is king." This means that quality programming is what both viewers and Internet users want, and therefore the future of the Internet would be in combined efforts with traditional content producing media. Introducing the Microsoft–NBC partnership, Gates said:

> Content is where I expect much of the real money will be made on the Internet, just as it was in broadcasting. The television revolution that began half a century ago spawned a number of industries, including the manufacturing of TV sets, but the long-term winners were those who used the medium to deliver information and entertainment …
>
> The Internet also allows information to be distributed worldwide at basically zero marginal cost to the publisher. Opportunities are remarkable … For example, the television network NBC and Microsoft recently agreed to enter the interactive news business together. Our companies will jointly own a cable news network, MSNBC, and an interactive news service on the Internet. NBC will maintain editorial control over the joint venture …

The idea that "content is king" was also the underlying rationale in the high-stakes bet on a partnership between America Online and Time Warner CNN. In 2000, the stock value of AOL had inflated to the point where it was used to buy Time Warner CNN, then one of the word's largest media content companies and owner of Warner Brothers studio, Cable News Network (CNN), and the *Time* publishing empire. It was the largest merger in business history, as noted above.

The "content is king" idea was really an endorsement of the "top-down" media structure at a time when a grass-roots media revolution was just beginning to sprout. Instead of merely watching TV over the Internet, people wanted a more interactive approach to going online.

5.2 Browsers and search engines

When the World Wide Web became widely available to consumers in the mid-1990s, a dozen browsers were available: among them were Opera, Arachne, Cyberdog, HotJava, Lotus, and the popular Mosaic. After Marc Andreessen left the University of Illinois, he founded Netscape Corp. with venture capital expert Jim Clark in 1994. Netscape's Navigator browser became the most popular on the web in the mid-1990s, but trouble was on the horizon.

Microsoft licensed Mosaic from the University of Illinois in 1995 and released their version of it as Internet Explorer 1.0 with the first Microsoft Windows operating system. Microsoft's browser caught up with Netscape around 1998 and took about two-thirds of the market by 2000. Finding it difficult to compete, Netscape was acquired by America Online (AOL) in 1998, and the browser software code was released to the Mozilla Foundation, which opened the code to all programmers.

Microsoft's Internet Explorer was widely used because it was bundled with Microsoft Windows. Even though Microsoft gave Explorer away, a complex new twist on century-old anti-trust laws against "tying" and "refusal to deal" became evident. With around 90 percent of all computer system software, Microsoft was already a monopoly in fact. By tying of products together, Microsoft allegedly violated antitrust laws. Another serious allegation involved Microsoft's alleged altering of application programming interfaces (APIs) to favor Internet Explorer over other web browsers when used with Microsoft's system software. This was seen as a "refusal to deal," similar to the way newspapers once refused to carry radio ads in the 1950s (as noted in Chapter 3).

The US Justice Department sued Microsoft in 1998, alleging that the company abused its monopoly power, but the department dropped most of the lawsuit when the Republican administration of George W. Bush took office in 2001. A similar lawsuit was settled in Europe. Meanwhile, the Mozilla Foundation took Netscape's basic code and, through the open-source process, created the Thunderbird and Firefox browsers in 2004.

The overall problem, according to some observers, was that Microsoft was composed of technological idealists who were slow to appreciate the political implications of some of its technology decisions (Auletta 2010). The lesson for large engineering-oriented companies was that they could find that they had overstepped legal or ethical boundaries without always knowing how serious those boundaries had been when applied to traditional media.

The story of the most popular search engine of the twenty-first century, so far, goes back to 1996 when a pair of young Stanford University computer students, Larry Page and Sergey Brin, started research on the link structure of the World Wide Web. By 1998, their research had become Google, a new kind of web browser. At the time, most web searches were based on the number of times the search term was found on a web page, and it was easy to optimize web pages for searches by simply repeating the terms over and over again (often this would be done in hidden meta tags).

Another approach was to see how often a web page was linked from another web page. These links were in effect votes by other users for the content of the web page, Page and Brin realized. By creating a map of weblinks, they created the basis of a new kind of search engine that would be more likely to turn up useful information than competing search engines. Also at the time, other search engines like Yahoo and Ask Jeeves were positioned as " portals" to the web. Their strategy was to be "sticky," to slow users down so they would find other items of interest (and advertising) on the way to getting the information they were looking for. Google, with a rapidly responding, light-graphics front end, was designed to speed users on their way to the pages they wanted to find.

By the second decade of the twenty-first century, Google was by far the world's leading search engine with one million servers in data centers around the world, over a billion

Figure 11.15 Google founders—Sergey Brin and Larry Page were interested in mapping the web as a Stanford University graduate project in computer engineering when they realized that their web maps provided a better basis for a search engine than others already on the market. Photo by Joi Ito, Creative Commons.

hits per day, and two-thirds of US search engine traffic. The Google phenomena includes dozens of other products, such as YouTube, and auxiliary services such as translation and collaborative documents that can be shared.

Google also developed the Chrome browser which, by 2015, knocked Microsoft's Internet Explorer and Firefox out of the market (GlobalStats 2015). Google's $66 billion dollar income in 2014 came mostly from advertisers who want to reach people already in the market. For example, retailers can advertise on search pages that come up for people who are looking for specific products. The entire process is automatic through Google Ad Sense. There are no advertising salesman, no middle-men, no contracts.

"There are sound reasons for traditional media to fear Google," said Ken Auletta in his book about Google. "Today, Google's software initiatives encroach on every media industry from telephone to television to advertising to newspapers to magazines to book publishers to Hollywood studios to digital companies like Microsoft, Amazon, Apple and eBay" (Auletta 2010). By 2015, Google's web browser, Chrome, had 50 percent of the market, with Microsoft's Internet Explorer and Mozilla's Firefox down to about 20 percent each.

6 The Free Web

6.1 Communications Decency Act

The idea that the web would become just another channel for externally generated content was not what many of the original visionaries had in mind. They wanted a more inclusive future, and they disagreed with the idea of a marriage between the Internet and traditional media.

They also strongly disagreed with government regulation that became law in the 1996 Telecommunications Act, especially the portion called the Communications Decency Act (CDA), which attempted to impose heavy content restrictions on indecent language and images on the Internet and web. Under the law, the word "breast" could have been illegal, even if it referred to cancer research, while other potentially indecent words and ideas could have also been criminalized.

Reacting to the restrictive vision inherent in the CDA, John Perry Barlow, a Grateful Dead lyricist and one of the founders of the Electronic Frontier Foundation, wrote "A Declaration of the Independence of Cyberspace":

> Governments of the Industrial World, you weary giants of flesh and steel, I come from Cyberspace, the new home of Mind. On behalf of the future, I ask you of the past to leave us alone. You are not welcome among us. You have no sovereignty where we gather. We have no elected government, nor are we likely to have one, so I address you with no greater authority than that with which liberty itself always speaks. I declare the global social space we are building to be naturally independent of the tyrannies you seek to impose on us. You have no moral right to rule us nor do you possess any methods of enforcement we have true reason to fear …

Barlow's argument for free speech on the Internet and web struck a strong chord, and many others joined him to argue for unrestrained freedom of speech on the internet for a variety of reasons. For example, in court testimony about the value of internet freedom, Howard Rheingold noted the importance of virtual communities to people who felt socially isolated by their values or orientations. "If you were, for example, a gay teenager in a small town who felt that maybe you were the only person in the world who had certain feelings … [You would be among] a number of people like that who are at risk of suicide and depression." Heavy regulation of the Internet would mean that, "they might be unable to participate in discussions with others who might be able to tell them that they're not alone" (Rheingold 1996).

Others noted that the rationale for government regulation was quite different from broadcasting. The structure of broadcasting, and the allocation of radio and television channels, needs to be done by government in the public interest because the electromagnetic spectrum is a limited public resource (as we have seen in Chapter 8). Given this scarcity argument, the rationale for content regulation is that children may inadvertently be exposed to obscenity and indecency because there are so few channels. On the other hand, there is no particular physical limit to the size of the Internet, nor any particular need to regulate its structure or content.

In 1997, the US Supreme Court endorsed the idea of free speech and struck down portions of the CDA in the *Reno v. ACLU* case. The court said:

> Unlike the conditions that prevailed when Congress first authorized regulation of the broadcast spectrum [for radio and television], the Internet can hardly be considered a "scarce" expressive commodity. It provides relatively unlimited, low cost capacity for communication of all kinds. Through the use of chat rooms, any person with a phone line can become a town crier with a voice that resonates farther than it could from any soapbox. Through the use of Web pages, mail exploders, and newsgroups, the same individual can become a pamphleteer …

Figure 11.16 Independence in cyberspace—John Perry Barlow, lyricist for the Grateful Dead music group, wrote a widely circulated call for independence in cyberspace as a reaction to congressional attempts to control internet content in the 1996 Communications Decency Act. Photo by Joi Ito, Creative Commons.

The result was that the Internet and web in the US was considered to be protected media under the First Amendment, like print, which meant that they were free and open to nearly all content, like print, photography, and film media, and not regulated by a federal agency, like radio and television.

Part of the CDA that did stand up to court scrutiny involved liability for defamation and copyright violations. Internet Service Providers (ISPs), the court said, would not be held responsible for defamatory statements (libel) and copyright violations made by others who were simply using the ISP as a common carrier.

6.2 The free software movement

Computer hackers of the 1970s and 1980s were noted both for their idealism and their anti-authoritarian culture. One important idea was that digital media had unique characteristics, and trying to make it follow old media rules would just hold it back. "Information wants to be free" was the motto; working together on information software was their obsession.

In the words of free software advocate Richard Stallman:

> The copyright system grew up with printing—a technology for mass-production copying. Copyright fit in well with this technology because it restricted only the mass producers of copies. It did not take freedom away from readers of books. An ordinary reader, who did not own a printing press, could copy books only with pen and ink, and few readers were sued for that. Digital technology is more flexible than the printing press: when information has digital form, you can easily copy it to share it with others. This very flexibility makes a bad fit with a system like copyright. That's the reason for the increasingly nasty and draconian measures now used to enforce software copyright. (Stallman 1994)

Figure 11.17 Free software advocate—Some of the most important network and system software has emerged from the free software movement led by Richard Stallman, a leader of the hacker culture and a programmer who worked on artificial intelligence at MIT. Stallman also urged Wikipedia founders Jimmy Wales and Larry Sanger to try an open encyclopedia. Photo by Sam Williams, from the O'Reilly book *Free as in Freedom: Richard Stallman's Crusade for Free Software*. Creative Commons.

The idea of open-source software may seem idealistic and far-fetched at first, since it lacks even the most rudimentary business model. And yet, some of the most important software applications in computing—for instance, the Unix operating system, the Apache web server, and the Mozilla (Firefox) browser—have been based on the open source concept. Unix, the application at the base of most mainframe computers—along with Apple system 10, Linux, and others—was developed at the University of California, Berkeley, by Bill Joy, Kevin Thompson, and others in the 1970s and 1980s. The important contribution was not just the software, according to tech writer and historian Andrew Leonard. "It was the way Berkeley created software," he said. A core group would coordinate the contributions of a far-flung network of hackers, creating a template for open-source software development. "The Berkeley hackers set up a system for creating free software," he said (Leonard 2000).

This was the same approach taken in the mid-1990s when the web started outgrowing the NCSA/Mosaic web. A group of developers around the San Francisco Bay area formed a group to patch the NCSA web server software, and the original name, "A patchy" sever, quickly evolved into Apache. Today the software is used by at least 50 percent of web servers, leading Microsoft and other proprietary software systems. It was developed using the same open-source approach. Apache developers said, "We believe the tools of online publishing should be in the hands of everyone … We realize that it is often seen as an economic advantage for one company to 'own' a market … This is typically done by 'owning' the protocols through which [software] companies conduct business, at the expense of all those other companies. To the extent that the protocols of the World Wide Web remain 'un-owned' by a single company, the Web will remain a level playing field for companies large and small."

The Free Software Foundation, founded in 1985, continues to advocate free software, free media formats, the GNU system, and open "general public license," also known as "copyleft." It also organizes activist campaigns against what it sees as threats to user freedom in traditional computer operating systems and digital rights management of eBooks and movies.

"The free software movement is one of the most successful social movements to emerge in the past twenty-five years, driven by a worldwide community of ethical programmers dedicated to the cause of freedom and sharing … and teaching … about the danger of a society losing control over its computing" (Brown 2010). Not surprisingly, the Free Software Foundation is frequently at odds with the Business Software Alliance, which represents Microsoft, IBM, Dell, and other electronics firms in large-scale networking standards issues.

6.3 SOPA and Internet protests

In 2012, a Texas congressman proposed a bill called the Stop Online Piracy Act (SOPA) that would have granted far-reaching powers to government agencies in order to fight online copyright piracy. A similar bill, the Protect IP Act, or PIPA, was introduced in the US Senate. Infringing websites and domain names could be quickly banned and blocked from the Internet, and this, proponents said, would provide a better intellectual property environment for writing, research, products, and services. Many of the proponents were from the same Hollywood interests that had long opposed video recording technologies and demanded heavy penalties for minor copyright infringements.

Free speech advocates reacted with alarm. They saw SOPA as a way to close down entire domains due to minor or supposed infringements. They also feared copyright "enforcement" behind the scenes for things that had nothing to do with copyright.

"Imagine if the U.K. created a blacklist of American newspapers that its courts found violated celebrities' privacy," said tech blogger Jerry Brito. "What if France blocked American sites it believed contained hate speech?"

Legal experts and other free speech advocates from around the world also weighed in. As the uproar grew in January 2012, Google, Wikipedia, and thousands of other websites shut down in protest for a day, and the SOPA bill was withdrawn.

The lesson, said Jimmy Wales of Wikipedia in a *Washington Post* opinion piece, is simple: while giant technology companies continue to consolidate their influence over the world wide web, advocates of freedom have to speak out.

Figure 11.18 GNU—Logo of the free software movement. Creative Commons.

7 Net Neutrality, International Net Justice

7.1 Common carriers

Under many ancient laws, anyone who carried trade goods by sea or land was responsible for their safe arrival. A similar principle is found in European common laws, stretching back many centuries, in which all members of the public were entitled to the services of anyone who carried goods in wagons or barges, or who kept an inn, or who practiced an expert trade. For example, a blacksmith could not turn away a traveler whose horse had lost a shoe, even if he didn't like the traveler's religion or politics. The law required anyone whose profession served the public to serve the entire public (Speta 2002).

In the United States, regulation of railroads, telegraph, and telephone in the late nineteenth and early twentieth centuries was based on the "public nature and obligations of the carrier, and the right of the people, through the Governmental authority, to have a voice in the management of a corporation which performs a public function" (Cullom 1886). This obligation held not only for monopolies but also as part of the corporate obligation to the general public interest (Speta 2002).

The 1934 Federal Communications Act reinforced the obligations of telecommunications companies to serve without discrimination when it came to simply carrying the signal from one customer to another. There was no confusion with that principle for over sixty years. However, when the Internet and web started to become available to the average person, Congress passed the Telecommunications Act of 1996 with the idea of opening up a variety of markets to competition in areas ranging from value-added network services to content creation. Companies like Verizon that were providing a neutral "common carrier" telephone service were encouraged to invest in all kinds of content-related businesses that would be separate from their status as common carriers.

But the question concerning net neutrality is how far into network services the common carrier obligations extend. Could Verizon legally block content from sites it does not prefer, or slow the delivery speed (throttle back) content from providers who did not pay what Verizon demanded? According to some tech analysts, this was already happening, as Verizon took advantage of the 2014 ruling and slowed down Netflix and other services (Fung 2014).

Internet Service Providers (ISPs) already benefit from common carrier status in many respects. They are not responsible for libel, obscenity, threats, copyright violations, or invasions of privacy from third parties, that is, people who don't work for Verizon or the recipients of the content. (These benefits come from the "Good Samaritan" section of the Communications Decency Act and from the Digital Millennium Copyright Act.)

Advocates of the net neutrality approach include computer and web innovators Vint Cerf, Tim Berners-Lee, and Reed Hastings, along with Netflix, Vimeo, the Electronic Frontier Foundation, and many others who want a free and open internet. Opponents of the idea include the telecommunications and cable companies like Verizon and the cable industry. The telecommunications industry says that government regulation will stifle competition and prevent profit-making that is needed for infrastructure.

What the telephone and cable companies would like to do, argues Michael Wolff, is return to the days of near-monopoly media, when broadcasters and publishers enjoyed large profits because demand for information and entertainment far exceeded supply. "The social and commercial advantage here was in having extremely profitable businesses that could make big investments in content and maintain a stable media world," Wolff said. "The disadvantage for consumers was that the menu was limited. The disadvantage for upstart companies was that it was hard to break into this closed world" (Wolff 2014).

Verizon won the first round in 2014, in the *Verizon Communications v. FCC* case, when a federal court said that broadband was not originally regulated like a common carrier, and therefore most net neutrality regulations were not applicable. But net neutrality advocates won an important February 2015 ruling by the FCC that placed broadband Internet services into the common carrier category. "The Internet is simply too important to allow broadband providers to be the ones making the rules," FCC Commissioner Tom Wheeler said prior to the vote.

7.2 International net justice

A long time ago, when the Internet was very young, one guy in an office in southern California assigned all the Internet domain names and numbers. Things started getting pretty busy for computer science researcher Jon Postel around 1996, and in 1998, the US Department of Commerce created the Internet Corporation for Assigned Names and Numbers (ICANN).

The original domain names were based on organizations initially setting up Internet services. These included: com, net, org, edu, gov, and mil for (respectively) business, network, non-profits, universities, government, and military. Other domain names were given to countries, such as uk for Britain and ca for Canada.

The slow response to expanding these domain names has been one of the complaints about the US management of the global Internet. Only in 2010, for instance, were the first non-Latin alphabet scripts used for top-level domain names. So "eg" was available for Egypt, but not an Arabic lettered country code. By 2011, a much broader system was in place that allowed the equivalent of ".com" or any other domain name in most of the world's languages. This proved controversial in the US among retailers who feared that their brands and trademarks would be diluted in a global flood of domain names. A Coalition for Responsible Internet Domain Oversight (CRIDO) was organized to fight the ICANN's top-level domain international expansion, but the coalition lost the first major round in 2011. Still, it reflected a narrow and parochial view of the Internet among powerful US corporations.

"The Internet is often seen as a generous gift to the world's people, promoting free speech, free markets, and democratic values, helping to end oppression and poverty," said Richard Hill, president of a Swiss-based NGO. "Useful services and applications such as search engines, email and social networks are considered to be 'free' services ... Despite evidence to the contrary, the US takes the view that the Internet is different: it can be a competitive market and therefore should not be regulated nationally, and much less internationally. But the Internet is now dominated by a handful of mostly US-based companies (Apple, Amazon, Google, Facebook, etc), with the exception of the Chinese market where comparable home-grown companies (such as Alibaba, Baidu, Tencent) dominate domestically" (Hill 2014).

Another group, called the Just Net Coalition, issued a declaration in 2014, saying:

> Existing governance arrangements for the global Internet are inadequate. They suffer from a lack of democracy; an absence of legitimacy, accountability and transparency; excessive corporate influence and regulatory capture; and too few opportunities for effective participation by people, especially from developing countries. The situation can be remedied only through fundamental changes to the current governance arrangements.

What the international net justice advocates want is to place the global Internet under the governance of the international body that handles other international communications issues—the International Telecommunications Union (ITU) based in Geneva, Switzerland. How the ITU and the others work together with even larger issues will be considered in the next chapter.

Laws of Network Value

A "law" in economics or technology is simply a theory based on observations about repeating patterns. It's not to be confused with the kind of law made by a legislature or parliament. There are several "laws" of networks that have been warmly debated, but the recent ones show that the one-to-many relationship of the broadcaster to the audience (Sarnoff's law) is less insightful than the new ideas about relationships among computer network users in the many-to-many systems.

Sarnoff's law—David Sarnoff, the president of NBC radio and RCA from the 1920s to the 1950s, said that a broadcast network is valuable in proportion to the number of people in its audience. This "top-down" model values each individual once. A network of five would be half as valuable as a network of ten.

Metcalfe's law—Robert Metcalfe, inventor of ethernet, said the value of a network was the square of the number of users. A network of ten users would be four times more valuable than a network of five users (e.g. 5 x 5 = 25; 10 x 10 = 100).

Reed's law—David P. Reed said the value of a network doubles every time a user is added. A network of five users would have a value of 32, while a network of six users would have a proportional value of 64, and a network of ten people would have a value of 1024.

Beckstrom's law—Rod Beckstrom said the value of a network is in the way it saves on the costs of transactions. A more concrete economic law than Metcalf or Reed's laws, Beckstrom's idea is simply that the money a person saves in a network transaction is the value of that network to that person. If a book costs $25, but it can be purchased for $15 on a network, then the network is worth $10 to that person based on that one transaction. The overall value of the network is how it saves money in all transactions.

For additional reading, discussion questions, links to video, and other suggestions, see www.revolutionsincommunications.com.

12

Global Culture

> As man advances in civilization, and small tribes are united into larger communities, the simplest reason would tell each individual that he ought to extend his social instincts and sympathies to all the members of the same nation, though personally unknown to him. This point being once reached, there is only an artificial barrier to prevent his sympathies extending to the men of all nations and races.
>
> Charles Darwin, 1871

> Choosing a world that favors connection over disconnection is a set of political battles, large and small, fought everywhere from the scale of national politics to the decisions we make as individuals when we open our web browsers.
>
> Ethan Zucherman, 2013

Two decades into the twenty-first century, the digital media revolution was well under way, destroying the barriers of time and space, creating major shifts in media structures, and sparking dramatic social change. For the first time in human history, computer networks allowed billions of people to communicate across national boundaries, instantly, at no cost, in any media format—from text to video—with the help of instant translation technologies.

Through global media culture, information about an earthquake in Asia, violence in Africa, or a protest in Latin America could be shared instantly and with little effort. People were exchanging the best in art, cinema, music, and literature. They were finding a million ways to share the human experience. Collaborations in education, health, culture, environment, and trade sprang up across the world. Social media included networking, user generated content, trading and marketing, and gaming experiences (Van Dijck 2013). The sympathies of all people were extending to all nations and races, just as Darwin predicted. In all of human history, the prospects for peace and understanding were never brighter.

Yet if global culture was a blessing, it could sometimes be a curse. Virtually every sort of business and communication function around the planet was disrupted in one way or another, and often sooner rather than later. Some of the effects were almost trivial: existing hotels and taxi companies didn't much like new sharing technologies like Lyft and Airbnb. Some were difficult, such as exchanges of personal privacy for social capital, or the collapse of old media business models.

Some of the effects seemed almost apocalyptic, such as the information wars between conflicting ideologies in the Middle East, where, in one of history's most macabre ironies, the terrorists who wanted to return the world to a medieval mindset had themselves become adept at twenty-first-century video sharing of gruesome public executions.

Ideas about how to regulate the new global media environment proved contentious, as Europe and the US championed individual rights while others saw more reason for concern about collective rights and defense of cultures. And yet, despite vast differences in outlook, a permanent international dialogue on communication rights, involving both the powerful and the disenfranchised, was underway by the second decade of the twenty-first century.

1 Collaborations

One of the most important things that new media enhance is online collaboration between groups of people working at the same time on larger projects. Call it the "wikipedia effect," or the application of "cognitive surplus," or perhaps a new moment in the sun for civic technology, this new media capability is among the most profound impacts on the culture. Writers, musicians, artists, software designers, and others can now work together on projects no matter where they live or what their daily schedules.

1.1 An encyclopedia for the global village

The basic idea of an encyclopedia has always been revolutionary. Not only does it codify general knowledge, but more importantly, it reorganizes our worldviews, and helps us re-examine how we know what we know.

The first encyclopedia, organized and edited by French philosopher Denis Diderot in 1751, was written with this reorganization in mind, and it set the stage for the European Enlightenment. "The Encyclopedia was virtually a protest against the old organization, no less than against the old doctrine," said historian John Morley more than a century ago. "Broadly stated, the great central moral of it all was this: that human nature is good, that the world is capable of being made a desirable abiding-place, and that the evil of the world is the fruit of bad education and bad institutions" (Morley 1905).

The English-language *Encyclopedia Britannica* was first published in 1768, and went through fifteen printed editions until the final 2010 edition with about 40,000 articles. The *EB* still exists in online editions, with perhaps 120,000 articles.

Another type of revolutionary encyclopedia that reorganized worldviews called the *Whole Earth Catalog* arrived in 1968. Publisher Stuart Brand's idea was to provide "access to tools" and help the reader "find his own inspiration, shape his own environment, and share his adventure with whoever is interested" (*WEC*, 2015).

1.1.1 Wikipedia

There has never been anything quite so revolutionary as the digital collaborative encyclopedia known as Wikipedia, founded in 2001 by a group of web entrepreneurs led by economist Jimmy Wales and epistemologist Lawrence Sanger. By 2015, Wikipedia had over 4.7 million articles in English, and 34 million in 288 other languages, according to Wikipedia. This is 100 times more than the 32-volume, 15th edition of the *Encyclopedia Britannica*.

Figure 12.1 Encyclopedic entrepreneur—What started as a use of new media to simplify communications among scholars turned into a collaborative encyclopedia where users and readers would make the contributions. According to co-founder Jimmy Wales, no one thought it would amount to much more than an experiment at first, but Wikipedia's volunteer spirit has made it the sixth most popular website in the world, with over 35 million articles (4.8 million in English) by 2015. Photo by Manuel Archain, Creative Commons.

The story behind the phenomena is that Wales and Sanger were putting together an encyclopedia for the web called "Nupedia" in 2000 when the dot-com bubble burst, dashing their hopes for a paying project. Nupedia wasn't a wiki. In fact, contributors had to qualify by faxing in their diplomas, and their articles had to go through a seven-stage review process.

"As you might expect, it was a complete failure," Wales said. However, a side project that was originally meant to help Nupedia, an open wiki site, was attracting some interest. So, with encouragement from Richard Stallman, Wales and Sanger decided that if Nupedia wasn't going to attract investment during the dot-com bust, they would focus on the open source side. They had been watching the growth of the open source software movement, Wales noted, so they decided to take a similar approach, to remove the barriers and to see what would happen (Blodget 2010).

Over the long term, Wales and the Wikimedia Foundation hope to create a free encyclopedia that can be accessed by every person on earth in every language. "It means a lot more than just building a cool website," Wales said. "We're really interested in all the issues of the digital divide poverty worldwide, empowering people everywhere to have the information that they need to make good decisions."

"We Are the Media," Wales said. This of course contrasts rather directly with Marshall McLuhan's deterministic aphorism, "The Medium is the Message," and gives a sense of the extent to which social construction is the key approach in creating popular global media. But who are "we?" As historian Jose Van Dijck has noted, Wikipedia aims for objectivity and neutrality, but its officials are not elected. Some people dislike its non-democratic socio-technical control, but others appreciate the openness to many contributions, and the transparency about each entry on associated pages (Van Dijck 2013).

1.1.2 Origin of wiki software

A wiki is an application that allows many users to create and edit pages on a website through their browser windows. Software designer Ward Cunningham from Portland, Oregon, came up with the first wiki in 1995 as a way for lots of people to contribute to a software repository. He picked the word "wiki" as the Hawaiian language word for "fast," and the idea was that a wiki could be a quick and simple way for many people to make changes on web pages (Leuf 2001). Wiki software is unusual in that it provides a single-step process for creating branched, indexed, footnoted information structures.

Small-scale collaborative wikis proved useful for software designers and businesses, but they did not seem useful for bigger projects at first, since wide open editing could undermine a website. That openness would seem to be the last thing you might want for an encyclopedia, which is supposed to be a well-vetted reference guide produced by experts. "One of the most important keys to success," Wales observed, "is to genuinely trust people, and give them the tools to do things they are proud of."

Other approaches to creating a common record have sprung up in the wake of Wikipedia, for example in wiki-map sites, political wikis, health wikis, cookbooks, game wikis, and many more. There are also collaborative sites where musicians in different locations can record separate tracks to a song that can then be put together in one place.

1.1.3 The Wikipedia effect

Why would people want to pitch in to create a definitive world encyclopedia, without any thought of reward? That mystery has been called the "Wikipedia effect" and it's a useful form of crowd psychology. We usually think of crowd psychology as negative, but there is also a strongly positive side, argues James Surowiecki in *The Wisdom of Crowds*. A diverse collection of independent-minded people is likely to make certain types of decisions better than the experts (Surowiecki 2004). Similarly, in *Smart Mobs*, Howard Rheingold noted that new digital technologies could help people assemble quickly to get things done (Rheingold 2002). And media theorist Clay Shirkey has argued that the Wikipedia effect is an example of people using their free time constructively, using a "cognitive surplus" to accomplish larger things (Shirkey 2010).

The question of accuracy comes up frequently with Wikipedia. One 2005 study published in *Nature*, a scientific magazine, asked experts to review forty-two articles in both Wikipedia and *Encyclopedia Britannica*. In both encyclopedias, four serious errors were found in each group, while Wikipedia had 32 percent more minor errors or omissions than *Britannica* (Giles 2005). The editors of *Britannica* disputed the findings, especially the conclusion that the accuracy rates were close (*Encyclopedia Britannica*, 2006). In response, Wikipedia noted that its open digital technology makes it possible to quickly correct errors as well as make them.

One major Wikipedia error involved a biographical entry for journalist and *USA Today* editor John Seigenthaler. The entry falsely alleged that he had been involved in a plot to assassinate US President John F. Kennedy and his brother Robert Kennedy in the 1960s.

The information had been planted by a malicious prankster and stayed in place for four months. Seigenthaler saw it as an example of the weakness in the system. "I had heard for weeks from teachers, journalists and historians about 'the wonderful world of Wikipedia,' where millions of people worldwide visit daily for quick reference 'facts,' composed and posted by people with no special expertise or knowledge—and sometimes by people with malice … We live in a universe of new media with phenomenal opportunities for worldwide communications and research—but populated by volunteer vandals with poison pen intellects" (Seigenthaler 2005).

In response, Wikipedia required registration for page edits on controversial topics and reinforced its civic technology framework to catch errors. Wikipedia's technology now makes it possible for flagging and corrections to be made more quickly. The idea is not that errors will be prevented, but rather, that when they occur, they can be reported and repaired as part of the collaboration between readers and editors.

1.2 WikiLeaks: Secrets of the global village

In 2006, the success of Wikipedia and the versatile wiki software led Julian Assange and other journalists to open what was, in effect, a global drop box for "leaks" (anonymous disclosures) of business and governmental secrets. Leaks to the press have been common for as long as there has been a press, and the new technology was not initially seen as anything revolutionary. The idea was to protect whistleblowers and leakers from retaliation by the government and the theme was a continuation of the sorts of labor and public interest press that had been at work since at least the English Civil War (Assange 2011).

WikiLeaks quickly made a name for itself by leaking information about offshore banking, oil industry scandals, illegal toxic waste dumping, and the secrets of Scientology. In November 2011, WikiLeaks published the first 200 of over 250,000 secret diplomatic cables leaked from the US military by Pvt. Chelsea Manning. Most world governments, including China, the United States, and European nations, took serious steps to close down access to WikiLeaks. Overt pressure on web hosts and covert attacks by data intelligence companies were among these steps.

The WikiLeaks disclosures tended to be embarrassing rather than threatening, and free speech advocates wondered why government reactions were so punitive. "This is the first time we have seen an attempt at the international community level to censor a website dedicated to the principle of transparency," said global press freedom group Reporters Sans Frontiers. "We are shocked to find countries such as France and the United States suddenly bringing their policies on freedom of expression into line with those of China" (Apps 2010).

Despite its usual defense of Internet freedom, the response of the United States to WikiLeaks was widely seen as contrary to its own traditions. American courts have long prevented the government from censoring similar leaks of classified information to major media, for example in the Pentagon Papers case of 1971, *United States v. New York Times*. In that instance, a secret history of the Vietnam War could not be repressed by the government, the courts ruled, merely because it was embarrassing.

Similar cases, such as the courts' refusal to allow former president Teddy Roosevelt to sue Joseph Pulitzer's *New York World* in 1909, are found throughout US history. The standard for prior restraint censorship has been the prevention of "imminent" violence. None of the leaked documents directly advocated violence. WikiLeaks editor Julian Assange even insisted that his organization worked to corroborate all of the leaked documents and that they offered to work with the United States government to edit materials that could harm individuals. But still, Assange became a hunted man. Following a set of charges in the US and Sweden—charges which supporters say were trumped-up—Assange found asylum in the Ecuadorian embassy in London.

While the leaks were not supposed to provoke violence, rioting and military coups took place across the Middle East and North Africa between 2011 and 2012 during the "Arab Spring." The first riots broke out when the leaked cables showed corruption around former Tunesian president Zine El Abidine Ben Ali and his wife's family in 2011. "In one incident of corruption revealed by WikiLeaks, the son-in-law of the president purchased a 17 percent share of a bank just before it was to be privatized and then sold the shares at a premium," said economics professor Basel Saleh. The protests that followed the revelations drove Ben Ali from office (Saleh 2011).

Figure 12.2 WikiLeaks editor—Julian Assange, editor of the WikiLeaks whistleblower website, was both reviled and praised for enabling the release of hundreds of thousands of secret diplomatic cables that triggered popular revolts in the Middle East starting in 2011. When a variety of private web providers refused to host WikiLeaks, open-access advocates began disseminating the documents across a wide spectrum of the Internet in what was described as the outbreak of an "information war." Assange also faced a wide range of retaliatory legal charges as a result of the release. Photo by Espen Moe, Creative Commons.

The WikiLeaks Arab Spring revelations of 2011–12 were overshadowed in 2013 by disclosures from a US intelligence analyst, Edward Snowden. Most alarming was evidence that after the 2001 terrorist attacks, the US government began wholesale monitoring of telephone, internet, banking, and location records of most of the world's population. These wholesale invasions of privacy not only help track down actual terrorists, but also provide detailed information about the lives of people who clearly were not terrorists. Even online games like World of Warcraft were being monitored by the spy agencies.

The information gleaned by the US government provides political leverage over nearly anyone and any country whose interests may not align exactly with those of the US. The combined effects of the WikiLeaks and Snowden revelations have been to seriously damage the original argument that internet structures, such as the Internet Corporation for Assigned Names and Numbers, are best located in United States due to its high standards for protecting freedom of speech.

1.3 Collaborative journalism

If collaborations of cognitive surplus can work for encyclopedias and investigations, wouldn't that approach work for news organizations? So far, there's not enough experience to answer that question one way or the other.

Originally, the hope for digital news was simply that readers and viewers would have more personal choice. In his 1995 book, *Being Digital*, MIT Media Lab director Nicholas Negroponte said it would be possible to produce a "Daily Me" sort of newspaper where a personal agenda would guide the use of top-down information. In a non-structured sort of way, that has already taken place.

What no one anticipated was that greater efficiencies in news distribution and advertising would rapidly crash the old penny-press business model, cutting revenues by more than half and putting more than 30 percent of journalists out of work in the 2003–12 time frame (Jurkowitz 2014). And because media organizations spent virtually nothing on research when they were profitable around the turn of the twenty-first century—unlike most types of industries—only a few of the alternative business models have had even the most cursory trials. Most media organizations, now at greatly reduced staff levels, have been left guessing as to their next best moves.

The model for collaborative journalism still assumes that some sort of editorial infrastructure remains in place to guide development, just as Wikipedia has dozens of professional editors and programmers along with thousands of volunteers. These positions are crowd-funded through appeals on Wikipedia, which is similar to the telethon approach used by public radio stations. Some argue that because news about public issues is a public good that cannot be captured in the marketplace, then government should fund public media more (McChesney 2010).

"Public goods need to be supported by public funds," said Craig Aaron. Publicly funded media like PBS and NPR are needed because the market failure leads to an externalities and public goods problem. "Positive externalities are values created by a product that are difficult for the private producers of those products to capture in a transaction. Since journalism, accountability and the general consciousness of accurate information are all benefits to society that cannot be captured, or monetized, the private sector does not invest sufficiently to produce them, and society is denied their value" (Aaron 2011). As compelling as these arguments may be, powerful forces have been working to shut down public media, and expanding it is an uphill battle.

"How can strong independent journalism thrive when independent outlets can't afford to pay reporters, writers or producers a living wage?" asks journalist Bill Moyers. "A free press … doesn't operate for free at all. Fearless journalism requires a steady stream of independent income" (Moyers 2015).

Experiments in citizen journalism range from automatic blog sites for all subscribers to non-journalism volunteers recording civic meetings to student and journalism school supported projects. Most of these have been short lived, and none have discovered a new business model.

One possibility involves member-supported cooperatives. In Berlin, Germany, a daily newspaper named *Taz.de* organized a member cooperative in 1992 to capitalize its building and infrastructure. Then it rewarded members by providing volume discounts for consumer items like books, bicycles, and coffee to members. Similar proposals on a smaller scale, involving service to community groups, have been made in the US.

In Manila, Philippines, journalists are using social media to fight corruption. "We're living through a time of creative destruction, and it will get worse if you hold on to the past," said Maria A. Ressa of Rappler.com. "There is a bright side. Technology gives journalists new power. Instead of fearing the dramatic shifts in our industry, we celebrate it because it provides new ways of solving age-old problems that allow journalists to go far beyond storytelling. In a country like the Philippines, where institutions are weak and corruption is endemic, we can capture the zeitgeist of a frustrated society, push action and help build institutions bottom-up." Rappler has four main initiatives linked to crowd-sourcing and social media: (1) BudgetWatch: How can we stop corruption? (2) ProjectAgos: Climate change adaptation; (3) HungerProject; and (4) WhipIt, dealing with women's rights.

Meanwhile, at the *New York Times*, someone leaked an anemic document called the "NYT Innovation Report"—an action plan for the future. Noting a drop from 150 million web page views per year in 2011 to 80 million in 2013, the *Times* planned to enlist readers as loyalists. For the most part, the focus was on promotion, packaging, and using the existing resources to maximum commercial effect. Despite its many accomplishments, and the goodwill built up over many decades of journalistic service, the idea of innovation at the *Times* boiled down to self-promotion. It was not their finest hour.

"Face facts," said Jason Stverak in an *Online Journalism Review* article. "Traditional media have put journalism last for at least a decade, cutting thousands of jobs and [then] wondering why readers, viewers and listeners flee." America lost a generation of professional journalists, Stverak said, and that is a serious threat to self-government. "How will we replace them?" (Stverak 2010).

Some are wary of the concept of citizen journalism. "As a bit of a reality check, when was the last time you encountered a 'citizen doctor' … took off in a plane flown by a 'citizen pilot' or saw justice meted out by a 'citizen policeman'?" asked James Farmer in an article in *The Age*, an Australian newspaper (Farmer 2006).

Actually, it's not hard to find free clinics, amateur pilots, and neighborhood watch programs. All of these reflect a changing relationship between the public and professionals who find it harder to remain cloistered. Although medicine and piloting require licenses and performance to professional standards, the media is (and should be) far different. People from all walks of life can write, perform music, shoot film, record sports games, and program computers at a professional level without having to work for professional pay. They're often called "Pro-Ams" or professional amateurs (Leadbeater 2004).

In the end, what the new media needs to find is a working business model that continues momentum up through Lippmann's four stages of the media. As noted in Chapter 3, these are: (1) Totalitarian; (2) Partisan (e.g., Republican/Democrat); (3) Commercial—Penny Press; (4) Organized Intelligence. Some news organizations have regressed into the partisan model, but others, with imagination, will find a way to approach organized intelligence on behalf of the public interest.

2 Conversations in the Global Village

2.1 Facebook and MySpace

Before the era of web applications, a "face book" was a reverse yearbook with the photos, names, majors, and home towns of incoming university freshmen. The idea was to help them get accustomed to their new university homes and introduce them to the campus and to each other. When universities starting putting their "face books" online, entrepreneurs saw a chance to do the same on a popular level. SixDegrees and SocialNet were among the first in the 1990s, but both were ahead of the market. When computer programmers Jonathan Abrams and Chris Emmanuel founded Friendster in 2002, the name was a take-off on the music-sharing site Napster. A year later, a group working in the same company as Friendster founded another social networking site called MySpace.

Users who joined these sites would be able to post pictures and videos and comments and just statements about how they were feeling today or what music they liked best. The postings would be read by anyone who was a friend of the poster.

MySpace was the leading social media site at first, and at its peak around 2009 had 95 million users and $12 billion in value. It looked like an attractive investment to Rupert Murdoch, head of Fox News and its parent company, and it was purchased for $580 million in July 2005.

Facebook was founded by a Harvard student named Mark Zuckerberg whose first foray into social media was a "hot or not" ranking system for photos of female Harvard students. The crude sexist joke was not appreciated, and the university called him on the carpet for unauthorized use of the photos. In 2004, Zuckerberg dropped out of Harvard to create "thefacebook.com." Like Google, Facebook did not try to capitalize immediately with heavy advertising that would slow down the functions of the site.

Facebook also allowed third-party programmers to create applications, while MySpace kept all its programming work in house. MySpace also had relatively poor technical performance.

As of 2015, Facebook has about 1.4 billion users and is the second most visited website in the world, after Google, according to web metrics company Alexa. MySpace is down to less than one million and was purchased for $35 million in 2013.

Controversy and lawsuits surrounding the creation and success of Facebook were partly described in a 2010 movie called *The Social Network*. Questions about privacy policies for Facebook and other social media sites have also been raised by groups like the Electronic

Privacy Information Center. It's not likely that Facebook will always dominate the market for social networking software. One question is whether the way users value a network can peak and then decline if the network's size or complexity makes it too unwieldy. So far, Facebook hasn't faced that dilemma.

Figure 12.3 Social media mogul—Mark Zuckerberg and three other Harvard students started Facebook in 2004 and expanded it as social media became increasingly useful. By 2015, Facebook had 1.44 billion users. Photo by Guillaume Paumier, guillaumepaumier.com, CC-BY, 2011, Creative Commons.

In April of 2015, Zuckerberg and Facebook introduced a global plan to provide free access for billions of people to a site called "Internet.org." Telecommunications companies such as Nokia, Ericsson, Qualcomm, and Samsung are collaborating on the project, which provides access to free basic services such as health, education, and news. Others are skeptical.

"Internet.org's goals are based on a real problem: the digital divide," said David Bogado of the Electronic Frontier Foundation. But the effort is being structured so that poor people will have free access only to parts of the Internet approved by corporations and governments. "Internet.org users will be cut off from the 'ocean' of the Internet," Bogado said, and will be confined to a "fishbowl" Internet.

Net neutrality supporters in India and Brazil have petitioned telecom companies to give up on the plan, pointing out the controversial nature of closed-off systems. But Zuckerberg and Facebook say that privacy rights will be respected and that simple services are all that is needed for an on-ramp to the Internet.

2.2 Twitter: The bulletin board, and pillory, of the global village

If the "Wikipedia effect" of volunteering to write encyclopedia articles seems mysterious, consider the "culture of generosity" sometimes found within the Twitter universe. Twitter was originally a way for programmers to catch up with each other in the mad hacking environment of Silicon Valley, where it was typical to work for forty hours straight followed by a few days off.

In this environment, employees at Odeo, a start-up search engine for audio and video, were finding it difficult to plan meetings in 2006. They could text each other by phone, but that became confusing when more than a few people were involved. So they created a mini-blog where someone could post a short text message and anyone in a small group "following" that person could read it, either on the website or on a cell phone (Israel 2009).

Twitter was originally named twttr, a take-off on Flickr, the name of a photo-sharing website. An interesting feature of Twitter, according to writer Shel Israel, is the "culture of generosity" among its users. Twitter has been useful in situations ranging from life-threatening emergencies to simply chatting about the best restaurants in town, but in many cases, the willingness to share and to experience community seemed to be a hallmark of Twitter users, Israel said in his book *Twitterville* (Israel 2009).

Twitter took off in 2007 when it proved useful at several conferences, notably the South by Southwest conference held every year in Austin, Texas. People in crowds found it easy to assemble small groups and compare notes with Twitter, and since the application was free, and easily used on any cell phone or digital assistant, its use quickly expanded at these conferences

By early 2010, over 50 million Twitter messages (tweets) were being posted daily. Five years later, by 2015, this grew to 340 million, and Twitter was the world's eighth largest web application. Once again, an accidental discovery paved the way for a communications innovation.

Controversies about Twitter don't involve the company so much as what users do with its product. For example, in 2013, Justine Sacco, the public relations director of a charity, sent out a Twitter joke saying that she wouldn't have to worry about AIDs because she was white. Although in poor taste, Sacco faced a very public shaming and immediate firing from her job, just because of her Twitter post. Thousands of "tweets" from people far outside her immediate network responded to her joke with comments like: "disgusting racist tweet." The furor was not just a reaction to her apparent racism, joke or not, but also a very public form of shaming. So many other Twitter controversies have come up that Wikipedia has created a page just for them.

The use of media for shaming is hardly new. It was typical in Soviet Russia when individuals exceeded their ration allowance or got caught jumping a subway turnstile. One woman was depicted with a pig's body in a Moscow newspaper after trying to save a few rubles in the subway. But the controversy died down after a few weeks. Tweets and web postings, on the other hand, can live forever.

The point is not that the culture of generosity has instead become a culture of shaming. Rather, both of these social activities, and many more, are elevated, amplified, and preserved in the digital amber of the global village.

3 Yard Sales in the Global Village

3.1 eBay and Craigslist

The world's largest garage sale is an online auction site founded by Pierre Omidyar, a computer programmer who worked at an Apple Computer subsidiary in San Jose, California. He was inspired to write the basic code for what was first called AuctionWeb over a long weekend in 1995. According to some accounts, the first item sold on eBay was an apparently useless broken laser pointer at the price of $14.83. Worried about the transaction, Omidyar emailed the buyer to explain that the pointer was broken. But the buyer explained that he wanted it—he collected broken laser pointers.

The incident amazed Omidyar, who realized that millions of collectors were waiting for a service that would help them buy and sell their particular obsessions. In 1997, with an infusion of venture capital, the site's name was changed to eBay. Like Amazon or Netflix, eBay is a "long tail" marketing service, but with the difference that sales do not move from a central point to outlying buyers, but rather can be made between individuals across the network. Both buyers and sellers register products, negotiate bids, and finalize sales through the site. By 2009, eBay was grossing nearly $9 billion in revenue per year and operating in thirty nations.

The sophisticated eBay operation stands in sharp contrast to a website known as Craigslist, which receives a similar number of unique web visitors but operates on a minimalist non-profit basis. Craig Newmark started Craigslist the same year as eBay, in 1995. An iconoclastic San Francisco programmer, Newmark began a free email list service in 1995 that featured local events, and a year later, wrote code to turn the emails into a web page. Within fifteen years, Craigslist had become the world's leading site for what newspapers once called classified advertising: cars, pets, real estate, and other items for sale. Most of these can be advertised for free on Craigslist. The organization's relatively low revenue stream comes from fees to post "help wanted" ads in major cities. With personals and discussion forums, Craigslist also qualifies as a social media site.

Figure 12.4 eBay founder—Peter Omidyar, founder of eBay, 2007. Photo by Joi Ito, Creative Commons.

Craigslist is perhaps the main reason for the precipitous drop in newspaper classified advertising revenue in the early twenty-first century. Newmark is not apologetic about his role in undermining newspaper publishing. He distrusts journalists and says that badly informed reporting led to the war in Iraq (Usborne 2005). Ordinary people are "ready to take over the newsroom," he says, although at this point, Newmark has only gotten as far as the classified advertising department.

With sites for 570 cities in fifty countries, Craigslist is by far the largest job and community bulletin board in the world. But the site is prone to spam and uses a minimalist design reminiscent of the earliest web pages. Despite profits that probably range into the hundreds of millions per year, Craigslist has a light management style with only thirty-two employees (in contrast, eBay has 15,000 employees). *Wired* magazine called it the "tragedy of Craigslist," equating the site's somewhat chaotic state with the "tragedy of the commons," a bio-ethical concept about overuse of common resources (Wolf 2009). But Newmark's idea of a social service is to connect people and then step back. He doesn't want 15,000 employees. Perhaps the interesting thing about the new digital media is that both eBay and Craigslist auction sites are thriving, despite radically different approaches to business, with respective ranks of 8th and 12th in the US, and 18th and 62nd worldwide (Alexa 2015).

3.2 The sharing economy and disruptive technologies

One of the hallmarks of a new media technology is the potential for disruptive impacts in unexpected areas. Sometimes crowd-sourced services can generate fights even with such mundane businesses as taxi and hotel companies, as new information services redistribute buyers and sellers in new areas.

While private car and apartment sharing are nothing new, wholesale disruption of the old markets means that millions of people can access private resources as public services. The old public services—such as hotel and taxi companies—are not happy because the new services mean that unregulated, unlicensed, and unqualified businesses are now competing for their customers.

Bed and Breakfast (B&B) establishments used to be known as guesthouses

Figure 12.5 Craigslist creator—Craig Newmark, founder of Craigslist, is proud to be providing a free service even if it has cut into newspaper advertising revenues. The site, running on twenty-first-century servers in over 700 cities worldwide, has retained its 1990s design and its 1960s peace logo. Photo by Gene X Hwang, Orange Photography, San Francisco.

or boarding houses. Typically they would offer overnight accommodation and a breakfast, but no other meals. They are usually operated by someone who has an extra room or two and could use some extra income from travelers. The travelers benefit because the B&B is less expensive than a hotel.

So when Brian Chesky and a group of friends started Airbnb.com in 2008, the website offered (for a small commission) to match travelers and those who had extra accommodation, which could be a bargain for both sides. By 2014, the company had 800,00 listings all around the world, and was valued at $10 billion. Some have called it an example of collaborative consumption, but others say it violates rules designed to protect consumers. And, according to critics who built a site called InsideAirbnb.com, the company is helping people keep housing off the market through short-term low-cost leasing. "Airbnb has permeated New York City's housing market and its impact has been parasitic," said Murray Cox, an independent digital storyteller and community activist.

A similar sort of controversy hit the shared ride services Uber (founded in 2009 as a limousine service) and Lyft (founded in 2012). Both were started as ride-sharing services, a way for people who had extra seats for their commute to share with others. But eventually, both grew into businesses for a largely unlicensed group of freelance drivers who work for cash. Regular taxi companies, which are required to have licenses and driver training, have cried foul. California state prosecutors have filed lawsuits over some of the activities of the crowd-sourced ride-sharing companies, and state regulatory agencies are trying to balance innovation against regulation.

3.3 Tethered apps and generative technologies

One of the most important shifts in the digital world has been the move from the wide-open web to semi-closed platforms that use the Internet and web like the airwaves and a television set. It's top-down media driven primarily by the rise of the iPhone model of mobile computing.

According to law professor Jonathan Zittrain, digital technologies came into the market while they were still incomplete, leaving open the potential for further improvements. That was the only way they could compete with the big computer and media companies. The Unix/GNU operating system and Apache server software are examples of collaborative

Figure 12.6 Free culture advocates—Jonathan Zittrain and Lawrence Lessig, both professors at Harvard University Law School, question the way copyright and communications law often stifles creativity and freedom. Photo by Andrew Feinberg, Capitol Valley Media, Creative Commons.

open system approaches. The more these applications spread, the more they improved, until a virtuous circle pushed them from the creative margins into the mainstream.

"This is the story of the PC against information appliances, and it is the story of the Internet against the proprietary networks," Zittrain said. It's a legacy that Zittrain and others hope can be kept alive, a social construction of technology that is quite different from the static and deterministic corporate model.

What worries Zittrain is a new generation of "tethered" one-way information appliances, such as the Apple iPad, iPhone, and other mobile units. "The iPhone is sterile," Zittrain said. "Rather than a platform that invites innovation, the iPhone comes preprogrammed. You are not allowed to add programs to the all-in-one device that Steve Jobs sells you. Its functionality is locked in" (Zittrain 2010).

At one point, former Apple CEO Steve Jobs said his intent was to move beyond the PC market long dominated by rival Microsoft. That has been accomplished, now that Apple is at least twice as big as Microsoft. "The iPad is clearly going to affect notebook computers," he said. "This is a new model of computing."

Traditional media hope that it is a new business model for professionally produced top-down media as well. *Wired* magazine's editor Chris Anderson sees the "app" economy helping to build value for publishers. "You can retain everything that makes the magazine great and then add these new things: the videos, the animations, the interactivity, a social media layer," Anderson said. "You can have more pages, and little things people don't think about—the idea of a jump page makes no sense in an app. A lot of the bugs in the linear medium get sort of fixed now in a two-dimensional or three-dimensional medium like the iPad" (Anderson 2010).

The financial side of top down media is also attractive. "You can only make money with scarcity," Anderson said. "In the 20th century, that scarcity was printing plants and trucks and crazed oligopolies over the powers of distribution. The rise of the specialized devices in the app economy is a way to ... raise the barrier to entry, to create scarcity, both by taking content off and also more production going into the content you put on."

Traditional media enthusiasm for the "app" economy waned slightly in February 2011 when Apple announced highly restrictive rules governing the use of their mobile technologies. Apple said it would allow publishers like the *New York Times* and *Washington Post* to charge for their subscriptions to their "apps" for the iPad, but only after Apple took a 30 percent share. News organizations would not be able to refer customers directly to their advertisers, nor would they know who their subscribers were (Kane 2011). This did not make publishers happy. Meanwhile, Google announced a 10 percent no-strings-attached deal, while electronics companies like Samsung, Motorola, and Sony moved quickly to market pads using the open Android operating system developed by Google in 2005 (Tsukayama 2011).

By 2015, the digital revolution seemed to be moving in two technical directions. On the one hand, open source civic technologies had already shown that new digital media could be socially constructed in ways never before imagined. On the other hand, traditional media was re-bundling content in dedicated mobile "apps" with information appliances like the iPad. The new apps business model would (theoretically) encourage more professional content and restore some profitability for top-down professional information. Both approaches will probably coexist in the new media of the twenty-first century, but it is important to ensure that top-down media do not drown out civic media.

3.4 The long tail of the web

One of the most significant innovations that the World Wide Web makes possible is a way to serve special needs and niche markets. This is known as "long-tail marketing," a concept that can be applied to mass media, products, services, and social networks.

Long-tail marketing is more or less the opposite of mass marketing or mass media. In order to appeal to a mass market, the most popular 20 percent of items must be available in volume to the buying public. For a retail bookstore, this can mean stocking the shelves with best-sellers and popular books but not serving smaller niche markets.

Two important examples of successful long-tail marketing in mass media are Amazon.com and Netflix. Jeff Bezos, a financial analyst who left his job with just an idea of an online book company, started Amazon.com in 1994 at a time when selling books through the web was difficult. "Investors thought he was crazy," said a *Time* magazine profile (Ramo 1999). By 2014, Amazon revenue was $89 billion.

Figure 12.7 Amazon Books founder—Jeff Bezos founded Amazon.com online bookstore as an early test of "long-tail" marketing to serve large numbers of small niche markets. Photo by James Duncan Davidson/O'Reilly Media, Inc., 2005, Creative Commons.

A similar long-tail venture was started by Reed Hastings, a computer engineer who left the Marines for the Peace Corps. Hastings founded Netflix in 1997 after being laid off from his job and worrying about overdue fees at a local video store. By 2013 the company was bringing in $4.37 billion in revenue and providing an on-demand video movie service that had become a threat to the major cable providers.

While niche marketing is nothing new, the Internet presents new kinds of opportunities for people who see the potential. Chris Anderson, editor for *Wired* magazine, sees the future of business in long-tail marketing through the Internet since the volume of all the low popularity items can be greater than volume of highly popular items (Anderson 2008).

4 Communication Rights in the Global Village

The digital revolution's most contentious issue involves individual rights to freedom of expression within and across national boundaries. To understand these issues, we consider, first, the original principles of international law; then, the historical expectation that new media technologies would enhance freedom; next, some of the issue areas in free speech such as religious and political speech across borders; and finally, international conventions on communications rights and responsibilities.

When we speak about communication rights, it's important to distinguish between typical real-world constraints on expression and those in cyberspace. Social norms, commercial markets, and basic architecture are also factors.

Take unwanted email solicitations—spam—for example. In the non-digital world, a commercial solicitation has to go through a post office and must pass through advertising regulation; it can't be socially outrageous; it costs money to send, so it has to have some potential value to the sender; and it's easy for the recipient to deal with because it only arrives once a day. The digital equivalent, emailed spam, has little regulation, no social constraints, is sent without cost, and arrives constantly through an architecture that is governed by computer code.

Figure 12.8 Netflix founder—Reed Hastings got tired of driving videos back to the store late at night to avoid late fees. He founded Netflix in 1997 as a way to exchange DVDs through the mail, and later developed a streaming video service. Photo by James Duncan Davidson/O'Reilly Media, Inc., 2005, Creative Commons.

Law professor Lawrence Lessig argues that in the case of spam and other free speech issues, the key to good policy is a balance of constraints, not a single silver bullet. "We choose how we want to treat [values] in cyberspace," he says. So, continuing with the example of spam, the aim should be to allow the receiver to regulate the way he or she wants to communicate about commercial propositions in a content-neutral manner.

Political speech is far more difficult. Since World War II, Lessig argues, the United States has insisted on the First Amendment as the approach to international communication:

> Many have criticized this conception: Some found it too extreme, others not extreme enough. Repressive regimes—China, North Korea—rejected it directly; tolerant regimes—France, Hungary—complained of cultural decay; egalitarian regimes—the Scandinavian countries—puzzled over how we could think of ourselves as free when only the rich can speak and pornography is repressed. This debate has gone on at the political level for a long time. (Lessig 2006)

In addition, European nations regulate the kind of "hate speech" that would be legally permitted, if socially and commercially discouraged, in the United States under the First Amendment. When it comes to television, many countries control the percentage of US programming that can be shown, and they also insist on programs produced in their countries during certain times of day. Arab nations are particularly concerned about speech that attacks religious beliefs, and have advocated international blasphemy laws, as we will see.

In some cases these regulations are within the scope of the European Enlightenment ideals. In others they are not. But all of these areas were regulated before the digital revolution, and rarely did they create the kind of conflicts that are now seen in the early twenty-first century.

> As if under cover of night, we have now wired these nations with an architecture of communication that builds within their borders a far stronger First Amendment than our ideology ever advanced. Nations wake up to find that their telephone lines are tools of free expression, that e-mail carries news of their repression far beyond their borders, that images are no longer the monopoly of state-run television stations but can be transmitted from a simple modem. (Lessig 2006)

To understand approaches to this multifaceted problem, we turn to some of the original principles of international communication law.

4.1 Basics of international communications law

International principles of communications law are found in the United Nations Declaration of Human Rights, adopted globally in 1948. Two points apply to most of the current debates: Article 7, about freedom from discrimination, and Article 19, which is the global equivalent of the First Amendment. But individual rights may conflict with Article 29, which concerns morality and public order, sometimes called community rights.

- Article 7: "All are equal before the law and are entitled without any discrimination to equal protection of the law. All are entitled to equal protection against any discrimination in violation of this Declaration and against any incitement to such discrimination."
- Article 19: "Everyone has the right to freedom of opinion and expression; this right includes freedom to hold opinions without interference and to seek, receive and impart information and ideas through any media and regardless of frontiers."
- Article 29: "Everyone has duties to the community in which alone the free and full development of his personality is possible. In the exercise of his rights and freedoms, everyone shall be subject only to such limitations as are determined by law solely for the purpose of securing due recognition and respect for the rights and freedoms of others and of meeting the just requirements of morality, public order and the general welfare in a democratic society."

These are the bedrock principles, and it should be obvious that imposing a prison term or a death sentence for political speech is a gross violation of Article 19 and basic human rights. And yet, at the same time, social norms and concepts of morality and public order vary greatly from country to country, and are recognized in Article 29.

According to Freedom House 2015 report, the number of free countries in 2014 stood at 89, which was 46 percent of 195 nations and 40 percent of the world's population. While democracy and free speech were still on the rise, the report said that, "authoritarian regimes were beginning to abandon the quasi-democratic camouflage that allowed them to survive and prosper in the post-Cold War world." China, Cuba, Russia, most of the Middle East, and large parts of Africa are not free.

4.2 *Technologies of Freedom*

Throughout the digital revolution, the idea of liberation through technology has been an important motivating force. Vannevar Bush's 1949 argument that a Memex machine would simplify basic research is one example. We've also seen the approach to "computer liberation" by idealists like Ted Nelson in the 1970s and Steve Jobs in the 1980s. John Perry Barlow's Declaration of the Independence of Cyberspace of 1996, noted in Chapter 11, is another example.

The ideas are not unique to the digital revolution. The idea that satellite and electronic communication would have an impact on human rights was articulated by Ithiel de Sola Pool, whose 1983 book, *Technologies of Freedom*, predicted a "convergence" of electronic and print technologies in a digital sphere:

> In the coming era, the industries of print and the industries of telecommunications will no longer be kept apart by a fundamental difference in their technologies. The economic and regulatory problems of the electronic media will thus become the problems of the print media too. No longer can electronic communications be viewed as a special circumscribed case of a monopolistic and regulated communications medium which poses no danger to liberty because there still remains a large realm of unlimited freedom of expression in the print media. The issues that concern telecommunications are now becoming issues for all communications as they all become forms of electronic processing and transmission. (Pool 1983)

As technologies were converging and shrinking the world, Pool insisted that the only rational basis of a civil society was to continue expanding free speech and free press in the broadcast and digital technologies as well. It would be a "political error," he said, if free speech values did not apply to all technologies:

> Technology will not be to blame if Americans fail to encompass this system within the political tradition of free speech. On the contrary, electronic technology is conducive to freedom. The degree of diversity and plenitude of access that mature electronic technology allows far exceed what is enjoyed today. Computerized information networks of the twenty-first century need not be any less free for all to use without hindrance than was the printing press. Only political errors might make them so. (Pool 1983)

Another scholar who endorsed de Sola Poole's views at the time was Ray Kurzweil, who predicted in 1987 that that the Soviet Union "would be swept away by this growth of decentralized communication." And, in fact, the end of Russian domination of Eastern

Europe and the dismantling of the Berlin Wall in 1989 owed a great deal to changing international communications.

Looking back on that time, former Polish president Lech Walesa noted:

> Rapid development of satellite television and cell phones ... helped end communism by bringing in information from the outside. It was possible to get news from independent sources; stations like the BBC (British Broadcasting Corporation) and VOA (Voice of America) were beyond government control. During '50s and '60s, the communist government put people accused of listening to these stations in prison ... It's hard to believe that things like that actually happened from today's perspective. (Scheeres 2002)

In 2013, Kurzweil followed up with this note: "People thought it was ridiculous that this mighty nuclear superpower would be swept away by a few clandestine hackers with teletype machines, but in the 1991 coup against Gorbachev that ended the Soviet Union, that is exactly what happened." Communication empowers, Kurzweil says. "So while the world may seem chaotic, people today have far greater knowledge and power to shape events and respond to problems" (Kurzweil 2013).

John Perry Barlow's declaration of Cyberspace, in retrospect, seems focused on government regulation to the exclusion of social norms and computer code. "It's not just governments that have grown more powerful online," said author Jacob Silverman. "Companies have used the notion of an independent Internet to justify calling themselves its sovereign authorities." They may think they are handmaidens to emancipation, he says, but they are even better than governments at collecting data (Silverman 2015). Barlow, for his part, says libertarianism has taken a hit. When everything is deregulated, there is little to stop commercial powers from controlling cyberspace.

4.3 Political and religious speech in the international arena

As de Sola Pool hoped, the internet and web were afforded the highest levels of free speech protection in the US following the *Reno v. ACLU* Supreme Court decision in 1997. But how far can the US First Amendment be applied when international free speech issues emerge?

For example, during the 2012 Arab Spring, when thousands of Egyptians rioted over a US-made video that was deliberately designed to be insulting to the Islamic religion, the Obama administration said the video was an abuse of free speech. In response to the president's statement, the *Denver Post* said, "Sorry, provocative speech is not an abuse of free speech. It is precisely the speech the First Amendment exists to protect" (*Denver Post* 2012). Of course, the First Amendment applies to Americans who made the deliberately insulting video in America. But how does it apply to Egypt? The dilemma for global culture is that these issues are being judged by a variety of standards.

Some governments are defiant about the potential for liberating technologies. Take, for example, this statement by Turkish president Recep Tayyip Erdoğan: "We'll eradicate Twitter. Everyone will witness the power of the Turkish state" (Puddington 2015). Turkey is also exploiting the "war on terror" to treat journalists as "threats to national security," according to a 2014 report by Reporters Sans Frontieres. Overall, the RSF world press freedom index was only slightly higher than the year before. The usual problems with repression in China, Russia, and the Middle East were compounded by the US hunt for security leaks around the WikiLeaks and Snowden revelations (RSF 2015).

China's Internet dictatorship is, according to both Freedom House and RSF, among the world's worst. Limits to internet access and punishment for disparaging China's political leadership are endemic, and an enormous system of censorship, known as the "Great Firewall of China," exists to keep over 650 million internet users in line.

Political protests, advocacy of separation (for Tibet, for instance), any mention of the word "democracy" or "Tiananmen Square" or even "June 4, 1989" can bring anything from internet banning to a jail sentence.

For example, according to an Association Press article, Chinese blogger Shi Shusi posted a note in 2013 that simply said, "Remember June 4." Moments later, all of his posts were erased and he received a note saying that he had engaged in "inappropriate publicity" (*New York Times*, June 1, 2014).

Google has had particular problems in China. In 2000, Google began offering Chinese language web searches from its US base, but found it was being slowed or blocked at the border by the hardware and software of the "Great Firewall of China." China's use of 30,000 internet police, its blocking of "harmful" content like the words "freedom" and anti-government protests, and its imprisonment of journalists and dissidents are well known abuses of internationally guaranteed freedoms.

Deciding that it was better to engage than remain out of the picture, Google began offering search engine services through a Chinese version of Google, Google.cn, in 2006. The company was criticized in the United States and Europe for cooperating with Chinese censors but a spokesman said Google.cn was faster, more reliable, and provided better search results for all but a handful of politically sensitive subjects.

"Self-censorship, like that which we are now required to perform in China, is something that conflicts deeply with our core principles," said Google spokesman Elliot Schrage in congressional testimony. "This was not something we did enthusiastically or something that we're proud of at all" (Schrage 2006; Martin 2007).

Then in January 2010, Google said it had come under a highly sophisticated hacking attack in China and would no longer cooperate with the censors. It redirected searches to Google.hk (Hong Kong), which is part of China but under a somewhat different legal system.

China is not the only country with a "great wall" around the Internet. Many countries block websites that are deemed illegal. For example, Saudi Arabia has two firewalls, one for indecent content and the other for politically offensive content. According to an annual Reporters Without Borders report, *Enemies of the Internet,* the worst violators of freedom of expression tend to be Saudi Arabia, Burma, China, North Korea, Cuba, Egypt, Iran, Uzbekistan, Syria, Tunisia, Turkmenistan, and Vietnam.

"We are rapidly entering into a new world of hyperconnectivity," said Carl Bildtis, foreign minister of Sweden, in a July 5, 2012 *New York Times* op-ed:

> We cannot accept that the Internet's content should be limited or manipulated depending on the flavor-of-the-month of political leaders. Only by securing access to the open and global Internet will true development take place. The governments of the Human Rights Council now for the first time have confirmed that freedom of expression applies fully to the Internet. A global coalition for a global and open Internet has been formed ... The challenge now is to put these words into action to make sure that people all over the world can use and utilize the power of connectivity without having to fear for their safety. This work is far from over.

4.3.1 Religious traditions and freedom of expression

Until the late twentieth century, it would have been almost impossible for people in the Middle East to be exposed to sacrilegious cartoons in European magazines. But increased global commerce, satellite communications, and, in recent decades, Internet and web communications have brought the world's religious cultures into an uncomfortable proximity. Despite the goodwill created by increased communication between the cultures, points of friction also stand out:

- In 1988, Salmon Rushdie, a British-Indian novelist and essayist, was sentenced to death in absentia for his book *The Satanic Verses*, which contained a storyline that many Muslims believed was blasphemous. Rushdie went into hiding to avoid assassination, and controversy continues to swirl around the sentence.
- In September of 2005, a Danish newspaper, *Jyllands-Posten*, printed editorial cartoons depicting the Islamic prophet Muhammad in an unfavorable light. The cartoons led to riots that left more than 100 people dead in Pakistan and other parts of the Middle East. In 2010, five men were arrested while beginning to carry out an attack on the building.
- As noted above, in July 2012, violent protests with over fifty deaths took place in Egypt and other Muslim nations in response to a fictional narrative video entitled *The Innocence of Muslims*, which associated the prophet Mohammed with wrongdoing. The American producer was found guilty of fraud and jailed for a year and put on probation for four more years, but the conviction had nothing to do with the actual content of the video, which was still available on YouTube as this book went to press in 2015.
- On January 7, 2015, two members of al-Qaeda killed fifteen journalists and police officers in the Paris offices of *Charlie Hebdo*, a satirical weekly magazine known for crude humor aimed at almost everyone, including people of the Muslim faith. One lamentably crude cartoon, for example, depicts the head of a Moslem emerging from the rear end of an Islamic cleric with the title "Where Moslems come from." Ironically, this same theme, under the heading of "where priests come from," was employed in an equally crude engraving distributed by Protestants in the 1500s.

Leaders of Muslim, Christian, Jewish, and other faith traditions expressed shock and dismay over all of these incidents. The Organization of Islamic Cooperation, a major voice for the world's 1.4 billion Muslims, has repeatedly condemned incidents of terrorism like the *Charlie*

Hebdo attack. "Such acts of terror only represent the criminal perpetrators … Violence and radicalism [are], indeed, the biggest enemies of Islam and [go] against all its fundamental principles and values" (OIC 2015). These voices of tolerance are far stronger in Arab culture, and not heard often enough in the West, argues Marc Lynch in Foreign Policy (Lynch 2012).

What can be done? One answer, according to the OIC, involves laws against blasphemy, which used to be in force in Europe and the US as recently as sixty years ago and are still on the books in thirty-three countries (including twenty-one Muslim majority nations). For years the OIC has asked the United Nations to consider non-binding resolutions along those lines.

Most of the international diplomatic debate has taken place around the International Convention on the Elimination of All Forms of Racial Discrimination (ICERD), a treaty convention established in January 1969. Within this context, disparagement of Moslems and Islam has been the basis of OIC resolutions.

But enforcing a United Nations resolution against religious discrimination is not a realistic option for Western democracies since freedom of religious expression has long been held as a fundamental freedom in the West. After all, Victor Hugo depicted the Catholic Church in the worst possible light in *The Hunchback of Notre Dame* in 1831. So did Martin Luther in his Theses in 1518. Europe and the Americas have a long tradition of religious criticism, and it's understood that this is not about to change. As the Center for Law and Democracy said in a recent paper:

> There have been numerous academic attempts to distinguish hate speech from merely offensive speech. One line of reasoning, which is helpful at least conceptually, is to distinguish between expression targeting ideas, including offensive expression, which is protected, and abusive expression which targets human beings, which may not be protected. In … [one European case] the European Court of Human Rights seemed to support this approach, holding that the impugned speech was not a gratuitous attack on religion but, rather, part of a clash of ideas ("débat d'idées"). (Mendel 2010)

4.4 International communications commissions

Although the US and Europe are hardly perfect, it has been clear all along that they will not compromise on any international agreement that curtails basic human rights and free expression within their own borders or in cyberspace. But this doesn't mean there is no room for discussion.

Global communication issues need to be discussed, and it's important to note in this context that laws protecting freedom of speech can differ from country to country. Not all the world needs, or must have, a US First Amendment, or is happy with the ways that US law support US business. For example, hate speech and fascist symbols are illegal in Europe but legal in the US, since the theory is that the best remedy for bad speech is good speech. The US is different in other ways, too. Copyright punishments are far more draconian in the US than in the rest of the world. US laws restrict foreign content in US broadcast networks, but Hollywood studios complain about restrictions on US television programs that can be used in European and African television networks.

So at some point, a more global perspective is needed. That was the idea that Jean D'Arcy, director of the UN radio and TV services, had in 1969 when he suggested that the right to communicate was inherent in the UN Declaration of Human Rights. The idea was taken up by policy analysts and academics and became part of the Communication Rights in the Information Society (CRIS) campaign.

The CRIS group saw many problems in the concentration of media ownership, the flow of news and what was called "cultural imperialism," that is, the domination of less developed cultures by cinema, TV, and news services from powerful nations.

The problems were part of the global division between the rich "north" and the poor "south," but in the 1970s and 1980s, the debate was sidetracked into a Cold War confrontation between the US on the one hand and the USSR (Russia) and China on the other. The real North–South problems involve structural concerns as well as protections for content, and these are seen very differently in different parts of the world.

This is one of the main points made in the 1980 report *Many Voices, One World*, by the Commission on International Communication for the United Nations Educational, Scientific and Cultural Organization (UNESCO) chaired by Nobel Laureate Seán MacBride. The commission said that the unequal flow of global communication was making developing nations dependent on the industrial West. Centuries-old customs, time-honored cultural practices, and simpler lifestyles were being threatened.

At the same time, the industrial nations were not making an effort to understand the rest of the world. News about the developing world in North America and Europe was dominated by spot reports on disasters and military coups, but the underlying realities and developments were being ignored. As a result, Americans and Europeans were developing a cartoon version of the world that had little to do with global realities.

Many of the recommendations were not controversial. There was a need for more professional international training for journalists on both sides of the North–South divide. Other recommendation involved protection of journalists and freedom of the press. Another recommendations included that small nations should foster internal media development, have more control over the cultural processes of modernization, and find ways to reduce the commercialization of communication. These recommendations amounted to an international theory of social responsibility for the media—a Hutchins Commission report on a global scale.

But the recommendations, and subsequent proposals for a New World Information and Communication Order, were seen at the time as opening the door to increased media regulation by non-democratic nations, especially in the Soviet bloc, and the International Federation of Newspaper Publishers (FIEJ), among others, issued strong denunciations of the NWICO. The US and Britain withdrew from UNESCO in protest in 1984 and 1985 (although they later rejoined in 2003 and 1997, respectively).

Although not successful in bridging some of the gaps, the MacBride report's authors "had the foresight to hope for a kind of 'globalization' that, rather than signify divisions among citizens of the world, acknowledged our common humanity," said Andrew Calabrese in a 25th anniversary article on the report. "With all of its flaws, for which progressive communication activists understandably have distanced themselves over the past twenty-five years, the MacBride Report projects a spirit of hopefulness about how a better world is possible, [and] about the continued importance of public institutions as means to ensure global justice" (Calabrese 2005).

4.4.1 Discussing the future of global communication

New technologies spurred United Nations ITU officials to propose a World Summit on the Information Society, and meetings took place in 2003 and 2005 in Geneva and Tunis. While 175 countries and thousands of people took part, the summits did little more than point up major disagreements in world communication policy.

Governments were not even able to agree that the Universal Declaration of Human Rights would be the basis of a summit declaration. Nor could they agree on the demand that ICANN (the Internet Corporation for Assigned Names and Numbers) be removed from US jurisdiction to an international body like the ITU, which already coordinates broadcast frequency allocation and technical standards. In addition, the summit at Tunis was badly marred by attacks on journalists and refusals to include some organizations critical of the human rights records of China and other countries.

But the summit did agree on the creation of an Internet Governance Forum, a multi-stakeholder forum for policy discussion on issues like domain names, Internet security, copyright, and development issues. In 2014, the IGF proposed a NetMundial Initiative that would place ICANN under international control, although some nations such as Russia, China, Iran, and India want to exercise their own control over domain names and protocols rather than leave it to an international body. Opponents of the idea, both in the US and in the international arena, fear that this will make it even easier for totalitarian states to control their areas of the Internet. The proposal seemed destined for a stalemate for the foreseeable future.

In the end, harmonization of communications law between various systems does not mean forcing the same laws on every country, but rather, reducing the differences and creating minimum standards. Given the enormous differences between political and cultural systems in the world, the current potential to minimize conflict and bridge cultures seems small compared to the potential to generate conflict. And yet, there is reason for optimism.

"We can build new tools that help us understand whose voices we're hearing and whom we are ignoring," said Ethan Zuckerman in a 2013 book, *Rewire*. "We can make it easier to understand conversations in other languages, and to collaborate with people in other nations ... We can build a network that helps us discover, understand, and embrace a wider world. We can, and we must, rewire" (Zuckerman 2013).

The point has been widely acknowledged for many decades. "The future of the new democracies will depend in part on the development and strengthening of free, independent and pluralist media in both the public and private sectors," said UNESCO Director Federico Mayor in 1997 (Demers 2007).

5 Conclusion

In the early twentieth century, W. E. B. Du Bois predicted that the problem of the twentieth century would be the problem of the "color line," which is to say, the sharp distinction between races (Du Bois, 1903). At the dawn of the twenty-first century, the problem and opportunity seems to be the blurring of lines and distances that once separated entire cultures around the world.

In that light, it's useful to recall the principles that guided the mass media from its inception in early modern Europe over five centuries ago. The principles of individual freedom of expression and access to uncensored information took many generations of bitter struggle before they formed the modern bedrock of global human rights policies. These principles are found in the First Amendment to the United States Constitution, the European Convention for the Protection of Human Rights, and the United Nations Charter of Human Rights. While they are too often violated, they can never be repealed. Under democratic theory, human rights are natural rights that are not granted by governments but rather are innate in human nature. Thus, people will never stop defending and expanding their freedom, and no wholesale attempt to close down the marketplace of ideas can be rational or even effective in the long run.

The corollary to the principle of freedom of speech and press is the principle of social responsibility, as noted in the Nuremberg Principles following World War II, the Hutchins Commission in the United States in 1947, the United Nations MacBride Commission in 1980, and recent decisions by the United Nations International Court of Justice. Incitements to violence and hate speech directed against people or cultures are prime examples of a lack of social responsibility.

However, as is often the case, law and social conditions do not keep pace with technology. Whether the Internet and web will remain free and continue to be liberating technologies, despite occasional misuse, and be free to encourage social responsibility and bridges between cultures, is a question that the genius of the twenty-first century will address.

As historian Wilbur Schramm once said, language and writing were the tuition paid by humanity for its own education. By the same token, we could view mass media as the new open university of the world. Since the advent of printing, each media revolution has had enormous social impacts. The global digital revolution is a quantum leap forward into this process, and it is quite possible that humankind was not entirely prepared. But it hardly matters now. The walls are down, and this university is now wide open to both the lowest and the highest aspirations of humanity.

With the future at our feet, what will we do? With a vast new power of worldwide networking, how will we envision the future? Will we use the media to lift and protect and diversify the human spirit? What will global culture become in a decade, or a century? It's a question of social construction, not simply one of technological momentum.

The ability to shape the way technology is used, to serve the public interest, is the twenty-first century's truest badge of freedom.

For additional reading, discussion questions, links to video and other suggestions, see www.revolutionsincommunications.com.

Bibliography

For additional reading, discussion questions and suggestions for video and multimedia links, go to www.revolutionsincommunications.com

Abramowitz, Rachel. "Avatar's Animated Acting." *Los Angeles Times*, February 18, 2010.

Action for Children's Television v. FCC (*ACT × FCC*), 821 F.2d 741, 1987.

Acton, Lord. "The History of Freedom in Christianity." Address to the Bridgnorth Institute, May 28, 1877.

Acton, Lord. "A lecture on the study of history." June 11, 1895. London: MacMillan, 1895.

Adams, Henry. *Autobiography of Henry Adams*. Boston: Massachusetts Historical Society, 1917.

Adams, Samuel Hopkins. "The Great American Fraud." *Collier's Weekly*, October 7, 1905.

Aitken, Hugh. *Syntony and Spark: The Origins of Radio*. Princeton, NJ: Princeton University Press, 1992.

Alexa, "The Top 500 sites on the web." www.alexa.com (accessed February 18, 2011).

Alpert, Jesse, and Nissan Hajaj. "We Knew the Web Was Big ..." *The Official Google Blog*, 2008.

American Academy of Child and Adolescent Psychiatry. "Children and TV Violence." November 2002.

Anderson, Chris. *The Long Tail: Why the Future of Business is Selling Less of More*. New York: Hyperion, 2008.

Anderson, Chris. "How Web Video Powers Global Innovation," TED, September 2010. Available online https://www.ted.com/talks/chris-anderson-how-web-video-powers-global-innovation

Anderson, Chris and Michael Wolf. "The Web is Dead." *Wired*, August 2010.

Anderson, Kevin B. and Peter Hudis. *The Rosa Luxemburg Reader*. New York: Monthly Review, 2004.

Andreessen, Marc. Message forwarded by Tim Berners-Lee, New "XMosaic" World-Wide Web browser from NCSA, message to comp.infosystems, January 23, 1993. http://www.bio.net/bionet/mm/bio-soft/1993-February/003879.html (accessed March 17, 2015).

Apache Software Foundation. "Apache http sever project." 2010. http://httpd.apache.org/ABOUT_APACHE.html (accessed March 17, 2015).

Appel, Joseph H. "A Case Study of an Advertising Agency and Some Observations on Advertising in General." *Bulletin of the Business Historical Society* 13, no. 4. (October 1939): 49–57.

Apple, R. W. "Lessons From the Pentagon Papers." *New York Times*, June 23, 1996.

Apps, Peter. "WikiLeaks Stirs Debate on Info Revolution." *Reuters*, December 6, 2010.

Arango, Tim. "How the AOL-Time Warner Merger Went So Wrong." *New York Times*, January 10, 2010. http://www.nytimes.com/2010/01/11/business/media/11merger.html?pagewanted=all (accessed March 17, 2015).

Arthur, W. Brian. *The Nature of Technology: What It Is and How It Evolves*. New York: Free Press, 2009.

Attar, Rob. "Interview with Neil MacGregor." BBC History Extra Podcast, October 23, 2014.

Auletta, Ken. *Googled: The End of the World as We Know It*. New York: Penguin, 2010.

Australian Broadcasting Corporation (ABC). Interview with Arthur C. Clark, 1974. https://www.youtube.com/watch?v=OIRZebE8O84 (accessed March 17, 2015).

Axelrod, Toby. *Hans and Sophie Scholl: German Resisters of the White Rose*. New York: Rosen Publishing Group, 2001.

Bacevich, Andrew. "The Golden Age of Special Operations," Moyers & Company, May 29, 2012. Available online http://billmoyers.com/2012/05/29/the-golden-age-of-special-operations/

Baker, Carlos. *Hemingway*. Princeton, NJ: Princeton University Press, 1972.

Baker, Kevin. "Stabbed in the Back! The Past and Future of a Right-wing Myth." *Harper's Magazine*, June 2006. http://www.harpers.org/archive/2006/06/0081080 (accessed March 17, 2015).

Balboni, Philip S. "Documentary Journalism Vanishes from Network and Local Television." *Nieman Reports*. Fall, 2001.

Balio, Tino. *United Artists: The Company that Changed the Film Industry*. Madison, WI: University of Wisconsin Press, 1987.

Barbrook, Richard. *Imaginary Futures*. London: Pluto Press, 2007. http://www.imaginaryfutures.net/book/ (accessed March 17, 2015).

Barnouw, Eric. *The Image Empire: A History of Broadcasting in the United States*. New York: Oxford University Press, 1970.

Baudrillard, Jean. *The Illusion of the End*. Palo Alto, CA: Stanford University Press, 1994.

Bawker, R. R. "Great American Industries: A Printed Book." *Harper's Magazine*, July 1887.

Beard, Charles A., *An Economic Interpretation of the US Constitution*. New York: MacMillan Co., 1913.

Beard, Charles A. "Time, Technology, and the Creative Spirit in Political Science." *American Political Science Review* 21, no. 1 (February 1927).

Beasley, Maurine H., and Sheila J. Gibbons. *Taking Their Place: A Documentary History of Women and Journalism*. College Park, PA: Strata, 2003.

Benjamin, Walter, Michael W. Jennings, Brigid Doherty, and Thomas Y. Levin. *The Work of Art in the Age of Its Technological Reproducibility, and Other Writings on Media*. Cambridge, MA: Harvard University Press, 2008.

Bentley, L., and M. Kretschmer, eds. Court of Cassation. Supreme Court on Photography. 1863, Primary Sources on Copyright. 1450–1900). www.copyrighthistory.org (accessed May 21, 2010).

Berners-Lee, Tim, with Mark Fischetti. *Weaving the Web: The Original Design and Ultimate Destiny of the World Wide Web*. New York: Harper, 1999.

Berry, S. Torriano and Venise T. Berry. *Historical Dictionary of African American Cinema*. Lanham, MD: Scarecrow Press, 2007.

Billington, James. *Fire in the Minds of Men*. Piscataway, NJ: Transaction Press, 1999.

Black, Edwin. *IBM and the Holocaust*. New York: Time Warner Paperbacks, 2002.

Blackwood, William. "The Press." *The Times*, July 23, 1834, 7.

Blackwood, William. "The New Art of Printing." *Blackwood's Edinburgh Magazine*, January 1844, 45.

Blodget, Henry. "Interview with Jimmy Wales: How Wikipedia Became a Monster." *Business Insider*, May 3, 2010.

Blondheim, Menahem. "Rehearsal for Media Regulation: Congress versus the Telegraph-News Monopoly, 1866–1900." *Federal Communications Law Journal* 56, no. 2 (2003–4).

Blondheim, Menahem. *The Toronto School of Communication Theory: Interpretations, Extensions, Applications*. Jerusalem: Hebrew University Magnes Press, 2007.

Blumberg, Stephen J. *Wireless Substitution: Early Release of Estimates From the National Health Interview Survey, January–June 2013*. Atlanta, GA: US Centers for Disease Control, 2013.

Bly, Nelly. *Around the World in Seventy-two Days*. New York: Pictorial Weeklies, 1890a.

Bly, Nelly. *Ten Days Inside a Madhouse. New* York: Ian L. Munro, 1890b.

Bogart, Humphrey. "I'm No Communist." *Photoplay*, March 1948.

Bolter, J. David. *Turing's Man: Western Culture in the Computer Age*. Chapel Hill, NC: University of North Carolina Press, 1984.

Boorstin, Daniel J. *The Image: A Guide to Pseudo-Events in America*. New York: Harper Colophone, 1961.

Bord, Matthew de. "The Crisis in Crisis PR: Why the Dark Art is in Meltdown." *The Big Money*, July 20, 2010.

Borkin, Joseph. *The Crime and Punishment of I. G. Farben. New* York: Free Press, 1978.

Bourke-White, Margaret. "Dust Changes America," *The Nation*, May 22, 1935, 597.

Bowman, Shayne and Chris Willis. *We Media: How Audiences Are Shaping the Future of News and Information*. Reston, VA: American Press Institute, 2003.

Brecht, Martin. *Martin Luther*. Trans. James L. Schaaf. Philadelphia: Fortress Press, 1985–93, 1:204–205.

Brendon, Piers. *The Life and Death of the Press Barons*. New York: Atheneum, 1983.

Brian, Dennis. *Pulitzer: A Life*. Hoboken, NJ: John Wiley and Sons, 2001.

Bricklin, Dan. *VisiCalc: Information from its Creators, Dan Bricklin and Bob Frankston*, 2010. http://www.bricklin.com/visicalc.htm (accessed March 17, 2015).

Briggs, Asa and Peter Burke. A Social History of the Media: From Gutenburg to the Internet. Cambridge: Polity Press, 2010.

Brinkley, Alan. *The Publisher: Henry Luce and His American Century*. New York: Knopf, 2010.

British Library. *Treasures in Full, Caxton's Chaucer*. http://www.bl.uk/treasures/caxton/english.html (accessed March 17, 2015).

Bronowski, Jacob, *The Ascent of Man*. London: Random House, 1976, 198.

Brown, Horatio, *The Venetian Printing Press. An Historical Study*. New York: G. P. Putnam, 1891.

Brown, Peter. "Free Software is a Matter of Liberty, Not Price." Free Software Foundation, December 27, 2010. http://www.fsf.org/about (accessed March 17, 2015).

Brown, Robert E. and Katherine Brown. *Virginia 1705–1786: Democracy or Aristocracy?* East Lansing, MI: Michigan State University Press, 1964.

Browne, Malcolm W. "The Fighting Words of Homer Bigart: A War Correspondent Is Never a Cheerleader." *New York Times*, April 11, 1993.

Bryce, James. *Report of the Committee on Alleged German Outrages*, 1914. Originally published by the British government. http://www.gwpda.org/wwi-www/BryceReport/bryce_r.html (accessed March 17, 2015).

Bucholz, Robert O., and Newton Key. *Early Modern England 1485–1714: A Narrative History.* Hoboken, NJ: Wiley, 2009.

Burnett, James. "Stewart Closes Rally with Biting Critique of Media." *Rolling Stone*, October 30, 2010. http://www.rollingstone.com/culture/news/17389/228438 (accessed March 17, 2015).

Burrough, Bryan and John Helyar. *Barbarians at the Gate: The Rise and Fall of RJR Nabisco.* New York: Harper & Row, 1990.

Burrows, Edwin G. and Mike Wallace. *Gotham: A History of New York City to 1898.* New York: Oxford University Press, 1999.

Bush, Vannevar. "As We May Think." *Atlantic*, August 1946.

Bush, Vannevar. *Modern Arms and Free Men: A Discussion of the Role of Science in Preserving Democracy.* New York: Simon and Schuster, 1949.

Butterfield, Herbert. *The Whig Interpretation of History*. London: G. Bell, 1931.

Bytwerk, Randall L. *Julius Streicher: Nazi Editor of the Notorious Anti-Semitic Newspaper* Der Sturmer. New York: Cooper Square Press, 2001.

Calabrese, Andrew. "The MacBride Report: Its Value to a New Generation." *Quaderns del CAC* 21 (2005).

Cambeau, Don. *Modern Marvels: The Telephone*. History Channel documentary, 2006.

Campbell, Joseph. *The Hero with a Thousand Faces*. 1st edn, New York: Bollingen Foundation, 1949; 2nd edn, Princeton, NJ: Princeton University Press, 1968; 3rd edn, Novato, CA: New World Library, 2008.

Campbell, W. Joseph. *Yellow Journalism: Puncturing the Myths, Defining the Legacies*. Santa Barbara, CA: Praeger, 2003.

Campbell, W. Joseph. *Getting It Wrong*. Los Angeles, CA: University of California Press, 2010.

Cappo, Joe. *The Future of Advertising: New Media, New Clients, New Consumers in the Post-Television Age.* New York: McGraw Hill, 2005.

Carey, James W. *Communication as Culture: Essays on Media and Society.* New York: Routledge, 1992.

Carpenter, E. and M. McLuhan, eds. *Explorations in Communication: An Anthology.* Boston, MA: Beacon Press, 1960, Intro. Sec 3, xi.

Carr, David. "So Plentiful So Cheap." *New York Times*, February 7, 2010.

Cha, Ariana Eunjung. "Mobile Coupons Help Retailers Track Customers." *Washington Post*, June 27, 2010.

Chakravorti, Robi. "Marx the Journalist." *Economic and Political Weekly*, September 4, 1993, 1856–9.

Chaplin, Charlie. *My Autobiography.* New York: Simon and Schuster, 1964.

Christensen, Thomas. "Gutenberg and the Koreans: Did East Asian Printing Traditions Influence the European Renaissance?" http://www.rightreading.com/printing/gutenberg.asia/gutenberg-asia-1-introduction.htm (accessed March 17, 2015).

Clark, Stuart B. *The Sun Kings: The Unexpected Tragedy of Richard Carrington and the Tale of How Modern Astronomy Began.* Princeton, NJ: Princeton University Press, 2007.

Clifford, Stephanie. "A Fine Line When Ads and Children Mix." *New York Times*, February 14, 2010.

Conley, Scott R. "The Children's Television Act: Reasons and Practice." *Syracuse Law Review* 61, no. 1 (2010).

Conner, Clifford D. *A People's History of Science.* New York: Nation Books, 2005, 359.

Conquest, Robert. *The Great Terror: A Reassessment.* New York: Oxford University Press, 1990.

Cousins, Mark. *The Story of Film.* (DVD). Music Box Films, 2012.

Cousteau, Jacques. *The Silent World.* New York: Harper Brothers, 1953.

Cramer, Richard Ben, and Thomas Lennon. "The Battle Over Citizen Kane." *Frontline* documentary, Public Broadcasting System, 2000.

Crandol, Michael. "The History of Animation: Advantages and Disadvantages of the Studio System in the Production of an Art Form, Digital Media FX." http://www.digitalmediafx.com/Features/animationhistory.html (accessed March 17, 2010).

Creelman, James. "The Real Mr. Hearst." *Pearson's Magazine*, May 1906, 257.

Cringley, Robert X. *Accidental Empires: How the Boys of Silicon Valley Make Their Millions, Battle Foreign Competition, and Still Can't Get a Date.* New York: Harper Paperbacks, 1996.

Cronkite, Walter. "Hell 26,000 feet up." *New York Times*, February 27, 1943, 5.

Csillag, András. "Born in Hungary 160 Years Ago: Joseph Pulitzer and the Hungarians."*Americana* VI, no. 2 (Fall, 2008). http://americanaejournal.hu/vol4no2/csillag (accessed March 17, 2015).

Curtis, James. *Mind's Eye, Mind's Truth: FSA Photography Reconsidered.* Philadelphia, PA: Temple University Press, 1991.

Czitrom, Daniel. *Media and the American Mind: From Morse to McLuhan.* Chapel Hill, NC: University of North Carolina Press, 1983.

Darnton, Robert, and Daniel Roche, *Revolution in Print: The Press in France 1775–1800.* Berkeley, CA: University of California Press, 1989.

De Vinne, Theo L. *The Invention of Printing.* New York: Hart, 1878.

Demers, David. *History and Future of Mass Media: An Integrated Perspective.* Cresskill, NJ: Hampton Press, 2007.

Dentsu Information Institute. *Information Media Trends in Japan*, 2014.

Denver Post. "The Deadly Enemies of Free Speech," Editorial, September 12, 2012.

Dewar, James A. "The Information Age and the Printing Press: Looking Backward to See Ahead." Palo Alto, CA: Rand Corp., 1998. http://www.rand.org/pubs/papers/P8014.html (accessed March 17, 2015).

Dickens, A. G. *The English Reformation.* London and Glasgow: Fontana/Collins, 1978, 439–40.

Douglass, Frederick. "The Destiny of Colored Americans." *The North Star*, November 16, 1849.

Dregni, Eric, and Jonathan Dregni. *Follies of Science: 20th Century Visions of Our Fantastic Future.* Golden, CO: Speck Press, 2006.

Drout, Michael. *Rings, Swords and Monsters: Exploring Fantasy Literature.* Modern Scholar series. Prince Frederick, MD: Recorded Books, 2006.

Du Bois, W. E. B. *The Souls of Black Folks.* Chicago: A. C. McClurg, 1903.

Dunne, Finley Peter. *Observations by Mr. Dooley.* New York: R. H. Russell, 1902.

Ebert, Roger. "The Green Berets." *Chicago Sun-Times*, June 26, 1968.

Ebert, Roger. "Casablanca." *Chicago Sun-Times*, September 15, 1996.

Ebert, Roger. "Birth of a Nation." *Chicago Sun-Times*, March 30, 2003.

Editor & Publisher. "Generally Upbeat World Press Trends Report Highlights Regional Differences." *Editor & Publisher*, August 10, 2010.

Eisenstein, Elizabeth. "The Advent of Printing and the Protestant Revolt: A New Approach to the Disruption of Western Christendom," in Robert Kingdon, ed., *Transition and Revolution. Problems and Issues of European Renaissance and Reformation History.* Minneapolis, MN: Burgess Publishing Co., 1974.

Eisenstein, Elizabeth. *The Printing Press as an Agent of Change.* Cambridge: Cambridge University Press, 1980.

Eisenstein, Elizabeth. *The Printing Revolution in Early Modern Europe.* Cambridge: Cambridge University Press, 1983.

Elders, M. Joycelyn. *Preventing Tobacco Use Among Young People, Report of the Surgeon General.* US Government Printing Office, 1994.

Ellett, Ryan. "Amos 'n' Andy: The Chicago Defenders Response." *Old Time Radio Researchers,* 2010. http://otrr.org (accessed March 17, 2015).

Emery, Michael and Edwin Emery. *The Press and America: An Interpretive History of the Mass Media.* Englewood Cliffs, NJ: Prentice Hall, 1988.

Encyclopedia Britannica Inc. "Fatally Flawed: Refuting the Recent Study on Encyclopedic Accuracy by the Journal *Nature.*" *Nature,* March 2006.

Engelbart, Douglas C. *Augmenting Human Intellect: A Conceptual Framework.* SRI Summary Report AFOSR-3223, 1962. http://www.dougengelbart.org/pubs/augment-3906.html (accessed March 17, 2015).

Eyman, Scott. *The Speed of Sound: Hollywood and the Talkie Revolution, 1926–1930.* New York, Simon and Schuster, 1997.

Fallows, James. "How to Save the News." *The Atlantic,* June 2010. http://www.theatlantic.com/magazine/archive/2010/06/how-to-save-thenews/8095/1/ (accessed March 17, 2015).

Farmer, James. "Citizen Journalism Sucks." *The Age* (Melbourne, Australia), October 5, 2006.

Farnsworth, Stephen J., and S. Robert Lichter. *The Nightly News Nightmare: Television's Coverage of US Presidential Elections 1988–2004.* Lanham, MD: Rowman & Littlefield, 2007.

Febvre, Lucien and Henri-Jean Martin. *The Coming of the Book.* London: Verso, 1976.

Feldstein, Mark. "A Muckraking Model: Investigative Reporting Cycles in American History." *Harvard International Journal of Press/Politics,* Spring 2006.

Fenster, Julie M. "Inventing the Telephone—and Triggering All-Out Patent War." *American Heritage,* March 7, 2006.

Ferriman, Annabel. "Advertising Standards Authority Finds Against Nestlé." *British Medical Journal* 318.7181, February 13, 1999.

Fidler, Roger. *Mediamorphosis: Understanding New Media.* Newbery Park, CA: Pine Forge Press, 1997.

Fine, Barrett. *A Giant of the Press: Carr Van Anda.* Oakland, CA: Acme Books, 1968.

Folkerts, Jean and Dwight L. Teeter. *Voices of a Nation: A History of Mass Media in the United States.* New York, MacMillan, 1989.

Forbes, Jill and Sarah Street. *European Cinema: An Introduction.* Basingstoke: Palgrave Macmillan, 2001.

Franklin, Benjamin. "An Apology for Printers." *Pennsylvania Gazette,* June 10, 1731.

Freund, Gisele. *Photography and Society.* Boston, MA: Godine, 1980.

Friedel, Robert. *A Culture of Improvement: Technology and the Western Millennium.* Boston, MA: MIT Press, 2007.

Friedman, Jerome. "The Battle of the Frogs and Fairfold's Flies: Miracles and Popular Journalism during the English Revolution." *Sixteenth Century Journal* 23, no. 2 (1992): 419–42.

Friedman, Milton. *Capitalism and Freedom.* Chicago: University of Chicago Press, 1962.
Friedman, Thomas. *The World Is Flat: A Brief History of the Twenty-first Century.* New York: Farrar, Straux and Giroux, 2005.
Friendly, Fred. *Due to Circumstances Beyond Our Control.* New York: Random House, 1967.
Frontard, Raymond. "Standards Related Activities, The Global View," in *Friendship Among Equals.* Geneva, Switzerland: International Standards Organization, 1997. http://www.iso.org/iso/about/the_iso_story/friendship_equals.htm (accessed March 17, 2015).
Fukuyama, Francis. *The End of History and the Last Man.* New York: Free Press, 1992.
Fussel, Stephan. *Gutenburg and the Impact of Printing.* Surrey: Ashgate, 2005.
Gallup, 2015. http://www.gallup.com/poll/1654/honesty-ethics-professions.aspx (accessed March 17, 2015).
Gage, Beverly. "Terrorism and the American Experience: A State of the Field." *Journal of American History*: (June 2011) 73.
Garvin, Glen. "Walter Cronkite, 1916–2009." *Miami Herald*, July 19, 2009.
Gavin, Clark. *Famous Libel and Slander Cases of History.* New York: Collier Books, 1962.
Gates, Bill. *The Road Ahead.* New York: Viking, 1995.
Gates, Bill. "Content is King." January 3, 1996. http://www.craigbailey.net/content-is-king-by-bill-gates (accessed March 17, 2015).
Giles, Jim. "Internet Encyclopedias go Head to Head." *Nature* 438:7070, December 15, 2005, 900–1.
Gilliam, Terry. "The Ten Best Animated Films of All Time." *Guardian*, April 27, 2001.
Gilmont, Jean-Francois. *John Calvin and the Printed Book*, trans. Karin Maag. Kirksville, MO: Truman State University Press, 2005.
Ginzburg, Carlo, John Tedeschi, and Anne C. Tedeschi. *The Cheese and the Worms.* Baltimore, MD: Johns Hopkins University Press, 1992.
Gleick, James. *The Information: A History, a Theory, a Flood.* New York: Pantheon, 2011.
Godin, Seth. *Tribes: We Need You to Lead Us.* New York: Portfolio, 2008.
Goff, Leslie. "Univac Predicts Winner of 1952 Election." *CNNTech*, April 30, 1999. http: // articles.cnn.com/1999–04-30/tech/9904_30_1952.idg_1_election-returns-election-night-machine?_s=PM:TECH (accessed March 17, 2015).
Goldberg, Vicki. "Introducing the Poor to the Middle Class." *New York Times*, November 3, 1991, H35.
Goldstein, Tom, *Killing the Messenger: 100 Years of Media Criticism.* New York: Columbia University Press, 2007.
Goodman, Amy. "Media Giant John H. Johnson Paved the Way for Black-Owned Press." *Democracy Now*, August 16, 2005. http://www.democracynow.org/2005/8/16/media_giant_john_h_johnson_paved (accessed March 17, 2015).
Goodman, Amy. "The FCC & Censorship: Legendary Media Activist Everett Parker on the Revocation of WLBT's TV License in the 1960s for Shutting Out Voices of the Civil Rights Movement." *Democracy Now*, March 6, 2008. http://www.democracynow.org/2008/3/6/the_fcc_censorship_legendary_media_activist (accessed March 17, 2015).
Gordon, John Steele. "The Public Be Damned." *American Heritage* 40, no. 6 (September/October 1989).
Gosling, John. *Waging the War of the Worlds: A History of the 1938 Radio Broadcast and Resulting Panic.* Jefferson, NC: McFarland, 2009.

Gould, Jack. "TV: Topical Bonanza Racial Issue Treated on Western Series with Story of Negro Opera Singer," *New York Times*, April 27, 1964, 55.

Grabo, Carl H. "Review: A History of American Journalism." *American Journal of Sociology* 24, no. 1 (July 1918): 104–5.

Greeley, Horace. "The Philosophy of Advertising." *Merchant's Magazine and Commercial Review*, November 1, 1850, 580.

Greeley, Horace. *An Overland Journey from New York to San Francisco in the Summer of 1859*. New York: C. M. Saxton, Barker & Co., 1860.

Green, Abigail. "Intervening in the Public Sphere: German Governments and the Press, 1815–1860." *Historical Journal* 44 (2001): 155–75.

Greenberger, Martin. "The Computers of Tomorrow." *Atlantic Monthly*, May 1964.

Greenslade, Roy, "First World War: How State and Press Kept the Truth off the Front Page." *Guardian*, July 27, 2013.

Griese, Noel L. "AT&T: 1908 Origins of the Nation's Oldest Continuous Institutional Advertising Campaign." *Journal of Advertising* 6, no. 3 (Summer 1977): 18–23.

Gronow, Pekka. "The Record Industry: The Growth of a Mass Medium." *Popular Music* 3, Producers and Markets (1983).

Grunig, James. "Symmetrical Presuppositions as a Framework for Public Relations Theory," in C. H. Botan and V. Hazleton, Jr., eds., *Public Relations Theory*. Hillsdale, NJ: Lawrence Erlbaum Associates, 1989.

Guha, Ramachandra. "Gandhi the Journalist." *The Hindu*, June 8, 2003. http://www.hindu.com/thehindu/mag/2003/06/08/stories/2003060800320300.htm (accessed March 17, 2015).

Habermas, Jürgen. *The Structural Transformation of the Public Sphere*, trans. Thomas Burger. Boston, MA: MIT Press, 1991.

Halberstram, David. *The Best and the Brightest*. New York: Random House, 1973.

Halberstram, David. *The Powers That Be*. New York: Knopf, 1979.

Haley, Alex. *Roots: The Saga of an American Family*. New York: Doubleday, 1976.

Hallin, Daniel C. *The "Uncensored War": The Media and Vietnam*. New York: Oxford University Press, 1986.

Hammond, William M. *Reporting Vietnam: Media and Military at War*. Lawrence, KS: University of Kansas Press, 2007.

Hand, Richard J. *Terror on the Air!: Horror Radio in America, 1931–1952*. Jefferson, NC: Mcfarland & Company, 2006.

Hart, Roderick P., and Mary Triece, "US Presidency and Television." Museum of Broadcast Communication Encyclopedia of Television. http://www.museum.tv/debateweb/html/equalizer/essay_usprestv.htm (accessed March 17, 2015).

Hauben, Ronda. "From the ARPANET to the Internet." Online paper, Columbia University. http://www.columbia.edu/~rh120/other/tcpdigest_paper.txt (accessed March 17, 2015).

Hemingway, Ernest. *Men at War*. New York: Crown Publishers, 1942.

Herschthal, Eric. "The Other Guy with That Mustache." *Nitrateville*, July 31, 2008. http://www.nitrateville.com (accessed March 17, 2015).

Hiebert, Ray. *Courtier To the Crowd: The Story of Ivy Lee and the Development of Public Relations*. Sioux City, IO: Iowa State University Press, 1966.

Higgins, Marguerite. *Our Vietnam Nightmare*. New York: Harper & Row, 1965.

Hilmes, Michelle. *Only Connect: A Cultural History of Broadcasting in the United States. New* York: Wadsworth, 2006.

Hiltzik, Michael. *Dealers of Lightning: Xerox PARC and the Dawn of the Computer Age*. New York: Harper, 2000.

Hind, Arthur M. *A Short History of Engraving and Etching*. Boston, MA: Houghton Mifflin, 1908.

Hippler, Fritz. "Film as a Weapon." *Unser Wille und Weg* 7 (1937): 21–3. http://www.calvin.edu/academic/cas/gpa/hippler1.htm (accessed March 17, 2015). See also Fritz Hippler, Internet Movie Database. IMDb, August 2010.

Hirshberg, Peter. "On TV and the Web." *TED Talks*, 2007. http://www.ted.com/talks/peter_hirshberg_on_tv_and_the_web.html (accessed March 17, 2015).

Hoe, Robert. *A Short History of the Printing Press*. New York: Hoe, 1902.

Holt, Debra J., Pauline M. Holt, Debra M. Des Rochens, and Christopher R. Kelly. "Children's Exposure to TV Advertising in 1977 and 2004: Information for the Obesity Debate." *Federal Trade Commission*, June 1, 2007.

Holtzberg-Call, Maggie. *The Lost World of the Craft Printer*. Urbana, IL: University of Illinois Press, 1992.

Horan, James. *Mathew Brady: Historian with a Camera*. New York: Crown Publishers, 1955.

Horne, John N. and Alan Kramer. *German Atrocities, 1914: A History of Denial*. New Haven, CT: Yale University Press, 2001, Appendix I.

Horwitz, Robert B. "Broadcast Reform Revisited: Reverend Everett C. Parker and the 'Standing' Case. Office of Communication of the United Church of Christ v. Federal Communication Commission." *Communication Review* 2, no. 3 (1997).

Houseman, John. "The Men from Mars." *Harper's Magazine*, December 1948.

Howe, Daniel Walker. *What Hath God Wrought: The Transformation of America, 1815–1848*. New York: Oxford University Press, 2007.

Hudson, Frederic. *Journalism in the United States,* from *1690–1872*. New York: Harper & Brothers, 1873.

Hutchins, Robert M. Chair, the Commission on Freedom of the Press. *A Free and Responsible Press: A General Report on Mass Communication: Newspapers, Radio, Motion Pictures, Magazines, and Books*. Chicago: University of Chicago, 1947. http://www.archive.org/details/freeandresponsib029216mbp (accessed March 17, 2015).

Illinois/Inter-ocean Publishing Co. v. Associated Press, 184 Ill. 438, 1900.

Innis, Harold. *Empire and Communication*. New York: Oxford University Press, 1950, 7.

International Telecommunications Union, (ITM). *History of the ITU*, 2010. http://www.itu.int/en/history/ (accessed August 17, 2010).

Internet Advertising Bureau (IAB). "IAB Internet Advertising Report," 2010. http://www.iab.net/insights_research (accessed March 17, 2015).

Irwin, Will. "The American Newspaper." *Collier's Magazine*, January 1911. Series republished by Iowa State University, 1969.

Israel, Shel. *Twitterville*. New York: Penguin, 2009.

Jefferson, Thomas, to John Tyler, 1804. E-text, University of Virginia, ME 11:33. http://etext.virginia.edu/jefferson/quotations/jeff1600.htm (accessed March 17, 2015).

Johnson, Bradley. "Digital Media takes the jobs lead in new mainstream media." *Advertising Age*, October 31, 2011.

Johnson, Paul. *Birth of the Modern*. New York: HarperCollins, 1991.

Jung, Carl, and Marie-Luise von Franz. *Man and His Symbols*. New York: Doubleday, 1964.

Jurkowitz, Mark. "The Losses in Legacy." Pew Research Center, March 26, 2014. http://www.journalism.org/2014/03/26/the-losses-in-legacy/ (accessed May 1, 2015).

Kahn, David. *The Codebreakers: The Story of Secret Writing.* New York: Macmillan, 1967.

Kaiser, Robert G. "The Bad News about the News," *Brookings Essay*, October 16, 2014.

Kane, Yukari, and Russell Adams. "Apple Opens Door, Keeps Keys." *Wall Street Journal*, February 16, 2011.

Katz, John. "Bulletin Boards: News From Cyberspace." *Rolling Stone*, April 15, 1993, 35–77.

Kellner, Douglas. "Jean Baudrillard." *Stanford Encyclopedia of Philosophy.* (Winter 2009 edition), Edward N. Zalta. ed. http://plato.stanford.edu/archives/win2009/entries/baudrillard (accessed March 17, 2015).

Kelloway, Lucy. "BP is the Company We All Love to Hate." *Financial Times*, June 18, 2010. http://www.ft.com/cms/s/0/9c732c98-7b01-11df-8935-00144feabdc0.html (accessed March 17, 2015).

Kempton, Murray, "Return of the Luddites." *New Republic*, December 22, 1962, 6.

Kennan, George Frost. *Russia Leaves the War: Soviet–American Relations, 1917–1920.* Princeton, NJ: Princeton University Press, 1989 (1956).

Kennedy, Robert F. *Crimes Against Nature.* New York: HarperCollins, 2004.

Kershaw, Alex. *Blood and Champagne: The Life and Times of Robert Capa.* New York: St. Martins, 2002.

Kesterson, W. H. *A History of Journalism in Canada.* Ottawa: Carlton University Press, 1984.

Kielbowicz, Richard B. *News in the Mail: The Press, Post Office, and Public Information, 1700–1860s.* New York: Greenwood Press, 1989.

Kiplinger magazine, "Radio Listeners be Damned." February 1947, 7.

Klein, David, and Scott Donaton. "The Advertising Century, Advertising Age, 1999." http://adage.com/century/ (accessed March 17, 2015).

Kleiner, Art. "Telecommunicating," *Whole Earth Catalog*, Spring 1984.

Kluger, Richard. *The Paper: The Life and Death of the* New York Herald Tribune. New York: Knopf, 1986.

Knight, Charles, ed. *London.* London: Henry G. Bohn, 1851.

Knightly, Phillip. *The First Casualty: The War Correspondent as Hero and Myth-maker from the Crimea to Iraq.* Baltimore, MD: Johns Hopkins University Press, 2004.

Kochersberger, Jr., Robert C. *More than a Muckraker: Ida Tarbell's Lifetime Journalism.* Knoxville, TN: University of Tennessee Press, 1996.

Kovarik, Bill. "Publishing Technologies for Eastern Europe." Memo to the Center for Foreign Journalists, July 1990.

Kovarik, Bill. "To Avoid the Coming Storm: Hezekiah Niles Weekly Register as a Voice of North–South Moderation, 1811–1836." *American Journalism* (Summer 1992).

Kovarik, Bill. *Web Design for Mass Media.* New York: Pearson, 2001.

Kroeger, Brooke. *Nellie Bly: Daredevil, Reporter, Feminist.* New York: Three Rivers Press, 1995.

Kulash, Jr., Damian. "Whose Tube?" *New York Times*, February 19, 2010, A17.

Kulash, Jr., Damian. "OK Go on Net Neutrality: A Lesson from the Music Industry." *Washington Post*, August 29, 2010.

Kurtz, Howard. "In Lean Times, TV Reporters Must Be Jacks of All Trades." *Washington Post*, March 8, 2010.

Kurzweil, Ray. *The Singularity is Near.* New York: Viking, 2005.

Kurzweil, Ray. "Humans From Ourselves," Policy.mic, April 29, 2013. Available online https://mic.com/articles/37887/ray-kurzweil-artificial-intelligence-will-save-humans-from-ourselves

Lacy, Stephen, and Hugh J. Martin. "Profits Up, Circulation Down for Thomson Papers in 80s." *Newspaper Research Journal* 19 (1998).

Lafrance, Adrienne, "In 1858, People Said the Telegraph Was 'Too Fast for the Truth.'" *The Atlantic*, July 28, 2014.

Lange, Dorothea. "The Assignment I'll Never Forget: Migrant Mother." *Popular Photography* (February 1960).

Lanier, Jaron, *Who Owns the Future?* New York: Simon & Schuster, 2014.

Leadbeater, Charles, and Paul Miller, "The Pro-Am Revolution." *Demos*, November 24, 2004. http://www.demos.co.uk/publications/proameconomy (accessed March 17, 2015).

Leary, Kevin. "Joe Rosenthal: 1911–2006; Photo Was His Fame—His Pride 'My Marines,'" *San Francisco Chronicle*, August 21, 2006, A1.

Lee, James Melvin. *History of American Journalism.* Boston, MA: Houghton Mifflin, 1917.

Lembecke, Jerry. *Spitting Image: Myth, Memory and the Legacy of Vietnam.* New York: New York University Press, 1998.

Lenin, V. I. "Where to Begin." *Iskra* 4 (May 1901) in *Collected Works.* Trans. Joe Fineberg and George Hanna. Moscow: Foreign Language Publishing House, 1964.

Lenin, V. I. Speech at the Opening Session of the First Congress of the Communist International, March 2–6, 1919. Marxist Internet Archive. http://www.marxists.org/archive/lenin/works/1919/mar/comintern.htm (accessed August 17, 2010).

Leonard, Andrew. "BSD Unix: Power to the People, from the Code." *Salon*, May 16, 2000. http://www.salon.com/technology/fsp/2000/05/16/chapter_2_part_one (accessed March 17, 2015).

Lerner, Daniel. *The Passing of Traditional Society: Modernizing the Middle East.* New York: Free Press, 1958.

Lessig, Lawrence. *Free Culture: The Nature and Future of Creativity.* London: Penguin, 2005. See also TED 2007 talk: "Larry Lessig on laws that choke creativity." http://www.ted.com/talks/larry_lessig_says_the_law_is_strangling_creativity.html (accessed March 17, 2015).

Lester, Paul Martin, ed. *Images That Injure: Pictorial Stereotypes in the Media.* New York: Praeger, 1996.

Leuf, Bo and Ward Cunningham. *The Wiki Way.* Boston, MA: Addison-Wesley, 2001.

Liebling, A. J. *The Press.* New York: Pantheon, 1981.

Lienhard, John, *Engines of our Ingenuity*, University of Houston radio series, 1987–2014. http://www.uh.edu/engines/ (accessed March 17, 2015).

Life magazine. "Speaking of Pictures." April 21, 1951, 19.

Linder, Doug. "The Trial of John Peter Zenger: An Account." Famous Trials, 2001. http://www. law.umkc.edu/faculty/projects/ftrials/ftrials.htm (accessed March 17, 2015).

Lippmann, Walter. *Public Opinion.* New York: Harcourt Brace, 1922.

Litchfield, Richard Buckley. *Tom Wedgwood, the First Photographer.* London: Duckworth, 1903.

Lloyd, Caro. *Henry Demaerest Lloyd, 1847–1903.* New York: Knickerbocker Press, 1912.

Lord, Walter. *A Night to Remember.* New York: Holt, 2004 (1955).

Low, A. M. "Wireless to Rule Our Lives, British Professor Predicts." *New York Times*, August 30, 1925, XX7.

Luxon, Norval Neil. *Niles Weekly Register: News Magazine of the Nineteenth Century*. Baton Rouge, LA: Louisiana State University Press, 1947.

Lynch, Marc. "The Failure of #Muslimrage," *Foreign Policy*, September 21, 2012.

Macauley, Thomas. *The History of England, from the Accession of James II*. Philadelphia, PA: Porter & Coates, 1848.

Manchester, William. *The Glory and the Dream*. New York: Bantam Books, 1974.

Marchand, Roland. *Creating the Corporate Soul: The Rise of Public Relations and Corporate Imagery in American Big Business*. Los Angeles, CA: University of California Press, 1998.

Markoff, John. *What the Doormouse Said: How the 60s Counterculture Shaped the Personal Computer*. New York: Viking 2005.

Markoff, John. "When Big Blue Got a Glimpse of the Future." *New York Times*, December 11, 2007. http://bits.blogs.nytimes.com/2007/12/11/when-big-bluegot-a-glimpse-of-the-future/ (accessed March 17, 2015)

Marshack, Alexander, "The Art and Symbols of Ice Age Man." in David Crowley and Paul Heyer, eds., *Communication in History*, 4th edn. Boston, MA: Allyn & Bacon, 2003.

Martin, James B. *Mass Media: A Bibliography with Indexes*. New York: Nova Science, 2002.

Martin, Kirsten E. "Google Inc., in China." *Business Roundtable*. Washington, DC: Catholic University, 2007.

Martin, Michel. "Star Trek's Uhura Reflects on MLK Encounter," *National Public Radio*, January 17, 2011.

McCabe, Charles, ed. *Damned Old Crank: A Self-Portrait of EW Scripps from His Unpublished Writings*. New York: Harpers, 1951.

McCauley, Anne. "'Merely Mechanical': On the Origins of Photographic Copyright in France and Great Britain." *Art History* 31, no. 1 (February 2008): 57–78.

McChesney, Robert. *Telecommunications, Mass Media and Democracy: The Battle for Control of US Broadcasting, 1928–1935*. New York: Oxford University Press, 1994.

McChesney, Robert. *The Death and Life of American Journalism: The Media Revolution That Will Begin the World Again*. New York: Nation Books, 2010.

McDonald, Hamish. "Freedom of Speech Is Still Something of a Trial in China." *Melbourne Australia Age*, November 2, 2005.

McGrath, Alister. *In the Beginning: The Story of the King James Bible and How It Changed a Nation, a Language, and a Culture*. New York: Anchor Books, 2001, 15.

McLeod, Elizabeth. *The Original Amos 'n' Andy: Freeman Gosden, Charles Correll, and the 1928–1943 Radio Serial*. Jefferson, NC: McFarland & Co., 2005.

McLuhan, Marshall. *The Gutenberg Galaxy*. London: Routledge, 1962.

McLuhan, Marshall *Understanding Media: The Extensions of Man*. Signet, 1966

McLuhan, Marshall *The Global Village: Transformations in World Life and Media in the 21st Century*. New York: Oxford, 1992.

McLuhan, M., and B. R. Powers. *The Global Village: Transformations in World Life and Media in the 21st Century*. New York and Oxford: Oxford University Press, 1989, 68.

McLuhan, M., and B. R. Powers. *Laws of Media: The New Science*. Toronto: University of Toronto Press, 1992.

McLuhan, M., and B. R. Powers. *Understanding Media*. Cambridge, MA: MIT Press, 1994.

McMurtrie, Douglas, *The Gutenberg Documents*. Oxford: Oxford University Press, 1941, 93.

Melvern, Linda. *Conspiracy to Murder: The Rwandan Genocide*. London and New York: Verso, 2004.

Mercado III, E., L. M. Herman, and A. A. Pack. "Song Copying by Humpback Whales: Themes and Variations." *Animal Cognition* 8 (2005): 93–102.

Meyer, Philip. *The Vanishing Newspaper: Saving Journalism in the Information Age*. Columbia, MO: University of Missouri Press, 2009.

Miller Center, Project on Media and Governance. *Old Media, New Media and the Challenge to Democratic Governance.* Charlottesville, VA: University of Virginia, 2010. http://millercenter.org/public/debates/internet (accessed December 17, 2010).

Miraldi, Robert. "Scaring Off Muckrakers with the Threat of Libel." *Journalism Quarterly* 65, no. 3 (Fall 1988): 609–14.

Mitgang, Herbert, ed. *Spectator of America: A Classic Document about Lincoln and Civil War America by a Contemporary English Correspondent, Edward Dicey.* Athens, GA: University of Georgia Press, 1989. http://www.mrlincolnandnewyork.org/inside.asp?ID=38&subjectID=3 (accessed March 17, 2015).

Moore, Gordon E. "Cramming More Components onto Integrated Circuits." *Electronics Magazine*, April 19, 1965, 4.

Moritz, Scott. "How Yellow Colored an Era." *Editor & Publisher*, September 28, 1996.

Morris, Erol. "Which came first, the chicken or the egg?" *New York Times*, September 25, 2007.

Morris, Roger. *Richard Milhous Nixon: The Rise of an American Politician.* New York: Henry Holt, 1991.

Morse, Samuel Finley Breese, and Edward Lind Morse. *Samuel F. B. Morse: His Letters and Journals.* New York: Houghton Mifflin Company, 1914.

Mott, Frank Luther. *American Journalism, a History: 1690–1960.* New York: Macmillan, 1966.

Motte, Dean de la. *Making the News: Modernity & the Mass Press in Nineteenth Century France.* Boston, MA: University of Massachusetts Press, 1999.

Moxon, Joseph. *Mechanick Exercises: Or, the Doctrine of Handy-Works Applied to the Art of Printing.* London: Atlas, 1683.

Moyers, Bill. "Journalism Must Survive the Pressure Cooker of Plutocracy," *Salon,* May 30, 2015.

Munro, John. *Heroes of the Telegraph.* London: Religious Tract Society, 1891.

Murray, Michael D. *Encyclopedia of Television News.* Phoenix, AZ: Oryx Press, 1999.

Murrow, Edward R. Speech to the Radio TV News Directors Association, 1958. http://www.rtdna.org/pages/media_items/edward-r.-murrowspeech998.php (accessed March 17, 2015).

Museum of Broadcast Communications (MBC). "Civil Rights and Television," 2010. http://www.museum.tv/eotvsection.php?entrycode=civilrights (accessed March 17, 2015).

Nassaw, David. *The Chief: The Life of William Randolph Hearst.* New York: Houghton Mifflin, 2001.

National Academy of Engineering (NAE). "Greatest Achievements: Computer History." 2010. http://www.greatachievements.org/?id=3985 (accessed March 17, 2015).

Nelson, D. L., U. S. Reed, and J. R. Walling. "Pictorial Superiority Effect." *Journal of Experimental Psychology: Human Learning & Memory* 2 (1976): 523–8.

Nelson, Ted. *Literary Machines.* San Antonio, TX: Project Xanadu, 1981.

Nelson, Ted. *Computer Lib/Dream Machines.* Redmond, WA: Tempus Books of Microsoft Press, 1987 (1974).

Neuzil, Mark. *The Environment and the Press: From Adventure Writing to Advocacy*. Chicago: Northwestern University Press, 2008.

Neuzil, Mark and Bill Kovarik. *Mass Media and Environmental Conflict.* Thousand Oaks, CA: Sage, 1997.

Nevins, Allan. *The Gateway to History.* New York: D. Appleton-Century, 1938.

New Republic, "A Woman in History—The Wonderful, Horrible Life of Leni Riefenstahl." March 14, 1994, 30.

Newspaper Association of America. NAA. "Advertising Expenditures, 2010." http://www.naa.org/TrendsandNumbers/Advertising-Expenditures.aspx (accessed March 17, 2015).

Newth, Mette. "The Long History of Censorship, 2001." http://www.beaconforfreedom.org/about_project/history.html (accessed March 17, 2015).

New York Times, "Marconi future of radio." February 25, 1928, 4.

New York Times, "Radio and the Press." April 25, 1931, 11.

New York Times, "Seeking a Code." November 20, 1938, 174.

New York Times, "FCC Decree Bars Bias on the Radio." January 18, 1941.

New York Times, "Guard Listeners Denny Tells Radio." October 24, 1946, 45.

New York Times, "New Code is Urged on Broadcasters." September 18, 1947, 50.

Nicholson, Michael. "Strict military censorship covered up much of what was really happening in the trenches." *Daily Telegraph*, August 5, 2014.

Niemi, Robert. *History in the Media: Film and Television.* Santa Barbara, CA: ABCClio, 2006.

Novick, Peter. *That Noble Dream: The Objectivity Question and the American Historical Profession.* Cambridge: Cambridge University Press, 1988.

O'Brien, Frank. *The Story of the Sun.* New York: Doran Co., 1918.

Office of Communication of the United Church of Christ v. FCC, 359 F. 2nd 994; 1, 1966.

Olasky, Marvin. *Corporate Public Relations: A New Historical Perspective.* Mahwah, NJ: Lawrence Earlbaum Associates, 1987.

Ong, Walter J. *Orality and Literacy: The Technologizing of the Word.* 2nd edition. London and New York: Routledge, 2002 (1982).

Organization of Islamic Cooperation, "IPHRC strongly condemns …" January 18, 2015. http://www.oic-oci.org/oicv2/topic/?t_id=9698 (accessed January 20, 2015).

Outlook. "Birth of a Nation." April 14, 1915, 854.

Palmer, Samuel. *A General History of Printing, from the First Invention of it in the City of Mentz to its Propagation and Progress.* London: n.p., 1733.

Parish, James Robert and Gregory Mark. *The Best of M-G-M, The Golden Years: 1928–1959.* Westport, CT: Arlington House Publishers, 1981, 143.

Parsons, Frank. *The Telegraph Monopoly.* Philadelphia, PA: Equity, 1899. [See also Arthur Mann, "Frank Parsons, the Professor as Crusader." *Mississippi Valley Historical Review* 37, no. 3 (December 1950): 471–90].

Parton, James. *The Life of Horace Greeley.* New York: Mason Brothers, 1855.

Parton, James. *Life and Times of Benjamin Franklin.* Boston: Ticknor and Fields, 1867.

Parton, James. "Samuel F. B. Morse." *Scientific American*, December 3, 1870.

Parton, James. "The Battle of New Orleans," in Rossiter Johnson, ed., *Great Events by Famous Historians, The National Alumni* XV, 1905, 343.

Paul, Annie Murphy, "Your Brain on Fiction." *New York Times*, March 18, 2012. http://www.nytimes.com/2012/03/18/opinion/sunday/the-neuroscience-of-your-brain-on-fiction.html?pagewanted=all (accessed March 17, 2015).

Pauline M. Holt, Debra M. Desrochens, and Christopher R. Kelly. "Children's Exposure to

TV Advertising in 1977 and 2004: Information for the Obesity Debate." *Federal Trade Commission*, June 1, 2007.

Pauly, Philip J. *Biologists and the Promise of American Life: From Meriwether Lewis to Alfred Kinsey.* Princeton, NJ: Princeton University Press, 2000.

Pearson, Drew. "Washington Merry-Go-Round." Washington, DC: American University, December 8, 1943. Drew Pearson online archive: http://www.library.american.edu/pearson/ (accessed March 17, 2015).

Pershing, Ginny. "Cybertelecom Project," 2010. http://www.cybertelecom. org/notes/att.htm (accessed March 17, 2015).

Petersen-Perlman, Deborah. "Texaco's Support of the Metropolitan Opera Broadcasts." *Journal of the Northwest Communication Association* (Spring 1994): 65–90.

Peterson, Iver. "Newspapers End Network for Web Sites." *New York Times*, March 11, 1998, D-6.

Pew Project for Excellence in Journalism, "State of the news media," 2014. http://www.journalism.org/files/2015/04/FINAL-STATE-OF-THE-NEWS-MEDIA1.pdf (accessed July 1, 2015).

Pew Research Center for People & the Press. "Internet Overtakes Newspapers as News Outlet." December 23, 2010. http://people-press.org/report/479/internet-overtakes-newspapers-as-news-outlet (accessed March 17, 2015).

Photographic Times. "A Bit of History." December 1910, 483.

Plattner, Steven W. *The Standard Oil N.J. Photography Project.* Austin, TX: University of Texas Press, 1983.

Playboy. "Marshall McLuhan, A Candid Conversation with the High Priest of Popcult and Metaphysician of Media." *Playboy*, March 1969.

Popkin, Jeremy D. *Media and Revolution.* Lexington, KY: University of Kentucky Press, 1995.

Postman, Neil. *Amusing Ourselves to Death: Public Discourse in the Age of Show Business.* New York: Penguin, 1985.

President's Commission on the Accident at Three Mile Island, US Government Printing Office, 052–003-00734–7, 1979.

Press, Bill. "Progressive Radio is Alive and Well," 2010. *Huffington Post*. http://www.huffingtonpost.com/bill-press/progressive-radio-is-aliv_b_432621.html (accessed March 17, 2015).

Price, Derek J. de Solla. "An Ancient Greek Computer." *Scientific American* (1959): 60–7.

Princeton University Library, Mudd Manuscript Library, Ivy Lee collection, *Biography of Ivy Lee*. http://diglib.princeton.edu/ead/ getEad?id=ark:/88435/m039k489x#bioghist (accessed June 17, 2010).

Pyle, Ernie. *Home Country.* New York: Wm. Sloane & Associates, 1935.

Pyle, Ernie. *Brave Men.* New York: Henry Holt, 1944.

Pyle, Ernie. *Ernie's War: The Best of Ernie Pyle's World War II Dispatches*, David Nichols, ed. Norwalk, CT: Easton Press, 2000.

Pyle, Richard. "19th-century Papers Shed New Light on Origin of the Associated Press." *AP News Release*, January 31, 2005.

Ramo, Joshua. "Jeffrey Preston Bezos: 1999 Person of the Year." *Time*, December 27, 1999.

Recording Industry Association of America (RIAA). "Piracy: Online and on the Street," 2010. http://www.riaa.com/physicalpiracy.php (accessed March 17, 2015).

Reed, Harry. "My Life with the ENIAC—a Worm's Eye View," in *Fifty Years of Army*

Computing: From ENIAC to MSRC, Symposium Proceedings, Aberdeen Proving Ground, US Army Research Laboratory, November 13–14, 1996.

Reed, John. *Ten Days that Shook the World.* New York: Penguin Books, 1977 (1919).

Rehak, Joan. "Tylenol Made a Hero of Johnson & Johnson: The Recall That Started Them All." *New York Times*, March 23, 2002.

Reichardt, Rolf. "Die stadtische Revolution als politisch-kultureller Prozess," in Rolf Reichardt, ed., *Die fran- zosische Revolution*. Frankfurt: n.p., 1988.

Reid, T. R. *The Chip: How Two Americans Invented the Microchip and Launched a Revolution.* New York: Random House, 2001.

Reid, Whitelaw. "Newspapers." *Encyclopedia Britannica.* London and New York: 1911, 546.

Rhees, David J. "A New Voice for Science: Science Service Under Edward Slosson, 1921–29." Master's Thesis, University of North Carolina, 1979.

Rhees, David J. "The Chemists Crusade." Ph.D. Dissertation, University of Pennsylvania, 1987.

Rheingold, Howard. "The Virtual Community." *Homesteading on the Electronic Frontier*, 1993. http://www.rheingold.com/ (accessed March 17, 2015).

Rheingold, Howard. Testimony, *Reno v ACLU*, April 1, 1996. http://www.ciec.org/transcripts/April_1_Rheingold.html (accessed March 17, 2015).

Rheingold, Howard. *Smart Mobs: The Next Social Revolution.* New York: Basic Books, 2002.

Rhodes, Chloe. "25,000 tomorrow." *Daily Telegraph*, May 23, 2006. http://www.telegraph.co.uk/culture/3652606/25000-tomorrow.html (accessed March 17, 2015).

Richardson, Brian. *Printers, Writers and Readers in Renaissance Italy.* Cambridge: Cambridge University Press, 1999.

Roberts, Gene, and Hank Klibanoff. *The Race Beat: The Press, the Civil Rights Struggle and the Awakening of a Nation.* New York: Vintage, 2007.

Robinson, Eugene. "Lena Horne: A Glamorous Revolutionary." *Washington Post,* May 11, 2010.

Rokicki, John. "Advertising in the Roman Empire." *Whole Earth Review* (Spring 1987). http://findarticles.com/p/articles/mi_m1510/is_1987_Spring/ai_4806053/ (accessed March 17, 2015).

Roosevelt, Theodore. "Reform through Social Work: Some Forces That Tell for Decency in New York," *McClure's*, March 1901.

Roselle, Mike. "Dragline: The CGZ Interview." *Appalachia Watch*, January 26, 2010. http://www.appalachiawatch.org/2010/01/dragline_25.html (accessed March 17, 2015).

Ross, Corey. *Media and the Making of Modern Germany.* New York and London: Oxford University Press, 2008.

Rossetto, Louis. "Cyberpunks Anticipate a New Digital Culture." *Wired*, September/October, 1993.

Rossetto, Louis. "In a Letter to His Kids, *Wired*'s Founding Editor Recalls the Dawn of the Digital Revolution." *Wired* magazine, May 19, 2008. http://www.wired.com/ techbiz/media/magazine/16-06/ff_15th_rossetto (accessed March 17, 2015).

Rothenberg, Randall. "The Advertising Century." *Advertising Age*, Crain Communications, 1999. http://adage.com/century/index.html (accessed March 17, 2015).

Royal Commission on Newspapers. Ministry of Supply and Services, Canada, 1981.

Rusbridger, Alan. "I Was Shown the Media's Future 16 Years Ago: Now with the iPad, It's Here." *Guardian*, April 11, 2010.

Saerchinger, Cesar. "Radio, Censorship and Neutrality." *Foreign Affairs,* January 1940, 337.

Saffo, Paul. "Farewell Information, it's a Media Age." December 2005. http://www.saffo.com/essays/index.php (accessed March 17, 2015).

Sagan, Carl. *Cosmos.* New York: Random House, 1980.

Sagan, Carl. *The Demon-haunted World: Science as a Candle in the Dark.* New York: Random House, 1995.

Saleh, Basel. "Tunisia: IMF 'Economic Medicine' has Resulted in Mass Poverty and Unemployment; Protest by Suicide as a Symbol of Resistance." Center for Research on Globalization, December 31, 2010. http://www.globalresearch.ca/index.php?context=va&aid=22587 (accessed March 17, 2015).

Sampson, Anthony. *The Seven Sisters.* New York: Viking, 1975.

Sampson, Henry. *A History of Advertising from the Earliest Times.* London: Chatto and Windus, 1875.

Sarnoff, David. "The Birth of Television, Address at New York World's Fair, Flushing Meadows, New York, April 20, 1939," in *Looking Ahead: The Papers of David Sarnoff.* New York: McGraw Hill, 1968.

Savage, William. *A Dictionary of the Art of Printing.* London: Longman, Brown, Green and and Longmans, 1841.

Scheeres, Julia. "Lech Walesa: Tech Freedom Fighter." *Wired,* June 19, 2002. http://www.wired.com/politics/law/news/2002/06/53299 (accessed March 17, 2015).

Schickel, Richard. *Charlie: The Life and Art of Charles Chaplin.* Warner Brothers video, 2003.

Schickel, Richard. *The Essential Chaplin: Perspectives on the Life and Art of the Great Comedian.* Lanham, MD: Ivan R. Dee, 2006.

Schrage, Elliot. "Testimony before the House Committee on International Relations Subcommittee on Asia and the Pacific and Subcommittee on Africa, Global Human Rights, and International Operations." February 15, 2006.

Schramm, Wilbur. *The Story of Human Communication, from Cave Painting to Microchip.* New York: Harper and Row, 1988.

Schudson, Michael. *Discovering the News: A Social History of American Newspapers.* New York: Basic Books, 1978.

Schudson, Michael. *Advertising, the Uneasy Persuasion: Its Dubious Impact on American Society.* New York: Basic Books, 1986.

Segaller, Stephen. *Nerds 2.0.1: A Brief History of the Internet.* New York: TV Books, 1998.

Seigenthaler, John. "A False Wikipedia Biography." *USA Today,* November 29, 2005.

Seijas, Rasfael Fernando and William Lindsay Scriggs. "To the London Times." Atlanta, GA: Franklin Printing Co., 1896.

Seldes, George. *Witness to a Century.* New York: Ballantine Books, 1987.

Shafer, Jack. "Newspaper Death Foretold by Warren Buffett." *Slate,* April 27, 2009. http://www.slate.com/id/2217014/ (accessed March 17, 2015).

Shannon, Warren. "Confronting the Nazis: Americans and German Propaganda." Ph.D. Dissertation, Washington State University, 1995.

Sheehan, Neil. *A Bright Shining Lie: John Paul Vann and America in Vietnam.* New York: Vantage Press, 1988.

Shein, Edgar H. *DEC is Dead.* San Francisco: Berrett-Koehler Publishers, 2004.

Sherman, Scott. "The Long Goodbye," *Vanity Fair,* November 30, 2012.

Shirer, William L. *The Rise and Fall of the Third Reich: A History of Nazi Germany*. New York: Simon and Schuster, 1960.

Shirer, William L. *Gandhi: A Memoir.* New York: Pocket Books, 1986.

Shirkey, Clay. *Institutions versus Collaboration*. TED Video, July 2005.

Shirkey, Clay. *How Social Media Can Make History*. TED Video, June 2010.

Siebert, Frederick. *Theodore Pederson, Wilbur Schramm, Four Theories of the Press*. Urbana, IL: University of Illinois Press, 1963.

Sinclair, Upton. *The Jungle.* New York: Doubleday, Page & Co., 1906.

Sinclair, Upton. *The Brass Check: A Study of American Journalism.* Pasadena, CA: Published by the author, 1920.

Sinha, Shall. "Mahatma Gandhi the Journalist." 2010. http://gandhi4peace.com/journalist.htm (accessed March 17, 2015).

Smiles, Samuel. *Lives of the Engineers*, New York: Harper, 1862.

Smiles, Samuel. *The Huguenots.* New York: Harper, 1867.

Smiles, Samuel. *Men of Invention and Industry*, New York: Harper, 1884.

Smith, Jeffrey A. *Printers and Press Freedom: The Ideology of Early American Journalism*. New York and London: Oxford University Press, 1988.

Smith, Sally Bevell. *In All His Glory: The Life and Times of William S. Paley and the Birth of Modern Broadcasting.* New York: Simon & Schuster, 1990.

Smith, W. E. and A. M. Smith. *Minamata.* London: Chatto & Windus, Ltd, 1975.

Snyder, Louis L. and Richard B. Morris. *A Treasury of Great Reporting.* New York: Simon & Schuster, 1962.

Softky, Marion. "Building the Internet: Bob Taylor Won the National Medal of Technology for Visionary Leadership in the Development of Modern Computing Technology." *The Almanac*, October 11, 2000. http://www.almanacnews.com/morgue/2000/2000_10_11.taylor.html (accessed March 17, 2015).

Sola Pool, Ithiel de. *Technologies of Freedom.* Boston, MA: Belknap Press of Harvard University Press, 1984.

Sontag, Susan. "Looking at War." *New Yorker*, December 9, 2002. http://www.newyorker.com/magazine/2002/12/09/looking-at-war (accessed July 1, 2015).

Sontag, Susan. *Regarding the Pain of Others.* New York: Picador/Farrar, Straus and Giroux, 2003.

Sperber, A. M. *Murrow: His Life and Times.* New York: Fordham University Press, 1998.

Sriramesh, K., James Grunig, and David Dozier, "Observation and Measurement of Two Dimensions of Organizational Culture and Their Relationship to Public Relations." *Journal of Public Relations Research* 8, no. 4 (1996): 229–61,

Standage, Tom. *The Victorian Internet: The Remarkable Story of the Telegraph and the Nineteenth Century's On-Line Pioneers.* New York: Walker & Company, 1998.

Starr, Paul. *The Creation of the Media: Political Origins of Modern Communications*. New York: Basic Books, 2004.

Stephens, Mitchell. *The Rise of the Image.* New York: Oxford University Press, 1998.

Stephens, Mitchell. *A History of News.* New York: Oxford University Press, 2007.

Stephens, Mitchell. "A Call for an International History of Journalism," 2011. http://www.nyu.edu/classes/stephens/International%20History%20page.htm (accessed March 17, 2015).

Stevenson, William. *A Man Called Intrepid.* New York: Ballantine Books, 1978.

Story, Louise. "New Advertising Outlet: Your Life." *New York Times*, October 14, 2007.

Strauss, Neil. "The MP3 revolution." *New York Times*, July 18, 1999.

Streible, Dan. *Fight Pictures: A History of Boxing and Early Cinema.* Los Angeles: University of California Press, 2008.

Stverak, Jason. "The pros and pros of 'Citizen Journalism,'" *Online Journalism Review*, March 9, 2010. http://www.ojr.org/ojr/people/stverak/201003/1830/ (accessed March 17, 2015).

Suite101. "The Communications Revolution in Early America." http:// americanhistory.suite101.com/article.cfm/the-communications-revolution-inearly-america#ixzz0tJxp7d9a (accessed March 17, 2015).

Sumner, Charles A. *Then and Now.* San Francisco: Bacon & Co., 1876. http://archive.org/stream/thennoworationby00sumnrich/thennoworationby00sumnrich_djvu.txt (accessed July 1, 2015).

Surowiecki, James. *The Wisdom of Crowds: Why the Many Are Smarter Than the Few and How Collective Wisdom Shapes Business, Economies, Societies and Nations.* New York: Little, Brown, 2004.

Swanberg, W. A. *Luce and His Empire.* London: Scribners, 1972.

SXSW 2010. Richard Rosenblatt interview: "Content On Demand," 2010. http://www.youtube.com/watch?v=8diEYt-g0xY (accessed March 17, 2015).

Talese, Gay. *The Kingdom and the Power: Behind the Scenes at The New York Times: The Institution that Influences the World.* New York: Random House, 1966.

Tallentyre, S. G., aka Evelyn Beatrice Hall. *The Friends of Voltaire.* New York: G. P. Putnam's Sons, 1907. [See also *Saturday Review*, May 11, 1935, 13: http://en.wikiquote.org/wiki/Evelyn_Beatrice_Hall (accessed August 17, 2010)].

Tebbel, John, and Mary Ellen Zuckerman. *The Magazine in America.* New York, London: Oxford University Press, 1991.

Telephony, "The Kellogg Company: Dismal Failure of Five Years' Strenuous Efforts to Deceive Independents." *Telephony* XIV (September, 1907): 136.

Thomas, Isaiah. *The History of Printing in America.* Worcester, MA: The Press of Isaiah Thomas, 1810.

Thoreau, Henry David. *Walden: Or, a Life in the Woods.* Boston, MA: Beacon Press, 2004 (1854).

Timberg, Bernard. *Television Talk.* Austin, TX: University of Texas Press, 2002.

Time, "The Formula Flap." July 12, 1976.

Time-Warner. "America Online and Time Warner Will Merge to Create World's First Internet-Age Media and Communications Company." Press Release, January 10, 2000. http://www.timewarner.com/corp/newsroom/pr/0,20812,667602,00.html (accessed March 17, 2015).

Tocqueville, Alexis de. *Democracy in America*, 1835. http://xroads.virginia.edu/~HYPER/DETOC/home.html (accessed March 17, 2015).

Toops, Diane. *Food Processing*, July 1, 2005.

Tosh, John. *The Pursuit of History: Aims, Methods, and New Directions in the Study of Modern History.* Toronto: Longman, 2000.

Trenchard, John, and Thomas Gordon. "NO. 15. Of Freedom of Speech; That the same is inseparable from publick Liberty." February 15, 1721, in *Cato's Letters: Essays on Liberty, Civil and Religious, and Other Important Subjects.* London: London Journal, 1720–3.

Tsukayama, Hayley. "The Year the Tablet Market Grew Up," *The Washington Post*, November 25, 2011.

Tuchman, Barbara. *The Guns of August.* New York: Macmillan, 1962.

Tuney, Michael. Online Readings in Public Relations, Northern Kentucky University, 2010. http://www.nku.edu/~turney/prclass/ readings/3eras2x.html (accessed March 17, 2015).

Twain, Mark. *A Tramp Abroad*. Hartford, CT: American Publishing Company, 1880.

Twain, Mark. *Mark Twain's Sketches, New and Old*. Hartford, CT: American Publishing Co., 1882.

Twain, Mark. *Mark Twain's Speeches*. Ithaca, NY: Cornell University Press, 2009 (1920).

Ungar, Richard. "Has Rush Limbaugh finally reached the end of the road?" *Forbes Magazine*, April 15, 2014.

United States Bureau of Labor Statistics (BLS), *U.S. Department of Labor, Occupational Outlook Handbook*, 2014–15 edn. http://www.bls.gov/ooh/media-and-communication/ reporters-correspondents-and-broadcast-news-analysts.htm (accessed January 26, 2015).

United States Holocaust Memorial Museum. "The Press in the Third Reich." *Holocaust Encyclopedia*. http://www.ushmm.org/ wlc/en/?ModuleId=10007655 (accessed March 17, 2015).

United States House of Representatives, "The Transmission of Telegrams." Hearing on HB 3010, May 24, 1912.

United States Senate, Report No. 48-577, 1884.

United States v. New York Times Co., 403 U.S. 713, June 30, 1971.

Usborne, David. "Entrepreneur Taps Mistrust of Media for New Venture." *Sunday Independent*, November 23, 2005. http://www.independent.co.uk/ news/world/americas/ entrepreneur-taps-mistrust-of-media-for-new-venture-516533.html (accessed March 17, 2015).

Van Dijck, Jose. *The Culture of Connectivity: A Critical History of Social Media*. Oxford and New York: Oxford University Press, 2013.

Van Doren, Carl. *Benjamin Franklin*. New York: Viking Press, 1938.

Varian, Hal. *Newspaper Economics Online and Offline*. Palo Alto, CA: Google, 2010. http:// www.scribd.com/doc/28084224/030910-Hal-Varian-FTCPreso (accessed March 17, 2015).

Vaughn, Stephen L. *Encyclopedia of American Journalism*. London and New York: Taylor & Francis, 2008.

Voltaire. *Lettres Philosophiques*. c. 1778, Modern History Sourcebook. http://www.fordham. edu/halsall/mod/1778voltaire-lettres.html (accessed March 17, 2015).

Waldrop, M. Mitchell. *The Dream Machine: J. C. R. Licklider and the Revolution That Made Computing Personal*. New York: Viking Penguin, 2001.

Ward, Hiley. *Mainstreams of American Media History*. Boston, MA: Allyn & Bacon, 1996.

Warren, Donald. *Radio Priest: Charles Coughlin, The Father of Hate Radio*. New York: The Free Press, 1996.

Washburn, Patrick Scott. *A Question of Sedition: The Federal Government's Investigation of the Black Press During World War II*. New York: Oxford University Press, 1986.

Washington Post. "JW Mack Under Fire." February 28, 1928, 1.

Washington Post. "Peril to Press Freedom Seen in Radio Bill." June 19, 1947, 15.

Washington Post. "Crisis at Three Mile Island, 1999." http://www.washingtonpost.com/ wp-srv/national/longterm/tmi/whathappened.htm (accessed March 17, 2015).

Watson, Thomas. *Exploring Life, the Autobiography of Thomas A. Watson*. New York: D. Appleton and Co., 1926.

Wattercutter, Angela. "35 Years after Star Wars, Effects Whiz Phil Tippett is Slowly Crafting a Mad God." *Wired Magazine*, May 24, 2012.

Waugh, Alec. *The Lipton Story.* New York: Doubleday, 1950.

Weber, Eugen. *Europe since 1715: A Modern History.* New York: Norton, 1972.

Weber, Johannes. "Strassburg, 1605. The Origins of the Newspaper in Europe." *German History* 24 (2006): 387–412.

Weiser, Philip J. "The Ghost of Telecommunications Past." *Michigan Law Review* 103, no. 6 (May 2005).

Wells, H. G. *When the Sleeper Awakes.* London: *The Graphic* Illustrated Newspapers Ltd, 1898. http://www.gutenberg.org/files/775/775-h/775-h.htm#2HCH0009 (accessed March 17, 2015).

Wells, H. G. "World Brain: The Idea of a Permanent World Encyclopedia." *Encyclopédie Franaise*, August 1937.

Whelan, Richard. *Aperture* (Spring 2002). http://www.pbs.org/wnet/americanmasters/episodes/robert-capa/in-love-andwar/47/ (accessed May 17, 2010).

White, Thomas A. *United States Early Radio History.* http://earlyradiohistory.us (accessed March 17, 2010).

Winston, Brian. *Media Technology and Society.* New York: Routledge, 1998.

Wolf, Gary. "The Tragedy of Craigslist." *Wired*, September 2009.

Wolf, Maryanne. *Proust and the Squid: The Story and Science of the Reading Brain.* New York: Harper, 2008.

Wolfe, Tom. *The New Journalism.* New York: Pan, 1975.

Wolff, Michael. *Television is the New Television: The Unexpected Triumph of Old Media in the Digital Age.* London: Portfolio, 2015.

Wood, James. *The Story of Advertising.* New York: Ronald Press Co., 1958.

Woods, Oliver, and James Bishop. *The Story of the Times.* London: Michael Joseph, 1985.

World Association of Newspapers, "World Press Trends Report," October 2014.

Zinn, Howard. *A People's History of the United States.* New York: HarperCollins, 1980. http://www.historyisaweapon.com/defcon1/zinncol1.html (accessed March 17, 2015).

Zittrain, Jonathan. *The Future of the Internet and How to Stop It.* New Haven, CT: Yale University Press, 2010.

Zoglin, Richard, and Elaine Dutka. "Cinema: Lights, Camera, Special Effects!" *Time*, June 16, 1986. http://www.time.com/time/magazine/ article/0,9171,961611,00.html (accessed March 17, 2015).

Zuckerman, Ethan. *Rewire.* New York: W. W. Norton & Co., 2013.

Index